The Ethics of Discernment
Lonergan's Foundations for Ethics

In *The Ethics of Discernment*, Patrick H. Byrne presents an approach to ethics that builds upon the cognitional theory and the philosophical notion of self-appropriation that Bernard Lonergan introduced in *Insight*, as well as upon Lonergan's later writing on ethics and values.

Extending Lonergan's method into the realm of ethics, Byrne argues that we can use self-appropriation to come to objective judgments of value. *The Ethics of Discernment* is an introspective analysis of that process, in which sustained ethical inquiry and attentiveness to feelings as "intentions of value" lead to a rich conception of the good.

Written for those familiar with Lonergan's ideas and for those with an interest in theories of ethics but only a limited knowledge of Lonergan's work, Byrne's book is the first detailed exposition of an ethical theory based on Lonergan's philosophical method.

(Lonergan Studies)

PATRICK H. BYRNE is a professor in the Department of Philosophy and director of the Lonergan Institute at Boston College.

PATRICK H. BYRNE

The Ethics of Discernment

Lonergan's Foundations for Ethics

UNIVERSITY OF TORONTO PRESS
Toronto Buffalo London

Reprinted in paperback 2017

ISBN 978-1-4426-3286-8 (cloth)   ISBN 978-1-4875-2223-0 (paper)

∞ Printed on acid-free, 100% post-consumer recycled paper

Lonergan Studies

Library and Archives Canada Cataloguing in Publication

Byrne, Patrick H. (Patrick Hugh), 1947–, author
The ethics of discernment : Lonergan's foundation for ethics /
Patrick H. Byrne.

(Lonergan studies)
Includes bibliographical references and index.
ISBN 978-1-4426-3286-8 (cloth). – ISBN 978-1-4875-2223-0 (softcover)

1. Lonergan, Bernard J. F. (Bernard Joseph Francis), 1904–1984 –
Criticism and interpretation. 2. Ethics. I. Title. II. Title: Lonergan's
foundation for ethics. III. Series: Lonergan studies

BJ404.L663B97 2016   170'.4   C2015-908169-6

University of Toronto Press acknowledges the financial assistance to its
publishing program of the Canada Council for the Arts and the Ontario Arts
Council, an agency of the Government of Ontario.

Canada Council   Conseil des Arts
for the Arts   du Canada

Funded by the   Financé par le
Government   gouvernement
of Canada   du Canada

Canada

*To Martha and Hugh Byrne,
my parents,
who first showed me by word and deed
what it means to live ethically.*

Contents

PART III: WHY IS DOING THAT BEING ETHICAL?

Preface

This book has been many years in the making. It grew out of a different project begun in 2003, intended to bring Bernard Lonergan's ideas to bear on the then very hotly debated topic of physician-assisted suicide, and especially the role played by the principle of autonomy in that controversy. Some proponents of physician-assisted suicide argued that autonomy guarantees persons the right to determine the story of their own lives and that there is no greater right than the determination of how that story will end. Lonergan himself wrote that human choices and actions are "the work of the free and responsible subject producing the first and only edition" of his or her life.[1] And yet there can be little doubt that Lonergan would have vigorously opposed physician-assisted suicide. So my original intention was to explore how the principle of autonomy evolved from its classic formulation by Immanuel Kant into its currently accepted usages, and then to show how Lonergan's work could shed new light on the controversy.

Originally I intended to present a narrative of the dialectical development of the understanding of autonomy in the main body of the book, assigning the summary of Lonergan's approach to an appendix, which could be referenced by the reader as needed. However, the appendix grew to well over 100 pages, still far from complete. It then became clear that the appendix would have to be a book in its own right; the book now in your hands. However, before I could complete that project, I agreed to serve for seven years as chairman of the Philosophy Department at Boston College, and the administrative responsibilities of that role did not allow me the time I needed to complete this book.

The delay has been providential, in my view. I learned many things in the intervening years that have made this a better book than what I could have written over a decade ago. In particular, I learned a great deal from other Lonergan scholars who have written about ethical topics during that period, and I have tried to acknowledge their contributions to my own thinking in the body and references of this book. I fear, however, I have not done justice to every such contribution. I also wish to express my gratitude to over 200 students who over the past decade have enrolled in my classes, "The Foundations of Ethics" and "Kant and Lonergan on Ethics," where I tried out earlier versions of some chapters of this book. Their responses and feedback helped me understand how better to communicate my ideas. I also am grateful to the dozens of fellows and faculty who have participated in the Lonergan Post-Doctoral Fellowship Seminars at Boston College where I also presented some drafts of chapters. I am especially indebted to Brian Braman, Charles Hefling, Fred Lawrence, J. Michael Stebbins, and the late Joseph Flanagan, SJ. Not only the particulars of my work on this book but my appreciation for the depth of Lonergan's thought is the result of ongoing conversation, illuminating questions, and criticisms in a spirit of deep friendship that I have shared with them over several decades. In addition, I am also grateful to four anonymous reviewers of the earlier draft of the whole manuscript of this book for University of Toronto Press, to the press's humanities editor Richard Ratzlaff, and especially to Mr. Christopher Berger. Their numerous and meticulous comments led to a great many improvements in this text. Finally, but most importantly, I wish to thank my wife, Joan, for her love, patience, and support through the years that it has taken me to write this book.

The Ethics of Discernment
Lonergan's Foundations for Ethics

Introduction

When Bernard Lonergan's work began to be known in the 1960s, it was received with enthusiasm for its emphasis on both the dynamism of human knowing and the dynamism of the world. It was seen as a fresh alternative to the dominant epistemological and metaphysical views that reigned in secular and Catholic circles – logical positivism and scholasticism, respectively – which felt lifeless and static. Lonergan became best known for his innovative contributions to the theories of human subjectivity and human knowing – cognitional theory, as he called it – that appeared in his major work, *Insight: A Study of Human Understanding.*[1] Both in *Insight* and in his writings from that period, he showed the fruitfulness of his approach to all kinds of topics.

By comparison, Lonergan's interest in ethics seemed quite muted. While he intended in *Insight* to develop an ethics that "prolongs … self-criticism into an explanation of the origin of all ethical positions and into a criterion for passing judgment on each of them," the book actually contains only one chapter devoted to ethics, which was circumscribed by the larger project of *Insight.*[2] Some of his most important ideas of ethical import came in the writings that followed *Insight* as he worked his way towards *Method in Theology.*[3] Yet his later writings that touched on ethics were never given an integrated presentation comparable to his earlier treatments of cognition, human subjectivity, philosophy of science, history, and God. My own readings of his post-*Insight* writings that touched on ethics were deeply illuminating, but they also gave rise to many difficult questions which he did not himself answer explicitly, or that he addressed elliptically or in confusing ways. I gradually learned through my conversations with others that they shared many of the same questions and also found them difficult to answer.

This book presents the answers that I have come to after years of wrestling with such questions as: Why does he call hunger a "non-intentional" feeling, when it seems perfectly clear that the feeling of hunger does have an intentionality? What exactly did he mean in saying that feelings respond to values? Why did he say that feelings are "intermediate" between judgments of fact and judgments of value? Why did he say that ethical deliberation does not arrive at a grasp of the virtually unconditioned? What justifications can be provided for his pronouncements on the invariant structure of the human good? What support can be offered for his characterization of a transcultural scale of value preferences? In order to answer these and many other questions, I found it necessary to go beyond what Lonergan actually wrote, all the while endeavouring to take seriously what he did say about these matters. For this reason I have subtitled this book "Lonergan's Foundations of Ethics." This book, therefore, intends to round out an approach to ethics on the foundations that Lonergan began in his own writings.

In seeking answers to these and other questions, I have endeavoured to remain faithful to his approach to philosophy in general – what he called "self-appropriation." Self-appropriation can be likened to the contemporary philosophical method of phenomenology – returning to the things themselves (*zu den Sachen selbst*, as Edmund Husserl put it) by discovering the correlations between the objects that appear to consciousness and the diverse activities of consciousness that constitute these as objects for consciousness. For Lonergan this meant that each person would pay careful attention to the activities that actually occur when he or she is endeavouring to know anything. In particular, Lonergan held that the roles of insight and inquiry had been shockingly overlooked or misunderstood throughout most of Western philosophy, and he set himself the task of reacquainting people with the prevalence of these activities in their own processes of knowing. He likened his method of self-appropriation to an experiment: "The crucial issue is an experimental issue, and the experiment will be performed not publicly but privately. It will consist in one's own rational self-consciousness clearly and distinctly taking possession of itself as rational self-consciousness."[4] This means paying careful attention to one's own experiences of coming to know (what Lonergan called the "data of consciousness"), endeavouring to understand those experiences and critically scrutinizing and correcting one's understandings of those experiences. As with Husserl and other phenomenologists, Lonergan held that a person gains ability to resolve a host of philosophical and other conundrums, once he or she has taken the time for this kind of self-scrutiny.

Following Lonergan's approach has been very beneficial in appropriating my own endeavours to know and to criticize what I thought I knew. So I endeavoured to follow this approach also in answering the further questions pertaining to ethical knowing and acting, questions about ethics raised not only by Lonergan's writings, but also by the writings of many others, as well as questions that arose for me simply in trying to find my way towards thinking and acting ethically. In other words, I endeavoured to pay attention to my experiences of the various acts of consciousness that went into my efforts to think and act ethically, to understand those experiences, to critically evaluate my understandings, and to consider what courses of action I should take in light of this self-knowledge. All the while these efforts were enriched by my readings of the writings of Lonergan and many other authors. In turn, what I gradually learned about my own activities of trying to be ethical also transformed my readings about ethical matters as well.

The chapters of this book came out of this interaction between self-appropriation and reading. I have chosen to characterize the approach to ethics that resulted as "the ethics of discernment." Chapter 1 explores the notion of discernment in general. It situates Lonergan's approach of self-appropriation in relation to discernment as understood by some of his most important predecessors – principally, Aristotle, St. Paul, and St. Ignatius of Loyola. Self-appropriation, however, could only be given a preliminary sketch in this first chapter. Still, this preliminary sketch is needed in order that the reader might begin with some understanding of what I mean when I speak of the "ethics of discernment." A more complete account of self-appropriation is presented later, especially in chapters 3 and 10, and will serve to refine the reader's initial understandings. The remainder of the book is devoted to explaining in much greater detail just what discernment as self-appropriation means when extended into the realm of ethical thought and action, what some of its consequences are, and how this relates to the idea of a method in ethics.

Part I of this book is devoted to "Preliminaries." In addition to the chapter on "Discernment," chapters 2 and 3 treat Lonergan's philosophy of cognition. Chapter 2 is intended mainly for those who are new to Lonergan's approach to the phenomena of human knowing, although those already familiar may also find some things worthwhile there as well. It offers a summary of Lonergan's best known contributions to philosophy. Because it is a summary of a major philosophical achievement, this is a dense chapter. Readers new to Lonergan's thought are encouraged to make use of the excellent and more expansive treatments of most of the same material by other scholars recommended in chapter 3.

Chapter 2 itself is cast in the form of extended answers to Lonergan's three questions: What am I doing when I am knowing? (cognitional theory); Why is doing that knowing? (epistemology); What do I know when I do that? (metaphysics or theory of being). He himself never stated explicitly what he regarded as the answers to these questions, so that chapter is original at least in making those answers explicit.

The central topic of the chapter is his approach to the problematic of objective knowledge, which also provides the background for much of the remainder of the book in two ways. First, Lonergan himself stressed that factual knowledge of reality is indispensable to authentic knowledge of ethical values and actions. Second, objectivity and normativity in ethics are among the greatest contemporary concerns, and Lonergan's approach to objectivity of factual knowing provides a unique and fruitful model for approaching the problem of objectivity in ethical knowing and acting.

No doubt many will contend justifiably that the greatest moral problem is not in knowing the right thing to do, but in actually doing it. But we live in an age where that deep ethical problem is masked and rationalized by a skepticism that there cannot be any objective knowledge of what is right, and a hyperbolic suspicion that every claim of objectivity in ethical matters can be nothing other than a cloaked effort to gain or maintain power. When such attitudes prevail, doing what is right has little chance of succeeding. So objectivity in ethical matters is of great importance at present and perhaps perennially.

Chapter 3 presents the notion of self-appropriation insofar as it pertains to factual knowing. That is to say, it presents what Lonergan called the "self-affirmation of the knower," and also offers a guide for readers to appropriate for themselves what they are doing when they are knowing. Self-appropriation does not consist in merely believing some statements about what knowing is on the authority of Lonergan or the words of this book or anyone else. Just as personal, self-reflexive knowledge is indispensable to the notion of discernment discussed in chapter 1, this is also true for self-appropriation of one's own processes of knowing.

The three major sections of this book (parts II–IV) are organized around three questions: What am I doing when I am being ethical? Why is doing that being ethical? What is brought about by doing that? These three questions are modelled on Lonergan's own three questions concerning knowing, objectivity, and reality.

The opening chapter of part II (chapter 4) forms the core of this book. There I offer my account of the expanded structure of ethical intentionality that includes but goes beyond the structure of cognitional intentionality presented in chapter 2. Perhaps many readers will be satisfied that this book has reached its goal in chapter 4. However, it took me a very long time to work out, on the one hand, the structure of conscious activities involved in ethical knowing and doing and, on the other, their relationships to what Lonergan called "feelings as intentional responses to value." The role of such feelings, then, could only be given a preliminary sketch in chapter 4.

It takes several additional chapters (5 through 9) to analyze more fully those feelings and their proper (and improper) roles in ethical thought and action.

Since it is widely assumed that ethics and values are merely matters of subjective opinion, much of this book (parts II and III) is an extended argument that values, and especially ethical values, can be known objectively. This argument depends upon Lonergan's revolutionary approach to objectivity in the realm of factual knowing. He eschewed the idea that factual objectivity consists in accurate representation – that is, matching an idea formed in the mind with how things actually stand "already out there now" in the external, real world. Instead, he argued that factual objectivity results from authentic subjectivity – that is, faithfulness in answering all the questions posed about whether or not things really are so. Part III ("Why is Doing That Being Ethical?," chapters 8–10) therefore explains how this notion of objectivity can be expanded to incorporate a faithfulness in answering all questions about value and the good and what ought to be done. The argument for the possibility of objectivity in ethics builds upon the previous chapters, which detail the structure of ethical intentionality, but now focuses in greater detail on the role played by the horizon of feelings in reaching judgments of value.

Because feeling responses to value play such a central and indispensable role in knowledge of ethical values, the objectivity of such knowledge depends utterly upon the character of our feeling lives – upon the structure of our "horizons of feelings." Yet both cultural and personal events massively influence how our feelings come to be structured. Unless our feeling lives are restructured so as to empower authentic judgments of value, ethical knowledge and action will be distorted and lack their proper objectivity. Lonergan used the term "conversion" to designate the changes in the structuring of our feelings necessary for us to be capable of objective judgments of value. The first two parts of this book explain what Lonergan meant by three kinds of conversion, and why they are so essential to objective and authentic ethical knowing and living.

Chapter 7 argues that each person's horizon of feelings determines what questions will be regarded as needing answers in order to substantiate a judgment of value. Chapter 8 argues that two fundamental feelings – the unrestricted notion of value and the experience of unrestricted being-in-love – are permanent sources of tension and self-transcendence in those horizons. These two feelings, I propose, provide standards for assessing a person's own horizons of feelings that are internal to that horizon itself. When the composition of the rest of the feelings in a horizon is in harmony with those two fundamental feelings, then the further questions regarded as pertinent, and the subsequent judgments and actions that follow from that horizon, will be objective in the unqualified sense. However, when there are unresolved tensions in the feeling horizon arising from the unrestricted notion of value and unrestricted being-in-love, then judgments of value and subsequent actions will be objective only relative to that horizon. The tensions that arise in each person's horizon of feelings from the unrestricted notion of value, unrestricted being-in-love, and the normative scale of value motivate transformations (conversions) of horizons of feelings that will resolve these tensions. The transformed horizons of feelings that the tensions orient towards are horizons out of which objective judgments of value and ethical actions come forth.

The composition of every horizon of feelings will contain some scale of value preferences, at least implicitly. I refer to this *de facto* scale as a person's existential scale of value preferences. Chapter 9 offers illustrations of how we make *comparative* judgments of value, in order to bring to light these existential scales of value. The chapter argues further that, in addition to the existential scale, there is also a normative, invariant, transcultural scale of value preferences. This normative scale also makes its presence felt within a person's horizon of feelings, *even though* a person's individual, existential scale may deviate from it in significant ways. There will also be tensions in the horizon of feelings that betray this deviation. These tensions testify to the existence of a scale of normative value preference that can provide grounds for objective judgments of comparative value.

It is one thing to argue that *a* normative hierarchical scale of values reveals itself in human thinking, deciding, and acting, even when it is being violated. It is another thing altogether to formulate accurately the hierarchical organization of that scale. Because Lonergan relied on the works of Max Scheler and Dietrich von Hildebrand for his idea of a scale of value preference, their differing accounts of the elements in the scale are compared. Yet the question of the accuracy of Lonergan's own account is postponed until chapter 14 because it presupposes the discussion of Lonergan's account of the good.

This book reaches a certain climax in chapter 10, "Self-Appropriation, Part II: Why Is Doing That Being Ethical?" This chapter explores in detail the fuller meaning of self-appropriation. Much of what is promised in chapter 1 is fulfilled at that point. All that comes afterwards – especially regarding Lonergan's theory of the good and a model for method in ethics – depends upon what is gathered together in chapter 10.

Since the objective of this book is to provide an integrated view of Lonergan's disparate ideas about ethics, the topics in part IV ("What Is Brought About by Doing That?," chapters 11–14) are explorations of his ideas about the good. It shows the implications of the expanded account of ethical intentionality and objectivity for a comprehensive theory of the good.

Contemporary philosophical schools of ethics tend to divide into those based upon deontological notions of right action and proper procedures on the one hand (and their "thin" theories of the good), and those based upon on a more robust (or "thick") theory of the good or value on the other hand. For the ethics of discernment, this is an unnecessary dichotomy. The structure of ethical activities (the most basic, perhaps "thin" ethical procedures) implies a surprisingly rich account of the good, including the diversity of natural goods, the goodness of the natural universe as a whole, the structure of "the human good," Lonergan's approach to the problem of evil, and the relation of all these things to transcendent goodness. For this reason, part IV is much more technical than the rest of the book. It works out in careful detail just how the structure of ethical intentionality entails a fundamental, pre-choice commitment to a structure of the good and a scale of values that is not limited to mere subjective preference, or even to the specificities of particular cultures or epochs.

These accounts of the good and of ethical knowing and acting provide a basis for entering into the very difficult ethical disputes of our time. Part V (chapters 15 and 16) therefore, explains how Lonergan's idea of the "eight functional specialties" can be used to make unusual but much-needed contributions to those disputes. I argue that this is a method that integrates these functional specialties and meets the challenge Lonergan set for himself in *Insight* but never fully met: a method in ethics that would be comparable to his work on method in metaphysics and theology. Those final chapters do not, however, actually apply the method to such disputes, but rather offer tools that can be used fruitfully by those engaging in such controversies.

Throughout this book I have provided concrete illustrations of unfamiliar and technical ideas either from literature, world events, or from my own experiences. Much of the length of this book is due to those illustrations, as well as to the effort to bring all of Lonergan's ideas touching on ethical concerns into a coherent whole. I hope that the clarity gained from these illustrations will more than compensate the reader's patience with the length.

PART ONE

Preliminaries

1 Discernment and Self-Appropriation

It is only through [our] movement towards cognitional and moral self-transcendence [that we] can hope to discern the ambivalence at work in others and the measure in which they resolved their problems. Only through such discernment can [we] hope to appreciate all that has been intelligent, true, and good in the past even in the lives and the thought of opponents. Only through such discernment can [we] come to acknowledge all that was misinformed, misunderstood, mistaken, evil even in those with whom [we are] allied. Further, however, this action is reciprocal. Just as it is one's own self-transcendence that enables one to know others accurately and to judge them fairly, so inversely it is through knowledge and appreciation of others that we come to know ourselves and to fill out and refine our apprehension of values.

– Bernard Lonergan, Method in Theology

1.1 Introduction

This book was written out of the conviction that discernment is of fundamental importance to ethical thinking and living, and that the work of Bernard Lonergan, SJ, casts considerable light upon that importance. Accordingly, this chapter endeavours to provide a context for thinking of what Lonergan called "self-appropriation" as a form of discernment. It begins with reflections on uses of the word "discernment" in ordinary English usage. It then explores writings of Aristotle of Stagira, Paul of Tarsus, and Ignatius of Loyola, in part because of their historical importance, and in part because scholars have used "discernment" to translate their ideas originally expressed in Greek, Latin, Basque, or Spanish. Ignatius is a natural choice, because Lonergan encountered his ideas about discernment in his training as a Jesuit. Ignatius, in turn, was profoundly influenced by St.

Paul. Although there is no direct line of descent from Aristotle through Paul and Ignatius to Lonergan, Aristotle's acute observations about discernment cast much light upon the ideas of all three, and reveal the generalized importance of discernment outside of an explicitly Christian religious framework. Although a more detailed exposition of what Lonergan meant by self-appropriation and its relevance to thinking and acting ethically will be taken up in several of the succeeding chapters, the concluding sections of this chapter begin that exploration.

Hence, this chapter does not aim to prove the direct influences of Aristotle or St. Paul on Lonergan's notion of self-appropriation. Rather, the intent is to explore how their ways of thinking about discernment illuminate what Lonergan called self-appropriation. On the other hand, Ignatius did have a direct influence on Lonergan, and a later section of this chapter endeavours to show how that influence might have influenced his approach to self-appropriation.

1.2   The Notion of Discernment

Discernment involves going beyond ordinary perceptiveness. Discernment means keen perception or judgment and derives from the Latin *discernere* – to separate. Discernment is the process of identifying something of value by separating it from other phenomena that obscure it and compete with it for our attention. Discernment is required in order to make out a figure on the horizon at twilight; or to recognize an exceptional jewel or painting amidst a collection of similar items of lesser worth; or to notice a subtle anxiety underlying someone's self-assured conversation. Discernment implies that some sort of extra effort and expertise is needed to get things right.

Discernment is therefore a refined form of attention. We speak, for example, of a discerning listener and a discerning buyer. This language identifies people who are better than average at listening and buying. They are not merely passive receptacles for sounds or advertisements. They are people who bring something extra to their listening or buying. That something extra enables them to sift through a clutter of stimuli and to pick out sounds of significance from background noise, or to locate items of value within a marketplace of lesser offerings and hollow promises.

We all bring some sort of interest or concern to our listening or purchasing, as well as to our visual and other sensations. There is no such thing as completely passive experiencing; all attention is structured by prior interests or concerns. But the something extra that discerning listeners and buyers bring is their sense of worth – what is worth listening to or what is worth buying – along with their skill in detecting that worth. What separates discerning attention from ordinary attention is the sophistication, the refinement, the depth, and the accuracy of this sense of worth (and all that this presupposes) that discerning persons bring to their activities of attending. People of discerning attention are simply better at their type of attending. Discerning attention does the work of attending better because of this refined sense of what is worth attending to, and the skill of attending to it.

Discernment also implies a kind of double-intentionality – attentiveness to the matter at hand, but also attentiveness to one's own way of being attentive. Only by self-consciously and deliberately drawing upon one's refined sense of worth and engaging in the skillful extra effort can discernment of subtle differences be accomplished.

Discernment, therefore, is no mere matter of just seeing or hearing what is out there to be seen or heard. Discernment presupposes a development or even a transformation of the person engaged in discernment. Practices in discernment are designed to bring about this sort of development and transformation. The more this development advances, the more discerning the person becomes. What develops is discernment of subtleties, and only by being made subtle can one discern subtleties. In particular, only by being developed into a discerning person can one truly discern subtleties of value.

When sports commentators announce, "That was a split-fingered fastball," or "That was a double Salchow," they do so on the basis of their abilities to notice subtle but significant differences that most of us will have missed. When critics remark on a creative and innovative musical performance, something in them has permitted a difference of worth to stand out in their attention, but not in ours. Of course, in response to any such comment, some people can and do say, "I didn't hear or see anything special. You are just making that up." Some may even hold this attitude obstinately in all situations. But most of us, sooner or later, acknowledge that some people's discernment in some area is more refined than our own. These are instances where we recognize someone as more discerning in listening to conversations or musical performances or in identifying economic opportunities, baseball pitches, or excellence in competitive ice skating. Recognizing discernment in others can sometimes be the beginning of transformations in us, towards something of value previously beyond our horizon.

Sometimes we acknowledge someone's expertise after having learned from them how to notice these differences of value for ourselves. Sometimes we acknowledge expertise in discernment because we recognize personal qualities of the expert that convince us she or he must truly possess this expertise. Sometimes we acknowledge expert discernment because third parties "in the know" accept this person as an expert. How and why we recognize others as especially discerning are questions that we are not in a position to probe further at this point. For the present, I merely wish to draw attention to the readers' own memories of such instances, in order to initiate deeper reflection on the phenomenon of discernment.

To summarize, then, discernment is a refined form of attentiveness guided by exceptional knowledge of value and by knowledge, even transformation, of oneself as a discerner.

I have chosen the title for this book, *The Ethics of Discernment*, in order to underscore the something extra that is involved in authentic ethical knowing, choosing, and living. This something extra means that the ethics of discernment also involves double-intentionality – more specifically, awareness of the value about which we deliberate, accompanied by a kind of reflective attention to that something extra about ourselves as we deliberate. This means discovering how we are already consciously intending matters of ethical value, and using those very same powers of intending in order to discriminate among our various ways of intending. The ethics of discernment, then, is about learning to pay attention to that something extra – what is deepest and best within us – and about learning to act ever more consistently in fidelity with what is deepest and best.

In this sense, the ethics of discernment is equivalent to the common adage, "Let your conscience be your guide." Although the common adage may be more familiar, understanding it properly is no easy matter. Knowing what it means to let your conscience be your guide is no simpler a task, certainly, than understanding what is meant by the ethics of discernment. Knowing what "conscience" really means (and does not mean) is exceptionally difficult. We can easily be deceived, and deceive ourselves, about what our conscience is "telling" us. And even when we are clear about the promptings of conscience, following those promptings is seldom easy. Hence the meanings of the common adage, as well as that of "ethics of discernment," stand in need of considerable explication.

Such explication is the objective of this book. The explication of the ethics of discernment is intended to lead you, the reader, to a refined understanding of the genuine meaning of conscience. This book will propose that this refined understanding is crucial to the foundations of ethics. Yet merely understanding alone, no matter how refined, cannot be sufficient as a foundation of ethics, and so ethical discernment not only requires but goes beyond understanding. Ethics is not a concept merely to be understood; it is rather a way of life to be lived. Those who actually do live out the ethics of discernment – those who do act in fidelity with what is deepest and best in them – are the genuine foundation of ethics. This foundation is people, both individually and in concert, who actually live in this discerning way. To understand the foundation of ethics, then, is to understand how these people discern values and how their discernment governs their way of life.

Given that there are many conflicting opinions about ethics, following the approach offered by this book comes with risk. There can be no argument in advance that can prove to the reader that it is worth the risk to take seriously this notion of the ethics of discernment. There can be no demonstration in advance that following the approach of this book will lead to authentic ethics. This book is offered in hope – a hope that the reader will try this approach and will find that it offers successful guidance to thinking and living ethically, including how to find one's way among the many competing voices about what it means to live ethically. Listening and responding to what others say and do in matters of ethics is itself inevitably part of ethical living. Listening and responding well to those voices requires discernment.

I have found that the work of Bernard Lonergan offers especially valuable resources for this kind of exploration. Because Lonergan's treatment of "self-appropriation" (as he called it) provides such a wealth of detail and subtlety, it is especially enlightening for the exploration of the double-intentionality that is central in ethical discernment.[1]

1.3   Aristotle of Stagira

Aristotle drew attention to the importance of discernment in the context of his discussions of dialectic, especially in his *Topics, Sophistical Refutations* (*De Sophisticis Elenchis*), and *Rhetoric*. In those works, Aristotle carefully delineated the notion of dialectic in general, as well as its subtle varieties and related disciplines. Dialectic, as he understood it, originated with Socrates and was taken up, deepened, and given a dramatic portrayal by Plato in his dialogues. Aristotle later modified and presented dialectic in an expository form.

Before the rise of modern empirical science, the pre-eminent method in philosophy and theology was dialectic. Dialectic begins, not with empirical data as do the modern sciences, but with the opinions (*endoxa*) that people hold. It uses the tools of argumentation and logic to explore and clarify the implications of those opinions. It moves from unexamined opinions towards refined knowledge about a variety of issues, such as justice, happiness, nature, and even the kind of knowledge that deserves to be called "science" (*epistêmê*).

In his *Rhetoric*, Aristotle thoughtfully stated his own reasons for taking opinions as the methodological point of departure:

> It belongs to the same faculty [*dunamis*] to discern [*esti dunameos idein*] what is true and what is like the truth, and human beings are sufficiently well orientated towards the true by nature and mostly hit

> truth. For which reason being good at aiming for reputable opinions belongs to the person who is also disposed in the same way toward the truth.[2]

In other words, dialectic can begin with reputable opinions because there is a kernel of truth already contained in those opinions, or at least in those that hold the opinions. For this same reason, dialectic can also progress towards more refined and even unexpected truths and towards deeper understandings of truths. To modern readers formed by practices of criticism and suspicion, the assumption that there is even a ghost, let alone a kernel, of truth in the opinions of others, and especially of our predecessors, will seem a naive and even a dangerous point of departure for any serious philosophical investigation. But for Aristotle, discernment has less to do with the kernel of truth within an opinion than with the potency (*dunamis*) for and orientation towards the truth in the person holding the reputable opinion. Moreover, this discernment is possible insofar as the practitioner of dialectic recognizes the very same disposition "towards the truth" within himself or herself. Moreover, being "good at aiming for reputable opinions" is made possible by the self-reflective recognition within oneself of that which inclines towards truth. This self-reflective recognition is the "something extra" that makes discernment possible.

The crucial factor here is the potency (*dunamis*) for truth shared by the interrogator and interlocutor alike. This potency is the standard of truth. Discernment in Aristotle's sense, therefore, has this double-intentionality. Discernment of this standard of truth as it actually operates within people forms the basis for discerning the differences between reputable and disreputable persons, which underlies the repute of their opinions.

Therefore, mere logic alone will not suffice for the effective practice of dialectic. Something beyond logic – discernment – is required if one is even to begin dialectic and head towards the deeper aspects of things, whether in the realm of ethics or elsewhere.

Yet beginning with persons and opinions that are reputable does not by itself establish those opinions as beyond question. In fact, this is exactly what dialectic adds to opinions that possess a kernel of truthfulness. It subjects them to vigorous, even aggressive, questioning. It uses techniques (*topoi*) including logic to draw out consequences of the various opinions held by interlocutors, and then poses these consequences as further questions for agreement or disagreement to the persons who held the original opinions themselves. Further consequences of these answers are drawn until, as C.D.C. Reeve has put it:

The questioner succeeds if he forces the answerer to accept a proposition contrary to the one he undertook to defend ([*Sophistical Refutations*,] 2 165b3–4). The questioner fails if the answerer always accepts or rejects premises in a way consistent with that proposition. To a first approximation, *dialectic* is the art or craft (*technê*) enabling someone to play the role of questioner or answerer successfully. ([*Topics*,] I 1 100a18–21, VIII 14 164b2–4)[3]

Aristotle traces in meticulous detail the ways that different kinds of dialectic can draw out different consequences, always presenting the interlocutor with radically alternative options. He explores, for example, the ways that valid deductions can proceed from what look like (but are not) reputable opinions, or how arguments that look like valid deductions (but are not) can work on genuinely reputable opinions (*Topics*, I 1 100b23–5). He also shows how someone who has genuine scientific knowledge can fall victim to, and can avoid, clever sophistical arguments against their positions.[4]

Aristotle classifies the several different ways in which dialectical reasoning can be used. Still, the most important objective of dialectic is to bring the interlocutor to a point where he or she has to choose between a logical consequence drawn from one of his or her opinions and the consequence drawn from another equally cherished opinion. At the finale of his *Topics*, Aristotle describes the situation when this sort of confrontation takes place:

> Where knowledge and philosophical wisdom are concerned, the ability to discern [*sunaron*] and hold in one view the consequences of either hypothesis is no insignificant tool, since then it only remains to make a correct choice of one of them. But a task of this sort requires *euphuia*. And true *euphuia* consists in just this – the ability to choose the true and avoid the false. For people with *euphuia* are the very ones who can do this well, since they discern [*krinousi*] correctly what is best by a correct love or hatred [*philountes kai misountes*] for what is set before them.[5]

No matter how skilled someone is in the techniques of logic and dialectical argument, this can lead only so far and no further. It leads up to the point of discerning what is at stake, and what the available options are, but it "'remains to make a correct choice of one of them.'"[6] The power that allows us to make that choice correctly is *euphuia*. The word does not easily translate into English, but is probably best translated as "good disposition" or, better, "disposition towards the good,"[7] which is grounded in a correct love or hatred for the alternative consequences that are produced by the logical operations of dialectic. Discerning which of the two alternatives is choiceworthy, then, is founded upon an even deeper discernment of proper love for the true and the good.

Reeve remarks that *euphuia* is the power philosophy has and dialectic lacks, and he points out that this is a power that Aristotle explicitly connects with ethical choice in his *Nicomachean Ethics*:

> A person doesn't aim at the end [the good] through his own choice; rather, he must by nature have a sort of natural eye to make him discern (*krinei*) well and choose what is really good. And the person who by nature has this eye in good condition is *euphuês*. For it is the greatest and finest thing ... and when it is naturally good and fine, it is true and complete *euphuia*. (III 5 1114b5–12)[8]

The love of what is really good and true is natural in the sense that the potency for this resides in every human being. Yet that power can remain dormant and undeveloped or, worse yet, perverted into a distorted love for lesser goods in place of greater good. If the potency for what is genuinely good and true is developed into a disposition (*hexis*), it becomes like a second nature, as do the virtues of courage, generosity, wittiness, or moderation. People who have developed their potency ("natural eye") into a habitual disposition are those called *euphuês*.

In the end, therefore, the logical operations of argument can lead up to the ultimate objective sought by dialectic, but cannot reach it on their own. Something further is needed to discern and choose truly among the radical alternatives with which dialectic confronts us. To discern and choose well requires special kinds of persons, *euphuês*, who come to be discerning as a result of a self-reflective, personal development. As we will see, Aristotle's notion of *euphuia* bears striking similarities to what Paul and Ignatius call discernment, and to what Lonergan called self-appropriation.

1.4 Paul of Tarsus

Like Aristotle, St. Paul was concerned with the problem of discerning truth amidst conflicting claims. In particular, he counselled the need for discernment when it came to sorting out the authenticity of the proliferating prophesies issuing forth from various members of the fledgling Christian community.[9] Paul shared with Aristotle the abiding concern over discernment of ethical behaviour – discerning between good and evil inclinations, for example.[10] Again, just as with Aristotle, Paul recognized that a special ability was needed in order to make good discernments.

Of course, the context for Paul's reflections on discernment was dramatically different from that of Aristotle, and this inevitably led Paul to write about discernment in ways that were quite different from the terms used by Aristotle. Most significantly, for Paul the primary focus had to be discerning the will of God,[11] whereas Aristotle wrote about discernment in terms of choosing the true and avoiding the false. Paul, of course, would claim that this is precisely what he meant as well.[12] Yet Aristotle's observations about discernment took place within the context of the nascent dialectic originated by Socrates, whereas the context for Paul's reflections was the emerging early Christian community. That context was framed by Paul's own Jewish rabbinical training, his conversion, and his encounters with members of the Christian community who had been formed by their direct encounters with and memories of the sayings and deeds of Jesus. Hence Paul was bound to speak of discernment explicitly in relation to the will of God as it was coming to be understood in that community.

Furthermore, against this background, Paul identified that special ability of discernment as a gift from God. According to Paul, the fundamental gift is "the love of God that has been poured out into our hearts through the Holy Spirit that has been given to us."[13] This indwelling of divine love within Paul and others formed the basis for their capacities to discern whatever else is spiritual. As Paul puts it, "There are different kinds of spiritual gifts but the same Spirit."[14] He counts "discernment of spirits" among other spiritual gifts such as leadership, prophecy, healing, and the ability to speak with wisdom and knowledge.[15] That is to say, a person can discern what is of the Spirit only because the Spirit as divine love has become operative within that person. It takes a spiritual gift to discern what is from the Spirit among the many things clamoring for endorsement or commitment.[16] For Aristotle as well, the capacity for genuine discernment rests upon "a correct love or hatred" for whatever competes for a person's choice. Of course, Aristotle does not explicitly identify this love as a gift from the God of Jewish or Christian revelation, but the similarities are there nonetheless.

Beyond the similarities, there are of course differences. Biblical scholar David M. Stanley traces the Christian tradition of discernment back to the writings of St. Paul, remarking that "it is no surprise the expression 'the discernment of spirits' comes from Paul's pen."[17] According to Stanley, the intensity of Paul's conversion and subsequent spiritual experiences, and his brilliant, practical intelligence, made him keenly aware and exceptionally capable of analysing the subtleties of the dynamics of the spiritual life. Stanley is emphatic that for Paul the gifts of the Spirit do not obliterate human reason. Rather, they supplement the natural human capacities for reasoning. He observes that "Paul's approach to the Christian life may be characterized as eminently rational and practical, provided such qualification be understood within the context of faith and love and hope." He adds that while faith empowers the believer to share in the wisdom of God concerning things that exceed human reason, it "does not destroy his reason, nor lessen his obligation to act as a responsible person":[18]

> This discernment, which is to be made by the Christian in every concrete situation of his existence, is carried out effectively with the help of the indwelling Spirit of God, whose dynamic presence provides the certainty that a correct moral judgment has been made. Thus in every individual action which he performs, the Christian must decide the issue for himself, and assume responsibility for it.[19]

This practical reliance upon both natural reason and spiritual gifts is evident in Paul's response to an ethical problem faced by the Corinthian Christian community. Much of the meat for sale in ancient Corinth would have been used in pagan sacrifices before arriving at the marketplace. Since consuming meat originating from these sacrifices would seem to imply participation in idol worship, this posed a moral dilemma. Paul's response was twofold. First, he distinguished the knowledge that is a spiritual gift from the superficial "knowledge" that generated false scruples about this issue. In virtue of the spiritual gift of knowledge, "we know that 'there is no idol in the world,' and that 'there is no God but one.'"[20] In other words, a person who has genuine spiritual knowledge will know that he or she cannot possibly be worshipping a god that does not exist by consuming sacrificed animal flesh. Second, Paul turns to what both ordinary human reason and the gift of discernment will recognize as the real issue – whether consuming or not consuming sacrificed meat will scandalize others in the community, some of whom are still struggling to shake off the effects of previous religious practices. This concern will be evident to ordinary, practical understanding which comprehends the good of a harmonious community, along with the considerable difficulties of maintaining that harmony. Paul's spiritual discernment also recognized the further good of union of the community with God – and the many ways that value can also be sundered. Paul recognized, therefore, that it requires both discernment as a gift, as well as practical reason, to know how to act ethically in regard to something as seemingly trivial as whether or not to consume sacrificed meat.[21]

As with Aristotle, Paul understood discernment as dependent upon a special capacity for sophisticated self-understanding, though Paul also understood this capacity to be given by God. Just as Aristotle saw the self-reflective knowledge of *euphuia* as essential to the effective practices of the *euphuês* themselves, something similar is also the case with Paul. Spiritual discernment depends upon understanding oneself as gifted with the Spirit. For Paul, that self-understanding grew out of his intense awareness of how different a self he was before and after his conversion. His reflections on those differences developed in him the capacity to pronounce normatively not only upon the spiritual significances of dietary practices, but upon a whole host of other topics as well. He was aware of how easy it is to be misled in spiritual and ethical matters, especially among those he recently converted from pagan religions. This led him to emphasize how essential the presence of members possessing this gift of discernment would be to the life of Christian communities.

1.5   Ignatius of Loyola

Aristotle and Paul both focused on the need for a special capacity in order to practise discernment well, but they devoted little if any attention to how to acquire or enhance this capacity. That was, however, a fundamental concern for Ignatius of Loyola. He elaborated what he meant by discernment in the context of his "spiritual exercises," which were intended to help develop people's capacities for discernment. Hence if we are to properly understand what Ignatius meant by discernment more generally, it is necessary to describe Ignatius's spiritual exercises and the place of discernment in them.

The Ignatian spiritual exercises are one form of a religious retreat, where a person withdraws from ordinary daily commitments for a limited period of time in order to pursue spiritual enrichment. Ignatius recommended that a person making the spiritual exercises withdraw for a period of thirty days and engage in a series of activities under the guidance of a director of the exercises, although he also made provisions for people who were not able to leave commitments for such a lengthy period.[22] The director guides the person making the exercises according to *The Spiritual Exercises*, a text of meditations, prayers, and contemplative practices compiled by Ignatius. Drawing upon his own experiences and insights into spiritual dynamics, he spent almost twenty years revising and refining his text.

Although he articulated his view of discernment in the context of these spiritual exercises, Ignatius did not intend that discernment should be confined to a retreat period. He expected that after the retreat, people would use in their daily lives what they had discovered about discernment and decision making. As Edouard Poussset has put it, these practices of discernment are

> valid not merely for the macro-decision that involves an entire life, nor even merely for the decision of a moderate magnitude that plans a reform. They are also suited for directing the multitude of choices implied in the running of a household, the carrying out of a profession and all our relationships with others, even if it is only a question of saying or not saying a *word*.[23]

The primary objective of the exercises is to assist a person in making decisions in conformity with God's will. But just what does it mean to speak of "God's will"? In his scholarly studies of Ignatius's spiritual writings, Jules Toner argues that according to Ignatius, God's will is "to give us greater glory," which means God wills for us to participate in, and indeed to be in union with, the unconditional love and goodness that is the very being of God – the "uncreated glory" that God is.[24] Ignatius's exercises were constructed to help retreatants discover that this really is also their own deepest desire, that this is what they themselves most profoundly wish to freely choose as well. At bottom, God's will is what humans would will freely, if liberated from ignorance and distorting biases. In this way, Ignatius shares with Aristotle the view that most people are misled about the happiness that they truly desire, and that special efforts are needed to overcome these deceptions.[25]

Toner argues further that Ignatius understood God's will to be highly specific to each individual in her or his uniqueness. God's will is specially matched to the qualities as well as biographical and cultural specificities of each individual person, and to the specific decision he or she is considering. What might be God's will for one person in one concrete situation will not necessarily the same for another person in different circumstances. As Toner puts it,

> Ignatius is not proposing a way of finding any universal moral principle ... Ignatius is rather proposing a way of finding God's will for this particular person with this temperament and character, with these gifts or limitations of nature and grace, at this certain stage of development (physical, intellectual, emotional, moral, religious). God's will thus understood involves this person's relationship with God and with other humans in this present situation with all its circumstances of place, time, culture, social structures, customs and so on.[26]

From these observations, it follows that the uniqueness of God's will for each individual person is deeply connected to the glory of God in still another way. In choosing to act in accord with the glory that God wills for the person individually, that person chooses to play her or his unique role in the construction of social relationships, institutions, cultures, and history, through which the glory of all humankind is being brought about. Any particular human decision, no matter how seemingly insignificant, is to be viewed as "God's positive will regarding something to be done *by* that person."[27] If the person actually chooses to act in that way, this decision contributes to the realization of God's glory in the whole history of humankind, and indeed of the evolving of all creation. Once again, Toner comments:

> The greater glory is not to be thought of merely in terms of the immediate consequences of a choice or even in terms of the clearly envisioned long-range consequences, but in terms of the consequences for the ultimate glory to be achieved through the whole of history.[28]

Thus, for Ignatius, God's will is situated in the context of "an incomplete universe, an unfinished created glory" which is brought to realization through "the great glory of persons who have the amazing destiny and dignity of being [God's] intelligent, loving and free co-workers."[29]

But how could a person ever possibly know whether or not the decision he or she is considering would be a contribution to the glory of the whole of human history and the universe? Toner observes that this is certainly beyond the bounds of ordinary human knowledge. In his books, Toner sets himself the task of showing how Ignatius dealt with this problem in the composition of *The Spiritual Exercises*. By way of anticipation, I would add that neither Ignatius nor Toner developed a rigorously grounded philosophy of history that would enable them to respond to further questions about how the spiritual exercises could possibly meet this challenge. However, Bernard Lonergan devoted his life's work to developing just such a philosophy of history. One of the objectives of this book is to show how Lonergan's work can provide answers to these sorts of further questions.

Ignatius was convinced that God does make it possible for individuals to know how they are called to act for God's glory in history through the special promptings, or "movements" or "spirits," given to each human being within her or his consciousness. In his *Exercises*, he provided guidelines ("rules for the discernment of spirits") to assist people in how to discern these movements, in order to make decisions in conformity with God's will.[30] What Ignatius calls "rules" are not so much rules in the usual sense at all – directives to perform (or not perform) certain actions, often accompanied by sanctions for failures to obey.[31] Many are, rather, descriptions intended to aid the discerner (with the guidance of a director) in noticing subtleties in her or his consciousness.[32]

For example, Ignatius described what he called a "third time of election," a process leading up to a choice.[33] He characterizes this process as "a tranquil time" when a person freely uses her or his "natural powers" such as "insight, reason, imagination, memory, and will ... finding the significant facts and reasoning correctly."[34] By "tranquil" he means two things:

first, the use of these natural powers of human thought and reason are exercised under the guidance of actually and explicitly desiring to know God's will (i.e., "to serve God and save one's soul");[35] second, and as a consequence of the first, "tranquility" means without disturbance by feelings or impulses that would distract the processes of natural reasoning from the goal specified by the desire to serve God's greater glory. This does not mean that no feelings whatsoever accompany human reasoning during this third "time." For one thing, tranquility is itself a feeling. For another, the *desire* to know God's will is also a feeling and is indispensable to this way of using one's reasoning processes. Without such desire, the natural powers would lack direction and orientation as to what kinds of facts sought by reasoning would count as significant. Furthermore, as Toner points out, Ignatius understood that this desire itself is a gift from God, and thereby has the power to give the proper orientation to such thinking. Any feelings or impulses that deviate from the direction of this gift of desire will disrupt true feeling of tranquility, and therefore will not contribute to knowledge of God's will.[36]

The Ignatian *Exercises* also famously include "rules" for the discernment of what he called "spiritual consolations and desolations."[37] Toner claims that Ignatius built his discernment of spiritual consolations upon the ordinary meaning of the word "consolation" as meaning "feelings of peace, gladness, sweetness, well-being, and the like, replacing or easing a feeling of disturbance, depression, bitterness, distress, and so on." He continues, "We find consolation in religious contemplation, in philosophical study, in making love, in playing music, in drinking and chatting with boon companions."[38] Ignatius presumed this familiarity with ordinary kinds of consolations as a stepping stone towards discerning *spiritual* consolations. What distinguishes consolations as spiritual in Ignatius's proper sense is that the consoled becomes "aflame" with the love of God, and by loving each finite, created thing not in itself but rather as caught up within this love of God.[39]

By way of contrast, we also commonly experience feelings of desolation "because of a broken friendship, death of a beloved one, frustrated ambition, loss of status," and so on. In discerning spiritual desolations, a person comes to notice that they share the emotional tone of these common feelings, but run even deeper to include "a loss of faith, hope, and charity as opposed to increase of these; tepidity as opposed to warmth; a feeling as if separated from God as opposed to the sense of union; dryness or coldness toward God and spiritual things as opposed to inflamed love."[40]

In Ignatius's view, the spiritual consolations properly understood can offer support to choosing God's will, while the spiritual desolations tend to threaten and to undermine such choices. Hence he offered his "rules" to help the director and the retreatant to identify these movements, and offered advice as to how best to respond to them.

Among the consolations, Ignatius singled out a special group that he called "consolations without preceding cause." The "preceding causes" that Ignatius had in mind are "a person's own acts of understanding and will," such as "any previous perception or understanding of any [finite] object."[41] Ignatius held that when consolations occur without any prior promptings by the person or any other creature, they can only come immediately from God. As such, according to Ignatius, they are immune from any deception. So it might seem that courses of action inspired or endorsed by consolations without preceding cause are infallible signs of God's will for that person.

However, Toner argues in great detail that this would be a serious misinterpretation of Ignatius's teachings about the discernment of spirits. He points out, first, that Ignatius says that consolations without preceding cause are only *without deception,* but nowhere says that they are surefire confirmations of a course of action.[42] Second, Toner points out how difficult it is, with regard to any given experience of consolation, to be absolutely certain that it is indeed *without* preceding cause and is therefore directly from God. Third, he shows further that Ignatius's main reason for addressing consolations without preceding cause is in order to alert people about serious misdirections that can follow even such profound experiences of God's grace. For this reason, he advises that it is important to carefully distinguish between the periods of time when one is actually in the throes of consolation without preceding cause from "the following time, in which the person is still glowing and graced by the residue of consolation that is now over with."[43] For while judgments and decisions made solely on the basis of, and within, the period of consolation without preceding cause are free of delusion, judgments and decisions made in the period of afterglow do not automatically enjoy the same immunities. Ignatius drew upon on his keen insights into his own intense experiences of consolations and desolations and counselled that, especially during this afterglow, "these purposes and opinions are in need of prolonged and careful examination before full assent is given to them or they are put into execution."[44]

Even desolations can play an important part in this growth in the love of God and commitment to discerning and doing the will of God. In fact, most of the "rules" for discernment focus upon the desolations. They explain how the sources of desolations can be evil spirits, and therefore the "counsels" of desolations are not to be trusted. Ignatius advises, for example, that "desolation is no time at all to change purposes and decisions with which one was content the day before … or the decisions with which one was content during the previous consolation."[45] But, perhaps surprisingly, Ignatius held that desolations can come from the divine Spirit as well. Even "a good person has dimensions of his or her personality not yet set toward God. When the good spirit touches on these there can be disturbance."[46] With sophisticated discernment and the assistance of an experienced director, therefore, a person can learn to recognize such desolations as revelations of unconverted dimensions of her or his personality, and invitations to reverse these to promote more harmonious growth in love of God.

Therefore, consolations, whether with or without preceding cause, are not a substitute for discernment. They are, rather, points of departure for discernment, or, to be more precise, they are no more than components in the more comprehensive practices of discernment of spirits. Such discernment is the prolonged and careful examination of the proposed judgments and decisions that arise in conjunction with consolations and desolations.

This brings us to one of the most important assumptions underlying Ignatius's directions for discernment – the kind of person engaging in the spiritual exercises. As Toner puts it, "All else in discernment depends first on knowing what sort of person is experiencing the diverse motions" from the Spirit of God as well as from ignoble sources.[47] Knowing the kind of person is basic because Ignatius recognizes that a person moving towards God will experience as consolation what a person moving away from God will experience as desolation – and vice versa. Toner is emphatic that directors of the spiritual exercises, before "attempting to interpret the inner motions [of retreatants must] always try first of all to know not only where the other *is* spiritually, but much more importantly, whether the other *is progressing or regressing* spiritually, maturing or decaying."[48]

Yet in order to make such judgments objectively, directors must themselves have come to self-knowledge about their own periods of progress and regression as they themselves moved gradually towards maturity in discernment. They have to understand their own development to guide another's. But the *Spiritual Exercises* does not provide any "rules to guide directors" in making these sorts of judgments about the orientation and present development of retreatants; rather, it assumes that such judgments have already been made prior to employing Ignatius's "rules for discernment." Some kind of prior discernment of the orientation (progress or decline) of persons determines how the rules for discernment are to be applied. Ignatius presupposed that a decent upbringing, human reason, and the teachings of the Church offer the guidance needed by the director in order to judge whether or not a retreatant is advancing or declining. Or, to be more accurate, prior discernment facilitates judgments concerning what dimensions of a person are advancing and what dimensions are still pulling away from God. The parts that are advancing will receive movements from the Spirit in consolation, while other parts will experience them as desolations.

But this raises the question of a wider background field of discernment. Ignatius's genius was in understanding the subtle and conflicting dynamics within the consciousnesses of people genuinely attempting to grow in their commitment to follow God's call. But those directions are effective only within a larger setting that provides effective answers to such questions as "What is reason?" and "What is progress or decline?" and "How and when has the Church been able to work its way towards ever more refined understandings of God's revelation?" These are the kinds of questions addressed by discernment in Bernard Lonergan's sense of self-appropriation. Although the details of how Lonergan approached these various issues will be taken up in subsequent chapters, the next section provides a preliminary sketch of how Lonergan's notion of self-appropriation is connected to these prior notions of discernment.

1.6   Bernard Lonergan

The term "discernment" only appears twice in Bernard Lonergan's masterwork, *Insight* – once having to do with discernment of subtle systematic patterns in seemingly random data, and again in connection with the need for discernment to account for all that needs to be considered in reaching judgments of fact and belief.[49] Nevertheless, I think it is possible to see the notion of self-appropriation that he set forth in *Insight* and later works as an extension of Ignatian discernment. Robert Doran in particular has drawn attention to the "tone" of *Insight*, and to the experiences of consolation that several people have had in their readings of the book. As he puts it:

> This consolation is related to an illumination that *Insight* can effect: in fact this world *is* intelligible, things *do* hold together, we *can* make sense of the universe and of our lives, we *can* overcome the fragmentation of knowledge, we *can* make true judgments, we *can* make good decisions, we *can* transcend ourselves to what is and to what is good.[50]

Cynthia Crysdale likewise explores the consolation and liberation that come from discernment – the "discovery of discovery" of one's own agency and capacity for knowledge. This is especially true, she argues, for women and others who find themselves marginalized. She selects a telling remark from a series of interviews of women: "I didn't think I had the right to think."[51] Crysdale shows how this lack of self-knowledge plays a key role in patterns of injustice and victimization. For this reason, personal discernment of one's very own activities of understanding, knowing, valuing, choosing, and acting bring about major life transformations: "Each must work out his or her own salvation in fear and trembling. Surely a community can and should guide its members toward forgiveness and healing. But communities can only facilitate *discernment*, and the discovery of discovery is a potent resource on the road to salvation."[52]

This is not to say that Lonergan explicitly thought of himself as widening the scope of Ignatian exercises. There are, however, indications that Lonergan's involvement as a Jesuit with the spiritual exercises influenced how he approached philosophy and theology.

He wrote about the spiritual exercises in at least two places. One came rather late in his career when Lonergan had a momentous insight into the nature of discernment. He described that insight in a letter that he wrote in support of an academic promotion for fellow Jesuit, Harvey Egan, SJ. In that letter he referred to an address that Egan gave to the Jesuit community on the topic, "Consolation without a previous cause." Lonergan wrote,

> I had been hearing those words since 1922 at the annual retreats made by Jesuits preparing for the priesthood. They occur in St. Ignatius's "Rules for the Discernment of Spirits in the Second Week of the Exercises." But now, after fifty-three years, I began for the first time to grasp what they meant … What I was learning was that the Ignatian *examen conscientiae* might mean not an examination of conscience but an examination of consciousness … I was seeing that "consolation" and "desolation" named opposite answers to the question, How do you feel when you pray? … I was hearing that my own work on operative grace in St. Thomas … brought to light a positive expression of what was meant by Ignatius when [he] spoke of "consolation without a previous cause." In Aquinas, grace is operative when the mind is not a mover but only moved; in Ignatius consolation is from God alone when there is not conscious antecedent to account for the consolation.[53]

Through the presentation by Egan, Lonergan came to recognize in a new way connections between his philosophical explorations of human consciousness and the Ignatian spiritual exercises. He discovered in himself something that had been going on for a long time, but this was not something that he had adverted to explicitly or understood with clarity, nor was it something for which he had the proper words to express. With the aid of Egan's talk, Lonergan was able to do all three. He was able to identify certain feelings in the interiority of his own consciousness, and to recognize that the practical writings of Ignatius and the theoretical writings of Aquinas provided him with a correct understanding of those experiences. Lonergan came to recognize that the form of philosophy – self-appropriation – that he originated and practised most of his life was very much in the spirit of the practices of discernment that Ignatius intended in the *Spiritual Exercises*. However, this fact had long been hidden from Lonergan because of the decadent state in which those exercises were communicated to him during the early years of his Jesuit life.[54]

This was not the first time that Lonergan reflected on Ignatius's spiritual exercises. Three decades earlier, in notes entitled "Grace and the Spiritual Exercises of St. Ignatius," Lonergan sought to understand how a revitalized theology might illuminate the place of grace in the spiritual exercises.[55] Drawing upon his studies of Aquinas's theology of grace, Lonergan proposed that the spiritual exercises are concerned with the grace that makes people "more and more fully *and* [ever] more consciously living members of Christ Jesus."[56] According to Lonergan, this seemingly evident fact had been obscured by the state of theology of that day, which had lost its ability to illuminate scripture or life "due to the influence on it of conceptualism."[57]

Already at this early stage of his career, then, Lonergan was aware that the Ignatian exercises and discernment had to do with consciousness and that the theology of that time needed a great deal of rejuvenation in order to deal with this fact. But these notes were probably composed at the time he was writing *Insight*, and perhaps he had not yet fully appreciated the links between the project of self-appropriation and the activities of discernment that he performed during the exercises. Among other things, self-appropriation as set forth in *Insight* did not yet extend to the place of feelings and values in the structures of consciousness. Nevertheless, the insights and details set forth in these notes reveal that Lonergan had been deeply influenced by the Ignatian practices of discernment by the time he was composing *Insight*. It should not be surprising that his philosophical work demonstrates the skills of discerning his own consciousness that he acquired through the spiritual exercises. It is perhaps not a coincidence, therefore, that he would characterize "the book *Insight* [as] therefore a series of *exercises* in self-appropriation."[58]

1.7   Self-Appropriation as Discernment

The remainder of this chapter will indicate how what Lonergan called "self-appropriation" functions as discernment in the senses outlined in the preceding sections. The chapters which follow will, first of all, elaborate in much greater detail what is meant by self-appropriation (especially chapters 3 and 10), and then show the implications that discernment as self-appropriation holds for ethics.

In brief, *self-appropriation begins in coming to know what it is to know, value, and decide for oneself. It continues on to affirm the value of one's own knowing, valuing, and deciding. Self-appropriation reaches its culmination in freely choosing to live in fidelity to that value.*

As with Ignatius, discernment as self-appropriation works with the internal experiences of consciousness. In the first stages of self-appropriation, people pay attention to the experiences of activities in their own consciousnesses that play key roles in knowing, valuing, and deciding. They may have previously noticed some of these activities, but few have noticed all of them. Frequently, people experience this intensified self-awareness with a great sense of exhilaration.[59] Self-appropriation next turns to the more challenging tasks of properly understanding and appreciating the broadened experiences of these activities. Even for those who are more familiar with the diversity and rhythms of their interior experiences, few will have appreciated their full importance and interconnections. In this way, growth in self-understanding and self-appreciation adds on to what increased self-awareness only begins.

Again, as in the Ignatian spiritual exercises, people engaged in self-appropriation gradually discern that among the many activities in their own consciousness, a select few play a more significant role in knowing, valuing, and deciding than do the others. Subsequent chapters will show that the most significant of all such activities are those inquiries arising from the unrestricted desire to know and value, and the act of unrestricted being-in-love. Recognizing their presences and roles intensifies the sense of value not only of these most fundamental acts of consciousness but of everything they influence as well.

Once this deepened sense of self-appreciation emerges, a person is then confronted with the challenge of choosing whether or not to foster that value. This is a challenge because it frequently intensifies awareness of how much of a person's living has been at odds with this newly won self-appreciation, and how difficult it will be to give up old ways and to form new ways of thinking, valuing, and deciding. The choices that this new self-appreciation presents to a person are the choices for or against what Lonergan called conversion (in its several forms). Self-appropriation pursued persistently, then, tends to foster these forms of self-transformation or conversion towards living in fidelity with the value of authentically being a knower, valuer, and decider.[60]

Self-appropriation does not teach people how to perform the activities of knowing, valuing, or deciding. Rather, self-appropriation begins from experiences of knowing, valuing, and deciding that people have been performing all along. As the later chapters of this book will endeavour to show, these activities of knowing, valuing, and deciding are also the activities of trying to live ethically (and even of trying to avoid ethical living) that people have been doing for a long time, well before anyone ever embarked upon any explicitly guided exercises in self-appropriation. But self-appropriation does add "something extra": it adds intensified awareness, better understanding, deeper appreciation, and strengthened commitment to the performance of what is best in the activities that people have been performing all along. For while almost everyone has been performing the activities of ethical thinking and acting for some time, few people have been doing these activities well, and fewer still doing them to perfection. As Immanuel Kant put it so keenly, "Innocence is indeed a glorious thing; but, unfortunately, it does not keep very well and is easily led astray." Hence he offered a "critical examination of our reason" in order to elucidate, refine, chastise, and strengthen its spontaneous but untutored goodness in ordinary living.[61] Aristotle also recognized that dialectic supplemented by the virtue of discernment (*euphuia*) contains a dimension of self-knowledge that is essential to the enhancement of ordinary judging and choosing – a dimension that is essential to authentically pursuing what is true and good. In like manner, discernment as self-appropriation adds to our already operative efforts at ethical living. It adds new levels of self-awareness, self-understanding, self-appreciation, and resolute commitment that will deepen their ethical worth.

Again, as is the case with Ignatian discernment, the success of self-appropriation depends on a community of conversation that includes at least some members who are more advanced in self-appropriation, tracing to Lonergan himself, and beyond him to his own mentors, especially Newman, Aquinas, Aristotle, and Plato.[62] Initially Lonergan seemed to think that the book *Insight* by itself would be sufficient guidance for those undertaking the project of self-appropriation; in fact, this is seldom enough. I cannot imagine that I myself would ever have achieved the level of self-understanding that I have without the assistance of genuine friends who were both patient with me and wise in the kind of self-understanding and self-appreciation that was needed to afford me reliable guidance.

This means, therefore, that discernment as self-appropriation, like Ignatian discernment, is also a socially, culturally, and historically situated phenomenon. Lonergan recognized that any and all of the ethical activities of knowing, valuing, and deciding inescapably arise out of and then contribute to the building up of social relations, social and cultural institutions, and ultimately to the unfolding of human history. To appropriate oneself ethically as a knower, valuer, and decider, therefore, can only be carried out completely if one also appropriates oneself as intrinsically constituted through social relations and as inescapably playing a role in the drama of history.

Still, those already familiar with Lonergan's work might find it puzzling that I place his notion of self-appropriation in line with discernment in the Pauline and Ignatian senses. After all, the book *Insight* is almost completely devoted to the self-appropriation of strictly human cognition – the very sorts of acts of consciousness that Ignatius characterizes as the "natural powers" of "a person's own acts of understanding and will." The invitation issued in *Insight* is to self-appropriation of knowing in the ordinary human modes of common sense, the natural and human empirical sciences, philosophy, and aesthetics (along with the "natural," merely analogical knowledge of God that is possible within the limits of human cognition). This no doubt seems a far cry from learning to discern the movements in consciousness produced directly by the divine Spirit, with the ultimate objective of knowing and doing the greater glory of God. Yet a careful reading of *Insight* reveals that, in his theory of strictly human cognition and the corresponding account of natural reality, Lonergan was setting the stage for a proper theological method – a methodology for knowledge, value, and choice in relation to supernatural realities – God, grace, and revelation.[63] This objective of extending discernment towards God's activity was for the most part carried out in what Lonergan wrote after *Insight,* especially in *Method in Theology.* (See the epigraph to this chapter.) But discernment in this broadened sense never did presuppose anything dogmatically. It broadened the project of the self-appropriation of knowing elaborated in *Insight* to also integrate the conscious activities of feeling, valuing, and deciding, including feelings and thoughts that arise from unrestricted being-in-love. While Lonergan as a Christian theologian would identify this latter set of acts and experiences as from the Spirit, this identification is not presumed in his phenomenological descriptions of them as they occur in consciousness and influence other acts of consciousness.

Lonergan's notion of discernment as self-appropriation in this extended sense, among other things, helps to supply the prior level of discernment presupposed by Ignatius's spiritual exercises – the level that Aristotle referred to as *euphuia.* Aristotle acutely identified both the fact and the all-too-rare presence of *euphuia* in human beings, but he did not go on to specify the activities involved in *euphuia,* or how it can arise through self-appropriation – the application of the operations of knowing, valuing, and deciding to the experiences of those very activities. But something like *euphuia* is presupposed in order to begin Ignatian spiritual exercises with an assessment of the state of a person as headed towards or away from God, for *euphuia* is the something extra that selects the right judgment from the dialectically refined alternatives. Self-appropriation also provides an account of how people know whether their prospective courses of action are wrong or evil – one of the prerequisites for genuine discernment of God's will.

Thus Lonergan's broadened sense of self-appropriation reveals a connection between Aristotle's notion of *euphuia* on the one hand, and the perquisite for Ignatius's spiritual exercises on the other. This is because mature self-appropriation recognizes that all human inquiry headed towards knowledge and commitment to truth and goodness is headed towards God. Likewise, mature self-appropriation also recognizes that all bias against one's own inquiring spirit is also headed away from God. Lonergan derives his account of intellectual and ethical development (progress) from self-appropriation. He also derives his account of the devastating consequences of intellectual and ethical decline from the manners in which biases distort knowing, valuing, and deciding. Together, these provide the self-appropriated basis for a dialectical analysis and for objective judgments about the orientation of a person entering into the spiritual exercises.

Of course, such judgments do not become automatic or infallible just because they are pronounced by people who have achieved some degree of self-appropriation. Rather, genuine and mature self-appropriation has the effect of making people ever more circumspect, cautious, and humble when faced with the task of making such judgments about other people, or even about themselves. What self-appropriation adds is a much more keen and accurate awareness and understanding, and greater sensitivity to the values at stake, and to the large number of things that would have to be taken into account in order to make objective judgments about whether a person is advancing or degenerating spiritually – or more specifically, in which ways this particular person is advancing or declining.

Nor does the matter end there. As Ignatius recognized, the movements of God's grace come mixed together with many other natural, human movements of perception, inquiry, bias, understanding, feelings, and reason. It is quite difficult to notice them all and to distinguish them from one another. It is particularly difficult to notice and clearly distinguish acts that originate from human powers from those that are immediately moved by God. This is accomplished only gradually and with guidance. Where Ignatius provided important guidance for discerning supernatural movements in consciousness, it might be said that Lonergan provided guidance for discernment of the movements of natural human cognition in consciousness. The two forms of discernment complement each other.

1.8   Conclusion

It has not been my intention in this chapter to build a case for the direct influences of Aristotle, St. Paul, or Ignatius on Lonergan's thinking about discernment. Rather, I have endeavoured to show that Lonergan's understanding of self-appropriation is connected at the deepest levels with the thinking of all three about discernment. It is the objective of the rest of this book to elaborate more precisely what Lonergan means by self-appropriation, and to make explicit its great importance for ethics.

As a first step towards that elaboration, the next chapter examines Lonergan's account of factual knowledge and its "intrinsic objectivity," as he called it. That chapter will both explain what he meant by these terms, and why he held that objectivity in knowing facts is indispensable to objectivity in knowing and acting ethically.

2 Objectivity and Factual Knowing: Lonergan's Three Questions

---

What is obvious in knowing is, indeed, looking. Compared to looking, insight is obscure, and the grasp of the unconditioned is doubly obscure. But empiricism amounts to the assumption that what is obvious in knowing is what knowing obviously is.

— Bernard Lonergan, *Insight*

2.1 Introduction

Ethical action requires more than good will. Much harm has been done by well-meaning people who have lacked genuine knowledge of the facts of their circumstances. As Lonergan himself put it, "It is quite true that objective knowing is not yet authentic human living; but without objective knowing there is no authentic living."[1] And again,

> The judgment of value presupposes knowledge of human life, of human possibilities, proximate and remote, of the probable consequences of projected courses of action. When knowledge is deficient, then fine feelings are apt to be expressed in what is called moral idealism, i.e. lovely proposals that don't work out and often do more harm than good.[2]

Objective factual knowledge is therefore most fundamental to ethical authenticity. Lonergan devoted his most vital years to working through the difficult problems associated with factual objectivity. Following Lonergan's lead, then, I begin by offering an overview of his account of objective knowledge of facts.

This starting point should not be taken to imply that I believe that ethical precepts can be derived from knowledge of facts. A remarkably diverse range of philosophers that includes David Hume, Friedrich Wilhelm Joseph von Schelling, and G.E. Moore have long insisted that it is impossible to derive "ought" from "is." I am in fundamental agreement with this emphatic claim. However, the relationship between knowledge of facts and knowledge of values (including the ethical or moral value of the ought[3]) is more complex than has been commonly assumed. The common understandings of this relationship rest upon assumptions about the nature of factual knowledge – assumptions that are ultimately untenable. These flawed assumptions about factual knowledge tend to infiltrate our ways of thinking about knowledge of ethical value. In particular, such assumptions have led to the view that there is no such thing as objective knowledge in the realm of values, including ethical values.

Hence, while I agree with the basic assertion that "ought" cannot be derived from "is," I do not subscribe either to the reasons usually given for the assertion, or to the accounts of ethical knowledge and action based upon those reasons. As will become evident in the chapters that follow, Lonergan's distinctive way of resolving the problem of factual objectivity clarifies the kinds of relationships that actually do hold between knowledge of "is" and knowledge of "ought." It also provides a more reliable basis for approaching the even more knotty question of objective knowledge of value, especially in ethical matters. As a first step, therefore, this chapter offers an overview of Lonergan's philosophy of factual knowledge – what he called "cognitional theory" or theory of cognitional structure.

2.2   Lonergan's Three Questions

On several occasions, Lonergan wrote that his philosophy of knowledge was primarily concerned with answering three fundamental questions: What am I doing when I am knowing? Why is doing that knowing? What do I know when I do that?[4] Although his answers to those three questions are implicit in his writings, to the best of my knowledge he never answered them explicitly as such. The overview offered in this chapter endeavours to make those answers explicit, and is therefore organized along the lines of those three questions. As will become clear, Lonergan's answers reveal that the achievement of objective factual knowledge demands a great deal of discernment on the part of the knowing subject.

2.3   Inquiries, Questions, and Wonder

Inquiry, or questioning, is at the heart of Lonergan's philosophy of cognition. Occasionally I quip with my students that *Inquiry* would have been a more appropriate title for Lonergan's masterwork than *Insight*.[5] I say this because in order to really understand what Lonergan meant by "insight" – to really appropriate one's own acts of insight – requires that one also recognize the ineliminable connection between insights and questions. Insights come as answers to questions. They release the persistent and sometimes even unbearable tension of inquiry that yearns to understand what one does not yet understand.[6]

This tension of inquiry is called by many names: question, problem, puzzlement, quandary, dilemma, and so on. Inquiry is precisely a yearning for knowledge. The tension of an inquiry will not be quelled until the sought-for insight or judgment releases that tension and brings a temporary rest to the soul. Rest does come when the knowledge desired by the inquiry arrives, but that rest is only temporary. When one question is answered, new questions crop up almost instantaneously.

In this way, an inquiry or a question sets a standard. There can be many efforts at answering a question, but unless the efforts really do answer the question, they will not satisfy the desire or resolve the tension of the inquiry. The question is a conscious desire that cannot be satisfied in just any arbitrary way. Questions are tenacious. They can be diverted for a while. They can be stifled or ignored. We can be distracted or flee from the tensions they introduce. But questions will lurk at the periphery of our consciousness, and reassert their tensions when our guards are down. The only thing that can really dismiss the tension that an inquiry introduces is the item of knowledge that it actually desires. All of our attempts at knowledge have to live up to the standards that are inherent in our questions and inquiries. In this sense, it is even misleading to speak of "our questions." It is not so much that we possess the questions; rather, they possess us, pulling us out of the complacency of our prior achievements of knowledge in an unending process of self-transcendence into the unknown, towards ever new knowledge.

I will use the terms "question" and "inquiry" to refer to the pre-linguistic cognitional tension that we endeavour to express linguistically using the interrogative grammatical form. By "pre-linguistic" I do not mean that our inquiry is completely independent of language. Language permeates our very being, as many philosophers from a variety of approaches showed so convincingly in the twentieth century. So of course our inquiries arise in the midst of the flow of our languaged communications, with others and with ourselves. Moreover, our ability to discern nuances among the different kinds of tensions in our inquiry is conditioned by the level of our linguistic competence. A sophisticated level of linguistic competence is the condition for the emergence of sophisticated levels of inquiry.

Nevertheless, most people have had the experience of finding it difficult to put questions and inquiries into words. Before we have words to communicate our questions to others – or to clarify them for ourselves – we experience the intellectual tensions of inquiries. Those intellectual tensions not only set the standards for what will count as proper answers; they also set the standards for the adequacy or inadequacy of our interrogative forms of grammatical formulation. Those intellectual tensions are the prior, fundamental meanings that we subsequently formulate and pose linguistically. I would argue even further that the pre-linguistic phenomenon of questioning or inquiry is one of the indispensable conditions for the very possibility of the emergence of language in human beings.

Lonergan spoke of this pre-linguistic experience of inquiry as "pure question": "[Pure question] is prior to any insights, any concepts, any words; for insights, concepts, words have to do with answers, and before we look for answers we *want* them; such *wanting* is the pure question."[7] However, in order to avoid confusion between the linguistic expression and the phenomenon upon which it depends, I will use either "inquiry" or "question" to refer to the pre-linguistic desire (wanting) for cognition, and "formulated question" (or some variant) to refer to the linguistic expressions of questions.

There are, of course, some uses of interrogative expressions that are not direct expressions of a genuine cognitional inquiry seeking an unknown answer. So-called rhetorical questions are examples of formulated questions that are not direct expressions of genuine inquiries. Yet even these forms of interrogative expressions depend upon the more original meanings of questions that reside in the pre-linguistic tensions of inquiry. In courtroom interrogations, for example, questions are frequently asked when the attorney already knows the answer. As such, she is not expressing her own tension of inquiry, because she is not actually experiencing a desire for knowledge that corresponds to the interrogative expression. But even when interrogators already know the answers, the meaningfulness of their utterances still rests upon the primordial phenomenon of this conscious tension of inquiry about and desire for an answer that is as yet unknown to the hearers of their interrogative speech. Such formulated questions are asked in the presence of and for the sake of others who do not know the answers – jurors, for example. Their dramatic import depends upon the fact that the linguistically expressed question evokes the pre-linguistic experience of inquiry in the jurors. Something similar happens in the cases of formulated questions posed to students by a teacher, or to an audience by a public speaker. When lecturers pose rhetorical questions in such circumstances, the speaker already knows the answer. Nevertheless the meaningfulness of his or her rhetoric depends upon the primordial phenomenon of this conscious tension towards and desire for an answer that is experienced as unknown by at least some in the audience.

This does not mean that the listeners do not frequently respond in unexpected and very novel ways to questions posed by police officers, lawyers, teachers, lecturers, and others. Of course they do. When they do, they reveal to the interrogator that the linguistic formulation of the question can simultaneously express an inquiry different from the one originally intended. When this happens, the language of the response reflects back and reveals a new pre-linguistic tension of inquiry to the interrogator.

Through all these variations in interrogative expressions, the phenomenon of questioning underpins and constitutes the meaningfulness of these grammatical forms. Throughout all of these variations, the standard set forth by the tension of inquiry is ever present.

It follows that Lonergan's three questions express three inquiries about inquiry. As the next sections will endeavour to show, Lonergan's answers to his three questions reveal that many other conscious activities are underpinned, knitted together, and constituted as cognitional by the phenomena of questioning and inquiry. Those sections (as well as the next chapters) will explore how the primordial wonder that underlies all inquiries differentiates into many different kinds of questions. They will explore how those different kinds of questions seek different kinds of answers known through different kinds of conscious activities. They will further explore how the differentiated kinds of questions serve to link together the diverse answers and acts of consciousness. This linked sequence of questions and answers forms what Lonergan called "cognitional structure."

2.4 Cognitional Structure: What Am I Doing When I Am Knowing?

The answer to Lonergan's first question – "What am I doing when I am knowing?" – is given in his account of cognitional structure itself. That account begins with a list such as that given in his classic essay, "Cognitional Structure": "Now human knowing involves many distinct and irreducible activities: seeing, hearing, smelling, touching, tasting, inquiring, imagining, understanding, conceiving, reflecting, weighing the evidence, judging."[8]

The list is meant to be suggestive, not exhaustive. Many other terms could be added almost indefinitely to the list, referring to additional activities or drawing attention to fine distinctions among activities falling within the broad categories included in the list. Still, Lonergan's objective was not the impossible goal of exhaustively listing all manner of cognitional activities; rather, his objective was analysis of the *structure* within which these activities occur. His answer to "What am I doing when I am knowing?" is "I am performing a structure of activities." It is the essential and dynamic structure of relations among the activities that are the true heart and soul of Lonergan's cognitional theory because, in Lonergan's view, no one of these activities alone constitutes human knowing. Rather, human knowing is a *structure* of many activities. Hence each particular activity is at best a partial contribution to the whole of human knowing. His objective, then, is to draw attention to the whole of the structure, making certain that none of the most fundamental constituent activities is overlooked in the account of the whole of knowing.

The word "structure," however, itself can be misleading. Structure has static connotations of fixity and rigidity. Lonergan attempts to undermine those connotations by means of an oxymoron, insisting that human knowing is a "dynamic structure."[9] In some ways, it might have been preferable to speak of a stream or flow of activities.[10] Yet these alternate phrasings have their own limitations as well. To speak of a stream or flow makes it sound as though the activities are carried along in a stream of internal time consciousness that is somehow given prior to and apart from those activities – as in, say, Newton's Absolute Time as a pre-given foundation for the universe, or time as an a priori condition of the possibility of all experiencing (i.e., a form of intuition). A flow or stream of activities of consciousness can, therefore, suggest a dynamic order imposed by an alien stream in which the activities are mere passengers along for the ride. Then the order of their sequence would be merely coincidental. In a stream of consciousness in this sense, there need not be any intrinsic relationships among the succession of activities.

Lonergan, on the other hand, insists that in human knowing each of the activities in the sequence has intrinsic and dynamic relationships to other activities. It is this set of dynamic relationships that constitutes the structure as a whole, and thereby constitutes each of the activities as a contribution to knowing. While not denying that there is a temporal stream of consciousness, Lonergan emphasized a further and more fundamental dynamic structuring of consciousness[11] – hence his preference for the phrase "dynamic structure."

In Lonergan's analysis, therefore, inquiry plays the central role in structuring the various activities of consciousness. The activities of inquiry determine how the entire assembly of the remaining activities is organized and structured. In addition, since acts of inquiry introduce intellectual tension into knowing, they are also the sources of the dynamism in the structure. One could think of the activities of inquiry as the dynamic relations and the other activities in the list as related to one another by the inquiries.

2.4.1 *The Patterned Stream of Experiencing, Remembering, Imagining*

The first group of activities in Lonergan's list – seeing, hearing, smelling, touching, tasting – are familiar acts of sense experiencing. Most obviously missing from his list are acts of experiencing bodily posture and motion –

what might be called bodily kinesthetic experiencing. Also missing are sense experiencings such as feeling pain, heat, cold, itchiness, and so on. The list could be further expanded; for instance, each of the terms could be further subdivided – hearing a blaring horn differs from hearing a lark's song. Not only do the contents (sounds) heard differ, but also the qualities of the acts of hearing differ. This list could be extended indefinitely not only for hearing but for all other acts of sense experiencing. Soon, the effort to enumerate such differences and nuances reaches a point of diminishing returns. Most of these acts are already familiar to most readers, and that is part of the point to elaborating Lonergan's list – to direct readers' attention to conscious activities such as these. But again, Lonergan's main objective was not to provide an exhaustive list of all activities of sense experiencing. Rather, he sought to draw attention to the relations among the acts of sense experiencing and other acts of consciousness. Hence I will move along to other acts of consciousness in his list that are perhaps less familiar.

Next in Lonergan's list is "imagining," but "remembering" should also be added. What I mean here by acts of remembering are acts that recapitulate the contents of previous acts of sense experiencing. In the modern West, at least, we tend to think of remembering previous visual contents – remembering a face, a sunset, an automobile accident. Still, a little reflection will reveal that we also have rich auditory memories – memories of a friend's voice, a song, a clap of thunder. We also have occasional memories of tactile sensations, bodily movements, tastes, odours, etc. While the latter are less obvious to most of us, some people develop highly sophisticated abilities to recall such sensations – choreographers, dancers, skaters, and other athletes, for example, can recall bodily movements with great nuance.

If remembering is recapitulation of past sensory content, then acts of imagining in Lonergan's sense are constructive extensions of sense contents into images that one has never had before – or, at least, imagining involves creative modifications of previous sense contents (e.g., imagining a purple cow or imagining a straight line in an empty plane with no other surrounding objects). As with memory, imagination in this specific sense is usually associated with visual constructions. Yet talented musicians and poets develop sophisticated abilities to imagine sounds, and others with effort are able to develop abilities to imagine movements, tactile sensations, and perhaps even tastes and smells.

Because the contents of acts of imagining and remembering are very similar to the contents of acts of sensing, young children begin to recognize these distinctions only slowly, haltingly, and with difficulty. Very young children easily confuse remembering with imagining. They also occasionally confuse both remembering and imagining with sensing – becoming frightened by a memory or fantasy of a frightening thing or event, as though it were right there, present in the room with them. The earliest stages of discernment are accomplished in early childhood as accurate recognition of these distinctions becomes more stable and reliable. Since, however, other acts besides those of sensing, imagining, and remembering are also mixed into the streams of consciousness, later stages of discernment are also needed. These later stages of discernment do not occur as spontaneously or frequently as do the childhood stages of discriminating between sensing, remembering, and imagining. In part, this book is intended to assist readers in moving through these further stages.

I have been using the terms "imagining" and "remembering" in somewhat specialized and restricted ways. They seem to exclude wide ranges of connotations commonly associated with both imagining and remembering. People speak of creative imagination and of imagining a world in which everyone lives in peace and harmony. Richard Kearney, for example, has explored rich dimensions of imagination.[12] St. Augustine and Henri Bergson give much richer accounts of memory than the one I offered above.[13] The authors of *Habits of the Heart* speak of "communities of memory."[14] All of these discussions of imagination and memory go well beyond the mere recapitulation or constructive expansion of the contents of sense experiences. They offer wider accounts of memory and imagination infused with meaning, feeling, comprehension, value, wonder, awe, and even terror. However, I am deliberately using the terms for imagination and memory in limited and technical senses. In doing so, I am not unaware of the important, non-sensate dimensions that permeate imagination and memory in these wider senses; rather, I am aiming at a more refined degree of discernment. Phrases like "creative imagination" or "remembering a childhood" do not refer to single acts of consciousness – rather, they refer to a compound of conscious acts. "Creative imagination" includes acts of sense-like imaginative contents, but also includes acts of wondering, understanding, feeling, and valuing. "Remembering a childhood" includes recapitulated sense contents, but also adds concomitant acts of feeling (such as nostalgia), imaginative reconfiguration, understanding, critical assessment, and acts of relating past sensations to present circumstances and future hopes or anxieties. There is usually a tacit recognition of the multilayered compounds of different sorts of acts that are implicit in these richer, ordinary uses of the terms "imagining" and "remembering." However, frequently, there is a tendency to collapse or overlook these differences within the whole that is the compound structures of acts and to speak of imagination or memory as though they were single acts rather than compound acts. Usually this poses little difficulty, but in certain contexts the failure to discern the differences among the constituents of a creative imagination or a rich memory can lead to various distortions. Hence, Lonergan found it valuable to introduce a more nuanced and technical meaning of "imagination" (and, implicitly, "memory") as just the acts that parallel those of sense experiencing.

These distinctions among sensing, imagining, and remembering in the strict sense are not obvious at the outset. Activities of sense experiencing, imagining, and remembering do not occur in isolated packages, nicely wrapped and tagged with appropriate labels. These acts of consciousness come mixed together in flows and streams of consciousness (in "patterns of experiencing," as Lonergan refers to them[15]). Among the elements making up our patterned stream are the wide range of experiences that arise from touch, breathing and blood circulation, muscular tensions and relaxations, posture, and balance (from the sensory apparatus of our inner ears). This means that our experiencing is always embodied.

While the numerous elements of sense experience arising from our physical bodies always surround visual and auditory experience, they often do so in very muted ways. Elements of sight and sound are frequently more intense and occupy the focus of our attention in sensory experiencing. The prominence, or lack thereof, of these bodily elements in our patterned flow of experiencing depends upon the sets of interests and concerns, as well as linguistic and cultural influences, that contribute to the structuring of that flow. Neither external stimuli nor the biochemical processes in our neurophysiology completely determine the exact contents or the patterned arrangement of our sensing, remembering, and imagining. Our interests and concerns as mediated by cultures select what will actually rise to the level of conscious presentation from among the vast range of possibilities available from our neural functionings. Although there is always a correspondence between what is happening in our nervous systems and what enters the flow of experience, that relationship is not one-way from below upward. Our conscious experiencing, then, is never a bare, unmediated contact either with the state of our nerve-impulses or with the external world that stimulates them. We will return to the ways in which our interests and concerns, and language and cultures, determine what enters into our actual conscious experiencing in the next section, as well as in later chapters.[16]

Learning to notice the distinctions among acts and contents of sensing, remembering, and imagining in the limited senses is the work of discernment. Discernment is also needed in order to detect the presence of intellectual, affective, judgmental, and evaluative elements in what are called experience, memory, and imagination in broader senses. In addition, discernment is called for to identify the kinds of interests and concerns that are actually involved in determining what does and does not come into our consciousness. By introducing these various distinctions, it was my intention in the present section to stimulate the interest of the reader in developing this level of discernment.

2.4.2 *Questions for Intelligence and Acts of Understanding*

According to Lonergan, cognitional inquiries or questions divide into two basic types: questions for intelligence and questions for reflection.[17] First, questions for intelligence are expressed in sentences using words such as "what," "why," "how," "where," "when," "who," "how many," and "how often." Such questions arise in reference to the contents of acts of experiencing. In fact, what constitutes the acts of sensing, remembering, and imagining, discussed above as cognitional acts of experiencing in Lonergan's technical sense, is that their contents give rise to this first type or level of questions. In Lonergan's analysis, it is their capacity to elicit questions for intelligence that *constitutes* them *as* experiencing with a properly cognitional valence.[18] Moreover, inquiry in its elemental sweep can even be responsible for the selection of the experiential elements that actually come to consciousness precisely *as* contributions to cognition.[19] Hence, inquiries constitute and structure the cognitional dimension of our experiencing.

Questions for intelligence stand intermediary between acts of experiencing (which are inquired about) and acts of understanding or "direct insights" (which are sought after by these inquiries). Lonergan regards these acts of understanding or insights as the fundamental acts of human intelligence. As such, questions for intelligence serve to dynamically relate direct insights to acts of experiencing. Inquiry in this sense is the elementary instance of human self-transcendence. By inquiring, a human subject is pulled beyond merely experiencing towards something that lies beyond experiencing – namely, understanding (insight) and its unique and distinctive content (which Lonergan termed "intelligibility"). Such inquiries also endow acts of understanding with a special status among other acts of consciousness. Direct insights are the conscious activities that release the tension of inquiry present in questions for intelligence, and thereby answer the questions of what, why, how, etc. By their very nature, this is what direct insights (or acts of understanding) are: activities that answer questions for intelligence and dissipate their tensions. Because a question for intelligence introduces the tension and thereby establishes the standard that its answer must meet, only an intelligent act of direct insight is capable of meeting that standard – by definition, as it were. Acts that do not fully and adequately resolve that tension are not at all answers to that question. This is why Lonergan refers to questions of this first type as questions for intelligence.

Hence, while activities from Lonergan's list other than direct insights are indispensable to the structured process of cognition, they are not the acts that questions for intelligence seek. When other activities (e.g., sensing, remembering, or imagining) occur in inquiry-structured cognition, they are structured to be auxiliaries that assist the emergence of insights.[20] Hence questions for intelligence structure a multitude of acts of sense experiencing, remembering, and imagining into dynamic relationships with acts of understanding.

Almost hidden in Lonergan's list of cognitional activities is "understanding," although he certainly considered intelligent acts of understanding to be of supreme importance in human knowing. In his usage, the terms "understanding" and "insight" are equivalent and interchangeable. He complained about the "little attention" that insights had received in the history of philosophy because they seem "so simple and obvious."[21] Perhaps the best way to approach the task of highlighting the act of insight is by means of an example. The example I offer is the well-known story by Friedrich August Kekulé regarding his discovery of the circular structure of the benzene molecule:

> I was sitting, writing on my textbook; but the work did not progress; my thoughts were elsewhere. I turned my chair to the fire and dozed. Again the atoms were gamboling before my eyes. This time the smaller groups kept modestly in the background. My mental eye, rendered more acute by the repeated visions of the kind, could now distinguish larger structures of manifold conformation: long rows sometimes more closely fitted together; all twining and twisting in snake-like motion. But look! What was that? One of the snakes had seized hold of its own tail, and the form whirled mockingly before my eyes. As if by a flash of lightning I awoke; and this time also I spent the rest of the night in working out the consequences of the hypothesis.[22]

This vignette provides much more than a description of a single act of insight. It is, rather, a narrative that situates that act of discovery ("flash of lightning") amidst several other prior and subsequent activities: the underlying tension of inquiry, the vividly varying flow of acts of imagining, and the subsequent activities of working out the consequences.

While it is unlikely that any reader has been puzzling about the structure of the benzene molecule, it is almost certain that she or he has been carrying around one or another inquiry as Kekulé did. Insights do not occur only in the realms of science and mathematics; inquiries and the insights that release their tensions are common experiences. People have insights every day into how to get an appliance to work, how to cheer up a friend, how to plan a trip, or how to organize their finances. Insights and their distinctive ("intelligible") contents abound in everyday life, in artistic creativity, in the labours of erudite scholarship, and in other areas as well.

Because they are so mundane, these more common insights are initially difficult to discern. Discernment of one's own insights is also made difficult by this distinctive nature of their contents. In his conception of the phenomenological method, Edmund Husserl introduced a powerful and useful analytic tool: the relationship between an act of consciousness (*noesis*) and the content or object of that act (*noema*).[23] Knowledge of this relationship can aid in discerning the different kinds of acts of consciousness by means of their contents. For example, a *noetic* act of seeing is that which makes conscious the *noematic* contents of shape and colour. Using a phenomenological method, one can begin with the *noematic* sense-content and work back to its constituting *noetic* activity or activities of sensation. But the *noetic* acts of insights are distinctive because they do not share any of the *noematic* contents of sensing, imagining, or remembering. The contents of insights are *sui generis*; they are not at all like sensible or imaginable contents.[24] Lonergan thus adopted the term "intelligibility" to designate the *noematic* contents of insights.[25]

But this dramatic difference between the intelligible contents of insights and the more familiar sensible or imaginable contents of the other acts of consciousness makes it difficult to begin with the intelligible *noematic* content as a means of heightening our awareness of the *noetic* act. When people exclaim, "Oh, now I see the answer," they are in fact referring to acts of insight. What they precisely are *not* doing is *seeing*. They are instead having an insight that grasps a non-visual intelligible content. Ordinary language, therefore, often mistakenly conflates insights and their *noematic* contents with much more familiar contents of visual sensation which usually accompany insights. As Lonergan put it, "What is obvious in knowing is, indeed, looking. Compared to looking, insight is obscure, and the grasp of the unconditioned is doubly obscure. But empiricism amounts to the assumption that what is obvious in knowing is what knowing obviously is."[26]

In opposition to this empiricist and commonsense position, Lonergan held that each insight has a distinctive, intelligible content that is irreducible to the acts or consciousness of sensing, remembering, or imagining.

Precisely because questions for intelligence and insights are so frequent and common, and because their intelligible contents are neither visible nor tangible, the insights that are most noticeable and most easily discernable for a beginner are those that come "suddenly and unexpectedly"[27] as dramatic releases to especially intense tensions of inquiry. The path towards more refined discernment begins with the dramatic instances but then moves gradually towards an ever greater refinement of the ability to notice the ever more subtle inquiries and insights that make up the fabric of one's everyday knowing and living.

2.4.3 *Questions for Reflection, Judging, and Reflective Understanding*

There is also a second, distinct type of cognitional inquiry, namely the type expressed in a grammatical form such as "Is it so?"[28] Lonergan refers to these somewhat misleadingly as "questions for reflection." Questions for reflection do not really "look back" at anything, as the term seems to suggest. Unlike questions for intelligence, questions for reflection arise, not in direct relation to the sensible contents of acts of experiencing, but in direct relation to the intelligible contents of acts of understanding. The "it" in "Is *it* so?" refers back to the *noematic* content of a direct insight. It is about such an intelligible content that one asks an "Is it so?" type of question. Hence, just as questions for intelligence presuppose acts and contents of experiencing, so also questions for reflection presuppose acts and contents of direct understanding.

Questions for reflection also confer a special status upon acts of judging, for only in acts of judging are the tensions of reflective inquiries finally brought to rest. Like the what, why, and how questions, the tension of "Is it so?" questions also establishes a standard that their proper answers, that is to say, judgments, must meet. Such acts of judging are either acts of affirming (expressed linguistically as "yes") or denying (expressed as "no") in response to "Is it so?" questions. One or the other of those activities is what questions for reflection seek. In the end, only affirmative or negative judgments are capable of meeting that standard unconditionally. By their very nature, then, acts of judging in Lonergan's strict sense are those acts of consciousness capable of bringing resolution to questions for reflection.

However, people can and often do verbalize affirmative and negative judgments on fairly arbitrary grounds. Arbitrary affirmations and denials verbalize mere opinions; they are not judgments in the full and proper sense, because they do not ultimately settle the tension of inquiry experienced when a person genuinely entertains a question for reflection – "Is it so?" Any question that has not really been answered will linger in consciousness, perhaps at its periphery or in a submerged form. Yet a discerning mind will be aware of tensions of inquiry that linger and have not been resolved adequately. The cognitive tensions present in questions for reflection can be dulled, but they cannot be completely obliterated by merely arbitrary assertions. Rather, the tension raised in an "Is it so?" question is genuinely resolved only when the affirmation or denial emanates from cognizance of reasonable grounds for that act of judging.

Lonergan carefully analysed the processes by which human knowing arrives at cognizance of reasonable grounds. Those processes consist of interconnected series of acts of consciousness that he referred to, variously, as "marshaling the evidence," "weighing the evidence," or generally "reflecting." He used the term "reflective understanding" (or "reflective insight") to denote the acts that come at the end of these reflective processes and that achieve cognizance of reasonable grounds (or "sufficient reason") for the acts of judgment. The process of reflecting begins with awareness that the content of a direct insight is merely "conditioned" – that is to say, the intelligible content of any direct insight is initially no more than an interesting idea. All human direct insights are merely contingent, merely hypothetical. As such, they are not automatic, direct intuitions of the essences of existing things. A question for reflection stimulates a reflective process that intends to find out if the intelligible content is more than just an interesting idea. As reflection proceeds, it thinks out the "link between the conditioned and the conditions"[29] – that is to say, acts of reflecting endeavour to figure out under what sorts of conditions the conditioned intelligible content could be reasonably affirmed and thereby truly answer the "Is it so?" question. (Or, on the other hand, reflecting might determine under what conditions one could reasonably deny the intelligible content.) Once cognizance of this link is established, reflecting then proceeds to determine whether or not those requisite conditions are indeed fulfilled ("marshaling and weighing the evidence"). If successful, reflection arrives at an act of "reflective understanding," which then understands the same intelligible possibility that direct understanding understood, but it understands that intelligibility in a radically new way. It no longer understands the intelligibility as a mere possibility, but as a conditioned possibility whose conditions happen to be fulfilled. Reflective insight understands the intelligibility not only as intelligible, but also as a virtually unconditioned intelligibility. Reflection grasps that there is sufficient reason for affirming (or denying) that the intelligibility is (or is not) so.

The preceding remarks stand in need of further clarification. The processes of reflection are seldom simple. Processes of reasonable reflection can be quite complex and extended. While there is no single formula or simple set of rules to follow in the search for reflective understanding, there are several recurring patterns of reflection.[30] Among Lonergan's most important contributions to philosophy is his way of directing our attention to these different patterns. In what follows, the reader might be assisted by bearing in mind an example such as a juror faced with the task of arriving at a verdict, or a scientist endeavouring to verify a hypothesis, or an insurance investigator determining the cause of damage.

First, sorting out links to possible fulfilling conditions can require considerable creativity and ingenuity. Next, determining whether or not such conditions are fulfilled may require gathering further data from additional acts of experiencing. More often than not, sober processes of reflection discover that fulfilling the conditions for judging has become problematic. Frequently, attempts to find the most obvious sorts of supporting evidence fail once one becomes serious about the matter. The initial path towards linking a conditioned intelligibility with conditions has to be abandoned in favour of ever more complex, subtle, and ingenious ways of finding other such links. Difficulties encountered may be overcome by developing special techniques or technical instruments to supplement the evidence of ordinary experience. New possibilities and questions arise as reflection advances. Frequently, reflection either leads to outright abandonment of the original insight or to its modification into a more refined, more carefully qualified, or more sophisticated intelligibility – one whose conditions actually can be fulfilled. In other words, the reflective process is often a self-correcting process that substitutes a more mature and nuanced idea for an initially promising one.

Processes of reflection can last seconds or can continue for days, months, years, and occasionally even centuries. Most often they are the work of a single person, but with surprising frequency they involve collaborative effort (e.g., it took generations of mathematicians over three centuries of extended reflections to finally establish Fermat's famous "last theorem" as virtually unconditioned[31]). The duration and degree of complexity of any series of reflective acts depends entirely upon the complexity of the intelligible content under consideration. But no matter how extended or complex, all the acts composing a process of reflection are assembled under the guidance of the originating question – "Is it so?" – and its orientation towards a final answer in a judgment of affirmation or denial.

When reflecting eventually does determine that the requisite conditions are indeed fulfilled, it then grasps a unity of the intelligible content as conditioned along with its conditions as actually fulfilled. Lonergan calls this grasp of unity the "reflective understanding of the virtually unconditioned."[32] Grasping an idea not only as intelligible, but also more profoundly as virtually unconditioned is equivalent to grasping that there is sufficient reason for affirming this intelligibility as really so (or for denying that it is really so). In summary, then, reflective understanding arises once the inquirer has grasped the intelligible content of an insight to be "virtually unconditioned." An insight is known to be virtually unconditioned when (1) it is known to be conditioned (which happens as soon as the inquirer wonders, "Is it so?"), (2) a link is discovered that connects the conditioned insight to conditions that would have to be fulfilled in order to affirm (or deny) the intelligibility in question, and (3) the conditions are known to be fulfilled.[33] Put less technically, the grasp of a virtually unconditioned involves "knowing" what one would have to "know" in order to reasonably affirm a proposition, and "knowing" that one "knows" that.[34]

2.4.4 *Judging the Correctness of Insights*

Of particular importance for later discussion of judgments of value and ethical judgments is Lonergan's analysis of the pattern of reflection devoted to judging the "correctness of insights into concrete situations."[35] There is a kind of naive view of how one might go about checking the correctness of an insight. According to that view, one would compare the intelligible content of an insight with sensible data from the external world in order to see if what is actually there corresponds to the insight in one's mind. But, in fact, this would amount to comparing the intelligible content of one's insight with the sensible contents of one's sense perceptions – a sort of checking to see if the intelligibility "matches" up against the sensible reality.

When stated in this more precise fashion, however, the fallacy of this naive view becomes apparent. Precisely because an act of insight "supervenes" and goes beyond any act of sense, imagination, or memory,[36] its intelligible content also goes beyond and is incomparable with any sensible or imaginable content. Intelligibility is, therefore, intrinsically non-sensible and unimaginable. It follows that there is no possible way of holding it up against a sensible or imagined content to "see" if it matches. Insights are beyond "picture thinking" and representationalism. For this reason, any attempt to determine their correctness by means of a direct comparison or correspondence with a sensible presentation is doomed to failure. This would be like trying to determine which shade of red matches the number forty-seven. In the purely intelligible content of an insight, there are no sensible qualities whatsoever which could be made to fit on top of the data of sensation. Many other authors have criticized this form of representational-correspondence theory of knowing; Lonergan joins their ranks.

The metaphor of reaching a judgment by matching an intelligibility against experience is therefore an unhelpful and misleading way of thinking about how we arrive at judgments about the correctness of insights. Lonergan suggests that at the root of representational-correspondence theories of knowing is the perhaps unacknowledged assumption that human knowing is fundamentally a matter of taking a look, at least metaphorically. But the incommensurability of experiential content with intelligible content reveals both the assumption and the metaphor to be vacuous. Once again, as Lonergan puts it, this is the mistaken "assumption that what is obvious in knowing [i.e., looking] is what knowing obviously is."[37] Discernment therefore requires going beyond what seems obvious about human knowing, towards the full, nuanced comprehension of what human knowing actually is.

Lonergan's own analysis pays closer attention to what we actually do when we attempt to judge the correctness of our insights. For example, how do we recognize someone as the same person we met yesterday? As we head towards a judgment in answer to this question, some of the conditions that need to be fulfilled are indeed drawn from sense experiences of empirical data – shapes and colours of face, hair, and body, as well as tones of voice. But sensation, memory, and imagination do not supply all of the requisite conditions for answering such a question. This is because today's sense experiences of a person never are exactly the same as they were yesterday, and if they are not exactly the same, how do we recognize the person as the same? How do we know which differences in our sense experiences are insignificant and can be ignored in recognizing a person again today? Hair might be groomed differently, facial expressions might be more fatigued or more animated, and so on; a voice might be hoarse. Exact sameness of visual and auditory data is not one of the conditions for judging these to be sensible data about the same person.

When we know someone to be the same person, what is the same is the intelligible unification of those different sense data. And the conditions that must be fulfilled to judge sameness of intelligibility are different from sameness of sensible data.

This kind of issue crops up in scientific investigations as well. How do scientists know that the lab animal or plant specimen they work on today is the same as the one they began to prepare many days or months ago? It is not by the same empirical data, for the organism's growth will have changed its data over the intervening time period. In fact, the scientist usually hopes that there will be at least some data that differ at the end of the experimental period; otherwise, the experiment will yield a null result. So it is not by means of identical empirical data that we know sameness – it is by identical intelligible organization that we know sameness. But if we do not know intelligible sameness from empirical evidence, how do we know it?

It might be objected that in controlled experiments, lab animals and plant specimens are tagged, and the marks on the tag are identical empirical data after all. But how does the investigator know for sure that tags were not forged, or that the experiment is not being sabotaged by someone who switched the original tag to a specimen that looks exactly the same, but has had a different preparation?

Notice the flow of questions that occurs whether we consider this problem of insuring the integrity of an experiment or the problem of judging personal identity. In his penetrating analysis Lonergan reveals the cognitional significance of this flow of further pertinent questions that arise spontaneously with regard to any question for judging the correctness of insights into concrete situations.[38]

Every bright idea (direct insight) is followed spontaneously by a flow of questions. Some of these inquire about the sensible contents that would provide some of the conditions needed to regard the insight as virtually unconditioned. Not a representational match, but whether the sense data serve as fulfilling the conditions set by inquiry is the standard that matters.

Yet even when sensible data are found that meet the reflective criteria of fulfilling conditions, these are seldom the complete or sole set of conditions that must be fulfilled. Still further questions arise about the insight itself. These further questions lead to further insights, some of which correct, complement, criticize, modify, revise, or even replace the original bright idea with a more sophisticated and more tenable understanding. If this cyclical process of questioning and revised understanding arrives at a limit where there are no further questions pertinent to the correctness of a given insight, then the modified understanding is "invulnerable" to further correction. This absence of further correcting questions, Lonergan argues, is recognized by reflective understanding to be the fulfillment of conditions for judging an insight to be a correct understanding. Until this limit has been reached, one has conditions only for the judgment, "I think this is so, but I am not yet certain." On the other hand, once the intelligible content of an insight has been corrected to the point where there are no questions to correct it further, it is reflectively recognized as a fully correct, virtually unconditioned intelligibility. This recognition is what Lonergan calls a reflective act of understanding, and it becomes the ground for a reasonable affirmation of the correctness of the intelligibility. Lacking such reflective understanding, judgments about the intelligible content would not be reasonable. Rather, they would be merely arbitrary.

It may seem impossible to reach the limit where there are no further questions pertinent to our inquiry about the correctness of an insight. In fact, however, over and again, we actually do reach the point where we confidently acknowledge that this is indeed the same person with whom we interacted previously. At some point, scientific investigators do know that the specimen today is the same as the one prepared previously. In these and similar cases, intelligible sameness is known in a virtually unconditioned fashion precisely because there are "no further pertinent questions."

The criterion is not just that I do not *think* there are any further pertinent questions. Nor is it is just that I don't *notice* the further pertinent questions. The criterion for judging the correctness of an insight into intelligible sameness, or the correctness of the intelligible content of any insight, is that there *are* no further pertinent questions, period. This criterion sets a challenge for discernment. It is the challenge to become ever more discerning in noticing the subtle traces of lingering questions that need to be considered before one commits oneself to the correctness of a proposition (and the intelligibility that it expresses). It is a very demanding criterion for discernment.

Again, further questions about one's understanding of sameness may be posed out of an attitude of hyperbolic skepticism or an abnormal paranoia. But these are sources of further questions with agendas other than the standard set by the question "Is it so?" Once all the questions have been answered that are indeed pertinent to knowing whether this or that intelligibility really is so, then we have reached the virtually unconditioned, reasonable ground for making a very limited judgment about the correctness of our understanding of something.

2.4.5 Summary

In brief, then, this is Lonergan's answer to "What are we doing when we are knowing?" What we are doing is dynamically assembling a structured whole of conscious acts under the guidance of intelligent and reflective inquiry. Every act of judgment in that structure responds to some "Is it so?" question for reflection, which in turn presupposes some intelligible content as the "it" being asked about. These intelligible contents, in their turn, come to consciousness in acts of direct insights (and only in such acts), and these acts of direct understanding always respond to questions for intelligence. Again, questions for intelligence presuppose experiences that they ask about; hence these various acts (of experiencing, sensing, imagining, remembering, intellectual inquiring, understanding, reflective inquiring, reflecting, reflectively grasping the virtually unconditioned, and judging) are assembled into a dynamic structure of interrelationships by inquiry. The acts of inquiring relate the acts to one another, and thereby constitute a structure of cognition. This, according to Lonergan, is what we are doing when we are knowing.

2.5   Objectivity: Why Is Doing That Knowing?

It is one thing to agree that human beings, including oneself, actually do perform the conscious activities that Lonergan enumerates – or even that they are performed in and constituted by the dynamic structure that he claims they are.[39] But one may well ask, "Why does the execution of these activities in this dynamic structure deserve to be called 'knowing?'" – or as Lonergan himself puts it, "Why is doing that knowing?"

2.5.1 *Lonergan's Answer*

Perhaps the most straightforward definition of objectivity is "cognizance of how things really are." Now, if knowing is indeed the compound, dynamic structure of activities that culminates in unconditionally affirming (or denying) that something truly is so (or not), then knowing in this sense is *intrinsically* objective, for it fits exactly the definition of objectivity. This is because, in making affirmative judgments ("Yes, it is so."), we attain unconditioned cognizance of how things are.

But judgments by themselves alone cannot confer upon themselves their unconditional status. They are unconditioned only in virtue of the contributions made by the earlier activities in the structure – reflective acts of understanding which grasp virtually unconditioned and reasonable grounds for judging some intelligibility to be so (or not). In other words, since this structure culminates in *unconditionally* grounded judgments about what is or is not, when performed normatively and without distortion, then "doing that" is intrinsically a matter of knowledge about what is (as well as knowledge about what is not). Such performance is therefore intrinsically objective.[40]

This is what Lonergan meant when he wrote that "genuine objectivity is the fruit of authentic subjectivity."[41] Authentic subjectivity in this case means faithfully being oneself as a knower, faithfully participating in the dynamism of cognitional structure, and faithfully following the standards and guidance laid down by our own questioning that underpins that structure. Faithful performance of this pattern of acts is therefore the most fundamental meaning of both the authenticity and the objectivity of human knowing. Our factual judgments are objective if they are correct. They are correct only if we have successfully corrected faulty insights. We do this by taking into account everything that needs to be taken into account (i.e., the "conditions" for reasonable judging), and especially following the lead of the further pertinent questions for reflection. Our judgments are correct, then, when they affirm or deny the intelligible content of some insight as virtually unconditioned.

Implicit in the exhortation to authentic subjectivity, of course, is the possibility of inauthentic subjectivity. If performance of the pattern of cognitional activities in conformity with the normativity of questioning is *intrinsically* objective, still there can be all sorts of *extrinsic* interferences with such faithful performance. Those extrinsic interferences are responsible for failures of objectivity. This issue of extrinsic interferences with objectivity will be addressed in section 2.5.5.

2.5.2 *Contending Notions of Objectivity and the*
"Epistemological Theorem"

Not everyone, however, will find the simple answer to Lonergan's second question completely satisfying. Many will view it with puzzlement if not strong resistance. The reason for such incomprehension and resistance, I would suggest, is that everyone already has some prior, less or more explicit notion of what objective knowing ought to be like, and Lonergan's account does not seem to match that notion very well.

Lonergan anticipated such objections. He also anticipated the deepest source of discomfort shared by many different kinds of objection. That source is implicit in the way he formulated the challenge to his own position: "Why should knowing result from the performance of such *immanent* activities as experiencing, understanding, and judging?"[42] The word "immanent" is the crucial word in Lonergan's question, and he suspected it was the crucial concern behind resistance to affirming that this structured set of activities amounts to knowing.

"Immanence" implies confinement to the interior, while, by way of contrast, it would seem that reality lies "out there" in the exterior. When posed in this fashion, the problematic of objective knowledge is "the bridge problem": the seemingly unsolvable problem of bridging the chasm between the immanent activities of consciousness "in here," and the way things really are "out there now." Quite likely with Kant in mind, Lonergan posed the question more explicitly: Why is performance of the acts of cognitional structure "not restricted to the immanent content of knowing, to *Bewusstseinsinhalte*"?[43] In other words, how does one get from the contents inside consciousness (*Bewusstseinsinhalte*) to the outside, the already-out-there-now real world? How does one overcome this subject-object divide? This is one way of stating the fundamental modern epistemological problematic of objective knowledge.[44]

Lonergan responded to the impasse of this problematic by drawing attention to the self-transcendence that is already and always operating in cognitional structure itself. This is the reason for Lonergan's repeated emphasis that the structure of human cognition is *dynamic*. The dynamism of human cognition is our questioning and our inquiry. Our inquiry means that we are never content with, or limited to, what is already immanent in our minds thus far. Our inquiry is a desiring for what we are not yet and what we do not yet comprehend. It is a leading beyond what we already have in mind towards what we do not yet have in mind. Most importantly, our inquiry leads us beyond whatever we thus far think or believe or opine or hypothesize to be the case. We ask not merely what we think is so or might be so – we do not merely ask what is immanent in our minds; we also ask about what truly is so. When we do so, we are *already* in the process of self-transcendence – transcending beyond mere *Bewusstseinsinhalte.*

With the act of unconditional judgment that process of cognitional self-transcendence is realized. In judging unconditionally that this or that is the case, cognitional structure manifests its self-transcendence by going beyond merely conditioned understanding of what appears to be or might be to judge what is so. Furthermore, this cognitional self-transcendence does not suddenly appear for the first time in an act of reasonable judgment; self-transcendence has already been operative in the earlier stages of the cognitional process when questions for intelligence go beyond mere experiences, and insights go beyond mere questions for intelligence. Even more profoundly, self-transcendence operates in the subsequent processes of reasonable reflection that move beyond the grasp of merely conditioned intelligibilities towards the grasp of the links with their conditions, and onwards still towards a reflective grasp of a virtually unconditioned. Cognitional self-transcendence is especially manifested in the "Is it so?" question that stimulates and animates the whole reflective process, for in raising that question human consciousness already goes beyond the mere *Bewusstseinsinhalte* of a bright idea; in other words, the whole of cognitional structure is a self-transcending dynamism that reaches its cognitional culmination when it affirms, reasonably and confidently, unconditioned results – namely, that some intelligibilities really are so.

The root of this human capacity for cognitional self-transcendence is what Lonergan called the "unrestricted desire to know." Because of this unrestricted desire, reasonable reflection has the capacity to ask everything about everything. There is no further pertinent question that is beyond its capacity to ask. The human capacity to reach an unconditioned result (reflective understanding of a virtually unconditioned) rests upon the dynamic self-transcendence of unrestricted human wonder. Because human inquiry is intrinsically unrestricted, human beings *can* raise every question that they would need to answer before they could reasonably judge something to be so unconditionally. By this same unrestricted intention, they have awareness of when some of those pertinent questions remain unanswered, and so can reasonably refrain from affirming what they do not yet grasp to be virtually unconditioned.

Because of this self-transcending and inquiring dynamism, our cognitional activities are never merely immanent *Bewusstseinsinhalte*; rather, our cognitional activities are always already caught up in and constituted by the dynamic that leads beyond themselves and heads towards what is. We achieve objective knowledge of what is to the extent that we allow inquiry to play itself out all the way, without interference.[45] This, Lonergan argues, is why "doing that" (faithfully following the dynamic lead of cognitional structure) is indeed a performance that is properly called objective knowing.

Lonergan elaborates his argument in terms of what he calls the "epistemological theorem" that human knowing is "intrinsically objective" because it "rests upon an unrestricted intention and an unconditioned result."[46] By "unconditioned result" he means a judgment grounded in a reflective understanding of an intelligibility as virtually unconditioned. By "unrestricted intention" he means the pure, unrestricted desire to know that is the source of, and is manifested in, *all* questions for intelligence and reflection.

It is evident that objectivity results from the "unconditioned result" of judgments grounded upon reflective grasps of insights as virtually unconditioned. If an intelligibility is virtually unconditioned, then one is reflectively cognizant of all conditions requisite for affirming that it is so (or denying that it is so). When one affirms (or denies) on this basis and this basis alone, one's judgment is precisely about what is or is not so. This is the basic notion of objectivity – that our thinking about something is identical with what really is so.[47]

However, serious doubts have been raised by countless thinkers about our ability to reach any such so-called unconditioned result. It is for this reason that Lonergan also asserts that human objectivity rests upon an "unrestricted intention" – upon an *unrestricted* desire to know, which is "manifested in questions for intelligence and for reflection."[48] His claim that all humans have an unrestricted desire to know, and that this is the source of all our cognitional questions, is perhaps the most crucial assertion in all of his philosophical writings.

Why does human objectivity depend upon the persistence of an unrestricted desire to know? Because if there were any questions that we could not raise, then we would be stuck with insights that are incorrect and fallacious, and we could never be aware of them as incorrect. We would reach the natural end of restricted human questioning, and our questioning would be satisfied (because no further tension of inquiry would remain) even though our ideas remained incorrect. But our "is" questioning should not be satisfied with truncated questioning, because the animating question was supposed to be about what *is* so, not about what some finite human desire finds satisfying. We would be able to reach a reflective understanding of some intelligibility as virtually unconditioned, only if we could ask and answer *all* further questions pertinent to the pursuit of that understanding as a correct understanding of how things really are. But if there were some questions inherently beyond the reach of human consciousness – if there were some questions that could not be raised – then it would be impossible in principle to raise all of the requisite further questions. There would be no way to know that all objections to our understandings of things had been addressed. Or, there would be no way to attain the further insights needed to modify a fallacious understanding into a correct understanding.

So the attainment of the "unconditioned result" (i.e., the reflective understanding of the virtually unconditioned) depends absolutely upon a capacity to raise all questions pertinent to the correctness of our understandings. It depends, in other words, on the unrestricted intention of the pure unrestricted desire to know. Contrary to the hypothetical state of affairs where human beings would have only a finite capacity for inquiry, Lonergan claims that our capacity for inquiry is in fact unrestricted. Our desire to know is unrestricted. *On this claim rest all of the other achievements of his philosophical work.*

Of course, in so many cases we are unable to answer further questions that are pertinent to the attainment of correct understanding. In those cases, the objective judgment would be, "I do not know for sure." Objectivity consists just as much in knowing what we do not know as it does in knowing what we do know. Notice, however, that the statement for judgment has shifted: from the statement "X is so," we have shifted to the statement "I do not know for sure whether X is so." While the persistence of further unanswered pertinent questions makes it impossible for us to say that all the conditions for affirming X have been fulfilled, simultaneously the very same persistence of those questions is the fulfillment of the conditions for saying correctly and unconditionally, "I know that I do not know whether or not X is so."

Human objectivity does not depend upon having answers to all questions. If that were the case, then of course there could be no objective human knowledge, since no human has ever had the answers to all questions. Rather, objective human knowledge depends upon the fact that every human being has a pure wonder, an unrestricted desire that is the source of an endless stream of questions concerning everything about everything. Our objectivity depends, not on having answers to every question, but on the capacity to entertain every question. That capacity resides in the unrestricted desire. Even if the only objective judgments we ever reach are of the form, "I know that I don't know whether X is so," such objective judgments rest upon the unrestricted desire. But, of course, those are not the only objective judgments we do in fact make.

If human questioning really is unrestricted as Lonergan claims, then that means there is no question for intelligence or reflection that is beyond the capacity of human consciousness. This means further that it is humanly possible to be aware of *all* further questions that are pertinent to sustained reflection on the question "Is this intelligible content really so?" Human cognitional objectivity, therefore, depends upon a desire for knowing everything about everything, which manifests itself in an intrinsically limitless flow of questions for intelligence and reflection.

2.5.3 Is Human Questioning Unrestricted?

Lonergan's most crucial claim is that the desire to know that issues forth into questions is *unrestricted*. Here "desire" means no more and no less than something that is manifested in the tension of questions for intelligence and reflection. It is the desire that stimulates, accompanies, and constitutes inquiring, questioning, asking, wondering, being puzzled, and so on. Lonergan observes, "Because it differs radically from other desire, this desire has been named pure. It is to be known, not by the misleading analogy of other desire, but by giving free rein to intelligent and rational consciousness."[49]

Among the ways that the desire to know differs radically from other desires is that it is unrestricted. Desires for other satisfactions – for food, pleasure, sex, comfort, honour, or power, for example – are desires for identifiable objects. Once those objects are possessed, the desire for them is satisfied and its tension is quelled. The desire to know, however, cannot be satisfied by anything short of knowing everything about everything. While we can identify what our other desires desire, we would not be able to identify what our desire to know desires unless we already knew everything about everything – unless we already had answers to all of the questions that flow from this unrestricted desire. This is among the reasons why analogies with other desires prove misleading in attempting to think about the "pure" desire.

Instead, Lonergan contends, this unrestricted desire to know is best "known" by giving it free rein – that is to say, "knowledge" about the desire to know cannot be attained in the fully human sense of knowing that takes place through the cognitional structure. In order to know the desire in this fully human sense, we would have to understand correctly everything that the desire desires to know, and then say this is the desire that once desired to know those now-knowns. But that would amount to already knowing what the desire desires – in which case, the experience of this desire would already have vanished. Rather, the least inadequate way in which we can "know" the unrestricted desire is by participating in its sweep, by giving ourselves over to its throe.[50] We can experience the desire as drawing us ever beyond ourselves by letting ourselves be drawn. We do this in a limited fashion whenever we immerse ourselves, as children do, in a lively flow of questions and answers. But soon we withdraw from that immersion, caught up by other desires and cares that push the unrestricted desire to the margins of our awareness. It takes considerable formation in the ethics of discernment to sustain awareness of and participation in the unrestricted desire, which unrelentingly draws our knowing and our living ever onwards.

If we best "know" our unrestricted desire by experiencing and practising it, it does not follow that we know that it *is unrestricted* by such practice. Yet the claim that it is indeed unrestricted – that there is no question beyond human capacity – is of the greatest importance to Lonergan's philosophy of knowledge and, I shall argue later, of the greatest importance to ethical thought and practice as well. How do we know that the desire is unrestricted? We cannot know the unrestrictedness of our desire in the direct fashion of experiencing, understanding, and judging for, once again, that would require correctly understanding everything about everything. Knowledge of the desire as unrestricted must therefore be somehow indirect.

Lonergan takes this indirect approach by pointing out that the question about the unrestrictedness of the human desire to know can be formulated in different ways.[51]

For example, if we ask whether there might not be something beyond the desiring of the desire to know, the very question itself is a manifestation of the desire. The very question itself manifests the desire to know about something which, it is purported, it does not desire to know. Indeed, the desire to know by definition is precisely that which is manifested in questions for intelligence and reflection. Hence to ask whether there is some restriction to the desire, whether there are some things that it cannot ask about, reveals that it not restricted to limited forms of knowing after all.

As a second example, Lonergan comments,

> It will be objected by many that they have no desire to know everything about everything. But how do they know that they do not already know everything about everything? It is because so many questions can be asked. Why do they not effectively will to know everything about everything? Because it is so troublesome to reach even a few answers that they are completely disheartened by the prospect of answering all the questions they could ask.[52]

Lonergan here reveals an equivocation on the word "desire" that is at the heart of this form of this objection. Those who object that they have no unrestricted "desire" to know everything about everything mean "desire" in a subtle but oddly familiar sense. "Desire" here means a willing commitment resulting from a decision. "Desire" in this sense is perhaps more evident in another equivocal statement such as "I no longer desire to study English literature." The statement reveals a prior willingness to pursue answers to the questions that issue forth in the study of English literature, followed by a decisive act of turning away from that willingness. But preceding both the willingness ("desire") and the turning away from it there is a prior desire that issues forth the bewildering flow of questions that reveal one's humiliating ignorance before the wealth of English literature and the vast domain of its scholarly studies. Desiring in this more primordial sense is different from "desiring" in the secondary and derivative sense that is the result of the subsequent decisions that led first to willingness and then to unwillingness to pursue what questioning desires. That desire is ultimately unlike the "desires" that result from decisions. The objection that one does not have an unrestricted "desire" to know, then, in fact means that one has abandoned willing pursuit of what one cannot help but desire in the primordial sense – the desire that is manifested in questioning. The decision not to take interest in so many questions presupposes their prior occurrence; that is to say, the prior manifestation of the desire to know results in so many (or so many unpleasant) questions, and people make decisions to sequester that desire. Far from proving they do not have or never had such a desire, a lack of "desire" in the derived sense presupposes the unrestricted desire to know in the primordial sense. Otherwise, "how do they know that they do not already know everything about everything?"

There are other ways of raising the question about whether the desire that is the source of questions is truly unrestricted, and individual readers will need to try out different alternatives before they can arrive at their own virtually unconditioned judgments that the desire to know, the source of their questioning, is truly unrestricted. Pursuits of these alternative questions about the unrestrictedness, however, all have very similar forms: the attempt to formulate a question or objection about the unrestrictedness will inevitably manifest the very unrestrictedness about which it asks. Careful analysis of the various formulations will reveal the reflexive character of this question about questioning – and that it thereby fulfills the conditions for affirming its unrestrictedness.

2.5.4 Ongoing Criticism

If we humans were not intrinsically constituted by an unrestricted desire to know, human knowing could not be self-correcting, as Lonergan claims it is. It would therefore be necessary to invent something that performed the function of the unrestricted desire – or to hope that some such thing would come from outside human invention. This is because of the persistent problem that human thought about realities becomes complacent and stagnant. History is rife with examples of social groups, no matter how creative, critical, and progressive they were at one stage, inevitably entering into subsequent periods where there is a drying up of critical questions needed to address new and important issues. Prejudicial assumptions about the virtues of members of in-groups and the deficiencies of members of marginalized groups become entrenched and ossified. This loss of the dynamism of inquiry extends to theoretical positions as well. For example, Newton's doctrines of absolute space and absolute time were criticized sporadically, beginning with George Berkeley, but the criticisms were not taken seriously in the scientific community until Einstein's work over two centuries later.[53]

The unrestricted desire to know, however, stands in tension with any imperfect or indeed any limited set of answers to questions for intelligence and reflection. Were the human capacity to question not unrestricted, human thought would be irretrievably entrapped in these stagnations. Indeed, there are thinkers who believe human thought is all social construction and that there is no possibility of effectively criticizing these constructions and moving beyond their limitations. The question of *effective* criticism from *within* a social context is a knotty one, to which this book will return in part IV. For the moment, I wish to underscore that even effective criticism from outside a social group presupposes an unrestricted desire to know that permeates human consciousness. For if there were some questions that were beyond human capacity to raise, then neither the in-group nor the out-group could raise the questions needed to criticize the shortcomings and point towards innovations and reforms required to go beyond social stagnation. In this vein, Lonergan observes that "by raising still further questions for intelligence and reflection, it excludes complacent inertia."[54]

2.5.5 *Biases: Mere Subjectivity vs. Authentic Subjectivity*

To claim that this desire or wonder is intrinsically unrestricted does not mean, of course, that it cannot be overridden or repressed or distorted extrinsically by willful indifference, apathy, anger, *ressentiment*, bias, malice, prejudice, fear, passion, etc. The desire is unrestricted in its desiring, but not omnipotent in its effectiveness. During his or her lifetime, each human being experiences a deluge of tensions of inquiry, only to ignore and brush aside many without good cause. But such avoidances of questioning only testify further to the fact of this persistent flow of questions, against which bias must continually and ingeniously struggle. Bias must constantly devise new strategies in order to ignore questions or to convince the biased individuals that imperfect answers really are correct.

In Lonergan's lexicon, "bias" means precisely *interference* with inquiry and with the self-correcting sequence of questions and answers that constitutes the dynamism of the cognitional structure.[55] Being "merely subjective" in the pejorative sense means failure to adequately address all the demands that our inquiry poses for us. It means allowing other desires, fears, interests, concerns, or preferences to take precedence and to interfere with the normative guidance that comes spontaneously from our unrestricted inquiry.

We don't have to *make* ourselves raise questions. We don't need to say to ourselves, "I must raise more questions! I have to work at this questioning thing harder!" Ever further questions will arise naturally and spontaneously. What we do need to do, rather, is to let go of the things that interfere with our spontaneous questioning and attend to it more carefully.

If objectivity is the fruit of *authentic* subjectivity, this amounts to saying that authenticity, and therefore objectivity, is difficult and that it is approached only through prolonged, deliberate efforts of discernment dedicated to making inquiry (rather than bias) become the effective core of one's thinking and living. But it is important to emphasize what bias means in this context. Bias is *not* the previous acquisition of experiences, insights, feelings, or judgments, *unless* they happen to interfere with the self-correcting trajectory of the unrestricted desire to know. To the contrary, previously acquired insights may actually hold parts of the answers to the further pertinent questions that we face, or they might accelerate the raising of still more questions pertinent to the topic at hand. Lonergan criticized the notion that all previously acquired knowledge must be automatically prejudicial as the "Principle of the Empty Head."[56] According to the Empty Head Principle, to be an expert in any area of judgment, a person would have to be completely ignorant not only of that field, but in every field. Suffice it to say that, on Lonergan's account of objectivity, human beings are neither constitutionally incapable of objectivity, nor automatically excluded from being objective in virtue of having been observant and thoughtful prior to asking of a new idea, "Is it so?" Human beings are only excluded from objectivity by inauthenticity, by the failure to be discerning – the failure to be attentive and faithful to the calling of their own unrestricted questioning. *Being attentive and faithful to the promptings of our questioning constitutes a significant portion of what I mean by the ethics of discernment.*

There are of course numerous extrinsic interferences with the proper and normative sense of human objectivity. Lonergan identified and discussed at length several (but by no means all) major and recurring strategies for evading the call of unrestricted inquiry. He grouped these under the headings of dramatic bias (e.g., psychological repression), individual bias (self-centredness), group bias (e.g., racism, sexism, ethnocentrism, religious prejudice, prejudice based on economic class, etc.), and general bias (bias against the seeming impracticality of theoretical pursuits).[57] Authentic subjectivity does not occur automatically; it occurs only by facing the harsh fact that just about every human being is the victim of some forms of bias, then confronting those sources of interference with the pursuit of questions, and then taking measures to marginalize or eliminate those influences.

In this process of facing biases, one thing is certain: whatever biases can be easily recognized by someone, those are not the biases that are most pernicious to that person's own striving towards objective knowing. If someone can name race, gender, ethnic, or religious bias as what they are trying to overcome, it is likely those are not the most worrisome distortions of his or her objectivity. The most troublesome biases are the ones we have not yet even learned to recognize or name.

Among the various well-known strategies of bias, Lonergan singled out one that is especially intransigent and is a perennial source of disorientation in philosophical discussions and in human thinking in general. Most people think of individual or group bias as the most pernicious kinds of bias, because the immediate consequences of these biases are so evident to those who suffer from them. But Lonergan regarded another kind of bias as the most worrisome, precisely because its negative consequences can take generations to develop incrementally, and in the meantime people adapt so completely to those increments that they tend to rationalize them as natural.

According to Lonergan, this most devastating interference ("general bias," which might be termed an "ontological bias") derives from the disparity between our animality and our search for answers to questions for intelligence and reflection. Human animality includes a deeply seated heritage from our evolutionary history, which often interferes with our unrestricted inquiry. This is not the distorting influence from our animal desires that is usually cited (e.g., "inclinations" by Kant). Lonergan does not have in mind primarily the ways that animal desires can conflict with moral standards.

Rather, according to him, the even more fundamental and problematic source of confusion and disorientation about objectivity stems from the fact that human beings share in the animal advantages of sense perception. As animals, we benefit from the evolutionary inheritance of various forms of sensation that have biological significance. The basic characteristic of all animal sensitivity, Lonergan argues, is extroversion: "Outer senses are the heralds of biological opportunities and dangers."[58] Sensation gives each species of animal a specific kind of evolutionary advantage in its basic biological tasks of feeding, reproducing, and securing shelter and protection. For this reason, evolutionary advantage privileges a certain kind of realism that is associated with extroversion. The realities that can contribute to survival and reproduction must pass the muster of what is "already out there now."[59] After all, biological opportunities and dangers reside in the externally present here-and-now. By way of contrast, what is merely "in here" (i.e., the *Bewusstseinsinhalte* inside consciousness in memory or imagination or in fanciful ideas) lacks any immediate relevance for the biological functions of nourishing, avoiding harm, or reproducing. Whatever further qualities must be added to the "already out there now" to insure its significance for survival depend upon the particular organism. For example, nutrition for a Koala must not only be present for it to eat, but must also look, taste, and digest like eucalyptus leaves. But in every case, those species-specific qualities are over and above the primary animal characteristic of the real – being already-out-there-now. The reality that could be beneficial or detrimental for survival must at least be capable of being sensed as present in space and time. What counts as possibly real for animal survival must be at least already-out-there-now, whatever other qualities the organism would further recognize as real for its survival.

This is a healthy, evolved biological sense of objectivity. In principle, it does not necessarily preclude a distinctively human way of knowing and sense of reality, grounded not in extroversion but in understanding correctly. Even so, while it does not logically exclude another sense of reality, this biological sense of the "already out there now" reality nevertheless competes forcefully with, undermines, and becomes a recurring source of prejudice against the distinctively human notion of reality. In order to consistently pursue objectivity in a serious fashion, therefore, this domination by the evolutionary-biological sense of reality has to be overcome in a radical way. Lonergan came to speak of "intellectual conversion" in order to underscore the radicality of this overcoming of the biological sense of reality.[60]

Objectivity, therefore, like discernment, is both the quality of a person as well as something achieved by such persons. Objectivity as the quality of a person is the deliberate, sustained fidelity to unrestricted inquiry as the core of one's thinking and living. Objectivity as an achievement consists in the acts of judgment and decision made by such persons, who will settle for nothing less than reflective understanding of the virtually unconditioned as the motivations for the judgments they make. This reflective understanding in turn rests upon the absence of further pertinent questions.[61] Hence such judgments authentically know what is, how things are, what they are really like – and this is what is meant by objective knowing in the unqualified sense.

The answer to Lonergan's second question – "Why is doing that knowing?" – is therefore the following: "Doing that is knowing because authentic human knowing is a process of self-transcending that leads to unconditional judgments that affirm what is."

2.6   Reality: What Do I Know When I Do That?

2.6.1   *The Simple Answer*

The simple answer to Lonergan's third question follows directly: when we "do that," we know *what is*. In performing cognitionally structured acts of consciousness, we know reality, being, what is – or more precisely, we know something real; some piece of reality is what we know when we complete a full cycle of the cognitional structure in one of its limited, unconditioned judgments of fact. This is because "doing that" (i.e., following the normative lead of inquiry through the pattern of cognitional structure) terminates in unconditioned acts of judgment. In a virtually unconditioned affirming, judgment affirms that something *is* – and the totality of what is (i.e., being) is reality. No human judgment grasps everything about being (reality), but each reasonable judgment grasps something about reality (including what is not real). Each act of affirming affirms the membership of some intelligibility in the community of being. Each act of denying tells us what is not included in reality.[62] Each act of affirming or denying is therefore a limited contribution towards knowing all that is, all of being, all of reality.

Hence, it is Lonergan's position, his response to his own question, that reality (being) is what is known in understanding correctly.[63] Reality is what we know when we "do that" – when we faithfully follow the path of our questioning through the execution of our own cognitional structure.

2.6.2   *Contending Notions of Reality*

That is the simple answer to "What do I know when I do that?" The fuller answer, however, is complicated (just as is the case with objectivity) by the notions about reality that compete within us for our allegiance.[64] To say that we know reality through the operations of the cognitional structure will no doubt strike many as strange, if not incredible. Lonergan himself famously referred to this as a "startling strangeness."[65]

This alien sense of strangeness about the claim that reality is what is known through the cognitional structure arises because we actually have several notions of reality. There are several contenders for our sense of reality (for what Heidegger called our *Vorverstehen* of being) vying for acceptance within most of us. One or more of them will have already gained a secure foothold within us long before we contemplate the idea of reality as what is to be known through unconditionally answering "Is it so?" questions. These contenders include (but are not limited to) the biological, the pragmatic, and the narrowly scientific notions of reality, over against the notion of reality that is implicit in our unrestricted desire to know. To fully accept that reality is what we know when we judge our understandings to be correct will require that we wrench free of the strong grip that these other senses of reality have upon us. This is why Lonergan used the term, "intellectual *conversion*" to characterize the process of turning away from and being freed from the limitations of these other notions of reality.

Insofar as our evolutionarily inherited biological sense of reality holds the upper hand, what we know by understanding and affirming is bound to seem ethereal, ephemeral, and abstract. If, on the other hand, our primary allegiance is to a sense of reality tied up with the spirit of accomplishing things in the world of "getting and spending," the notion that reality is the understood and affirmed will seem idealistic and pragmatically unrealistic. Again, to someone whose sense of reality is closely tied to the methodical procedures of the hard empirical sciences, the insights and virtually unconditional affirmations of humanists and philosophers will seem to be no more than soft opinions about vagaries – certainly not tough knowledge about the really real.

There is no simple response to this variety of ways in which people tend to resist the implication that reality is what we know in understanding correctly. Still, some of the disquiet can be addressed. One part of a response consists in drawing the objectors' attention to the fact that the reality of experiencing, understanding, and judging is already implicit in their own sense of reality, whether pragmatic or scientific. Practicality is successful because it is insightful, because it regards ideas as standing in need of the tests of further questions, and because it will not settle for half-answers to very pragmatic questions. In other words, the pragmatic attitude itself implicitly endorses the normativity of cognitional structure, but only up to a point. The pragmatic attitude is concerned with insights that are unconditioned in virtue of having withstood the tests of pragmatic questioning, but it regards questions and ideas that are non-pragmatic as unrealistic. In fact, just what counts as pragmatic and why, and whether there are any deficiencies in a completely pragmatic attitude, are questions seldom asked. These are just not pragmatic questions to ask, but they *are* among the questions of concern to the unrestricted desire to know.[66]

Science, on the other hand, is scientific because its methods guide both the formation of scientifically intelligible hypotheses and also guide the further questions that lead to experimental tests. It is scientific because its methods push beyond the mere gathering of data towards the understanding of how data are related. In this sense, the concerns of scientific questions and insights are different from the concerns of the pragmatic attitude. They seek to understand a very broad range of relationships among observable data – not just how the data relate to pragmatic interests. Yet empirical science, like pragmatic common sense, is committed to asking and answering only certain kinds of questions – namely, only those that can be settled by its methods.

The earlier section on biases discussed how our evolutionary inheritance gives us a persistent source of expecting reality to be "out there now." Reality in that sense is what is known by immediate and direct contact, through sight and touch. From the perspective of our animal sense of reality, what is not present in space or time to our immediate contact is just not real. It has no relevance to survival or reproduction. For Lonergan, this evolutionary, animal sense of reality is the most elemental and the most stubborn of all of our competing notions of reality. It is the source of our deepest doubts that reality can be what we know by understanding correctly. Its grip on our allegiance to its notion of reality – what is present – is the most difficult to loosen.

Reality is neither "out there" nor "in here," as some renderings of idealism and solipsism seem to hold. Reality just "is." Some realities might also be "out there," and some might also be "in here," although the sense of these spatial metaphors would need to be examined carefully. But neither the "out there" nor the "in here" are the criteria of reality. "Is" is the criterion of reality, and we know what is, neither by extroversion nor by introspection. We know what is by understanding correctly – by arriving at virtually unconditioned judgments about the correctness of our understandings.

Animality, pragmatic common sense, and empirical science are therefore committed to certain notions of reality, but none of these is reality in the full and unqualified sense. Each of these senses of reality is only the part of reality that is of concern to the unrestricted desire to know. The reality of what is present is all that is of interest to biological survival and evolutionary success. Pragmatic and scientific practices also regard reality only insofar as it is proportionate to their limited concerns. But when people commit exclusively to these other concerns and limited notions of reality, serious distortions ensue. The unrestricted notion of reality that flows from the unrestricted desire to know will seem unreal to those notions of reality determined by these lesser concerns. Making the unrestricted notion of reality seem strange and alien is chief among the distortions that ensue from such substitutions. Unrestricted questioning has a broader notion of reality that incorporates but goes beyond the notions intended by pragmatic attitudes and scientific methods. In fact, it is our most primordial and natural sense of reality. But this broader, unrestricted notion of reality – especially its correlative commitment to the intelligibility of reality – is strange and foreign to the more limited pragmatic and scientific attitudes. Ultimately, then, the resistances to this broader sense of reality as incorporating but going beyond restricted notions of reality have to be overcome in a radical way. This radical intellectual conversion requires a serious self-encounter and self-appropriation.[67]

2.6.3 *Reality as Intelligible*

Contributing mightily to the sense of strangeness about reality is the fact that intelligibility is the reality known through the exercise of human cognitional structure. Because human knowing is structured, every act of reasonable, unconditioned judging always affirms (or denies) some intelligible content that it "borrows" from prior acts of understanding (insights).[68] "Is" is said of some intelligibility or other that is the *noematic* content of an insight. It is the intelligible content that is affirmed (or denied) as real. Hence, in every case where some reality is affirmed, that reality is intelligible.

This means that the answer to the question "What do we know when we do that?" has the strange and even startling implication that reality is completely intelligible. It is a strange implication, because intelligibility *as such* has no sensible qualities. Intelligibility as such is both invisible and intangible – quite literally, neither visualizable nor touchable. This absence of visual or tangible qualities from reality as intelligible makes it seem quite unreal to people with other kinds of commitments about reality – commitments that they know realities only because they can see or touch them. To most people, saying that we know reality in affirming as correct the intelligible content of our understanding of what we see and touch – as well as what we neither see nor touch – will likely seem unsatisfactory, if not downright incredible.

Early on, Lonergan himself struggled with the seeming unreality of the notion of reality implicit in the affirmation of intelligibilities as virtually unconditioned. During his student days, he came to the conclusion that human reasoning is discursive, rather than intuitive – that is to say, he became convinced that human reason is a process, and later he eventually formulated what he thought was the correct understanding of that process of reasoning in his cognitional theory.

But his early conviction that reasoning is discursive initially posed a problem for him. What he understood to be its rival, reasoning as intuitive, entailed some form of direct access to reality. The correspondence between reasoning as intuitive and reality was guaranteed by these direct contacts. But Lonergan could not initially see how reasoning as discursive could lead to knowledge of reality, because it lacked any such direct contact. How could discursive reasoning lead to reality? How could "the performance of such immanent activities" lead to knowledge of "external" ("out there") reality?

The basic idea that eventually led him to the resolution of this dilemma came from his study of Plato's philosophy. Although he would later criticize Platonism for also harbouring a subtle form of intuitive reasoning ("knowing by confrontation"[69]), his studies of Plato led him to the realization that reality itself is intelligible.[70]

In their own ways, the animal, pragmatic, and scientific attitudes mistakenly assume that they have some form of direct access to reality, and that this privileges their notions of reality. In fact, however, sensations do not give direct access to reality. Instead, empirical data are important to knowledge of reality only insofar as questioning and discursive reasoning make use of them to fulfill conditions needed to arrive at virtually unconditioned knowledge of reality.[71] As Lonergan puts it,

> It is not true that it is from sense that our cognitional activities derive their immediate relationship to real objects; that relationship is immediate in the intention of being [i.e., the unrestricted desire to know]; it is mediate in the data of sense and in the data of consciousness inasmuch as the intention of being makes use of data in promoting cognitional process to knowledge of being.[72]

Knowing reality through authentic performance of our cognitional structure is knowing that the content of our understanding "is." The content of our understanding is intelligibility,[73] and therefore each instance of knowing is knowing that some intelligibility is. Each affirmation is the affirmation of the reality of an intelligibility. The totality of reality is therefore the totality of all intelligibilities so known. It is the totality to be known in asking and answering all questions for intelligence and reflection, the totality of all intelligibilities so affirmed. In other words, reality, being, is completely intelligible.[74] Reality is not what we "know" by direct contact with the senses, however difficult it is to accept this fact at first. However strange it may seem, reality is intelligible.

2.7   Conclusion

In this chapter, I have presented an overview of Lonergan's cognitional theory – his philosophy of knowledge and reality. I have relied upon his three questions to organize this overview. Cognitional structure – the performance of a set of cognitional activities structured by the dynamics of unrestricted questioning – is the answer to his first question: What am I doing when I am knowing? The answer to his second question is that "doing that" is knowing because performance of that structure of activities in fidelity to the guidance of our questioning leads us to virtually unconditioned cognizance of what is and what is not. This is what is meant by genuinely knowing. To the third question, Lonergan answers that reality is what we know when we "do that" – despite the startling strangeness of the intelligibility of reality that confronts us if we take seriously the implications of "doing that."

These answers to Lonergan's three questions have profound implications. They mean that a habit of discernment – of keen attentiveness to one's own inquiring spirit – is the condition for becoming a good judge of correctness of our understanding. This habit of discernment is not easy to develop or sustain, yet it is of paramount importance. As Lonergan puts it, "it is not enough to say that no further questions occur *to me*."[75] The criterion is, rather, that there *are* no further questions. There may be a whole host of interferences responsible for the fact that no further questions occur to me or to you. There may indeed be subtle stirrings of questions about our insights, but because these stirrings are not particularly strong, or because we are so enamoured of our brilliant ideas, we simply might not pay any attention to these subtle further pertinent questions. Or we might be tired or sick or have dulled wits. We might be lazy or complacent. We might be victims of one or several forms of the biases that Lonergan analyzes. Lonergan fully recognizes the multiplicity of ways that interferences can obscure the awareness of further questions in the consciousness of any particular person. But the possibility and the facts of such interferences do not negate the legitimacy of Lonergan's answers to his three questions and their implications. Rather, the almost universal human evidence of such interferences simply points to what is being interfered with – unrestricted inquiry – and therefore points also to what is demanded if we are to be objective about correctness of understanding. We would have to discern the presence of biases, endeavour to minimize and eventually eliminate them, and develop an intensified, subtle discernment of, and fidelity to, the promptings of further questions. Fidelity to the lead of questioning is what Lonergan meant by "authenticity" in the most fundamental sense. This is why he claimed that objectivity is the fruit of authentic subjectivity. In other words, one has objective knowledge of reality by becoming an objective judge of the correctness of one's understandings. One does this just to the extent that one is discerning and authentically open to and attentive to the subtle promptings of one's own unrestrictedly inquiring spirit.

3 Self-Appropriation, Part I: Self-Affirmation of Cognitional Structure

The crucial issue is an experimental issue ... It will consist in one's own rational self-consciousness clearly and distinctly taking possession of itself as rational self-consciousness. Up to that decisive achievement all leads. From it all follows. No one ... can do it for you.

– Bernard Lonergan, *Insight*

3.1 Introduction

This chapter brings together the themes of the two preceding chapters. Chapter 1 proposed that what Lonergan meant by self-appropriation is intimately related to practices of discernment. Chapter 2 presented Lonergan's way of answering the question, "What am I doing when I am knowing?" The two are connected, because genuine discernment includes knowing when one knows and when one doesn't. Of course, there is more to discernment, and more to self-appropriation, than knowing when one truly is knowing. Nevertheless, grappling with Lonergan's three questions is indispensable to discernment and self-appropriation in their fuller senses. Hence, this chapter focuses on the first stage of self-appropriation – the "self-affirmation of the knower," as Lonergan referred to it. Discussion of self-appropriation and discernment in the more complete sense will be resumed in chapter 10.

Still, even self-appropriation as self-affirmation involves more than merely accepting Lonergan's or anyone else's answers to the three questions about knowing solely on the basis of authority. Self-appropriation means that one has to answer those questions for one's own self, and especially the question "What am *I* doing when *I* am knowing?"

Attempting to answer such questions draws one into practices of discernment. This is because attempting to answer these questions requires one to discern the differences between when one actually knows and when one does not. It requires attention to the activities one performs as one comes to know something, as well as to the activities that lead one astray. It requires distinguishing activities that genuinely contribute to knowing from the welter of other activities. (These include both activities that are purported to be the ways we come to knowledge, but really are not, as well the many other activities one performs, which are simply irrelevant to the pursuit of knowledge, although this is not apparent at the outset.)

But if one does not yet already know the answer to "What am I doing when I am knowing?," upon what basis will one distinguish the activities that do contribute to genuine knowing from those that do not? Chapter 1 argued that the ability to discern the differences among experiences of internal conscious activities requires the attainment of heightened levels of commitment and skill on the part of a person trying to discern – in this case, to discern the differences between activities of knowing and not knowing. It also faced the difficulty that guidance of a special sort is required in order for anyone to attain such a capacity for discernment. Otherwise, the task of properly distinguishing among so many different experiences and activities and opinions about them will be overwhelming. But such guidance has to be just that – guidance, not persuasion or subtle manipulation. The first chapter also argued, therefore, that the proper kind of guidance must come from people who have themselves already attained self-knowledge and genuine openness through the processes of maturation in discernment.

So while a person taking up the challenges of self-appropriation as self-affirmation cannot and should not accept Lonergan's answers merely on the basis of his authority, Lonergan did offer *his* own answers in the spirit and hope of guiding others to appropriating *their* own activities of knowing. Do Lonergan's answers indeed offer valuable assistance as one grapples with the question oneself, or not?

Perhaps by this point some readers have already discerned amidst the internal experiences of their conscious activities which ones contribute to their knowing, and how they come together. Perhaps these readers have already affirmed for themselves that Lonergan's account expresses a correct understanding of their own conscious experiences of knowing. If so, then much of what follows may be redundant. But for those readers who have not yet reached that stage, I hope that what follows will be of assistance.

3.2   Self-Appropriation and Self-Affirmation

Lonergan regarded self-appropriation as the great cornerstone to his life's work. He regarded self-appropriation as the "essential benefit" that he gained from his early years of studying Thomas Aquinas – because in order to comprehend Aquinas, he had to encounter and come to terms with his own self.[1] He carried over into his later work the importance of what he learned about himself as a knower through his encounter with Aquinas, saying emphatically that this was his principal objective in his writing of *Insight*.[2] When he finally arrived at what he regarded as the proper approach to theological method, self-appropriation continued to play the most fundamental role. He organized that method so as to (1) lead the investigator towards self-appropriation, (2) show how self-appropriation, once acquired, enhances further theological research, and (3) further reveal the implications of results achieved by this method for the improvement of the world.[3]

Lonergan described self-appropriation in *Insight* as "one's own rational self-consciousness clearly and distinctly taking possession of itself as rational self-consciousness."[4] By "rational self-consciousness" he meant to include not only the acts of cognitional structure discussed in the previous chapter, but also the additional acts of consciousness that have to do with deliberating, valuing, deciding, and acting. Self-appropriation in this more complete sense is clearly a major undertaking that requires time and patience, and that passes through several stages before reaching its mature state. The present chapter focuses only on the first stages of self-appropriation that focus just on the activities of cognitional structure. These first stages of self-appropriation culminate in what Lonergan called the "self-affirmation of the knower."

3.3   Self-Affirmation as Conditioned

Self-affirmation of the knower is an affirmative judgment of fact. It is a limited judgment that affirms as correct a certain set of insights that answer the question "What am I doing when I am knowing?" The previous chapter offered an overview of what Lonergan thought human beings do in knowing. It offered an understanding of these interesting, complex, and theoretical relationships among cognitional acts of consciousness. But Lonergan did not intend his cognitional theory to be merely a possible, interesting, or plausible theory; he presented it as a correct understanding of human knowing and of the implications that this understanding holds for one's views about objectivity and reality.

Was he right? Does his theory present the correct understanding of what actually happens in your own conscious activities? This is the question for self-affirmation of oneself as a knower.

A first observation is that although this question is complex because of the complexity of Lonergan's account of cognitional structure, it is still only a very limited question. As Lonergan put it, "by 'knowing' I mean no more than performance [of such activities] as sensing, perceiving, imagining, inquiring, understanding, formulating, reflecting, grasping the unconditioned, and affirming."[5] Hence the question of self-affirmation of the knower asks only the limited question of whether or not one performs those activities in that dynamic pattern. This is not a question about knowing oneself completely and without qualification; what is sought in this question is not total knowledge of everything about oneself. This question only seeks a limited self-knowledge – knowledge of whether or not one is a knower in Lonergan's specific sense.

If one judges that in fact one is a knower in this sense, that does not settle the vast number of further questions about oneself: "Will I be happy? Will I be rich?," as the popular song asks. It does not settle whether the larger context in which one performs the activities of sensing, imagining, remembering, understanding, judging, and so on is a context of noble motives or evil motives. It does not answer whether or not one's self-identity is solely one's own doing, or whether that identity is largely constituted by involvements in gender, family, social, cultural, racial, ethnic, or religious groups. It does not answer whether or not the estimate of one's self-worth is sober and objective, or whether one is self-deceived.

While all these further questions are crucial to self-knowledge in the fuller sense, self-affirmation is a much more limited form of self-knowledge. Self-affirmation is merely an answer to the question for reflection and judgment as to whether or not one performs the activities in the dynamic cognitional structure.

Yet, while this is a limited judgment, it is a crucial and strategic judgment. If the answer is, "Yes, I am a knower in precisely this sense," then the answer implies that whatever remains to be known about oneself will come about by performing the cognitional structure with fidelity. It also implies that if one deviates from performance of the structure in attempting further self-knowledge, the result will be self-deception rather than authentic self-knowledge. The answer to the question for self-affirmation therefore will influence in profound and pervasive ways how one goes about answering other questions for self-knowledge in the fuller sense.

A second observation is that the question of self-affirmation of the knower is a question about an intelligibility. Hence this question is on the same footing as every other question for judgment. It entertains something as a conditioned intelligible possibility – that there is an intelligible order in the way one goes about achieving knowledge (i.e., the order articulated in section 2.4 of the previous chapter). This means that the proposition "I do perform these activities in this intelligibly ordered way" is a conditioned proposition. This conditioned proposition will be grasped as virtually unconditioned only once a link to requisite fulfilling conditions has been identified, and only when those conditions have been fulfilled. In this regard, Lonergan remarked,

> The link between the conditioned and its conditions may be cast in the proposition "I am a knower, if I am a concrete and intelligible unity-identity-whole, characterized by acts of sensing, perceiving, imagining, inquiring, understanding, formulating, reflecting, grasping the unconditioned, and judging." The fulfillment of the conditions is given in consciousness.[6]

3.4   Self-Affirmation of the Knower as Hermeneutical

Perhaps some readers have no difficulty with Lonergan's remark that they do indeed have internal, conscious experiences of the activities that contribute to their knowing. Such readers may find that these experiences "given in consciousness" are sufficient conditions for affirming the correctness of Lonergan's account.

However, Lonergan's claim that the fulfillment of the conditions is "given in consciousness" will likely be viewed as problematic by readers who have delved into the set of problems concerning consciousness and immediacy that have been raised by contemporary philosophers, psychologists, literary critics, and theologians. This section is addressed to some of the most basic of these issues.

First, then, Lonergan is using the term "consciousness" in a rather unconventional sense, and this difference is likely to cause misunderstanding. Second, he vastly oversimplifies the situation, for while the fulfillment of the conditions for the judgment of self-affirmation of knowing does indeed include experiential elements from the field of consciousness, those do not exhaust all of the fulfilling conditions. Like most other judgments of fact, there are many additional pertinent questions that must also be answered as part of the fulfillment of the conditions for the judgment of self-affirmation. Third, at first glance, Lonergan seems to be ignoring the wide range of philosophical discussions that have arisen about experiential givenness in general. More particularly, he seems also to be overlooking the difficulties that have been raised regarding the immediacy of consciousness as a subject's privileged mode of access to the subject himself or herself. He seems to be overlooking the fact that our reflections on consciousness already take place within the context of language, and that language mediates or interprets our acts of consciousness.

It is clear, however, that Lonergan himself was aware, at least to some extent, of the mediations of consciousness that self-affirmation requires. He noted that "*Insight* may be described as a set of exercises in which, it is hoped, one attains self-appropriation."[7] In other words, fulfillment of the conditions for affirming ourselves as knowers in Lonergan's precise sense is a mediated fulfillment. Access to the givenness in consciousness of our cognitional acts is a mediated, not an immediate, access. If we are to judge whether or not we actually perform our acts of consciousness in the cognitionally structured way, we first need to work through a set of exercises, directing our attention to certain acts of consciousness and to the relationships among them. These exercises will help bring into relief the experiential data necessary to arrive at a virtually unconditioned judgment on the question of self-affirmation.

Moreover, these exercises are guided by the language of *Insight*, which must first be understood in order to perform the exercises properly. But in order to understand what Lonergan means by the keywords in his special vocabulary, such as "experiencing," "inquiry," "insight," and "judgment," one must also have insights into those experiences. This interdependence of language and access to acts of consciousness form, therefore, a hermeneutical circle. But has Lonergan overlooked the hermeneutical problems involved in knowing what knowing is?

All of these concerns – the meaning of consciousness, the wider pattern of further questions, and the philosophical criticisms of the immediacy of subjectivity – intersect with one another. They form the hermeneutical problem of self-affirmation. These are the topics of the next sections.

3.4.1 *Consciousness as Experience*

When Lonergan says that the fulfillment of conditions for self-affirmation of knowing is given in consciousness, he has a very specific notion of consciousness in mind. At first, his way of thinking about consciousness may seem very strange, but eventually it comes to make eminent sense.

Commonly, consciousness is thought of as "consciousness of": consciousness of objects, consciousness of the ego, consciousness as the medium of access to objects by subjects. Consciousness in this sense is identified completely with intentionality *towards* some object or content of consciousness. To recall a point made in the previous chapter, intentionality is the irreducible relationship between an intending act (*noesis*) and an intended content or object (*noema*). To be intentionally conscious is to be oriented towards something. So there would have to be a non-identity involved in being conscious of an act of consciousness. Consciousness of an act of consciousness in this sense would be the intending of one conscious act by another.

Lonergan, on the other hand, distinguished "consciousness" from "intentionality." He meant something more primordial by "consciousness" – something he called "consciousness as experience."[8] By this he meant that consciousness is the experience that accompanies the performance of intentional activities such as seeing, hearing, inquiring, getting insights, reflecting, judging, etc. In order for *noetic* acts to have intentional relationships to *noematic* contents, the acts themselves must have the more primordial characteristic of being experientially conscious – that is to say, not only must the acts be intentional (i.e., have the property of being related to a *noematic* content), but they must also be the experiences of a subject who is performing them.

Conscious activities in Lonergan's senses are not like natural events that can occur whether or not a being ever experiences them. The prehistoric impacts of meteors on the moon's surface could and did occur without any accompanying conscious experiencing of those impacts, either by the meteors or the moon or anyone else. On the other hand, events like seeing, hearing, inquiring, and understanding can only occur if they occur consciously – that is, only if a subject experiences them. The emphasis here is on the events (the acts), not their contents. It is true that in seeing, there is an intentional experience of the object seen. But it is likewise true that there is also a conscious experience of the act of seeing itself. Without that accompanying conscious experience, these acts do not occur at all. Consciousness as experience is constitutive of the very being of conscious *noetic* acts. Moreover, without that conscious experience accompanying and immanent in the *noesis,* the *noema* could not be intended at all.

Consciousness as experience is immanent in and indispensably constitutive of the acts comprised by cognitional structure. This means that conscious experience of these acts happens simultaneously with those acts whenever they happen. It is not necessary to direct one's intentional attention to those acts in order to become conscious of them – one can direct one's attention to them only *because* they are *already* part of the field of one's experiencing. If one directs one's intentional attention towards one's own *noetic* act of hearing, this transforms the *noetic,* conscious experience of hearing into the *noematic* intentional content of a second act of attending to one's hearing. The ability to perform this kind of intentional attending presupposes that the act of hearing would already be part of one's field of experiencing, in order that it could then be made into an object of the act of attending.

Attending, however, can also have a more subtle and more primordial meaning. It can mean heightening the intensity of some experiences and diminishing the intensity of other experiences. If I attend (in this second sense) to what you are saying to me, I have to decrease the intensity of my experiences of the background conversations and the noises from the ventilation system and the traffic outside. But when I do so, I do not need to make my experience of hearing into the object of a second act of attending, in order that I may better hear your voice, nor do I have to bring the sound of your voice into intentional consciousness by my very act of directing my attention to it. Rather, because that sound was already the content of my act of hearing, I can re-pattern the field of my conscious experiencing, so that my hearing of the sound of your voice becomes prominent, while my hearing of the distracting sounds subsides.

In this re-patterning and heightening of my field of consciousness as experience, I do not make myself conscious of my act of hearing by directing my attention (in the first sense) towards that act. Rather, heightening my awareness or consciousness of my act of hearing presupposes that the conscious experience of hearing is already part of the field of my experience, and that I re-pattern that field in order to grant the experiential consciousness of my hearing greater prominence in that experiential field.

Each of us is already skilled to a greater or lesser extent in this kind of re-patterning the field of some kinds of conscious experiencing, although we may not have noticed ourselves doing this. This consists of a set of skills of being attentive that we have acquired long ago, probably beginning early in childhood. We develop such skills when parents, teachers, and others implore us to "Pay attention!" This kind of heightening of our experiences, then, has become second nature to us because we have developed these skills. But doing something similar for other experiences of *noetic* acts (such as inquiring, having insight, reflecting, grasping the virtually unconditioned, and judging) does not come spontaneously or easily to most people. In order to do so, one needs to acquire new sets of skills of re-patterning and heightening the intensity of experiences of these kinds of acts. These are elemental skills of discernment. So the first stage of self-affirmation (i.e., self-appropriation in the limited sense) is a matter of acquiring these new skills in heightening awareness of the experiences of one's cognitional *noetic* acts.

I have deliberately adopted the metaphor "experiential *field*" in order to emphasize that, in its most primordial state, our experiencing is a homogeneous and undifferentiated realm. There is no privileged experiencing *qua* experiencing within that field. In particular, there is no privileged experiencing of the self (ego) or of its *noetic* acts, over against other experiences, such as the *noematic* contents of seeing, hearing, feeling cold, etc. All distinctions and relations among our experiences are made by subsequent acts that supervene upon and interpret our experiencing. The distinction between the conscious *noetic* experiencing of seeing and the intentional *noematic* experience of the thing seen is a distinction made by insights and judgments subsequent to the field of experiencing as such.[9]

Of course, by the time you read this paragraph, you have already patterned your experiential field by means of a whole host of previous acts that constitute your own ongoing concerns and interests (acts that include but are not limited to inquiring, understanding, judging, feeling, valuing, believing, decisively committing, etc.). Your field of experiencing is no longer the purely homogeneous, undifferentiated field that it was in the earliest days of infancy. The prominence and persistence of certain elements in the ways that you pattern your experiential field is the result of those subsequent acts. The prominence of those elements in the stream of your consciousness is not a "given" that is imposed by something external to the experiencing subject – neither by the nervous system nor the outside world. Rather, what comes to the fore of attention is the result of your own activities of understanding, judging, feeling, valuing, deciding, and so on.

This means that there are already in place routines of attending that need to be modified if we are to embark successfully upon the process towards self-affirmation. If these routines are deeply entrenched, developing new skills of heightening the consciousness-as-experience of *noetic* acts will be especially difficult. As Lonergan remarked wryly, the act of insight "is so simple and obvious that it seems to merit the little attention that commonly it receives."[10] So some transformations of our routines of attending, re-patterning, and heightening of our experiential field are needed, in order to fulfill in consciousness the conditions for self-affirmation. The very fact that these prior routines were previously developed testifies to the great flexibility and plasticity in our ability to re-pattern our experiential field. Because this is not easily accomplished, however, some degree of guidance is needed for most people. We will return to consider this process and its guidance in greater detail in section 3.4.3.

3.4.2 *Cognitional Structure Applied to Cognitional Structure*

The first stage of self-affirmation of the knower (and therefore of self-appropriation more generally) involves efforts to heighten the experiential consciousness of the *noetic* acts. By themselves, the results of efforts at heightening consciousness of acts can be quite delightful and exhilarating. It can become tempting to spend all of one's time exploring this new domain of revelations about the wealth of one's consciousness as experience. But the exciting expansion of heightened awareness of one's *noetic* activities is only the beginning of the process of self-affirmation.

The process towards self-affirmation of knowing does not end or rest content with the achievements of the heightening of consciousness of *noetic* acts. The project of self-affirmation approaches experiential consciousness as more than just something to be experienced for its own sake. Moving to the next stage on the path towards self-affirmation involves inquiring into consciousness of oneself and one's acts as experience. It A person on that path wonders about the experiences of consciousnesses and conscious activities. He or she pursues all sorts of inquiries about consciousness-as-experience. The pursuit of self-affirmation of oneself as knower then seeks to answer the questions that arise from the heightened experiences of *noetic* acts. Those answers, of course, come in the form of insights, acts of direct understanding about those heightened experiences, about what they are like, about their differences from each other, and about the relationships among them. The project of self-affirmation moves still further as preliminary insights into consciousness as experience give rise to further questions, yielding more refined insights, which in turn also yield still further heightening of consciousness as experience. When experiences of the more subtle acts of consciousness are brought into greater relief, they give rise to still further questions and further insights that produce not only more discerning understanding of these acts of consciousness, but also an ever more discerning awareness of the consciousness-as-experience of *noetic* acts.

In other words, the process of self-affirmation involves applying the acts of cognitional structure to the consciousness-as-experience of performing those acts. The project of self-affirmation is a matter of a "reduplication" of the structure, as Lonergan put it.[11] Its ultimate objective is virtually unconditioned judgments about the correctness of one's understanding of one's own acts, how they are distinguished from one another, and how they are related to one another. If Lonergan is correct, then judgments of self-affirmation will lead to the conclusion that one's own acts of affirming follow upon the performance of a series of prior acts structured and underpinned by questions for intelligence and reflection about one's own conscious experiences.

The very acts involved in these later stages of self-affirmation are themselves conscious. As one performs them, the consciousness-as-experience of them becomes part of one's experiential field. The inquiries, insights, reflections, and judgments that make up the activities of self-affirmation themselves have experiential dimensions precisely because they too are conscious activities. The conscious experiences that accompany these activities also invite inquiry, understanding, reflection, and judgment. In this fashion, cognitional affirmation is cognitional self-affirmation – it endeavours to affirm what one is when one is affirming what one is doing.

3.4.3 Mediated Givenness

When Lonergan writes that the "fulfilment of the conditions is given in consciousness," the term "given" can suggest unexamined and misleading connotations. It can suggest that the data of consciousness are a special, foundational realm through which the subject has immediate, privileged access to himself or herself, unlike its access to any other realm. Jürgen Habermas gave voice to a widely shared post-modern critique and suspicion about any such approach when he wrote, "The paradigm of the philosophy of consciousness is exhausted." His comment comes towards the end of his evaluation of Michel Foucault's critique of subjectivity, and he continues, "the objectifying attitude in which the knowing subject regards itself as it would entities in the external world is no longer *privileged*."[12]

For Habermas, then, the paradigm of the philosophy of the givenness of consciousness has to do with the special privilege attributed to self-knowledge. Either this special privilege is thought to derive from some special, immediate access to consciousness, in opposition to the "from a distance" access to the "external world," or self-knowledge is held to become especially privileged when it imitates the kind of objectifying attitude thought to be appropriate to objects in the external world. We have already seen that Lonergan sharply dissociates his philosophy from this notion of external objectification. Furthermore, the dependence of self-knowledge upon fulfillment of conditions from the data of consciousness does not make it any more certain or privileged than knowledge whose conditions are drawn from data of sensation. The certitude of every judgment is grounded solely in a grasp of the virtually unconditioned. Every such judgment is just as certain as every other, irrespective of whether the fulfilling conditions are drawn from the data of sense or the data of consciousness or both. Both consciousness and sensation equally can be sources of data that may or may not contribute to the conditions for some particular instance of a virtually unconditioned judgment.

As Habermas rightly observes, virtually all attention to experience (whether sense experience or consciousness as experience) is mediated and structured.[13] Many other twentieth-century philosophers have also underscored the fact that our experiencing is not purely immediate. They have argued that our experiencing is overwhelmingly mediated and structured by language – that our observations are "theory laden," for example.[14] This is no less true of attention to data of consciousness than of attention to data of sense. From the fact that linguistic and other factors are involved in the structuring of experience, many have concluded that there is no such thing as the objectively given – that there are only constructions (structurings) which are purely human fabrications.

However, this conclusion does not necessarily follow, because the structuring of attention constitutes what might be called a "mediated immediacy." What is "given" in human experience is a mediated givenness. The given of experience is not had, as Lonergan puts it, by "mere passivity"; rather, the given "occurs within [experience's] own dynamic context."[15] It is a highly selected and patterned givenness. As Lonergan notes, self-appropriation requires a "reversal" that mediates the immediacy of consciousness as experience.[16]

That this is so, however, does not eliminate the given altogether. The fact that givenness is mediated means that experiencing retains an element of givenness nonetheless. Consider the example of someone pointing out and describing a special rock formation in a canyon to a companion. The spoken linguistic expressions used in pointing out the formation neither fabricate nor substitute for the other person's visual experiences of the formation. Rather, they guide the listener in the heightening of visual experiences. They assist the listener in bringing some visual experiences to the fore, and in letting others recede to the periphery, in hopes of achieving what has been called a "Gestalt shift." The linguistic clues highlight subtle differences among colours and shapes that were unnoticed at first. What is given in the contents of the listener's experiences before, during, and after the description (including the sights of the rocks and the sounds of the speaker's voice) differs because the description itself has stimulated a restructuring of experience. Still, in each stage of this transformation of experiencing, there are contents given in the experiences, however much that givenness varies from one moment to the next, and however much that givenness is facilitated by linguistic expressions. That the given elements of experiencing and attention vary according to mediating and structuring activities does not eliminate the fact that those elements, once mediated, are given in consciousness as experience.

Not only are the contents of sensations given, but the contents of memories, imaginations, optical illusions, hallucinations, and dreams are given as well.[17] Again, not only do the contents of sense, memory, and imagination have elements of givenness, but also the experiences of the acts themselves are given in consciousness insofar as a conscious subject is actually performing those acts. Yet the givenness of data (whether of sensation or of consciousness) in no way guarantees that there is "something really out there (or in here)" that is impressing itself on one's consciousness. This is not what is meant by the givenness of experience – that there is something out there, independent of consciousness, which guarantees givenness. The difference between sensation and hallucination is not that sensations are given while hallucinations are not; both are given (otherwise one would not actually be hallucinating). Rather, the sorting out of givens into sensations, memories, imaginations, illusions, dreams, hallucinations, etc., is not settled by the given as given. This sorting out is the subsequent work of inquiry, understanding, reflection, and especially unconditioned judgment. These subsequent acts intelligently comprehend and reasoningly distinguish among the various kinds of mediated givens. Likewise, settling whether or not there is anything independent of consciousness from which the given is derived is a matter not of givenness as such, but of subsequent acts of inquiry, understanding, reflection, and judgment about what is given in mediated experiences. Again, even though a given content is the result of prior mediation, even though the intelligibility of the given is only known by subsequent activities, still some content is given, whether in sensation or in hallucination. If there were no given content, there would be neither sensation nor hallucination.

In light of these considerations, then, how should we construe Lonergan's remark that the "fulfillment of the conditions is given in consciousness"? Clearly the remark should not be construed as some simple matter of immediate introspection and comparison. Arriving at a judgment about whether Lonergan's cognitional theory is a correct understanding of your own consciousness as experience is not a matter of turning your attention towards some unmediated givenness in the interior of your own consciousness, and then comparing Lonergan's account of cognitional structure with those internal experiences to see if they match. As was argued in the previous chapter, this metaphor is of no use.[18] The intelligible content of an act of understanding cannot be fitted up against contents of sense experience. Neither can it be fitted upon data of consciousness. Hence self-affirmation is no matter of introspection and comparison in this naive sense – something else is involved. The something else is sorting out what conditions would have to be given and what kinds of mediations deliver those givens reliably, and then determining whether in fact those conditions are fulfilled.

The issue of mediations is raised by yet another critic of the "philosophy of consciousness," Paul Ricoeur. In his reflection on Nietzsche's critique of Cartesianism, Ricoeur remarks that "the philosophy of subjectivity had utterly disregarded the mediating factor of language in the argumentation of the 'I am' and the 'I think' ... Nietzsche brings to light the rhetorical strategies that have been buried, forgotten, and even hypocritically repressed and denied, in the name of the immediacy of reflection."[19]

Taken at face value, Lonergan's claim that "conditions are given in consciousness" seems to fall victim to this line of criticism. It seems to bypass the fact of linguistic mediation in favour of immediate access to conditions fulfilled in consciousness.

Yet Lonergan himself was keenly aware of the indispensability of mediation, linguistic and otherwise, to the task of self-appropriation. In addition to his comment that *Insight* is a set of exercises in order to assist the reader towards self-appropriation, he also remarks that the conditions to be fulfilled in consciousness "have *become familiar* in the course of this investigation," namely the investigation of *Insight* itself.[20] Elsewhere he observes that "the process of self-appropriation occurs only slowly, and, usually, only through a struggle with some such book as *Insight*."[21] In other words, the mediating language and exercises from a text such as *Insight* itself are required in order to become familiar with the data of consciousness. However, *Insight* was aiming at several objectives all at once,[22] and this tends to diminish its effectiveness as a guide to heightening consciousness of the important acts of consciousness. Better yet, the reader will find fine assistance from the texts and exercises aimed at this heightening experiences of the key acts of consciousness, such as Peter Beer's *An Introduction to Bernard Lonergan,* Brian Cronin's *The Foundations of Philosophy,* Joseph Flanagan's *The Quest for Self-Knowledge,* and Mark Morelli's *Self-Possession: Being at Home in Conscious Performance,* among others.[23] The later chapters of the present book are also intended to assist the reader in heightening experiences of acts of consciousness that go beyond those having to do with factual knowing (cognitional structure), and fall into the more encompassing structure of ethical intentionality.[24]

To Lonergan's recognition of the factors of language and exercises involved in mediating the givenness of conditions in consciousness, I would add an observation of my own: the heightening of consciousness of the acts of consciousness that are the foci of self-affirmation (as well as of self-appropriation in the fuller sense) usually requires participation in a community of conversation. Written words can be taken to mean many things, but the multiplicity of meanings can be pruned, modified, and corrected by the insights and judgments of others who have struggled with the tasks of self-affirmation and self-appropriation. A community of conversation, along with texts and ensuing exercises, are needed to properly heighten the reader's attention to the givenness of consciousness as experience.[25] This sort of apprenticing within a community also takes place in the scientific and medical fields, where novices are instructed in how to take a blood pressure reading, properly use a microscope, or notice significant features on a CAT scan. Likewise, good conversation and instruction can guide novices towards refined awareness of the experiences they are having of their own *noetic* acts, so that consciousness-as-experience of acts like inquiries and insights can be discerned over the clamour of other experiences that were initially more intense and more familiar. The mediating work of text, exercises, and community – as well as the mediating influences of one's own inquiring, understanding, reflecting, and judging – are required if one is to learn how to pay attention to the data of consciousness. They are also needed to assist the novice in discriminating between experiences of consciousness and experiences of sensation. Finally, they are also needed to assist in discerning within the experiences of consciousness those subtle differences among activities of seeing, hearing, inquiring, insight, reflecting, judging, and so on.

No doubt these comments about the role of community in developing skills of attention and discernment will elicit serious worries about indoctrination. Is it only by belonging to a certain community that one can "see the light"? Is self-affirmation and self-appropriation a cult phenomenon? These concerns are very legitimate and must be faced. Still, the ways in which they need to be faced are not simple. Critique of a community of practices from outside overlooks the problem of critiquing the community by means of which the critic himself or herself was formed. The examples above from scientific and medical fields draw attention to the fact that skills of observation and criticism are nurtured and perfected in communities of expertise. However, proper discussion of the complex problem of self-criticism of communities and traditions of expertise, especially in the field of ethics, has to be deferred to chapters 15 and 16, as it depends upon prior discussion of a number of other topics. For the present, it is possible to say that as long as the guiding principle of such communities of expertise is the unrestricted desire to know, then these will not be communities of in-group indoctrination. As long as one is oriented by unrestricted inquiry, what is said by interlocutors or in texts in a community will not be ultimately determinative of what is affirmed about one's own cognitional processes. The challenges of realizing this critical orientation will be discussed in the ensuing chapters.

3.4.4 *Correctly Understanding Consciousness-as-Experience as Hermeneutical*

The givenness of the conditions for self-affirmation is an unavoidably and massively mediated givenness. To admit as much acknowledges the legitimacy of objections such as those of Habermas and Ricoeur. However, this admission need not jeopardize the givenness in consciousness as conditions for self-affirmation. Still, if those conditions are not just "already in here now" – if they are instead mediated by thought and language use – exactly how can they be relied upon as conditions for unconditional self-affirmation of ourselves as knowers?

The way to answer this dilemma is to observe that Lonergan overstated the reliance on the givenness of conditions in consciousness. They are necessary, but not sufficient conditions for cognitional self-appropriation. By emphasizing givenness in consciousness, Lonergan emphasized something crucial to the task of self-affirmation, namely that there is an indispensable experiential, given dimension to the conditions that must be fulfilled in order to reach a virtually unconditioned ground for affirming oneself as a knower in his precise sense. Unless the activities are experientially conscious, they are not being performed by any subject, and then there is no possible way to correctly affirm that one is actually performing such acts. But in emphasizing this givenness in consciousness, Lonergan also tended to downplay other conditions that are also required for affirming the cognitional structure as a fact of one's own consciousness. These additional conditions include, importantly and indispensably, a long sequence of inquiries, insights, reflections, and judgments that began with the acquisition of linguistic competence and eventually converged on the interplay between language of texts and consciousness-as-experience. The acquisition of linguistic competence began in childhood and includes the inquiries, insights, and judgments that form the background for competent use of such words as "experience," "question," "desire," "understanding," and "judgment" that are brought to the task of heightening consciousness and the project of self-affirmation.

This becomes evident in any attempt to read a text like *Insight*. Whatever the reader's previous linguistic inheritances, anyone who attempts to read such a text will quickly find himself or herself puzzled. The text soon elicits questions that lead beyond the previously accumulated linguistic competences that the reader initially brought to the text. Nor are these experiences of questions and puzzlement elicited by the text tangential to the project of self-affirmation. Lonergan's text includes the self-revelatory proclamation that it is "written from a moving viewpoint"[26] – in other words, it is a text explicitly written to provoke new questions and elicit new insights and judgments. Some of the questions, insights, and judgments elicited by the text draw the reader beyond the text itself into new questions about the reader's now heightened personal experiences of acts of consciousness. As Lonergan puts it, "the meaning of all these sentences" is to be grasped fully only by "going beyond" the linguistic elements in the text towards one's own field of conscious experience.[27]

As with any text, studying a text about self-appropriation such as *Insight* entails reading and rereading, where the rereading gradually extends to include the "text" of one's own experiences of acts of consciousness, along with experiences of the written marks of the printed text. In other words, the linguistic mediation of what is given in consciousness means that the self-correcting cycle of questions and answers gradually enlarges the field of experience to be interrogated. If one carefully reads this kind of text, one's field of experience gradually shifts and expands from the base provided by the visual data of the "spatially ordered marks"[28] on paper, to include the data of one's own consciousness-as-experience.

In this interplay, preliminary insights regarding a written text or spoken instructions restructure attention to experiences. Restructured experiences give rise to new inquiries and insights that suggest new readings of the text (or new understandings of the spoken words), which in turn further restructure attention to the data of one's own consciousness. This cyclical process is hermeneutical. It is a cyclical process of learning how to begin to heighten the conscious experience of one's *noetic* acts, leading to new questions, new insights, a more refined heightening of consciousness, more questions, and so on. But this hermeneutical circle is not self-enclosed; each repetition of the cycle leads to transformations of experience, understanding, and judgment. This cyclical process does not come to a rest until all the further pertinent questions are answered, when one recognizes and affirms that her or his *noetic* acts really do occur in this structure of cognition underpinned by inquiry. It is not merely the consciousness-as-experience of acts of consciousness that form the conditions for affirming oneself as a knower in this precise sense. It is also the absence of further questions pertinent to the question, "Do I really perform such activities as sensing, perceiving, imagining, inquiring, understanding, formulating, reflecting, grasping the unconditioned, and affirming in this cognitionally structured way?"

While the process towards self-affirmation of oneself as a knower can be detoured into an unproductive and self-reinforcing obsession, it will be productive and normative when it is guided and structured by the unrestricted desire to know how things really are. Insofar as it is guided by the desire to understand the facts of one's own knowing correctly, it becomes a self-correcting exercise in self-transcendence, as the relentless sequence of further questions gradually converges on the fulfillment of all conditions that such an inquiring spirit requires – conditions fulfilled both insofar as experiences of *noetic* acts are given in consciousness, and insofar as there really are no further questions pertinent to self-affirmation of the knower.

In the end, the conditions that are needed to ground the judgment, "Yes, I do perform those activities in that structured way," include but go beyond the givenness of experiences of those acts in consciousness. Those conditions do not consist in some passive "always already in here now" given in consciousness. They are, rather, experiences of one's own acts – not only given, but also confidently known to be not merely imagined or hypothesized or invented by means of processes of mediation guided by unrestricted inquiry. Those given elements in experience as consciousness become conditions for the judgment of self-affirmation only once they are also correctly understood. In this synthesis of givenness and correct understanding of the experiences of one's own acts as conscious, one appropriates oneself (i.e., makes oneself one's own) truly and genuinely as a knower. One objectively knows oneself as a subject who is a knower. This is the achievement of self-affirmation of the knower, of cognitional self-appropriation.

As chapter 2 explained, cognitional theory has important implications for philosophical positions on objectivity and reality (being). Therefore, once cognitional structure is affirmed to be true of one's own experiences, one also possesses the grounds for affirming those further philosophical positions. They can become, in Lonergan's sense, a "verified" philosophy of knowing, objectivity, and being for you.[29]

3.5   A Decisive Act

Certainly it is difficult to commit oneself to the affirmative judgment of self-affirmation that "I do actually perform such activities as sensing, perceiving, imagining, inquiring, understanding, formulating, reflecting, grasping the unconditioned, and affirming." Nevertheless, Lonergan points out that at least the negative answer has to be excluded.[30] The negative answer is itself a judgment. If it is not just an arbitrary judgment, then the person uttering it must have an answer to the question of whether or not there are sufficient reasons for committing to this judgment. The judgment, its prior question, and the recognition of sufficient reasons (reflective understanding) and the relations among them are among those things that, according to the negative judgment, never happen. Again, the judgment that "I really do not perform such activities as sensing, perceiving, imagining, inquiring, understanding, formulating, reflecting, grasping the unconditioned, and affirming" presupposes some understanding of what these words mean, and this in turn presupposes some questions about experiences that led to the understandings of those words. But the negative judgment denies having ever had either inquiries or insights.

Hence, while one may not yet be certain about the affirmative answer to the question about whether one is a knower in Lonergan's sense, the negative answer, "No, I do not perform these activities in this way," is simply a performative self-contradiction. It denies in words what it performs in the meaningful utterance of those very words.

Still, the positive self-affirmation of oneself as a knower is ultimately something that each person can do only for himself or herself. At this point, this text can go no further. The language offered in this chapter, the texts recommended (including *Insight*), the communities of conversation, and the exercises can facilitate efforts, but they can go only so far. Without one's own efforts, they remain mere words. The next steps are up to the reader.

It is no accident that Lonergan calls self-appropriation a "decisive act."[31] However well the reader may have followed and understood the words in this chapter, in Lonergan's writings, or in those of the other authors mentioned here, one has to *decide* to take up the project of self-affirmation.

This means that self-affirmation is incapable of standing alone. Taking the next step means deciding that it is valuable and worthwhile to undertake the tasks of heightening one's consciousness-as-experience, to engage in the prolonged self-correcting hermeneutical circle towards correctly understanding that heightened field of experience, and to reach an affirmative judgment about that understanding. But self-appropriation of what is involved in valuing and deciding is not included under of the self-affirmation of oneself as a knower. The challenge of self-affirmation, therefore, invites a decisive commitment to engage in the stages that progress towards self-affirmation. The achievement of the factual judgment of self-affirmation itself will also confront one with decisions to take up the further fundamental philosophical questions about knowing, objectivity and being that self-affirmation implies, and then the further decision about whether or not to let one's thinking be guided by such implications. This last is a decision for or against what Lonergan called "intellectual conversion."

Still, decisions to embark upon the work of self-affirmation, as well as the decision that is intellectual conversion, fall outside of what is affirmed in self-affirmation of the knower. Such decisions are activities of a self that is wider and deeper than the self as a knower. The remainder of this book endeavours to spell out what is involved in making such decisions responsibly, and how this is related to decisions called "moral conversion." To that endeavour we now turn.

PART TWO

What Are We Doing When We Are Being Ethical?

4 The Structure of Ethical Intentionality: Three More Questions

They mistake what is most obvious in ethics (i.e., choice) for what ethics obviously is.
– Anonymous

4.1 Introduction

The previous chapters were devoted to exposition and affirmation of the human cognitional structure – the structure of factual knowing – as Lonergan presented it. This chapter begins the expansion of the themes of those chapters in the direction of ethical thought and action by first taking up the question of the more encompassing structure of ethical intentionality.

In *Insight*, Lonergan referred to this more encompassing structure as the "dynamic structure of knowing and doing."[1] He further claimed that just "as a metaphysics is derived from the known structure of one's knowing, so an ethics results from knowledge of the compound structure of one's knowing and doing."[2] However, he never stated explicitly just how he conceived of this more encompassing structure,[3] nor did he explicitly carry through on his promissory note about showing how that structure could be elaborated into an ethics parallel to the way he developed his metaphysics.

Moreover, unlike his thinking about cognitional, epistemological, and metaphysical issues, Lonergan's thinking about ethics underwent considerable evolution after the publication of *Insight*. This evolution included (1) his recognition of a "transcendental notion of value" and a consequent level of consciousness that was quite distinct from anything he had treated in *Insight*, (2) his discovery of a genus of feelings that intend values and disvalues, and (3) his discovery of a second direction in the dynamism of consciousness complementary and inverse to the dynamism of inquiry. The dynamism of inquiry he called "the movement from below upward," while the inverse dynamism he referred to as the movement "from above downwards."[4]

These developments considerably complicate the task of showing how the structure of knowing and doing implies an ethics. In order to do so, it first becomes necessary to revise whatever Lonergan might have thought about the structure of knowing and doing at the time of *Insight* in light of the significant changes in his thought that occurred afterward. Unfortunately, Lonergan himself did not explicitly address these issues.

In this chapter and the next three I will offer an interpretation, a plausible synthesis, that pulls together various sources into an integrated account of what I will call "the structure of ethical intentionality." While I believe this account represents Lonergan's mature position, I will not attempt to argue that claim. The path that Lonergan followed as his thought on ethics and values evolved is a worthy subject for a book in its own right. But instead of attempting to support my account by reconstructing the path of Lonergan's thought, I will appeal instead to the reader's own experiences of endeavouring to think and act ethically. In other words, I will appeal to self-appropriation as the arbiter of the benefits and defects of my own account of ethical intentionality. Self-appropriation in this broader and deeper sense will be the subject of chapter 10. But before the appeal to self-appropriation can be made, it is necessary, first, to set forth the account of the structure of ethical intentionality itself and its implications.

In chapter 2, I approached the structure of cognitional intentionality by means of Lonergan's three questions: What am I doing when I am knowing? Why is doing that knowing? What do I know when I do that? Similarly, I have organized most of the chapters of this book by means of three parallel questions. The answer to the first question (What am I doing when I am being ethical?) will occupy the present chapter along with chapters 5–7. Chapters 8–10 are devoted to the second question (Why is doing that being ethical?). The third question (What is brought about by doing that?) is the subject of chapters 11–14. The question of the method of ethics is treated in the final chapters, 15 and 16.

My use of these three questions to explore ethical intentionality is parallel to, but slightly different from, those posed by Joseph Flanagan in his *Quest for Self-Knowledge*. There Flanagan structures his discussion of ethics around the three questions: What am I doing when I am deliberating? Why do I decide? And what do I choose when I make a choice?[5] Flanagan's discussion is important and rich. In particular, I have found his reflections on the ways that elemental desires and fears, cultures, symbolisms, and history all enter into the ethical life, and how the structure of ethical intentionality can serve as a basis for criticism and transformation of them to be of special importance. His ideas have influenced several important parts of this book. Still, I have chosen to formulate the three questions somewhat differently, for two main reasons. First, I formulated the questions in a way that I believe is a bit more congruent with Lonergan's three questions about human cognition. Second, Flanagan's focus on deliberation and choice is somewhat incomplete, since they lead up to but do not include action. That is of course implicit in Flanagan's account, but I believe it is preferable to use terminology that makes the wholeness of the ethical phenomenon as explicit as possible (recognizing that it can never be made completely explicit). So in my formulations I have adopted the traditional term "ethical," which does include, action along with deliberation, choice and numerous other acts of consciousness.

4.2   Structure of Ethical Intentionality: What Am I Doing When I Am Being Ethical?

Lonergan's answer to his first cognitional question – "What am I doing when I am knowing?" – began with a list of activities of consciousness. Likewise, answering the question about the structure of ethical intentionality – "What am I doing when I am being ethical?" – also begins with a list of activities. This list incorporates all of the activities in cognitional structure, but also expands upon it. To the list of cognitional activities – seeing, hearing, smelling, touching, tasting, inquiring, imagining, understanding, conceiving, reflecting, weighing the evidence, judging, etc. – the following activities must be added: feeling, practical inquiring, practical insight, value inquiring, value reflecting, reflective understanding of value, value judging, deliberating, choosing/deciding, and acting.[6]

As before, this expanded list is meant to be suggestive, not exhaustive. Many other terms could be added. What is at issue here is not the impossible goal of an exhaustive listing, but the analysis of the structure within which these activities occur. In human ethical living, each of the activities in the list has intrinsic dynamic relationships to other activities. Being ethical does not consist in performing just one or some selected few of these activities. Among other things, this especially means that being ethical entails much more than choice alone; rather, being ethical is performing the whole of the dynamic structure that comprises these many activities. Lonergan speaks of being responsible as one of his five "transcendental precepts."[7] Being responsible means being authentically ethical – and both mean thinking, feeling, deciding, and acting in fidelity to that dynamic structure as a whole.

As with cognitional structure, a special subset of activities in the expanded list plays the central role in dynamically structuring ethical intentionality. As with cognitional structure, this subset includes inquiries of various kinds. Unlike cognitional structure, however, it also includes the special category of feelings – feelings that Lonergan, following Dietrich von Hildebrand, called "intentional responses to value."[8] Feelings of this type, together with ethical inquiries, introduce tensions into consciousness. Together they form the dynamic relations that structure the whole of ethical intentionality. The other activities in the list compose the elements that are related. Feelings for values and ethical inquiries determine how the remaining activities are organized, structured, and related to one another. As a first approximation, it could be said that the inquiries are sources of what Lonergan called the movement from below upward, while intentional feelings are sources of the movement from above downward.

The fact that such feelings, as well as inquiries, constitute the structuring of ethical intentionality complicates matters considerably, and this affects the manner in which the account of the structure will proceed. For the sake of clarity, therefore, I begin with the structuring that results from ethical inquiry in this chapter, and will treat the role played in value reflection, deliberation, and deciding by feelings in chapter 7. This does not mean, however, that feelings enter into the structure of ethical intentionality at a later point in time, only after ethical inquiry, understanding, and judging have begun. Rather, feelings are basic and primary in ethical intentionality – and indeed in human consciousness in general.[9] Lonergan used to say that "feelings are the mass and momentum" of human living. Feelings as intentional responses are always operative throughout the entire dynamic structure of human consciousness. Still, the appropriation of such feelings and their roles in the functioning of our ethical intentionality is best approached after the structure of value inquiry has been clarified.

4.3   Basic Ethical Questions

The inquiries that characterize and structure ethical intentionality include those expressed in the following questions: "What is going on?" "What can be done?" "What could I do?" "What good is it?" "What is it worth?" "Would it be good (worthwhile) for me to do it?" "What should I do?" "How should I do it?" "Shall I do it?"[10] As was the case with cognitional structure, these inquiries divide into several basic types. However, where there were two basic types of cognitional questions (questions for intelligence and for reflection), now there are four basic types of ethical questions: questions about the situation, the practical possibilities, the worth and obligatoriness of the possibilities, and, finally, the question for decision. In one sense, the question for decision governs the entire flow and structure of ethical intentionality even though it comes last. The question for decision depends upon answers to all of the prior questions, and yet each of the prior questions is oriented so as to make a contribution towards answering the question for decision. In other words, all of the questions and the acts that they presuppose and that they lead to are situated within an overall dynamic structure that ultimately culminates in the acts of responsible, ethical deciding and acting.

In what follows, a separate section is devoted to each of these four basic types of questions and the acts that immediately and specifically answer to them. This does not mean, however, that there must always be a one-to-one correspondence between these basic inquiries and the linguistic formulations of questions. For example, if I were to ask, "What should I do?," I would be simultaneously expressing in a single sentence three closely related but distinguishable pre-linguistic inquiries: "what?," "should?," and "do?" (i.e., "What can I do?," "Should I do it?," and "Will I do it?"). Each of the discernable underlying inquiries establishes a distinct dynamic relationship towards something specific that it desires and seeks. With growing skill in discernment, the distinct tensions of inquiry underlying unified verbal expressions can be discerned. While such fine-tuned ethical discernment is not necessary in many ordinary situations, it is nevertheless essential in order to clarify the structure of ethical intentionality. Such clarification and discernment are needed in many areas where the resources of ordinary ethical reflection break down.

4.4   What Is the Situation?

Responsible ethical inquiry begins with the question "What is going on?" If ethical intentionality is to be more than naive or complacent moral idealism, it must incorporate genuine knowledge of the situation in which the ethical subject finds herself or himself. The important observation that opened chapter 2 bears repeating for emphasis: A great deal of harm has been done in the name of ethics and morality by well-meaning people who have failed to properly understand the real situation. As Lonergan himself put it, "One cannot do good without knowing the facts, without knowing what is really possible, without knowing the probable consequences of one's course of action."[11] In her criticism of the serious failures and deleterious results of urban planning, for example, Jane Jacobs asked, "How can you know what to try … until you know how the city itself works?" She continues, "It may be that we have become so feckless as a people that we no longer care how things work, but only what kind of quick, easy outer impression they give."[12]

Taking her own advice, Jacobs set forth her understandings of how and why cities function well and poorly in her book *The Death and Life of Great American Cities*. The book has become a classic in rethinking urban design. She thus provides a prime example of the point that objective knowledge of the situation in which the subject finds himself or herself is indispensable to ethical authenticity. Hence, one of the most important elements of ethical responsibility is responsibility for objective knowledge of the situation.

Knowing what is going on is the work of cognitional structure, which was discussed in chapter 2. This means, of course, that the question "What is going on?" is really a compact abbreviation of the structured inquiring of cognitional structure that operates in and through the acts of experiencing, questions for intelligence, insights, questions for reflection, and virtually unconditioned judging.

To a large extent, our knowledge of what is going on is the work of cognitional structure operating in the mode of what Lonergan called "common sense":

> [Common sense] remains completely in the familiar world of things for us. The further questions, by which it accumulates insights, are bounded by the interests and concerns of human living, by the successful performance of daily tasks, by the discovery of immediate solutions that will work. Indeed the supreme canon of common sense is the restriction of further questions to the realm of the concrete and particular, the immediate and practical.[13]

The dynamic of common sense consists in a "self-correcting process of learning" that wonders about how things are related to immediate experiences and concerns, that draws upon a "common fund of tested" insights of others, and that continually adds "at least one further insight into the situation at hand."[14] In doing so, each person draws upon a vast number of insights accumulated over a lifetime, many of which were insights that others have passed along in all sorts of informal and formal ways. Most of the questions pertinent to sizing up a specific situation have already been answered in advance by means of this inventory of accumulated insights. This accumulation constitutes a "person of experience" who is capable of arriving at sober, objective, commonsense judgments about what is going on, especially in social situations. This implies, therefore, that the first task of ethical intentionality is to acquire a substantial fund of commonsense insights and judgments needed to think accurately about the situation that one is in. The lack of accurate commonsense understanding of a situation sets the stage for blunders of fixing what is not broken and applying the wrong remedies to problems. Thoughtless blundering is hardly the paradigm for ethical responsibility. Developing the capacity for good commonsense judgments is indispensable to becoming ethically responsible.

As important as commonsense knowledge of the situation is, however, it alone is not sufficient for ethical responsibility. The situations in which people find themselves are related to far more than the individual person's immediate experiences, interests, needs, and concerns. Every concrete situation is also related actually and potentially to people and circumstances both present in space and time, as well as distant in space and in time, both in the future and in the past. The further these relations to people and circumstances stretch away from the immediate present, the more likely they are to lie beyond the horizon of individual or group interests and concerns. The obvious examples of environmental pollution and global warming serve to illustrate the general point. What were regarded as commonsense solutions to disposal of industrial waste products a century ago turned out to have had deleterious consequences for people today and in the future. These consequences were beyond the horizon of the commonsense concerns of people a century ago.

Thus while commonsense knowledge makes an indispensable contribution to answering the question "What is going on?," commonsense knowledge must be supplemented with another kind of knowledge that relates immediate situations to more distant situations. Lonergan variously used the terms "explanatory," "scientific," or "theoretical" to characterize this second type of knowledge. Whatever term one chooses, the concern of this second type of knowledge is with relations that go beyond what is immediate in place and time. Explanatory knowing does take into account the ways that things are related to a particular individual's or a particular group's interests, needs, and concerns as legitimate, but as only a part of a larger set of interrelationships. It recognizes that the virtually unconditioned answer to the question "What is going on?" also includes knowledge about how human actions affect what goes on in the non-human natural realm, and what will be going on in future generations as well. It is the business of scientific-theoretical knowing to correctly understand this wider realm of explanatory relations. For example, already in 1896 Swedish chemist Svante August Arrhenius predicted that increases in carbon dioxide emissions would lead to significant increases in global temperatures.[15] Even though he and other scientists already understood the fuller dimensions of the situation at that time, clearly commonsense practices remained ignorant or indifferent to those consequences. Even today, when far more people of common sense appreciate the long-term consequences of the continuing increase of the carbon dioxide content of our atmosphere, commonsense insights into what to do have yet to catch up to the explanatory understanding of these facts because, as was explained in chapter 2, general bias against theoretical ideas as "impractical" is a constant source of distortion of human knowing. Hence, fully answering "What is going on?" requires intelligent and complex syntheses of both commonsense practical and scientific theoretical specializations of factual knowing. Such syntheses require strategies to overcome the general bias that accompanies common sense.

Yet, as the phrasing of the question "What is going on?" suggests, this synthesis of commonsense and explanatory factual knowledge is not being sought just for its own sake. It is rather being sought within the context of a larger intention. Here factual knowledge is being sought within the anticipation of an eventual active response on the part of the inquiring subject.

This does not necessarily mean, however, that when the interests of ethical intentionality are introduced, they will distort the normative autonomy and objectivity of factual knowing. Distortions of cognitional structure of course do occur. The biases that distort cognitional structure even in its non-ethical modes do not disappear. Such biases can reappear and become more intense and far more intricate when factual knowledge is sought within the larger horizon of ethical intentionality. Yet biases are just as much distortions of the structure of ethical intentionality itself as they are distortions of cognitional structure. In other words, authentic ethical intentionality by itself and as such does not necessarily introduce alien interests that distort cognitional structure. Genuine ethical inquiry in itself desires to know what the facts really are, so that it can discover properly what should be done. It is rather the biased distortions of ethical intentionality that distort cognitional objectivity. On the other hand, to the extent that both cognitional and ethical intentionality are free of biases, the entirety of cognitional structure is incorporated (or "sublated") intact within the structure of authentic ethical intentionality. As Lonergan puts it, sublation in this sense, "far from interfering with the sublated or destroying it, on the contrary needs it, includes it, preserves all its proper features and properties, and carries them forward to a fuller realization within a richer context."[16]

How this can be so in the case of the sublation of cognitional structure by the structure of ethical intentionality will be explored in subsequent sections. Suffice it to say for the present that when cognitional structure is sublated by authentic ethical intentionality, its intelligent and reflective questions about facts continue to establish the norms and criteria that direct insights and reflective understandings of the virtually unconditioned and judgments need to satisfy. As Cronin puts it,

> The question of value sets the criterion which guides the process to a correct solution ... We know that in our past experience we have made good judgments of value and some mistaken judgments of value ... We have this strange ability to recognize a correct and a mistaken answer to the questions of value.[17]

This normativity is preserved within the structure of authentic ethical intentionality. Nevertheless, as we will see, the fact that the structured activities of factual knowing occur within the larger comprehending context of ethical intentionality does affect, in complex ways, which questions of fact are pursued and in what order.

4.5   Questions and Insights of Practical Import

Accurate knowledge of our situation is endowed with ethical significance as soon as we ask the question "What should I do?" As we have seen, "What should I do?" is really asking three things at once. It compresses into a single linguistic expression three distinguishable inquiries – "what?," "should?," and "do?" These inquiries incorporate the activities of our cognitional structure into the broader structure of our ethical intentionality. Each of these distinguishable inquiries constitutes a distinct phase and a further dynamic relationship within the overall dynamic structure of ethical intentionality. The present section treats the "what?" component; the other two components will be treated in the successive sections.

As is the case with all inquiries, the question "What can I do?" presupposes something and seeks something. It presupposes experience and knowledge of a situation (what is going on) in which the ethical subject finds herself or himself. It intends and seeks a practical insight (an idea or a plan) about a course of action that the inquiring subject could undertake.

Practical insights respond to "What can I do?" inquiries by grasping courses of action as intelligible possibilities. There is elemental inventiveness and creativity to even the most ordinary of human actions, which derive from the acts of intelligence that add "at least one further" practical insight to what the subject already knew. For example, selecting which tool or technique to use and understanding how to adapt it to the circumstances at hand are matters of practical insights. Likewise, planning what to serve for dinner and how to prepare it require new practical insights. Practical insights are involved in figuring out how to make the financial numbers "work" for a major purchase or a new business venture. Determining what to say and how to say it in a sensitive interpersonal situation are also matters of practical insight. Daily efforts at mediating and resolving ordinary conflicts, as well as the more specialized skills required to resolve intense conflicts, also require creative practical insights on the part of the mediator. Practical insights enable people to find ways around unexpected obstacles blocking their paths. Organizing and planning any cooperative human venture involves numerous practical insights.

"Practical" here is not restricted to courses of action whose consequences will be immediate and short term. Just as our situations are intelligibly related to other people and circumstances that are distant in time, so also the consequences of our actions can stretch across great distances and times. Practical intelligence, therefore, involves thinking about alternative courses of action along with their possible and probable outcomes beyond the range of merely immediate results. In order to achieve this, once again commonsense intelligence must be supplemented by explanatory insights that understand these possible long-term consequences.

These are but a few illustrations of the myriad of occurrences of new practical insights responding to the question "What can I do?" While authentic practical insights always rely and build upon the traditions of previously accumulated insights, merely doing things the way they have always been done, *just* because it is easier, can hardly be called ethical. That would, instead, be an example of the vice of laziness. Laziness ignores the fundamental call to be creative, a call issued intelligently by ourselves to ourselves by means of the question "What can I do?" In an important way, the call to be authentically ethical involves responding to the call to be continually and intelligently creative in ordinary situations. Ethical responsibility requires ongoing intelligent creativity of human subjects. Refusal of the call to be intelligently creative is a failure of ethical responsibility.

4.6   Questions for Ethical Reflection and Judgment[18]

Still, just because we have had a creative insight into a possible course of action, that does not mean that we ought to implement it immediately, without hesitation or further thought. As is the case with insights regarding matters of fact, practical insights reveal no more than intelligible possibilities – courses of action as indeed intelligible and understandable, but merely as possible. Whether the course of action revealed by the practical insight *should* be undertaken is a further ethical question – "Should I do it?" In this question, the "it" refers to the course of action as an intelligible possibility, as brought to consciousness by an intelligent practical insight. The question "Should I do it?" therefore always presupposes the structure of acts that culminate in practical understanding.

But the question also seeks to go beyond understanding of the course of action as intelligible. It seeks further comprehension of the course of action as *worthy of one's commitment,* indeed even as obliging that commitment. As such, the further question "Should I do it?" is closely related to the question "Is it worthwhile for me to undertake this course of action?" Both are questions of ethical value. "Is it worthwhile?" asks whether the course of action has sufficient value for me to undertake it. "Should I do it?" asks whether that value has the value of compelling obligation – not merely a valuable thing for me to do, but a value of moral obligation for me.[19]

As with questions for factual reflection, the tensions in questions of value in general, and in questions of ethical value in particular, are brought to final resolution only in acts of judging – acts of affirming or denying. But where questions of fact lead to affirmations or denials that X is so, questions of value ultimately seek judgments that affirm or deny that X truly has value V.[20] Questions of ethical value, therefore, seek judgments that a prospective course of action does or does not have the value of being worthwhile or obligatory.

But if judgments of value and judgments of ethical value are not to be merely arbitrary – merely subjective – then they cannot just come out of nowhere. Judgments of ethical value will be responsible judgments only if we have sufficient reasons for affirming or denying them, just as is the case in judgments of fact. Thus prior to finding satisfaction in judgments of value, questions of value set in motion processes of reflection that seek sufficient grounds for making the judgments of value. This is what value questioning really desires. Only value judgments based upon sufficient reasons will release the tensions of value questioning. This means that processes of value reflection in general, and ethical reflection in particular, bear similarities to the processes of reflection that occur within cognitional structure. Judgments of fact are reasonable only insofar as they rest upon reflective understandings of intelligible contents as virtually unconditioned. Analogously, judgments of ethical value are responsible in Lonergan's sense only insofar as they rest upon reflective understandings of possible courses of action as having virtually unconditioned value.

As is the case with reflective understandings of the virtually unconditioned in the realm of knowing facts, so also in the realm of value reflection, reflective understanding of the virtually unconditioned involves cognizance of a conditioned, a link to conditions, and the fulfillment of those conditions. In value reflection, the conditioned is the intelligible course of action in question. It is revealed to be conditioned by the very questions that ask whether it is worthwhile or ought to be put into action. If practical insights by themselves had already revealed a particular course of action to be unconditionally valuable, we would not be asking these further questions in the first place. We would know immediately, simply by having the insight, that it does or does not have ethical value. But in fact we do ask about courses of action once we have thought of them, and by asking we begin to seek whether there are sufficient conditions that would make our undertaking of the course of action unconditionally ethical.

Notably, the general form of the virtually unconditioned in the realm of values differs from the form it takes in the realm of reflecting about questions of fact. In most instances when we seek grounds for our judgments of fact, conditions are fulfilled to some extent by data given in acts of sensation. When it comes to judgments of value in general (and ethical value in particular), however, there are no data of sense on the course of action, precisely because the action has not yet occurred. This would seem to imply that it is impossible to grasp a virtually unconditioned in the matter of a question of ethical value. Indeed, Lonergan himself seemed to have drawn exactly this conclusion:

> When speculative or factual insight is correct, reflective understanding can grasp a relevant virtually unconditioned. But when practical insight is correct, then reflective understanding cannot grasp a relevant virtually unconditioned; for if it could, the content of the insight already would be a fact; and if it were already a fact, then it would not be a possible course of action which, as yet, is not a fact but just a possibility.[21]

But the absence of sensible conditions for virtually unconditioned value does not necessarily mean that there can be no knowledge of virtually unconditioned value. In chapter 2, we saw that even in reflection concerning questions of fact, the fulfillment of conditions usually also includes the answering of a number of further pertinent questions, in addition to the conditions given in sensation. Insights about facts are correct and true when they are invulnerable – that is, if they are incapable of further correction. Hence, the criterion of there being "no further pertinent questions" plays an important role in judgments of fact.

The absence of further pertinent questions is *the* central criterion when it comes to matters of value reflection. Value and ethical reflection are overwhelmingly matters of asking and answering further pertinent questions, until the intelligibility in question is grasped to be of invulnerable value. When ethical reflection is liberated to follow its normal course, it will proceed until there are no further pertinent questions that would lead to further insights to modify and correct a flawed idea about a course of action into one that would be genuinely, unconditionally worthwhile or obligatory.

Hence judgments of value are grounded in reflective understandings of virtually unconditioned value. Although Lonergan appears to have denied this in the passage just cited, in a later section of *Insight* devoted to believing, he took a very different position. There he identified "a reflective act of understanding that … grasps as virtually unconditioned the value of deciding to believe some particular proposition."[22] Elsewhere he also offers a lengthy list of further questions that occur during practical reflection.[23] This means that we must qualify his strong statement about reflective understanding not being able to grasp a relevant virtually unconditioned in practical reflection. If reflection seeks a judgment of fact about whether or not a course of action has occurred, then of course there is no virtually unconditioned until a choice is made and an action taken. But if reflection seeks a judgment about the value of undertaking a course of action, then a virtually unconditioned value can be grasped, provided the relevant further pertinent questions are all answered.

For the most part, the ethical processes of asking and answering of further pertinent questions about proposed courses of action is done in a commonsense mode. Beginning with consideration of the proposed course of action, we ask ourselves, for example, "what would happen if I did this?" The prior acquisition of commonsense insights from one's communities supplies many of the sought-for answers. An experienced person of common sense will know likely consequences: "The ladder will likely slip." "The motor will overheat." "That person's feelings will likely be hurt." "People witnessing my action would react in this way." "Word would get around. My friends would likely be shocked to hear that I had done what I am now considering." The commonsense insights about each of these likely outcomes will raise still further questions. We call to mind at least some of our culture's commonsense ethical and religious sayings about the values of such actions. We will ask whether these reactions and sayings are compelling or even relevant. We may seek the counsel of others, hear them out, try to understand them, and then ask about the pertinence of the advice received to the course of action under consideration. This process of asking and answering questions will continue until there are no further pertinent questions that could lead to modification or correction of our proposed course of action. Ethical discernment, therefore, involves learning to carefully discern the tensions of the subtle, further pertinent questions that remain to be answered as conditions for grasping a course of action as having unconditional value.

But what determines the pertinence of the further questions? In the case of judgments of fact, the formulation of the intelligible content of the insight reveals various links to various sets of possible conditions under which it can be reasonably affirmed or denied to be a correct understanding of the real.[24] In the case of judgments of ethical value, however – and indeed for all judgments of value – there is an additional component. The link for a judgment of value is not simply "Intelligibility I can be reasonably affirmed (or denied) to be so under conditions C," but "Intelligibility I can be responsibly affirmed (or denied) to have value V under conditions C," where fulfillment of conditions C here means that all further pertinent questions have been raised and answered. Here, more than anything else, it is the value V in question that determines the conditions – what further questions are pertinent – for the grasp of "I has value V" as virtually unconditioned.

But how do we arrive at the cognizance of value that enters into the link between the conditioned course of action and the grasp of it as having virtually unconditioned value? Our awareness of value *V* is not in the insight, for that is a grasp of intelligible possibility not yet known to have the value in question. Again, our awareness of value *V* cannot be in a judgment of value, because that is exactly what value reflection is striving for. Judgments of value presuppose a reflective understanding of courses of action as virtually unconditionally valuable. Those reflective understandings, in turn, can occur only if there is some prior awareness of value that enters into the value reflective processes themselves. So what is the source of the awareness of value that enters into our ethical reflection?

4.6.1 *Feelings and Ethical Reflection*

Some years after publishing *Insight,* Bernard Lonergan encountered a new way of thinking about values and feelings and their roles in the ethical life. This new way of thinking came to him through his encounter with the writings of certain phenomenologists, primarily Dietrich von Hildebrand and Max Scheler. Previously, he tended to regard feelings primarily as sense experiences that can be organized by insights into graceful living, or that can become sources of interference (bias) with the normative process of asking and answering all further pertinent questions.[25] Now it is certainly true that some of our feelings – what I shall call "somatic feelings" – are matters of sensation.[26] It is also true that these feeling sensations can be intelligently integrated into noble ways of living, or can be sources of interference that lead to great distortions. Yet his study of the aforementioned phenomenologists revealed to Lonergan entirely different kinds of feelings that make quite different, positive, and indispensable contributions in coming to knowledge of values itself. In a cryptic remark, he wrote, "Intermediate between judgments of fact and judgments of value lie apprehensions of value. Such apprehensions are given in feelings."[27]

In other words, our judgments of fact give us factual knowledge of the situations ("what is going on") that are the settings for our ethical actions. Our judgments of value are the basis for our responsible ethical decisions and actions. But what is meant by saying that feelings are "intermediate"? Somatic feelings at the level of sensation are not intermediate between judgments of fact and judgments of value. Somatic feelings generally precede both judgments of fact and judgments of value because they are elements of the situation that need to be correctly understood and properly evaluated.

I will argue that the intermediate kind of feelings are what Lonergan calls intentional responses to values,[28] and that these kinds of feelings are the sources of our cognizance of the values *V* that enter into the value reflective processes. I will also argue that feelings, along with value inquiries, endow judgments of value with their *unconditional intensity*, and constitute them precisely as judgments *of value*. I will further argue that these feelings of values determine what further questions count as pertinent for the grasp of virtually unconditioned value – that is to say, feelings as intentional responses set the criteria for what further questions must be answered in order to fulfill the conditions required to grasp intelligibility *I* as having value *V*.

A lengthy digression is required to explain what I mean by all of this. Rather than disrupt the overview of the overall structure of ethical intentionality at this point, however, I will defer the discussions and analyses of these claims to chapters 5–7.

4.6.2 *Judgments of Ethical Value*

Once we have answered all of the further pertinent questions that condition our affirmations (or denial) of "*I* has value *V*," we attain a grasp of a course of action as having virtually unconditioned ethical value. We then have sufficient grounds for objective value judgments of ethical responsibility. The ethical tensions originally raised with the "worthwhile" and "should" inquiries are brought to a temporary rest in value judgments of ethical responsibility. As with judgments of fact, judgments of ethical responsibility can be fully answered only in one of two ways. Acts of ethical judging, in the strict sense, are either acts of affirming ("Yes") or denying ("No"). One or the other of those activities is what is sought by questions of ethical worth and responsibility. In affirming and denying we are making judgments about what are or are not worthwhile or obligatory courses of action for us. Whether affirming or denying the course of action as having ethical value, these judgments of ethical value are objective (and therefore responsible) insofar as these follow upon and are grounded in a grasp of virtually unconditioned value.

It is only in virtually unconditioned judgments of value that values are truly known. *Ethical value is not known in any prior act, such as feeling responses that intend values.* In turn, what virtually unconditioned judgments of ethical value know is the value of some intelligible course of action.

4.7   Questions for Choosing, Deciding, Acting

Finally, the last of the four basic types of ethical questions is "Shall I do it?" We can objectively know what the situation is, can have found intelligent and creative ways to improve upon the situation that already is, and can know that the course of action is not only an intelligent but also a truly valuable course that we should follow. But none of this knowledge necessitates that we will do what an attentive, intelligent, and responsible person should do. This last question – "Shall I do it?" – presupposes all the aforementioned activities, but is not answered by any of them or even by all of them together. This last question in the structure of ethical intentionality can only be met fully and completely by a conscious act of deciding or choosing (consenting or refusing) to do what we have already judged to be of unconditional worth or even of obligatory value.

Like questions for judgment that seek one of the binary alternatives (affirming or denying), "Shall I do it?" also seeks one alternative between consenting and refusing. You can *say* that you both affirm and deny the same thing, but you cannot actually *do* the affirming and denying about exactly the same intelligible content. So also you could say that you both consent to and refuse the exact same content of a value judgment about the worth of a course of action, but you cannot actually both consent to and refuse the exact same value. The existential reality of human ethical responsibility is that we cannot have it both ways, no matter how we might wish that could be so, and no matter how much we try to make it be so. The question for choice places an either/or before us, and its existential tension can only be resolved by either consenting or refusing, but never both simultaneously.[29]

Beyond choosing or deciding, there is actually doing and carrying out one's decisions. Strictly speaking, deciding (consenting or refusing) is one thing and doing, acting, or carrying it out is another.[30] Choosing to build a house is not identical with building it. Yet in a more fundamental sense, can it be said that a person has really chosen to do something, even though she or he actually does not do it? If a person tells himself that he is going to go on a diet, and tells himself this every day for ten years, but all the while still does nothing whatsoever to bring this about, has he really chosen to go on a diet? Or has he only chosen to tell himself a distracting story?

The relationship between deciding and doing, for the most part, is a matter of how bodily movements result from decisions. Actions include large-scale movements of arms, legs, feet, and torsos to sit, stand, balance, walk, lift, push, throw, etc. Actions also include smaller-scale – but often much more significant – movements of mouth, tongue, facial muscles, and hands to produce a wide range of expressions. For a Cartesian, the problem of how acts of *res cogitans* (e.g., decisions) can cause movements of *res extensa* (e.g., bodily movements) is insurmountable. For Lonergan, however, Descartes's *res extensa* is fundamentally a counter-position about reality. It is a philosophical formulation of the animal-extroversion notion of reality as the already-our-there-now.[31] *Res extensa* fills up some portion of external space. Causality with regard to the *res extensa* occurs when one body takes over a spatial location, forcing out another body that previously filled up that space.[32] Since *res cogitans* (including thoughts and decisions) does not occupy space, it is difficult if not impossible to say how it could cause the motion of spatial objects such as legs, hands, or tongues.

In place of this Cartesian dilemma, Lonergan proposed both a different conception of reality and a different conception of the relationships among levels within reality. Physical reality is fundamentally intelligible, not some subdivision of the already-out-there-now. Human thought is likewise intelligible. Its intelligibility is in part known in self-affirmation. The deep Cartesian chasm, then, between two radically different kinds of reality is in fact a distinction within one kind of reality that is intelligible throughout. The distinction between physical reality and humanly conscious reality is, according to Lonergan, a distinction among successively higher generic levels of intelligibility that integrate the lower generic intelligibilities. Thus human thinking and deciding integrates "otherwise coincidental" neural and muscular events into intelligible and meaningful sequences of human courses of action. While a good deal more needs to be said about the intricate details of how ethical choosing and bodily movements are related, efforts to engage these issues will distract us from the present purpose of explicating the overall structure of ethical intentionality.[33] Therefore, we will focus instead on the act of choosing that is the basis for the acts of doing that carry it out.

While human choosing and acting are dramatic and distinctive acts, they are never radically isolated. Every action is related to the decision it enacts. Every decision always comes in response to a "Shall I do it?" question to which it is intrinsically related. In turn, every choice presupposes an "it" that it chooses to do. The "it" in the question refers back to the content of the judgment of value, and reveals the dynamic relation of choice to that judgment. "It" refers directly to the value affirmed in that judgment, and indirectly to the intelligible course of action, which was previously understood in a practical insight, then felt to have some value, and subsequently affirmed to have value in a judgment of ethical value. Intelligible courses of action respond to questions about what can be done in the actual, concrete situation in which one finds oneself. This, in turn, rests upon the activities of cognitional structure.

In other words, action and choice are always intrinsically and dynamically related to all sorts of prior acts of consciousness. Just as these acts are dynamically related to one another in a structure of ethical intentionality by inquiries, so also acts of choosing and acting are parts of that same structure because they are responses to the final question in the series – "Shall I do it?"

The prior acts of ethical intentionality may be carried out well or poorly. The prior questions that animate the structure can be ridiculed or ignored or short-circuited. But action and choice always presuppose some kind of thought about ideas and values, which they then actualize, no matter how well or poorly they have been thought through. Contrary to common opinion, choice is not the primary source of our consciousness of values. It is not as though values first pop into our consciousnesses in our acts of choosing. We do not choose in a vacuum. It is by choices and actions that we make values actual and that we make them our own. Nevertheless, our consciousness of the value does not first occur when we make a choice. Before we choose values, we know values in judgments of value, and before we know values in judgments, we have more primordial forms of value-consciousness in questions of value and feelings that are intentional responses.

Again, people often speak as though it is choosing that legitimates our values. They speak as though our values are to be respected solely because we chose them. But our choosing does not automatically guarantee that what we do choose will be *truly* valuable. Prior activities of ethical reflection and judgment perform that function, provided that they are done authentically – that is, we choose what is truly valuable provided that we perform the prior activities in complete fidelity to the standards of our own ethical inquiring. When ethical reflection is carried through incompletely or corruptly, its judgments offer to choice merely apparent values that fail to live up to the high standards inherent in the structure of ethical intentionality. Choice and action can only actualize values that prior ethical reflection delivers to it, whether they are known as virtually unconditionally valuable, or whether they are presented in flawed, distorted, or disfigured fashions. Choice and action can realize values only in conjunction with the prior acts of ethical intentionality. Choice and action derive their authenticity from the normativity of that structure. Choices are authentic when they choose judgments of ethical value that are produced by that structure operating in its full, undistorted movement. On the other hand, choices will be inauthentic when there is some failure in prior stages of the structure of ethical intentionality, or when they fail to choose what virtually unconditioned judgments of ethical value propose.

Frequently, people speak of the central problem of ethics as how to get people to do the right thing. That is to say, the problem is how to get people to do what they already know is the right and ethically valuable course of action. It is of course true that many times people know what is right and fail to choose and act according to their value knowledge. If we take this to be the principal ethical problem, then attention will inevitably focus on how to *make* people act ethically. This, however, is impossible. Securing behavioural compliance by means of threats of force (whether physical, financial, or psychological) can never produce ethical behaviour. Ethical behaviours are actions done on the bases of decisions grounded in virtually unconditioned judgments of value. Enforcing behaviour may be the correct or the only way to limit the damage that unethical people can inflict, but one can never force ethical behaviour of another (or oneself).

On the other hand, people frequently act unethically because something has gone seriously wrong at an earlier point in the structure of ethical intentionality. Ethical intentionality is spontaneously and naturally oriented towards decisions that enact true and objective judgments of ethical value. This is expressed already in the question "What should I do?" All human beings ask this question. The question itself already manifests the desire to do what is ethical and right. When decisions fail to do so, something has interfered with that natural, normative orientation. Frequently, the problem is located in corrupt judgments about what they should do, and this in turn can be traceable to failures to ask and answer all further pertinent questions, or to distortions in the horizon of feelings that guides the processes of ethical reflection. One of the central aims of this book is to offer guidance for discernment that will enhance the ethical reflective processes that ultimately ground choices.

Lonergan argued that choosing (deciding) is human freedom in its most radical, contingent form.[34] This radical contingency is perhaps most evident at those times when we do make decisions against our better judgments – against our judgments of ethical value about what we should do. With deplorable frequency, people fail to do what they have judged to be worthwhile or obligatory, or do anyway what they have judged to be not worth doing. Here feelings also play a role. In chapter 7, we will explore how tensions in our horizons of feelings play a major role in how we come to judge or misjudge values. Those same horizons of feelings also play important roles in our deciding and acting. We may be able to judge on the basis of one side of a conflict in our feelings, but nevertheless decide on the basis of the other side of that conflict. Indeed, our feelings influence in important ways how we develop our habits of deciding as well as our habits of judging.[35] Thus fully consistent ethical knowledge, choice, and action requires that underlying tensions in our feeling horizons be discerned and resolved.

Lonergan analysed this phenomenon by means of a distinction between essential and effective freedom. The analysis of the act of deciding reveals that it is intrinsically related to, but not absolutely determined by, the acts of consciousness that precede it. Neither our feeling horizons nor our virtually unconditioned judgments of ethical value completely determine our acts of choice. We can refuse to follow our responsible judgments. We can override our feelings. Human choosing is radically free in its intrinsic relationships to all other acts of consciousness. This is what Lonergan meant by essential freedom.[36]

Nevertheless, once specific habits of choosing have taken root in our lives, they can profoundly affect the probabilities of certain choices over others.

These habits determine our effective freedom. Our effective freedom is determined by the patterns of decisions we are likely to make, as distinct from the decisions we know we should make. Virtuous habits of deciding cooperate with unconditional judgments of ethical value. Vices are habitual deviations from such judgments. Lonergan even argues that in our world, where the "social surd" of unintelligibility, irrationality, and evil abounds, it is highly likely that every person will eventually adopt habits of choosing that corrupt her or his effective freedom. This is the phenomenon he called "moral impotence."[37] We will return to this problem in chapters 8 and 13.

Choice or decision, along with consequent actions, are thus the culminating acts in the structure of ethical intentionality. They presuppose the whole structured network of inquiries and acts of consciousness that lead up to them. Conversely, they are intended by the prior acts that are structured by that network of inquiries.[38] Choice and action give to those activities and their structure their *raison d'etre*. Choice and action are the most central of all human acts, the acts that constitute us as human in the most radical and existential fashion. But this is only so because they are intrinsically related to the whole network of acts that precedes them. Without that structure there would be no human choice or action in any real sense.

4.8   Value Knowledge and Belief

In the previous sections I elaborated what I take to be the structure of value knowing, deciding, and doing. The phrase "value knowing," however, must certainly sound strange to many. Surely, it will be contended, we can only have beliefs about values, never knowledge. After all, it might be alleged, knowledge rests upon sense experience, and we can never have sense data about which values are correct or best. Yet as the previous chapters argued, knowledge of facts does not rest upon sense experience alone. Rather, factual knowledge is a matter of judging, on the basis of a reflective grasp of a virtually unconditioned, that we have understood correctly. Sense experiences frequently contribute to the conditions needed to grasp a judgment of fact as virtually unconditioned, but they are almost never the sole conditions. The criterion of factual knowledge, then, is the virtually unconditioned, and this is not limited to sense experiences. The previous sections have endeavoured to show that it is also possible to grasp at least some value judgments as virtually unconditioned, and therefore to have value knowledge as well as factual knowledge.

Still, most people speak of values as a matter of belief rather than of knowledge. For example, we might say, "She stood up for her beliefs." Or we say, "I believe strongly in this value." According to the analysis of the preceding sections, in some cases at least we should be saying instead, "She stood up for what she knew to be of value," or "He stood up for what he knew to be the right thing to do (the ethical value)." Or, again, we should say, "I know this to be of higher value."[39]

Therefore, in order to meet the objection completely and to discern the differences between knowing and believing values, it is necessary to clarify just what is meant by believing. Although many philosophers have developed complex approaches to the question of belief in their epistemological theories, in this section I will be relying on Lonergan's account of the structure of believing.

Most of our acts of believing, Lonergan argued, are situated interpersonally, socially, and historically. In these cases, believing means believing person P about X. He spelled out this process of interpersonal believing along with the judgments of value that are its foundations:

> Five stages are to be distinguished, namely, (1) preliminary judgments on the value of belief in general, on the reliability of the source for this belief, and on the accuracy of the communication from the source, (2) a reflective act of understanding that, in virtue of the preliminary judgments, grasps as virtually unconditioned the value of deciding to believe some particular proposition, (3) the consequent judgment of value, (4) the consequent decision of the will, and (5) the assent that is the act of believing.[40]

In other words, acts of believing follow from decisions which in turn rest upon several prior judgments of value. These include judgments about the value of cooperation in general and of the results that can be achieved only by collaboration. They also include value judgments about the reliability of person P, and judgments of fact about the accuracy of one's understanding of P's expressions. These fulfill the conditions for the reflective act that understands the value of the course of action of accepting what P has communicated as true. These judgments of value and the subsequent acts of deciding and believing, then, proceed from reflective understandings of virtually unconditioned values.

This analysis of believing means that at least some of our valuing cannot be solely matters of belief. No doubt for many of the facts and values that we accept as true, we do so as a matter of believing. But it is no less true that our acts of believing something to be true (whether of facts or values) must rest upon knowing the value of doing so. Our beliefs can be responsible in Lonergan's sense only if there is knowledge of values that grounds those acts of believing.

To summarize, then, obviously there are beliefs about values as well as beliefs about facts. But there is also knowledge of values as well as knowledge of facts. If this were not so, there could be no legitimate believing at all, whether of values or facts.

Hence, our analysis of the structure of ethical intentionality points to a difficulty in assuming that all value judgments are merely matters of belief, and that such beliefs are solely a matter of choice. As I have argued, choosing is always an act of consciousness that occurs as part of the structure of ethical intentionality. It always comes in response to an explicitly acknowledged or implicit question of the form, "Shall I do it?" (in this case, "Shall I believe it?"), which in turn presupposes some judgment of value about a course of action as the "it" about which it asks. If this is the case, then the act of deciding to believe someone else's value judgment V always presupposes a prior judgment of value, V', of one's own. If all judgments of value were beliefs, then there would have to be an infinite regress of decisions to believe in value judgments. However, none of us actually do this.[41] This infinite regress can only be circumvented when we actually do affirm a value on some basis other than an act of choice or belief. Self-appropriation of the structure of ethical intentionality reveals that at least some objective judgments of value do not proceed from prior decisions or beliefs but instead proceed from acts of reflective understanding of values as virtually unconditioned. We will return to these issues in chapter 8.

To conclude this section, there are acts of believing facts as well as acts of believing values. But there are also acts of knowing values, as well as knowing facts. Were there no acts of knowing values, then neither acts of believing facts nor acts of believing values would have any objective basis. Both types of believing and both types of knowing can be objectively true, provided they are made by persons who are following the lead of the dynamism of the structure of ethical intentionality.

4.9   Summary

In summary, then, the answer to "What I am doing when I am being ethical?" is a structure of activities. What we are doing when we are being ethical is a network of acts of consciousness that is dynamically structured by questions about the situation as well as questions for practical intelligence, questions for practical reflection and questions for choice. That structure may be briefly summarized as follows: experiencing, inquiring, understanding, and unconditionally judging what is going on in the situation; feeling; inquiring about what can be done intelligently in that situation and coming up with creative practical insights; responsibly reflecting, unconditionally judging the value of what one should do; choosing to do so, and acting on that decision. This is a structure animated by ethical inquiries and by the horizon of intentional feelings that constitute one's felt intentions of value.

Being ethical is not performing one or another of these activities in isolation, but is rather performing all of them in their intrinsic, dynamic relationships to one another. This structure includes but also expands upon the cognitional structure of factual knowledge. Performance of this expanded structure in fidelity to the standards and norms of ethical inquiry is what we are doing when we are being ethical.

Central in this structure are the occurrences of judgments of value that rest upon reflective understandings of courses of action as having virtually unconditioned value. However, these reflective understandings themselves have complex relationships to the large class of feelings called "intentional responses to values." We now turn to investigate what these feelings are, and how they intersect with reflective understandings of value.

5 Kinds of Feelings

I would draw on Dietrich von Hildebrand and distinguish non-intentional states and trends from intentional responses.

– Bernard Lonergan, *Method in Theology*

5.1 Introduction

The previous chapter offered an overview of the structure of ethical intentionality. Central to that structure are the processes of ethical value reflection and judgment. In the course of that overview, I mentioned that after the publication of *Insight* Lonergan came to a new understanding of feelings and their role in the processes of value reflection. Because of its complexity, the account of feelings and their role in the structure of ethical intentionality was postponed. The next three chapters resume that account. This chapter surveys several different types of feelings and takes up the question of the intentionality of feelings. The intentionality of feelings in general, and their various roles in ethical thought and action, is not simple. The feelings that Lonergan referred to as "intentional responses to values" are of paramount importance, but his way of distinguishing feelings as intentional responses to values from other kinds of feelings needs some clarification. This chapter attempts to offer some clarification by way of a survey of different kinds of feelings, which endeavours to prepare the way for a more specific analysis of feelings as intentional responses in the next chapter. That analysis, in turn, will form the background for the discussion of the role that feelings as intentional responses play in ethical value reflection and judgment, taken up in chapter 7.

5.2   A Basic Division of Feelings

Consciousness of value is suffused with feelings, but the relevance of feelings to ethical reflection and deliberation depends upon what kinds of feelings they are. Feelings are grouped under many different generic headings: emotions, passions, sentiments, sensibilities, inclinations (e.g., Kant's *Neigungen*), aversions, stresses, affects, moods, and so on. The meanings of these terms vary widely.

I have chosen to use the word "feelings" rather than other terms such as "emotions" or "passions" for two reasons. First, it is the term that Lonergan himself used. Second, at least when used by Lonergan, Scheler, and von Hildebrand among others, "feelings" has a cognitive connotation (i.e., cognitive of values) that is missing from the connotations of other terms. For example, "emotion," as derived from its original Latin roots, refers to feelings as sources of movement and action (as when emotions rouse crowds to assemble in protest). "Inclination," "aversion," and other terms also tend to identify feelings as motivational. More recently, however, "emotion" has also come to mean a mental state of agitation that is directed towards a specific object and accompanied by physiological changes. The etymology of "passion," on the other hand, reveals core meanings of "to undergo," or "suffer" or "receive," and so tends to emphasize the passive dimensions of feelings as something that we undergo rather than as sources of action. Something similar can be said about the terms "sentiment," "sensibility," and "affect" as emphasizing the receptive dimensions of feelings. However, "passion" has also come to designate especially intense and powerful feelings, and as a consequence passions are also spoken of as sources of actions, as when we speak of crimes committed out of passion.[1]

The colloquial meanings for many of these terms for feelings tend to convey the impression of immediate relationships between inward experiences and outward stimuli or resulting actions. Sometimes the relationship between feelings and outer conditions or consequences is immediate – as when I experience a stabbing pain when stepping on something sharp. More often, however, there are varying levels and degrees of complexity that mediate between feelings and outer occasions or actions. The complexities and subtle nuances of feelings within each of these categories have been explored in rich detail by numerous poets, novelists, musicians, artists, philosophers, religious thinkers, psychologists, neurophysiologists, and others. This literature is so vast that it is impossible to even attempt a fair summary here. In the concluding chapter of this book, I will present some suggestions as to how a method in ethics can assist in the exploration and appropriation of the vast dialectical mixture of ethical ideas and expressions (which naturally include ideas about feelings and their places in ethical thought, choice, and action).

Lonergan's own way of classifying feelings begins with a basic division into two very broad classes of "non-intentional states and trends" and "intentional responses to values." As he puts it, "The states have causes. The trends have goals." As examples of non-intentional states, he offered "fatigue, irritability, bad humor and anxiety," while in illustration of non-intentional trends he listed "hunger, thirst and sexual discomfort."[2]

Lonergan derived this idea of non-intentional feelings from Dietrich von Hildebrand's category of "unintentional" feelings.[3] Von Hildebrand used the term to distinguish it from what he regarded as "intentional feelings." In doing so, he was relying on the prior work of Max Scheler who distinguishes between "feelings" (*Gefühle*) and "mere feeling-states" (*Gefühlszuständen*).[4] Scheler illustrates the difference by means of an example where a feeling responds to a feeling-state. Suppose a feeling-state or sensation arises from being touched. The sensible feeling-state of the touch can be additionally "felt" as repulsive or annoying or tolerable or endurable or welcome, etc. Even though the original felt sensation (feeling-state) of the touch can be identical in all these cases, the secondary feeling responds to it as having very different kinds of values. Hence feelings (*Gefühle*) in Scheler's sense always include a consciousness of value, while feeling-states do not. Scheler tends to characterize lower feeling-states by their capacity to be localized somewhere on or within the body,[5] but not exclusively so. On the other hand, von Hildebrand says that intentional experiences have a "conscious, rational relation between the person and an object." He goes on to say that pure states, such as

> being tired, being in bad humor, being irritated, and so forth ... do
> not imply the specific polarity of the person on the one hand, as
> against the object on the other ... We are not tired about something;
> tiredness is only a state, an experience of something qualitative
> related to our body, but it does not have a meaningful reference to
> an object.[6]

Clearly there are some differences between how von Hildebrand and Scheler understood unintentional feelings and feelings-states, respectively. These differences tend to originate from what each thinker is prepared to reckon as an intended "object" of a feeling. These differences lead to difficulties regarding the nature and status of what they meant by intentional feelings. Although Lonergan followed von Hildebrand and used "non-intentional" in order to sharply distinguish this class of feelings from intentional responses to values, it is not entirely clear why they should be called "non-intentional." Given the phenomenological sense of the term "intentional," it would seem that "non-intentional feelings" such as hunger or thirst would have to be *noetic* feeling acts, states, or trends which lack any *noematic* content.[7] This, however, is a questionable assumption.

Lonergan at least makes clear why he adapts von Hildebrand's terminology to his own purposes:

> The relation of the [non-intentional] feeling to the cause or goal is simply that of effect to cause, of trend to goal. *The feeling itself does not presuppose and arise out of perceiving, imagining, representing the cause or goal.* Rather, one first feels tired and, perhaps belatedly, one discovers that what one needs is a rest. Or first one feels hungry and then one diagnoses the trouble is a lack of food.[8]

The class of feelings that Lonergan calls non-intentional do not arise in response to the *noematic* content of another, prior *noetic* act. In other words, he is using the term "intentional" here to refer to the *noematic* object of some *act other than the feeling-act itself.* A more complete discussion of feelings as intentional responses in this particular sense will be the topic of chapter 6. But it does not follow that the feelings that Lonergan and von Hildebrand exclude from the category of intentional cannot have their *own proper noematic* contents. I shall argue to the contrary that most if not all such "states and trends" do indeed have *noematic* contents of their own, and that they, too, should be called "intentional feelings," although they will indeed differ markedly from what Lonergan calls intentional responses to values. I will, therefore, introduce a different distinction: namely, that between somatic feelings and feelings that are intentional responses that intend values.[9] This is not meant to be an exclusive either/or classification; there may well be other feelings that are neither somatic nor intentional responses that intend values in my precise terms. Although what these feelings might be has not yet occurred to me, I do leave that possibility open for further investigations.

5.3   Somatic Feelings as Grounded in Neural Processes

As the term suggests, somatic feelings are directly associated with the fact that we are embodied, sentient animals. Somatic feelings are sensations, along with seeing, hearing, smelling, tasting, etc. In the most primitive sense, somatic feelings are associated with the sense of touch – feelings of pressure, texture, roughness, smoothness, hardness, softness, sharpness, warmth, cold, moisture, dryness, and muscular feelings of ache and relaxation. They also include feelings of thirst, hunger pangs, cravings, being slaked or bloated, arousal, fatigue, feverishness, equilibrium, sensations of bodily movement, and feelings associated with breathing, including the movements of the lungs as well as the sensations of air as it flows in and out of the airways, and so on. Somatic feelings arise more or less directly from the states of our nervous system as it, in turn, responds to changes in our bodily states. This is one major way in which somatic feelings differ from feelings as intentional responses, which arise directly from other *noetic* acts (or their *noematic* contents). Intentional responses are, therefore, only indirectly correlated with our nervous and bodily states, and sometimes only very remotely. We will return to this topic in chapter 6.

Somatic feelings, then, do have a more or less direct correlation with states of our neural functioning. Our bodies are laced with billions of afferent nerve endings that are distributed throughout our muscular systems and epithelial layers, external as well as internal. Hence changes in our physiological states cause changes in our neural states. These in turn set the conditions for changes in our somatic feelings. This correspondence with neurophysiological states enables somatic feelings to perform their primary role as heralds communicating to consciousness the condition of bodily states.[10] When somatic feelings enter consciousness, they provide data to consciousness regarding the conditions of the tissues and organs that stimulate the remote nerve endings.

As the parts and organs of animal bodies became more differentiated and specialized through evolutionary processes, the nerve endings and their correlated pathways and interconnections also became correspondingly differentiated and specialized as well. The differentiations of nervous systems were in turn accompanied by the emergence of correspondingly differentiated somatic feelings that supervened upon them.[11] If the most primitive animal forms, such as cnidarians (hydra, jellyfishes, corals, sea anemones, etc.), have somatic feelings, it is likely that these would be very elemental feelings of contact or pressure (touch) upon the inner and outer layers of cells that cover their bodies.[12] But as animal organs and nervous systems became more differentiated through evolutionary processes, feelings of touch themselves became further differentiated so as to feel not only pressure and contact, but also cold and hot, sharp, smooth or rough, irritating or soothing or painful, and so on at various outer locations along the skin. For the internal organs, differentiations of nerve endings and pathways led to distinctions among feelings of different kinds of inner pains, but also to feelings such as tension, ache, relaxation and fatigue in muscles, hunger and thirst from the nerve endings that respond to changes in concentrations of glucose or sodium ions in the blood stream, feelings of discomfort and relief associated with the needs to urinate and defecate, and, of course, the feelings that arise from the neural functionings correlated with changes in sexual organs. It is also likely that even the non-feeling sensations themselves, such as seeing, hearing, tasting, and smelling, are correlated with highly differentiated neural structures that developed through evolutionary processes from the undifferentiated neural structures that originally underpinned primitive feelings of touch. In other words, organisms developed the capacities to feel not only the touch of physical contact, but also the "touch" of photons, sound waves, and aromatic molecules.

While they are indeed correlated with the states of our nervous and bodily systems, somatic feelings are not wholly determined by the nerve impulses themselves. We will return to this issue in section 5.5.

5.4   Somatic Feelings as Intentional

Some if not all of what Lonergan refers to as "non-intentional" feelings clearly are somatic feelings – fatigue, hunger, thirst, and sexual discomfort, for example. In one limited sense somatic feelings could be called non-intentional, but more generally they are properly called intentional.

Somatic feelings can be called non-intentional in the limited sense that Lonergan notes – their causes or goals are not intended in their *noematic* contents.[13] This is certainly true for human infants. Babies feel discomfort in response to changes in their digestive and excretory organs and their associated nerve cells. They also feel cold or pain in various parts of their bodies. These discomforts will be relieved and replaced by feelings of contentment, if the right actions are taken. But these infantile feelings of discomfort or urges emerge without any immediate awareness of what sort of relief is needed. Even knowing the feeling as discomfort or urge – let alone knowing what particular kind of action or intervention is needed for its relief – is the further work of insights, judgments, and decisions. Infants just cry in response to their discomforts and urges; parents use their intelligences and judgments to try to figure out and interpret what their babies need. Only after children acquire a sufficient number of insights are they able to properly comprehend their different kinds of feelings, and to communicate their causes or the needed remedies. Interestingly, children do gain fairly sophisticated understandings of at least some of their somatic feelings and what will bring them relief well before they are able to express any of this in language. And of course adults add still further insights to build upon their infantile insights to develop much more extensive understandings of the causes and objectives of their somatic feelings. But none of this is given as the *noematic* content of the somatic feelings as such. Lonergan, then, is correct in the limited sense that these somatic feelings as such do not intend their causes or goals as their *noematic* contents.

Nevertheless, most if not all of somatic feelings are intentional in the more general sense of having some kind of *noematic* content proper to the kinds of feelings that they are, even if those contents do not include causes, goals, or values. In fact, we tend to denote many somatic feelings by means of their *noematic* contents, especially when these arise in response to external causes. For example, we speak of feeling wet or feeling sharpness. It is true that physical moisture and sharp objects are sources of such feelings, but our terms for the feelings refer to *noematic* contents that are given in the feelings themselves, just as deep-purple is the content of an act of seeing, or C# the content of an act of hearing. The sharpness *as felt* in touching a razor blade, for example, is not at all the same as the physical, three-dimensional shape of the razor blade's edge. That physical sharp-shape does stimulate the sharpness-as-felt, but what is felt is not the three-dimensional spatial edge-shape that exists in space, whether or not someone feels it *as* sharp. The feeling of sharpness communicates to consciousness important data (*noemata*) about the razor's shape, but does not communicate the spatial shape itself. What is felt is a *noematic* content that in no way is the same as the spatially sharp edge as seen. Sharpness in this sense is the *noema* of the feeling, but we lack a distinct word for the *noetic* act of feeling itself. We simply use its *noematic* content to indirectly name the *noetic* act: the "*feeling of* sharpness." Similarly, we use phrases like "feeling a sting" or "feeling a prick" to name slightly different kinds of somatic feelings (*noetic* acts) by means of *noematic* contents that are slightly different in quality from the *noematic* content of razor-edge-sharpness.

Conversely, when the feelings originate from sources internal to the body, we tend to use words for the *noeses* but not their *noematic* contents – tension, irritation, pain, ache, contentment, and arousal are examples. In particular, feelings of internal pain are sometimes spoken of as though they were purely *noetic*, lacking any intentional *noematic* content. Indeed, the distinction between *noesis* and *noema* of internal somatic feelings can be difficult to discern. The pain-as-felt (*noematic* content) that one feels can seem almost completely absorbed into the pain-feeling (*noetic* act), but this is not quite correct. We can be misled in identifying the pain *noema* with its *noesis*, especially if we rely too heavily upon seeing to provide the paradigm for the intentional relationship between *noesis* and *noema*. Because the lenses of our eyes have a focal point slightly inside our skulls, we tend to think of the *noetic* act as occurring inside our heads, while the *noematic* content appears outside. But this focal-point phenomenon is peculiar to vision, and does not occur in other sensations, especially somatic feelings such as pain. Although the distinction of *noesis* and *noema* is not nearly as easy to draw as is the case with vision, that distinction is still to be found in the realm of somatic feelings.

In fact, we are able to discern the various bodily locations of somatic feelings of pain precisely because of the differences in their *noematic* contents. Again, in addition to containing data on location, the *noematic* contents of feelings of pain also differ qualitatively. The pain of a toothache feels differently from the labour pains of birth, or the pain of a sharp cut, a punch on the nose, or a broken leg. These differences are given as *noematic* pain-as-felt contents that make the subject aware of the *noetic* pain-feelings as different. In a few cases, we do have common names for the feeling acts as well as their intentional contents – such as the *noeses* of feeling chilled and feeling warmed, along with the *noemata* of cold and warmth respectively.

These cases serve to underscore the fact that somatic feelings are indeed intentional in the standard phenomenological sense. As feelings, they are *noetic* acts and they have *noematic* contents. It is therefore misleading to refer to these feelings as unintentional or non-intentional without qualification. Although their causes or goals are not their *noemata*, they do have intentional contents nonetheless.

Lonergan also relied upon von Hildebrand in order to distinguish between feelings that intend values and those that do not. However, von Hildebrand's way of making this distinction is problematic. For von Hildebrand, intentionality is primarily a matter of transcending from consciousness "in here" over to an object "out there" (e.g., "the specific polarity of the person on the one hand, as against the object on the other"[14]). He says, therefore, that feelings like fatigue are not "about" anything; they are just experiences of states of our body. Hence, they do not seem to have an "object" outside of consciousness. As he puts it, unintentional feelings "do not possess the character of transcending the realm of the mind."[15]

The motivation behind von Hildebrand's designation of these feelings as non-intentional was to distinguish them from feelings whose *noematic* contents are values (feelings as responses that intend values). Since somatic feelings do not intend values as their *noemata*, they are not intentional in that limited sense. However, von Hildeband's uses of both "unintentional" and "intentional" are rooted in what Lonergan would call the counter-position on subjectivity and objectivity.[16] According to the counter-position, objects are "already out there now real," while conscious subjectivity is "in here now." Thus the subjective side of intentionality (*noetic* act) intends an objective *noema* that is already out there now real. According to this counter-position, intentionality can be objective if and only if the *noetic* act attaches to a really-out-there object.

Clearly somatic feelings are not intentional in this counter-positional sense. For Lonergan, of course, both the experiences of *noematic* contents and consciousness as experiences of *noetic* acts are merely given. They are merely data for further inquiry, understanding, reflection, and virtually unconditioned judgments. Whether or not somatic feelings have *noematic* contents, then, does not depend on whether they intend objects that are "out there." It depends, rather, on whether or not there are intentional contents proper to the kinds of feelings they are in themselves. The relations of both the *noetic* feelings and their *noematic* contents to objective realities is a further question for judgments. Whether or not the noematic contents have any objective relationship to real objects is not given in the *noematic* contents of the experiences. Objectivity is rather a function of virtually unconditioned judgment.

Hence, in a genuinely phenomenological sense, somatic feelings are not really non-intentional after all. Just as a *noetic* act of seeing intends a *noematic* visual image, and a *noetic* act of tasting intends a *noematic* content of sweetness, so somatic feelings also intend *noematic* contents. All of this means, of course, that pains and other somatic feelings are indeed intentional. They do have intentional *noematic* contents. Their contents simply differ from other *noematic* contents, just as the *noematic* contents of acts of seeing differ from those of hearing, understanding, or factual judging, for example. For this reason, I have chosen to refer to these as "somatic feelings," rather than "unintentional" or "non-intentional" feelings. Still, von Hildebrand and Lonergan are certainly correct in this respect: the *noematic* contents of somatic feelings differ dramatically from the contents of feeling responses that intend value.

5.5   Somatic Feelings and Patterns of Experiencing

While somatic feelings do arise out of correlative neurophysiological states, still they do not arise solely from those states independently of everything else. Neural states alone do not automatically determine somatic feelings. Human beings, as well as higher animals, have a primal capacity for selectivity of what enters into consciousness. Just because networks of neural impulses are operating does not mean that their corresponding somatic feelings must emerge into consciousness. We allow only a limited selection of somatic feelings and other sensations into consciousness, according to the interests and concerns that are in play at the moment. It is true that neural functioning provides the indispensable basis for what can be selected for admission into what Lonergan called the "first level of consciousness." Where neural activity is impaired or absent, there can emerge no corresponding act of consciousness. The blind cannot see, the deaf cannot hear, the paralyzed cannot feel certain parts of their bodies. Hence nerve functioning is a necessary condition for somatic feelings. However, it is not a sufficient condition for the actual occurrence of somatic feelings in consciousness. Nerve functioning alone is not the sole factor in determining somatic feelings.

This becomes clearer when we advert to the concrete patterns within which somatic feelings actually do occur. Somatic feelings do not come to consciousness as isolated monads. Like other experiences, our somatic feelings always occur within streams and patterns of experiencing, as was discussed in chapter 2, section 2.4.1. Any given somatic feeling occurs simultaneously with other somatic feelings, as well as with other sensations such as seeing colours and shapes, hearing tones and timbres, and so on. Somatic feelings also intensify and fade away sequentially in streams along with other somatic feelings, sensations, memories, and imaginations. Given the vast number of nerve impulses every second, it is impossible that all such neural functionings could be communicated into consciousness simultaneously. This would result in a chaos of thousands if not millions of simultaneous somatic feelings and other sensations. Instead, at the most primal level, human beings exercise a pre-deliberative, pre-perceptual selectivity that selects a small portion from among these numerous matrices of nerve excitations. These are then allowed to emerge into consciousness as a manageable number of patterned somatic feelings and other sensations. This primal selectivity by our psyches determines how these feelings are to be arranged within the overall patterning of our stream of experiences, with varying intensities, combinations, and associations. Were this selectivity and patterning not the case, the trillions of nerve impulses that take place in our bodies each day would swamp our consciousness and reduce us to quivering, incoherent wretches.

Lonergan borrows from Heidegger the notion of "concern" (*Sorge*) in order to speak of the conscious factors that combine with neural functioning in determining what actually becomes present in consciousness and in which patterns.[17] Along with the states of our nervous systems that possess potentials for presentation in consciousness as somatic feelings, one or another "concern" determines which among them are to be admitted into consciousness, which are to be excluded, and how the admitted feelings and contents are to be arranged.

Even non-human animals exhibit something like the psychic selectivity of concerns in this sense. A dog playing ball with a child can be quite attentive to the ball's movements and the child's shouts. It is engaged in, "concerned" with, this child and this game. But if another dog happens along, the first dog's concern shifts suddenly and dramatically. The dog's attention is now riveted on the movements and postures and sounds and smells of its perceived foe. The child and ball game drop out of its awareness almost as if they have disappeared from the planet. Entirely different aggressive retinues of somatic feelings come to the fore, the playful feelings now relegated to the recesses of unconsciousness. Of course the dog's neural processes continue to register the light rays and sound waves emanating from the ball and child, but these no longer rise above the threshold into its consciousness.

Likewise in human beings, the actual awareness of sights, sounds, smells, tastes, and especially somatic feelings is determined not only by neural functioning but also by the concerns of the person. When a person is engaged in a practical task such as repairing something, she temporarily excludes from consciousness all sorts of stimuli that would interfere with her concentration, and includes the somatic feelings and other details necessary for successful repair. When a musician is deeply engaged in his performance, feelings of pressure of clothing upon his skin are excluded from consciousness, while on the other hand the selection and patterning of the somatic feelings of fingers and mouth connected with the instrument are concernfully patterned in service of a skilled musical performance. In deep meditation or in moments of extreme emergency, even severe pains will not be noticed. There are cases of emergencies where people have sustained serious injuries, but did not actually experience their pains for prolonged periods of time until the emergency was over. In times of intense anger, a person will exclude tender memories from consciousness, only to have them return with great regret at a later time when the anger no longer dominates concern. Lovers in passionate embrace and religious contemplatives immersed in prayer lose awareness of virtually all other experiences, since these would distract them from absorption with their beloveds.

In some cases, of course, impairments of nervous systems make it difficult for afflicted people to govern what enters their consciousness, as in attention deficit disorders. Even so, in all but the most extreme cases there is some degree of self-determination of what comes to consciousness. Lonergan uses the phrase "neural demand function" to identify this phenomenon.[18] Neural functioning exerts certain exigences for awareness, but these exigences are merely variables in a function. They can be accommodated by incorporating into, or excluding from, consciousness their associated somatic feelings and other experiences, according to which function (i.e., which concern) is operating. Changes in physiology can change the intensity of the exigences for awareness in the form of somatic feelings and other kinds of experiences that are posed by certain nerve structures, but the intensities alone do not determine which experiences emerge into consciousness.[19]

To cite one example, addictions of various kinds modify the dopamine receptors in neurons, sometimes permanently. These modifications give rise to intense somatic feelings (cravings) when the concentration of the drug molecules decreases. The intensity of such cravings makes it increasingly difficult for other experiences to enter into the stream of consciousness, including potentially countervailing memories or images. What is true for the intense somatic feelings associated with addiction can be true for other forms of somatic feelings as well. People who engage in regular regimes of running also alter the chemical constitutions and dopamine receptors of their nervous systems. When they have to refrain from running for long periods of time, they also feel powerful cravings. These somatic feelings tend to squeeze out images and memories that would occasion further corrective questions, insights, judgments, and feelings of values, which in turn would lead to alternate courses of action.

Nevertheless, even these powerful somatic feelings need not wholly determine the pattern of experience. Some addicts do recover. Other "concerns" arise that enable addicts to begin to re-pattern their experiences, including the intense somatic feelings associated with dopamine cycles. These changed patterns of experience make it possible for addicts to make a series of decisions (such as in twelve-step programs) that change their bodily states and somatic feelings to the point where they can resist the cravings.

Not only is there variability in the ways that many somatic feelings and bodily responses can be patterned, but the feelings themselves can be integrated into those patterns with greater or lesser degrees of intensity. In addition, the bodily responses to feelings can be patterned so as to occur only after delays. Some feelings of nervous functionings and bodily responses can even be blocked from consciousness for indefinite periods of time, if they would disrupt the orientation of a particular patterning of experiencing.

Hence we can only say that somatic feelings arise in a "more or less direct" correspondence with neurophysiological functioning. Their correspondence is indeed direct in one sense, for the primary role of somatic feelings is as heralds to consciousness of bodily states. Nevertheless, somatic feelings do not occur solely according to some automatic, Pavlovian stimulus-response mechanism. The mediating factor of some higher, governing concern is always also involved. It is the concern that determines the "more and less" of how somatic feelings emerge from the potentialities of neural functioning into conscious experiencing. The essential point, therefore, is that nerve functioning is a necessary but not sufficient condition for the actual occurrence of somatic feeling in consciousness.

Even though somatic feelings are subject to the influences of concerns, still they are quite distinct from feelings as intentional responses. Although concerns do influence what somatic feelings emerge into consciousness, somatic feelings do not arise in response to such concerns – as do the feelings comprised by the category of intentional responses.

5.6   Somatic Feelings in Ethical Life

The variability of the patternings of somatic feelings is directly related to their roles in ethical thought, decision, and action. Because somatic feelings signal to consciousness physiological states, they form an important part of the data about one's own bodily condition. Such feelings enter into ethical value reflection insofar as they contribute to correctly assessing "what is going on." As with other forms of human experiencing, somatic feelings are sources of questions for intelligence, reflection, evaluation, and decision. Accurate understanding of one's own bodily states and their relationships to the wider world is an essential component in the process towards authentic value judgments about oneself, and decisions concerning possible courses of action.

In recent years, there have been increasing numbers of scientific studies of the correlations between neural functioning and somatic feelings. These studies have greatly improved the accuracy of our understanding of our somatic feelings, supplementing our commonsense understandings of how our bodies feel with expanded and nuanced scientific understandings.[20] For example, when scientists discover that in certain people some somatic feelings are due to internal electrical or biochemical factors, rather than as a result of external stimuli as they are in other people, knowing this will change what counts as a proper, ethical response. Yet even the wealth of these scientific studies of somatic feelings is a further indication that nervous functioning cannot be fully determinative of which somatic feelings come to consciousness. If this were not so, scientists could not selectively pattern their own somatic feelings in ways that prevent these feelings from interfering with the sustained attention needed to insure objective outcomes of their studies.

Our somatic feelings constantly present us with challenges for accurate understanding and ethical response. Somatic feelings call for intelligent and ethical responses of nourishment, diet, exercise, rest, treatment of injuries and illness, and so forth. Hence, somatic feelings play an important role at an elementary level in the performance of one's structure of ethical intentionality and value consciousness.

Moreover, since most of our ethical actions involve bodily movements, these actions cannot occur without bringing about changes in somatic feelings. A chosen course of action can be carried out successfully only if the preceding and resulting somatic feelings are somehow harmoniously integrated into the pattern of experience that supports the action. This is possible because the somatic feelings that enter into consciousness are not wholly determined by bodily and neural states alone. If a genuinely ethical concern guides the patterning of somatic feelings into the pattern of experience, then one's body and nervous systems can support and cooperate with the ethical course of action.

It is sometimes claimed that giving free rein to somatic feelings of hunger, thirst, aggression, sexual drive, and fear is "only natural," and that all human ethical norms regarding these feelings are merely social constructions and therefore unwarranted restrictions on our natural bodily desires. It is true enough that some cultural norms have failed to fully and correctly understand somatic feelings and their ethical significance for care of the body. Still, the only thing that is natural at the level of neural functioning is that it occurs in accordance with the laws of physics, chemistry, and neurophysiology. Which of the cascade of nerve impulses are to be selected and allowed representation in consciousness in the form of somatic feelings is not determined by those "natural" laws alone. Rather, the reservoir of these neural functionings is open to a variety of selections, integrations, and patternings, some of which cooperate with ethical performance and some of which do not. The alleged "natural" patternings of unbridled somatic feelings are just that – patternings by unethical concerns, not something more natural than patternings by authentic ethical concerns.[21]

So far we have emphasized the positive, constructive, and necessary roles played by somatic feelings in ethical thought and action. However, philosophers and religious thinkers seem to have almost exclusively regarded feelings negatively, as threats that distort and corrupt ethical thought and action. Although this need not always be the case, still it is undeniably true that certain feelings – both somatic feelings and feeling responses that intend values – can and do interfere both with asking and answering all the questions required for authentic ethical thought and action, and with carrying out what one judges to be the right course of action. Even though somatic feelings can and do play positive roles in ethical thought and action, they certainly also can and do interfere with our ethical thinking and acting. Addictions and certain other intense somatic feelings screen out images, memories, and sensations that are needed to arrive at virtually unconditioned, objective judgments of fact and value and to make truly ethical decisions.

When somatic feelings interfere with the patterning of experiences and are no longer simply patterned by questions and concerns of ethical intentionality, they become obsessive sources of biases and profound barriers to authentic ethical living. Yet precisely because somatic feelings can be patterned and re-patterned in the streams of our experiences, this biased interference of somatic feelings is not inevitable. Families and other cultural institutions have developed highly sophisticated techniques for helping children develop appropriately ethical ways of patterning their somatic feelings. In addition, specialized therapeutic strategies have been developed that are effective in some cases for altering neural and behavioural functionings for addictions to alcohol, drugs, eating disorders, sexual obsessions, and so on. Once the neural functioning is normalized, somatic feelings can be more easily integrated into patterns that cooperate with ethical living. Some addictive feelings never entirely disappear, but their interference with the patterning of experience can be attenuated. Ascetic practices can also re-pattern less severe forms of biases that interfere with normative ethical living. This is why ethics includes instruction in practices that will sculpt our somatic feelings into patterns that cooperate with the normative functioning of the structure of ethical intentionality.

Yet decisions to submit to such therapeutic practices presuppose some kind of intervention that will overrule biased interferences and reorient the patterning of experiences into a different, healthier stream. This is something that cannot be produced by somatic feelings alone. Cooperation with therapeutic practices is the result of decisions. Such decisions, in turn, result from ethical reflections directed by different kinds of feelings – feeling responses that intend values. Thus we now offer a brief typology of somatic feelings and feelings as intentional responses, before turning in the next chapter to the fuller analysis of feelings that are intentional responses.

5.7   A Further Division of Feelings: Desires/Aversions, Affects, and Moods

In addition to the basic distinction between somatic feelings and feeling responses that intend values, there is another important and complementary categorization of feelings. This is the division among feelings as desires and aversions, affects, and moods.[22] This distinction applies to somatic feelings as well as to feelings that intend values. Hence feelings in general can be cross-divided (as is shown in Figure 5.1).

Feelings of desire and aversion are well known. They are feelings of need for satisfaction or relief of some sort. Somatic desires include hunger, thirst, fatigue, and sexual urges; they prompt pursuit of objects that will yield satisfactions. Feelings of somatic aversion include physical discomfort and pain, and these call for relief that involves withdrawal rather than pursuit. Intentional responses that are desires for values include ambition, desires for wealth, power, knowledge, recognition, respect, and for God. Intentional responses of aversion include being repulsed by ugliness, for instance by the sight of a disfigured or bloodied body, or by witnessing a person acting with cruelty or mean spiritedness. Most profound among the desiring intentional responses are the pure unrestricted desire to know and its prolongation

Figure 5.1. Cross-Division of Feelings

	Somatic Feelings	Intentional Responses
Desires/Aversions	Example: Thirst	Example: Ambition
Affects	Example: Quenched thirst	Example: Feeling beauty
Moods	Example: Bodily relaxation	Example: Joie de vivre

into the pure unrestricted desire for the good (the unrestricted notion of value), about which more will be said in chapter 8.

That there are somatic desires is evident enough. But perhaps some justification is needed for the claim that there are also desires that intend values. The criterion for classifying feelings as intentional responses is that they presuppose and arise out of prior acts of consciousness or their contents. Questions such as "What should I do?" and "What is the good of it?" are obvious instances of intentional-response desires, since they respond to the contents of prior acts of understanding and judgment, and their response is of a desire for something beyond those prior contents. Or again, we may witness, or merely hear about, the superlative performance of an athlete or a musician or a public speaker or someone's great philanthropic deed, and respond by desiring to be like that – or at least to meet this person, obtain an autograph, and so on. In all these cases, feelings of desire are intentional responses in Lonergan's sense. They respond to the contents that come to awareness through intentional acts. In general, desires as intentional responses arise from images, as well as from the understandings and judgments that we have about images. The advertising industry has developed very sophisticated techniques for exciting and inculcating these kinds of desires for all sorts of products by putting carefully crafted images before us.

Superficially, it may seem that all feelings are desirings or aversions, and certainly many have written as though this was the case. In addition to feelings of desire and aversion, however, there are other kinds of feelings. The most obvious examples are the somatic feelings that come as fulfillments of desires, such as feeling rested, feelings of having thirst, hunger, and sexual urges sated, and feelings of relief of itches, discomforts, or pains. Likewise, there are feelings as intentional responses that come as fulfillments to desires, such as the satisfactions of ambitions for power or knowledge or respect, the natural pleasures that accompany virtuous actions, as Aristotle puts it,[23] or the feeling that accompanies divine grace and fulfills the restlessness of the soul that Augustine identifies.[24] Likewise, there are feelings of relief that come to end feelings of fear or aversion, as the feeling of relief when a violent storm has passed or a war has ended.

There are also other intentional responses that are not so obviously satisfactions of desires. These include the feelings of appreciating something beautiful, or feelings of admiration of athletic prowess, intellectual achievement, or an exceptionally noble act, feelings of sympathy for someone grieving, or feeling awestruck before a natural vista. Such feelings do not necessarily come solely as responses to desires. I shall use the term "affect" in a technical sense for this broad class of feelings that dwell in appreciation of values, whether or not they arise in response to desires or seem to arise more spontaneously.

In addition to desires/aversions and affects, there are also moods. Desires, aversions, and affects tend to be limited in scope, while moods are more global. A muscular ache is localized in a particular part of the body, and its relief is also centred there. But relaxation is of the whole body, not just of some part. It is a somatic mood. Feverishness would be another example of a somatic mood.

Examples of moods that are intentional responses include feelings of contentment and being at peace with oneself and with the world. Likewise, feelings of discontent, depression, anxiety, or of a dour or pessimistic outlook are also intentional-response moods. All such moods are global in their range. They do not respond to just one specific intentional object, or to a limited set of intentional objects; once they have arisen, their moodiness extends to all objects that come to a person's consciousness. The whole world within one's purview is felt this way. Moods occur simultaneously with desires, aversions, and affects, and moods colour the context within which those feelings are felt.

"Mood" has been used to translate Heidegger's term *Befindlichkeit* in *Being and Time*.[25] Commenting on Heidegger's notion of *Befindlichkeit*, Robert Doran writes that it is "the way one finds oneself … the disposition or mood or self-taste that accompanies all our intentional operations."[26] This means that our moods are felt evaluations of the world, which are simultaneously the moods which contain our felt evaluation of ourselves. Our moods about the world are radically rooted in our moods about ourselves.

While the feelings of desire/aversion, affect, and mood that are intentional responses in Lonergan's sense can be correlated with neurophysiological processes, they are quite distinct from somatic feelings. Felt intentional responses respond to the contents that come to awareness through other intentional acts. They do not arise directly from states of our nervous system derived from states of our bodily organs as do somatic feelings. Although the distinctions among somatic versus intentional response feelings of desire/aversion, affects, and moods is frequently overlooked, they are nonetheless quite important distinctions. Without this distinction, it is difficult to properly appropriate the several different roles that feelings play in our ethical thinking, deciding, and living. In other words, discernment depends importantly upon a deep understanding and appreciation of the various forms of desire, aversion, affect, and mood, and their various roles in ethical living.

Much more could be said about somatic feelings, and about the correlations that obtain among all six categories of feelings and their underlying neurological processes. However, the objectives in this chapter were to clarify these basic distinctions, explore the relationships of somatic feelings to ethical thought and action, and to prepare the context for discussion of the class of feeling responses that intend values and their place in ethical thought and action. The next chapters, therefore, are devoted to the fuller exploration of such feelings.

6 Feelings as Intentional Responses and Horizons of Feelings

Intermediate between judgments of fact and judgments of value lie apprehensions of value. Such apprehensions are given in feelings.

– Bernard Lonergan, *Method in Theology*

6.1 Introduction

In the previous chapter we began to explore the complex issue of the intentionality of feelings. In this chapter we continue that exploration, this time focusing in more detail upon the feelings that do intend values as their *noematic* contents – what Lonergan called "intentional responses to value." Because of the complexity of the intentionality structure of feelings as intentional responses, this chapter proceeds in several stages. First, I offer a set of examples of such feelings. This is followed by a somewhat technical discussion of the multiple intentional objects of this kind of feeling. I then turn to illustrate these more abstract discussions with concrete examples, leading into the discussion of the horizons of feelings and their various internal tensions.

6.2 The Rich Field of Feelings as Intentional Responses

Feelings that are intentional responses form a wide and diverse class. They include feelings of delight, urgency, *joie de vivre*, anxiety, anger, religious awe, hostility, contentment, self-regard, despair, disgust, rage, compassion, envy, hatred, love, ecstasy, desires for possession of various sorts, respect, terror, revulsion, horror, empathy, sympathy, shame, and guilt. Lonergan himself offers a similar list:

> Because of our feelings, our desires and our fears, our hope or despair, our joys and sorrows, our enthusiasm and indignation, our esteem and contempt, our trust and distrust, our love and hatred, our tenderness and wrath, our admiration, veneration, reverence, our dread, horror, terror, we are oriented massively and dynamically in a world mediated by meaning.[1]

This broad class of feelings intends and reveals to consciousness a rich diversity of values or disvalues. These diverse feelings and their arrays of correlated values and disvalues may be gathered into very general categories, such as feelings of the values of comfort, usefulness, efficiency, vitality, orderliness, social worth, being cultured, responsibility, human dignity, or religiosity. The exact differences among these categories of intentional feelings depend to a certain extent upon the purposes of the authors using the terms and making these distinctions. (This, of course, is also true of the cross-division of feelings presented in the previous chapter.)

These lists and distinctions can be extended indefinitely. The lists are not meant to provide an exhaustive enumeration of all feelings that are intentional responses. They are offered as points of departure for the reader's self-appropriation of her or his own feelings of intentional response. The wide variety of terms used to classify feelings suggests the rich differentiation and diversity of values that are revealed in the great many concrete and specific feelings that people have over the courses of their lives, and that cultures manifest through their enduring histories. Heightened awareness and discernment of the differences among our many feelings are indispensable for fuller understanding of the intentionality of feelings.

The following example is offered in aid of this process of discernment. Consider the example of two people watching a sporting event. Both perceive more or less the very same set of visual images as the event proceeds. Suddenly one shouts in excitement, "Did you see that move! That was great!" The other sits in bored silence. The second spectator did indeed "see" the move, but had no feeling for it, and without that feeling there is no consciousness of its "greatness" – that is, of its value. The excitement of the first spectator is an intentional response that intends, reveals, and makes her aware of an athletic value. The first spectator is aware of the value in and through the feeling of excitement. She is aware of the value by feeling it. She could go on to describe the feeling, or to explain in some detail how that move compares with the athletic abilities of other players, or how it is a remarkably innovative use of the rules, and so on. But the value must be felt, and no amount of description or explanation can substitute for the feeling as the elemental source of consciousness of that value. In fact, any such descriptions will remain obscure to the second spectator, unless he also comes to share in some way these feelings of excitement. As it is, however, the second spectator has no consciousness of that value precisely because he has no feeling for it.[2]

Occurrences such as the one just described occur regularly in ordinary life. The analyses presented in the rest of this chapter are intended to promote discernment of the more subtle dynamic relationships between these regularly recurring feelings of intentional response and their intended values.

6.3   Intentional Responses to What?

Although Lonergan's use of the term "intentional responses to value"[3] was influenced by his readings of the works of von Hildebrand and Scheler, he gave it his own specific sense: "Intentional responses ... answer to what is intended, apprehended, represented. The feeling relates us, not just to a cause or an end, but to an object."[4] In this sense, intentionality concerns the relationship between acts of consciousness and their intended objects (or contents) – the conscious relationship between a *noesis* and its intended *noema*. Hence, to speak of human feelings as intending values means that values are the objects (*noemata*) of certain kinds of acts of consciousness (*noeses*).

There is, however, an ambiguity in Lonergan's brief remarks regarding the intentional objects of such feelings. Following von Hildebrand, he clearly held that values are the *noematic* objects of feelings: "Feelings that are intentional responses regard two main classes of *objects*: on the one hand, the agreeable or disagreeable, the satisfying or dissatisfying; on the other hand, values."[5] Yet he also speaks of feelings as having very different kinds of objects. Situations, occurring events, things, persons, and their qualities are also spoken of as the objects of such feelings:

> We have feelings about other persons, we feel for them, we feel with them. We have feelings about our respective situations, about the past, about the future ...
>
> In general, response to value both carries us towards self-transcendence and selects an *object* for the sake of whom or of which we transcend ourselves.[6]

Which, then, is the *noematic* object of intentional feelings – values, or something ontological such as a person or a situation?

There is further ambiguity in Lonergan's phrase "*response to* value." This phrase seems to suggest that values are already out there lying around somewhere, awaiting feelings that will respond to them. Values would be the *noematic* objects existing "already out there now" and feelings would be *noetic* acts that reach out to them ("intend" them) as they already are. This view certainly entered into the thinking of von Hildebrand when he remarked that unintentional feelings "do not possess the character of transcending the realm of the mind,"[7] as was noted in the previous chapter. He was quite concerned to provide a philosophical grounding for the objectivity of values. In doing so, he tended to construe conscious intentionality in general (and the intentionality of values more specifically) on the model of "knowing as taking a look."[8] According to this model, the objectivity of feelings as acts of value-consciousness would be guaranteed by their immediate contact with the objective, already existing values.

However, Lonergan's criticisms of the counter-position regarding knowing construed on the model of taking a look closes off this approach to value objectivity.[9] It is necessary, therefore, to reconsider more closely both the relationship of intentionality between feelings and values, as well as the question of value objectivity (and therefore the further relations among intentional responses, value reflection, and value judgment).

These puzzles regarding value-feelings can be resolved if we recognize that the intentional response of this class of feelings is a multiple intentionality – that is to say, feelings as intentional responses actually do have more than one object. Nor are the feelings of this kind the only instances of acts of consciousness that exhibit multiple intentionality; insights, acts of understanding, likewise have this characteristic.

6.4   The Multiple Intentionality of Insights[10]

The multiple intentionality of insights is brought to light most clearly in Lonergan's studies of Aquinas's writings about the "inner word" (the *Verbum* studies). Even though Lonergan wrote *Insight* in order to expand upon the basic breakthroughs that he achieved in those earlier studies, still they contain several nuanced points of analysis that are not to be found in *Insight*. There Lonergan traced Aquinas's accounts of the relationships between the *noetic* act of *intelligere* (insight/understanding) and its objects. He shows that Aquinas found not just one but four distinct kinds of objects of the act of *intelligere* – a fact that makes understanding a remarkable *noetic* act.[11]

First Lonergan distinguished between what he calls the "agent object" (or "moving object") and the terminal object.[12] Concerning this distinction he wrote, "This *intelligere* [insight] can be what it is only if there are objects to move it as well as the objects that it produces."[13] The agent object of *intelligere* is an image ("illuminated phantasm") that stimulates the emergence of an insight. Lonergan observed that we have the "universal experience that whenever we try to understand we construct images," and that these move us to have the insights that answer our questions.[14] In addition to the agent object of acts of understanding, "there is the terminal object of the inner word. This is the concept [or definition]."[15] While the agent object precedes and stimulates the emergence of an act of understanding, the terminal object follows, is produced by, proceeds from, and expresses the understanding.

There is also a third object of *intelligere*, intermediate between the agent object and the terminal object. According to Lonergan's reading of Aquinas, this is "the proper and proximate object of intellect … the *species intellecta* [intelligible form]."[16] That is to say, an insight has its own proper and distinctive intelligible content (object). This is the intentional object, the *noema* of the *noetic* act of understanding in the strict phenomenological sense. This proper intelligible object emerges simultaneously along with its intending insight, and it supervenes upon the lower agent objects (phantasms or images).[17] This supervenience means that the proper, intelligible content of the act of insight is the intelligibility *of that* agent image. But this does not mean that the image as imagined is intelligible, for the proper object of an insight is qualitatively distinct from its agent object (illuminated phantasm). Rather, the proper object of the insight is connected to and belongs to the agent object, which is the image, because the insight is into that image. Understanding thereby adds to and bestows its properly intelligible content upon what would otherwise be a merely sensible or imaginable content in the absence of the insight.

In addition, there is a kind of fourth object of insight – the "real object." Lonergan alludes to this only in *Verbum*: "Corresponding to this agent object there is the terminal object of the inner word; this is the concept, *and the first of concepts is ens [being]*."[18] In other words, Lonergan argues that for Aquinas the ultimate objective of each finite act of *intelligere* is correct understanding of how *all* things really are. This is because each finite, correct understanding is a contribution to the objective of knowing reality. Correct understanding of course is not reached automatically just because someone has an insight. An insight is not correct just because someone happens to have had one. Insights are known to be correct only when they are known to be virtually unconditioned as the result of the arduous, self-correcting process of reflecting and answering all the further pertinent questions. Only then can the proper, intelligible, *noematic* object of an insight also become known as a real object through a virtually unconditioned judgment.[19] Still, this does mean that insights have an objective that lies beyond their understandings of their proper intelligible objects. That objective is knowledge of something real, and ultimately of all reality, of being.

Finally, while the proper intelligible object of an insight is not by itself knowledge of reality, there is nevertheless *one* sense in which every proper object of every insight possesses a kind of objectivity. Lonergan calls this the "*per se* infallibility of intellect."[20] By this he does not at all mean that each and every insight we have is automatically correct. Rather, he means that *all* insights are "infallible" *with respect to the images* which are their agent objects. "No one misunderstands the things as he imagines them."[21] When we have an insight, it emerges from some image that is *its* agent object. This means that the proper intelligible content of the insight is connected to and belongs to that agent object (image, phantasm) which it understands. The insight thereby bestows its proper object (intelligible content) upon what would otherwise be the merely imaginable content of the image. This is what is meant by "insight *into* phantasm" – not that the intelligibility (proper object) is somehow hidden within or behind the image, but rather that the insight adds intelligent consciousness of the intelligibility proper to that image out of which it emerges.

Hence, the purely intelligible proper content of an insight is *always* the intelligibility of its agent object (image). The difficulty, of course, is that our imaginings can have more or less or virtually nothing at all to do with the way things really are. This is why the human capacity for reflecting and reaching the virtually unconditioned in response to questions of fact is one of the most profound dimensions of human self-transcendence. Reflection moves human thinking beyond the limitations and fascinations of our imaginations. Reflection also moves us beyond the merely provisional insights that are attached to our limited imaginations. It does this by relentlessly posing ever further pertinent questions. It goads us to take into account data not contained in our self-indulgent imaginings. It prompts us to consider alternative counterexamples, and to take into consideration prior insights and judgments, even those which may not conform to our imaginations. So, while every insight is "infallible" with regard to its agent image, in another sense every insight is very fallible before the tribunal of the further questions for reflection that press beyond that image. Every insight does understand something about its image, but that image (and understanding) may well diverge from reality, which is known fully only in virtually unconditioned judgments.

To summarize this section, in his investigations of Aquinas's writings about the inner word, Lonergan discovered that understanding (insight) has four different though related objects. First there is the proper object of understanding, which is its purely intelligible content. Such intelligible contents come to human consciousness in and only in acts of understanding. Without acts of understanding, there can be no human awareness of intelligibility. Second, there are also the agent objects of insights. These are "illuminated" phantasms – images constructed under the inspiration of intellectual inquiry. When inquisitive construction hits upon a suitable imaginative composition, an insight with its proper intelligible content emerges and supervenes upon this agent object with its imaginative content. The emergent insight bestows its own proper object of intelligibility upon the image, since, strictly speaking, the image as merely imagined has no intelligible content of its own. Third, there is the terminal object which is a concept or definition, and which expresses the pre-conceptual, intelligible proper object of an insight. Finally, there is the real object. The proper object of an insight in itself is only an intelligible possibility that may or may not be a real, objective intelligibility. If the rigours of reflection and further inquiry reveal the proper object to be virtually unconditioned, then it is also the objective intelligibility of some real object. Last, there is a sense in which the proper intelligible content is always "infallible" relative to the image that is its agent object, even though the image may ultimately prove to be irrelevant or distracting to attaining virtually unconditioned knowledge of intelligible realities.

This scheme of analysis of intentional acts and objects will prove helpful as we now turn to the task of sorting out the complex intentionality feeling responses, as well as the problem of how the intentionality of values can be objective. To that task we now return.

6.5   The Multiple Intentionality of Affect-Feelings

Discussion of desires, aversions, and moods as intentional responses will be taken up in the next section. This section focuses on affects as intentional responses. Recall that affects in my technical sense are feelings that dwell in and appreciate values, whether those feelings come in response to desires or arise seemingly more spontaneously. Affects can have multiple objects just as insights do. Affects as intentional responses also have proper objects, agent objects, expressive (or terminal) objects, and true objects. In addition, there is something in the realm of affective feeling responses that is comparable to the quasi-infallibility of insights with regard to their agent images.

6.5.1 *Value: The Proper* Noematic *Object of Affect-Feeling Responses*

As intentional, our affects directly intend their proper *noematic* objects, which are either values or disvalues. (Values or disvalues as the proper *noematic* objects of affects correspond to intelligibilities as the proper objects of insights.) An affect is the *noesis* and the value it feels is its intended *noema*. Such feelings make us conscious of values (or disvalues). They intend values immediately, *in* the very affects themselves. Aristotle says that when we feel angry, we feel what seems to be the injustice (disvalue) of a situation.[22] When we feel proud of our children and friends, we feel the value of what they have accomplished. When we wake up in the morning and feel great, we feel the value of being alive. Such feelings reveal values to our consciousnesses as their contents in the very acts of feeling them. In fact, feelings as intentional responses are our primordial access to any kind of value whatsoever. We do not have access to values by means of some other mode of consciousness that is completely disconnected from feelings.

The value that is the proper object of an affect is not somehow already out there, waiting to stimulate that feeling as a response to it. Values do not somehow already exist "outside" feelings ("in" the situation we know or "in" the morning we see), before feelings arise, catching a glimpse of those external values, so to speak. Affects do not arise by being stimulated by values already out there now in the external world (or up there in some sort of Platonic *noetic* heaven). The values *emerge* as *noematic* objects in our awareness simultaneously with the emergence of our *noetic* feelings of them. The example in the previous section illustrates how the value of an athletic feat is available only to someone who has an affect that feels the value.

Nor does our consciousness of values first come by means of some other mode of consciousness, such as perceiving or reasoning. It is not as though we first have a perceptual or conceptual representation of a value in some other way, and then add feeling for that value. We do not first have a perception of a value, or first logically argue ourselves into a conviction that something is valuable, for which we do not yet have any feeling. (A line of reasoning can serve as the agent object out of which a feeling for the value does emerge, but the line of reasoning alone does not yield consciousness of the value by itself.) Just as the value does not exist "out there" awaiting a feeling response to it, so also the value does not previously exist "in here" and then elicit a feeling response to it. We do not have consciousness of *any* value *qua* value prior to feeling it. There is no prior *noetic* act that makes us conscious of the value as *noema*, followed later by a subsequent *noetic* act of feeling that then responds to and thereby feels the value. Values emerge originally and primordially with and in feelings themselves. As Lonergan puts it, "the apprehension of values and disvalues is the task not of understanding but of intentional response. Such response is all the fuller, all the more discriminating, the better ... one is, the more refined one's sensibility, the more delicate one's feelings."[23]

In making these claims, I am following not only Lonergan, but also Max Scheler who remarked that "values are given first of all in *feeling*."[24] He continued:

> The actual seat of the entire value *a priori* (including the moral *a priori*) is the *value-cognition* or *value-intuition* that comes to the fore in feeling … This cognition occurs in *special* functions and acts which are *toto caelo* different from all perception and thinking. These functions and acts supply the only possible *access* to the world of values.[25]

The intentional, *noematic* objects of value or disvalue are originally given and revealed precisely as felt, immediately and for the first time in the very feelings themselves. Values are the proper *noematic* objects of these intentional feelings, and human consciousness of values does not happen apart from feelings that are intentional responses.

6.5.2 *Movers of Affective Responses*

Like insights, affects also have their agent objects. While affects do not respond to value-objects as if they were somehow already out there, nevertheless they always do respond to other contents and acts which are different from value-contents as such.

As with insights, affects respond to "phantasms." Quite frequently affects respond to the *noematic* contents of acts of sensation, memory, or imagination. People respond with awe to a vista seen from a mountaintop. They respond with revulsion to the sight of a badly wounded animal. They feel calmed in response to the rhythmic sounds of the surf, but respond with feelings of irritation to the sound of fingernails upon a blackboard. Or a person may become aware of the sensations of her or his own muscles in exercise, and then respond by feeling the vitality (the vital value) of those sensations. One person may respond affectionately to a touch upon his skin, while another may feel their personal space violated.[26] Upon remembering a favourite song, a person may feel nostalgia or grief for a lost friend. Or a person might become caught up in a fantasy and respond with humour to a scenario she herself has composed in her imagination.

Of course such sensations, memories, and imaginations do not occur in isolation; they occur in streams or patterns of consciousness. As such, particular sensations, memories, and imaginations appear as related to other *noematic* contents. Most often, intentional feelings respond not just to isolated images, but rather to these experiential complexes, replete with all of their concrete interrelationships. The concrete interrelatedness of these sensations, memories, and imaginations then becomes the complex agent object that moves affects. Most often, our affects respond to these more complex patterns, even though one or a few components stand at the centre of our attention. For example, the different affective responses to being touched depend importantly upon associated memories about being touched previously by this same person, or by other persons or things.

Hence, affects frequently respond to *noematic* contents on the first level of consciousness – the level of sensation, memory, and imagination – as their agent objects. However, unlike insights, the range of agent objects to which affects can respond extends well beyond this level. Feelings of awe, dread, anxiety, or fear can arise, for example, in response to our new questions for intelligence. Feelings of delight, surprise, excitement, or horror can arise in response to the new ideas grasped in new insights. Feelings of trepidation can arise in response to questions for judgment, while the judgments of fact themselves can move a person to feelings of admiration, sympathy, disappointment, or disgust. In the movie *The Godfather II*, Michael Corleone hears something that enables him to answer in a virtually unconditioned fashion all his questions about who was responsible for the betrayal of his brother, Sonny. He reacts with feelings of rage and vengeance in response to this judgment of fact. His feelings do not respond merely to the sounds that he hears. They respond to the virtually unconditioned judgment, for which the words heard, and their meanings, supplied the final fulfilling conditions.

In addition, decisions, once made, can move a person to feel regret, peace, or the weightiness of a new responsibility or destiny. When such feeling responses occur, a person feels the values or disvalues of the *contents* of those questions, insights, judgments, or decisions, even though these contents are not strictly speaking instances of what Lonergan meant by "phantasms" in his *Verbum* studies. Thus the range of movers of affects is much wider than the range of movers of acts of understanding.

Affective feelings may also be actuated in response to *noetic* acts of consciousness themselves, no less than by their *noematic* contents. There are feelings that revel in the joy of sensing as such. This is especially evident in a vacationer who, freed from the routine demands of working life, can simply enjoy the liberation of his or her powers of sensation as such. This is also evident in the feelings of a person who rejoices in the restoration of a lost sense of seeing or hearing or touch. Feelings may also respond to acts of intelligence as such. Young children laugh with delight at their insights, not just at the contents of those insights. They delight in the epiphany of their own intelligences as they rise above mere sensation, catching onto intelligible connections, and making inventive constructions. The "Eureka!" that accompanies an insight, especially an insight that comes after a prolonged search, is a feeling of the value of the act of understanding itself, over and above any other feelings about the value of its ideas grasped in that act. Such feelings reveal the value of intelligence as such – the value, as Lonergan puts it, of "the eternal rapture glimpsed in every Archimedean cry of 'Eureka.'"[27]

Feelings also respond to acts of rational reflection and judgment as well, and in so doing, those feeling reveal the value of the very acts themselves. Rationality and criticism are described as "cool and detached," which is mistakenly taken to mean a lack of feeling. Rather, the cool feeling of rationality is in fact a felt-recognition of the sublime value of rationality as such. It is a feeling of the austere importance of reasoning, and of the peace that comes in finally arriving at judgments of fact and value. These feelings feel the value of critical reflection as it transcends even the delight of insights about what might be, in order to stand in reverence of the mystery of existence and truth. Moreover, there are also feelings that feel the preciousness of human acts of moral self-transcendence and freedom, feelings that respond to the profundity of the human capacity to originate values. The actualization of freedom in particular acts of making choices can be accompanied by feelings that intend the preciousness of human freedom in its most radical appearance.

In the next chapter, we will explore in detail how feelings enter into the very formation of judgments themselves. Affects, however, do also respond to such judgments of value. This means that certain affects first inform judgments of value, which in turn give rise to still further affects. For example, the conclusion that someone has lied is not only a judgment of fact – it is also a judgment of value since lying is a value-laden category. Our very notion of lying arises from our earlier affects about the kind of disvalue that lying is. But once we have concluded that someone has lied, we then respond with further affects towards the person concerned. The quality and intensity of our affective responses varies in many ways. We feel differently depending upon the kind of relationship, or lack thereof, we have with the person. If the lie was told by a dear friend or a mere acquaintance, if it was done by someone holding an office of public trust, or someone we just read about in the newspaper: all these factors contribute to the detailed ways in which we feel affectively about the liar. In this way, affects entering into and following upon judgments of value constitute a self-reinforcing cycle of feeling development as the affects interact with their agent objects.

Furthermore, affects may respond to the experiences of the self as a whole person. Each of us is constantly being revealed to ourselves as a unique and whole human being through each and every one of our own numerous acts of consciousness, although we seldom attend to this fact. Feelings of being at peace with oneself or feelings of shame or self-loathing respond to our own awareness of our total selfhood. Children delight in the value of intelligence when they have insights, but more profoundly, they delight in the revelation of themselves as selves revealed in and through those insights.

Perhaps most importantly in the realm of ethical deliberation, feelings also respond to possible courses of action. When we deliberate about what to do, our imaginations, intellectual inquiry, and accumulating insights construct ideas of possible courses of action. All through this process, our feelings respond to these various alternatives. These constructed possibilities are the agent objects to which our feelings respond. We might feel the course of action as nice or silly, noble or disgusting, beautiful or ugly. We might feel the course of action as a worthwhile possibility for someone else to take, or we may feel it as obligatory, as an alternative that we must do, because of the needs of the unique situation. This might be because of our particular talents or background, but it might be because no one else is close enough at the moment to do what we feel must be done. All these factors come together to move our affective response to the possible course of action before us.

In all these various instances, the feeling response is to the object that moves the feeling to emerge. It is likely that there is no content or act of human consciousness incapable of eliciting an intentional response by one or another feeling. Strictly speaking, then, feelings do not respond *to values*, as von Hildebrand held, and as even Lonergan's phrase seems to suggest.[28] Rather, feelings respond *to* a vast range of *agent objects*. To say that affects respond to such objects means that they emerge from and supervene upon those objects. When affects emerge, they reveal values to consciousness. The values are the proper *noematic* contents of those affects. Because those feelings come in response to the agent objects, the affects endow those objects with the values as felt. The intentionality of affects, then, is not that they respond to values that are "already out there;" rather, affects respond to non-value agent objects. The proper value-objects are added to those agent objects by the responding affects. The responding affects thereby value those agent objects; affects endow them with value. Von Hildebrand seems to have overlooked this more complex relationship between these two distinct objects of intentional feelings.

6.5.3 Expressions as "Terminal Objects" of Affective Feeling Responses

What Lonergan calls the "terminal object" of an insight is its expression in a definition and its concepts. Likewise, affective responses may also be expressed in various ways, and these expressions might be called their terminal objects as well. These expressions express the values that are felt. Such expressions can be spontaneous and embodied – crying, or jumping for joy, for example. Lonergan offered an extensive reflection on the ways that feelings are expressed in smiles: "From smiles one might go on to all the facial or bodily movements or pauses, to all the variations of voice in tone, pitch, volume and in silence, to all the ways in which our feelings are revealed or betrayed by ourselves or are depicted by actors on the stage."[29]

Affective responses can also be expressed spontaneously in symbols. In fact, Lonergan goes so far as to define symbols by means of their expressive and evocative relationships to feelings.[30] This means, of course, that the proper interpretation of symbols must attend to the values revealed by the feelings they express. Felt values can also be expressed in ordinary, commonsense language when a feeling is described, and its corresponding value thereby tacitly implied. For example, "I feel like I am walking on eggshells around him," expresses the felt-valuation of his touchiness.

Perhaps the purest expressions of felt values are artistic. This is suggested by Lonergan's comment, "Poetry, according to Wordsworth, is emotion recollected in tranquility."[31] Artistic expression may have its origin in sensed or remembered experiences, imagined scenarios, insights, judgments, or profound moments of reaching decisions. Any of these could give rise to feelings of values. But because life throws many movers of feelings at us all at once, it takes times of tranquility and detachment, as well as artistic skill, to properly sort out and express just what values one has become aware of in the most intricate, subtle, and refined of feelings.[32] In this sense, perhaps artistic expression of feelings and values is analogous to the explanatory modes of expression that Lonergan attributed to the mature sciences.[33]

While the purest expressions of feelings might be in works of art, the most complete expressions of values as felt occur in human decisions, actions, and deeds. Values are most fully expressed through the full commitment to them by human beings who incarnate those values in their actions and in the ways they live their lives. In a profound sense, then, human action and its incorporation into the ongoing drama of human history is the most profound expression of feelings. History is the penultimate expression of human feelings.[34]

6.5.4 *True Values and the Quasi-Infallibility of Affects and Values*

Corresponding to the real objects of insights, there are the true objects of felt values. This brings us back to the question of the objectivity of values. With affects, just as with insights, the correspondence between the proper and true objects is only established by the work of reflection and judgment. While there can be no consciousness of values without feelings, feelings alone do not automatically yield consciousness of true values. True values are only known in virtually unconditioned judgments of value. Here Lonergan's discussion of the infallibility of insights can shed some light.

When we have an insight, the proper and agent objects of insights combine. The insight bestows its intelligibility upon its agent image and makes it intelligible. Something similar is also true of affects as intentional responses. They also combine their proper and agent objects. The proper object of an affect is the value that it feels. There can be no consciousness of that value apart from the contribution made by the feeling. Once a feeling responds to its agent object, it feels its proper value-object as the value of that agent object. The feeling endows its agent object with the value it feels. The feeling and its value are "infallible" with respect to the agent object in a limited sense. For example, when we feel the delight of a child's smile as we perceive it, that *perception* is delightful. It is our affect of delight that reveals that value of the smile as perceived by us. Affects feel the value, and recognize it as the value of their agent object. But if I look more closely, the pattern of my experiencing might become more nuanced. I might notice the trace of a mendacious smirk in that smile. If I do, I will no longer feel delight in this changed perception. I will feel perhaps disappointment or anger in response to it. Affects of disappointment or anger and their correlated values are infallible relative to the ways I now perceive the child's smile.

Again, I may feel admiration towards someone as generous in response to what I experience, understand, and judge of that person in limited settings. I may later have other encounters that change my judgments about the same person, and no longer admire him as generous. My original feeling of admiration was "infallible" with respect to the limited knowledge that was the original agent object of my affective response. Yet my original knowledge was not knowledge of the whole person, only of some limited actions, and my affect of admiration was not infallible with respect to the whole of the person's reality.

This infallibility of affects is a very limited and partial kind of value objectivity. Just as the infallibility of insights is only partial, so the infallibility of affects is also far from unconditioned. We can feel the value of some scenario we have constructed in our imagination, but that value can have little or nothing to do with reality. Our perception of the child's smile might miss a subtlety. Had we perceived this nuance more attentively, our feelings would not have responded with delight. The divergence between images and reality also occurs in the propaganda and rhetoric of commercial advertisements, politics, and war. During election campaigns, we are told that candidates are soft on crime, hate workers, are addictive spenders of public funds, or are insensitive to the plight of the poor, and so on. To the extent that such slogans go uncriticized, they inevitably elicit affects of antipathy towards the candidate. More ominously, prior to and during the Rwandan genocide, Tutsis were called cockroaches,

which conjured up images and associations that led to affects of murder-
ous hatred. During the Nazi Holocaust, Jews were portrayed as dwarves
resembling the treacherous Hagen in Wagner's *Götterdämmerung*.[35] Exag-
gerations, distortions, lies, and their associated images can be movers of
affects just as much as nuanced, balanced understandings and truths.
Were distorted narratives true accounts of facts, then the affects would
reveal accurate evaluations of real people. Affects are infallible only relative to their agent objects. Great injustices and horrors occur because the
real objects in no way correspond to the imagined objects that elicited
the affects. In such cases, the felt valuations have nothing to do with the
realities, only with the false appearances put forth. If the rhetoric is false,
then the felt valuations may be infallible, but the responding feelings are
not feeling true values.

True values (the true objects of feelings), therefore, are the proper
objects of properly ordered affects felt in response to true judgments
of fact. When judgments of fact are based upon a grasp of the virtually
unconditioned, reached through the relentless reflective processes of asking and answering all pertinent questions, properly ordered feelings will
spontaneously feel the true values of the realities known through these
true judgments. When properly ordered human feelings respond to what
is known in true judgments of fact, these feelings apprehend true values
objectively.

However, this is the case only when feelings are properly ordered. We
hear of shocking cases of cold-blooded murder, and of delight that aberrant
people have taken in torturing other people. Through these and other heinous cases, we know that not only imaginations and judgments of fact can
be distorted, but that feelings themselves can also be distorted. While these
are perhaps the most extreme cases, distortions of a lesser degree infect the
affectivity of a great many people. Certainly, these distorted affects cannot
be relied upon to intend true values, even if a person's judgments of fact
are impeccable.[36]

The possibility of fully objective knowledge of true values, therefore, lies
in part in our capacity to reflect and reach virtually unconditioned knowledge of the way things are, and in part in our ability to intend their values
in responses of well-ordered affects. In order to approach the larger issues
regarding the proper ordering of feelings, it is necessary to enlarge the
account of feelings as intentional responses. First, the relation of values
to desires, aversions, and moods as feelings of intentional response will
be considered. This will be followed by more concrete phenomenological descriptions of some complex examples of feelings and values. Finally,
the phenomenon of horizons of feeling and their proper ordering will be
discussed.

6.6   Desires, Aversions, and Moods as Intentional Responses

In the realm of feeling responses that intend values, desires/aversions and moods are like affects in that they all respond to acts, contents, or subjects of consciousness. Like affects, they also intend values, but they do so in ways that differ from the intentionality of affects. Clarification of the intentionality of desires/aversions and moods, therefore, can best be approached by focusing on the ways that they differ from affects.

6.6.1 Desires and Aversions

A concrete example will prove a useful point of departure for analysis of desires as intentional responses. Consider what happens when we have a desire for a meal. Our bodies may need nourishment before we become consciously aware of this in somatic desires of hunger. Somatic hunger emerges in some pattern of experiencing, and preoccupation with other concerns can defer feeling somatic hunger for quite some time. Many factors are involved in the patterning that eventually does allow somatic feelings of hunger into consciousness.[37] Among these may be actual sensations of the colours and smells of food items, but they can also include memories or pictures of food or even reading a menu or a recipe. Each of these is a possible agent object for other feelings that change the patterning of experiences.

These agent objects do more than open consciousness to the emergence of somatic hunger desires. They also elicit additional desires that are intentional responses proper. Somatic hungers can be non-specific. Researchers hypothesize that somatic hungers may be limited to desiring one of the basic taste groups: sweet, sour, bitter, or salty. But the desire for spaghetti with marinara sauce, or for lemon meringue pie, adds desires of intentional response to somatic desires and transforms them into a richer complex of desiring. What is desired is not just biological nutrition or even the sensations of taste that the body uses as its instrument to attain nutrition. What is desired is a meal replete with feelings of its richer values – of healthy eating, beauty of the presentation of the food, and the fellowship of a communal gathering. The agent objects elicit desires on several different levels that merge into a desire for a holistic experience suffused with affective appreciations of the complexity of the value of the meal. Yet neither those values nor the affective appreciations are given directly in desiring as intentional response, no matter how complex. The values and their affective appreciations are felt only indirectly – only as something absent yet desired.

This simple example highlights several features that are found in many other desires that are intentional responses. Such desires are feelings of attraction towards values or disvalues. By aversions, on the other hand, we are repelled by values or disvalues. Unlike affects, desires and aversions do not feel values directly; they feel values indirectly. Just as a question does not directly intend an answer, but only indirectly intends it by desiring to directly understand it, so also desires as intentional responses do not directly intend values but only desire them.[38] They yearn for affective feelings that feel those values directly. By way of contrast, affects are neither attracted towards nor repelled away from values or disvalues. Affects simply abide in feeling the values or disvalues directly. Affects are contemplations of values and disvalues.

Consider as a second example a desire to win an athletic competition. Such a desire arises in response to a complex combination of agent objects. The person desiring competitive success will have memories of seeing such competitions by other athletes in the past, hearing people talk about the winners, and perhaps visions of past award ceremonies and interviews with the victors. As these various components are fashioned into a complex image, a desire arises and yearns for the value of being that kind of a winner. The agent object of this desire may include a prior affect that first feels the athletic value achieved by others, but the desire itself could also be the very first felt apprehension of that value. The value felt by the desire itself is the value of "*being like* those victors," and it is felt in response to the complex assembly of the agent object – that is to say, the desire is not just a feeling of the value of this kind of victory as it actually happens to some people somewhere in the world, but a feeling for the value of the person himself or herself achieving that victory. It is a desire for being oneself the incarnation of that value. It is simultaneously a feeling of the absence of that value, of not yet possessing the value oneself. Desires are feelings of the value through the feeling of its lack, whereas affects are feelings of the value through feelings of its presence. The desire itself may grow and complexify in stages, as the desiring person grows in understanding of the sport, begins to exercise and acquire the physical and intellectual skills needed for success in this athletic field, and so on. But whatever its stage, the desire itself is a felt-apprehension of the value through feeling it as absent in one's own life.

Something analogous can be said for other kinds of intentional responses that are desires. One also can desire for another to be victorious in the athletic competition, and then feel as desirable the value of that victory through feeling its absence in the other. Or one can feel desire for success in intellectual, professional, legal, artistic, business, political, military, or ordinary family matters, and so on.

Of course, some of the most intense and all-consuming desires occur in the dramatic field of human sexuality. Here the differentiated somatic desires of sexual urges become defined and focused as they join with the other erotic agent objects that give rise to the full intensity of human sexual desires as feelings of intentional response. Most often it is the visual appearance of the other to which erotic desires respond in an intentional fashion. But sometimes it will be the voice, or a particular act of kindness, wittiness, intellectual brilliance, or exercise of power that will elicit the intentional response of erotic desire that incorporates somatic sexual urges into its intentional desiring-complex. Likewise, acts of sexual intercourse lead to alterations in neural processes and biochemistry, giving rise to intensified somatic sexual feelings that last well beyond intercourse itself. These somatic feelings, however, are not the entirety of sexual feelings, as they also combine with additional feeling responses that intend values. What we call sexual desire is not merely a somatic feeling; it is a complex of somatic feelings in combination with feelings that are both desiring and affective intentional responses. The complexity of sexual feelings is well-known, and this intertwining of somatic feelings with intentional responses is part of that complexity.

Desires are usually thought of as desires for possession – possessing the object of one's sexual desire, for example, or for possessing money or a car or a house or a title of accomplishment. Yet more basic than desires for possession are desires for attainment, desires for self-transcendence and self-transformation. That is to say, usually what seems superficially to be a desire to possess or own some object is often more fundamentally a desire to become something that one will value about oneself. Fully human sexual desire is not simply the desire for biological intercourse with the other who has excited that desire; it is simultaneously a desire to be valued as sexually desirable by the other as well. It is a desire to become valued by the other in that way, and most often it is a desire to be valued for more than one's sexual performance. Without attaining those richer and more complete levels of value, the sexual desire as intentional response is frustrated and not completely satisfied. Likewise, desires for material possessions are almost always part of larger desires as intentional responses – desires for comfort, for beauty, for recognition and admiration by others – and behind these, more broadly, lie desires to be *worthy* of such admirations. It is a perversion and a stunting of desire to try to force the full desired value V (e.g., intentional response as desire for sexual intimacy) into the lesser form V' (somatic desire for sexual intercourse) in an effort to avoid the call to self-transcendence. This is not real sexual desire, but the attempt to repress desire as intentional response. It is a perversion of desire as intentional response.

That said, desires can themselves also be perverse. It is possible to desire not only values but also disvalues. People can and do have desiderative responses to things that are objectively loathsome. This is because while desires as intentional respond to agent objects, they do so only within a larger, comprehending horizon of feelings and values. We will return to this in section 6.7.

Aversions are similar to desires in that they feel values and disvalues indirectly rather than directly. They are of course opposite to desires in their felt directionality. Like desires and affects, they respond to a variety of agent objects of greater or lesser complexity. But where desires respond to the agent objects by feeling attraction towards them, aversions respond to their agent objects as something repulsive and to be avoided. "Repulsive" here names the felt-direction of a feeling of aversion. While an affect may feel the agent object as a negative value (a disvalue), a feeling of aversion adds the felt sense of the disvalue of being near or being in contact with the disvalue, whether in a literal, physical sense, or in an analogous sense (i.e., wanting to avoid something that would "infect" one's value horizon). A feeling of aversion is not the same as a movement of bodily turning away, although felt aversions can be so strong as to elicit such movements almost automatically. Like desires, aversions can also be perverse, in that it is possible to feel aversion not only in response to disvalues but also towards values.

6.6.2 Moods as Intentional Responses

People speak of being in a good mood or in a bad mood. Good moods as intentional responses include feelings such as *joie de vivre*, confidence, happiness, joy, hopefulness, calm, consolation, and ecstasy. On the other hand anxiety, depression, stress, nostalgia, grief, desolation, and rage are examples of bad moods. Moods tend to be fairly long-lasting feelings, and individuals can even be characterized by moods that last virtually their entire lives. Moods are like affects in that they feel values directly, and therefore unlike desires and aversions that feel values indirectly. But unlike affects, which tend to confer the values they feel upon a specific object, moods range across a wide variety of objects. While moods can arise in response to a particular agent object, their felt valuations will tend to spread across the whole of a person's world. Particular affects, desires, and aversions may come and go without significantly altering a mood. The mood colours the way in which these more specific feelings evaluate their particular agent objects.

A person might become joyful in learning that his beloved loves him in return, but his joy is not limited to his beloved. His whole world and everything in it is experienced as bearing the value of being filled with joy. Or another person may become discouraged and depressed when she loses her job. Yet it is not just the job or the employer who terminated her, or even she herself, who is cast with the negative evaluation felt in depression – her whole world is felt as depressing. A mood like depression can also arise in response to seasonal changes as in the "winter blues." But it is not just the season that is experienced as depressing. Very little at all seems worthwhile when a person is in a mood of depression. Affects and desires that would otherwise feel the positive values are soured or blunted by this depression's felt valuation that these are not very important values after all.

Even when moods like depression have a significant neurophysiological basis, as they frequently do, they are not merely somatic feelings. Unlike somatic feelings, moods bestow value or disvalue upon a person's world, and that felt valuation can last a very long time.

6.6.3 *Questioning as Intentional Response*

The tensions of inquiry are themselves feelings as intentional responses. They are desires for *noetic* acts and *noematic* contents that are absent from one's consciousness. Inquiries arise in response to some *noematic* content as their agent objects – questions of intelligence respond to contents of experiencing, or questions for reflection respond to formulations of insights, for example. Inquiries sometimes even respond to *noetic* acts (as when we desire to understand what understanding is).

Questions of value are also examples of desires as intentional responses. Questions such as "Is it worthwhile?" or "Should I do it?" respond to the understood courses of action as their agent objects. They desire the value-knowledge to be known in judgments of value or the actual value be realized in authentic decisions. Yet transcending all desires as intentional responses, including all limited questions of value, there is the unrestricted desire for the good. It is a desire manifest in every one of our questions about what is good, what is of value. It desires the goodness and value intended in any particular question of value, but goes beyond to ask about still further values. It underpins and embraces all ethical questions about what one should do. It includes ethical questions, but goes beyond questions about the good that one can make or do oneself. It extends to eliciting questions about the goodness of what is beyond one's own doing – both the goodness of what other humans have accomplished before one arrived on the scene, as well as the goodness of natural events and things that were not produced by any human action at all. It extends, therefore, to all questions about the goodness, the value, of the entire universe and of all human beings and their activities within the unfolding of natural and human history. It even extends to questions about goodness that might transcend the human and natural orders. We will return to these issues in chapter 13.

6.7   Concrete Illustrations

The preceding sections have of necessity been comparatively abstract. It is now time to offer some concrete illustrations that reveal the utility of these abstractions for the purposes of discernment and self-appropriation in the field of ethics.

As a first example, I return to the scenario presented in section 6.1 of two spectators watching a sporting event. There I said that they perceive more or less the very same set of visual images. But in fact the visual images of the athlete's movements would not be exactly the same for these two spectators. The visual images of the athlete's movements are patterned by a certain background familiarity with the sport in the case of the first spectator. Her background understandings and judgments of fact help her notice subtleties – and the combination of those subtleties and the background contents give her a different agent object from that of her partner. While there might be little difference between what she and her partner actually see, these slight differences in the visual components of her agent object are made significantly different by her accumulated knowledge of the sport. These significant differences between the total agent object for the two spectators elicit significantly different feeling responses with correspondingly different valuations. The "greatness" felt in the excitement of the first spectator is the proper, intentional object that her feeling feels. In this feeling response, the first spectator becomes aware of the athletic move with its subtleties as having a very·concrete, perhaps even unique value: "That was great!" Her feeling of excitement acknowledges the value of greatness in the athletic movement as she saw, understood, and judged it. On the other hand, her partner was aware neither of the same agent object nor felt the value of its greatness.

As a second example, consider a parent who is furious at a two-year-old child for taking his aunt's expensive cosmetics and smearing them all over his body. The doting aunt simply laughs with delight. In the parent's fury, frustration, and embarrassment, there are felt apprehensions of disvalues: the waste of expensive cosmetics, the ruination of good clothes, the loss of valuable time now needed to clean up the mess, and perhaps deeper down, a desire to be a good parent, a worry of failing at that goal, worries about how the aunt is judging the parent, or underlying moods of anxiety or lack of self-worth. The aunt, by contrast, in her feelings of delight, feels values: the comic value of the child's artistry, the marvel of the surprising creativity in a mind so young, the unconditional worth in this nephew as a marvellous and unique human being, and perhaps a tinge of feelings of superiority or relief that she does not have to bear the burden of parental responsibility for the child's mess.

These descriptions can be used to communicate the disvalues and values that the feelings intend. But such words can communicate effectively only to someone who has had such feelings. It is not as though the parent and aunt first know these values by means of concepts or reasoning, and then somehow respond to the conceptually grasped or reasonably affirmed values by having feelings for them only after the fact. Nor do the parent and aunt first have the feelings as experiences, and then have insights into them – and only then, by understanding these feelings, become conscious of values for the first time through the insights into the feelings. The values are already the *noematic* proper contents of their feelings, even before there is any understanding of the feelings. Ideas (intelligibilities) are the *noematic* contents of insights (understandings), not the contents of feelings. Acts of understanding can add further intelligible contents to the value-contents as felt. Those insights into the feelings can themselves be the agent objects of subsequent additional feelings that lead to refinements of feelings and nuanced feelings for values. But the intelligible contents of those insights cannot substitute for the awareness of values and disvalues that comes primordially in feelings.

In a sense, of course, both the parent and the aunt are "right" in their feelings. There are both disvalues and values to be discerned in this ordinary yet complex situation. The parent is more attentive to certain parts of the scene, the aunt to somewhat different parts. Their individual attentiveness and their individual patterning of their experiences constitute different agent objects, which in turn condition the emergence of different feeling responses. This plurality of feelings and values that pertain to a single situation raises further questions. The questions as to which feelings and values ought to prevail are not, however, answerable by feelings alone. They are questions for judgments of comparative value, which go beyond the values as felt and head towards true value objects. Even so, those further questions and further judgments of comparative value presuppose, and cannot replace, the feelings that make the values conscious.[39]

As a third example, I offer the contrast between the great thinker about cities, Jane Jacobs, and her nemesis, the czar of New York City urban renewal, Robert Moses. In her book *The Death and Life of Great American Cities,* Jacobs sets before the reader rich descriptions of urban social life at its best. She uses the term "lively" to signify the rich panoply of social values that she feels so intensely in her love for the good of urban life (when and where it is good). She also explains how ill-conceived decisions destroy these social values and leave in their wake "dull, grey" urban regions. By contrast, where Jacobs "saw" social values, Robert Moses "saw" only chaos and messiness that interfered with the efficient movement of traffic and commerce. He oversaw the destruction of closely-knit neighbourhoods in New York and their replacement by vast, multi-lane, limited-access highways.[40]

To be more precise, of course neither Jacobs nor Moses "saw" values or disvalues. They *saw* many of the same visual features of buildings and roads, as well as automobile and pedestrian patterns of interaction. But they actually entertained significantly different agent objects, because of the backgrounds they brought to their acts of seeing. Their different images, understandings and judgments about urban life were the different agent objects of their intentional feelings. Consequently, they responded differently and felt differently about what they saw, understood, and judged. But their affective feeling responses to city life as they saw and understood it were also accompanied by very different desires and moods. Although Jacobs was able to face soberly and with detachment the evils of human thoughtlessness, carelessness, and injustice that are undeniable parts of urban life, she nonetheless embodied moods of humour and hopefulness throughout most of her life. Moses, by contrast, carried quite different desires and moods and attitudes about people throughout his career. In those different feelings, these two people intended different values. Their feelings beheld dramatically different values in the complexities of urban life. What came to consciousness in their feelings were the proper, intentional objects – the values or disvalues – of the agent object of urban life as they perceived and understood it. In turn, as they grew within Jacobs and Moses, these felt valuations of city life further patterned their selective experiencing, occasioned their further questions, insights, and judgments of fact. Their cycles of intellectual learning and feeling for values intertwined and reinforced each other.

In all three cases, feelings as intentional responses constitute a composite consciousness of values by their unification of the agent and proper objects. Intentional feelings both respond to something (X, a complex agent object) and intend some concrete value V. In doing so, intentional feelings feel X as having value V. The proper object of an intentional feeling is the value V that it intends (feels). The agent object X is that to which the feeling responds.

Because the three examples are concrete, they also illustrate the complexity of the agent objects to which intentional feelings respond. This is also true even for seemingly simple symbolic images because they carry with them rich retinues of associations that may reach back many years, often many generations. The simple symbol may have a focal image (a hand wave, a ring, a cross, a veil) but that image does not exist in a vacuum. The entire agent object can include stories, interpretations, and traditions of the symbolic image that expand and enrich its meanings. The vivid sensible appearance of a symbol can mislead us into overlooking the full concrete historicity of its associations and meanings that constitute the fullness of it as an agent object. Likewise, the intentional responses to complex or even simple agent objects can themselves be compound feeling responses. The parent and the aunt each have not just one feeling response, but many to the child's antics. The same was certainly true of Jacobs and Moses as well.

These complex compositions of feeling responses also imply correspondingly complex evaluations of the agent objects. Concrete situations do not have just one conceptually simple value. Their values are correspondingly concrete and complex. The concreteness of our feelings as intentional responses reveals the intricacy of our feelings and valuations – a fact that is easily and commonly overlooked, unless special effort is made to discern what we are doing when we are feeling. The next section will endeavour to become still more concrete in aid of discerning the complexity and concreteness of our feelings and valuations.

The preceding examples also do more than illustrate this general, structural relationship between the proper and agent objects of feelings as intentional responses. Because of their concreteness, the examples also illustrate the divergence of feelings and values in response to agent objects. In each example, two different people responded with different feelings and different evaluations to the same situation. Closer analysis revealed that subtle differences between the two people in their sensations, imaginations, memories, background understandings, and judgments about the situations constituted significantly different agent objects. In a sense, then, each member of the three pairs was "objective" in her or his valuation of the agent object – because the agent objects themselves were different.

The differences in value perspectives in the three examples might seem to provide further justification for the prevailing view, which says that everyone has different feelings and different values, and that there is no such thing as objectivity regarding values. Yet this is a limited and ultimately unsatisfactory response to the problem of the objectivity of feelings and values as responses to agent objects. Almost everyone who claims to be a committed value relativist inevitably surfaces passionate commitments about at least a few values. Among other things, they tend to be people who are passionate that everyone has a right to value relativism. That passion and sense of right is inconsistent with their professed relativism. These inconsistent relativists spontaneously expect others to agree with their valuations, and can become quite indignant with people who do not share their valuations. In these passionate commitments they are performatively feeling and acting as though these select values are absolute and not at all relative.

This suggests that while human felt responses to concrete situations differ in complex ways, it does not follow that there is no such thing as objectivity in the realm of feelings as intentional responses and values. What does follow, however, is that whatever kind of objectivity is to be had in this realm, it must be rather complex. The problematic of value objectivity will be addressed again in chapter 8. In order to prepare for that discussion, we turn in the next section to still more concrete phenomenological descriptions of feelings and values, this time in the phenomenon of the clustering of feelings to form value horizons.

6.8   Horizons of Feelings as Intentional Responses

Initially I treated feeling responses somewhat abstractly. The first example in the previous section treated the feeling of excitement as though it were isolated from other feelings, in order to draw attention to the relationship between its proper object (value) and its agent object (athletic move). While the emphasis in that example was a necessary step in the analysis, it can leave the misleading impression that feelings occur independently of one another. We may tend to think of joy or sadness or fear as forces bursting upon the scene independently, pushing aside prior feelings to make room for themselves. We may tend to think of such feelings as alien intruders coming from outside of us (or from our nervous system inside but still alien), as separated from the influence and responsibility of ourselves as whole persons, as existential subjects. These would be misleading impressions.

In fact, intentional feelings always occur in contexts of other associated and interconnected feelings. That context is established by the character of the whole person herself or himself. Because feelings are diverse and subtle, we notice perhaps only the most dramatic and imperious of our feelings as they rise to the fore of our consciousness. Nevertheless, even the most intense feelings arise as always already part of a connected network of feelings. (The second and third examples in the previous section begin to make this apparent.) Anger may be tempered by mercy, and compassion tinged with frustration, annoyance, and grief. The passion of falling in love can be tinged with guilt about other felt-values one also holds dear and that may have to be forsaken for one's beloved. The felt-valuation of the nobility of courage is elevated precisely because it is felt along with the fear of death which it overcomes. In this section we become even more concrete by describing the manners in which feelings and their intended values interact in complex ways.

Any identifiable feeling is in fact always felt in the company of other feelings. I will adopt a term commonly used in phenomenology – "horizon" – in order to characterize the assembled, interrelated totality of feelings as concretely experienced by an individual.[41] "Horizon" is itself a visual metaphor, suggesting the spatial surroundings of an object or activity. Those surroundings contribute to the *de facto* concrete, visual appearance that something has to a conscious subject. The scene of sky, clouds, ground, trees, and stream affects how the deer in the foreground appears visually. The same deer appears quite differently, however, if it is walking down a city street. Likewise, in the realm of intentional feelings there is also a background network of accompanying feelings, always present but perhaps less noticed, that modulates and constitutes the ways that even our most vivid feelings are felt. Horizons of subtle background feelings give the more prominent foreground feelings their special, concrete valences. These surrounding horizons affect *how* we feel sorrow or joy or fear, for example.

In doing so, the horizon of feelings also modulates and nuances the values that are felt. The concrete values intended in the feelings are complex values because the feelings themselves are made more complex by their horizons. The feeling of disappointment over losing a competition can be elevated by feeling genuine joy for a friend's victory. The loss, therefore, is not felt as so great a disvalue as it would be without the joy over the value of the friend's achievement. Or again, one's feeling for the value of an architectural masterpiece can be corrupted by feeling the contempt for its greedy and arrogant designer. Or one's intense anger at what seemed like an inexcusably unjust action may become moderated as new feelings emerge when one learns more about the background and details of the case.

Horizons of feelings are complex constellations of a great many feelings. Each feeling in the constellation is affected and modified by the other feelings. The radiating influence of the whole horizon constitutes an orientation into the realm of values that goes beyond any single feeling itself. This horizon of feelings also permeates and guides our other acts of consciousness such as the cognitional activities and patterns of experiencing, inquiring, insight, reflecting, and making judgments of fact. Our horizon of feeling most especially influences our value inquiries, value reflections, deliberations, judgments of value, and choices, which will be explored in chapter 7.

In addition to the visual metaphor of horizon, other metaphors can also serve to illuminate the constellations of our feelings as intentional responses. A horizon of feelings may also be likened to an archer's target, with some one feeling most vivid at the present moment constituting its centre. Just as the peripheral rings of an archer's target highlight and focus how a target's bull's-eye is perceived, so also other feelings that are felt as more or less peripheral affect how a central feeling is felt. Consider for example a person filled with excitement upon learning that he has received a job offer. At the centre of this target is the feeling of the accomplishment – feeling the value of achieving this professional goal. At the same time, and closely associated, is the feeling the person has about himself as esteemed by the one who hired him. Slightly farther from the centre are numerous feelings of joy, disappointment, and indignation that accompanied the many preparatory stages of achievements and set-backs that led up to this moment. Perhaps more central or perhaps more peripheral are feelings of gratitude for all the acts of kindness by those who assisted and supported him along his way. Finally, perhaps at the very periphery are feelings of anxiety and self-doubt about the great responsibilities that lie ahead, and the possibility that he may not really be able to perform the role well. All of these feelings reinforce, undermine, and modulate the central feeling about the offer of this professional role. The person does not just feel that this is a good (valuable) job. He feels it as a very complex value nuanced by the ways that the surrounding "target circles" of values reinforce or temper the "bull's-eye" feeling of accomplishment. Each of these surrounding feelings affects the central feeling according to how "closely" or "remotely" it is felt in relation to that central feeling. In doing so, these surrounding feelings combine with the central feeling to give the very personal, concrete, modulated value that this new job will have for him.

Again, someone might feel an annoyance at the weakness of another person's repeated failure to keep his promise as central in the bull's-eye. Yet that annoyance can be moderated by feelings of compassion, patience, and even sorrow, developed perhaps by knowledge of the serious trauma that is the source of this character flaw. The annoyance does feel the disvalue of the repeated failure; but it feels its disvalue in a specific way, as a negative value made less severe by the exculpating values that are felt as connected to it.

The interconnection among intentional feelings may be further likened to a vertical scale or ladder. For as Lonergan, Scheler, and von Hildebrand have said, intentional feeling responses are also felt as related in some order of preference[42] – as comparatively "higher" or "lower" values, following the suggestion of this spatial metaphor. One person may feel compassion as "higher," in preference to revenge as "lower," while another person's felt-preferences may be exactly inverted. This felt-ordering of feelings carries and establishes a hierarchy of value priorities, ranging from highest (most valued and esteemed) to lowest (least valued, most despised). When compassion is felt as higher than revenge, the value of the other person's repentance is felt as more valuable than the value of repaying an injustice or defending honour. On the other hand, when honour is felt as higher, repentance is felt as perhaps mere weakness. Or again one doctor may feel the health of her patients as surpassing all other values, and sacrifice time with her own family or even her own health for the sake of her patients. Another doctor may concretely feel monetary reward above all else, even temporarily leaving a patient on the operating table in order to make a banking transaction.[43]

These preferences are *not* primarily matters of choice – that is to say, these preferences are not *chosen* as higher or lower (even though the history of a person's choices will profoundly affect how this scale becomes organized). Rather, these are primarily *felt* preferences and priorities of values. Our choices both precede and follow from our felt scales of preference, but our choices do not constitute these scales of values as such. The scales are constituted by preferences and priorities as felt.

An alternate spatial metaphor, exactly reversed, can also illuminate scales of feeling preference. Where the ladder metaphor suggests as a contrast between "higher" and "lower" values, another metaphor can be invoked to contrast "deeper" and "surface" or "superficial" feelings towards values. The point of the metaphors is that some values are in fact being *felt* as greater or weightier than others. Moreover, whether the priority is described as higher or deeper, the vertical ordering of feelings need not correspond to the horizontal ordering suggested by the target metaphor. The feelings that occupy the most central place at a given moment in a person's horizon are not necessarily the same as their highest (or deepest) feelings. A feeling of anxiety about economic security might be the central feeling at a specific moment in a person's life, even though the affect of appreciation for the value of great artistic creativity persists as a person's highest (or deepest) felt priority.

Horizon, target, ladder, and depth are all spatial metaphors. Each metaphor has the strength of highlighting a distinct aspect of the interrelationships among our feelings. All four, however, suffer from being merely static, spatial metaphors, for our feelings are dynamic. Some of our feelings are fleeting. Others endure for a long time and underpin commitments we make for our entire adult lives. As Lonergan observes,

> I must add that [feelings as intentional responses] are not merely transient, limited to the time that we are apprehending a value or its opposite, and vanishing the moment our attention shifts. There are, of course, feelings that easily are aroused and easily pass away. There are too the feelings that have been snapped off by repression to lead thereafter an unhappy subterranean life. But there are in full consciousness feelings so deep and strong, especially when deliberately reinforced, that they channel attention, shape one's horizon, direct one's life.[44]

Among the feelings that are deep, strong, and endure through a whole lifetime are the unrestricted desire for all value, and the feeling of being-in-love in an unrestricted fashion. We will return to a fuller discussion of these and their roles in our horizons of feelings in chapter 8.

In addition to feelings that intend values as such, there are also feelings that intend the relationships among values. We feel not only the disvalue of something ugly, but also the relation of ugliness to beauty. We feel not only the value of a genuinely courageous deed, but its relations to the ordinariness of most deeds, as well as its relation to the cowardice of other deeds. Max Scheler notes that certain kinds of persons (whom he calls "common") are only able to feel the value of something by means of feeling comparisons and contrasts. Others, whom he calls "noble," Scheler says first feel the values themselves directly, and then come to feel their relations to one another. This, he says, is because the noble person feels "his own value and the fullness of his being, an obscure conviction that enriches every conscious moment of his existence, as if he were rooted in the universe."[45] Whether one first feels the values or the relationships among values, these relations among values come to consciousness in other kinds of feelings themselves, not in insights or concepts or judgments. Whether one has a noble or common or another kind of character, every person's horizon of feelings will include feelings of relations among values, as well as for the values themselves.

Among the relations that we feel, there can be and usually are persisting, unresolved felt tensions within our constellations of feelings – felt tensions between their horizontal target-like orderings and their vertical scale-like orderings, for example. A person may well feel that generosity is a higher value than financial acquisition, even though feelings about financial success seem to be constantly at the forefront of her or his attention. It is not a question that the person *says* he values one thing (generosity), but *really* values another (financial success). Rather, the person really values both generosity and financial success through feeling them, but does so in ways that are in conflict and really are felt in tension with one another.

Another metaphor, that of a web or net, can be helpful in illustrating yet another aspect of the constellation of intentional feelings. A spider's web, for example, is a network of interconnected nodes and threads. When a particular node in that network is stimulated, the whole network resonates with a frequency and pattern that is characteristic of that particular stimulation. The vibration pattern of the whole web is determined both by the specific stimulus at some specific point, as well as by the whole web's network which situates that specific point. (Spiders are able to identify the location of a trapped insect by means of the different resonances of the whole web.) In a similar fashion, feelings respond to particular conscious acts or contents as their agent objects. But feelings do not respond as separate, isolated acts of consciousness; rather, it is the person's whole web of feelings that responds.

A particular feeling such as anger, delight, sorrow, or worry may be touched off by some event. Yet the felt response is not just anger but anger as concretely resonating with the felt preferences and proximities that constitute that person's actual web of feeling life. The way in which the whole network of feelings resonates makes the person conscious of the value of the agent object with all the specific concreteness with which he or she actually does feel its value. That value need not be either the central or the highest value in the subject's horizon of values. Yet those central and highest values will play the key roles in determining how the value of the agent object is felt. *How* that value is felt determines *what* that value is for the subject who feels it in that way. Hence, taken as a whole, any individual person's concrete horizon of feelings not only determines how each particular constituent feeling is felt, but also determines the concrete values that are bestowed upon particular agent objects.

Each of the spatial metaphors – horizon, target, scale, ladder, depth – draws attention to certain dimensions of the complex interconnections within a horizon of feelings as well as the relationships among their intended values. Still the variations in duration, and the dynamic shifting of tensions among our feelings as intentional responses, point us towards a final metaphor – that of composition, as in the composition of a piece of music, a painting, or a work of literature. Composition is a much more complete metaphor for the concrete constellation of a person's actual feelings. Nor is this comparison accidental; great works of art express the complexities of felt experiences of values in all their personal concreteness. In a painting the elements of colour, line, and shape, or again in music the elements of tone, intensity, and rhythm; are put together into complex and nuanced visual or auditory relations with one another. These compositions relate the elements together to produce an overall whole, while the whole gives special subtlety and poignancy to particular visual or sonorous elements. Each particular colour or tone is like a particular feeling intention of some particular value.

Each person's horizon of feelings is like the whole of an artistic composition. By means of the concretely composed arrangement of feelings, a person feels values not in a vacuum but as related and modulated. By means of that composition of feelings, a person situates herself or himself within a world of values, with concrete intensities, emphases, preferences, nuances, and ambiguities.

In order to further illustrate how these various metaphors assist in discerning the arrangement of feelings in a horizon, consider the example of a person for whom receiving honour from "important" people is both the central and the highest value. The person is working on a speech for an important audience. An "unimportant" neighbour comes by and asks for a favour that really cannot be deferred – her car won't start and she urgently needs a ride. The person's feeling horizon as a whole will respond to the request. Precisely because honour by important people is paramount, the feeling response will at least be tinged with annoyance. The more precise feeling response (and therefore the precise felt-evaluation) will depend in complex ways on how other feelings are felt in relation to one another in the person's feeling horizon. Which feelings are more central or more peripheral? Which are higher and lower, deeper or shallower? And so on. Perhaps in the past some action by the neighbour has elicited specific feelings of compassion, or of anger, or perhaps the person's parents inculcated feelings of duty to help neighbours. Perhaps the person especially admires those parents, or perhaps is alienated from them. All these concretely interrelated feelings enter into the overall feeling resonances to the neighbour's request. As a whole, they determine how the value of that request is felt. This example illustrates how at any particular moment in time a person's horizon of feelings determines how they intend values in their felt responses.

A concrete horizon of intentional feeling responses as a whole also constitutes the feeling-*orientation* of that individual, existing person – that is to say, a person's feeling horizon puts her or him on a life trajectory, a "project" for life. In doing so, that horizon massively directs the consciousness of its subject. It directs the subject's attention towards experiences, towards sights and sounds and memories, towards questions, towards the search for insights, towards reflections for the sake of reaching judgments and decisions. For example, feelings of compassion have an orientation to them. In general, compassion feels the value (or disvalue) of another person's plight. It orients or directs attention to the person, to her circumstances, to the questions to be considered, to insights into the possible means of remedy. This feeling also excludes all sorts of considerations irrelevant to compassion. But compassion never occurs in general. It occurs only in the consciousness of some individual subject. As such, compassion is concretely situated in a horizon of other feelings that feel the disvalue of someone's plight in a more complex way. It is this complex manner of feeling compassion that directs the attention of the conscious subject. The manner in which compassion is surrounded by other feelings fine-tunes the direction of compassion's orientation. Unconditional compassion will attend to slightly different sensations, memories, questions, etc., than will compassion tinged with a touch of pride in one's capacity for compassion.

Any given person's affective horizon, her or his concrete constellation of feelings, can change gradually and incrementally, or suddenly and radically. Changes in feelings can form sequences that result in growing sensitivity and nobility, or they can form downward spirals into apathy or brutishness or bitterness or *ressentiment*. Yet, no matter what the trajectory, at each stage in her or his life every person has some particular and concrete horizon, some constellation or composition of feelings. That constellation forms the horizon for almost everything else that occurs in a subject's consciousness.

These metaphors also suggest ways of thinking about the well-known phenomenon that feelings do not seem to obey the laws of logic. People experience conflicting and even contradictory feelings about the same thing simultaneously, and this seems to defy logic. Yet from another point of view, there is no violation of logic here at all. Conflicting feelings are indeed felt as conflicting. The feeling-conflict is precisely how these feelings are related in a person's horizon. To the extent that a person's horizon of intentional feelings comprises conflicting feelings, that horizon may well respond to some particular agent object with felt-conflict. In such cases the valuation of that object will indeed be felt as a value-conflict. As this suggests, horizons of human feelings frequently, perhaps always, have internal tensions embedded within them.

6.9   Summary

In this chapter I have explored the nature of the broad class of feelings that Lonergan referred to as intentional responses. Although his terminology (following that of von Hildebrand) seems to suggest that these feelings respond to values as if they were "already out there," I have argued that there are four distinguishable objects of such feelings. These feelings only truly "respond" to their agent objects – whether to images in sensations, imaginations or memories, or to ideas from insights, or to facts as known in virtually unconditioned judgments, or to deeds, or to acts of consciousness or to persons. With respect to values, intentional responses do not so much *respond* to them as *bring* them to consciousness. Values emerge in our consciousnesses simultaneously with and through the agency of feelings as intentional responses. I have argued that feelings do not respond to values that first came to consciousness in some other way, such as through reasoning. Reasoning about feelings and values is of the utmost importance. However, such reasoning presupposes the kind of consciousness of values that can only come first in feelings. The next chapter will explore in detail processes of reasoning about values and their resultant judgments of value.

This chapter also situated feelings of values in their concrete contexts, what I have termed "horizons of feelings." Such horizons have been described in some detail. This analysis led to the claim that we feel values with a kind of infallibility, a *limited* form of objectivity *relative* to the concrete compositions of our horizons of feelings, and also *relative* to concrete agent objects that move our feeling responses. The analysis ended with the observation that there are tensions within our horizons of feelings. These tensions tend to destabilize our horizons of feelings. In chapter 8, we will return to a fuller exploration of these tensions as well as to the problematic of value objectivity. It will be argued there that every person's horizons of feelings has deep and permanent sources of tensions, which can only be resolved by what Lonergan termed "conversion." That chapter will also argue that resolution of those tensions through conversion holds the key to what might be meant by full (not merely relative) objectivity of judgments of value in general and judgments of ethical value in particular.

7 Feelings and Value Reflection

7.1 Introduction

Chapter 4 offered an overview of the structure of ethical intentionality. That structure begins to operate when questions arise about what we should do. These questions arise out of our experiences and our prior understandings and judgments of fact. They initiate the dynamism of the structure of ethical intentionality. That structure begins with questions seeking to objectively understand the factual situation in which one finds oneself. It then progresses to questions seeking practical insights into possible intelligible courses of action. It continues through value reflection, the grasp of virtually unconditioned value, and consequent judgments of value. It ends with decisions concerning those judgments, and actions that implement those decisions.

Judgments of ethical value and how we arrive at them are therefore of central importance in the structure of ethical intentionality. These judgments have the form, "Intelligible, possible course of action I has value V," where I is supplied by a practical insight and V is supplied by a person's horizon of feelings. Because of the complexities surrounding the intentionality of feelings, their role in arriving at judgments of ethical value could only be sketched earlier in the chapter 4. Since those complexities were explored in some detail in the intervening chapters, it is now possible to expand upon that abbreviated sketch.

Judgments of ethical value about a course of action as worthwhile or obligatory make up only a part of the much broader range of judgments of value in general. We do not judge only the values or disvalues of actions we contemplate undertaking. We also make judgments about values that we have had no part in realizing. We make judgments about the values of the natural wilderness and the natural behaviours of animals, about the medicinal value of pharmaceuticals, about the aesthetic values of works of art, music, and literature, about the fruitfulness of competing lines of scientific research, about governmental programs, and about the platforms of political parties and candidates. We also make judgments about the value of daily events, about the people we encounter, and their characteristics and flaws. These judgments of value do not necessarily extend into decisions and actions. Many processes of value reflection are content to rest once they reach virtually unconditioned judgments about the value of something or someone.

Asking and answering further pertinent questions is central to all processes of value reflection. As I proposed in chapter 4, feelings determine what further questions will be regarded as pertinent. Feelings play this role not only as we endeavour to reach judgments of ethical value, but also in our efforts to reach true judgments of value in general.

This chapter will explore the ways that feelings function in the process of arriving at value judgments in general, and then turn to what is specific to judgments of ethical value. First, we will explore how questions of value and of ethical value arise in the first place, and the roles played by feelings in their emergence. Then we will consider how the processes of value reflection proceed once such questions have arisen. Following the discussion of value reflection and value judgment in general, we will turn to look more closely at the process of ethical reflection and judgment. The chapter then turns to the ways in which processes of value reflection determine which questions are selected for serious pursuit, and the role played by feelings as intentional responses in these processes. These analyses will surface the problem of order and disorder in our horizons of feelings. As I will argue in the next chapter, the problem of the objectivity of values (including the problem of objective ethical values) is intimately connected with the problem of tensions and order in our horizons of feelings.

7.2   Habitual Valuing and Questions of Value

We move through our daily lives with greater or lesser awareness of a broad range of values. Most of the time, our value awareness operates without being disturbed by new questions of value. Yet questions of value do arise at various times, and without them we would not reach the virtually unconditioned judgments in which values are known in the fullest sense. So we ask, under what circumstances do questions of value arise?

In his intentionality analysis of a simple judgment of fact, Lonergan himself noted that our knowledge of facts is largely habitual. This habituality is only occasionally punctuated by new questions about facts. Lonergan offered the example of someone returning home, finding his house in disarray, and asking the mundane question of whether something had happened. Lonergan observed that the "question is asked, not in its full generality, but with respect to concrete situations that diverge from our expectations and by that divergence set us a problem."[1] He continued his analysis, noting that our commonsense knowledge of what is to be expected is constituted by a host of previously acquired insights and judgments. In other words, as long our prior understandings and judgments of facts continue to make sense of our flow of sensible experiences, new questions for judgment of fact do not arise. The absence of those further questions is the condition for the objectivity of our habitual, factual knowledge of these new experiences that we encounter. But when we encounter something that does diverge from our habitual knowledge, or notice something we previously overlooked, questions for intelligence and reflection arise spontaneously. Once these questions do arise, the resulting processes of factual reflections will not be put to rest until we reach satisfactory answers to all the further pertinent questions that ensue, and reach new virtually unconditioned acts of understanding and judgments of fact.

Something similar happens with respect to our knowledge of values. Most of the time our valuing is habitual and new questions of value do not arise.[2] We take for granted the values (and disvalues) that we have come to know regarding the broad range of images, situations, events, things, and persons that we encounter regularly. We can become complacent about altogether too many of these values. We tend to forget the lustrous moments when first we experienced feelings for those values. We seldom recall the careful mental processes that we went through on the way to our measured judgments of value about them. We tend to forget also how many value judgments we have taken on as our own through thoughtful and thoughtless decisions to believe. But even if we have become complacent about the values we have embraced in previous feelings, judgments, and beliefs, that embrace persists in the form of a habitual mentality about our values.

Moreover, just as our experiences can and do diverge from our habitual factual knowledge of what to expect, so also our encounters with novel experiences, ideas, facts, and persons can diverge from our habitual valuing. When something diverges from our habitual valuing, new feelings respond and new questions for judgments of value arise spontaneously. When a new situation diverges from our habitual valuing, it provokes in us new questions for practical insights – how are we to respond? And if we come up with a new practical insight into what would be a new potential course of action for us, spontaneously we respond to both the insight and the situation with new feelings and new questions for value judgment that depart from the habits of valuing that have been in place up to now.

Exactly what, then, is this habitual valuing? For the most part, this habituality is a complex synthesis of our previous judgments of value, beliefs, and our horizon of feelings. Our habitual embrace of values develops over many years through our acquisition of previous feelings of intentional response, prior judgments of value, and earlier decisions to believe assertions about values. Just as our accumulation of insights and judgments of fact assemble into habitual knowledge of our world, so also our accumulation of value judgments, beliefs, and their associated feelings forms into habits of valuing the things, events, and persons that we encounter.

The interconnections and roles played by the various components in our habitual valuing, and circumstances that lead to new questions of value, can be made clearer by an example taken from Jane Austen's novel *Pride and Prejudice*. Austen's protagonist, Elizabeth Bennet, rises above almost all the other characters of the novel in terms of her intelligence and her ethical stature. This is particularly true in comparison to other members of her family, consisting of her parents and four sisters. Elizabeth's mother speaks rashly in public and makes bad decisions, to the point of endangering one of her daughter's health and another's reputation. Her father has tired of his wife's foolishness, and has abdicated much of his family responsibility. He withdraws to his library, and most of his interactions with his family have been reduced to occasional sarcastic comments. Three of Elizabeth's sisters are immoderate or socially awkward. Only her sister Jane has an honourable character, although she lacks Elizabeth's intelligence and shrewd judgment of people, and her somewhat excessive modesty eventually leads to misunderstandings. For the first half of the novel, only Elizabeth's friend Charlotte appears to have qualities comparable to those of Elizabeth.

Gradually we learn that understandable anxiety lies behind Elizabeth's mother's lack of moderation. The family's home and income depend upon a behest, which will terminate upon the death of Mr. Bennet. Given the social and economic vulnerability of women of her class in England at that time, Mrs. Bennet knows full well that the well-being of her daughters – and indeed her own well-being in her elder years – depends upon them marrying well. Although others in similar situations did not always act with the imprudence displayed by Mrs. Bennet, Austen reveals the difficulties that women had to face and to negotiate in those social and historical conditions.

Elizabeth is also well aware of the financial and social vulnerabilities of the family's situation. Still, because of her nobility she is unwilling to accept the proposal from a Mr. Collins. Although marriage to Mr. Collins would have secured her financial and social future, Elizabeth judges his character negatively: "Mr. Collins was not a sensible man," among other things.[3] This, even more than her lack of romantic love for him, is the reason she refuses his proposal. Well aware of what she is risking with this rejection, she nevertheless is unwilling to compromise the value of her own character, which she maintains unflinchingly. She could not "have sacrificed every better feeling to worldly advantage."[4]

Elizabeth is therefore quite upset when Charlotte accepts Mr. Collins's proposal of marriage on the rebound only three days later. Charlotte held exactly the same judgments of Mr. Collins's character as did Elizabeth. When Elizabeth tries to talk her out of her decision, Charlotte points out that she lacks the physical attractions and social graces of Elizabeth, and has therefore much more to risk in refusing Mr. Collins's proposal.

In the meantime, Elizabeth has been approached by two other young men: Fitzwilliam Darcy and George Wickham. Elizabeth judges Mr. Darcy to be haughty and quickly forms an overall negative valuation of him. Wickham, on the other hand, is a soldier who is more handsome, intelligent, and witty than Collins, and less aloof than Darcy. Wickham tells Elizabeth that Darcy has treated him unfairly, preventing him from receiving a pension promised by Darcy's deceased father. Elizabeth believes him, and this increases her negative evaluation of Darcy.

It is therefore a shock to Elizabeth when Mr. Darcy himself arrives with an offer of marriage. Darcy himself can hardly believe what he is doing, and he pulls no punches in stating his undiplomatic proposal: "In vain have I struggled. It will not do. My feelings will not be repressed. You must allow me to tell you how ardently I admire and love you." Austen's narration continues:

> He was not more eloquent on the subject of tenderness than of pride. His sense of her inferiority – of its being a degradation – of the family obstacles which judgment had always opposed to inclination were dwelt on with a warmth which seemed due to the consequence he was wounding, but was very unlikely to recommend his suit.[5]

That Elizabeth refuses his proposal comes as no surprise. It is perfectly consistent with her set of values thus far. She explains to him the particulars of her refusal, including his alleged mistreatment of Wickham.

This is the background for the points I wish to illustrate. The foregoing description summarizes the state of Elizabeth's habitual valuing. She has formed an exceptionally mature set of judgments of value, and has arrived at them according to her own insights in meeting the requirements of her own further questions. She has believed only some of what she has been told, and only after first thinking carefully about the conditions that need to be fulfilled before deciding to believe. She also had a nobly balanced and principled horizon of feelings, where her feelings for pleasure and security were felt as of considerably less value than her feelings about her personal integrity and her feelings about the character of other people. This symbiosis of judgments, beliefs, and feelings is the habit by means of which she evaluates the daily events in her life. The maturity of her habitual valuing is her source of virtuous pride, an object of exploration announced in the novel's title.[6]

It is out of this habit of valuing that new questions of value arise for Elizabeth.[7] The next day she receives a letter from Darcy. In it he defends himself against the complaints she enumerated in her refusal, including the accusation that he had treated Wickham unfairly. The letter enumerates facts incompatible with Elizabeth's habitual valuing, including the details of how Wickham had manipulated the affections of Darcy's fifteen-year-old sister and talked her into eloping, in order to gain access to her fortune.

Austen narrates that Elizabeth initially has difficulty accommodating all the implications of Darcy's letter, and has to read it a second time. As she does, she realizes that her decision to believe Wickham was based upon flawed value judgments and distorted feelings: "When she read with somewhat clearer attention a relation of events which, if true, must overthrow every cherished opinion of [Wickham's] worth ... her feelings were yet more acutely painful and more difficult of definition."[8] A friend had previously told her that Darcy had good reasons for his treatment of Wickham, but Elizabeth chose to believe Wickham rather that the friend.[9] Darcy's letter confronts her not only with new facts but also new feelings, and the relationships among her feelings begin to shift dramatically.

The new question about Wickham's worth opens up an intense period of value reflection, where many further pertinent questions arise under the guidance of her new feelings of "astonishment, apprehension, and even horror," among others.[10]

The new questions and feelings begin to form a new "concern" that transforms her pattern of experience. She begins to become aware of things that had previously eluded her notice: "She perfectly remembered everything that had passed in conversation between Wickham and herself in their first evening ... She was *now* struck with the impropriety of [his] communications to a stranger, and wondered it had escaped her before."[11]

Her period of value reflection leads her to arrive at an objective, negative judgment of value about Wickham. She begins to believe Darcy. Gradually her evaluation of Darcy turns positive. But most significantly of all, new feelings, new questions, and new judgments of her own self-worth emerge for Elizabeth from out of her previous habits of valuing:

> "How despicably I have acted!" she cried [to herself]. "I, who have
> prided myself on my discernment! – I who have valued myself on my

abilities! Who have often disdained the generous candor of my sister, and gratified my vanity in useless or blameable distrust ... Till this moment I never knew myself."[12]

This summary of these events does not do justice to the richness of Austen's remarkable narration of the complexity of value reflection. For that readers should turn to the novel itself. I hope that this summary has at least conveyed basic points of importance. Elizabeth's judgment that she never knew herself in this case of course refers to value-knowledge of her self-worth. Her new questions and new realizations bear striking similarity to Augustine's admission, "I have become a question to myself."[13] Augustine's judgments about his own self-worth eventually led him to profound choices that brought about his conversions. Something similar also happens in the remainder of *Pride and Prejudice* for both Elizabeth and Darcy. However, I have chosen this episode to illustrate not a decision that issues in conversion, but simply the kinds of circumstances when habitual valuing gives way to new questions of value and new processes of value reflection and judgment.

7.3   Value Reflection and the Horizon of Feelings

Once new questions of value do arise, they initiate processes of value reflection. Processes of value reflection can be quick or prolonged. They can comprise relatively few acts of consciousness or they can comprise thousands of such acts. In all cases, however, value reflections – as with reflections on their way towards judgments of fact – involve the asking of further pertinent questions until all of them have been adequately answered. In addition, value reflection is also suffused with feeling responses that intend values. Of course, questions of value are themselves feelings as intentional responses.[14] But other kinds of value-intending desires, affects, and moods also accompany questions of value in response to new situations. These new feelings enter into a person's horizon of feelings. As they do so, the feelings and the values they intend are modulated by the horizon. In turn, they modify the horizon itself.

Each person's value reflection takes place within this complex context of feelings and questions. The modified horizon of feelings both elicits further new questions, and establishes the criterion of the pertinence of the new questions of value. Value reflections are structured by the intimate interplays among questions of value and feelings that intend values. These concrete interplays select, call into play, and guide the re-patterning of sensations, as well as the additional memories, imaginative anticipations, insights, expressions, and judgments of fact that fill out processes of value reflection.

Austen's narrative of the episode from *Pride and Prejudice* is filled with details of the dynamics of one such process of value reflection – many more details than were provided in the previous section. Rather than elaborate further on that episode, I will offer some different cases that illustrate the complex interrelationships between questions of value, feelings as intentional responses, and other acts of consciousness that they structure on the way towards different types of judgments of value.

7.3.1 A Question of Vital Value

This first illustration is of a value reflection heading towards a judgment regarding a vital value. Suppose someone meets a friend whom she has not seen in six months. There is something about his changed appearance that moves her to feel its unhealthiness. This feeling does not occur in isolation; it occurs in conjunction with her feelings of affection for her friend, so that the impression of sickliness is intensified into a concern for his general well-being on many levels.

So far her feelings have a kind of infallibility. The complex way that her feelings respond to his appearance brings to her consciousness the disvalue of unhealthiness that seems to have befallen him. There is a natural trustworthiness to her feelings as far as his appearances go. But of course there is more to consider than appearances alone. Her feelings about his appearance prompt her to ask questions, and the questions are pursued with a certain urgency prompted by her feeling responses about how he looks. She wonders what changes in his appearance are making her feel this way. She then realizes that it is because his face seems slightly ashen and more gaunt. His bodily movements seem a little awkward. Soon she asks herself, is he all right?

Her questions for understanding and judgment of fact about his appearance are, therefore, soon followed by questions of value. She is seeking a judgment of vital value – a judgment about whether he is in good health or not. Also entering into her processes of value reflection are feelings about social and cultural values. She would like to say, "You look horrible. What is wrong?" But he does not look so horrible as to justify so great a departure from acceptable social and cultural values regarding casual conversations. So instead she asks the more innocuous, "How are you doing?" He responds, "I've made a big life change. I am on the Atkins diet." Never having heard of this diet before, she begins to ask him questions about it. He tells her it is an all-meat diet to help lose weight. "I was beginning to feel fat, so I decided to lose some weight." Her feelings shift and intensify in response to his remark, because her friend has always been quite slim. She asks him further questions, and later she begins to seek answers to other questions by reading about this diet, and about slim people who want to lose weight, and so on.

Her feelings lead her to ask a number of different questions of value, but for present purposes let us focus simply on the question pertaining to the vital value – Is he healthy? All sorts of further questions might be asked about this sort of diet. Some (e.g., "Is it expensive?") will be remote and have little or no resonance with the way she is feeling the disvalue of unhealthiness. Other questions pertinent to this judgment of value will not arise for her because she has already reflected and answered them in the past. Still other questions will be felt as quite alive and relevant. Regarding these latter questions, she may find some answers in the reports of biologists and medical scientists who have investigated meat diets and the various types and stages of human physiology. Her inquiry may lead her to discover that such diets under close supervision sustain normal biological functioning, but that a significant number of people misunderstand the diet and practise it in ways that lead to metabolic dysfunctions. Her questions may also lead her to look into the medical literature on eating disorders, and lead her to correct her previous belief that they are limited to females.

Notice that most of these are questions and answers about biological facts. Frequently, the further questions pertinent to a question of value are indeed questions of fact. While knowledge of facts alone never supplies all the conditions needed in order to fully answer questions of value, arriving at knowledge about facts is almost always essential in most processes of value reflection. True judgments of value are realistic. Genuine judgments of value are not about values one might wish were actual; rather, authentic value reflections face questions of fact objectively and arrive at unbiased, virtually unconditioned judgments about the true values or disvalues of those facts.

Thus, while not sufficient, answers to questions of fact are necessary for knowledge of her friend's new dietary practices as good or ill for his health. Scientists' investigations can supply some factual knowledge about the biochemistry and physiology of this kind of diet, and so on. Without the further, constitutive contributions played by feelings that intend values, however, this factual knowledge will not yet be knowledge of those facts *as* pertinent to the *value* of health. Those questions of and answers about facts can be given a new status as pertinent (or as irrelevant) to matters of value, by the manner in which health is felt as a value. The felt valuation of health will determine relevance and pertinence of these facts for the value of health. Once there are no further questions of fact or value that are pertinent to this value as felt, only then will she be able to make the virtually unconditioned judgment, "My friend is not healthy," where "healthy" derives its meaning from how she feels the value of health. In other words, this judgment is virtually unconditioned relative to value of health in the manner in which she feels it.

At this point, she will likely shift from the process of reflecting about a judgment of health value to ethical reflection about what to do for her friend. This question and her feelings for her friend will issue forth in a new series of questions seeking judgments of ethical value. She will consider how to convince him to consult with a reliable healthcare professional. But what constitutes "reliable" is itself a question for a still further judgment of value. In section 7.4, we will attend more closely to processes of value reflection where judgments of ethical value are sought for the sake of making ethical decisions.

7.3.2 *Questions of Social and Artistic Value*

For a second illustration, this time focusing on judgments of social value, we return to the investigations of Jane Jacobs. She clearly regarded "lively city neighborhoods" to be of great value in themselves. In light of her felt valuation of good urban neighbourhoods, she asked questions regarding the conditions that contribute to them. What are the means to such social values? What is useful to the promotion and sustaining of these valued patterns of social interaction? And so on.

She came to the conclusion that "diversity" is the key contributing factor. She gave detailed arguments as to what sorts of diversity were valuable for good city life, and why that is so. Diversity gives people many different reasons for interacting with one another. These interactions lead to various kinds of personal relations, which facilitate informal patterns of public surveillance and dissemination of information. Her investigations, her questions, her attention to details, her readings, her insights, were all guided by her feelings for the social values of neighbourhoods as lively. Likewise, her ability to identify factors that lead to what she called "dull, gray" neighbourhoods was motivated by her feelings for the disvalues of those kinds of social settings.

Her argument was not that diversity is a good in itself; rather, her judgment regarded the value of diversity as a means to the value of a good urban social life. In light of her valuing of urban social life, Jacobs gave convincing arguments that various forms of diversity (economic, ethnic, racial, architectural) are contributing means, which are therefore to be valued precisely for their contribution to the end-value of good urban life. Jacobs shares both these feelings for the social values of community as well as judgments about the values of conditions for such forms of social life with a tradition that includes such thinkers as Alexis de Tocqueville, Robert Bellah, and Robert Putnam.[15] Thinkers in this tradition have feelings for the values of human social interactions and community, which determine the further questions and researches they undertook. Those feelings determine the conditions that must be fulfilled if something is to be judged truly contributory to these social values as felt.

A third illustration pertains to judgments about artistic value. The realm of aesthetic judgment is vast and can in no way be treated adequately in this section. Here I limit myself to an example where a sophisticated critic is reflecting upon what she or he begins to feel is an exceptional masterpiece, and asks whether its value is truly exceptional. The critic will read or view or hear the artistic composition against the background of a highly developed and sophisticated habituation for noticing and valuing subtleties in the ways that compositional elements relate and interact. This habitual valuing will have been developed over many previous years of reading, viewing, listening, and exploring many other artistic works. As the critic begins to explore the new composition, new and ever more subtle feelings will add to the initial feelings about the artwork, yielding a more refined overall felt impression. Gradually, and perhaps imperceptibly, the effort devoted to feeling and appreciating the work will shift towards understanding and critiquing the work. The critic will entertain questions about technique, composition, and form. She or he will consider previous artistic influences and ask what subtle modifications and innovations the artist brought forth in this particular work, and how they alter sensory impressions and the consequent felt responses. The critic may consider the biography and historical context of the artist – finding that some questions about the artist's life and times lead towards a deeper understanding of the work's greatness, while others are inconsequential, reductive, or potential interferences with a sober critical judgment. Through all this, the critic's growing knowledge about the artist's techniques and historical situatedness is deemed as pertinent or irrelevant to judgments about their contribution to the work by the standard of the value of the masterpiece as it has come to be felt by the critic within the sophisticated horizon of her or his aesthetic feelings.

That horizon of feelings will situate the critic's aesthetic feelings in felt relations to other values as felt. Through these feelings, the critic will be aware of how the masterpiece relates to the vitality of nature and the goodness of human life, to the glories and miseries of human institutional arrangements, to the values and disvalue of human decisions, and to the absolute value of transcendence. A sophisticated critic will be considering this work of art not only as an isolated product of cultural value, but as a cultural value situated in a broader felt context of vital, social, historical, moral, and religious values.

As with vital and social values, judgments of aesthetic value require the asking and answering of a wide range of further pertinent questions. The pertinence of those questions, in turn, is determined by the refined horizon of feelings that the critic has developed over many years of studying, reflecting, and considering the aesthetic judgments of others.

By way of contrast, the term "aesthete" has been used to characterize a person for whom aesthetic values have become the ultimate values. The feelings of an aesthete respond to himself or herself and to everything else almost exclusively within a horizon of aesthetic values. An aesthete is not capable of feeling aesthetic values within the larger comprehending horizon of values as a whole.[16] All human and natural actions are valuated exclusively in terms of aesthetic excellence. What is of greatest importance to most people in their "ordinary" human affairs will almost always be felt as trivial and boring to someone who has the feeling horizon of an aesthete, since ordinary ways of life almost always fail to rise to the heights of artistic masterpieces. On the other hand, the value judgments of an aesthete will seem truncated and disturbing to a sophisticated art critic, whose judgments about works of art are situated in a wider horizon of feelings for values.

7.3.3 Feelings and Judgments of Value

These three examples offer but a small glimpse into the innumerable ways that we reach judgments of value about things, events, persons, and situations that already exist. In the first, we considered how a woman might seek an unconditioned judgment about a vital value *in itself* concerning the current state of health of a friend. In the second, we considered how Jacobs arrived at judgments about certain kinds of diversity as values *auxiliary* to the value of the urban neighbourhood communities that she identified as well-functioning. She had previously arrived at judgments about their social values in themselves, and proceeded to reflect upon the auxiliary values that contributed to those social values. In the third case, we considered how a sophisticated critic might come to a judgment of *comparative* value in the realm of cultural values. The judgment concerned an already completed work of art and its value in comparison to other works – whether it stood above most and in the small assembly of genuine masterpieces. In all three cases, feelings for a particular though complex value guided the asking and answering of the further pertinent questions needed to reach the acts of reflective understanding and to ground several different kinds of value judgments as virtually unconditioned.

In all three cases, people arrived at judgments of value of the form, "This is (or is not) a value (health, social utility, or a cultural masterpiece)." However, their judgments might not exactly qualify as "virtually unconditioned" in Lonergan's most basic sense. When he analysed the phenomena of invulnerable insights, he wrote,

> It is not enough to say that the conditions are fulfilled when no
> further questions occur to me. The mere absence of questions in my
> mind can have other causes. My intellectual curiosity may be stifled
> by other interests. My eagerness to satisfy other drives may refuse the
> further questions a chance to emerge.[17]

In the cases just considered, however, did not their feelings for values function as other interests or drives, which stifled intellectual curiosity and restricted what questions could be deemed as pertinent? It might seem, therefore, that feelings as intentional responses will always vitiate the possibility of attaining Lonergan's high standard for objective, virtually unconditioned judgments of value. It may seem that all judgments of value are merely relative to the ways in which a given individual happens to feel those values.

Because this is a complex problem, part of the response is offered here, while the fuller response must be deferred to the next chapter. First, then, intentional feelings for values are not necessarily "other interests or drives" that stifle intellectual curiosity, simply because they are feelings. They do not necessarily interfere with the asking and answering of all further questions merely because they are feelings. Rather, because the further questions are precisely about some value, some form of value-consciousness is required in order to determine which further questions would be pertinent to that value. In previous sections I have argued that, in its most basic form, consciousness of value comes in the form of feelings as intentional responses. Hence such feelings actually form the necessary conditions for the raising of the further questions pertinent to values. Such feelings are not necessarily antithetical, then, to the asking all further pertinent questions simply because they are feelings.

Second, what does, however, interfere with the openness of value questioning and reflection is *how* values are felt. Values can be felt obsessively or openly. They can be felt possessively or in a hospitable manner. Feelings for values can be relaxed or stressful. They can be felt in ways that openly welcome further questions for the sake of value, or defensively in ways that regard further questions as threatening to the values. Thus interference with intellectual curiosity and value reflection arises not just from feelings as intentional responses as such, but from the manner in which such feelings intend their corresponding values.

Third, the openness or interference of feelings is a function of the feeling horizons within which they occur. In all three of the preceding examples, attention was drawn to a larger horizon that situated the principal values by feeling them in relation to other values. It is these larger horizons of feelings that determine *how* the value is actually felt, whether the value is felt in an open or closed, in a normative or a distorted fashion. This larger horizon may be felt with greater or lesser intensity and awareness, but it is always felt. The fact that feelings for values always occur within this comprehending horizon, and that this horizon determines what will count as further pertinent questions, points to further considerations that must be addressed before concluding to the relativity or objectivity of judgments of value. These issues will be taken up in the next chapter.

Let me conclude this section by connecting these observations with the theme of discernment. In the context of judgments of value, discernment means, first of all, expanding our awareness of how many judgments of value we actually do make. In a culture that continually tells us, inconsistently, that it is bad to make value judgments, we may have deluded ourselves into thinking that we have successfully avoided making such judgments. But paying attention to the frequency with which we do, and indeed must, ask and attempt to answer questions of value is a corrective to this cultural deception. Discernment also involves learning to notice the sometimes subtle further pertinent questions that await our responses as we attempt to reach unconditioned judgments of value. It also entails increasingly committing ourselves to refraining from making judgments of value until all the further pertinent questions have been answered adequately. In addition, discernment also involves attending to and correctly understanding our feelings, both somatic feelings and feeling responses that intend values. Furthermore, discernment involves not only attending to individual feelings, but also noticing our encompassing horizons of feelings, and especially noticing their various tensions. Finally, discernment means understanding both the feelings and the tensions among them correctly, and becoming aware of the questions for decisions that arise from an ever deeper understanding of these tensions. We will return to this issue also in the next chapter.

7.4   Reflection about Questions of Ethical Value

In the previous sections we explored the ways in which judgments are reached regarding values of things, events, situations, or persons that already exist. By way of contrast, questions of ethical values always have to do with possible courses of action that have yet to be realized. As was the case with knowing the value of actualities, some portion of our knowledge of ethical values is habitual. Were we to encounter a situation exactly the same in all respects as one we encountered before, we would not have to raise questions such as "What can I do?" or "Should I do it?" If the circumstances were truly identical, our responses and value-reasons for responding in those ways would already be available in our habitual knowledge of values. We would not deliberate anew about what to do or whether to do it. We would already have asked and answered all the further questions pertinent from the perspective of our horizons of feelings.

However, it is extremely rare that two sets of circumstances (including the current states of our own bodies, knowledge, skills, wisdom) would be identical. Even when circumstances are fairly familiar and differ only slightly from the routine, frequently we will find ourselves presented with questions about how to respond intelligently, reasonably, sensitively, and responsibly to even slight changes in circumstances. When we do ask basic ethical questions such as these, they in turn set in motion processes of ethical value reflection. These reflective processes also will include the feelings we have in our initial responses to the slightly changed situation, with all its natural objects and human meanings.

Our questions seek new insights into how to adapt our previous understandings of how to act in accordance with these changed circumstances. These new insights bring us ideas about a modified course of action. We might use these new insights to construct in our imaginations how things would go if we acted on these insights. Our feelings will respond freshly to the newly conceived and imagined courses of action. We may respond with feelings that value the course of action positively. It may be felt as harmonious with the constellation and orientation of our horizon of feelings. But it might also be felt as a silly or ridiculous or embarrassing or wicked course of action. These feelings will arise in tension with the other feelings and values of our horizon. The unsettled feelings will prompt asking further pertinent questions, such as "Why am I feeling this way" and "What do these feelings mean?" These feelings influence whether we pursue further questions. Our feelings contribute to whether we will pursue this possible course of action further, or seek further insights into other possible options that will not have outcomes with such unsettling felt values. Our feelings may elicit questions that lead us back to reconsider courses of action we initially rejected. We may ask whether we really want to give priority to the feelings that led us to reject them, in favour of values we feel deserve to be given priority.

The feelings and further questions together will lead us to seek new insights into other possible courses of action. These, too, will be played out in our imaginations, raising further pertinent questions and further feeling responses that intend other values. We will ask such further questions as "What are the likely outcomes?" "Will they be agreeable?" "Will they promote or detract values such as health, social welfare, or nobility?" "Will anyone be offended or hurt?" "Are there overriding concerns that make these potential harms acceptable or even obligatory?" "Should I do it?" "Is it worthwhile for me to do it?"[18]

This interplay of insights into possible courses of action, imagination, felt intentions of values, and further questions form a self-correcting cycle similar to what takes place in reflections headed towards judgments of fact.[19] Here, however, felt intentions of values play the leading role. Such feelings reveal the values or disvalues of the various alternative courses of action. These feelings and their felt-tensions with other components in our horizon of feelings determine which questions and insights will be pursued further, and which ones will be ignored. In these intricate and concrete ways, our horizons of feelings determine the pertinence of further questions as we head towards judgments of ethical value, and the subsequent decisions and actions that can be based upon them.

In order to illustrate more concretely the ways that questions, feelings, and other acts of consciousness are structured into processes of ethical reflection that arise from such questions, I again offer a series of examples.

7.4.1 *The Ethics of Ordinary Life in* Northanger Abbey

The first is taken from a chapter of another Jane Austen novel, *Northanger Abbey*.[20] In this episode, the protagonist, Catherine Morland, is staying in Bath, and has promised to go for a walk with Eleanor Tilney and her brother Henry. Although a brief rain shower has prevented the sister and brother from arriving at the agreed upon time, Catherine waits knowing that it is likely they will still come for the agreed upon walk. As she waits, her friend Isabella Thorpe arrives with her brother, John. He is an impetuous, boorish, and ridiculous young man, and a compulsive prevaricator, oblivious to almost everything but his immediate impulses. At this point in time, however, Catherine herself has not yet arrived at these value judgments. John insists that Catherine accompany them on a carriage drive to Bristol, and tells her the grandiose plans that he and Isabella have for this ride. Isabella tells her that this scheme "darted into our heads at breakfast-time."

Catherine raises questions as to whether so much could be done in a single day, and also explains that she has made a prior commitment to the Tilneys. John dismisses Catherine's social commitment and boasts about how much ground he can cover with his carriage in a single day. He then mentions that they could visit Blaize Castle. Suddenly Catherine's commonsense judgments and feelings shift and intensify. In the background of this episode are the novels that Catherine and Isabella have been reading and discussing together. These are the gothic romances by Anne Radcliffe, especially *The Mysteries of Udolpho*. These novels have had considerable influence upon young women of the time, and Austen shows this influence in Catherine's horizon of feelings. Udolpho is a gloomy castle where intrigues take place, and the mention of Blaize Castle moves a response in the feeling horizon that Catherine has been developing through her absorption in these novels. These novels have intensified certain of Catherine's feelings, and diminished the intensity of others. In particular, Austen reveals how Radcliffe's novels have influenced Catherine's image of herself as a heroine, not in an entirely salutary way. This elevation of some feelings over others has had a profound effect upon the things Catherine notices and the things she ignores, especially her lingering questions about John Thorpe's proposal.

Although she is now intrigued, Catherine still objects that she must wait for the Tilneys. In reply, John Thorpe lies to her, saying that he saw them driving away from town on his way to visit her. Catherine is bothered to hear of this, but she ignores further questions she should have asked, because of her feelings of fascination with the castle and the expected pleasures of seeing the countryside in lively company. She gives in and agrees to accompany them without leaving any message for the Tilneys.

> Catherine's feelings, as she got into the carriage, were in a very unsettled state; divided between regret for the loss of one great pleasure, and the hope of soon enjoining another, almost equal in degree, however unlike in kind. She could not think the Tilneys had acted quite well by her, in so readily giving up their engagement, without sending her any message of excuse … to feel herself slighted by them was very painful. On the other hand, the delight of exploring an edifice like Udolpho, as her fancy represented Blaize Castle to be, was such a counterpoise of good as might console her for almost anything.[21]

Austen describes some of the sources of the unsettlement in Catherine's feeling horizon. At this point, her horizon is largely focused on the superficial pleasures that preoccupied members of her social class. She is still a self-centred young woman, although not nearly as much as the Thorpes. In the context of a different feeling horizon, she would have paid attention to and reflected about her own questions concerning John's report about the Tilneys. Is this really consistent with what she knows about the Tilneys – that they are people of their word? Is it possible John is not being truthful, as he had already exaggerated several times in just a few minutes? In addition, the excitement she feels about the castle is in tension with her very real, though not very strong, feelings about the value of keeping promises. Her exaggerated feeling of being hurt by what she imagines as a snub by the Tilneys is covering over these deeper disturbances in her feeling horizon. The further questions she counts as relevant – and those she ignores as irrelevant – are dictated by the self-centred constitution of her horizon of feelings and the titillating feelings she has about the image of a gothic castle.

Almost as soon as they set out, of course, they see the Tilneys walking towards Catherine's lodging to meet her. An intense and different set of feelings now course through Catherine's consciousness. She realizes that John's report was not only mistaken but a lie. She immediately feels the shame of having broken her promise to the Tilneys and leaving no message. She insists that John let her out of the carriage. He ignores her request and speeds off. She feels betrayed, but more deeply ashamed of allowing herself to be betrayed. These feelings stay with her for a considerable time – while such feelings are completely beyond the Thorpes' horizons. Predictably, the trip turns out to be quite disappointing, since indeed they did not have nearly enough time to reach Bristol, let alone Blaize Castle. The next day she seeks out the Tilneys and with some awkwardness manages to make a sort of apology – although she does lay all the blame on John Thorpe. Because of her apology and the good will of the Tilneys, the relationships are set on a new footing and gradually develop to reach considerable depths during the remainder of the novel.

Just before her decision to ride with the Thorpes, Catherine makes a judgment of value and consequent decision on the basis of the state of her horizon of feelings at that point. Given the values as felt through her feeling horizon, the few further pertinent questions that actually do occur to her are brushed aside. The difficulty, of course, is that hers is not a very mature or stable horizon. The feelings that are most forcefully at the centre of that horizon determine the values about which she will reflect, what means she will use to realize those values, and what will count as pertinent questions. But the episode also shows how she comes to discern something about her feelings. She shifts to give certain feelings greater preference in her horizon, and thinks and acts somewhat differently as a result of these realizations and revaluations. Of course, she is only just beginning to discern the deeper felt tensions that surround her superficial values, and to make judgments and decisions that take into account the deeper value intentionalities. Although she has a long way to go, her feeling horizon shifts and matures in a small way through her discernment of her feelings in this episode. For one thing, she is much more circumspect about John Thorpe and more firm in her commitments to her social values, which becomes apparent in the way Austen narrates her progress.

This episode is an important moment in the ethical maturation of Catherine Morland, but not the only one. There are further episodes, and the powerful hold that Radcliffe's novels have over Catherine's horizon of feelings shows up later in even more embarrassing ways. Catherine is not the strong or complex character that we see in other Austen novels (such as Elizabeth Bennet, Elinor Dashwood, or Anne Elliot), although each of them also undergoes significant ethical development marked by major shifts in their horizons of feelings.

Like Catherine Morland, we are the agents of our own development into the kinds of persons we become through the very ordinary judgments of value and decisions we make day in and day out. I deliberately chose this episode because of Austen's astute attention to the high ethical stakes of very mundane, ordinary decisions. A student of mine once complained that Austen's novels are superficial because they are only concerned about women gaining husbands. To the contrary, Austen is profoundly observant and ironic about the frequent pettiness and superficialities of the social scene and courtship practices of her society. But she also lays out for the attentive reader the deep value consequences that are at stake even in seemingly frivolous, ordinary decisions, such as the one in this episode.

7.4.2 Ethical Reflection in Jury Deliberation

The second illustration comes from one of my own experiences as a juror. In this case, I was empanelled to serve on a double-homicide trial. Three young people who lived in the apartment where murders took place were present at the time of the crime. One of the victims was a female college student, the mother of a small child. Another victim was a male of the same age. The third person was also a young male who survived the attack.

The survivor testified at the trial. From him we heard that the two murdered victims had been shot when two intruders broke into the apartment wearing masks and wielding a gun. The murdered young man was a drug dealer, and the intruders came to rob him of his supply of drugs and his money. The crime took a deadly turn when the young woman recognized one of the intruders despite his mask. She appealed to him and spoke his first name. Apparently based on their previous surveillance, the intruders did not expect anyone but the drug dealer to be present. When they encountered the other two people unexpectedly, they bound and blindfolded all three. Because she recognized him, the young woman was shot to death by one of the intruders, who then also shot and killed the drug dealer. The intruder then attempted to shoot the third victim, but had run out of bullets. The survivor could not identify the masked perpetrators, but he relayed the words of the murdered young woman.

Once I realized I would be serving on this jury, my feelings about the seriousness of the responsibility intensified. In addition, I soon felt awed by the ways my fellow jurors, without exception, also took their responsibilities seriously, and these feelings further intensified my own sense of the seriousness of what I was being called to do. All of us underwent shifts in our feeling horizons, placing seriousness about the trial at the centre, while moving more to the margins the other concerns we had from our very diverse backgrounds. Even before we were able to put it in words, we felt the importance

of the values at stake. We felt horror at the brutality of the crimes. We felt
the value of protecting the public from potential future violence, but also
we felt the importance of not sending innocent people to jail, and so on.

It is sometimes said that a jury just determines the facts of the case –
whether or not a crime has been committed, for example. However, my
reflections on this trial revealed to me that while service on a jury does
require objective judgments of fact, it is more profoundly an ethical practice that goes beyond merely judging the facts. Ultimately, jurors have to go
from judgments of facts to judgments of value, to decisions, and to actions.
Voting "guilty" or "not guilty" are actions that follow upon decisions. These
votes express judgments of value that are born of a special kind of value
reflection. People can and do form value judgments about people accused
of crimes based upon news reports alone. Many people express their opinions based on such reports. But ultimately a jury has the unique status that
its public expression of its judgment of value will have serious consequences
for the accused as well as for society at large – and for their own consciences
as well. When the judge asks, "Has the jury reached a verdict?," the action
of the publicly spoken answer is more than intellectual. The jury's answer
makes effective in the social order a new value in a way that almost no one
else's judgments and expressions can.[22] Jurors also have the responsibility
to enter into mutual deliberation, to be open to the arguments from fellow
jurors, and to present counter-arguments to them. Ultimately, however, the
question at stake for each juror is a question for a decision: "Should I vote
to condemn or exonerate the accused of this crime?" What makes jury duty
an ethical matter is not just that the crimes under consideration are ethical
matters. In addition, jury duty is also an ethical matter because jurors have
to make decisions about the crimes, and their decisions are themselves ethical matters of great value. In order to make such decisions ethically, jurors
have to arrive at a virtually unconditioned ground for making each of these
decisions. And this means that they have to answer a host of questions that
are pertinent to the values of justice as felt.

We were conscious of all this, though not explicitly in these terms, as we
began our jury service on this particular trial. Our shared and intensified
feeling horizons patterned how we listened, looked at, and thought about
the evidence brought before us during the trial. Although I believe my fellow jurors had similar experiences to my own during this trial, my account
in what follows is limited to my own experiences.

We heard testimony from the survivor and a considerable number of others: family and associates of the accused and the victims, law-enforcement
officers, crime-lab specialists, store clerks, and so on. We were shown videos
and photos of the crime scene and the victims as well as other physical
items. We also heard CD recordings of the police interrogations of the two

young men accused of the crime, who had been read their rights against self-incrimination, and to legal representation. Initially, every piece of evidence seemed to me potentially relevant to the verdict. I asked myself questions and thought about each piece of evidence or testimony. I tried to understand its relevance and formed several hypotheses. I had to refine, revise, or reject most of my hypotheses. Sometimes this was because a later piece of evidence could not be reconciled with my initial hunch. Sometimes I caught myself allowing something prejudicial to infiltrate the formation of my hypothesis. Gradually I came to realize that much of what was presented in evidence was not relevant to the conditions that needed to be fulfilled to reach one or another of the mutually exclusive alternative judgments (i.e., guilty or not guilty).

One piece of physical evidence came to light that put an end to any further pertinent questions as to whether one of the defendants was at the scene of the crime. In fact, his own attorney stipulated that he was there, and presented a different line of defence on his client's behalf. Based merely on the testimony of the survivor, however, it was possible that this defendant was not the shooter. Still, no *physical* evidence provided the conclusive, fulfilling condition to judge that the other defendant was there – and he himself seemed to be quite assured about this. The physical evidence and testimony presented answered a great many pertinent questions about his motives and likely involvement. I reflected a great deal about whether each of the witnesses should be believed, and reached judgments by taking seriously my questions about their credibility. But there remained some further questions that prevented me from reaching a virtually unconditioned judgment about the involvement of the second defendant. In another context, I might have brushed such questions aside and just fired off an unsubstantiated opinion. But my feelings about the serious values at stake were guiding my questioning and intensified my awareness that these questions remained unanswered.

However, as I listened to the CD of the second defendant's interrogation, suddenly one statement hit me. The interrogation was a long, circuitous cat-and-mouse game between the police detectives and the second defendant. The defendant knew they had no physical evidence and that the survivor could not identify him, and was cocky in his responses. After a very long time, one of the detectives said to the defendant, "What if I told you that someone identified you by name at the scene of the crime?" I remembered that the survivor had testified that the woman victim had spoken a first name which was the same as the first name of the second defendant. In response to the detective's question, the defendant quickly shot back a response. He asked the detective, "Did she say _______ _______?" speaking both his first and last name, with emphatic verbal stress on his last name. In rapid succession

I had an insight, and realized I had no further pertinent questions. This was followed immediately by a judgment of fact and then a judgment of value and a decision. I would vote him guilty of the crime.

Only afterwards would I be able to partially formulate for myself and for my fellow jurors the contents of the reflection and judgment of value that grounded my decision. The woman victim had not spoken his last name. He knew that. He knew there were millions of people who shared his first name, but very few who had the unusual combination of his first and last name. If she had spoken both his names, he knew that this, combined with the other particular characteristics and circumstances revealed in the other evidence and testimony, would single him out uniquely. So he was confident that knowing only his first name in combination with the other evidence would fall short of a virtually unconditioned – would not be "beyond a reasonable doubt," as the juridical terminology puts it.

But his statement revealed that he knew the woman victim had spoken his name, but had not spoken his last name. He could only have known this had he been there at the time. My horizon of feelings had heightened my attentiveness, and made it possible for me to notice this slight slip-up by a very clever defendant. For me, this was the last condition in a long series of fulfilling conditions needed to reach the virtually unconditioned judgment of fact that he had been there and had shot two people to death. My judgment of fact about what he did, and judgment of value about his guilt, in turn, provided the conditions for my further judgment of value that I should vote him guilty – and further that I should explain to my fellow jurors how I came to my judgments.

The foregoing narrative only partially captures all of the conditions that were fulfilled and that formed the grounds for my judgments of fact and value. Many of the other conditions were the results of evidence and testimony I heard, what I noticed, the many questions that arose for me, the many hypotheses I formed and rejected. Some conditions were supplied long ago through the experiences, insights, judgments of fact and value, and feelings about justice that were imparted during my upbringing in the culture of the United States. It is exceedingly difficult, probably impossible, to put into words *all* of what we know that has bearing – is a fulfilling condition – for the complex judgments of fact and value that we make in concrete circumstances. It is their very concreteness, their complex intertwining of factors (their *concrèscere*), that makes it virtually impossible to put into words all that is pertinent and that we draw upon when we make such judgments as virtually unconditioned.

Whether or not I came to virtually unconditioned judgments in this case is certainly open to question by the reader. That I perhaps did so may be given further credibility by what happened next. As is the practice, we were instructed not to talk about the case with anyone, not even our fellow jurors, until all testimony and final statements were completed and we were sent to deliberate together. The prudence of this became evident as the case proceeded. Had I ventured my vulnerable hypotheses at any earlier stage, I might have become defensive and held onto them unreasonably. Or I might have prematurely influenced others in ways that interfered with their attentiveness or their pursuit of answers to further questions. But once the closing statements were presented, we were instructed to deliberate together. There were actually multiple charges in addition to the homicides, and we were required to deliberate about all of them. This took us many days. Our foreperson was uncommonly skilled in disentangling the complex issues and in making sure everyone was heard. Whether or not it is the case for every jury, ours was pervaded with a remarkable atmosphere of respect for each other during the entire period of deliberation. We went back over evidence and testimony in careful order, and many jurors expressed various uncertainties. Through our conversations it gradually became evident that not everyone had noticed the crucial statement in the interrogation of the second defendant. Together in the jury room we eventually listened once again to the recordings of both interrogations. When we heard for the second time the question that the second defendant posed to the police officer, the postures and facial expressions of most of my fellow jurors changed dramatically. Although they would not have used these words, everyone recognized that this was the crucial remaining condition that needed to be fulfilled in order for them to reach virtually unconditioned judgments of fact and value about the guilt of the second defendant. One of the jurors noticed something I had missed. This juror said, "He said 'Did *she* say…'" The interrogating officer had not disclosed the gender of the person who identified him by name. How did the defendant know it was a female? This had escaped my notice. For me, this became further confirmatory evidence, but for my fellow jurors, it became the condition that put an end to further pertinent questions.

During our jury deliberations, we shared with one another many other questions that occurred to us concerning the great amount of evidence and testimony that was presented during the trial. We wondered about the backgrounds of some of the witnesses that appeared, about how the family members felt, about why it took so long for this case to come to trial, and so on. But our horizons of feelings about the decisions before us – how should we vote about the crimes with which these men were charged – determined for us that these other questions were not pertinent to the judgments and decisions at hand. During our deliberations we helped one another recognize that some of these questions were irrelevant, and this was accomplished by appealing to the values (i.e., feeling horizons) at stake.

7.4.3 Summary

In offering these two examples, I have endeavoured to bring to light several things that are illustrative of the general process of arriving at judgments of ethical value that ground ethical decisions. First, ethical reflection begins with a question – "What should I do?" – and ends with a decision and action that are the ultimate answers to that question.

Second, although the reflection begins with the question, it has already borrowed some of its meaning contents from prior stages. The answer to the "what" part is an intelligible, possible course of action that comes to consciousness in a prior act of insight.[23] In the two cases above, the courses of action were whether or not to go for a ride with the Thorpes, and whether or not to vote a guilty verdict. But the "what" in the question for decision is not just the intelligible arrangement of a series of actions. Those intelligible arrangements also move feelings to respond, thereby endowing them with certain valuations. The "what" and the "should" in this question combine to yield an object for choice that is a compound of the intelligibility of a possible course of action as understood along with its potential value as felt. In the case of Catherine Morland, the value of going for a ride included the pleasure and excitement of encountering a gothic castle setting, but the actual governing value as felt was tinged with annoyance at the Tilneys and a deeper unsettlement about not being true to her own social values. In the case of the trial, the course of action to vote was given a complex valuation by sorrow over young lives cut short, horror at the brutality of the murders, and feelings about public safety as well as about the defendants as persons of value in themselves and as deserving fairness in our deliberations.

Third, the deliberations leading up to the judgments of ethical value involved attention to sensations, memories, ideas, previous judgments, and feelings, but especially to the further questions and to feelings that arise. Those feelings determine what further questions will be entertained seriously. Our horizons of feelings can elicit questions about those feelings in their own right, but they also select among other questions those that will be taken into consideration during evaluation and deliberation. Our *noetic* feelings "model" for us, so to speak, the values (*noematic* contents) about which we reflect. Our feelings are the sources of our consciousness of the values that we contemplate ourselves as realizing. During our contemplations, those feelings intend the values under consideration and include unresolved tensions. Therefore we will feel these value conflicts in our contemplations. Those tensions may shift and resolve during our ethical reflections, but they might not.[24] If they do not, we may indeed end up actualizing conflicting values through our decisions. But if we do arrive at the point where there are no further pertinent questions to be answered, we have arrived at a reflective grasp of an ethical value as virtually unconditioned – that is to say, we have come to understand that this concrete, particular course of action has the value as we feel it, and that it should be realized. In the ordinary course, a decision and appropriate actions will follow – although as I pointed out in chapter 4, some people have characteristics that interfere with the spontaneous movement from a virtually unconditioned judgment of value to the consequent decision. However, barring the impediments that arise from vices of indecisiveness, when we choose, our action brings about an intelligible reality with its correlated value as judged and chosen.

7.5   The Double Intentionality of Ethical Reflection, Judgment, and Decision

Ethical reflection and judgments differ from other forms of value reflection and judgment in several ways. We have already discussed one of those differences – namely, that we reflect and make judgments of ethical value about events that do not yet exist, potential courses of action that we could choose and put into effect. By way of contrast, other forms of value reflection and judgment are about already existing persons, items, or situations. While these other forms of value reflection reach their proper terms in virtually unconditioned judgments of value, ethical reflection does not come to rest with ethical judgments alone. Since ethical judgments have the form "Yes (or No), this is (not) worthwhile for me to *do*," or "Yes (or No), I should (not) *do* this," they have an intrinsic orientation beyond the judgments themselves towards decisions and actions. We may have answered "Yes, I should do this," but we have not yet answered "Shall I do it?" until we decide and act. The intentionality of ethical thinking and reflecting extends all the way through this last question towards these acts of completion.

There is also another difference between judgments of ethical value and other kinds of value judgments. In chapter 6 we explored the intentionality of affects that are intentional responses. Although this broad class of feelings has multiple objects, only one of those (the value intended in the feeling) is the proper *noematic* object in the standard phenomenological sense. However, ethical reflections and their intended acts of deciding always have two simultaneous *noematic* objects that are inextricably intertwined. On the one hand, we begin our processes of ethical reflection when we ask about the value of the external course of action that would become a reality and therefore an actual value if we were to decide and carry out the action. We ask whether our action would produce the value as we intend it – a value such as a healthy outcome, an intellectual achievement, the justice some person deserves, something that will benefit or bring joy to another person, a work of artistic excellence, an improvement in an institution's functioning, a new business organization, or a pleasant meal. Most often our value reflections are focused almost exclusively upon the values of these external outcomes.[25]

These, however, are never the only outcomes of our decisions. When we decide, we also simultaneously produce ourselves as the person who made this decision.[26] In deciding, we make the value of ourselves at the same time as we produce something of value in the world.

This is a restatement in the context of intentionality analysis of the ancient Greek distinction between *poesis* and *praxis* given prominence in the ethical writings of Aristotle. According to him, *poesis* has to do with outcomes that are apart from the deciding and acting person. *Praxis* on the other hand is the reality that is identical with and comes about in the person by his or her actions.[27]

Ethical reflection therefore extends inevitably into self-knowledge and self-evaluation. We might ask the question "Would this course of action be worthwhile for someone to pursue?," but that is different from asking "Should *I* do it?"

The asking and answering of all further pertinent questions may lead to a reflective understanding that it would be unconditionally worthwhile and valuable if this course of action were undertaken by someone. This is a necessary, but not a sufficient, basis for affirming that *I* should do it. The "should" question is the question of personal responsibility and obligation. It seeks to know whether the course of action is of unconditional value for *my* choice and action. Beyond the affirmation of the value of the course of action in general, the "should I" question elicits still additional questions as pertinent. For the most part these additional questions demand an intense degree of self-knowledge and self-evaluation. Would it be worthwhile for *me* to take the steps needed to make the course of action a reality? What steps would be needed? Do I have the physical stamina for this course of action? (The answer to this question depends upon knowledge that derives from correctly understanding one's own somatic feelings.) Do I have the abilities, talents, and gifts needed to implement those steps? Not only my talents, but even my personal flaws and vices are called into consideration and ultimately into question. If I do not presently possess the requisite abilities, can I acquire them? How long would it take? Can I and should I enlist the cooperation of others, and how? What other possibilities will I have to abandon in following this course? Should I sacrifice those? If I choose this course (or refuse), how will that constitute the value that I thereby make myself to be?

As this series of questions makes clear, the "should" question is both a question of comparative value and a question of personal value. As a question of comparative value, it situates the value of the course of action and its consequences in relation to a wider range of values, both those that would be realized as a consequence of my performance of the action, and those that would be sacrificed by adopting it. It is a question that seeks knowledge of how the value of a possible course of action in the concrete circumstances of the here and now is situated within one's own wider feeling horizon of value priorities and preferences. As a question of personal value, it situates the value of that course of action in relation to the value that the subject herself or himself would become through the choice.

For the most part, the ways that those questions of comparative and personal value are resolved (which questions are pertinent and must be faced) are determined by one's horizon of feelings and one's habitual valuing. The feelings and preferences in our horizon of feelings enter into and inform the judgments and decisions about the values that the course of action would realize in the world distinct from ourselves. In addition, how we feel about the value of ourselves will also enter into the determination of what questions we count as pertinent, and the value we make ourselves to be through our decisions and actions. Our feelings guide us as we ask, for example, "Should I take this new job, though it would mean leaving my neighbours behind?" The way in which one's horizon feels the values of income and job status in relation to how one feels about one's neighbours will determine which further questions count as pertinent. At the centre of all this reflection about what one should do, there stands the manner in which one thinks and feels about the value of one's own life-story in relation to other felt values. The value of one's life may be felt as strongly connected with having fun, with having wealth, power, wisdom, with having status (in the eyes of particular others felt as especially significant), or with a mission to which one feels called to contribute. Each of these different felt priorities establishes horizons of feeling and habits of valuing that apprehend the value of one's own life.

The feeling for one's own life affects how one arrives at a virtually unconditioned basis for affirming (or denying) that it is one's own personal responsibility and obligation to commit oneself to a course of action. In effect, a hierarchy of values is already established by one's horizon of feeling, and one's feelings about oneself – one's personal value – play a prominent role in establishing that hierarchy. The questions for value reflection ask how the concrete, particular intelligibility of the possible course of action is situated with respect to that felt value hierarchy, and especially the value of oneself within that hierarchy. Clearly, then, the more personal, existential question about whether it is worth committing one's own self to that course is also determined by the extent to which one is operating out of a limited or an unrestricted horizon of feeling that feels the value of being oneself.

To reiterate, arriving at a judgment that it would be good for a course of action to be undertaken does not automatically mean that I should undertake it myself. In order to answer the latter question, I would first have to answer further pertinent questions about myself. Questions pertinent to this trajectory in ethical reflection include sober assessments of my own talents and limitations, as well as my virtues and biases. They will include questions about my ability to recruit others who would be needed to undertake courses of action beyond my own limitations and about my abilities to meaningfully contribute to cooperative efforts already underway. Still further questions will extend beyond those having to do with my own physical and intellectual abilities to consider also my willingness and capacities for commitment. And if those are found wanting, then ethical reflection brings forth questions about what I should do to make up the deficits. I would have to ask whether I have time to do this myself or even to work with others in cooperative courses of action. In other words, I would have to ask, of the many things of value that I could do, to which ones should I dedicate the time that is given to me?

These are not simply questions about which external values rank highest in my horizon and are therefore most deserving of my time. They are also questions about what kind (value) of person I will become in committing myself and my time to these various values. Moral value has to do with the values that we make ourselves to be as we simultaneously make an impact upon the world.

Permeating all of these reflections are the feelings we have about the value of ourselves as persons. These combine with other feelings in our horizons of values. They contribute profoundly to determining which questions we regard as pertinent in ethical reflection. Affective responses and moods intend the value of who we are. Desires and aversions anticipate values of who we might become. We not only respond to who we have become, but also to the images that we have constructed of ourselves. Most profoundly, however, our feelings respond to our experiences of ourselves as engaging in the activities of ethical inquiring, reflecting, judging, choosing, and acting. We spontaneously feel the value of ourselves as what Lonergan called "originating value" – the values of ourselves as the beings who make actual the value of ourselves as well as other values.[28] These feelings about ourselves as originating values enter into the constellation of our horizon of feelings. It may well be that our felt apprehensions of ourselves as instances of originating values are buried in the midst of other more intense feelings. Nevertheless, our feelings for our own worth as enactors of ethical reflections and choices will be experienced. Those feelings for the value of ourselves as originating values may arise only amidst deep tensions with the other feelings we have about who we have made ourselves, and what we imagine to be the realities of our value-identities. These tensions can be the sources of judgments of value and decisions that profoundly transform our horizons of feelings towards a more normative alignment. Or again, they could lead to further distortions in our feeling horizons that protect our fragile sense of value-identity from the reproaches of the normative ethical intentionality and objective value preference.

7.6   Habitual Deciding and Acting within Horizons of Feelings

There is a further matter to be considered – namely the habitual dimension of human deciding and action. Just as our valuing is largely habitual and only sporadically punctuated with new questions for judgments of value, so also our deciding and acting are overwhelmingly habitual.[29] We rise in the morning, prepare for our day, go about our day's work and our interactions with family members, friends, and associates largely in routines and patterns that we have come to perform habitually. We do not have to stop and reflect *ex nihilo* each time about what we should do or the value of doing so when we groom ourselves, kiss our loved ones good-bye for the day, journey to work, perform our tasks there, or chat with associates. We do not need to stop and persuade ourselves, or be persuaded by others, what or how to decide and act in each of these innumerable daily situations. For the most part we just do so habitually.

Nevertheless, these habits of deciding and acting were originally initiated and refined at times in the past when we did have to gain insights into how best to perform these operations, and to arrive at judgments about whether they were values to which we should commit ourselves not just once but habitually. With regard to the double intentionality discussed in the previous section, the value (or disvalue) that we decide to make of ourselves manifests itself most significantly in our habits of deciding and acting that are the inevitable consequences of our decisions about what kind of persons we will become. This means, of course, that our habits of deciding and acting result from and are modified by insights and judgments of fact we have formed, the practical insights, ethical judgments of value, and the consequent decisions we have made on numerous occasions in the past. We may think of our habits of deciding and acting as the capital that has accrued from the hard work of our ethical discernment in the past.

Or, at least we could think of them that way, if all of our decisions and actions in the past were solidly grounded in unconditionally objective judgments of fact and value. But this is not always the case. Thus our present habits of deciding and acting may also be the woeful, distorted burdens of our past decisions and actions. St. Paul puts it dramatically: "The willing is ready at hand, but doing the good is not. For I do not do the good I want, but I do the evil I do not want."[30] Our habits become burdens when they have been formed at least in part by decisions and actions that failed to conform to objective judgments of value, and this may happen in two ways. First, most often there are unresolved tensions within our horizons of feelings, and unless these tensions are resolved, our judgments of value will lack unconditional objectivity. Second, there are times when people do not do what they should, *even* when they know what they should do, and know the value for the sake of which they should do it. Human decisions are radically and essentially free. They are not even determined by judgments of ethical value that precede them, as we saw in chapter 4. We can choose and act in conformity with our judgments, or not. Tensions in our horizons of feelings interfere not only with our judgments of value. They can also interfere with the conformity of our deciding and acting to our knowledge of ethical values. The felt ordering of feelings for certain values (or disvalues) in our horizon of feelings can be so intense that it overrides our judgments of values. People can and do choose values as felt even when these stand in opposition to ethical values as known.

As well as our judgments of value, so also our choices and actions always take their bearings with respect to our horizons of feelings. When we speak of "difficult decisions" or "ethical dilemmas," this usually attests to conflicts and tensions among our feelings for values. When we decide and act in accord with objective judgments of ethical value, we take sides with one set of feelings for values against other feelings for values. We have to overcome the felt values and the attractions of the other courses of action. Such decisions have consequences to which our feelings also respond, adding the felt values of the consequences of our ethical actions to the prior constellation of feelings for values. This tends to reinforce the feelings that conformed with our ethical judgments, and to reduce the intensity of those that were in conflict with them. This transformation of our horizon of feelings supports the transformed habit of deciding and acting that was also modified by the decision.

However, when decisions deviate from objective ethical judgments, they also have their impacts on horizons of feelings and habits of choosing and acting. What was initially quite difficult for us to do, because we had to overcome both the knowledge that it was wrong and the feelings in support of that knowledge, becomes less difficult subsequently. The result of our unethical action can reinforce the feelings that attracted it to us in the first place, further distorting our horizon of feelings and inclining us towards repetitions of the action. Where some of our feelings at least supported our knowledge of the ethical course of action, now those feelings become muffled in the background. Moreover, this distortion of our feeling horizons begins to play a more prominent role in our future reflections about questions of ethical values. Decisions that deviate from our judgments of value, therefore, have profound consequences for the proper exercise of our structure of ethical intentionality.

We will return to the problems posed by unresolved tensions in our horizons of feelings in the next chapter. There we will take up the felt need for conversion, its relationship to our horizons of feelings, and its consequences, both for objectivity of ethical judgments, and for the responsibility of our decisions and actions. There it will be argued that only a transformation, a conversion, of the relationships among our feelings for values can ultimately overcome distortions in both our judgments about ethical values, and in our decisions and actions.

7.7   An Alternate Interpretation

Michael Vertin has argued for a different interpretation of the relationship between judgments of value and feelings as intentional responses. He does agree with Brian Cronin and me that judgments of value can be objective when there is a grasp of the judgment as virtually unconditioned, which is comparable to the act of reflective understanding that grounds objective judgments of fact. He adopted the term "deliberative insight" for this, while I have preferred to use "grasp of virtually unconditioned value" (where "grasp" means a value-reflective act of understanding, i.e., insight).[31]

The difference between Vertin's position and my own, however, is more than terminological, and his thinking on the nature of the deliberative insight has undergone some evolution. In a 1995 article, he argued that the deliberative insight is a feeling that is an intentional response: "The insight by which I grasp this unity [of conditioned and fulfilling conditions] is an act of *affective* cognition."[32] More recently, he proposed instead that feelings as intentional responses function as the primary fulfilling conditions for the deliberative insight that grasps a prospective judgment of value as virtually unconditioned, rather than as identical with the deliberative insight itself.[33]

In both cases, Vertin's account of the role played by feelings in the grasp of the virtually unconditioned grounding of judgments of value differs from my own. Although I agree with him that feelings emerge in response to various agent objects and thereby bestow upon them a felt sense of value,[34] I have argued that these feelings are components in our more encompassing horizon of feelings of values. As such, their role is to provide the criteria according to which the individual subject will regard further questions as pertinent to the judgment of value. This is the case whether the judgment of value pertains to an already existing reality or a possible course of action. Hence the feelings are not themselves the grasp of virtually unconditioned value, for that is the province of a kind of understanding or insight separate and distinct from either direct or factual reflective insights. Nor are feelings the fulfillment of conditions for the judgment of value, since that comes only when all of the further pertinent questions have been properly answered. Instead, the horizon of feelings determines what further questions will be felt as pertinent to the correctness of judgments of the values as felt.

Vertin rightly notes that Lonergan's writings on this topic are terse and open to many different interpretations. The correct determination cannot rest, therefore, upon Lonergan's writings themselves. Ultimately, the question of the correct role of feelings in reaching correct judgments of value has to be settled by an appeal to self-appropriation of one's own experiences of the phenomena themselves.[35] Both Vertin and I have done our best to discern how feelings enter into judgments of value. It remains to the readers' own efforts at self-appropriation to determine which, if either of us, comes closer to a correct understanding of these phenomena.

Finally, in spite of these differences, I agree completely with Vertin on three points. First, I agree that feelings as intentional responses contribute to the objectivity of judgments of value only if the feelings themselves are self-transcending.[36] Second, I agree also that the conversions provide the deepest sources of objectivity in judgments of value, and that feelings are completely self-transcending only in the horizons of feelings of people who are converted.[37] Finally, in an unpublished conversation, Vertin commented that feelings come after decisions to "confirm" the correctness of the decision. Decisions can be among the agent objects that elicit feelings, and certainly when we feel satisfied, relieved, ecstatic, regretful, guilty, etc. after having made a decision, such feelings reveal values of our decisions, often values to which our unconverted horizons of feelings were insensitive to beforehand. However, feelings also operate to guide the reflective processes leading up to the decisions, and a genuinely converted feeling horizon would have led to an objective judgment of value and decision before the confirmation by subsequent feelings.

7.8   Summary

This chapter has been devoted to explorations of how feelings affect the ways that we arrive at judgments of value in general and of ethical value in particular. Judgments of value presuppose the emergence of questions of value. Such questions of value do not emerge as long as we rely upon our habits of evaluation as we encounter the circumstances and people that come our way, drawing upon the resources of our previous judgments, beliefs, and horizons of feelings. But when some new encounter diverges significantly from the expectations of this habitual valuing, new questions of value do arise. They set into motion processes of value reflection that are directed both by a series of further questions and by feelings for values that determine the relevance and urgency of those further questions. Feelings and value inquiries endow judgments of value with their *unconditional intensity*, and constitute them precisely as judgments *of value*.

Earlier we emphasized that ethical intentionality is spontaneously and naturally oriented towards decisions that enact true and correct judgments of ethical value, even though people do not automatically act in conformity with what they know to be the right and ethically valuable thing to do.[38] People do act, however, in accord with their horizons of feelings, no matter how distorted or normative. Our horizons of feeling imbue our judgments with the values, the sense of importance, even urgency, that they affirm (or deny). This influence extends into the ways that our feeling-infused judgments motivate our decisions and the decisions with which we actualize values. The depth and urgency (or lack thereof) of commitment in our decisions and consequent actions derives ultimately from the apprehensions of value contained in our horizon of feelings. Judgments do affirm this is the course of action we will undertake. But the quality, priority, and intensity of the value itself come from our feelings.

The examples offered in this chapter attempted to illustrate how the pertinence of further questions is determined by the horizon of feelings. It was the intention of these illustrations to aid the reader in discernment – in personally appropriating the processes of value and ethical reflection with greater discernment. Many other examples could have been offered, but it is hoped that these examples have been helpful.

Our judgments of value can be virtually unconditioned *relative* to values of our horizon of feelings. In other words, if we ask, for example, about whether we should choose to embark upon a course of action, we will be asking whether it would be a realization of values in the ways that we have come to feel them. When there are no further questions pertinent to the concerns of our horizon of feelings, then we will form judgments of value that are objective, relative to that constellation of feelings and values – that is to say, the pertinence of further questions is determined by our horizon of feelings. At any moment, each of us has some horizon of feelings, in which certain feelings stand at the fore and feel their *noematic* values as having some ranking within a felt scale of value preferences. The foregrounded feeling is modulated and nuanced by its relations with the other feelings for values in the horizon of feelings. The foregrounded feeling with its nuances constitutes what counts as of value for us at the moment. Pertinence will be settled by this complex of value feelings. These are simply facts about the structure of ethical intentionality.

These facts about the way that a subject's feelings determine his or her value reflections clearly raises a problem about what makes value and ethical reflection authentic. Take for example persons whose horizons are dominated by feelings of vengeance, like Dantès in Alexander Dumas's *The Count of Monte Cristo*. Their attention to sensations and memories is directed by those feelings. Their interpretative insights and judgments about the motives of others are fueled by vengeance. Their intellectual inquiry and efforts to attain insights become absorbed and preoccupied with schemes of revenge. But are these schemes of unconditional value? As long as vengeance holds sway, such persons feel as distracting and irrelevant any further questions that would undermine their path of vengeance, such as, "Who else might be hurt?" "What will happen to one's own reputation?" "Will I lose the love of my life?" The stronger the vengeance, the less will further questions about such consequences be regarded as really pertinent. The "truly" pertinent questions will be those whose answers most efficiently realize vengeance. These questions may lead the vengeful soul to conclude that he or she can best succeed through guile – by actions that lead others to believe the injury has been forgotten. They may even lead to deep self-deception where the person comes to believe he or she actually has forgiven the offence – although episodically, caustic remarks and spiteful deeds belie the pretense. The course of action under deliberation will have a value, and it will be the value of vengeance, in the way it is felt to have the highest priority in the person's horizon of feelings. For such persons, responsibility becomes identical with carrying out acts of vengeance. This phenomenon can be generalized in a social group that develops a "Code of Honour" of reprisals and pay-backs. It can lead to self-perpetuating cycles of feuds where children are formed in the vengeful horizons of their parents.

The foregoing example is a different kind of illustration of how reflection arrives at a judgment about a course of action. It does so under the sway of these persons' horizons of feelings. If real-life examples of such ruthless people are relatively few, instances of people whose vengeance distorts their better judgment are more numerous.

Clearly there is something disturbing about the example of Dantès, and it was deliberately chosen to elicit this disturbing sense. The intent of the example is to heighten awareness that authentic responsibility depends profoundly upon living in an authentic horizon of feelings. Such a realization can lead to total despair about the possibility of authentic responsibility. If the exercise of value reflection is so utterly dominated by the horizon of feelings, how can anyone ever arrive at objective judgments about genuinely worthwhile courses of action? Is not our capacity for responsible reflection imprisoned within the confines of our horizons of feeling? It surely seems that if value reflection is determined by feelings, there can be no way to think one's way out of an inauthentic horizon of feelings.

Is all value knowledge therefore relative to one's merely subjective horizon of feelings? The answer is complicated, for all human value knowledge is indeed relative to one's horizon of feelings and the constellation of the values it intends. Values as known are affirmed in judgments that have the form, "*X* has value *V*," where *V* is supplied by the person's horizon of feelings. But it is not the case that all horizons of feelings must be *merely* subjective. There is a possibility, though not easily realized, of normative horizons of feelings that would ground absolutely objective judgments of value. The possibility of such horizons is the topic of the next chapter.

Why Is Doing That Being Ethical?

8 Horizons of Feelings, Conversion, and Objectivity

Genuine objectivity is the fruit of authentic subjectivity.
– Bernard Lonergan, *Method in Theology*

8.1 Introduction

In this chapter we turn to the question of whether there are objective judgments of value in general and of ethical value in particular. I will propose that judgments of value can be objective under certain conditions, although fulfillment of those conditions is no easy matter.

Doubts about the possibility of objectivity in matters of value have been widespread for quite some time. These doubts derive in part from certain assumptions about what objectivity requires. Lonergan's criticism of what he called a "counter-position" regarding objectivity goes to the heart of these doubts. Insofar as knowing is construed on the mistaken model of "taking a look," then objectivity is "seeing what is out there to be seen." Obviously values are not out there to be seen, so they could not be objectively known, according to this counter-position. The philosophy of positivism is one clear illustration of this counter-position, and it rejects the notion that there can be objective knowledge of values. Again, although certainly not a positivist, Max Weber famously articulated an influential version of the fact/value distinction. He argued forcefully that values had no place in the realm of scientific research (*Wissenschaft*), and he also issued grave warnings about introducing matters of value into teaching in universities.[1] His concerns are understandable in the context of the ideological conflicts that were growing in German universities at the time. Nevertheless, his powerful articulation of the deep division between objectivity that pertains to factual knowledge on the one hand, and commitments to values on the other, has had an influence that has grown far beyond its original context.

Neither Weber's account of scientific research nor positivism aligns with Lonergan's "position" on knowledge. Lonergan's "position" holds that knowledge is "understanding correctly"[2] – that is to say, knowledge consists in judging the correctness of one's understanding on the basis of a grasp of the prospective judgment as virtually unconditioned. Commonly this occurs when an insight is recognized to be correct because of the absence of any further pertinent questions, which would otherwise lead to further corrections of the insight. If the absence of further pertinent questions is the "positional" criterion of objectivity, then the fact that values are not "out there" to be seen is not a good enough reason for denying that value judgments can be objective in principle. In practice, however, actually attaining objectivity in the realm of value judgments is exceptionally challenging.

The preceding chapter led to a more complicated way of posing the question about the objectivity of value judgments. There we explored how feelings enter into our processes of value and ethical reflection. I argued that all of our judgments of value are conditioned by the state of our horizons of feelings. In particular, I argued that our horizons of feelings determine what further questions we will regard as pertinent to the prospective judgment, "X has value V."

But doesn't this involvement of feelings inevitably undermine the objectivity of our value judgments? We may indeed take the time and care required to answer all questions pertinent to a judgment of the form "X does have value V," but it has been the burden of the preceding chapters to show that value V comes to consciousness in our horizons of feelings, and that those horizons determine what questions will be regarded as pertinent to this value judgment. Therefore, if our judgments of value in general and ethical values in particular are objective when we consider and answer all further pertinent questions, they attain only a limited form of objectivity. Even when our judgments of value are indeed virtually unconditioned judgments, they are so only relative to the sense of values as determined by the concrete constitutions of our horizons of feelings. That is to say, values as we judge them are objective relative to the ways that our feeling horizons guide our lines of questioning and determine which questions are to be regarded as pertinent to the values as felt, and which are considered irrelevant.[3]

This leads to questions about those horizons themselves. Should we rely upon their guidance? Are they reliable standards for judgments of value? Should we not seek a standard for our judgments and decisions that is more objective and more detached than our horizons of feelings?

Even in raising such questions, we seem to be confronted by a vicious circle. Since these are questions about what we should do, they are questions of ethical value. But if our analysis so far has been correct, then we inescapably ask these questions about the horizons on the basis of our own horizons of feelings themselves. It would seem, then, that we must presuppose the reliability of our horizons of feelings in order to judge them as either reliable or unreliable. Since this would indeed be a vicious circle, it seems that we are trapped within our horizons of feelings, with no standards by means of which we could assess them objectively. This would mean, in turn, that there would ultimately be no standards by means of which we could assess the objectivity of any judgments of value that depend upon our horizons.

The situation is indeed serious, but not desperate. There are ways of breaking this vicious circle. But the ways out do not come in the form of some sort of reasoning that can detach itself from, and stand outside of, our feeling horizons. The opening, rather, is already available within horizons of feelings themselves. In this chapter and the next, we take up the problem of evaluating horizons of feelings by examining them more closely from within. In doing so, we will discover that immanent within those horizons there are tensions which make it possible to transcend the limitations of the horizons themselves, tensions that offer standards for what would count as a normative horizon of feelings.

Still, the fact that each person's horizon already contains such standards does not at all mean that their horizons are automatically exercising their normativity in practice. It does mean, instead, that the tensions already immanent and operative within each person's feeling horizons are potentialities inviting responses that would transform existing constellations of feelings into actually normative horizons.[4]

Identifying the sources of these tensions is not easy. Finding them is the work of discernment, and discernment is a challenging undertaking. Furthermore, even when we have identified these sources, our work is far from done. Proper discernment of the sources will require careful understanding of the tensions they produce in their relationships with other dimensions of our feeling horizons. If our value and ethical reflections are to be objective in the fullest sense, then these felt tensions will have to be resolved by bringing our other feelings into harmony with these sources of normativity. These kinds of changes in feelings are difficult, and they can take many years if not a lifetime to achieve, so the initial discernment of these tensions and sources will call us into an ongoing reorientation of our feeling horizons.[5]

This chapter and the next will be devoted to exploring these sources, the kinds of changes needed, and, ultimately, the question of objectivity of value judgments. These explorations will make it possible in chapter 10 to address the second ethical question: "Why is doing that being ethical?"

8.2   Tensions in Feeling Horizons and Value Objectivity

Even when the limited, relative form of objectivity is achieved, there likely remain further subtle, unsettling tensions within our feeling horizons themselves. Because of these tensions, the relative form of objectivity will not be ultimately or deeply satisfying. People remember with embarrassment or regret the judgments and decisions they made at earlier stages in their own lives when their feelings were insensitive or shallow or distorted. They wonder how they could have failed to attend to the intimations already present in those feelings.

Clearly our horizons of feelings are not static. There are subtle tensions in our horizons of feelings that are the dynamic sources of transformations of those horizons. In some cases, those transformations lead to horizons of feelings open to a more complete appreciation of values. When this does happen, it underpins a more profound kind of objectivity in judgments of value.

Such tensions therefore prompt us towards reorientations of our feeling horizons that will genuinely and fully resolve these tensions. Resolution of these tensions can only come ultimately from what Lonergan called "conversions" of our feeling horizons.

Although Lonergan did not describe horizons of feelings in the manner or detail of the preceding chapters of this book, his writings reveal that he was profoundly aware of their phenomena as well as the deep tensions within them. He wrote, for example, that "there are in full consciousness feelings so deep and strong, especially when deliberately reinforced, that they channel attention, shape one's horizon, direct one's life."[6]

This section will focus on two profound dynamic sources of tension internal to every person's horizon of feelings. The first is the pure, unrestricted desire to know and value everything that is good. The other is what Lonergan referred to as the "basic fulfilment" of this desire, which he also spoke of as "being in love in an unrestricted fashion." *For Lonergan, these are the two genuine foundations of ethics.* His most important contributions to the analysis of horizons of feelings and their roles in value intentionality comes in his identification of these two fundamental sources of tensions in our feeling lives. Neither of these sources is a product of our own efforts; both are given in and to consciousness. Because both are unrestricted, they can be deeply unsettling. Both trouble any limited horizon of feelings and goad it towards unlimitedness. This is so even if one or both of these unrestricted feeling sources is merely at the margins of a person's feeling horizon. Precisely because they are unrestricted, they are perennial sources of disequilibrium in every person's affective horizon.

These two sources can prompt profound changes to occur in our affective horizons. If they do, they also yield equally significant changes in ethical reflection and its regard for what count as questions pertinent to what courses of action are worthwhile. These two unrestricted feeling sources are the grounds of the possibility that a person's ethical reflections can escape imprisonment within limited horizons of feelings. They are the sources that make possible a "conversion" decision towards an unlimited horizon that constitutes genuine authenticity and responsibility.

8.2.1 *The Transcendental Notion of Value*

Lonergan remarked that he came to recognize a distinct, transcendental notion of value quite late in his career, well after the publication of *Insight*. He likened the transcendental notion of value to the transcendental notion of being.[7] In fact, he proposed that the transcendental notion of value "is the fuller flowering of the same dynamic principle [as the notion of being] that keeps us moving toward ever fuller realization of the good."[8] Our transcendental notion of being is our desire to know all that is – to know everything about everything. It is an unrestricted cognitional desire that is manifested in our unrestricted stream of questions for intelligence and reflection that seek understanding and factual judgment.[9] Likewise, our transcendental notion of value is our desire for everything good that is the source of our questions for value reflection, choice, and action.

Just as our notion of being is a notion and not a concept of being because we do not yet understand and know everything about everything that we desire to know, so also our notion of value is a notion and not a concept of value because we have not yet judged and embraced everything good, which we desire. As a notion of value, it is only an intentional response of desiring value. As desire, it does not itself know values nor does it make values firmly its own. Knowledge of values in the full sense comes only in objective value judgments, and values become fully our own only when we freely choose what we know objectively to be of value. (We make values our own when we choose their goodness, even if we do not possess them. For example, I can choose to accept the value that I have come to know in a judgment regarding an athletic performance, a work of art, an intellectual achievement, or a noble action, even if it is not something I personally possess or did.) Still, the transcendental notion of value precedes objectively knowing and choosing values. Like the notion of being, the notion of value is manifest in an unrestricted stream of questions – in this case, questions for evaluation, deliberation, and choice. Because judgments of value and choices are always responses to questions that arise from the transcendental notion of value, it is the condition of their possibility.

Lonergan remarked that the notion of value intends values through "questions for deliberation, just as the intelligible is what is intended in questions for intelligence, and just as truth and being are what are intended in questions for reflection."[10] Agreeing with Lonergan's point that values are intended in questions for deliberation, it is necessary to generalize his formulation and say that the notion of value is manifest also in questions for evaluation, as well as questions for deliberation. As we saw in the previous chapter, sometimes we do ask questions about the values of qualities, events, things, situations, and persons without further deliberating in order to also decide or do anything in direct response to these judgments of value. Some of our value questions are simply for the sake of knowing values without any immediate intention to make decisions or undertake actions on the basis of these judgments of values. Deliberating, on the other hand, always carries the connotation of considering a course of action to be undertaken. Deliberating in Lonergan's sense is what I have been calling "ethical reflection" – the process of seeking judgments of ethical value for the sake of choosing and acting on the basis of those judgments. Thus, when he defines the notion of value solely in terms of questions for deliberation, Lonergan seems unnecessarily to restrict the notion of value to the values that are to be realized through human choice and action. It is more accurate, therefore, to say that the transcendental notion of value is manifest in all questions for evaluation as well as for deliberation – not only questions regarding ethical values, but also questions regarding all values in general.

As a desire for judgments of value, decisions, and actions, the transcendental notion of value is itself a feeling of intentional response. Unlike the feeling responses of affects, this desire intends values through its questioning – that is to say, through its desire for answers. The transcendental notion of value raises questions about whether something is "truly or only apparently good."[11] Moreover, because there is no limit to what we can ask about goodness and value, our transcendental notion of value is an unrestricted desiring. This transcendental notion remains dissatisfied with any limited images, ideas, judgments, feelings, or attainments of value. Because of our notion of value, we cannot rest until we have affirmed, chosen, and accepted everything towards which this desire impels us – namely, everything good. Likewise, it impels us to negate (i.e., to objectively judge negatively) and reject everything that is a disvalue. Our transcendental notion of value will be satisfied only in the embrace of everything good about every good thing – and *only* by what is good.

Underpinning every specific question of value, therefore, is a desire that intends value prior to knowledge or choice of values. Prior to judgments and conceptions of the good, human consciousness is intrinsically oriented towards the good, and indeed towards the unlimited, unrestricted good. The human desire for the good precedes all human conceptions and judgments of the good. It also outlasts and goes beyond all such conceptions and judgments. For human beings, all conceptions of and judgments about the good are limited, while the desire for the good is unrestricted. Through their questions of value, human beings transcend their previous achievements and conceptions and judgments regarding the good, and head towards values that are as yet unknown and unchosen. Questions of value, therefore, are fundamental modes of human participation in the quest for unlimited, unrestricted value and goodness.

The fact that we have an unlimited desire for the good that goes beyond any of our conceptions of the good poses a problem. If this is the case, how are we to talk about the good? Although we need to express to ourselves and to others what we mean by the word "good," still we cannot adequately talk about it by means of any of our conceptions of the good, because these all fall short of its full meaning. We can, however, talk about the good indirectly and heuristically. We can talk about the good in its relation to our unrestricted desire for the good. It is possible to talk about the good as that which the unrestricted desire desires – to talk about the good as the objective of this unrestricted desire of which we are aware. That desire is evident and available and manifest in the value-inquiring spirit of each and every human being. Hence it is possible to talk about the good as the objective of the totality of all questions of value – as what is intended not in any particular question of value, but in the overall, ongoing, dynamic process of value inquiry. We will return to this topic in chapters 11–14.

Clearly, then, our unrestricted notion of value is also a feeling within our horizon of feelings, because it is an intentional response of desiring values. Furthermore, because its desiring is unrestricted, this desire is a permanent source of tensions in the horizon of human feelings. Our questions for deliberation, evaluation, and choice leave us discontented with whatever finite goods we have thus far known and chosen, and even less content with the ways that biases have infiltrated and distorted our value knowing and choosing. The questions that arise from the transcendental notion of value lead us to make better what already is good in limited ways, and to overcome, heal, rectify, and restore whatever corrupts and destroys value.

The tensions introduced by the unlimited desire for value are not only directed towards evaluating and perfecting the external natural and human worlds. Our transcendental notion of value is also, and perhaps most primordially, directed towards our own selfhood. It is directed especially towards our horizons of feelings because our horizons are profoundly constitutive of the identity and value of who we are. Because it is unrestricted, as almost no other feeling is, the transcendental notion of value is a source of permanent tension towards self-correction and self-transcendence – what Lonergan calls "moral self-transcendence."[12] This means that, ultimately, we can never rest content with anything less than a feeling horizon that is in harmony with the intentionality of this unrestricted, inquisitive desire for value.

Hence, whenever our feeling horizon feels the value of anything as it does in its concrete and complex way, it is always permeated by the tensions that arise from our unrestricted transcendental notion of value. This means, among other things, that within our horizon of feelings there always resides a desiring intention of value that calls into question any imperfections of that horizon itself. We need not go outside of our own horizon of feelings to seek a criterion for a kind of objectivity that is neither limited nor merely relative. That criterion is always already embedded in our own feeling horizons themselves. It is manifest in the tensions that arise from the unrestricted notion of value. The other affects, desires, and moods that make up the intentional responses in our horizons of feelings do combine to feel values in limited ways. But because they feel those values in the context of the horizon of feelings, those limited feelings of value are always felt, at least peripherally, with the awareness of their limitations. They are felt alongside the aspiration to feel those values from the viewpoint of a horizon of feelings that has no such limitations.

The ethics of discernment, therefore, is centrally a matter of learning how to attend to the tensions in our own horizons of feelings that arise from the transcendental notion of value, learning how to understand those tensions correctly, and learning how to respond to them authentically. Value objectivity in the fullest sense depends upon achieving refined levels of such discernment.

In principle, then, we are capable of raising every sort of value question, including questions about the imperfections of our own horizon of felt value priorities and questions as to what we should do about the limitations of that horizon. Effectively, however, we are only able to sustain such inquiry if the unrestricted notion of value plays the central role it should, and is not eclipsed by other feelings that interfere with its efficacy. This question of how effective a role can be played by our unrestricted notion of value is a question about what Lonergan called "moral conversion." We return to that question in section 8.3.3 below.

8.2.2 Is the Notion of Value Unrestricted?

Much depends upon the claim that the transcendental notion of value is unrestricted – that is to say, it is possible to evaluate and to transcend the imperfections of our horizons of feelings only if there is no limit to what we can ask about goodness and value. Further pertinent questions seek value-objectivity regarding values in general, as well as our own particular proposed courses of action, our horizons of feelings, and indeed the value of the lives we lead. This process of value-questioning has the potential for value-objectivity only if there is no limit to its questions. This is possible only if the source of those questions, the transcendental notion of value, is truly an *unrestricted* desire for goodness and value. Yet is this really so?

We faced a similar question in chapter 2 when we asked about the notion of being – the desire to know what is. There I followed Lonergan in affirming the unrestrictedness of the desire for knowledge of what is. I also explored the special difficulties involved in arguing for this affirmation. We face similar difficulties in making the case for the unrestrictedness of the transcendental notion of value.

First, then, like the notion of being, the transcendental notion of value is not known adequately by the "misleading analogy of other desires."[13] This is because "desire" in the case of the transcendental notion of value means no more but no less than that which reveals itself through questions about what is good – questions for deliberation and questions of value. For this reason, the notion of value differs not only from somatic desires, but also from other desires that are intentional responses. Where the objects of these desirings are identifiable, the notion of value desires first and foremost something unknown and as yet unchosen. The notion of value reveals its desiring through the ceaseless flow of questions about value – about what is good and what could be better. It desires to know and to choose everything of value in the totality of correct value judgments. Once the objects sought by the other desires have been attained, their tensions dissipate. The satisfactions of these desires, however, do not satisfy the more fundamental tension of notion of value. Even the successful fulfillments of these limited objects of somatic or intentional-response desires tend to be followed spontaneously by further questions of value. In some cases, after attaining what we once desired intensely, we might find ourselves surprisingly troubled by further questions as to whether these attainments were really worthwhile after all. Whether the answer is "yes" or "no," spontaneously we will still wonder: Could we have done something better? What more could we have done? Is there more that we might still be able to do? What other projects is it worthwhile for us to do? Far from completely satisfying the notion of value, the satisfaction of any particular desire tends to become the occasion for a further manifestation of the unrestrictedness of this notion's desiring. No single satisfaction, no single answer to a question of value or deliberation will satisfy the notion of value. It presses beyond particular judgments of value, and even beyond decisions and actions, with ever further questions about what we might yet do to make the world a better place. As long as we continue to ask such questions, we are not yet in a position to identify what it is that is desired by our notion of value.

Thus we can identify the finite objectives that our other desires desire. However, we would only be to able identify what our transcendental notion of value desires if we already were in possession of the complete set of correct judgments of value – if we already knew everything valuable about everything. This is part of the reason why analogies with other desires prove misleading in attempting to think about the kind of desiring intentional response that is characteristic of the transcendental notion of value.

As with the notion of being, the best way to "know" the transcendental notion of value is to give it free rein. This requires discernment – learning to become ever more attentive to the stirrings of our questions about what is truly good and what good should be authentically chosen. It also means deciding to cooperate with its inquisitive desiring, and to undertake practices that will give the desiring of the notion of value the place of priority in our horizon of value, in conjunction with unconditional being-in-love. In other words, the notion of value is best known in the wake of decisions for the conversions. We will return to a fuller discussion of this in section 8.3.

Still, if we best "know" our notion of value by attending to it and practicing it, it does not follow that we know it *as unrestricted* through such attention or practice. Nor can we know the unrestrictedness of our notion of value in the direct fashion of experiencing, understanding, and judging. That would again require us to have already come to know and to have decisively committed ourselves to the objective that it desires through the totality of judgments of value and choices that answer to the totality of all questions of value. Only if we had already attained the totality of judgments of value could we then conclude that the objective was indeed unrestricted. Hence knowledge of the notion of value as unrestricted cannot be obtained directly; we must find a suitably indirect approach, as did Lonergan in arguing for the unrestrictedness of the notion of being.

As one such indirect approach, suppose we were to ask whether there might not be something of value beyond the desiring of the transcendental notion of value. The very question itself, however, is a manifestation of that notion, since by "transcendental notion of value" is meant the desire that manifests itself in questions for evaluation and deliberation. The very question itself manifests the desire to know about something of value which, it is purported, lies beyond the desiring of the notion of value. Hence to ask whether there is some restriction to the values that the desire for values desires is to ask whether there are values that it cannot ask about. This reveals that it is not a restricted intending of values after all.

A second indirect approach also parallels another of Lonergan's arguments. No doubt some people will insist that they have no desire for everything of value – that they are perfectly content with what they have, or at least that they scorn what certain other people find of value. But as we saw in chapter 2, such an objection pivots on an equivocation on the word "desire." Those who object that they have no unrestricted desire to value mean by "desire" a willingness that has resulted from a prior decision to forego certain things of value. That decision rests upon prior judgments, feelings, and questions about those values. Those prior questions about values that one turns from are manifestations of the more primordial desiring of the transcendental notion of value. Prior to the willingness ("desire") that results from the decision, there is that prior and primordial desire that sends forth the bewildering flow of questions of value, including questions about the goods that lie beyond one's own limited choices and commitments. Desiring in this primordial sense is different from "desiring" in the secondary and derivative sense that is the result of a subsequent decision. Here again we see that it is misleading to think about the desiring of the transcendental notion of value by relying on the analogy with some other type of "desire." The notion of value is ultimately unlike desires that are somatic feelings and also unlike the "desires" that result from decisions. So the objection that one does not have an unrestricted "desire" for value means that one has willingly abandoned pursuit of some things that one already knows to be worthwhile because one cannot help but desire to value them in the primordial, inquisitive sense – the desire that is manifested in questioning. Far from proving one does not have or never had such a desire, "desire" in the derived sense presupposes the unrestricted desire for value in the primordial sense that is the source of the questions and judgments of value that one has experienced and chosen not to "desire."

There are of course many other ways of raising questions about whether the notion of value is truly unrestricted. Once again, individual readers will need to resolve their own lines of inquiry, asking and answering all their further pertinent questions before they can arrive at their own virtually unconditioned judgments that the transcendental notion of value, the source of questions of value, is truly unrestricted. Pursuits of these alternative questions about unrestrictedness, however, will all have very similar forms; the attempt to formulate a question or objection about the unrestrictedness will inevitably reveal the very unrestrictedness by being asked. Analysis of the various formulations of the questions about the unrestrictedness of the notion of value will reveal the reflexive character of this question about questioning – and that it thereby fulfills the conditions for affirming its unrestrictedness.

In conclusion, then, just as the our notion of being (manifest in questions for intelligence and reflection) amounts to an immediate "knowing" of all that is (being) by desiring it, so also an unrestricted notion of the value revealed in questions for evaluation and deliberation is an immediate "knowing" of and desire for all that is good, all that is of value. Because of the immediacy of the good that is made conscious by the aspiration of our notion of value, practical insights are sought, practical reflection and deliberation are undertaken, virtually unconditioned grasps of value are reached, judgments of value and choices are made, and horizons of feelings are criticized, re-evaluated, and reformed. To the extent that our judgments of value are arrived at under the sway of horizons of value that are in harmony with the unrestricted notion of value, those judgments will be unconditionally and not just relatively objective. And to the extent that the decisions and actions follow from these objective judgments of value, they will realize instances of genuinely unconditional value and goodness.

8.2.3 *Unrestricted Being-in-Love*

Lonergan identified a second feeling, which is also a perennial source of tensions within our horizons of feelings. Like the unrestricted notion of value, this feeling is also unrestricted, and for that reason it is extremely difficult to find language by which to adequately define or describe it. In order to accommodate this difficulty, Lonergan proposes to characterize this feeling, however inadequately, by its essential relationship to the unrestricted desire to know and to value. He identifies this feeling as the "the basic fulfilment" and "the proper fulfilment" of all our questioning.[14] But this feeling is only a *basic*, not a complete, fulfillment of our notion of being and value, because it leaves all particular questions unanswered, especially all of our questions about what is good and valuable. It is basic in the sense that it is a feeling of unshakeable reassurance that all of our questions have answers (especially all of our questions for evaluation, deliberation, and choice), before we find out just what those answers are.

Clearly, the intentionality of this feeling of unrestricted, basic fulfillment is different from that of the intentionality of the transcendental notion of value, to which it is intimately related. The latter intends values indirectly by anticipating them. Through its irrepressible questioning, the notion of value desires all judgments of value, choices, and actions. These judgments, choices, and actions are particular and partial fulfillments of what the notion of value intends only by desiring them. By way of contrast, the feeling of basic fulfillment is a "dynamic state" that intends the whole of values directly. It does not intend just some particular values, as do particular value judgments, decisions, and actions, nor does it intend the totality of values by anticipating it, as does the desiring of the unrestricted notion of value. It intends the wholeness of value by a basic fulfillment of that desiring.[15]

Hence the intentionality of the feeling of basic fulfillment intends values in a way that is similar to our moods as intentional responses – but without their finite limitations. This similarity to the intentional responses of finite moods is suggested by Lonergan's use of peace and joy to characterize the feeling of basic fulfillment. In an unrestricted fashion it intends all values unconditionally in all their objective value-relationships to one another. It does so by intending the unconditional whole within which abide those conditioned values and relationships. It feels everything good about every good thing without qualification or limit. Nevertheless, it intends this whole of all values directly without knowing it, just as finite affects and moods intend particular values without yet having arrived at corresponding judgments of value. Just as finite feelings of intentional response intend values primordially before values are intended more fully in judgments and decisions, so also the feeling of basic fulfillment intends the unlimited wholeness of value and good without yet knowing or deciding for the wholeness of value.

According to Lonergan, this feeling of basic fulfillment is primordially an experience that is not yet formulated: "To say this dynamic state is conscious is not to say that it is known. For consciousness is just experience, but knowledge is a compound of experience, understanding, and judging."[16]

Still, something more is wanted than just the language that attempts to characterize this fundamental feeling by its relationship to the unrestricted notion of value. Lonergan himself interpreted this experience in terms of his Christian religious tradition, and used the phrases "being in love in an unrestricted fashion … without limits or qualifications or conditions or reservations" and "being in love with God"[17] to characterize this experience of unrestricted fulfillment. Even to say that the being-in is a "being-in-love" is to go beyond the experience as experienced, and to add understandings and judgments drawn specifically from the Christian religious context. Among other things, the use of the term "love" invites the question "With whom am I in love?"

Although Lonergan drew upon his own religious tradition to talk about this second perennial source of tensions within our horizons of feelings, he also held that the experience is universal across all traditions, and he endorsed the authenticity of the many ways of interpreting it within different religious traditions. Prior to any attempt to formulate this experience, it is just a being-in. It is for this reason that Lonergan also defined unrestricted being-in-love by means of its intrinsic, intimate relationship to the unrestricted notion of value.

Lonergan further characterized unrestricted being-in-love by saying that it is experienced as a "dynamic state of love, joy, peace, that manifests itself in acts of kindness, goodness, fidelity, gentleness, and self-control."[18] But prior to Christian or other interpretations of the experience, there is just the being-in, where distinctions between lover and beloved are not yet drawn:

> This relationship is not subject-to-object but subject-to-subject …
> total, and so otherwordly, being-in-love … [which] puts the existential
> subject in a personal relationship to God. It is not a relationship to God

> as object, for it is prior to all objectification, whether in judgments of value or beliefs, or decisions or words or deeds … this being-in-love determines the horizon of total self-transcendence by grounding the self and all its self-transcendence in the divine lover whose love makes those he loves in love with him, and so with one another.[19]

In itself, therefore, the experience of unrestricted being-in-love does not contain understandings or expressions or judgments or decisions or actions. But it can become the foundation "from which flow one's desires and fears, one's joys and sorrows, one's discernments of values, one's decisions and actions" along with new questions, insights, expressions, and judgments. Still, in itself, being-in-love in an unrestricted fashion does not know what it loves, nor does it know its own *ordo amoris* – that is, it does not know in detail the ordering among values that it feels. It does not yet know what hierarchy among values it feels or which values are higher or why. So the experienced feeling of being-in-love in an unrestricted fashion can reside within and permeate our horizons of feelings without being explicitly attended to, understood, affirmed, or deliberately accepted.

This bears emphasis: oddly, we can feel unconditional being-in-love without yet deliberately deciding to love unconditionally. To actually love everything about everything by choice, to embrace without conditions or restrictions or qualms or *ressentiment* all that is and all that should be is an act that is almost beyond contemplation. It would mean comprehending and loving the value of a universe over 13 billion years old and everything intelligible that has taken place in the past and present, and will take place in the future. It would mean decisively loving the values of vast numbers of minuscule, strange elementary particles and of remote stars and galaxies that seem to have no relevance whatsoever to the rich realm of our own intimate loves. It would mean loving a seemingly wasteful and senselessly violent world in which over 99 per cent of all the living creatures that ever existed became extinct. It would mean loving a world in which the glories of human beings so often seem to be massively overwhelmed by their stupidities and hideous abuses of themselves, their fellow humans, and the natural world. Any deliberate choice to love unconditionally would have to face all of these issues and come nevertheless to some kind of unconditional knowledge of all values and all that needs to be accepted and forgiven for the sake of the value of the unconditionally valuable whole that unconditional being-in-love beholds.

A deliberate act of unconditional love certainly seems beyond human attainment. But unrestricted being-in-love itself is not yet a deliberate choice of unconditionally loving. It is, rather, a prior, felt apprehension of the wholeness of all that is of value. While unrestricted being-in-love is not yet a fully deliberate act of loving that whole, it is, however, the condition of the possibility that human beings could ever make such a choice.

Late in his career, Lonergan held that unrestricted being-in-love in fact does reside in the consciousness of each and every human being, and forms the foundation of every authentic religious tradition.[20] Even though Lonergan used a term, "love" (*agape*), that came from his own Christian religious tradition, he argued that the reality referenced by that term transcends the capacity of any human tradition to formulate it exhaustively. So other authentic religious traditions have also identified and interpreted this reality by means of languages and practices different from those employed by Christians.

If Lonergan is right, then unrestricted being-in-love abides in the conscious feeling horizons of everyone. However, such being-in-love can only flourish to the extent that it is attended to, understood, affirmed, deliberately accepted, and reinforced: "There are in full consciousness feelings so deep and strong, especially when deliberately reinforced, that they channel attention, shape one's horizon, direct one's life. Here the extreme case is loving."[21]

Unrestricted being-in-love directs and channels our experiencing, questioning, understanding, and judging of facts and values to a lesser or greater extent, depending upon how it is situated within our horizons of feeling. If it is deliberately accepted and reinforced through authentic spiritual exercises and practices, then it will play a more prominent role in directing and channeling the operations of our ethical intentionality. If not, then it will be experienced more as a source of discomfort and annoyance rather than a welcome orientation in our horizon of feelings.

Chapter 1 explored the notions of discernment found in the writings of Paul and Ignatius. There I proposed that, for the most part, Lonergan extended their notions of discernment so as to focus on discerning the love of truth abiding in and directing what they called "natural powers." However, with his reflections on attending to, understanding, judging, and deliberately reinforcing the experience of unrestricted being-in-love, Lonergan joined Paul and Ignatius in their endeavours to discern the gifts of the Spirit. In light of his Christian tradition, this experience of unrestricted being-in-love is the principal movement given by the Spirit.

No matter how peripheral that being-in-love is, it inevitably introduces tensions – "consolations" or "desolations," in Ignatius's terminology. Our feelings can and do arise and merge in ways that create tensions with unrestricted being-in-love, even when it is not strong or central or highest in our horizons of feelings. Nevertheless, because that being-in-love is unrestricted, its presence can never be fully repressed. Unrestricted being-in-love makes its presence felt through the tensions it stimulates.

Some thinkers have held that self-preservation is the most basic of our feelings. Freud argued that what he called the sex drive (*eros*) is the most fundamental feeling drive, and later in his career added the death wish (*thanatos*) as equally fundamental. Nietzsche and his followers have regarded both the will to power, and *ressentiment* against it, as the most fundamental sources of tensions in our feeling horizons. There is no doubt that each of these is indeed a powerful dimension in our horizons of feelings; nor is there doubt that each of these can and has become both the focus and the highest preference in the concrete feeling horizons of many people. Certainly Lonergan never doubted that these primordial feelings do exist in people's horizons, or that they have come to dominate the lives of many people, but he would not agree that they are the most fundamental of our feelings. Precisely because our notion of value is an unrestricted desire, it is the source that not only asks about itself ("What good is it to have an unrestricted desire for the good?") but also calls into question every other feeling – whether desires for self-preservation or sex or power or anything else. The unrestricted notion of value, therefore, goes beyond and is more basic than any other felt valuation. Likewise, because unrestricted being-in-love is intimately related to the unrestricted notion of being as its basic and proper fulfillment, it too goes beyond all other feelings of value by its feeling for the whole of values beyond limitation or condition. Whatever may be true about the depth or persistence of other feeling-sources of tensions in our horizons, the transcendental notion of value and unconditional love are permanent and ineliminable feeling sources of tension in our horizons. Hence, the transcendental notion of value and unconditional being-in-love are the sources of the tensions that are responsible for whatever degrees of unconditional value objectivity we are able to attain.

Although Lonergan himself clearly affirmed the reality and indeed the universality of being-in-love in an unrestricted fashion, still he introduced it more or less as a hypothesis. In other words, he introduced the idea of an experience, a feeling, defined by its intrinsic relationship to the unrestricted notion of value as its "basic" and "proper" fulfillment. It would be the feeling that intends unconditionally the whole of all values in their objective scale of relationships to one another. Whether or not such a feeling exists in any particular person, any groups of persons, or all human beings are further questions to be answered in virtually unconditioned judgments of fact. This task becomes complicated because the experience as such is prior to, and the ground of, expressions. People can understand and interpret this experience accurately or inaccurately. People can use Lonergan's language to say that the experience they are having is indeed the proper and basic fulfillment of the unrestricted notion of value, but they can be mistaken in this interpretation. People can say they have never had such an experience, and also be mistaken. Some people can use languages of the various religions to give accurate and authentic expressions of unrestricted being-in-love, while others might apply almost exactly the same expressions to different, and possibly completely incompatible, experiences.

This implies that correctly interpreting and identifying the experience of unrestricted being-in-love is not an easy task. It is possible only through an extensive self-correcting process. Individuals will be more likely to reach such objective judgments if they participate in communities and traditions that have developed inventories of insights and judgments and practices to aid in such discernments. The discussion of Ignatius's spiritual exercises in chapter 1 highlighted his great contributions to such practices. It also emphasized that in addition to methods, practices, and exercises, such communities will need wise and good people who can correct oversights, eliminate the dominance of aberrant feelings, and winnow out mistaken judgments and beliefs that are used in such discernments. In chapters 15 and 16 we will return once again to the question of methods and practices of discernment.

8.3   Conversions and Horizons of Feelings

Therefore unrestricted being-in-love, along with the unrestricted notion of value, are permanent sources of disequilibrium in our feeling horizons. They introduce the most profound tensions into our feelings. In different fashions the notion of value and unrestricted being-in-love conspire to prompt us towards changes in our feeling horizons.

In principle, these changes could be instances of what Lonergan calls "development." A development is a sequence of stages with an intelligible orientation[22] – an intelligibly connected sequence of transformed horizons of feelings in this case. In developmental sequences the tensions of one stage lead to its transformation into a successor that partially resolves those tensions in the form of a more differentiated and more complex, integrated stage.[23] In embryological developments, the organism at one stage changes its chemical and cellular constituents until the form of organization at that stage can no longer function as it had been. If the transformation is truly part of a developmental sequence, then demise of the former stage is followed by the emergence of a new stage that can successfully integrate the changed chemical and cellular components into a more differentiated organism.

When our horizons develop in this sense, their constituent feelings become more refined. At an earlier stage we might have been incapable of having feelings for more subtle kinds of values or subtle differences among values, whereas in a later stage of development our feelings make it possible for us to discern such differences. For example, at an early stage we might have been incapable of distinguishing among different kinds of wrongs and might have only been able to respond with the same intensity of anger to a wide range of wrongs. Later, however, our feelings of anger become differentiated so as to discriminate different degrees of wrong. We may even be able to respond with laughter at the foolishness of certain wrongs – such as John Thorpe's ridiculous bragging in *Northanger Abbey*. However, because the unrestricted notion of value and unrestricted being-in-love are unrestricted, the tensions they introduce motivate a series of stages towards ever further refinements of feelings.

In most cases, however, the changes in our feeling horizons are not along pure lines of development; in most cases our horizons include commitments to feelings that are fundamentally opposed to the guidance of the notion of value and unconditional being-in-love. Because both of these feelings make infinite demands that defy our finite understanding, we can respond with fear, dread, horror, disgust, or desires for power and control. Our horizons of feelings may include tensions and conflicts so deep that they cannot be resolved merely by developmental transformations. The changes in horizons that respond to these constellations of feelings simply redistribute these fundamental conflicts without really resolving them. Lonergan calls these kinds of changes dialectical:

> Let us say that a dialectic is a concrete unfolding of linked but opposed principles of change. Thus there will be a dialectic if (1) there is an aggregate of events of a determinate character, (2) the events may be traced to either or both of two principles, (3) the principles are opposed yet bound together, and (4) they are modified by the changes that successively result from them.[24]

Feeling responses are one such series of events bound together in a horizon of feelings. When a horizon contains deep feelings that are fundamentally, albeit imperceptibly, opposed to the calls of the notion of value and unrestricted being-in-love, our feeling responses may shift the quality of that opposition without truly resolving the conflict. Changes in feelings prompted by the notion of value and unrestricted being-in-love are met by other changes from the feelings of opposition and rebellion. The fundamental conflicts remain but change their manifestations. Such conflicts do not lead to refined or integrated feelings; instead, disturbances and insults early in life fester and grow. They can be displaced and take on new forms accompanied by newly imagined reasons for holding onto resentments.

These deep conflicts and tensions really seek changes more radical than can be achieved by these dialectical movements – changes that Lonergan called "conversions."[25] Conversions are radical types of decisions. Yet, at least in Lonergan's technical sense, conversions are not arbitrary decisions; rather, they are authentic decisions that respond to the tensions in our horizons of feelings. They are normative responses to objective values as they are intended in unrestricted value questioning and unrestricted being-in-love.

Conversions begin processes of fundamental reorganization of our horizons of feelings. Conversions move us towards properly ordered horizons of feelings. Still, decisions of conversion are only the beginning points for sustained resolutions of the fundamental tensions in our horizons of feelings.[26]

Conversion in Lonergan's sense is not the same as conversion in the more familiar sense – conversion to a particular organized religious group or to a political cause, for example. Conversion in his special sense could eventually lead to joining some such group, but that is not his basic meaning of conversion. Conversion in the more fundamental sense begins with an act of choice. It is a decision to follow the lead of the transcendental notion of value and being-in-love in an unrestricted fashion. Often enough the decision for the unrestricted value and love comes in the form of a decision against something that stands in opposition to them. Renouncing one's own bitterness about a past deed can be the expression of a decision to live according to the transcendental notion of value and unrestricted being-in-love. The act of renunciation is itself accompanied by feelings for the value of such an act, and these lead to further modifications in one's feeling horizon. These new feelings introduce new tensions calling eventually for still further decisions. Conversion is a decision we have to keep on making.[27]

Lonergan identified three kinds of conversions: intellectual, moral, and religious.[28] Robert Doran identified a fourth that he termed "psychic conversion," which Lonergan also acknowledged.[29] Of Lonergan's three conversions, his accounts of intellectual and religious are fairly straightforward, but moral conversion is the least clear.

8.3.1 Intellectual Conversion

Intellectual conversion begins with self-affirmation of the knower,[30] the judgment that cognitional structure is the correct account of how we really do know. Self-affirmation also includes knowledge of the most basic and profound consequences regarding objectivity and reality that follow from affirming that we truly do know by performing the cognitional structure.

Intellectual conversion builds upon self-affirmation by adding judgments of value and decisions that follow upon the affirmation of oneself as in fact operating with the cognitional structure. The judgments of value affirm the value of cooperating with the norms of questioning that are embedded in cognitional structure. Intellectual conversion as such, however, is a decision that follows upon the judgment of value. It is the decision to begin cooperating more fully with the exigences of cognitional structure. This means embracing inquiry and the grasp of the virtually unconditioned as the sole criteria for what one will count as knowledge. It is a decision to accept as real whatever and only whatever is to be known in virtually unconditioned judgments.

Typically, intellectual conversion also involves not only decisions that turn towards, but also decisions that turn away. The latter decisions come in a recurring series of renunciations of "the exceedingly stubborn myth … that knowing is like looking," along with all the implications regarding objectivity and reality that follow from that myth.[31] The myth is so stubborn because the notion that reality is what can be seen or touched is accompanied by feelings of security. To lose visibility and tangibility as criteria for reality will evoke anxieties. As long as one's horizon of feelings contains feelings of security and dread attached to mistaken notions of knowing, objectivity, and reality, these feelings will be in tension with the normative desires to understand correctly. Since understanding what is going on correctly is the first stage of ethical intentionality, sooner or later the absence of intellectual conversion will lead to false judgments of fact about what is going on. False judgments of fact will vitiate the objectivity of judgments of value when feelings respond to the supposed facts they falsely allege. False judgments will offer mistaken starting points for ethical reflection about what should be done in response to those false facts. Hence intellectual conversion is needed if our horizons of feeling are to be properly oriented not only towards factual truth but also towards true values.

8.3.2 *Religious Conversion*

Religious conversion is likewise a decision, a "total and permanent self-surrender without conditions, qualifications, reservations"[32] to the vocation of unrestricted being-in-love. Lonergan observes that just as being-in-love in an unconditional fashion is expressed in different ways, so also religious conversion as the decision to live out that gift is "interpreted differently in the context of different religious traditions."[33] Hence, as we noted above with regard to expressions of unrestricted being-in-love, Lonergan himself uses terms from the Christian tradition – such as "God" and "love" – while other traditions will employ different expressions in referring to religious conversion. Thus while religious conversion almost always occurs in the context of some religious tradition, and usually involves a subsequent decision to seek guidance in living out one's decision within some religious community, religious conversion in Lonergan's sense is more fundamental and is the foundation of any subsequent decisions to embrace a religious community or tradition – or not.

As a Christian theologian, Lonergan identifies God as the source of unrestricted being-in-love, and uses theistic language to characterize decisions of religious conversion for the sake of those who share his religious tradition: "There recurs the question of God in a new form. For now it is primarily a question of decision. Will I love him in return, or will I refuse? Will I live out the gift of his love, or will I hold back, turn away, withdraw?"[34]

Decisions of religious conversion also commonly include decisions of turning away from something. For example, a religious conversion can involve a sorrowful leaving behind of activities and acquaintances that are now understood to be obstacles to growth in a dedication to unconditional love. Then feelings of remorse and sorrow join with feelings of peace and fulfillment to introduce new dynamics into the horizons of feelings. More generally, religious conversion as the decision to grant unrestricted being-in-love the place of highest priority "dismantles and abolishes the horizon in which our knowing and choosing went on and it sets up a new horizon in which the love of God [i.e., being-in-love unconditionally] will transvalue our values and the eyes of that love will transform our knowing."[35]

Since the two basic sources of tensions in feeling horizons are unrestricted, and since they both thereby intend the totality of *all* that is of value, a decisive commitment to the vocation of unconditional love is needed to resolve the deepest disorienting tensions in our horizons of feelings.

8.3.3 *Moral Conversion*

What Lonergan had to say about moral conversion is less clear than what he said about either intellectual or religious conversion, so it is necessary to consider the several things he did say and to propose an interpretive synthesis.

At one point he characterized moral conversion as a change in "the criterion of one's decisions and choices from satisfactions to values,"[36] or as Doran puts it so keenly, "from impulse to value."[37] This, however, is only a partial account of moral conversion, for while a person may chose values over satisfactions, still her or his felt sense of value might be distorted. She or he might have feelings for only some values while oblivious to others, preferring false values over true ones, base values over more noble ones, and especially placing feelings for finite values ahead of feelings for the unlimited good intended by the transcendental notion of value and unrestricted being-in-love.

A more complete understanding of moral conversion can be drawn from Lonergan's accounts of what he calls "the existential discovery." He writes, for example, that

> the development of knowledge and the development of moral feeling lead to the existential discovery, the discovery of oneself as a moral being, the realization that one not only chooses between courses of action but also thereby makes oneself an authentic human being or an unauthentic one. With that discovery, there emerges in consciousness the significance of personal value and the meaning of personal responsibility.[38]

The double intentionality of each human decision that Lonergan mentions was discussed earlier.[39] But this passage focuses on what happens when a person *realizes* the fact of this double intentionality, along with the value dimensions that follow from this fact. Realization of the fact comes in a judgment of fact. Realization of the value dimensions comes in the feelings that respond to the fact known in that judgment. Those feelings reveal the awesome value of responsibility that is part and parcel of being a being who has the capacity to determine the value of her or his own life. Hence moral conversion begins both with the realization of a fact and with a major, accompanying shift in feelings.

In the passage, Lonergan points out that there are at least two distinguishable moments in this process. The first moment is the realization of the fact and value that in each of our decisions we are "producing the first and only edition" of ourselves, as he puts it.[40] This idea certainly did not originate with Lonergan. The esteem for human self-determination played a prominent role in the rise of modernity. It became the central preoccupation of the works of the existentialists, whose influence has lasted several generations. The existentialists' writings confronted readers with their own inauthenticity, unmasking the blatant or subtle ways in which we assign the blame for who we are to the deeds of others or the forces of nature, rather than accepting responsibility for ourselves. For many in the generations influenced by the existentialist authors, this was a bracing revelation. This existential discovery led many people to abandon previously comforting illusions about their responsibilities. Existentialist writings had also a most important influence on Lonergan's thought as well.[41]

Still, there is a second moment, for the realization that we determine who we are to be through our own choices is not yet moral conversion. Existentialist literature is filled with heroes resolutely accepting the fact that they alone decide their fates, but who choose selfish or nihilistic courses of action with no norms whatsoever to govern them. Frequently this pits the authentic existential hero against a society shown to be inauthentic by its lack of self-knowledge and self-determination. But it is also quite possible to make this existential discovery, and still decide to be a despicable person, because what matters is not society but *self*-determination. What matters is that *I* decide, not *what values* I decide upon. If the norms are all in my deciding alone, and nowhere else, then it does not seem to matter what I decide, only that I do so resolutely. It only matters that I am free of "bad faith," not blaming others or society or nature for who I am. People can accept this existential reality, and yet still choose according to a distorted set of values. As Lonergan puts it, "the paradox of the existentialist subject extends to the good existentialist subject."[42] In other words, just realizing that it is up to oneself to decide what to make of oneself does not guarantee that one will choose to be a good subject, especially if one thinks that one's own deciding is the only factor that determines what "good" is.

Cynthia Crysdale expands upon this point. She notes that moral conversion frequently begins with "the stark realization that even such heavily loaded and morally sanctioned pleasures may be, in fact, not coextensive with true value. The deepest desires of our hearts may be reaching for something else, something more (w)holly [*sic*] human." But such a realization is only a beginning. "Still, however thrilling such a discovery may be, it comes with the choice to engage in a long journey of discernment."[43]

There is, then, a second moment required for moral conversion. This second moment comes with the more complete understanding of just what it is we are doing when we are deciding, for deciding does not occur in a vacuum; it is not an act isolated from everything else. As I have been endeavouring to show thus far, deciding comes as the penultimate act in a structure of ethical intentionality. This means that deciding is what it is in virtue of its dynamic relationships to other acts of ethical intentionality, such as experiences, practical insights, feelings as intentional responses, ethical reflection, and virtually unconditioned judgments of value. Decisions are always realizations of practical insights and judgments of values. Furthermore, decisions proceed from ethical reflections that are surrounded by horizons of feelings for values. The unrestricted notion of value and unrestricted being-in-love, however, play the fundamental roles within our horizon of feelings. In the second existential moment, then, there is a fuller realization that the deciding that is up to oneself is a deciding to be the self that is always already caught up in the dynamics of feelings for *all* that is of value. Moral conversion is the culmination of this second moment. It is a decision to accept the fact that deciding always occurs within the structure of ethical intentionality with its unrestricted intention of all values. *Moral conversion is the decision to cooperate with this dynamic structure of activities in its rich pursuit of all values.*

The realization and acceptance involved in moral conversion situates one's own deciding, and indeed the personal value of one's life as one determines it, within a larger universe of values:

> Moral conversion goes beyond the value [of factual] truth, to values generally. It promotes the subject from cognitional to real self-transcendence. It sets [him or her] on a new, existential level of consciousness and establishes [him or her] as an originating value … Now [the] pursuit of [factual truth] is all the more meaningful and significant because it occurs within, and plays an essential role in, the far richer context of the pursuit of all values.[44]

One does not become morally converted by focusing exclusively upon the value of the person one is becoming while ignoring what seem to be the unrelated values, for moral conversion is a decision which will culminate in the personal acceptance of all values, including, for example, the values of health and athletic excellence, of virtuoso musical and dramatic performances, of masterpieces of fine art, of great discoveries in science and scholarship, of both great and ordinary acts of human kindness, of achievements in human social organization, of sacrifices for the sake of justice, of the all-surpassing value of the sacred, and so on.[45] Those who say they are committed to being authentic persons, while at the same time saying they care nothing for athletics or science or politics, are not morally converted. They are self-deceived.

Moral conversion places one's own decisions and other acts in a much larger whole universe of values, replete with its true rankings of value priorities. The questions that set ethical ("real") self-transcendence in motion are questions about true rather than apparent values. Morally converted persons have more and different questions about every potential course of action. Such persons do not ask merely whether this course of action will yield pleasure or even physical well-being. They go on to ask about and consider seriously how it would contribute to the improvement, preservation, or corruption of their society, their culture, their personhood, or the sanctification of the world. Such persons ask not merely how a course of action will affect them individually, or even how it will affect their immediate family and friends. They ask with seriousness about the implications for nature and for human beings distant on the globe and distant in the future. Morally converted ethical questioning challenges satisfaction and complacency, and moves us onwards towards judgments about true values. It therefore sometimes brings us to difficult judgments about our own selves, about the ways we have been living, about how our feelings have prioritized values, and about the need for profound and difficult changes. Questions about true values pursued without restriction bring up the questions about which values are truly and objectively greater or lesser. In particular, we raise questions about the value of ourselves as agents of moral self-transcending activities, and where we are situated in order of importance in relation to other values (and disvalues).

Moral conversion, then, is the acceptance of oneself as valuable and the realization that it is up to oneself to decide whether that value will be lived out authentically. But moral conversion is also situated within a whole realm of other values. What Lonergan says about moral conversion and the value of factual truth – that it "is all the more meaningful and significant because it occurs within, and plays an essential role in, the far richer context of the pursuit of all values" – can be equally said of the pursuit of personal (i.e., moral) value, for moral conversion also reveals "the significance of personal value and the meaning of personal responsibility."[46] Hence moral conversion has a very peculiar kind of reflexivity. On the one hand, the decision for moral conversion is the basic realization of moral self-transcendence – the choice of one's own value as the originator of one's own value. On the other hand, this decision also commits one to the understanding and value judgment of oneself as sublating all other values, and yet as standing within, but not at the pinnacle of, the realm of all values in its true and objective scale of value priorities. Moral conversion chooses what it knows from the comparative judgment of value that one's own personal value, grand though it be, is not itself the highest or most comprehending value.[47]

As with intellectual and religious conversions, moral conversion involves decisions that turn away, as well as those that turn towards, the full range of all value. In theory, moral conversion will involve repudiating any limited feeling and value that was previously functioning as the ultimate determination of a person's horizon of feelings. This could have been money, power, physical exercise, sex, scientific research, scholarly research, socializing with friends, or maintaining law and order.

In fact, it is often the case that pleasure, comfort, and avoidance of pain function as the highest values in people's value horizons, even when they would claim otherwise. This means that by means of their feelings as intentional responses such people take delight in, and give the highest felt preference to, the contents and acts of somatic feelings of pleasure and comfort, and respond to somatic feelings of pain, discomfort, and death with feelings that make decisions to avoid them at all costs the highest priority. Ethical writers frequently identify sensations of somatic pleasure and pain as the antagonists to ethical thinking, choosing, and living. But it is rather the ways that intentional feelings respond to the somatic feelings that are the sources of ethical corruption. Somatic feelings of pleasure and pain in themselves are natural and valuable components in human life. They provide data for questions about what should be sought and what should be avoided. Certainly extreme pains should be avoided – but not at *all* costs. We judge as heroes those who risk extreme pain and even death for the sake of genuinely higher values.

The proper values of various pleasures and pains in any human life are known only in judgments of value – provided those judgments are arrived at through processes of ethical reflection that are guided by a horizon of feelings that intends the whole of values in their proper relationships. Wherever our horizons of feelings have been dominated by any feelings for value that intend anything that falls short of the total range of all values, moral conversion begins a very difficult and unpleasant process of reorientation of one's horizon of feelings.[48]

Moral conversion, therefore, is a decision that originates from a judgment of fact and a shift in feelings. It is also a decision that fosters still further shifts in feelings, which tend towards the complete realignment of one's horizon of feelings so that the unrestricted notion of value and unrestricted being-in-love become central in that horizon, and that the actual, existential scale of preference in one's horizon becomes aligned with the objective, normative scale of values.

8.3.4 Moral Conversion and the Scale of Values

Moral conversion, then, is a decision to align one's horizon of feelings according to the ranking of the objective scale of values: "Not only do feelings respond to values. They do so in accord with some scale of preference. So we may distinguish vital, social, cultural, personal, and religious values in ascending order."[49]

Not only values but also their degrees of value importance are felt. The criterion of moral conversion, then, is feelings, judgments of value, decisions, and actions that are attuned to the objective scale of value preference. Though Lonergan seems to imply here that this ascending scale of value preference is a given in the consciousness of every human being, he later observes that it is achieved only through considerable effort and practice:

> But, once [feelings] have arisen, they may be reinforced by advertence and approval, and they may be curtailed by disapproval and distraction. Such reinforcement and curtailment not only will encourage some feelings and discourage others but also will modify one's spontaneous scale of preferences.[50]

At any moment, each of us feels values in relations of greater and lesser importance through the *de facto* ranking of our own horizons of feelings. As we have seen, the felt preferences for values within horizons of feelings can differ tremendously from one person to another. Yet there are always tensions, especially those introduced by the unrestricted notion of value and unrestricted being-in-love, that unsettle our consciousness of preference. The implication of Lonergan's remarks is to the effect that the objective scale of values that he proposes is a major source of those sets of tensions. Moral conversion is complete when we achieve full attunement with the objective scale of values. This attunement resolves those tensions.

When we deliberately decide to commit ourselves to the unrestricted notion of value and to unrestricted being-in-love, we thereby also commit ourselves to the normative scale of value preference. This is because both of these unrestricted feelings intend the whole realm of values in all their objective relationships to one another. If we do make this fundamental decision of moral conversion, then we embark along the path towards a horizon of feelings that begins to resolve these fundamental tensions and to reorient our value priorities.

Of course, our decision for moral conversion is only the "basic" actualization of our moral self-transcendence. As Lonergan puts it,

> Such conversion, of course, falls far short of moral perfection. Deciding is one thing, doing is another. One has yet to uncover and root out one's individual, group, and general bias. One has to keep distinct its elements of progress and its elements of decline. One has to keep scrutinizing one's intentional responses to values and their implicit scales of preference. One has to listen to criticism and protest. One has to remain ready to learn from others. For moral knowledge is the proper possession only of morally good [men and women] and, until one has merited that title, on has still to advance and learn.[51]

In other words, moral conversion is a decision that begins a path towards ever better moral living, in which discernment of one's questions, biases, intentional responses, and implicit scales of value plays an indispensable role.

People can and do make real and genuine decisions of moral conversion, with all that implies – that is to say, people can decide for values over against satisfaction and decide to cooperate with their innate desire to know and choose true versus apparent values. They can decide to live according to all values, not just some, and live those values in their real and objective scale of preference. Although each of these implied components may become clear only gradually, and decisions in favour of them may not come all at once, people nevertheless can and do make such a decision really and genuinely. Still, it can take the rest of a person's life to do the hard work of discernment and making the subsequent decisions required to readjust the actual horizon of feelings and scale of preferences about values that one had acquired up to the point at which the decision for moral conversion was made. In some sense, then, moral conversion is always an ongoing process, and there will be struggles to remain firm in one's resolve. Most people will fail, even fail miserably at times. Those failures can become so discouraging that for a time such people will give up on the effort of moral renewal. Most, however, will eventually recover and renew their commitment to live a life of authentic moral conversion and discernment.

As people grow in the reorientation that is the fruit of the decision for moral conversion, they begin to develop horizons of feelings that settle pertinence of further value-reflective questions in an unrestrictedly normative way. To the extent that through their feelings they prefer values according to the normative hierarchy of the objective scale of values, their virtually unconditioned judgments will reflect that normative order of values.

However most who have made the initial decision for moral conversion find that complete attainment of that goal is difficult. As Lonergan observes, "moral knowledge is the proper possession only of morally good" people.[52] Most of us remain short of this attainment, and as long as that is the case, our moral knowledge will be imperfect. Ultimately, then, objectivity in judgments of value in general and of ethical value in particular is something attained by people only to the extent that they have completed the difficult maturation process that is begun by their decisions for moral conversion and continued through sustained discernment. "Objectivity is the fruit of authentic subjectivity," as Lonergan puts it.[53]

Since the normative scale of value preference plays such a fundamental role in value objectivity, we need to explore that scale further, and this will be the topic of the next chapter. There in particular we will examine the phenomena of comparative judgments of value, and the decisions that follow from them. We will also consider what sort of justifications can be offered to support Lonergan's account of the ascending order of the scale of values. This analysis will enable us to fill out more fully what is meant by "moral conversion." Once the character of moral conversion has been clarified more fully, it will be possible to address the second of the questions posed in chapter 3: "Why is doing that being ethical?" This will be taken up in chapter 10.

8.3.5 *Illustrations of Moral Conversion*

Because Lonergan has been least clear about moral conversion, some concrete illustrations may help to clarify the discussions of the previous two sections. A number of examples of moral conversion can be found in literature. Perhaps the most famous is that narrated by Augustine in his *Confessions*. There he explains how his encounter with Platonic writings led him to profound realizations about good and evil. Much of what he had counted as evil in the world was not evil after all: "Evil, the origin of which I was trying to find, is not a substance, because if it were a substance it would be good."[54] He now realized that *whatever is,* is good, which opened before him the realm of the wholeness of value and being, replete with its objective scale of value: "Because [God] did not make them all equal, each single thing is good and collectively they are very good, for our God made his whole creation *very good* ... the sum of all creation is better than the higher things alone."[55]

Still, this was not yet moral conversion. Even though he had an intellectual realization about the wholeness of values, and even though he actually did love God, existentially Augustine was still prideful, choosing the value of his own self-authoring at the pinnacle of the scale of values. Only when he fully chose to accept where his personal value actually stood in the scale of values, and especially in relation to God, could he make the decisive commitment that was his moral conversion.[56]

A second illustration can be found in Dostoevsky's *Crime and Punishment*. Early in the story, Rodion Raskolnikov murders two women, and most of the novel probes the inner workings of his conscience in the wake of his crime. Although he could have offered many excuses and motives for his deed, in full honesty he confesses to Sonia, the woman who loves him, that in fact he just did it as a pure act of will, to show that he, like Napoleon, would stop at nothing to do whatever it took to be a great man. He had elevated his own personal value – his own value as an originator of values – over social and cultural values, even over the values of the vitality of life and the natural world. He has no real feelings for any other values than his own power of will.

Raskolnikov's path to moral conversion is long and tortuous. In the end it is Sonia's love for him that opens up his feelings to the values. But unconditional love working through Sonia has not finished its work. Rosemary Haughton writes that "Real knowledge of oneself is something that people can only dare to accept when love has broken through."[57] Haughton means especially that clear and unflinching knowledge of one's own evils – and the good that one *truly* is in spite of them – is only possible when a person knows himself or herself to be loved unconditionally. Dostoevsky traces how Sonia's love for Raskolnikov irresistibly wears down his final layers of self-deception and self-alienation.

After many years, Raskolnikov finally makes his converting decision, which is to love Sonia in turn, and all that she herself loves. Life now was not only sweet but abundant to the full. "Life had stepped into the place of theory and something quite different would work itself out in his mind."[58] Much earlier in her life Sonia had decisively committed to the whole realm of value with its objective scale of value hierarchy through her love of God. By his decision to love her, Raskolnikov has in fact chosen to love God and the whole order of value as God values it, just as Sonia had done earlier. His love of Sonia is simultaneously his religious and his moral conversion. Raskolnikov and Sonia recognize, though not with complete clarity, that much remains to "work itself out" as moral and religious conversion become his new principles of life.

A third example comes from the concluding section of *Pride and Prejudice*. The second half of the novel is devoted to the consequences of Elizabeth Bennet's discovery of her own prejudice (see section 7.2 of the previous chapter). In addition to narrating her maturation in objectivity and humility, the novel gradually reveals as well the true nobility of many of Darcy's deeds. But Darcy himself was also brought to a self-discovery and a change of feelings through Elizabeth's rebuff of his marriage proposal. Towards the novel's end, echoing the realizations of Augustine and Raskolnikov, he says to Elizabeth,

> I have been selfish all my life ... As a child I was taught what was *right,* but I was not taught to correct my temper. I was taught good principles, but was left to follow them in pride and conceit ... to care for none but my own family circle, to think meanly of the rest of the world, to *wish* at least to think meanly of their sense and worth compared to my own ... Such I might still have been, but for you ... You taught me a lesson, hard indeed at first, but most advantageous.[59]

The context makes it clear that Darcy has made some decisions about himself that brought about quite significant changes. He has now learned to situate the good moral principles he learned intellectually within a horizon of feelings that feels a much broader range of values – in fact, the value of "the rest of the world" that previously was beyond his valuing. This decisive broadening of his feeling horizon to embrace the whole of values is moral conversion.

Austen studies the events of moral conversion in *Pride and Prejudice* in isolation from intellectual, religious, and psychic conversion. For most people, however, moral conversion is intertwined with religious conversion, as it is in both the *Confessions* and *Crime and Punishment.* There are three reasons for this. First, moral conversion is a decision in favour of the whole of the realm of values intended by the unrestricted notion of value and unrestricted being-in-love. But unrestricted being-in-love is what Lonergan means by "religious experience," which he characterizes as being in love with God. Therefore, a moral conversion that commits to the realm of values intended by unrestricted being-in-love inevitably involves a religious conversion. Second, at least in Lonergan's rendering, the highest level of the scale of values is that of religious value. Therefore, if one embraces the whole realm of values in their objective relations to one another, commitment to religious values will at least be implicit in the decision of moral conversion. Third, the major obstacles to moral conversion in the examples given above were the biases and prejudices that blocked felt appreciation of the wholeness of values; moral conversion, then, can only be accomplished by turning away from those biases. According to Lonergan, Haughton, and numerous other religious authors, only the acceptance of unrestricted being-in-love can reveal such biases in all their ugliness and simultaneously heal them by casting light upon the far more attractive splendor of the whole realm of values. A decision that accepts unrestricted being-in-love is religious conversion, and seems to be the necessary condition for people to really turn away from such biases. Religious conversion, therefore, whether thought of explicitly in those terms or not, seems to be a condition for moral conversion. For Christians, of course, this is among the most fundamental of doctrines.

8.3.6 *Psychic Conversion*

Robert Doran identified a fourth type of conversion, which he called "psychic conversion." Doran explains that his idea about psychic conversion grew out of his simultaneous studies of Lonergan and Heidegger. Doran was struck by two things in this comparison. The first was Heidegger's statement in *Being and Time* that *Verstehen* (understanding) and *Befindlichkeit* (usually translated "state of mind," "disposition," or "mood") are equiprimordial in the constitution of the existence of a human being, *Dasein*. The second was that Lonergan's account of understanding was dramatically different from that of Heidegger. Still, Heidegger's claim about the fundamental relationship between *Verstehen* and *Befindlichkeit* led Doran to suspect that there had also to be something that stood in the same kind of relationship with Lonergan's unrestricted desire to know.

Doran has argued that the other pole in this fundamental relationship is the "sensitive psyche," which performs the role of selecting neural processes for conscious representation, admitting them into consciousness and organizing them into dynamic patterns of experience. He argues that in most people there has been a rupture of the spontaneous, natural collaboration between the unrestricted desire to know and the functioning of psychic selection and patterning. He became especially interested in the patterning of experiences and images that takes place in dreaming. He realized that dream images met Lonergan's definition of "symbol": "an image … that evokes a feeling or is evoked by a feeling."[60] He also agreed with Lonergan's analysis of the basic function of symbols: to provide communication between body, mind, and heart (i.e., what I have called the "horizon of feelings").[61] Since dreaming takes place beyond the effective control of our habitual knowing and valuing, dream symbols have the potential to initiate the major transformation that he called "psychic conversion":

> This fourth conversion establishes or re-establishes a link that should never have been broken, the link between the intentional operations of understanding, judgment, and decision, and the tidal movement that begins before consciousness, emerges into consciousness in the form of dream images and affects, continues to permeate intentional operations in the form of feelings, and reaches beyond these operations and states in the interpersonal relations and commitments that constitute families, communities, and religions.[62]

Psychic conversion, therefore, is another movement towards wholeness in which the resources of our neurophysiology are patterned in ways that promote ethical reflection under the guidance of the unrestricted notion of value and unrestricted being-in-love. As with the other conversions, this turning towards wholeness also involves a turning away. It involves breaking with the limitations of our previous patternings of experiences, as well as the limitations of our habitual knowing and valuing.

8.4   Conversion and Objectivity

At the beginning of this chapter, I proposed that judgments of value can be fully objective under certain conditions, although fulfillment of those conditions is not easy. In this chapter I have argued that conversion is the fulfillment of those conditions, and decisions that radically transform a person's horizons of knowing, feeling, valuing, and loving will clearly not be easy.

I have argued for the foundational character of the conversions in response to the problem posed by the role that our horizons of feelings play in our value reflective processes. It is possible to ask and answer all the questions that are pertinent to reaching a virtually unconditioned judgment of value. However, pertinence is determined by the ways in which our feelings are organized within our horizons of feelings. This means that our virtually unconditioned value judgments are objective *relative* to that constellation of our feelings. It can seem, therefore, that there could be no fully objective judgments of values unless there were some way to step outside our merely subjective horizon of feelings in order to gain access to some other ground for making unconditioned judgments of value.

In response to this problem, I have argued throughout this chapter that there are sources of tensions within our horizons of feelings themselves that point towards a foundational horizon for objective value judgments. That foundation is not attained by stepping outside of horizons of feelings altogether; rather, that foundation lies in radical transformations – conversions – of our horizons of feelings themselves. These conversions are radical because they are decisions to accept the normativity of the feelings of the unrestricted notion of value and unrestricted being-in-love – and by implication, to accept also the normative scale of value preference. Such decisions alone can begin to resolve the tensions in our horizons of feelings that arise out of these two fundamental feelings.

Because the unrestricted notion of value intends the whole realm of values, it serves as a source of criticism of the imperfections of our proposed courses of action, of our imperfect judgments of value and decisions, and even the imperfections in our unsettled horizons of feelings themselves. Because it is intrinsically related to the unrestricted notion of value, unrestricted being-in-love makes us conscious, not as a desire, but as a kind of mood, of the wholeness of the entire realm of values. Because the conversions are decisions in favour of these feelings as the ultimate standards for our value judging, converted horizons are the standards by which objective judgments of value and decisions can be arrived at.

This may strike the reader as excessively demanding as a standard for unqualified objective judgments of value and decisions. The reader might object that the conversions are such lofty standards that no human being could be expected to really make such decisions. It might be further objected that, surely, many people make objective judgments of value all the time, so something as rare as the conversions cannot really be the foundation of their judgments and ethical living.

I would respond by saying, first, that fully realizing and choosing to accept what deciding means – to accept oneself as self-determining within a wider realm of values – has already been achieved by many people without reliance upon the language used in this book. There are people who have made and continue to make decisions for moral conversion without using the sophisticated language of intentionality, analysis, and conversion. They also make the difficult decisions that continue the process by repudiating their falsely elevated values. They do so admirably without needing the complex analyses presented in this chapter. That analysis is needed, however, when mistaken ideas and resulting confusions arise concerning just what is involved in human deciding.

I would respond further that, apart from the individuals who actually do achieve the high standards of conversion as the foundation for their ethical thoughts, actions, and living, many more people make objective value and ethical judgments and decisions within the contexts of their families, friendships, work settings, societies, and cultures. Chapters 11 and 12 will explore how virtually unconditioned judgments and consequent decisions bring about human patterns of cooperation, institutions, and cultures. These patterns of human interaction embody intelligible forms of cooperation grasped by practical insights and values affirmed in the value judgments of their actors. These interactions form the situations from which ethical reflection takes its points of departure. The interactions also form the actors who participate in them. This means, among other things, that people share horizons of feelings for values with others.

When our feelings are shaped by cultural influences, we can be objective relative to that culture. We can share feelings and value judgments with a vast majority of members of our own culture. The values that we bring about will be recognized by others as objectively valuable contributions to the culture, because the value judgments and decisions will be underpinned by horizons of feelings that we share with them. But when our horizons conform to cultural norms, we can only be as objective as our culture is. No culture that ever has existed is a fully converted culture. So a person could be objective relative to a culture, without being completely objective.

Hence asking and answering further pertinent questions will lead to value judgments and decisions that are objective relative to the social and cultural situations, because they are also objective relative to the horizons of feelings that contributed to the value-constitution of the social situations themselves. In other words, people can make judgments of value and decisions that are virtually unconditioned in a social or cultural setting, because they have come to share the feelings for the values that are embodied in those social or cultural institutions. (Of course people can and do misunderstand and misjudge the values of their society. But then they would not be virtually unconditioned understandings and valuings.)

Thus when it is objected that people make objective value judgments and decisions without being converted in the senses discussed previously, it is possible to agree that indeed there are judgments of value that are objective relative to the social setting. But social and cultural settings can themselves be called into question. The standard for reaching virtually unconditioned judgments about cultures themselves cannot be a superior cultural context. The standard is, rather, converted persons who have arisen within some cultural context. This topic will be addressed at length in chapters 15–16. For the present, however, let me bring to a close the discussion of the objectivity of judgments of value and the decisions and actions that follow from them.

9 Judgments of Comparative Value and the Scale of Value Preference

9.1 Introduction

The previous two chapters explored tensions that are present in our horizons of feelings and how they enter into our processes of value reflection. These tensions in our feelings may be so intense that they dominate our consciousness to the point of paralysis. Or they may be so subtle that they are noticeable only by those who are exceptionally discerning. The previous chapter also led to the conclusion that objectivity in judgments of value and ethical value in the fullest sense depends upon moral conversion, which begins the process of resolving the most fundamental tensions, those arising from the ways our other feelings conflict with the unrestricted notion of value and the experience of unrestricted being-in-love. Moral conversion is a decisive commitment to a horizon of feelings that embraces the whole range of values.

Yet within this totality, our feelings and the values that they intend are not all of the same kind. Some values are felt to be more precious than others. Some disvalues are felt to be greater evils than others. This comes to light especially when we must choose among values. Moral conversion is thus also a decisive commitment to feelings of preference that accord with the objective hierarchy or scale that obtains among the values themselves. Such feelings of preference will accord with that hierarchy when they are also in harmony with the unrestricted notion of value and with unrestricted being-in-love. Then judgments of value made within such a horizon of feelings will be objective in the unqualified sense, because the unrestricted notion of value and the unrestricted being-in-love intend the totality of values in all their dimensions.

Each of us unavoidably prefers some values over others. While each of us has a horizon of feelings that is structured by one or another scale of value preference, that scale is not automatically the normative, objective scale. Deviations from the objective scale leave traces in the form of unresolved, often subtle tensions, which point us towards the persistence of still more primordial feelings of preference for the objective scale of values.

Moral conversion begins the realignment of feelings of value preference that resolves these tensions, but it is only a beginning. Moral conversion initiates the reorientation of our own, personal existential scale of feelings of preference towards feelings that prefer values in accord with the objective scale. This reorientation is prompted by the set of tensions within our feeling horizons that pertain to our feelings of value preference in particular.

In this chapter I delve more deeply into these tensions that exist within our feelings of value preferences in order to explore that objective scale of value preference. In doing so, I take advantage of the access to personal existential scales of value preferences afforded by the phenomena of judgments of comparative values. Felt scales of value preference play especially significant roles when we endeavour to reach judgments and decisions concerning value comparisons – that is, when we judge and choose some values over others. This chapter begins, therefore, with exercises in intentionality analysis of judgments of comparative value and their correlative acts of consciousness. Thereby the exploration of ethical intentionality becomes much more concrete, since virtually all ethical judgments and decisions are matters of comparative value. Once the feelings of preference and their unresolved tensions are brought to light, the chapter then proceeds to explore their relation to the objective scale of values through Scheler's analysis of *ressentiment*. I then compare Lonergan's account of that scale to those of Scheler and von Hildebrand, who influenced Lonergan's thinking on this topic. Finally, I consider how Lonergan's own account of the objective scale of value preference can be used to better understand the movements and tensions in our feelings of preference and our judgments and decisions of comparative value.

9.2   Judgments of Comparative Value and Scales of Preference

While our deliberations constantly involve scales of value preference, this is not always so evident to us. We do not always notice their presence or understand how they are influencing our ethical thinking and choosing. Thus I offer some exercises to facilitate attention to and understanding of their roles in our deliberations. These exercises focus on the concrete and complicated processes of deliberating about comparative values, in order to better discern feelings of value preference and their tensions. This section begins with some general comments about the processes of coming to judgments of comparative values, and then offers some concrete illustrations to help readers better understand what they are doing in making such judgments. In particular, the illustrations are intended to aid the reader in understanding the roles that feelings of value preference play in reaching such judgments and decisions, and the tensions that accompany feelings of value preference.

9.2.1 *Reflections on Value Comparison in General*

Lonergan comments only briefly regarding judgments of comparative value: "Judgments of value are simple or comparative. They affirm or deny that some *x* is truly or only apparently good. Or they compare distinct instances of the truly good to affirm or deny that one is better or more important, or more urgent than the other."[1]

His remarks imply a two-stage process for deliberation: first we come to judge courses of action as truly worthwhile, not just apparently so; second, we then reflect further in order to judge and decide which among these true values is better, more important, or more urgent.

In order to appropriate what he means, we must make our focus more concrete, and no longer think of deliberation as though it were concerned exclusively with judging and choosing values singly. Most often our ethical reflections concern comparisons of values. Most often we are confronted with more complex situations of conflicts not only between good versus evil, but also between what is better or worse. Hegel wrote, "The real tragedy of existence is not the conflict between right and wrong but between right and right."[2] At the other end of the spectrum, President Kennedy was quoted as saying that the most important choices are between bad and worse.

Most often we deliberate about which value is better or more important or more urgent. When we do so, our own scale of value preference is operating, even if we are not attending to it. The great ethical dilemmas that capture public attention almost always have to do with questions of what is the better thing or the least harmful thing to do. These dilemmas will remain difficult to resolve as long as the nature and function of feelings of value preference remain obscure.

9.2.2 *Some Illustrations of Reflecting about Value Comparisons*

It is better, therefore, not to turn attention initially to the most dramatic, earth-shattering, life-changing choices that have affected the courses of our lives. These momentous decisions not only depend upon, but also radically transform, our scales of value preference. Such decisions follow upon very complicated deliberations about value comparisons and are therefore not well suited to initial exercises in discerning the various activities within these deliberations. Fully appropriating the notion of a scale of value preference will eventually require turning attention to such major decisions, including decisions of conversion. However, that is not the best place to start.

It is better to begin instead by paying attention to some mundane, everyday moments of deliberation, opening with questions along the lines of "Should I choose this or that or some other valuable possible course of action?" The deliberations then proceed through a series of further questions, the pertinence of which is established by feelings of value preference. Noticing what is going on requires discernment – in this case, making efforts to recall in slow motion mental activities that often occur in a few seconds or less of real time.

Consider, for instance, the following illustrations of some instances of such deliberating from my own recent past:

- Whether to order entrée *A* or *B* from a restaurant menu.
- Whether to vacuum the living room or to read a philosophy book.
- Whether to stick daily to an exercise time early in the morning, or to allow academic work to impinge upon that time.
- Whether to attend a lecture co-sponsored by my department in my official role as chairperson of the Philosophy Department or to attend my son's high school soccer game.
- Whether to attend my own uncle's funeral service, or to give a presentation at a national conference.
- Whether to babysit my grandson, or to attend a meeting of the parish council of which I was a member.

Each of these examples is presented as a binary either/or, and often our deliberations do come down to two final options. But sometimes our deliberations are among several alternatives. No doubt the reader also can identify similar instances of common daily judgments and choices among competing alternative courses of action and their values. The following comments about my own deliberations are offered with the intention of highlighting certain features that I believe are present in most people's ethical reflections and deliberations about value comparisons.

9.2.3 *Time and Comparative Values*

Space and especially time are almost always key parameters when we reflect and deliberate about comparative values. We often juggle our schedules and parcel out our time so as to choose several courses of action as valuable.

We decide to undertake one course of action now and plan to do others at later times. But there are concrete circumstances determined by considerations of space and time which dictate that only one of the alternative values can actually be chosen. In all of the cases mentioned above, I affirmed both alternative courses of action as worthwhile, and in the abstract I could have decided in favour of both. Concretely, however, it was only possible for me to use my time in realizing just one out of each of the pairs of values that I listed. By choosing to move or place my body in a certain way at a specific time, I was realizing one value and committing myself to it in preference to the other.

In *Insight*, Lonergan speaks of the "data" of experience. Data comes from the Latin word *datum* for "what is given" – in this case, given to us. Lonergan makes it clear that while time and space may not be exactly equivalent to prime potency (the most basic of all givens), they are nearly so.[3] Of all the basic and precious gifts that we are given, time and space are among the most elemental. When we choose between values, then, we almost always choose what we are to make of the most elemental and precious of our gifts, especially our time. We use the metaphor of "spending" our time and in doing so tacitly acknowledge this most basic phenomenological fact. Our time is given to us that we may commit ourselves to values in the realm of the good proportionate to human reflection and choice. We can realize these choices only by giving form (i.e., an intelligible course of action) and value to the pure potency of our gifts of time. When we do so – when we spend our time to be with friends or families, to study or exercise, to enjoy entertainment, to serve a community or an organization, or pray to God – we realize *this* value in particular rather than any of the many other possible values upon which we could have spent our time.

When Lonergan commented that comparative judgments of value involve affirming or denying that one value is more urgent than another, he was adverting to the temporal dimension of making judgments and decisions of value comparison. Some values can only be realized in a narrow span of time, and to miss that window of opportunity would be to forsake that value. Life is a prime example of a value that becomes urgent in comparisons. When a life can be preserved only by an action performed in the nick of time, the value of that life becomes urgent in comparison to all other values.

When time allows us to choose only one course of action over others, which one do we choose? What value priorities do those courses of actions actually have for us, and what priorities did the actions forsaken actually have? Time provides the surest measure for identifying our actual scale of value priorities, the scale with which we actually operate, rather than the ones we proclaim to ourselves and others. Soberly and honestly recalling a series of such moments of decision will help us begin to notice and understand the scale of felt value preference that actually operates within our ethical reflections – what I will call our existential scale of value preferences.

9.2.4 Felt Scales and Concrete Deliberations

As I deliberated about the everyday choices that I listed above, numerous acts of consciousness entered into the mix. For example, I had previously made the decision to co-sponsor the lecture mentioned above in my capacity as department chairperson. In doing so, I expressed to the primary sponsor – the director of another program at my university – that not only did I personally value the speaker and the topic of the lecture, but also, as chairperson, I expressed the endorsement of my department as well. If, as chairperson, I now decided not to attend the lecture, I asked myself, how would the primary sponsor react? Would she conclude that I did not value the lecture as much as she did, and not as much as I should have? I was pretty sure she would. Would she conclude that the support of my department was empty? Would this compromise my department's ability to undertake future cooperative endeavours? As I was asking myself these questions, my feeling preferences for all these values (and disvalues) came into play as I deliberated.

On the other side of the comparison, my son played many soccer games. Would he feel let down if I missed just one? He repeatedly told me that he would not. But of course, I had to be attentive, intelligent, and critical about what he did *not* say, as well as what he did say. Would he be accepting on the surface, yet feel a deeper disappointment that he could not articulate? Other important questions entering into this concrete decision included the fact that all the rest of my son's home games conflicted with my class times. I asked myself whether I might cancel a class in order to attend one of his other home games. But in my own scale of feeling preference, holding classes as promised ranks very high, and this preference determined that the question of cancelling a class for this purpose would not be pertinent. This is especially so because, while I feel the value of fulfilling job responsibilities very highly, I feel the value of education even more highly. Also important in my decision were the memories and feelings about my own father making sacrifices, often taking time from work, to attend the school athletic contests of myself and my brothers. While we would have understood that he could not take time away from work, it nonetheless meant a great deal to us that he did come. We *felt* the way he valued us by being there for us.

All of these factors – the flow of questions, recollections, insights, feelings, prior judgments, etc. – entered into my reflections about this particular judgment and decision as I deliberated about this question of comparative value. In the end, I went to my son's game. The primary sponsor was quite unhappy with my decision, as I expected, and I felt badly about her reaction – that is to say, I could feel the way she felt the disvalue of my non-attendance, and I felt the disvalue of my diminishment in her esteem. In the end, it was my felt scale of preference that determined which questions and insights were, and which were not, pertinent to this judgment and decision of comparative value. That scale determined where the value of attending that lecture stood in comparison with the values of attending my son's game and of keeping to my class schedule, among the other values I have mentioned.

I felt no regret about my decision to attend my son's soccer game. There were no remaining unresolved tensions in the feelings of value preference that guided my reflections, judgment, and decision. I felt the normativity of the scale of values that informed my ethical reflections in this case. Although I did feel tensions about my changed relationship with the program director, those feelings pointed towards future actions I would need to take in order to build a new relationship with her. But those felt tensions did not cause me to regret the decision I did make.

Likewise, in the other examples of deliberating about comparative values and choices, very concrete sequences of conscious acts took place. I did decide to decrease my physical exercise time, and this was in part influenced by the fact that I would usually be exercising all alone early in the morning, and my feeling for the vital value of healthy exercise was not strong in comparison to my desire for the social value of companionship. In my feelings, I was preferring certain other values over the vital value of exercising – a value preference that, in this specific and concrete case, involved unresolved tensions. I did give up exercise for a while, but as I now reflect I recognize that my feelings were not entirely at ease with that decision.

In another case, my deliberations about whether to attend the national conference or my uncle's funeral included memories and feelings of a once warm relationship that had grown distant, along with present feelings of close personal relationships and deeply shared goals with members of the national organization. I also considered the question of the money already spent on my airfare to the conference, but realized this was really not pertinent to the judgment and decision at hand. I now regret that I chose the conference over the funeral. My feelings of regret after the fact helped me discern the conflicts and inconsistencies in my existential scale of values. These tensions were already present prior to the decision I made. Had I been more discerning, I would have paid closer attention to these tensions and I would have been more disturbed by them beforehand. As it was, the feelings of regret that arose from the decision itself revealed not only that this was not the better course of action, but also revealed the disturbances in my own personal feelings of value preference. That regret and recognition led to subsequent revision of my feelings of preference.

In one further case, I did choose to babysit my grandson, because his parents had an important commitment to keep. In my felt sense of preference, the importance that this commitment had for them, and the importance that all three of them have for me, outweighed the importance of attending the parish council meeting. Did this mean I was choosing a personal or some other value over a religious value? In one sense, yes – but in another sense, no. As I look back, I detect no unresolved tensions in my feelings of value preference that were in play at the time, and I have no regret about that decision.

I do not offer any of these examples as models of normative ethical orientation. I present them as honestly as I can, as aids to readers in appropriating felt scales of value preference, and how they operate in comparative value judging and deciding.

9.2.5 *Ethical Reflection and Feeling Preferences in* Middlemarch

Further access to the role of feelings of value preference in judgments and decisions of comparative values can be had by attending to great works of literature. Although many other works certainly could be chosen, here I offer a brief reflection about an episode in the novel *Middlemarch* by George Eliot (Mary Ann Evans). Among other things, *Middlemarch* is a masterpiece in the discernment of ethical reflection, self-deception, and human behaviour. Although the chief protagonist of the novel is Dorothea Casaubon (née Brooke), the episode here concerns the internal struggles of one of the other main characters, the doctor Tertius Lydgate.

When Lydgate arrives in the provincial town of Middlemarch, he is passionately devoted to developing a new scientific approach to medical care. He prefers, therefore, to care for the poor whose illnesses are more interesting, as opposed to the ailments of the rich which are "monotonous, and one has to go through more fuss and listen deferentially to more nonsense."[4] Because his approach is so radical a departure from then prevailing medical practices, he incurs the enmity of the community's established doctors and has difficulty gaining the wealthy patients he would need in order to earn a comfortable living. Even so, his practice slowly grows.

Initially, he intends to defer marriage for some time in order to pursue his medical career, but he soon becomes attracted to Rosamond Vincy. He does not realize the wider social consequences of his flirtations with Rosamond – "the flower of Middlemarch"[5] – because he is almost willfully indifferent to the social conventions and the intense network of scrutiny and gossip in this local community. After being partly manipulated by various townspeople, Lydgate unexpectedly falls deeply in love with Rosamond and finds himself proposing to her with almost no prior deliberation. His decision is made within a horizon of feelings suddenly dominated by this new passion for Rosamond.

This decision is a dramatic departure from his previous resolutions. It is not supported by the kind of ethical reflections and judgments that took place within the context of his earlier, more staid horizon of feelings. Among other things, he did not ask or answer a wider set of questions regarding Rosamond's character, nor how marriage to her would affect his long-standing commitments to science and care for poor patients.

Rosamond was spoiled in her upbringing and was very self-indulgent. In his efforts to indulge her, Lydgate spends excessively on rent for a home and purchase of furnishings to begin their marriage. Within a few years he finds himself in debt well beyond the capacity of his practice to repay.

Lydgate deliberates about various possibilities, now much more soberly. He judges that the least objectionable option is to obtain a loan against their belongings, possibly including Rosamond's jewellery, from a local merchant. In addition, he also judges that they would have to severely curtail their spending to have any hope of meeting their debts.

Eliot describes Lydgate's state of mind as he deliberates about communicating this news to Rosamond: "Having been roused to discern consequences which he had never been in the habit of tracing, he was preparing to act on this discernment with some of the rigor (by no means all) that he would have applied in pursing experiment."[6]

The horizon of feelings within which Lydgate conducts his ethical deliberation shifted from one dominated by his medical and scientific concerns at first, then to one dominated by his love for his wife, and then to one in which anxieties about his financial situation loom large. Eliot describes the tensions and discontents permeating Lydgate's horizon: "It was the sense that there was a grand existence in thought and effective action lying around him, while his self was being narrowed into the miserable isolation of egoistic fears, and vulgar anxieties" about his financial situation.[7]

Unfortunately, Rosamond has been so spoiled that she is constitutionally incapable of understanding the desperateness of their financial situation. She first rebukes Lydgate for not really caring or trying hard enough, and then she attempts some foolhardy manoeuvres of her own, which have disastrous repercussions. Finally, she even suggests that he change his medical practice, adopting treatments that he knows to be ineffective, so as to pander to the rich. Lydgate finally expresses his rage at her responses to their situation, but immediately stops to think about where things are heading. Eliot reveals her keen powers of discernment as she narrates his reflections:

> It was as if a fracture in delicate crystal had begun, and he was afraid of any movement that might make it fatal. His marriage would be a mere piece of bitter irony if they could not go on loving each other. He had long ago made up his mind to what he thought was her negative character – her want of sensibility, which showed itself in disregard both of his specific wishes and of his general aims. The first great disappointment had been borne: the tender devotedness and docile adoration of the ideal wife must be renounced, and life must be taken up on a lower stage of expectation, as it is by men who have lost their limbs. But the real wife had not only her claims, she had still a hold on his heart, and it was his intense desire that the hold should remain strong. In marriage, the certainty, "She will never love me much," is easier to bear than the fear, "I shall love her no more." Hence, after that outburst, his inward effort was entirely to excuse her, and to blame the hard circumstances which were partly his fault. He tried that evening, by petting her, to heal the wound he had made in the morning, and it was not in Rosamond's nature to be repellent or sulky; indeed, she welcomed the signs that her husband loved her and was under her control. But this was something quite distinct from loving *him*.[8]

That Lydgate compared giving up his fantasy of "the ideal wife" to losing arms or legs does not recommend his character to contemporary sensibilities that have been formed by feminist critiques. Yet while Eliot does present this consideration with full irony, she also characterizes Lydgate as a genuinely decent, virtuous, and loving man, who in spite of his biases is far nobler than most other males in Middlemarch. He has not stopped loving "the real wife" despite his feelings of disappointment, and his dismay at her selfish obtuseness. He realizes that his feelings of anger at her obstinacy and of urgency about the practical realities that must be faced have introduced tensions into his feelings of value priority – tensions that threaten his love for Rosamond. Eliot provides a vivid expression of that grave threat with her compelling image of an impending fracture of a delicate crystal. Although threatened, Lydgate's love for Rosamond remains the highest of all his feelings for values, even surpassing the value of being loved in return – "The real wife had not only her claims, she had still a hold on his heart, and it was his intense desire that the hold should remain strong." His decision to do whatever it takes to sustain his love reinforces the feelings of comparative value in line with this supreme value.

Lydgate feels the value of his love for Rosamond as the highest of all values, and he makes his judgments of values and choices accordingly. His subsequent reflections, judgments, and decisions flow from this even more firmly felt scale of value preferences. These begin with his decision to excuse Rosamond (in his own mind) from any responsibility for his financial plight and the injury to his reputation, although he does not entirely face responsibility for his own poor decisions, blaming instead "the hard circumstances" that led to his financial woes.

Later in the novel he finally decides reluctantly to approach Rosamond's wealthy banker uncle Bulstrode for help. Lydgate knows that Bulstrode is disliked in the community, in part because of his wealth, in part because of his manipulations in local politics, and in part because he is highly judgmental and moralistic. Bulstrode also committed a crime which for a long time remains hidden from other characters in the novel, though not from readers.

Although he does not yet know of Bulstrode's crime, Lydgate nevertheless has formed quite an objective judgment about his character. He feels repelled by Bulstrode and prefers to have little to do with him. But Bulstrode offered him the superintendency of his newly established fever hospital, which would give him a unique opportunity to serve the poor and to explore treatments scientifically. Lydgate tries to convince himself that he can confine his relationship with Bulstrode solely to this professional arena, but the association taints Lydgate's reputation in the eyes of society.

Lydgate overcomes his repugnance at forming any further association with Bulstrode because of the overriding value of maintaining his loving relationship with his wife. Initially Bulstrode refuses Lydgate's petition, but later changes his mind when he fears that Lydgate might have learned damning information from a patient (though in fact he had not). When the information does become public, Lydgate is unjustly suspected of conspiring with Bulstrode in a dastardly crime, although he is completely innocent. He realizes that because his financial relief from Bulstrode is public knowledge, any attempt on his part to defend himself will only intensify the suspicions. In retrospect, Lydgate knows that his ruined reputation could have been avoided had he attended to the tensions in his feelings for Bulstrode and given them proper priority in relation to his love for Rosamond. They leave Middlemarch. Lydgate gives up his ambitions to develop scientific medicine, and builds a more conventional and more lucrative practice. Nevertheless, writes Eliot, "he always regarded himself as a failure: he had not done what he once meant to do."[9]

But, in another sense of course, he did exactly what he intended to do – love Rosamond with his whole heart, no matter the cost. That love determined the scale of the rest of his values. No doubt many would fault Lydgate for subjugating and ultimately abandoning his scientific values in order to sustain love for his wife. Eliot, however, is more concerned with the fate of a decent man in a corrupt society who loves not wisely but too well.

My brief summary and analysis of this episode in *Middlemarch* does not do justice to Eliot's subtle discernment of the many levels and tensions in human feelings of value preference. The novel explores in depth the feelings and actions of a broad range of ordinary, even petty lives (its subtitle is "*A Study of Provincial Life*"). Eliot lays before the reader the feelings of her many characters, and what follows from their different scales of felt preference as they collide with one another. The novel invites criticisms of those various scales of values.

Each of us has some felt scale of value preferences. This very fact raises questions: Is my own scale of value preferences correct? Are there others? What are they? Which if any, are correct? If none are correct, which are at least better than the others? Which ones are defective? Is there a scale of value preference by means of which I can adjudicate various scales of value preference? Is there any scale of feelings of value preference that is the correct and objective one?

We will return to these questions later in this chapter and again in chapter 14. The present goal has been to offer a concrete illustration of the tensions and movements among the feelings of preference, judgments, and decisions of value-comparison that occur in ordinary life. The reader's own discernment will be aided much more by careful reading of the whole of *Middlemarch* as well as other such masterful literary studies of inward reflection.

9.3   Scheler on Intimations of the Objective Scale

The previous sections have illustrated how individual or existential scales of felt value preference guide ethical reflection in reaching comparative judgments of value. In this section I turn again to the work of Max Scheler in order to explore the manner in which feelings for an objective, normative scale of values may be said to be present and operative in every individual's horizon of feelings. He argued that these feelings of normative value preference are present, no matter how much someone's individual, existential scale of value preference may deviate from this objective scale.

In particular I will focus on Scheler's study of *ressentiment*. *Ressentiment* is arguably the most severe form of distortion of feelings of value preference. My proposal is that if the objective scale still makes itself felt even in the consciousnesses of people deeply mired in *ressentiment*, then the normativity of that scale is also accessible through the tensions experienced in the horizons of feeling of people with less severe distortions in their feelings of preference.

Scheler devoted considerable attention to the phenomena of felt scales of value preference – what he referred to as the *ordo amoris*, borrowing from Augustine.[10] The acuity of his discernment regarding these phenomena is especially prominent in his book *Ressentiment*. There Scheler considers Nietzsche's claim that *ressentiment* is the most important root of Western and Christian morality. While Scheler agrees with Nietzsche that *ressentiment* is indeed a powerful dynamic in Western culture, he disagrees that it is the real root of Christian morality. Instead, he argues that there is a normative scale of value preferences, and that *ressentiment* is a secondary, although profound distortion of that scale in our feelings. Nietzsche, of course, would not have agreed with the full range of Scheler's scale of values, or that *ressentiment* is an inversion of that scale. He held, instead, that the *ressentiment* of Western and Christian morality was a distorted revolt primarily against vital values.

Scheler and Nietzsche both retained the French word *ressentiment* as it has no exact equivalent in German (or English for that matter). While *ressentiment* might be translated "re-feeling," it is specifically a form of re-feeling that is directed towards past feelings of injury or perceived injury, or feelings of inadequacy or failure, recalling feelings of one's own impotence in the face of value challenges and brooding with an inability to let go of those experiences. One keeps reliving and rehearsing them, causing the feelings to swell and fester. The torment of such a re-feeling can be great indeed, and as Scheler notes, "the painful tension demands relief."[11] He observes that people tend to overcome "any strong tension between desire [for a higher value] and impotence by depreciating or denying the positive value of the desired object."[12] In other words, once our feelings have been tricked into feeling that the desired value is not so great after all, the experience of inability to attain that value no longer feels so demeaning. This felt depreciation of values spreads, however, in some cases resulting in an inversion of the whole scale of values.

With his acute discernment, however, Scheler recognized that the psychic strategy of *ressentiment* is never completely successful: "*Ressentiment* man … now feels 'good,' 'pure,' and 'human' – at least in the conscious layers of his mind. He is delivered from hatred, from the tormenting desire of an impossible revenge, though deep down his poisoned sense of life and *the true values may still shine through the illusory ones*."[13]

Scheler recognized that there are subtle self-deceits involved in these inversions of feelings of preference. No matter how advanced *ressentiment* may have become – no matter how "good" we may feel within this feeling dis-orientation – there remain felt tensions which are the traces of its origin as a departure from the fundamental and normative scale of values. In other words, *ressentiment* is always felt as a secondary reaction in relation to the normative felt value scale from which it arose. When Scheler uses the phrase "shine through," he is referring to these subtle, unresolved tensions in our horizons of feelings between our actual scales of value preference and the objective scale. Stated differently, in *ressentiment,* actual feelings of value preference are a compound of the spontaneous and normative feelings of preference for the objective scale of values on the one hand, and the secondary reactions that modify and distort those primordial feelings of preference, on the other. Such secondary reactions are in tension with the retained primordial feelings which they modify and the scale they intend. These unresolved tensions are also felt, and therefore point back to the objective scale of value preference, providing an internal access to that scale, and to standards according to which any account of that scale must be judged from the viewpoint of anyone with *ressentiment*-oriented feelings of value preference. There is no need to appeal to criteria foreign to such a person's horizon of feelings; these unresolved tensions are themselves the criteria for such an appeal.

Ressentiment is a severe and relatively widespread form of deviation from the objective scale of value, but it is by no means the only such deviation. Other less pernicious deviations also exist – deviations where one value is undeservedly ranked highest without necessarily inverting all the rest of the scale. Yet even less extreme deviations also give rise to tensions that are traces of their *departures from* the objective scale. In all such cases the more primordial objective scale also "shines through" – for example, in disproportionate flairs of defensiveness or anger or dogmatic attitudes, or when people show excess emotion in explaining or defending their value preferences. These are usually signs of unresolved tensions between their individual, existential scales of feeling preferences, and the primordial normative scale.

We will discuss what Scheler regarded as the objective scale of values in the next section. For present purposes, however, Scheler's observations point out that there are criteria always immanent and operative in the feeling horizons of every person, no matter how perverse, which point to the objective scale of value preference.

Lonergan's work adds to that of Scheler the idea that the tensions felt in *ressentiment* and other deviations from the objective scale ultimately derive even more fundamentally from the unrestricted notion of value and unrestricted being-in-love. Because they are unrestricted, these two fundamental feelings intend the whole realm of values along with the objective hierarchical relations among them. Objective feelings of value preference arise from these two sources. The primordial feelings of preference for the objective scale are grounded, therefore, in the notion of value and unrestricted being-in-love. This means that the objective scale is not merely a social or cultural construction; nor is this set of value priorities imposed from without by authority. Rather, the adequacy of various authorities must be evaluated in the light of the scale already evident in the tensions in horizons of feelings, even in the consciousnesses of people with grossly distorted actual scales of value preferences.

I do endorse Scheler's claim that there are the felt traces of the normative scale in every person's horizon of feelings. It is the task of discernment, therefore, to pay attention to the tensions among feelings for values, then to understand these tensions fully. This would include asking whether one's individual scale of values shows traces of defensiveness or a dogmatic attitude that point beyond one's own scale to another scale more deeply felt.

9.4   Lonergan, Scheler, and von Hildebrand Compared[14]

Still, it is one thing to say that the unresolved tensions in our feelings of value preference attest to this objective scale of values; it is quite another to give an accurate formulation to the structure of that scale. Lonergan offered his own terse formulation of that scale: "vital, social, cultural, personal, and religious values in ascending order."[15] His proposed scale is likely to be at some variance with the ones we actually use, but his is certainly not the only such formulation. It appears to differ from the scales of value hierarchy held in many different cultures, as well as those formulated by numerous philosophers. While the task of comparing Lonergan's formulation with all other contenders is not possible here,[16] it will prove instructive to at least compare it with those of Scheler and von Hildebrand, who most influenced Lonergan's thought on the topic. It is noteworthy that the formulations of scales of value preference espoused by Scheler and von Hildebrand differed from each other, just as Lonergan's differed from both of theirs. Both add a wealth of detail that is absent from Lonergan's discussion, and our understanding of the scale will be enhanced by consideration of these details. This comparison will provide further assistance in noticing and understanding the dynamics of our own feelings of preference and judgments of comparative values. It will also prepare the way for a later discussion of the justifications that might be offered in favour of Lonergan's formulation.

9.4.1   Scheler's Account of the Scale

Scheler approaches the scale (or "rank") of values by means of a kind of multidimensional coordinate axis system, rather than by a single, one-dimensional linear scale as Lonergan does. He distinguishes between "bearers" of values and value "qualities" (or "value-modalities"),[17] each forming something like a distinct axis within the realm of values. In addition, Scheler says that each value quality has its own proper feeling-functions and feeling-states. Scheler's scale of qualitative values is somewhat similar to that of Lonergan. Yet Scheler also identifies further subdivisions among the qualitative values themselves, which Lonergan does not attempt to do.

Scheler's scale of qualitative values is basically as follows: In ascending order, there are the values of the useful, the agreeable (i.e., the pleasant or enjoyable), the vital (e.g., the noble and ignoble), the spiritual, and the holy.[18] He is emphatic that there are positive and negative values at each level – for example, that the negative value of the ignoble is at the level of vital values along with the positive value of nobility.

Scheler explores subdivisions within the qualitative values in extensive but sometimes confusing detail. For example, his subdivisions of spiritual values include cognition, beauty and other aesthetic values, cultural values (which are said to include science and art), and ethical/moral values. He draws a further, keen distinction between the value of the *"pure cognition of truth"* in philosophy, in opposition to that of "positive 'science,'" which he claims is guided by the aim of controlling natural phenomena.[19] In addition, he groups utility and pleasantness together as "material values," but pleasantness is still ranked higher than utility with this grouping.[20]

Though rich in details, Scheler is not as clear or forthright as Lonergan in expressing the exact hierarchical ordering of his scale of qualitative values and subdivisions. His convoluted discussions make it difficult to derive a single, consistent formulation. I summarize Scheler's discussions of the scale (or ranking) of values in Figure 9.1.

Figure 9.1. Scheler's Scale (Ranking) of Values

Bearers of Values	Scale of Qualitative Values	Subdivisions
Persons/Things/Living Beings	Holy/Unholy	
Oneself/Others	Spiritual	Spiritual values: holiness, cognition, moral, beauty, cultural, social
Acts/Functions/Reactions		
Moral Tenor/Deeds/Success	Vital	Vital values: economic, nobility, ignobility
Intentional Feelings/States of Feelings	Material: Agreeable	
Terms/Relations/Forms of Relations	Material: Useful	
Individual/Collective		
"Self-Values"/Consecutive Values		

The entries in the column for "Bearers of Values" should not be thought of as corresponding one-to-one with the entries under "Scale of Qualitative Values." Rather, these two columns should be regarded as two independent axes orthogonal to one another, so that several value qualities may apply to each of the categories of value-bearers. The entries in the third column, on the other hand, do correspond to those in the second. This chart should be regarded as only approximate because of the many ambiguities in Scheler's discussion.

9.4.2 *Von Hildebrand's Account of the Scale*

Von Hildebrand was greatly influenced by Scheler, but departed from his formulation of the scale in significant ways. Still, like Scheler and Lonergan, von Hildebrand is emphatic that there is a unique, normative scale of feelings of value preference and that it is foundational in our consciousness of values.[21] Von Hildebrand also offers a multidimensional schema with four axes: ontological values, "capacities" or "parts" of entities, "domains" or "families" of qualitative values, and "types" of values within families.

In ascending order, his account of the scale of ontological values is things, plants, animals, and persons (including God). The scale of qualitative values likewise arranges the families or domains in a hierarchy: vital, aesthetic, intellectual, and moral. Interestingly, he does not explicitly include religious values or the value of the holy in his scale, although they permeate his discussions. He also drops from his scale Scheler's qualitative value of the useful, apparently because he regards the useful as an equivocal term.[22]

Furthermore, and most significantly, von Hildebrand drops Scheler's lowest level – that of the pleasant/unpleasant, the agreeable/disagreeable. He insists that the difference between satisfactions of the agreeable/disagreeable, on the one hand, and values, on the other, is not at all a matter of value rank. He says that the mere satisfaction derived from attending a party, for example, is not at all comparable to any value. According to him, a person oriented towards what is "merely subjectively satisfying" is "not even interested in the question of whether something is important [i.e., of value] in itself or not."[23] Therefore, the agreeable or satisfying is simply not on that scale of values in any way whatsoever. He chastises Scheler for missing this fundamental difference.[24]

Von Hildebrand further claims there is also a hierarchy within each of the families or domains of values: within vital values, sight is higher than taste; within intellectual values, depth is higher than acuteness; and within moral values, humility is higher than reliability. Unfortunately, he offers only a few examples such as these, and he does not propose any rules or criteria for thinking about why one of these pairs is higher than the other.[25]

Figure 9.2 presents a summary of von Hildebrand's discussion of the scale of values.

Figure 9.2. von Hildebrand's Scale of Values

Ontological Values (Values of existing entities)	Capacities and Parts	Qualitative Values (Domains/Families)	Types within Domains/Families
Persons (including God)	Will > Instinct Intellect > Sensation	Moral Intellectual	Humility > Reliability "Depth" > Acuteness
Animals		Aesthetic	Sight > Taste
Plants		Vital	
Non-living Material Things			
		Agreeable*	

*Not in the scale of values at all.

9.4.3   Similarities and Differences

These three thinkers all emphatically agree that there is one, normative scale of value despite the many human deviations from that norm, but all emphatically disagree with one another as to the details of this scale (see Figure 9.3). Scheler seems to be following Nietzsche and prior thinkers in classifying nobility as a vital value, where Lonergan would tend to call this a personal value. Lonergan also sharply differentiates between social and cultural values, and assigns a prominence to this distinction that is missing from the formulations of his predecessors. Likewise, he explicitly includes personal values on one and the same linear scale with the others, while Scheler and von Hildebrand treat these values as belonging to a completely distinct axis ("bearers" or "ontological values"). Lonergan places religious values highest on the scale, unlike von Hildebrand, who does not carve out a definite place for religious values.

On the other hand, both Scheler and von Hildebrand draw attention to many differentiations (or qualities, domains, or families) within what Lonergan regarded as a single generic level of value. These further subdivisions could be useful in further refining the appropriation of our own feelings and reflections about comparative values. Unfortunately, neither Scheler nor von Hildebrand offers much assistance in understanding why any of these subdivisions within a level should be regarded as higher or more choice-worthy than another, which limits the usefulness of their observations.

Finally, the comparison of the formulations of the scale of values by these three thinkers of course raises the question "Which, if any of these, is the correct or at least the most accurate formulation, and why is that the correct one?" This is a question to which we will return in chapter 14. Before doing so, however, it is necessary to first elaborate further Lonergan's account

Figure 9.3. Scales of Values Compared

Lonergan	von Hildebrand	Scheler
Religious		Holiness
Personal	Moral	
Cultural	Intellectual	Spiritual
Social	Aesthetic	
Vital	Vital	Vital
		Agreeable
		Useful
Agreeable*	Agreeable*	

* Not in the scale of values at all

of the scale. This clarification will set the stage for considering how his scale can be useful in discerning the operations of our acts of comparative judgments of value, and how his ranking can be justified as objective and normative.

9.5   Elaboration of Lonergan's Scale of Values

Lonergan's own account of the objective scale of value preference was introduced briefly in chapter 8. Once again, regarding that scale of values, he wrote, "Not only do feelings respond to values. They do so in accord with some scale of preference. So we may distinguish vital, social, cultural, personal, and religious values in ascending order."[26]

The words that Lonergan used in articulating his scale of values are familiar enough, and many of his readers have responded with enthusiastic endorsement of his way of articulating the normative scale. Yet he himself said very little about his scale or about what he meant by the words he used in this passage. It is necessary therefore to supplement what he explicitly said about the levels of values in his hierarchy. A fuller account of what he meant has to be inferred from other sources, and this will be taken up in chapter 14. For present purposes, I will rely upon his brief comments from *Method in Theology* for some provisional definitions to be used in this chapter.

Before going into the details for each of the particular levels in the scale, something needs to be said about the relations among the levels as such. First, the levels do not so much regard particular values but rather *orders* or *realms* of values. Nutrition is a vital value. So is procreation. Orderliness, reliability and efficiency all fall in the realm of social values. It is not primarily this or that value that is preferred over another, but orders of values as such that are preferred. Instances of values are preferred one over the other only derivatively, on the foundation of the relative preference of their genus.

Second, when we choose, we select a particular course of action and its value, and we thereby exclude others. But the scale of value preference is not a matter of preferring this *particular value* over that one; rather, it is a preference for one *order of values* over another. Still, this does not mean preferring one order of values only and forsaking all the others. Rather, it is a matter of a lower order of values *as* taken up, integrated, and relativized into a preferentially higher order of purpose, a higher order of values. In preferring social values, then, we value vital values such as life, health, vitality, and fertility *both* as vital *and* for the roles they play within social values such as cooperation or efficiency.

Third, while this preferring is of orders rather than of particular instances of values, particular instances of value can nevertheless become the focal points for the preferring of orders. For example, in *Middlemarch*, Lydgate feels the preference of orders through particular instances of those orders. He feels preferentially the order of personal values (in the person of Rosamond) over the order of cultural values (as exemplified in the value of new scientific medicine). His feelings about these values are genuinely conflicted and he struggles with this conflict between the value (science) over the personal value of love for his wife, but ultimately chooses according to what his felt preference reveals to him as genuinely higher. Because the person he loves is so spoiled, this means that his decision to live out the vocation to love Rosamond will require that he endure great sacrifice and injustice. This is what is entailed in these concrete circumstances by his decision in favour of personal value through the loving of this person. His decision reinforces his felt scale of value preferences. Had he decided otherwise – to pursue his scientific career knowing this would alienate his wife and his love for her, for example – this would have rebounded in a shift in his existential scale of values. But it would not have altered deep-down his invariant feeling of preference for personal values over cultural values.

Fourth, higher orders of values determine *how* lower orders of value will be realized when lower values are incorporated within the realizations of higher values. For example, a preference for social values does not exclude vital values (unless *ressentiment* is operative, as Nietzsche observed). Rather, a preference for social values determines the kinds of social arrangements that will be acceptable ways of realizing and sustaining vital values such as nutrition and procreation. These and other vital values can be realized in different ways according to different arrangements of social values.

Hence, courses of actions and their values on a lower-level are preferred and chosen in such ways as to realize, promote, and maintain values at the higher level. More succinctly, lower realms of values are felt to be for the sake of values at the higher levels of the scale.

These relationships will become clearer by considering each of the levels in Lonergan's scale in greater detail.

(a) Regarding *vital values,* Lonergan offers nothing more than a short list of examples: health, strength, grace, and vigour. Since these are all terms associated with the optimal functioning of biological organisms, it would be appropriate to add others such as nutrition, growth, development, flourishing, and fertility as examples of the values of biological homeostasis, growth, and reproduction. Notably absent from this list is survival, perhaps because while mere biological existence (survival) is a value, optimal biological functioning is what moves us to feel value preference. These vital values are opposed to disvalues such as starvation, illness, disease, weakness, lethargy, sterility, and atrophy, all of which are assigned to the symptoms of biological dysfunction.

Lonergan goes on to say that vital values are "normally preferred" to the "work, privations [and] pains" required to acquire, maintain, and restore vital values. This means that although vital values come lowest in his scale of value preference, they are not merely the basement class of values where everything of value that is preferred, is preferred over them. Rather, they are already first in the order of preferring, and they are preferred to mere comfort or satisfaction in particular. Feelings of preference for vital values themselves already call us to ethical reflection, decisions, and actions by means of which we transcend self-satisfaction with our present level of comfort, in order to take responsibility for more vitally valuable ways of living.

(b) The phrase "*social values*" calls to mind the mores of a society – the norms of appropriate behaviour in various social settings. In fact, for most people, being ethical means living in accord with social mores. These norms are promulgated far more frequently and effectively through informal social exchanges than by formal laws and their enforcement mechanisms. Yet in Lonergan's terminology many of the values carried by the mores of a society correspond to what he means by cultural values, so further clarification is needed.

Regarding social values themselves, Lonergan offers but a single illustration – "such as the good of order which conditions the vital values of the whole community"[27] – while only mentioning without further comment that such values are therefore to be preferred to the vital values of individual members of the community. Yet even these brief comments reveal the contrast between individual instances of vital values and the value of a whole that goes beyond those individual instances and makes possible their regular replenishment. We might say that social values have to do with the emergence, maintenance, and improvement of that whole, and would include the values of cooperative effort, order, dependability, efficiency, justice-as-fairness, and social tranquility. Social value is of the worth of the intelligible coordination of activities among many people with a minimum of confusion, frustration, chaos or violence. The latter would threaten not only the intelligible social order itself but also a host of vital values that it ensures with some regularity. Traffic laws, norms governing uses and exchanges of property, and the mores and laws surrounding marriage and citizenship, among other such structures, all serve to promote such social values as justice and tranquility. More will be said about the good of order and its relation to social values in chapters 11, 12, and 14, but this much will suffice for present purposes.

(c) Lonergan had his own unique way of distinguishing between social values and *cultural values*, but it must be distilled from several different texts. Those texts point to cultural values as the standards by which people reflect upon their ways of cooperating and living together. That reflecting has two different but complementary functions: maintenance and development. First, cultures develop specialized institutions and methods for reflection on practices in order to "discover, express, validate," the cultural values that provide a community with the "meaning and value in their living and operating."[28]

If social values of harmonious cooperation are promoted by truth in advertising and exchange, still such social values and practices can be realized in many different ways of interacting. When a person walks into a shop in Paris, unlike in New York City, it is expected that the shopper will greet the shopkeeper, "*Bonjour*," and that the shopkeeper will reply in kind. The same social value of honesty about products and exchange of goods for money is honoured in both cities. But the differences in customs and demeanour in the shops reveal different cultural ways of living. These cultural differences are distinct from the value of justice in economic exchange. They symbolize the larger complex of values that constitute French versus American culture. Nevertheless, the regular recurrence of acts that realize a social value such as fair exchange requires commitments to higher cultural values (such as citizenship or ethnic belonging), which serve to sustain and maintain them.

Cultures are wholes that integrate different sets of cultural values. Gestures, cultural customs, and symbols receive fuller articulation in the ways that a people tells the story of its identity. Each such story communicates the cultural values of their specific, historical way of living together. As Flanagan puts it, "A culture sets the conditions for developing the character of its people, or a culture is the people writ large ... The 'generalized other' of the culture is mediated through the 'super-ego' of the parents, and both become the inner voice of personal and social conscience for the child."[29]

Second, cultures also devise ways of reflecting that "criticize, correct, develop, improve" patterns of acting, cooperating, and living together.[30] In other words, cultural values do not merely provide justification in order to maintain a society's practices. They also criticize and correct those practices in order to foster value growth and development of the society. In fact, I think it is fair to say that Lonergan regarded improvement and development as the *proper* functions of culture and cultural values. In an unpublished manuscript, for example, he wrote, "Just as the good of order [i.e., social value] guarantees the continual recurrence of particular goods, so does cultural good not only enable the constant fluctuation and change occurring in the order to avoid aberrations but also directs it towards steady improvement."[31] In *Insight* he also hints that the proper function of cultural values is criticism for the sake of promoting development: "Culture is [our] capacity to ask, to reflect, to reach an answer that at once satisfies [our] intelligence and speaks to [our] heart. Now if [people] are to meet the challenge set by major decline and its longer cycle, it will be through their culture that they do so."[32]

This means cultural values are authentic if they perform their proper function of promoting social and personal development. While Lonergan's understanding of "development" will be explored more fully in chapter 12, for the present it can be said that cultural values are authentic to the extent that they motivate and guide a society to cooperate with the long-term unfolding of the unrestricted notion of value in its finality towards the realization of all values. In chapter 14 we will return to the examination of cultural values in relation to the other levels in Lonergan's scale of value preference.

Finally, there are other cultural values that are expressed tacitly in the ways people behave. These behaviours and values may deviate from the lofty values explicitly esteemed in the stories a culture tells about itself. They may also deviate from the authentic trajectory of the unrestricted notion of value. When they do so, the operative cultural values are undermining, rather than maintaining, a society's way of life. Cultural historians, sociologists, and anthropologists employ critical interpretive methods to make explicit the cultural values and meanings that are implicit in actions and words, but that escape the reflective thematization of the society itself. These scholars also criticize the ideological functions hidden within traditional stories of a culture. Lonergan's discussion of the methods for criticizing both acknowledged and unacknowledged dimensions of a culture will be taken up in part V.

(d) *Personal value* answers to the question "What good am I, he, or she?," not "What is one good *at* or good *for*?" The question, rather, concerns the good of oneself as one is. Personal value is the value of the wholeness of a person as self-transcending. We exhibit our human self-transcendence whenever we go beyond our current state – when, for example, we awaken in the morning to become sensitively conscious, or when we go beyond mere sensitive consciousness in asking and answering questions for intelligence and reflection. Yet the fullness of our self-transcendence (what Lonergan calls "moral self-transcendence") occurs when we engage in the activities of ethical reflection, choice, and consequent action.[33] In such activities we draw upon our prior self-transcending activities of experiencing, intelligence, and reasonableness, and incorporate these into deliberations. It is by means of this incorporation of many acts of consciousness into our decisions and actions that the wholeness of our way of being is realized. Personal value is the value of this wholeness.

I am indebted to Brian Cronin for clarifying the relationship between moral value and personal value in Lonergan's approach. Cronin writes, "In its specific sense, moral value refers to the value of the person as a whole person sublating all other values, to the person as a centre of interpersonal relations, to the person as deciding freely and responsibly, to produce the first and only edition of himself."[34]

In principle, our mere capacity for moral self-transcendence is itself a value – personal value. That capacity is immanent and operative in us, even when we deviate from responding authentically to the further pertinent questions that issue from the unrestricted notion of value. It is in virtue of that capacity and its operations that we are personal values.[35] Still, that value is only realized fully as a personal value when we reach virtually unconditioned judgments about the values of courses of action, choose to realize the values of those courses of action, and act to follow through on those commitments. When we make such choices, we actualize the double intentionality of values discussed in chapter 7. Simultaneously, we actualize two values – (i) the vital, social, or cultural value of the course of action, along with (ii) the personal value of ourselves as doers of what we have objectively judged to be the right thing for us to do.[36] Moral value is realized in us as persons when we know the value of what we should do and actually do it.[37]

While we can offer philosophical and theological accounts of the value of the person as a whole, it is only in and through love that people actually come to consciousness of personal value – the value of a person as a whole – in the most complete and most concrete way.[38]

When two persons are completely in love, and so long as they remain completely in love, they are one. Being-in-love *is* their oneness, their wholeness, the wholeness of their value as persons. Yet being-in-love is not the merger or absorption of *one* person into the *other* – a merger that would obliterate the identity of the first person.[39] Rather, *both are in* one and the same complete loving. Each is simultaneously conscious of the value of the wholeness of the other as well as of her or his own value. The value of each is the value of being-in-love. The lover is conscious of the value of the beloved because the beloved *is in* the love, and the lover is in that same love. It is the gift of being-in-love that makes them objectively loveable to one another.[40] Falling in love is the discovery that the value of both the lover and the beloved person abides in their loving.

When humans are in love, their love may be unrestricted or not. Lydgate at first was in a limited love for an "ideal," illusory Rosamond. He later came to unrestrictedly love the real, self-centred Rosamond. Lovers may think their love is unconditional when it is not, or their love may be unconditional, even though they may not explicitly know this to be the case. Whatever love they are in, limited or unrestricted, it is this love that determines the value of personhood for them. The connections between unrestricted love and the value of personhood will be explored further in the next section.

(e) Finally, *religious value* in its primary, paradigmatic, and absolute sense is the value felt by being-in-love in an unrestricted fashion. Because this being-in-love is the basic fulfillment of our unrestricted notion of value, it itself is also therefore unrestricted. This means that it is impossible to adequately formulate the value felt in that sublime being-in-love. Christians and some others use the term "God" to refer to this unconditional religious value. Muslims call this supreme value "Allah." Jews reverentially speak *Adoni* (LORD), substituting it in place of the ineffable name. Others use terms such as "the sacred." The meanings of such terms are elaborated and interpreted through the practices and writings of religious traditions, but they are authentic elaborations only to the extent that they derive their meaningfulness from unconditional being-in-love. As Lonergan puts it, "religious conversion is the event that gives the name, God, its primary and fundamental meaning."[41] Religious conversion is a total and permanent self-surrender without conditions, qualifications, or reservations to the vocation of unrestricted being-in-love.[42] It is a decision for the transcendent value of the sacred, the divine, that is felt and intended through unrestricted being-in-love.

Insofar as they are authentic, religious traditions instruct and model how religious value is to be realized in concrete circumstances. Such traditions, practices, symbols, and writings take on religious value themselves insofar as they result from authentic and objective reflecting, choosing, and acting undertaken within a horizon of feelings where this paradigmatic being-in-love unrestrictedly is the highest, most preferred, central, and guiding feeling of value. Of course, many actual behaviours that resemble authentic religious practices have lost their connection with the reality of unrestricted being-in-love, even while their practitioners proclaim or think of themselves as truly orthodox. When such pseudo-religious behaviours become widespread, they contaminate the authentic meaning of the religious values in a tradition.

Personal values are taken up, integrated, and given their fullest valuation within the context of authentic religious value. Complete and unconditional love is the unified value that differentiates itself into persons. The differences among persons emerge as differentiations within the unity of love the persons are in and remain in unconditionally. The value of persons is most fully and completely the value of the unity of unconditional love, out of which they are called to be emissaries and agents. To love another person unconditionally is to become one consciously with the unconditional loveliness and loveableness which is the value of that person. Love intends the value of the person as a whole, a value that transcends the person's obvious or hidden faults, and even transcends the disvalues that mar the fullness of their moral value.

This unrestricted being-in-love is a oneness that is not limited to the one other person upon whom one's loving attention is centred. In complete love we become one with *all* with whom we *are* in-love, with all whose value is to-be-in-love. To love one person unconditionally is to become conscious of that person as a loveable member of the unified value that is the loveableness of the historical community of all persons.

However, while being-in-love is a consciousness of this comm-unity with all persons within the nexus of personal relations that constitute human history, it is not yet a knowledge or a free and deliberate embrace of that unity. Arriving at this high degree of explicit knowledge and acceptance requires considerable further developments in understandings, feelings, judgments, and decisions.

Jesuit Fr. Gregory Boyle brings this to light in his sensitive reflections on his work with gang members in Los Angeles. In his book *Tattoos on the Heart*, he witnesses to the loveableness of each and every person, even those who have been involved in heinous gang-related crimes. He reports how recognition of such love has been transformative of the lives of hundreds of people. This transformative power comes from

> the loving, caring adult who pays attention. It's the community of unconditional love, representing the very "no matter whatness" of God ...
>
> Sometimes resilience arrives in the moment you discover your own unshakeable goodness. Poet Galway Kinnell writes, "Sometimes it's necessary to reteach a thing its loveliness."[43]

Boyle attests that the loveliness of persons is constituted by the unconditional love of God. Falling in love unrestrictedly with another person is falling into that unrestricted love, and finding the value of the beloved in there as well. Of course, this does not necessarily mean that the lover thinks of the love that she or he is in as the love of God. Most often the lover's attention is directed towards the beloved, rather than towards the unrestricted love that they are in.

It is in love that the value of a person as a whole is revealed. Other feelings feel the value of a person's physical appearance, physical strength or healthy vigour, their intelligence, practical know-how, wit, generosity, courage, self-control, aesthetic creativity, compassion, nobility, and other such qualities. But beyond these values of persons there is the value of personhood as a whole, apprehended fully only in unrestricted being-in-love. Love of the value of the wholeness of someone as a person is not limited to love for her or his achievements. It is love of a wholeness that precedes and in fact is the condition of those achievements.

Tad Dunne remarks that in love "we appreciate the value of one another simply for being."[44] His phrase, "simply for being" is apt, and yet invites fuller expansion. The being of a human person is the existence of an intelligible "unity, identity, whole," as Lonergan puts it.[45] But ontologically a human person is not just any sort of intelligible unity. Human persons are special kinds of intelligible unities characterized by the special acts of consciousness that they perform. What makes our acts of consciousness special (and so also we as the persons who perform them) is the fact that they are constituted as oriented towards complete and unlimited value and goodness – the value of unconditional love.[46]

Thus the wholeness of the value of human personhood analysed in the previous section is intended most concretely and most completely in unconditional love. Von Hildebrand makes this point when he writes:

> In the case of great love, we experience the lovability of the beloved
> as the only reason of our love; his beauty and goodness come as
> a complete surprise. But at the same time we experience that the
> beloved is the fulfillment of everything for which in an indistinct way
> and with our entire being we have always longed.[47]

It is in love that the wholeness of personal value is neither just longed for nor argued for, but now brought to full consciousness. Falling in love unrestrictedly is the coming to awareness of what has always been true all along, though not recognized – namely, the sublime value of being a person.

The fact that the full value of our personhood is brought to awareness by falling in love unrestrictedly in no way guarantees that we will respond with decisions and actions that are worthy expressions of that value. Tragically, we can and do betray the value that we and others are as persons, not only before we come to consciousness of that fact by falling in love, but even afterwards. We can disfigure our personhood as well as that of others by decisions and actions that fail to meet all the questions requisite for fully authentic actions. Nevertheless, even these actions manifest our value as unconditionally beloved precisely as disfigurement *of* that value of unconditional love. This is why it is possible to love another person, even knowing full well their flaws, and even knowing the evils they have done. Loveableness as the value of a person is even the condition of the possibility that persons can deliberately betray and reject love.[48]

These observations seem to imply that moral conversion to the full range of all values in their objective ranking must entail religious conversion. Religious conversion is specifically a conversion to the order of values (and especially to its supreme value) that is intended through being-in-love in an unrestricted manner. But if moral conversion is to a scale that includes religious value, it would seem that moral conversion must presuppose or at least go hand in hand with religious conversion. Again, since personal value is felt most fully through being-in-love without restrictions, this suggests that other values also receive their fullest felt valuation in such loving. On the other hand, it is quite possible that a decision to live according to being-in-love unrestrictedly may not yet have decided explicitly for all the values and the objective relations among those values that are only implicit in the decision for religious conversion. Full moral conversion, therefore, seems to be dependent upon religious conversion, and religious conversion seems to call for moral conversion, in order that both can attain their completions.

Lonergan frequently remarked that moral conversion most often follows religious conversion (though there are rare exceptions). Religious conversion is the decision to accept the transcendent value of unrestricted being-in-love. But this choice alone is not sufficient to reorient one's entire scale of value preference towards the objective scale. One can make such a choice without immediately realizing its consequences for one's existential scale of value preference. One can continue to value for a while pleasure or at least a comfortable life above all else. One can temporarily continue to regard physical fitness or legal orderliness or aesthetic refinement as the highest of all values, in ways that could eventually eat away at and undermine one's commitment to unconditional being-in-love. As the late Senator Harold Hughes once put it, a person can be genuinely "born again," but initially be capable only of consuming baby food; people who are religiously converted may need considerable further maturation, including moral conversion, before they can feel and live out the totality of the normative scale of value preference.

Moral conversion usually comes, then, as a decision about the normative scale of value preference that furthers and deepens religious conversion. This is not always so, but is so most frequently. Moral conversion can be a deepening of religious conversion even in the lives of people who have not joined explicitly religious communities, but in fact really have chosen unconditional being-in-love as their highest value. But when moral conversion does take place apart from religious conversion, it is a commitment to the normative order of the first four levels in the normative scale, but not to the fifth level. However, this is an inherently unstable commitment. As long as the morally converted person remains open to unconditional love, she or he will be able to think and act in accord with the normative order of the first four levels of value. Sooner or later, however, such persons will be faced with the need to articulate their moral stances in relation to traditions that are explicitly religious in the authentic sense. If such articulations become defensive or stereotyped, this will begin to produce unresolved tensions in their horizon of feelings. The proper resolution of these tensions comes only in the further choice of unrestricted being-in-love as the highest of values. This choice does not reject the first four levels of values, but sublates and integrates them into the context of being-in-love. If such a choice is deliberately rejected, it will become increasingly difficult to live out the normative order of the first four levels. Almost inevitably, some lower value will become ascendant and supplant higher cultural and personal values. The initial genuine commitment of moral conversion will be undermined.

More will be said about the levels of values later in subsequent chapters. Among other things, we will then consider whether or not Lonergan has accurately assigned these five genera of values their proper places in the hierarchical scale of values. The purpose of this section, however, was merely to provide some preliminary working clarifications of his terms.

Against the background of these clarifications, we turn to illustrate their usefulness in analysing more carefully the actual existential scales of felt preference with which we operate, as well as the tensions present within our feelings of preference.

9.6   Concrete Instances in the Light of Lonergan's Scale

In the earlier sections of this chapter I drew attention to concrete instances where feelings of preference played key roles in ethical reflection about value comparisons. However, I did so without offering a formal interpretive framework to enhance the understanding of those scales of preferences. In this section I now use the terms from Lonergan's scale to highlight some further features of these processes.

In the list of my own mundane reflections and deliberations about comparative values, I attempted to include decisions that touched upon all the levels of values that appear in Lonergan's scale – vital, social, cultural, personal, and religious values – and even the agreeable/pleasant (e.g., the restaurant menu).[49] It might seem at first glance that in order to be ethical we ought always to choose the higher value over the lower.[50] But if we attend carefully to our activities of value comparison in light of Lonergan's categories, this will help us to discover, perhaps surprisingly, that this is not what we always do. Nor is it clear that we should.

Consider, for instance, that each of us is committed to several different social roles – for me, this includes teacher, parent, administrator, friend, parishioner and council member, citizen, juror, and consumer, among others. Yet frequently we choose to devote time to one social role at the expense of another – for example, a particular span of time devoted to parenting might just as well have been spent working overtime, or vice versa. Here we are giving preference to one social value over another. What is the basis of this preference within the order of social values?

Sometimes it seems that we are in fact relying upon a *scale within the scale*; we are tacitly feeling distinctions and preferences within the category of social values themselves, for example. Yet, in other cases, do we choose to play one social role over another (and thereby commit to one social value over another) on the basis of a value from a distinct, higher level – cultural, personal, or religious? So, for example, we might choose to change jobs in order to perform some service to our country or because of the greater aesthetic enrichment that accompanies the new job (cultural values), or because it is a more genuine way to live out our religious faith. We might choose parenting over other social responsibilities because of the special value attached to parenthood by our particular cultural traditions or because of something from the still higher level of personal values – for example, the felt sense that in this case parenting is the right (moral) way to authentically realize the value of my own personhood. Or the exact reverse might be the case – choosing to neglect a job or parental role for the sake of pursuing a cultural ideal – star athlete or musician, successful business person, creative artistic genius, etc. In such cases some cultural value is felt as higher than mere social values, such as those associated with the social roles.

When we feel preference for, judge, and choose one lower-level value (e.g., social) because of a value at a higher level (e.g., personal), the higher level sublates the lower[51] – that is to say, the lower-level value is endorsed but incorporated as a constituent of the higher value, so that when we choose, say, to perform a social role because of our preference for a personal and moral value, this larger moral value incorporates the social value as a component. Then the social value is realized in the realization of our personal value.

Consider the young mother who leaves in the middle of a worship service in order to attend to the biological needs of her infant. Is this choosing vital values over religious values? Not necessarily and not usually. Most often it is really a matter of choosing the vital value and personal value of her child within the larger context of religious value that regards love and care for the child with its biological needs as the fulfillment of religious values.

These are just some preliminary examples of how using Lonergan's scale helps us to reflect upon our own activities of value preferring. Our comparative valuations and choices are very specific and concrete. They are very detailed, minutely graduated, and finely tuned. Therefore it is not possible to list a priori how all values will be preferred by specific individuals, even by those who are morally converted. While the generic levels of Lonergan's scale offer a framework for interpreting many of our value preferences, still his account of the ascending order does not determine all the subdivisions or nuances, or even the distortions in feeling preferences or choices. We will consider what justifications can be offered for Lonergan's way of situating particular kinds of values at their specific ranks in his hierarchy later in chapter 14. For the present, it is worth pointing out that Lonergan's account of the scale helps direct attention to aspects of the actual, existential scales that we actually do use. It helps us notice that in some cases our preferences are between generic levels in a hierarchical scale, while in others there may be a more refined preferential scale *within* a generic level itself. Using this scale in these ways can aid in discerning the details of the feelings of preference that inform our deliberations, judgments, and choices of comparative values.

9.7   Reason and the Priority of Feelings of Preference

Using Lonergan's scale in attending to our ordinary acts of evaluating and deliberating about comparative values reveals that the phenomenon of feeling preference is primordial. Whether we focus on our deliberations regarding judging and deciding for one level of values over another, or deciding among values within a given level, feelings of preference are always in play. They are perhaps the most significant dimension of our horizon of feelings. *Whenever* we apprehend a value through an act of intentional feeling, we always also feel that value as positioned, as ranked in a hierarchical scale of values. We do not just intend one value in one feeling, and then another value in a second feeling, and then compare them with one another, and finally somehow logically deduce where these values stand in comparison to one another. Value preferring is equiprimordial with value intending.

Lonergan makes this point when he observes, "Not only do feelings respond to values. They do so in accord with some scale of preference."[52] Scheler is even more emphatic:

> The "feeling" of values has its foundation, by essential necessity, in "preferring" and "placing after." The feeling of values is by no means a "foundation" for the manner of preferring, as though preferring were "added" to the values comprehended in a primary intention of the feeling as only a secondary act … Only those values which are originally given [in preferring] can *secondarily* be "felt." Hence, the *structure of preferring and placing after circumscribes* the value qualities that we feel.[53]
>
> One must not assume that the height of a value is *"felt"* in the same manner as the value itself, and that the higher value is *subsequently* "preferred" or "placed after." Rather, the height of a value is "given," by virtue of its essence, only *in* the act of preferring.[54]
>
> Therefore the order of the ranks of values can *never be deduced or derived*. Which value is "higher" can be comprehended only through the acts of preferring and placing after. There exists here an *intuitive "evidence of preference"* that cannot be replaced by logical deduction.[55]

This means that all feelings of values already and always occur within a felt scale of value preferring within our horizons of feelings. Each of our feelings of values always carries within it a felt sense of its place within a ranking or scale of values. This felt sense of value ranking is prior to our reasoning about such matters.

By insisting on the priority of feelings and a felt scale of value preference, Scheler is criticizing the limitations of a "reason alone" approach to matters of valuing and morality (and he explicitly criticizes Kant in particular). One cannot use reason alone to comprehend values, to establish values, or to establish the proper priority of one value over another.

However, I hasten to repeat my earlier qualification: Scheler's claim about the priority of feelings in consciousness of values – and now its extension to the priority of a felt scale in consciousness of value hierarchy – does not imply that reason has no role whatsoever in value knowledge or in ethical decisions. This is perhaps Lonergan's most important contribution to the discussion of feelings and values. From Lonergan as well as Scheler we learn that feelings are indispensable to value knowledge in general and to ethical knowledge, decision, and action in particular. Yet feelings alone are not sufficient to constitute decisions and actions as ethical. Although our primary *consciousness* of value hierarchy comes through feelings of preference, this is not the same as *knowing* which values are objectively higher than others. We do not by feelings alone know just where this or that value is ranked in the scale of value preferences, nor do we know whether or not our feeling preferences are objective and free of tensions. Nor do we know what we ought to do with regard to contending values. We have to gradually figure all this out. We do so by asking and answering questions of intelligence, reflection, and value. Importantly, these questions and answers presuppose the feelings, but they also go beyond them. All inquiries that lead to acts of understanding and judging presuppose some experiences. The relevant experiences here include the intentional feelings that intend values and value preferences. Before we understand or critically judge our felt value preferences, we have to experience them. Before we can form objective judgments of ethical value in order to make responsible decisions about comparative values, we have to experience feelings of value priority. Yet we need to actively go beyond the feelings as such to understand and critically evaluate our feelings.

We go beyond our feelings of value preference when we use our "reason" to form objective judgments of comparative value and to make responsible decisions, where by "reason" Lonergan "would understand the compound of activities on the first three levels of cognitional activity, namely, of experiencing, of understanding, and of judging."[56] To this compound we can add the further activities of ethical intentionality – what would amount to "practical reason" in Lonergan's sense. Our reasoning can be applied in two directions. On the one hand, it is employed under the guidance of our horizons of feelings and their felt value preferences as we reflect and deliberate about which courses of action and values we should choose. On the other, our reasoning can also be directed towards the feelings of preference themselves. When we reason to judgments and decisions concerning comparative values, our reasoning is guided by the prior experiences of felt value preference.

First, then, decisions are guided by feeling preference, but not completely determined by feelings of preference. In addition to the preference of feelings, we have to ask and answer questions about possible and obligatory courses of action. Questions for decision and action always pertain to concrete circumstances. When we decide, we decide to alter those circumstances, yet almost no set of circumstances is identical with any other. So while the normative scale of values is invariant, how it is to be realized in concrete circumstances varies and is known only by asking and answering the further questions that arise in response to those circumstances. What is right in every circumstance is beyond classification, but not beyond concrete reasoning.

Again, it is not just some transcendental ego that has to decide and act in this vast array of concrete circumstances in accord with the scale of value preferences. Each concretely existing person has to act. Even if everyone has the same scale of preference, this does not mean that everyone must make exactly the same decisions. Each of us brings to these moments of decision a host of previously acquired knowledge, skills, and prior commitments which are included in "what is going on" – that is, in the concrete circumstances to which our ethical actions would respond. So, for example, while abstractly it might be of the highest value to immediately repair by surgery the heart of someone in life-threatening cardiac trauma, in fact few if any people would be acting ethically if they tried to do this, precisely because they would lack the requisite knowledge and skill. It is our complex and concrete ways of ethical reflecting that bring us to the refined and corrected insights about courses of action that would be the ethical thing for each of us to do concretely, taking into account who we are, what we are capable of, and what the circumstances call for. Reasoning, therefore, is required above and beyond feelings of value preference to determine objective, ethical courses of action.

Second, we go beyond our feelings of value preference when we use our "reason" to discern – that is to say, critically assess our feelings of value preference. Although our reasoning to judgments and decisions about comparative values is guided by our own existential scale of value preferences, this scale is not necessarily an objective scale of value preference. Often the guidance of our feelings of preference remains at the implicit level of feelings alone without the fuller refinement that comes from understanding and criticizing those feelings of preference. The need for discernment, for full knowledge of our scale, arises because lack of clarity, or more profoundly, distortions in that scale, induce accompanying tensions in our horizon of feelings that undermine the objectivity of our value judgments and choices.

In order to deliberate responsibly, to arrive at virtually unconditioned comparative judgments of value, to make truly ethical decisions, we have to figure out just what values we concretely value as higher and lower, and to discern whether or not there are unresolved tensions among those preferences. The unavoidability of making decisions and the existential import of our unrestricted notion of value impel us to employ our self-correcting processes of knowing.

Unfortunately, authentic discernment is rarely done well, if at all. Most often our felt ranking just remains implicit. All too frequently we choose and act without fully engaging our feelings of value and value preference with the full range of our structure of ethical intentionality. Only seldom do we apply to our feelings the self-correcting cycle of learning that Lonergan calls reasoning – and that is one of the most important dimensions of what I have been calling the ethics of discernment. To the extent that we are faithful to the transcendental notion of value, we gradually make explicit for ourselves and come to terms with our own actual, existential, feeling scale of value preference and its tensions.[57] Doing so confronts us once again with the challenge of moral conversion.

9.8   Comparative Value Judgments about Questions to be Pursued

Thus far I have focused upon the spontaneous ways in which questions of value and further pertinent questions arise, and how feelings determine their pertinence in processes of value reflection. Yet our further questions of fact and value are infinite. Once a question arises, must it be pursued relentlessly, no matter what?

There are two factors that determine which further questions will be pursued: feelings and decisions. Up to this point, the role of feelings in determining pertinence of further questions has been explored. Positively, as we consider whether or not to pursue a possible course of action, our horizon of feelings provides us with the values for the sake of which that action might be undertaken. Our further pertinent questions scrutinize whether or not the course of action as understood would be compatible with the values as felt.

On the other hand, feelings can also be negative sources of bias that interfere with the self-correcting processes that would otherwise move forward in value and ethical reflection. In dramatic biases, fear prevents the emergence into consciousness of images or memories that would result in unwanted insights and lead to disturbing judgments of fact and value. Privileging one's own desires and fears leads to ignoring questions about the desires and fears of others and prevents the self-correction that rejects courses of action that would solve one's own problems at the expense of depriving or afflicting others. Group bias results when affections for one's intersubjective community interfere with questions about the well-being of people beyond the reach of one's intersubjective affections. General bias against theoretical insights and judgments results from the animal feelings of security that hold tight to the sense of reality as what is immediately at hand in space and time.[58]

Besides feelings that model values to be pursued and feelings that interfere with normative value reflection, we also determine which questions to pursue and which to leave aside through our decisions. In fact, we do make decisions all the time about which of our spontaneously occurring questions to pursue. Such decisions are made on the basis of judgments of comparative value. We have experiences of the further questions that arise within our consciousnesses. We can also ask further questions about those initial questions. We can have insights into those initial questions, and we can develop some understanding of what would be required to answer those questions. We can form fairly accurate estimates of how much time it would require of us. We might realize that we would have to talk with other people, read articles or web-search the topic, attend a training workshop or lecture, take a course, get a new degree, join a research group, and so on. We make these time assessments not only for one question but for related sets of questions. We come to realize that we do not have enough time to pursue all questions that occur to us. Judgments of value about the urgency of some situations and the values at stake enter into our comparative judgments about which questions are more important and valuable to us to pursue, and which less so. We can reach virtually unconditioned judgments about the values of pursuing each question in comparison with the others. On this basis we can ethically decide to pursue some further questions and not others.

Emergency situations bring about a variation in the dynamics of how we ethically deal with the large number of unanswered further questions. In cases of emergency, we can judge objectively that it is best to take a course of action, which still has some unanswered further questions about the best course of action, because the alternative of doing nothing will certainly result in greater harm.

In circumstances such as this, there is subtle change in the course of action under deliberation. The original question might have been "Would it be worthwhile for me to do X to realize value V in a concrete situation S?" About whether it is worthwhile or obligatory for me to do X in situation S, I may have many further pertinent questions. But as time runs out and an emergency becomes immanent, the situation changes from S to S', where S' includes the immanence of danger and the knowledge that there cannot be enough time to pursue all the further pertinent questions. The question of value thus changes – from a simple judgment of ethical value – "Would it be *worthwhile* to do X in order to realize value V in situation S?" – to an ethical judgment of comparative value – "Would X (or even X') be the *best* available alternative in order realize value V' that avoids evil, given the emergency situation S'?"

In emergency situations, then, people do and ought to act without asking and answering all the further questions that would have been relevant under different circumstances. But to do so ethically means to come to a comparative judgment of value that knows objectively that the best available thing to do is to set aside the further questions pertinent to X, and to embark on course of action X (or X') in order to realize value V' (minimize harm).

Whether in cases of emergency, or in the more leisurely circumstances of choosing which questions to pursue given the finitude of our lives, this means that we have to ask and answer all the further pertinent questions *about* which further pertinent questions are comparatively more worth pursuing than others. We do so in light of the realities of the time available to us, our talents, and the degree of urgency attached to each line of questioning.[59]

This dynamic is very different from the dynamics of the biases, where questions are ignored for no good reason at all. The fear of understanding, or the arbitrary privileging of one's own fears and desires, or those of one's own intersubjective group, is done at the level of feelings alone, not at the level of decisions grounded in objective judgments of comparative value. Still, objective judgments of comparative value even in emergency situations presuppose moral conversion that brings one's own existential scale of value preference into alignment with the normative objective scale.

9.9   Moral Conversion Revisited

In chapter 8 I argued that instead of thinking of moral conversion as the break from satisfaction to value, it would be more accurate to think about it in terms of the distinctions within the normative scale of value preference – that is to say, moral conversion should be regarded not as a shift away from absolute indifference in feelings regarding all values, but as a shift within an individual's actual, felt structure of value preference. It would be a shift towards the normative scale of value preference within one's intentional feelings. So conceived, moral conversion would overcome partial or distorted value blindness, and would not be exclusively a matter of overcoming absolute value indifference. This shift in the scale of value preference can proceed along a number of different paths and pass through a number of stages.

A first path of moral conversion would be from a truncated to a full scale of value preference. For example, a fitness fanatic might be totally preoccupied with vital values and have no effective feeling for social, cultural, personal, or religious values. A religious fanatic might be indifferent to vital and social values. A business mogul might have intense feelings for the economic good of his or her business empire with no appreciation for cultural values. A certain kind of scholar might value the realm of her or his research to the exclusion of all else. The feelings of such people would be truncated in their effective capacity to feel the values in other levels of the normative scale. These, of course, are stereotypes; no one's actual scale of value preference is quite so simplistic or crude. These stereotypes are offered solely to indicate what I mean by a truncated scale of value preference, and how moral conversion could be thought of as an expansion of one's actual feelings of value preferring towards encompassing the full scale.

A second path of moral conversion would be a conversion of a person's actual felt sense of preference from a distorted, towards the objective, scale of values. In the most profound cases, this would involve turning away from *ressentiment*, and becoming free to feel the goodness even of values that one is not personally able to attain. In lesser cases, this might mean a shift in feelings from orientation towards lesser-level values towards values at a higher level. Perhaps the most common examples of this are people once driven by ambition to reach the highest utilitarian values (e.g., wealth) who suddenly become profoundly committed to what Lonergan calls social, cultural, or personal values.[60] A person's felt preferring already would include, say, social and cultural values, but these would be belittled in order to elevate vital values inauthentically. Or, on the other hand, social, cultural, or religious values might be verbally extolled as higher, but in fact function as no more than put-downs of vital values. They might be praised as higher, but genuine felt preference for these higher levels of values would be absent. The differences between these two types of moral conversion are no doubt subtle, and careful attention to particular cases would be required in order to discern these differences. Nevertheless, I think both kinds of distortions in value preference may be familiar to most readers.

A third way of thinking about the path of moral conversion is in terms of the stages that have been suggested by Elizabeth Murray. She argues that there is both a positive and a negative dimension to moral conversion.[61] Her analysis takes as its point of departure a remark by Lonergan:

> Just as there is development from a theory of knowledge in terms of intuition to a theory of knowledge in terms of intelligence and judgment, so also there is the moral development of the subject from an aesthetic sphere that is concerned with objects of appetite … There is the reversal, the conversion, the transformation, of that type of organization in the subject to bring [him or her] into harmony with the objective good of order.[62]

Murray proposes that there are two moments in moral conversion. In the first moment, there is a turning away from a life organized "around the satisfactions of one's appetites and interests." The second moment is a turning towards a life "organized around the good as known intelligently and reasonably – the objective good."[63]

These two ways of organizing ethical living run parallel to the first two levels in what Lonergan called "the structure of the human good."[64] Murray also identifies a third moment in moral conversion, having to do with the enrichment of the notion of value and the role of feelings in value consciousness.[65] Although she does not explicitly identify this third moment with the third level in Lonergan's structure of the human good, I think this is implicit in both her article and in Lonergan's writings. At this third level of the human good, activities are organized around values and the personal relations which embody those values.

Murray's important identification of three moments in moral conversion can, therefore, be developed in terms of the structure of the human good. Lonergan's account of the levels of the human good will be discussed in detail in chapters 11 and 12. Yet the implications of Murray's contributions regarding moral conversion are best taken up here. To anticipate the later discussion, Lonergan identified three levels in the structure of the human good: particular goods, institutional orders as good, and terminal values as good.[66] At a first, primitive stage, the good for newborns is limited to particular goods that satisfy their desires or allay their aversions and fears. Some people never rise any higher in their feelings for the good.

The next stage in moral conversion looked at in this way is a transitional stage. As people mature morally, they begin to appreciate the good of laws, rules, and institutional orders. They tend to evaluate these, however, in terms of particular goods. Institutions are only regarded as good insofar as they serve to provide particular goods that meet the needs presented by particular desires or fears. Laws are to be obeyed only because of the undesirable particular evils that result from their enforcement.

While some people never get beyond this transitional stage, the movement towards more complete moral conversion does take an important step to a second, full-fledged stage when people do understand institutions as good in their own right. Insofar as laws and institutional arrangements are truly intelligible (and not merely ideological cloaks that perpetuate unintelligible exercises of power), they have value in themselves. Genuinely intelligible institutions transform individualized efforts into larger, cooperative wholes. Being together and accomplishing projects together is a good that cannot be reduced to the mere aggregate of satisfactions of individual desires.

People at this second full stage of moral conversion will tend to work for the preservation of institutions because they recognize their goodness, which Lonergan referred to as the "good of order." But as Murray observes, if development of a person's moral conversion becomes frozen at this second stage, it can take on a "cold, vice-like grip on one's actions, to aim for nothing more than" moral rational consistency.[67]

Moral development, however, can transcend the limitations of this second stage. There is a still higher level in the human good that recognizes institutions as the means, not to particular goods, but rather to the good of the whole of human history. Earlier institutions set the conditions out of which new institutions can later grow. The whole sequence of such growth is itself a good that goes beyond the good of any limited institution or the limited satisfaction of individual desires. People at the third stage of moral conversion recognize that institutions can and do contribute to bringing about the good of the whole of human history. When people reach the third stage of moral conversion, they commit themselves to working with institutional orders so as to promote the good of history. They do not limit their further questions to their own immediate desires and fears, nor to the goods of intersubjective communities or currently functioning institutions. They are concerned for the well-being of generations and the state of the earth far into the future.

9.10   Objectivity and Lonergan's Formulation of the Scale

The preceding reflections reveal, among other things, that our own existential scales of value preference expand to include complex gradations within as well as across the levels of values that Lonergan enumerates. Hence scales of value preference are far more complex than Lonergan's simple formulation of the scale would seem to indicate. For that matter, they are even more complex than the scales proposed and discussed at much greater length by either Scheler or von Hildebrand. In fact, their complexity seems to defy complete and adequate formulation in words. If this is the case, then what is the point to these formulations of scales of value preference, which are so streamlined and schematic?

The answer to this question must be indirect. For what defies formulation in words – philosophical words at least – does not necessarily defy expression by symbolic and artistic means. Where philosophical language pales in comparison to the finely tuned details of our unarticulated feelings and felt preferences, art and symbol strive to explore and give rich and concrete expressions to this realm. Still, while symbolic and artistic expressions (such as George Eliot's *Middlemarch* and Jane Austen's *Pride and Prejudice*) can meet the need for expressing, slowing down, and exploring the richness and detail of our valuings as concretely felt, these forms of expression are not designed to meet other kinds of needs. Symbolic and artistic expressions draw their audiences into realms of imagination and feeling, and in doing so they evoke not only new feelings but also new questions ("What does this mean?" being the most common) that they themselves are not prepared to answer.

Hence symbols and art often need to be supplemented by philosophical and other kinds of interpretive expressions. Each type of expression provides a contribution to the exploration of feelings and felt horizons of value preference that the other modes do not and cannot provide. I propose that Lonergan's philosophical formulation of the scale of value preference is meant to play one such role. Its role is not the impossible task of formulating the unfathomable richness of felt value preferences; rather, its role is to provide a heuristic for interpreting and reflecting on these feelings and the various attempts to give expression to them.

As we attempt to appropriate and make explicit how our felt scale of value preference really functions in our deliberating, we will be surprised (or perhaps not so surprised) to find that our actual, implicit scale of values may be different from what we believed that scale to be. Indeed, our own existential scale of value preferring may differ from what we think it ought to be. We might very well believe that our feeling and choosing of comparative values aligns perfectly with the objective scale, but on a regular basis we may very well not notice or understand that in fact we are choosing certain values over other values in ways that violate the objective scale and give rise to tensions in our feelings of value preference. Our own, personal, felt scale of value preferences is revealed in the ways it actually directs our concrete patterns of comparative choices and in the comparative judgments of value that stand behind those choices. In order to notice and understand the divergence between the actual scale of preference to which we are existentially committed and the objective scale, we need some sort of guidance. Lonergan set forth his formulation of the scale to provide such guidance.

This brings us back to the question of objectivity in judgments of value and ethical value in particular. Objectivity in judgments and decisions regarding comparative values rests upon the normativity of the feeling-scale of value preference or, to use Lonergan's own language, the objectivity of our judgments and decisions regarding comparative values rests upon the self-transcendence of our feelings,[68] and our feelings are self-transcending to the extent that our actual, existential scale of preference is aligned with the objective scale of value preference. We can only be as authentic and objective in making comparative judgments of value and choices as our own existential felt scale of value preference enables us to be. When we deliberate and reflect ethically, the "marshalling and weighing" of the further pertinent questions and other factors will be governed ultimately by our feelings, feelings which unavoidably prefer some values to others. If our actual, existential scale is biased or otherwise distorted, so also will be our judgments and choices. Hence the questions of what is *the* normative scale of value preference, and how to best bring oneself into harmony with it, are of the utmost importance.

The importance of Lonergan's formulation of the scale of value preference, therefore, is that it offers a standard of comparison. As such, it functions similarly to what Lonergan regards as the role of ideal types in historical and social-science investigations. Even though they are too generic for the complexity of concrete social and historical situations, they still direct attention to some things and also help us notice what might be otherwise overlooked.[69]

Such, I believe, is also the case with Lonergan's formulation of the scale of values. It is really a heuristic formulation of what might be called value *genera*.[70] Lonergan's formulation lacks the more specific details suggested by Scheler and von Hildebrand of the internal hierarchy of each value genus, but to expect something more detailed is perhaps to miss the point of Lonergan's way of formulating the scale. His formulation is not some mathematical algorithm – plug in the situation and it will print out for you a decision regarding which value to choose over the others. His formulation of the scale cannot substitute for the ongoing and difficult processes of growth in insights, in feelings, in discerning, in ethical reflection and judgment, or in responsibly deciding and action. His formulation is no substitute for the even more difficult processes of withdrawing from inauthenticity by attending to the unresolved tensions in our feelings of value preference, in trying to understand them, and in making decisions that will bring our actual feelings of preference more closely into alignment with the objective scale of values. As Lonergan put it, "One has to keep scrutinizing one's intentional responses to value and their implicit scales of preference."[71]

What his formulation does offer is a standard for comparison. Our own existential scales of values are subject to the gross distortions of *ressentiment* and less severe deviations from normativity. We catch some of these distortions from our cultures; others are of our own making. In either case, our own value preferences reverse and invert the proper order of value hierarchy. Such distortions and their resultant tensions can be brought to light by reflecting on something like Lonergan's formulation of the scale of values. When we begin to prefer vital values over social values (neglecting our job responsibilities in order to "buff up" our physiques, for example), Lonergan's scale can bring this to our attention. Or again, if we prefer to bury ourselves in the social value of mere work in order to evade developing, more refined cultural values, Lonergan's scale can point to this inversion and distortion. And if we choose, say, one social value over another, using Lonergan's scale helps us to notice this, even though it is not explicitly treated in his formulation.

Of course this task of bringing value distortion to light is also performed effectively and flexibly by the long traditions of commonsense value formation. Good traditions of parenting are far more effective in cultivating scales of value formation and in combating value distortion than a dozen books in philosophy or theology. Again, refined ascetic traditions of spiritual direction, meditation, and prayer (such as those of Ignatius) are especially effective in value discernment and formation, and in undoing value distortion. These traditions of spiritual practices are found throughout the history of world cultures and world religions. They often provide effective and practical guidance for heightening the very highest of religious values. That is to say, spiritual practices can be very effective in heightening our awareness of the indwelling gift of being-in-love in an unrestricted fashion. They can provide further guidance for contemplating other values in felt-comparison to this highest of values. In doing so, traditions effectively model and shape normative scales of value preferring in people's feeling lives.

Unfortunately, these traditions themselves can (and have) also become infected with distorted feelings of value preference. Among other things, therefore, I think Lonergan also offered his account of the scale of value preference in order that it might play a role in the critical mediation and correction of commonsense cultural traditions, as well as traditions of spirituality.[72]

Lonergan's way of articulating the scale of value preference is heuristic, but no more than heuristic. It makes strong claims about the proper axiological priority among value-genera, but leaves the ordering of the value-species to be worked out by people as they live their lives. It calls attention to unresolved tensions among feelings at different levels of the scale, but leaves it to individuals to respond to those tensions. It offers no more than a heuristic for the global orientation of the life of human feelings. Lonergan seems to be saying, "Is the *whole* of your feeling scale of preference attuned to this scale of values, or is it in rebellion against this scale?" He appears to be assuming that when this generic heuristic scale is intact, the other dimensions of a person's feelings of preference will gradually develop normatively because his or her horizon of feelings and its scale of value preferences is properly oriented. This need not mean, of course, that people for whom the scale of value preference is properly oriented will be completely free of biases or value distortions. In effect, however, Lonergan seems to be inferring that such distortions can be overcome.[73] The greatest distortions arise when *ressentiment* sinks in its vicious roots and perverts the generic order as such. The greatest of evils ensue when there are such major distortions of the generic scale of values.

In formulating this heuristic account of the scale of values, therefore, Lonergan intended to offer an important heuristic tool. Methodical use of this scale of values can enhance the capacity of individual persons, of cultural traditions, and of traditions of spiritual practices to notice and rectify distortions in value preference. It can provide them with anticipations of growth and development in valuing. Such, I believe, is the role that Lonergan meant his formulation of the scale to play.

If this is so, then of course the question of whether or not Lonergan's formulation accurately captures at least these broad dimensions of the objective scale of values is of utmost importance. This question will be addressed in chapter 14.

10 Self-Appropriation Part II: Why Is Doing That Being Ethical?

*Self-appropriation leads to a discovery that the self to be appropriated has to develop ...
It is the discovery that willingness is something that has to be developed to increase my
effective freedom.*

— Bernard Lonergan, *Understanding and Being*

10.1 Introduction

Chapter 4 proposed to pursue the ethics of discernment in terms of three
questions that parallel Lonergan's three questions about knowing and
being. Those three questions were "What am I doing when I am being ethical?," "Why is doing that being ethical?," and "What is brought about by
doing that?" Answering the first question proved to be surprisingly complicated. Initially we saw that the structure of ethical intentionality was similar
to cognitional structure, though more complex. We saw that the ability to
arrive at virtually unconditioned judgments of ethical value, and then deciding and acting in conformity with those judgments, is crucial to being ethical. However, the roles played by feelings in arriving at judgments of value,
virtually unconditioned or not, called for a lengthy examination of feelings,
their relations and tensions within horizons, and their roles in ethical and
value reflection, deciding, and acting. This led eventually to identification
of the two fundamental sources of dynamism in horizons of feelings, to the
notion of an objective scale of value preference, and to the need for conversion as the most fundamental standard for ethical judgment and action. We
could say, therefore, that the answer to the first question, compactly stated,
is this: *Being ethical is experiencing, inquiring, understanding, reflecting, grasping
the virtually unconditioned and judging what is going on, followed by inquiring*

about what could and should be done, further experiencing as re-patterned by such inquiries, getting insights into possible courses of action, reflecting, grasping values as virtually unconditioned, deliberating, deciding, and acting, all within a converted horizon of feelings for values that is in conformity with the notion of value, being-in-love, and the normative scale of values.

10.2   The Notion of the Ethical

Against the background of this complex answer to the first question, we now are in a position to consider the second question: Why is doing that being ethical? Initially, the question seems odd. It seems that the answer to the first question ("What am I doing when I am being ethical?") already stipulates by definition the meaning of the word "ethical," so that the second question seems redundant: doing that (performing that structured series of activities) *is* being ethical, by definition. But mere definition is not the point to either the first or the second question. The second question arises because the answer to the first is bound to strike the reader as odd – as somehow different from, if not strongly opposed to, some more familiar notion of the ethical. In other words, the second question asks how the structure of ethical intentionality is to be reconciled with notions of the ethical already present in more ordinary and familiar senses of what is ethical. Hence, just as Immanuel Kant endeavoured to show that his own highly theoretical account of morality was an apt "elucidation" of the ordinary understanding of duty,[1] so also it is necessary to show that the performance of the structure of ethical intentionality by a converted person fulfills the expectations of commonsense notions of ethics.

The second question, therefore, not only presupposes the preceding account of the structure of ethical intentionality; it also presupposes some notion of the ethical. There are, of course, many differing ways of *saying* what it means to be ethical. Yet it is axiomatic in Lonergan's approach to philosophy that before we are able to put many of our most important ideas into words, we already have a prior *notion* about them. For him a notion is an anticipation of what would be known or realized if the anticipation were to be fulfilled. He elaborates on the notions or anticipations of being, the thing, nature, development, and God, for example.

Likewise, everyone has some notion of the ethical, some anticipation of what it means to be ethical, that precedes their diverse linguistic expressions about the ethical. Those linguistic expressions can be more or less accurate portrayals of the pre-linguistic notion of the ethical. Still, each linguistic expression does reveal something about the notion of the ethical, and so comparing them to the linguistic expressions set forth in the preceding chapters is in order. There are, of course, many more ways of describing what is meant by being ethical than can be adequately addressed in this chapter. For the present, therefore, I begin with Aristotle's classic statement, and then consider the relationship of the structure of ethical intentionality to just eight additional, commonly held ways of saying what it means to be ethical.

10.2.1 Aristotle's Notion of the Ethical

I begin with Aristotle because he provided the classic etymology of the word "ethics" in his *Nicomachean Ethics.* There he writes that *êthikê* is derived from *ethos* because ethical excellence, ethical virtues (*aretai êthikai*),[2] come about as a result of habit (*ethos*).[3] Aristotle explained that our actions inculcate habitual ways of feeling and acting, and thereby determine our character:

> In our transactions with other people it is by action that some become just and others unjust, and by acting in the face of danger, and by developing the habit of feeling fear or confidence that some become brave or cowardly. The same applies to appetites and feelings of anger; some people become self-controlled and gentle, and others self-indulgent and short-tempered. In a word, characteristics develop from corresponding activities. For that reason, we must see to it that our activities are of a certain kind, since any variations in them will be reflected in our character.[4]

As the passage makes clear, not every kind of habit of acting and feeling deserves to be called an ethical virtue. Only those habitual ways of acting that consistently hit the median count as ethical virtues – e.g., consistently acting with neither too much fear nor too little, accepting honours with neither too much pride nor too little, and so on.[5]

Aristotle's focus is on actions, but it also extends to include the feelings that accompany and motivate our habitual performances of actions. The focus in this book has been on the process of ethical reflection that leads up to decisions and actions, and the roles that feelings play in that process. Building upon this analysis, chapter 7 argued further that our prior actions and horizons of feelings mould our habitual valuing, including our habits of ethical valuing, as well as our habits of deciding and acting. So just as "activities are of a certain kind" lead to ethical virtues and character according to Aristotle, so also actions that follow from faithful performance of the structure of ethical intentionality lead to genuinely ethical habitual valuing and acting.

Aristotle's standard for ethical action was therefore the character of the ethical person – a person possessed of habits of ethically virtuous acting and feeling. He recognized that there is so much irregularity to human life that it would be impossible to set out a code of rules that could prescribe the ethical thing to do in every situation.[6] Only a person possessed of ethical virtues would be able to adapt ethically to ever-changing situations. "In other words, acts are called just and self-controlled when they are the kind of acts which a just or self-controlled person would perform … in the way that just and self-controlled people do."[7]

Similarly, the account of the structure of ethical intentionality offered in the preceding chapters led to the conclusion that only converted people will arrive at unqualifiedly objective judgments of ethical value, make authentically ethical decisions, and act in genuinely ethical ways. The performance of actions that follow from such judgments and decisions, in turn, affect the feelings and habitual valuing that become the bases of our subsequent ethical thought and action.

More would have to be said about the relationships between Aristotle's account of the relationships between ethical thinking (*phronêsis*), feeling, action, and ethical habits (*aretai êthikai*) in order to make a stronger case for the affinities between Aristotle's notion of the ethical and the notion that is implicit in the structure of ethical intentionality.[8] But for the moment it is clear that there are affinities, if not an identity, between living in accord with the structure of ethical intentionality, and being ethical in Aristotle's sense.

10.2.2 Eight Commonly Held Ideas about the Ethical

Beyond the comparison with Aristotle's account of the ethical, I have to limit my discussion here to just eight of those common ways of saying what it means to be ethical. Being ethical, according to those common notions, means the following: (i) "Doing what one should"; (ii) "Doing what is right" (or "Doing the right thing"); (iii) "Acting for the good of others, not only for oneself"; (iv) "Obeying the law"; (v) "Doing what is authentic (not what others expect)"; (vi) "Standing up for what one believes in"; (vii) "Choosing the better over the less good course of action"; and (viii) "Doing no harm to others." These are some of the most common ways of saying what it means to be ethical in our society, though as I say, the list is not exhaustive. Just as I will show how the structure of ethical intentionality satisfies each in turn, I am confident that it will satisfy almost any statement we would recognize within our present social context as saying what it means to be ethical.

The above ideals do have some important commonalities of which we should take notice. First, then, all eight ideals of what it means to be ethical insist on doing and acting – and behind that, choosing to act. Being ethical means more than having noble beliefs and ideals, or talking a good story. It means even more than making good judgments of ethical value. Ethics means actually doing something. The structure of ethical intentionality begins with the question "What should I *do*?" and culminates in acts of deciding and acting. That structure remains incomplete until deciding and acting take place. Hence, the structure of ethical intentionality that I have endeavoured to portray in the preceding chapters conforms to the sense of the ethical and its emphasis on acting that is shared by all of these commonplaces about what is ethical.

Second, each of these eight common senses of what it means to be ethical emphasizes more than merely deciding and acting. After all, even a homicidal maniac acts. The kind of acting that is to be regarded as ethical acting is not just any acting whatever; it is acting that is qualified in some special way. Hence each of the eight common senses of being ethical provides some kind of specification of what kind of acting is acting ethically.

Third, each of these specifications can be understood in terms of the structure of ethical intentionality. Deciding and acting are qualified and specified by the structured activities that lead up to deciding and acting. In particular, deciding and acting qualify as ethical to the extent that they are realizations of the virtually unconditional value of intelligible courses of action. As difficult as it can be to choose and act ethically – to act authentically, to do what one should, to do the right thing – it can also be quite difficult to *know* what one should do, *know* what the right thing is, *know* what it means to be authentic in a particular situation. In the structure of ethical intentionality, the difficult work of ethical reflection is dedicated to providing such knowledge.

Fourth, the outcomes of our efforts at ethical reflection are profoundly conditioned by the horizons of feelings that surround them. To the extent that a horizon of feelings is ordered normatively, as it would be for a converted subject, then ethical reflecting and judging will be objective, and choosing and acting will be right, good, authentic. Insofar as the pertinence of our further questions are determined by the normative scale of values, we will judge objectively what is best for us to do in the concrete situation. And to the extent that we freely chose and act according to that judgment of value, we will make real what is the best improvement of or best response to the situation. We will also thereby simultaneously constitute ourselves as excellent and authentic instances of personal value. However, to the extent that our horizon of feelings is still troubled by unresolved conflicts that exist among our feelings for values, our exercise of the structure of ethical intentionality will be flawed, and our judgments, decisions, and actions will fall short of "moral perfection," as Lonergan puts it. Hence in answering the question, "Why is doing that being ethical?" we should always bear in mind that "doing *that*" means performing the set of acts as indicated by the structure of ethical intentionality within a horizon of feelings ordered in accord with the objective scale of values. Short of moral perfection, however, being ethical means the practice of that structure by a person who is morally converted and on a trajectory of refinement of feelings, though not yet morally perfect.

We now turn more specifically to the eight common ideas about being ethical, and show how each is underpinned by the extended structure of ethical intentionality as outlined above.

(i) Being ethical means "Doing what one should."

It is through the exercise of the extended structure of ethical intentionality that a person knows a concrete situation objectively, understands what is possible to do in that situation, and responsibly and objectively judges which (if any) of those possibilities would be worth realizing – and among those worthwhile options, which if any has the compelling value of what she or he ought to do (or refrain from doing). In addition, any exercise of the structure of ethical intentionality is not completed until the question "What should I do?" is answered fully by deciding and acting in accord with this judgment of value. Hence fidelity to one's own structure of ethical intentionality is the manner in which one both knows what one should do, and does it.

There is a notable contrast between this grounding of our notion that the ethical has to do with what we should or ought to do, and the Kantian grounding of the common understanding of duty.[9] For Kant, in order for anything to have the necessity and force of moral obligation, it must be a universal law. The content of what one should do, therefore, must be capable of formulation as a universal, categorical imperative that would be equally binding on all rational creatures regardless of circumstances. However, Kant's insistence on the universalizability of maxims leaves them insufficiently contextualized, and leads to the formulation of imperatives that seem monstrously unethical.[10] In the structure of ethical intentionality, by way of contrast, knowledge of obligation comes in a judgment of value that almost always is applied to a particular, concrete, course of action appropriate to a highly contextualized, particular situation. While the necessity of what one should do can be known through the exercise of the structure of ethical intentionality, that necessity need not be universal. The reason why Kant and others commonly expect that ethical norms must be expressible in universal propositions will be taken up in chapter 15, after the notion of the good, the structure of the human good, and the ontology of the good have been explored.

(ii) Being ethical means "Doing what is right" (or "Doing the right thing").

Exercise of the structure of ethical intentionality is precisely what is meant by knowing and doing "the right thing." Knowing what is right is a matter of objective judgments of comparative value. It is a matter of sorting through the many options that are intelligibly possible in the concrete situation, of asking and answering the questions about the value (or evil, disvalue) of those options. Such further questions will run up to and include questions about which options would be of unconditional value for me to commit myself to and enact. Knowing what is the right thing to do will result only when there are no further pertinent questions left for a person operating within a converted, rightly ordered horizon of feelings. Doing the right thing, then, is doing the option that I have judged to be the right, ethically valuable one for me to do in the situation.[11]

> (iii) Being ethical means "Acting for the good of others,
>   not only for oneself."

The range of further pertinent questions that arise during ethical reflection include others that would likely or inevitably be affected by one's potential course of action. To focus only on questions about how decisions affect oneself, ignoring questions about how those decisions affect others, and questions about the values of those effects, is not an exercise in asking all the further questions that a morally converted horizon of feelings would regard as pertinent. Moreover, the questions about others regarded as pertinent to a person whose horizon of feelings is completely ordered according to the normative scale of value preference will be completely open to the full range of values concerning others. To ignore questions about others, or to take into account only the questions about others deemed pertinent by a restricted or distorted ordering of values, would not be an exercise of genuine ethical reflection. It would be the exercise of only a truncated, distorted version of the structure of ethical intentionality. Hence faithful exercise of the structure of ethical intentionality includes reflecting, judging, and acting for the full good of others as well as for oneself.

> (iv) Being ethical is "Not breaking the law."

For the most part, ethical reflection takes place in the commonsense mode, where it draws upon the socially accumulated common fund of tested insights and judgments, adding the few further insights and judgments needed to answer the questions concerning what is unique in the present situation. At its best, human law codifies the accumulated commonsense fund of insights and judgments about what is intelligible and valuable to do in the regularly recurring social situations that make up the good of order.[12] At its best, human law educates people and sustains them in intelligible and valuable patterns of cooperating in order to meet recurring needs. At its best, human law anticipates recurring, unintelligent, and unethical acts that undermine the valuable and intelligible patterns of cooperation that constitute the human good of order, and prescribes commonsense measures to prevent or minimize their harm. At its best, human law makes available the wisdom of generations of women and men who have faced similar social circumstances in the past. At its best, human law supplies the commonsense insights and judgments, and helps to form the horizons of feeling that ground the possibilities of cooperation in the pursuit of common social and cultural values. At its best, human law is in the service of the community and its projects, as well as in the service of the flourishing of the personal values of its members and guests, for community is overwhelmingly life in common with others.

Respect for law at its best resides in a community's accumulated body of feelings and judgments that value the potential and likely relevance of the community's wisdom expressed in laws. At their best, the value of laws consists in the ways they can assist people in reaching further understandings and judgments of virtually unconditioned value about what is best to do in concrete social situations, situations which are frequently quite similar to many such situations that have occurred before. Respect for law in this sense means respecting it for its contribution to reaching understanding, judgment, and feelings about what is of virtually unconditioned value in cooperative action and living with others.

While laws and legal institutions at their best embody and communicate such wisdom, they need not be utterly rigid. Law always needs to be interpreted, because no matter how closely new social situations resemble their predecessors, they are almost never completely identical to them. Additional insights and judgments are always needed to answer the further questions that arise because of even subtle differences between similar situations.

Still, intelligently and responsibly interpreting and adapting laws is quite different from breaking laws. When human law is at its best, breaking the law means acting in an unintelligent and unethical way that undermines the valuable and intelligible patterns of cooperation that constitute the human good of order. Law-breaking entails dismissing whole ranges of further pertinent questions about others and the goods realized by intelligently and responsibly acting in cooperative arrangements.

Clearly, however, law is not always at its best. Laws can also be corrupt, unjust, and oppressive. But when laws are unjust, it is because they are not produced by the uninhibited exercise of the whole, normative structure of ethical intentionality as it responds to all further pertinent questions under the guidance of the normative scale of value preference. Laws are unjust when, instead, they result from biased, distorted, short-circuited, or fragmentary performances of that structure. The ethical solution to bad law is not to make things *worse* by breaking them for *one's own advantage*. The ethical solution is the long and difficult process of reforming or, in rare cases, overthrowing corrupt legal institutions and building up authentic new ones.

The line between breaking the law and reforming institutions becomes blurred in the case of civil disobedience. There are some cases when all other options have been exhausted and the only option left is to publically point out the injustice of the law by breaking it.

Law-breaking in acts of genuine civil disobedience are truly ethical actions. Acts of civil disobedience are ethical when they are undertaken to dramatically and vividly reveal the true injustices of laws and institutional structures that have been falsely accepted as just. Such acts of civil disobedience are ethical when they follow upon critical judgments that objectively evaluate the injustices of a situation, intelligent and creative insights that devise strategies to effectively challenge those injustices, and courageous actions and willing submission to the punishments prescribed by the laws, for the sake of dramatically portraying those injustices.[13] In cases of authentic civil disobedience, law-breaking would be profoundly ethical, because one would be confronting law that is far from its best, in the spirit of what law at its best is meant to achieve.[14]

However, from an ethical perspective, civil disobedience is a last resort. Working within the law to change the law will be the more common ethical solution (and will typically be more effective as well.) Hence obeying laws, when they are truly just and in service of intelligible and valuable patterns of human cooperation, is acting in accord with structure of ethical intentionality. This happens when those who act have (1) asked, understood, felt, and judged how laws foster and support the values of intelligible human cooperation, (2) asked and had insights about what can be done to intelligently act in ways that build upon or improve the intelligible order supported by the laws, (3) ethically reflected about the values of the impacts of these various possibilities upon that social order and, in light of a normative horizon of value preferences, reached virtually unconditioned judgments about the best values to realize in light of the laws, and (4) chosen to act in intelligently creative and valuable ways that build upon what the laws provide.[15]

> (v) Being ethical is "Doing what is authentic
>   (not what others expect)."

People who exercise a converted structure of ethical intentionality are asking their own questions and endeavouring to satisfy their own unrestricted questioning spirit with their own insights, their own judgments of value, and their own decisions and actions within a normatively ordered horizon of feelings that they have made their own by their own decisions of conversion. This is the very meaning of authenticity and autonomy

– of taking responsibility for one's own actions and not blindly following someone else or blaming someone else.[16] Authenticity here means responsibility to one's own unrestricted, restlessly inquiring and responsible spirit as it unfolds in the context of a horizon of feelings ordered according to the objective scale of values that has been made one's own, not forced upon one.

Still, this does not mean that what other people have to say about what is right and wrong must be ignored. Authenticity can never be merely a knee-jerk reaction to do the opposite of what others (society, "the herd") hold as valuable. Others may suggest or try to be persuasive about intelligible possibilities one had not thought of. Their suggestions may raise questions and pose difficulties one had not considered, but that indeed are pertinent to the values or disvalues of what one will do. Reflecting about what others say, and asking pertinent questions about them is also part of the exercise of authentic ethical intentionality. Whether or not their suggestions, advice, objections, and counsel, are really pertinent is ultimately settled by exercising one's own inquiry, taking responsibility for one's own feelings, and answering questions for oneself until there are no further pertinent questions. Authenticity and genuine autonomy, therefore, are the exercise of the wholeness of one's own agency – the *entirety* of the structure of one's own ethical intentionality, including the intelligent, critical, and normative evaluation of what others have to say about ethical matters.

(vi) Being ethical means "Standing up for what one believes in."

It is said that being ethical is a matter of standing by one's beliefs and not giving in to social pressures to betray those beliefs. But chapter 4 presented a nuanced account of knowing and believing that contains important distinctions relevant to this notion of one's beliefs and being ethical; there is both knowledge of fact and value, as well as belief regarding facts and values. We decide to believe both matters of fact and of value, but we also have knowledge of matters of fact and of value. Indeed, were there no knowledge of value, there could be no worthwhile or responsible acts of believing of either facts or values.

What is usually meant by standing up for my beliefs, at bottom, does not necessarily mean standing up for what someone else told me. Most often, it really means acting on the basis of my value *knowledge*, and especially on the basis of my virtually unconditioned judgments about the value of what I ought to do. Clearly, exercising of the structure of ethical intentionality does mean standing up for one's "beliefs," if by "belief" one really means "what is known in virtually unconditioned judgments of value about what one should do."

(vii) Being ethical means "Choosing the better
over the less good course of action."

Choosing the better over the less good course of action means choosing what really is better. But knowing what really is better is attained in the objective, virtually unconditioned comparative judgments of value by a person operating out of a converted horizon of feelings oriented by the unrestricted notion of values, unrestricted being-in-love. Consequently the existential scale of value for such persons is identical with the normative, invariant scale of values. Hence, choosing and doing what is truly better comes as the culmination of the exercise of this structure of ethical intentionality as it arrives at objective judgments of comparative value that form the basis of these choices and actions.

(viii) Being ethical means "Doing no harm to others."

The slogan that it is all right to do anything we please as long as we do not harm others is a commonplace in contemporary ethical discourse. It is seldom submitted, however, to the kind of critical scrutiny that the structure of ethical intentionality calls forth. "Not harming others" almost always carries with it an unexamined set of assumptions about what counts as "harm." If the deliberating person's actual scale of value preferences is restricted to vital values, then only questions of possible physical, bodily harm will be considered pertinent. But if the deliberator's actual scale is coextensive with the normative scale, then a vastly wider range of further questions will be felt to be pertinent. These will include potential harm at the levels of social, cultural, personal, and religious values, and questions about the concrete circumstances in which protecting and promoting one set of values unavoidably means harm to lower values. Hence taking the view that it is all right to do as one pleases as long as one does no harm to others will be ethical only if the meaning of harm is determined by rich, nuanced exercises of the structure of ethical intentionality by persons whose horizons of feelings are fully converted.

10.2.3 Summary

The second question of our study has been "Why is doing that being ethical?" It parallels the second question of Lonergan's study of cognition, "Why is doing that knowing?" Answering Lonergan's second question involves exploration of the genuine meaning of objective knowledge of what is. The answer to "Why is that being ethical?" entails the exploration of another kind of objectivity – "Why does doing that lead to genuinely ethical actions?"

This reformulation of the question focuses on one major difference between the two answers. Objective knowledge of what is terminates in judgments that are grounded in reflective grasps of the virtually unconditioned, whereas being genuinely ethical always terminates in decisions and actions. Nevertheless, as the preceding sections have made clear actions will be genuinely ethical only if they realize objective judgments of values. Not just any arbitrary actions will do. Moreover, as the preceding chapters have made clear, judgments of ethical value will be unconditionally objective only if they result from processes of value reflection and deliberation carried out under the auspices of horizons of feelings that have been converted to harmonize with the unrestricted notion of value, unrestricted being-in-love, and the normative scale of value preferences that follows from both. The answer to our second question, then, is "Doing that is being ethical, because 'doing that' means acting in such a way as to realize what is objectively valuable."

The preceding sections have attempted to show how knowing, valuing, deciding, and acting in this sense correspond closely with many, though not all, of the notions that people commonly hold about what it means to be ethical. I have endeavoured to show that the structure of ethical intentionality as outlined in the previous chapters of this book has the characteristics that most people have in mind when they think and speak of "being ethical." Just as importantly, considering these common notions of the ethical from the perspective of the structure of ethical intentionality brings to light some of their unexamined assumptions and limitations and, I hope, positive refinements in those notions.

I also hope that the brief examples offered in these sections can serve as models for entering into the more erudite contemporary debates and conflicting views about what is and is not ethical. Ethical and moral debates are taking place in a wide variety of academic, cultural, political, and religious settings. Many people have come to despair that they are capable of any sort of resolution. Chapters 15 and 16 explore the fruitfulness of Lonergan's idea of a method of "functional specialties" for entering into such debates. Behind that idea of a method of ethics stands the ideal of ethical authenticity – that is, morally converted thinking, valuing, deciding, and action, which takes place within a horizon of feelings converted and faithful to the immanent norms of the unrestricted notion of value, unrestricted being-in-love, and the normative scale of value preference. The method of ethics outlined in the concluding chapters shows how self-appropriation of converted ethical intentionality can clarify and refine and in at least some cases resolve otherwise intractable ethical conflicts.

This observation brings us to a question for existential choice – namely, the question about whether or not this is the way one should actually live one's own life.

10.3   Being Ethical and Choosing the Value of the Chooser: Self-Appropriation, Part II

There are many *ideas* about what it means to be ethical, but *being* ethical is something one has to actually do oneself. This fact returns us to self-appropriation, now in a deeper way. Chapter 3 introduced the notion of self-appropriation, but that chapter ended with the task unfinished. That chapter introduced the process of self-affirmation of the knower as comprising the first stages of self-appropriation, only to be faced with the fact that self-affirmation is something one must decide to attempt, or not. That chapter ended incomplete, because self-affirmation of the knower had nothing to say about the person as chooser who would have to choose to attempt the difficult, hermeneutical process of coming to know herself or himself as a knower. We can now resume the account of what is called for in self-appropriation in the more complete sense because in the intervening chapters the act of choosing has been explored and situated within the structure of ethical intentionality.

Self-appropriation in this more complete sense can be stated simply enough. Just as self-affirmation of oneself as a knower is knowing what we are doing when we are knowing, so also self-appropriation of oneself as ethical in the full sense is knowing and valuing what it is to be a knower, valuer, and chooser, and choosing to act in accordance with that valued structure of knowing, valuing, and choosing. Just as self-affirmation of the knower consists in a "reduplication" of cognitional structure as applied to one's own experiences of knowing,[17] so also self-appropriation in the full sense is the reduplication of the structure of ethical intentionality as applied to the experiences one has of being ethical by performing that very structure. In other words, self-appropriation in the more complete sense is deliberately choosing to value, choose, act, and live in accord with the very structure of activities that one cannot help but use in coming to this very decision.

This simple statement of what is meant by self-appropriation in the more complete sense is perhaps too simple. Therefore, the following sections endeavour to slow down and walk through the steps in this process of self-appropriation. I hope that doing so will lend clarity about what is meant by self-appropriation and will reveal its great importance as well.

10.3.1 Existential Discovery as Breakthrough to Self-Appropriation

The word "appropriation" comes from the Latin *appropriare*, meaning to make one's own. Self-appropriation therefore means, quite literally, making one's self one's own. From a strictly logical point of view, this way of speaking is quite odd and paradoxical. If I am not myself – not my own self – then whose self am I?

Although the problem of making oneself one's own may seem a logical oddity, it is nevertheless a very familiar human dilemma. It is the perennial problem of finding oneself determined by powers other than one's own. Those powers over oneself may be overt and easily identifiable, as in the violent force of a tyrannical regime or an abusive relationship, or they may be the more subtle psychological or ideological manipulations of one's thoughts, feelings, and beliefs that control how one understands and values oneself.

For almost everyone, then, the first step in appropriating oneself in the fuller sense is to find a way to break through the alienated self-understandings and self-valuings that have prevailed thus far. That break, as Lonergan understood it, comes with the recognition that it is up to each of us to determine what we are to make of ourselves – "the realization that one not only chooses between courses of action but also thereby makes oneself an authentic human being or an unauthentic one."[18]

Lonergan speaks of this knowledge as an existential moment of realization that many people come to, though they do not do so easily. Even before Lonergan, many existentialists described this moment, and dedicated their writings to provoking it among readers who had been drifting through life without such awareness.

10.3.2 Self-Appropriation: Factual Knowledge of the Structure of Ethical Intentionality

Yet this realization by itself is not yet self-appropriation in the fuller sense. It is a beginning, but only a beginning. If someone is to undertake self-appropriation in the fuller sense, she or he will have to build upon this beginning by following the lead of the host of further questions that arise in the wake of this existential realization. These include questions regarding the implications that this realization has for one's prior self-understandings and self-valuings.

If one embarks upon the journey of self-appropriation in the fuller sense, therefore, this will have to begin with an expanded form of self-knowledge. It begins with affirming the fact (the existential realization) that one is a chooser, and that this choosing has the double intentionality described in chapter 7. In each and every choice, we choose the value that we ourselves are to become, simultaneously with the values to be realized in the world distinct from our selves. We choose both simultaneously in one and the same act.

Knowing these things is a matter of correctly understanding some facts about our acts of choosing. This knowledge begins with our experiences of ourselves in the making of our choices. Going beyond these experiences of choosing, towards knowledge of choosing, proceeds through asking questions about those experiences of choosing, and then arriving at insights which present possible answers to those questions. It advances still further when we ask whether or not our understanding of those experiences of our choosing is correct – including questions about whether our experiences are in fact experiences of what people generally call "choosing" or "deciding." These further questions lead to further insights that correct the initial and provisional understandings of experiences of choosing, until all further pertinent questions have been answered.

Knowing ourselves factually as choosers who are self-determining, therefore, is an extension of self-affirmation from knowledge of the experiences of knowing to knowledge of the experiences of the acts of choosing. Self-affirmation of oneself as a self-determining chooser comes about through an application of cognitional structure to the conscious experiences of choosing.

Still, while many people do come to the existential realization and know this important fact about themselves and their own acts of choosing, there is far more to be known about acts of choosing. Some of the still further questions about what we are doing when we are choosing concern how our acts of choosing are related to other acts, including such questions as "Why do I make these choices?" Such questions concern the relations of our acts of choice to the values that motivated the choices. These, in turn, lead to still further questions about how we come to hold these values, questions about our experiences of ethical reflection, and judgments of ethical value. Correctly understanding ethical reflection and judgment gives rise to still further questions about their relationships to other acts in the whole of the structure of ethical intentionality – and, indeed, to questions about the whole of that structure and about ourselves as the agents of that structure.

Most importantly, these processes leading towards self-affirmation of one's own ethical intentionality manifest the ubiquity of the ethical questions that structure and guide the whole process. Self-affirmation then needs to confront the question as to whether or not there is any limit to the values that one can ask about. If the arguments presented in section 8.2.2 of chapter 8 are correct, then self-affirmation of ethical intentionality will affirm oneself as possessing an unrestricted capacity for questioning what is of value.

Just as self-affirmation of one's own cognitional structure is greatly facilitated by language and exercises set forth in texts such as *Insight,* so also the preceding chapters of this book have been offered in aid to those who choose to embark upon self-knowledge of the structure of their own ethical intentionality. It has been my intent to provide texts and illustrations that will heighten the reader's experiences of now this, and now that, act of consciousness and to propose ways that these experiences may be correctly understood in their relationships to one another – a network of relationships that constitutes the structure of ethical intentionality. The process of knowing one's own structure of ethical intentionality is, therefore, hermeneutical in the sense discussed in chapter 3. Attending to and understanding the acts are facilitated by the words and exercises, and the meanings of the words are refined through further attentiveness and understanding of the experiences of the conscious acts and structures themselves.

The question for self-affirmation of the structure of ethical intentionality, then, is this: Do you perform such acts as knowing what is going on, feeling, practical inquiring, practical insight, value inquiring, value reflecting, reflective understanding of value, value judging, deliberating, choosing, and acting, all of which are underpinned and guided by an unrestricted notion of value? Arriving at an affirmative answer comes as a *part* of the structure of ethical intentionality (cognitional structure) is applied to the *whole* of it, and involves the affirmation of oneself as the "unity, identity, whole" who performs these acts as they relate to one another in the structure of ethical intentionality.[19] Actually following through on all the further questions about what it means to be a chooser, however, and how this does or does not relate to what has been said in this or other books, is something that each individual can only do herself or himself.

10.3.3 Self-Appropriation: Valuing, Choosing, and Enacting Oneself

Still, even knowing oneself to be in fact a subject who does her or his choosing as part of a more encompassing structure of ethical intentionality is not all that comes about in the wake of the realization that it is up to each of us to decide for ourselves what we are to make of ourselves. As Lonergan puts it, along with this factual discovery, there also "emerges in consciousness the significance of personal value and the meaning of personal responsibility."[20] The significance identified here is the significance of value – the value of being a being who can and does make choices. This realization that it is up to each of us to determine who we are *feels* momentous, even startling and disorienting. Nietzsche used the image of standing before an "abyss" to characterize the feelings that accompany this realization: "And when you look long into an abyss, the abyss also looks into you."[21]

Our feelings spontaneously respond to this judgment of fact (as their agent object) and bring to our awareness the overwhelming value of being a free and responsible chooser (as the proper *noematic* object of these feelings). This judgment of fact and the ensuing feelings set in motion still further questions for judgment of value – "What good am I?" "Am I really a being having the profound value revealed in these feelings?" Answering these questions will bring into play a variety of further feelings about our own worth as a person. Many feelings that come into play will be those inculcated over a long lifetime – feelings acquired in childhood, in the extended family, in school, as well as from the larger contexts of friendships, societies, cultures, history, and religions. These feelings model for us what it means to be a worthwhile person and to live a worthwhile life. Our judgments about our own value can become frozen in the feelings evoked by the judgments by others about our worth. Such feelings arise in response, for example, to judgments made in the family setting about being a good or bad boy or girl, at play with friends about being good at games or sports, in school about being smart or stupid, at work and in social life about being efficient, lazy, nice, conceited, a leader, or a follower, and in a religion about being a sinner or a redeemed beloved, and so on. Still, the felt realization of the profound value of being a being who freely chooses what value she or he will become has the power to break through and reorient all these other determinations of self-value. When it does, it invites self-appropriation in the fuller sense.

Therefore, when we do realize the fact that it is up to us to determine the kind of person we will be, our feelings feel with awe the value of being a chooser. Yet these feelings are not limited to the *acts* of self-constituting choice that we perform; it is *we ourselves* as unity-identity-wholes whose value we feel with awe, and perhaps even with shame. We feel all that is implied in being a unity capable of choosing. This means, first of all, that we also feel the value of being alive. Were we not alive, we could not be choosers, or anything else. Thus our felt response to the realization of the fact of being choosers includes felt responses to ourselves as embodiments of vital values. It also includes felt responses to ourselves as constituted by social and cultural values that we inherited, which gave us specific capacities for choice we would not otherwise have. The social and cultural values we have acquired include language, scientific understanding, and the insights and skills for participating in the patterns of cooperation of our society in order to make decisions and carry out actions we judge to be ethically valuable and obligatory. Our feelings also feel the values of ourselves as being perceptive, intelligent, and reasonable – the values of ourselves as capable of objective factual knowledge. All these value dimensions are present as felt in each of us as a chooser. In addition, perhaps at the periphery, there will be the dawn of feelings about things we have thought and done that have betrayed our capacities for free and responsible self-determination. But beyond the values of these various constituents, there is also the value of each of us as a person who chooses, as a "subject in act, ecstatic, emergent, standing out [in our] own originating freedom."[22] This is the highest of the values that we feel in response to knowing the facticity of ourselves as choosers.

When we feel this complex of values, we do not yet fully understand what we are feeling – in fact, in our lifetime we might never fully understand the values of ourselves that we are feeling. Chapters 12 and 13 begin to elaborate some of what is to be understood about the values that we feel in the midst of this self-discovery of ourselves as responsible for what we are to make of ourselves. But for the present our focus is on how self-appropriation itself proceeds in the wake of those awakened feelings about the value we are.

Self-appropriation in the fuller sense, therefore, also endeavours to go beyond feeling value towards knowing more completely this personal value of being a chooser. More concretely, self-appropriation seeks to know the value of choosing as the culmination of the whole of the structure of ethical intentionality. In the more complete sense, then, self-appropriation pre-supposes self-affirmation of oneself as an agent of the structure of ethical intentionality, not merely as a possible structure that some people might sometimes follow, but as the structure that I myself do follow in and through acts that I perform consciously. Self-appropriation in this fuller sense then turns to discern in one's own feelings the values that such self-knowledge evokes, and moves through further questions for value reflection towards fuller and more profound judgments about the value of being the being who performs this structure.

Finally, complete self-appropriation raises the questions "What shall I do in light of this value-knowledge of myself as a self-originating value? Will I now deliberately choose to cooperate ever more consistently with the lead of my ethical questions? Will I endeavour to resolve the tensions in my feel-ing horizon in favor of the invitations of the unrestricted notion of value, being-in-love in an unrestricted manner, and the normatively oriented scale of feeling preferences for values?" Implicit in these questions is also the recognition, nascent or full-grown, that occasionally or perhaps frequently one has failed to act in accord with the fact and value of oneself as a self-determining chooser.

So self-appropriation in the fullest sense is choosing deliberately to oper-ate according to the norms always already operative in one's own structure of ethical intentionality. Self-appropriation in the fullest sense is an act of self-acceptance – choosing to accept the value of oneself as a chooser, along with choices to reorient pervious acts and habits that have been betrayals of that value. Complete self-appropriation therefore entails a decision for moral conversion. It is a decision to commit oneself to making that spontaneously operative structure of oneself truly one's own, and to take responsibility for ridding oneself from every influence that would undermine fully thinking and living that way.

Still, moral conversion is not equivalent to self-appropriation. There are many instances of morally converted people – people who have chosen to live lives seeking to know and act according to objective judgments of ethical value forged within a horizon of feelings ordered by the unrestricted notion of value, by being-in-love in an unrestricted manner, and by the normative scale of value preference. People make this decision without having the term "self-appropriation" for what they are doing. But self-appropriation in the complete sense means also knowing what one is doing when one makes this decision and strives to live accordingly. Complete self-appropriation combines self-knowledge of the structure of ethical intentionality with the decision to live in fidelity to it.

Even so, this or any book can only facilitate making such a decision and undertaking to know all that is implied in that decision. It cannot make that decision for anyone or implant that self-knowledge. What this book attempts, rather, is to situate that decision within a broader account of what is to be decided for or against.

Whenever we operate with this structure, whether in a fully self-appropriated way or not, what we think, value, choose, and do has consequences. In the chapters to come, we work out some of those consequences – what is brought about by "doing that."

10.4   Self-Appropriation and Discernment

Chapter 1 proposed that the approach to ethics resulting from what Lonergan meant by self-appropriation has strong affinities with the notions of discernment found in common speech and in the writings of Aristotle, St. Paul, and St. Ignatius. Now those affinities can be stated more precisely.

Commonly, discernment is understood to mean going beyond ordinary perceptiveness by distinguishing something of value from other phenomena that obscure and compete for our attention. This means that the very performance of our structure of ethical intentionality is itself an exercise in discernment. Like discernment, the patterning of our experiences by the unrestricted notion of value, unrestricted being-in-love, and the normative scale of value goes beyond ordinary perceptiveness in a direction towards refined values. So also the "supervening act of understanding"[23] goes beyond our experiences and discerns intelligibility to which mere sensation is blind. This is especially true when we come to understand feelings that we have been feeling, but whose meaning and significance has been obscure to us.[24]

But discernment comes into its own when we go still further by submitting our understandings to critically reflective processes which head towards judgments of fact and value and decisions understood to be virtually unconditioned. Only in such judgments and decisions do we arrive at truth and goodness,[25] the ultimate objectives of discernment as ordinarily understood. Hence the authentic practice of our ethical intentionality in and of itself leads us to discern and distinguish between what is truly of value and what is not.

Yet the *authentic* practice of our ethical intentionality cannot be taken for granted. Although that structure does not need to be taught, still contending ideas about knowing, being ethical, truth, reality, objectivity, and value can weaken people's confidence in and fidelity to their own intrinsic norms of truth and goodness. Discernment therefore becomes more assured, deeper, and more nuanced when it is performed self-reflectively. Because self-appropriation involves deliberately deciding with full understanding to accept oneself as a knower, valuer, and chooser, this clears away the interior static in our internal consciousness and makes our knowledge, evaluation, and choice of valuable courses of action in the exterior world all the clearer. This means, therefore, that self-appropriation adds the "something extra" that Aristotle, Paul, and Ignatius identified as the deeper sources of the discernment of truth and goodness.

For Aristotle, discernment is grounded in a special and even rare personal quality – *euphuia*. *Euphuia* is a quality or habit of being good at aiming for what is true and good in ethical opinions as refined by dialectical examination. *Euphuia* arises from the self-reflective recognition by dialecticians of the natural orientation towards truth and goodness that resides within themselves. This self-recognition is the "something extra" that makes possible their refined acts of discernment. It also means that they have chosen to operate in the light of this self-recognition, because Aristotle portrays such people as not just having, but also as using *euphuia*.

As with *euphuia*, self-appropriation is both self-recognition and choice to live in accord with the orientation towards objective value that operates in the structure of ethical intentionality. As self-recognition, it is the understanding and judgment of the orientation of one's own structure of ethical intentionality towards truth and goodness that comes from the unrestricted questioning spirit of the notion of value. As choice, self-appropriation is the commitment to pursue all pertinent questions that flow from this unrestricted notion of value. Aristotle's dialectical method itself is founded on just such a commitment. But the self-recognition of *euphuia* makes it possible to go beyond the questioning method of dialectic and to select the ethical stances that are in harmony with the orientation towards truth. In the same way, self-appropriated persons are able to discern what is true and good in what others say about ethical and other matters, by subjecting those sayings to the same standards for objective judgments of value and decisions to which they have become committed by their own self-appropriation.

Paul and Ignatius focused their attention on discernment of spiritual gifts of the divine Spirit, first among which they counted the gift experienced as unconditional love. They both held that these gifts build upon the natural powers of theoretical and practical reasoning and do not abrogate them. The gifts born of unconditional love add clarity and resoluteness about natural values, as well as reveal values that lie beyond natural reasoning. These spiritual gifts also elicit feelings which oppose feelings that distort values and stimulate bad courses of action.

Yet chapter 1 pointed out that Ignatius's rules and directors (and Paul as well) presupposed objective judgments of natural reason about whether a person was in a state of progress or decline. There I argued that this, in turn, presupposes broader practices of discernment that assist people in arriving at such objective judgments of fact and value. This, of course, was the focus of most of Lonergan's career – facilitating people in appropriating as their own norms the unrestricted notion of value and the normative scale of value preference. By comparison, Paul and Ignatius were concerned with appropriating the normativity of unrestricted being-in-love. For example, among the decisions that are compatible with notion of value, the specific way that a person is called by God to manifest God's glory, as Ignatius puts it, would correspond to a decision known on the basis of unrestricted being-in-love.

Both Paul and Ignatius counted as a gift from the divine Spirit the ability to discern the differences among the movements in feelings and thoughts that come from the Spirit and those that issue from either natural powers or evil sources. Ignatius went further, offering structured exercises to assist people in heightening their experiences of these movements in internal consciousness, understanding them by means of their relationships to the gospel narratives, affirming them, and making choices ("elections") in the light of these. Among the most important of all elections is the decision of conversion to the value of unconditional loving, and the consequent decisions to live in fidelity to that sublime value. This corresponds to what Ignatius meant by doing the will of God. It is not much of a stretch to say, therefore, that the Ignatian exercises in discernment help people to apply the structure of ethical intentionality to the structure of ethical intentionality itself, especially as informed and guided by the feelings of unrestricted being-in-love. We could say, therefore, that Lonergan's approach to discernment as self-appropriation focused primarily on what he called the way from below upward, while Paul and Ignatius directed their concerns to the movement from above downward.[26]

I have placed great emphasis on discernment, but there is great danger as well. My emphasis has been on making decisions on the basis of careful attention, intelligent understanding, and critical judgment of the movements and tensions in our horizon of feelings. But this emphasis has the obvious danger that people can be badly mistaken and even pathologically deluded about their feelings. This is especially true in the case of feelings about the true value of being and making oneself. For almost everyone the realization that it is up to them to determine what kind of person they will be occurs in a conflicting horizon of feelings. People can and do trust wrong feelings, disoriented and even horrendous feelings, as they form their judgments of value and decisions about what kind of person they will be. When a person's horizon of values is distorted, there is no guarantee he or she will choose to live according to the structure of ethical intentionality with its norms of the unrestricted notion of value, unrestricted being-in-love, and the normative scale of value preference.

Such a person needs a community that includes persons and traditions who have become mature in discernment. This means people who have learned for themselves the differences between ordered and disordered feelings, and who have also learned effective ways to assist others in discernment. It means people who have the wisdom to know what to say and to recommend, as well as how and when to chastise those less advanced in discernment, who have mistaken their biased feelings for a normative scale of value preferences. This can only be accomplished in a face-to-face community, because the concrete insights and judgments needed to assist specific individuals to grow in discernment can never be entirely captured in a written text.[27]

Paul and Ignatius are explicit about the need of a community for growth in discernment of the value that one is and is invited to accept, but this need is also implicit in Aristotle. This, of course, raises the question of how to address the problem of the potential or actual distortions in a community's shared horizon of feelings about values. We will return to this problem in chapters 15 and 16.

Finally, self-appropriation involves discernment and is the ground of discernment. Self-appropriation involves discernment because both begin with the messy combination of feelings and thoughts in internal consciousness that compete for our allegiance. Gradually, and with the guidance of a proper community, both progress towards enhanced and refined attentiveness to feelings and thoughts, improved understanding and judgment, refined feeling responses, and understandings of these, as they all enter into trying to figure out what is the best thing to do. Self-appropriation is the ground of discernment, since knowing what one is doing when one endeavours to be ethical brings clarity about what one should do in a host of concrete circumstances. Discernment as self-appropriation provides the "something extra" that makes possible discernment about what to do in concrete circumstances.

At its pinnacle, self-appropriation is a decision. It is a decision to be and live according to the discerning standards of ethical intentionality. Self-appropriation, then, is the decision to be discerning.

PART FOUR

What Is Brought About by Doing That?

11 The Human Good Described

In other words, while speculative and factual insights are concerned to lead to knowledge of being, practical insights are concerned to lead to the making of being. Their objective is not what is but what is to be done.

—Bernard Lonergan, *Insight*

11.1 Introduction

In chapter 4, I proposed that Lonergan's contributions to ethics can be explored profitably by means of three questions that parallel his three questions concerning cognition, epistemology, and reality. Once again, the three questions for ethics are "What am I doing when I am being ethical?" "Why is doing that being ethical?" "What is brought about by doing that?" An answer to the first question was offered in chapter 4. However, because feelings play fundamental, complex, and frequently misunderstood roles in what we do when we are being ethical, several additional chapters were needed to complete the answer to that first question. Again, because of the complexity of feelings, the answer to the second question required that in chapter 8 we first explore the phenomena of conversion in general and moral conversion in particular. These explorations led us to address in chapter 9 the issue of objectivity in judgments of value so that in chapter 10 we could examine how a morally converted person acting in accord with the normative structure of ethical intentionality could be truly said to be acting ethically.

In this chapter we turn to the third question: "What is brought about by doing that?" In other words, what is actualized when human beings act ethically – act as morally converted persons faithful to the structure of ethical intentionality?

The simple answer is that good is brought about. Authentic exercises of the structure of ethical intentionality culminate in human acts of choosing values known in objective judgments of value and acting upon those choices and judgments. This means that the values known in objective judgments of value are brought about by the corresponding acts of choosing and acting. Because objective values are good, good is brought about by "doing that."

In general, then, good is intended by the structure of ethical intentionality. Still, the good so intended is an integration of different kinds of goods. The structure of ethical intentionality is constituted and guided by the dynamism of our unrestricted notion of value. That notion is our desire for the good as manifested in our questions for practical insight, evaluation, and deliberation. Before we know the good, choose it, or enact it, we desire the good. That desiring guides our subsequent acts of seeking practical insights, ethical reflection, choice, and action. Whenever human beings think and act out of a converted horizon of feelings in accord with the structure of ethical intentionality, therefore, they authentically and objectively answer questions that arise from the unrestricted notion of the good. When human beings act authentically in response to this unrestricted desire for the good, they move from merely thinking about and even knowing what would be good, to bringing about what they know to be worth actualizing. But the questions that arise from this desire are differentiated and structured, and so they intend a structure of different kinds of goods. The most complete answers to questions from this unrestricted desire are the actions that actualize the values known to be worth actualizing. But because values so known are related to other components in the structure of ethical intentionality, ethical actions therefore actualize more than value alone; they actualize a structure in which value is the key component.

Hence the simple answer is too simple. What is brought about by authentic choosing and acting is good, but the good is not all of one piece. Most obviously values are brought about, but not only values. Choosing and enacting any value simultaneously realizes other distinct components of the good as well – the goods of both an institution, and the meeting of a particular human need, for example, might be realized simultaneously in a single choice of a value. While objective values are goods, so also are the components that are realized along with those values. In addition, what is brought about by human choice and action is a good dynamically structured in two ways. First, because all human ethical intentionality is dynamic, the good that results from its performance is also structured dynamically. Second, the good that results is also structured because much of the human good is brought about through collaboration – through the combined, structured, and coordinated actions of many individual persons. Those patterns of collaboration constitute social structurings of the good. Therefore, to fully answer what is brought about by "doing that" requires an elaboration of the various components and structuring factors that are constituents of the good.

There are other reasons to think that the simple answer is too simple. When human beings judge, choose, and act authentically, they bring about what Lonergan called the human good. But this human good is not necessarily all there is to the good. In addition to the questions about what goods human decisions and actions can actualize, we also ask about the values and the goodness of nature that precede and are actualized independently of human acting. For over a century, the conservation and environmental movements have been raising awareness about a goodness intrinsic to nature that is independent of human choices or utilizations. In addition, we can also ask still further questions about the possibility of a goodness that transcends both natural and human goodness. Since the unrestricted notion of value intends the good that is to be known by answers to *all* questions of value – not just the questions of value to be finally settled by human choice and action – the questions of the natural and the transcendent good also must be considered.

In *Insight,* Lonergan writes that for humans the definition of being can only be "of the second order."[1] That is to say, humans cannot define being as such, for definitions formulate acts of understanding, and to understand being, one would have to understand everything about everything. So instead Lonergan offers a second-order approach that defines being not on the basis of understanding what being is, but rather in terms of how it is to be known. In other words, "Being, then, is the objective of the pure desire to know [and] … can be defined, at a second remove by saying that it refers to all that can be known by intelligent grasp and reasonable affirmation."[2]

The same holds true for the definition of the good. Human beings could only define the good if they already knew everything good about every good thing. Therefore short of such omniscient understanding of value, a human definition of the good must also be defined indirectly, at a second remove. That second-order definition is the following: "The good is the objective of the unrestricted notion of value. The good is what is to be known in the totality of answers to the totality of questions of value."

Thus to say that what is brought about by human ethical action is good is true as far as it goes, but it lacks differentiation. The human good is part of the good, because the human decisions and actions that realize it rest upon objective answers to questions of value. But the human good is not the whole of the good. People ask, "What is the good of *that*?," but they mean many different sorts of things when they ask such questions. There are many kinds of goods, and people use the term "good" in various ways, sometimes even in equivocal, conflated, and conflicting ways. Indeed, just what sort of a good is a value? How does it relate to other conceptions of the good? Its goodness needs to be distinguished from and related to other kinds of goodness.

Therefore this and the following chapters explore the ways that our approach to the ethics of discernment opens out into a full, heuristic account of the good – an account that is expansive and open to the whole of the meanings of good. This chapter begins that exploration with a descriptive introduction to what Lonergan means by "the human good." Chapter 12 delves more deeply into the explanatory foundations for Lonergan's claims about the human good. In particular, it takes up takes up the question of why Lonergan claimed that the structure of the human good is *invariant*, and offers a justification for his claim. Chapter 13 explores the relations among the human good, the natural good, the transcendent good, and the normative scale of value. Finally, chapter 14 addresses the problem of a foundation for Lonergan's account of the normative scale of value preference.

11.2   Parameters of the Human Good

Lonergan's more specific answer to "What is brought about by people doing that?" is "the good in a human sense," or the human good.[3] For him the human good has both personal and social dimensions, as well as dynamic and structural aspects. Personally, it is the good of an individual person's life, while socially it has to do with the good of human relations and interactions. The dynamic aspect is the entirety of human history. The structural aspect is what Lonergan called the invariant structure of the human good. The following sections explain these parameters of the human good.

11.3   The Human Good as Personal: The Good of
an Authentic Human Life

The most elemental of all human desires is the unrestricted desire for the good, the unrestricted notion of value. Still, human beings fulfill their unrestricted desiring for the good not all at once but only one choice at a time. This inevitably means that the question about how best to live one's own life is never completely settled by any one decision. Every human choice raises, and is followed by, further questions about the good to be pursued by living and acting. For this reason human choices and actions form a sequence, with the earlier ones setting the stage for the later. The series of human choices is linked together into a sequence, a whole life, by ever further questions about the worthwhile courses of action to be followed.

Therefore, although the good that we human beings desire, love, and intend by our ethical activity is unrestricted, the limited good that we actually bring about most directly is the good of our own lives. As Lonergan put it, the life of an individual person "is the work of the free and responsible subject producing the first and only edition"[4] of herself or himself. By his metaphor, Lonergan rightly likens the work of human choosing to the composition of a literary work, to a story in which actions are assembled into a narrative that expresses the meaning and value of a human life. The good of a personal life, therefore, is a sequential, dynamic, narrative good. Still, a life is good only to the extent that the sequence is the result of constantly and authentically following the normativity of the structure of ethical intentionality. This means continually responding to the call of questions by objectively assessing one's situation, intelligently coming up with creative insights about what can be done, fostering a horizon of feelings genuinely open to all values in their objective scale, reflecting about questions of value persistently until knowledge of unconditional value is attained, and authentically choosing and acting on the value-knowledge of what one should do. This sequence of acts of ethical intentionality is also suffused with the person's horizon of feelings. It is the wholeness of that sequence of choices that is oriented by a felt horizon of values that forms what we mean by a human life. It is a fabric of interrelated choices and other acts that constitutes the whole life of the reflecting and choosing human subject. This is not a static wholeness, but rather a dynamic, developing wholeness. The good of a human life is the good of a developing whole of choices. The badness of a human life is the deteriorating whole that results from a sequence of choices that deviate from the normativity of the unrestricted notion of value, from being-in-love unrestrictedly, and from the normative scale of value preference. In such lives, early minor peccadillos establish an orientation towards rationalization and insensitivity to feelings of regret and guilt. If such an orientation is sustained throughout one's life, these early minor self-betrayals are followed later by increasingly bolder and more evil actions that corrupt the whole of a person's life.[5]

Therefore, our lives do not merit respect just because we freely choose our paths in life. The value of a life is constituted by *what* values are chosen and *how* the choices are arrived at and in what sequence. People can live lives that consistently weave new unconditional values into the fabric of the unconditional values that have made up their lives to the present. Or they can continually make choices that evade further pertinent questions for intelligence, factual judgment, and value judgment. Human beings choose ignoble as well as noble lives, evil as well as good lives. The mediocrity or waste of a human life is constituted by the forgone opportunities to realize objective values, or by the evils that have been chosen in place of positive values. In these cases, whatever good such lives might have is fragmented and broken, and the chaos of mounting problems and incompleteness increasingly threaten to overwhelm that good. The succession of inauthentic choices yields successively greater conflicts and chaos that, in the limit, head towards complete breakdown.

Yet no human life is completely determined by this or that particular choice. The reality of a human life is, rather, that of a *sequence* of choices. The good (or ill) of a human life is the good or ill of a whole sequence or pattern of choices. It is a developing good, a good on the way; it is never settled by any one decision in the sequence. At any stage in that sequence its goodness is always open to decline away from the limited goodness achieved thus far, or to rise above that limited goodness. A person can betray a previously decent life by making inauthentic judgments of value and decisions. Or conversely, the ill of a human life is always open to the reversal through a conversion, restitution, and to healing and rebuilding towards unrestricted goodness.

Hence there will be momentous decisions at one or more points in a life, decisions that largely, if not completely, determine the future sequence of other decisions. Such decisions may reverse a previous life of evasion. Such decisions will shift one's horizon of feelings towards fundamental concern for all values in their ascending scale. Such decisions of conversion shift the constellation of feelings in one's horizon of feelings. With decisions for conversion, the unrestricted notion of value and being-in-love unconditionally shift from the margins to the very centre of one's horizon of feelings, thus changing utterly the orientation within which ethical reflections and choices occur.

But there can also be momentous decisions that turn away from authentic reflection and choice, towards a life that begins to evade or drift or deliberately choose to negate values out of spite and *ressentiment* against an order of reality and values that one did not create oneself. To the extent that our choices are arrived at from anything short of a converted horizon, then our lives will be vitiated, to a lesser or to a greater extent, by the unintelligibilities and disvalues that constitute a "surd," an incoherent mixture of value and disvalue.[6] Since this surd, rather than perfect authenticity, characterizes the lives of most people, to a lesser or greater extent, it poses the profound question about the possibility of living a truly good, authentic life. It is related to Kant's famous third question: "In what may I hope?" The possibility of liberation from inauthenticity, therefore, leads beyond questions that are strictly ethical to questions that are inherently religious. That is to say, they lead to questions about the possibility of liberation from those things that vitiate authenticity and objective values. They lead beyond strictly ethical questions because the factors that vitiate an individual's decisions cannot be overcome by one's own vitiated decisions. The question of such liberation, then, is the question as to whether or not anything beyond an individual human being's ethical reflecting, deciding or doing is capable of setting her or his performance aright. This is a topic to which Lonergan devoted considerable attention throughout his career. It is a topic to which we will return in the section of chapter 13 devoted to the goodness of being and the problem of evil.[7]

11.4   The Human Good as Social

While human beings construct the wholeness and the value of their own lives one choice at a time, neither their choices nor the wholeness of their lives are closed in upon themselves. They are not isolated monads. Human choices and lives are massively situated. Not only are an individual's choices situated within the stream of her or his other choices that precede and follow them, they are also situated in the stream of questions and acts of practical insight, responsible reflection, horizons of feeling, and judgments of value that they presuppose.

For this reason our human choices are also situated in the midst of "what is going on." By virtue of our questions, our choices are related to our experiences of the concrete natural and interpersonal situations out of which those questions arise and to which those choices respond. We do not construct our lives in a vacuum or in Fantasyland. What we do with our lives is profoundly and inescapably conditioned by factors that we inherit or encounter, not only by the factors that we choose. The meaning of the sequence of our choices – the meaning of our lives – is always constructed in response to the givenness of the situations that form the contexts within which we make those choices. Moreover, by our responses we affect what will be "going on" in those situations after we choose and act.

Therefore, while the most direct and immediate good (or ill) realized by the performance of the structure of ethical intentionality is one's own authentic (or inauthentic) human life, other goods are also brought about by the very same acts of ethically reflecting and choosing. From one point of view, each human choice and action is related to the other choices and actions made by that individual to form the meaning and value of that person's life; but from another point of view, each individual choice and action is simultaneously related to the choices and actions of other human beings and, indeed, to its setting in the natural environment.

As Lonergan put it, "To a notable extent [human] operating is cooperating."[8] What Lonergan had in mind is the fact that most human choices are between courses of action that will enter into patterns of human interactions. This is so even when the individual does not explicitly think of her or his action as a matter of collaborative action. While this is most evident in the exceedingly intricate interdependencies of complex societies, it is also to be found in every social arrangement in human history.

What can seem like a purely individual decision – such as to get into one's own car and drive to the country or to purchase something – is in fact a choice to enter into patterns of cooperation. The ability to safely drive to one's chosen destination depends overwhelmingly on the cooperative efforts that build and repair roads, and upon thousands of other drivers who intelligently and freely follow traffic laws and customs, thereby maintaining a humanly constituted good of orderly highway transportation. Moreover, by driving according to those rules, the individual driver contributes to an order that serves other drivers as well, even though she or he may not have this intention explicitly in mind. More complex still are the manufacturing, commercial, and transportation networks that supply and resupply goods offered at sale at a store (or website), and the financial patterns that circulate money and credit to underpin those patterns.

Hence our decisions and actions enter into and have effects upon the social communities within which we act. Commonsense practical insights, judgments of value, and decisions overwhelmingly pertain to the concreteness of the social situations in which we participate. A concrete social situation can be profitably thought of therefore as a social ecosystem of individuals acting in and through institutions.[9] Every social ecosystem is composed of individuals playing now this role in this institution, and now that role in a different institution. For example, at the end of a workday a woman leaves her role in a business to take up her role in her family, and still later that evening she steps into her role as leader of a neighbourhood civic organization. Institutions and their roles form an interdependent and dynamic pattern of cooperation – a social ecosystem. At its best, a social ecosystem of interdependent institutions functions to intelligibly insure that the collective performance of tasks and roles makes possible the satisfaction of the collective needs of the group. In an intelligently ordered society, my responsible performance of my tasks in my role makes possible the satisfaction of the needs of someone else, while their responsible performances of their roles and tasks make possible the satisfaction of the needs of some third party, and so on in an extended, mutually conditioning network. The more advanced the social order, the more indirect and complex is that mutual conditioning.[10] Commonsense understanding and judgment of "what is going on" overwhelmingly pertain to correctly understanding in a concrete situation how to properly perform tasks and roles in order that the mutually conditioning good of an intelligible ecosystem can be sustained and renewed.

As Lonergan noted, an ecosystem of intelligent and valuable cooperation (or the "good of order," as he termed it) is effected through an institutional framework – a framework that links together the recurrent activities of various institutions, both formal and informal. Institutions, in turn, efficiently meet recurring needs by an intelligent division of efforts into roles. Yet while efficiency is a value, human beings do not live by efficiency alone. Efficiency can be pursued for the sake of, or at the expense of, vital, beautiful, friendly, and loving interpersonal relationships. Therefore, in addition to the various possible ways in which institutional frameworks can effectively meet recurring needs, there are also patterns of interpersonal relations that carry and constitute the horizons of value not of just any one individual but a whole society and culture. Human beings debate and struggle with one another to determine what kind of value (what "terminal value") their living together will have. That determination is worked out through the dynamics of their personal relations. The ways that people treat one another in their personal relations determine both what will be the value of their society and what value various persons will have in that society.

As individuals, we personally exercise the structure of ethical intentionality almost always within the concrete setting of our concrete social-cultural good. Our individual horizons of feelings are profoundly shaped by the stories, symbols, and personal relations of our cultural traditions. Through acts of believing, we draw upon the insights and judgments of fact and value gained by others in order to use them in our processes of ethical reflection. We draw upon them in order to understand and judge how best to place the satisfaction of our own needs and wants within the larger efficiency of the ecosystem of social cooperation, and in doing so we also contribute to the maintenance of those patterns. To the orderly, intelligible, and value-laden structure of the choices of others, we add our own insights into how to make things work and add our own valuations to the accumulated values of the social order in order to accomplish worthwhile purposes not just singly but cooperatively.

The foregoing is an abbreviated sketch of what Lonergan referred to as "the structure of the human good." Although he revised his account of that structure several times, he set forth his mature and final version of that account in *Method in Theology* in the form of the following diagram (see Figure 11.1):[11]

Figure 11.1. Diagram of the Structure of the Human Good

Individual		Social	Ends
Potentiality	Actuation		
capacity, need	operation	cooperation	particular good
plasticity, perfectibility	development, skill	institution role, task	good of order
liberty	orientation, conversion	personal relations	terminal value

The structure outlined in this diagram will be illustrated further in section 11.7 of this chapter, and will be examined in a more rigorous fashion in the next chapter.

11.5   The Human Good as Historical: The Corporate Good of Human History

In addition to the structural aspect of the social human good, there is also its dynamic aspect. In fact, our account of the human good cannot be considered fully concrete without including the dynamic aspect. A scientific account of the planet Mars would be incomplete if it included only an analysis of its geology but neglected to include the astrophysical account of its motion around the sun. Likewise, an account of the human good that focused only on its social and cultural structural dimensions but omitted its history would also be incomplete.

As human beings, we inquire and feel in response to the social situations that we inherit. We transform those situations by our choices and actions, individually and collectively, only to set the stage for further responses and transformations. Just as the whole sequence of individual choices and actions constitute the value of an individual, personal life, so also the sequence of collective human choices and actions constitute the whole, dynamic good of human history.

What Lonergan meant by the dynamic aspect of the human good – the "human good as developing object"[12] – is the entirety of human history, with all its glories and horrors, achievements and violence. Lonergan writes that the human good "is a history, a concrete, cumulative process resulting from developing human apprehension and human choices that may be good or evil. And that concrete developing process is what the human good in this life is, the human good on which depends [human] eternal destiny."[13] Lonergan spent much of his career thinking about the dynamics of human history, constantly refining his account. The details of his reworking of those ideas about the dynamics of human history are beyond the scope of this book. But throughout all those revisions, he continually identified three interpenetrating dynamics: progress, decline, and recovery (or redemption). Progress comes from authentic exercise of the structure of ethical intentionality. Decline results when biases or other distortions in the horizon of feelings undercut the proper unfolding of ethical intentionality. Recovery or redemption comes about when acts of resignation, forgiveness, or loving self-sacrifice heal the distortions brought into play by biases. While one or another dynamic can dominate during a certain historical period, all three operate and interpenetrate through every stage of history. In one period, collaborative creativity arising from ethical authenticity can predominate, in spite of the sporadic occurrence of acts of greed, corruption, and the violent abuse of persons. But in another period, biases can dominate social practices, so that disorder reigns and increases, and efforts at creativity and healing are marginalized (though not completely eliminated). In still another stage, acts of forgiveness, reconciliation, resignation, and loving self-sacrifice can reverse the dominance of biases even while those biases continue to chip away at the edges of recovery. (Consider, for example, the Truth and Reconciliation processes that followed the demise of apartheid in the Union of South Africa.)

The dynamic aspect of the human good can be viewed through the lens of institutions. It would be an oversight to think of institutions and their constituent roles as rigid and static. Institutions and roles are, rather, nodes within a dynamic, flexible, recurring flow (or social ecosystem) of many human actions. It is this dynamic social flow that serves needs from below and embodies values from above.

Moreover, institutions and roles are not merely situated within this dynamic flow, for they themselves are also dynamic. Roles and institutions are, after all, the constructs of commonsense intelligence, ethical reflection and judgment, and choice. Like the commonsense understandings and judgments that constitute them, roles and institutions are quite flexible. Without such flexibility they would soon perish. Their efficacious performance and the sense that these institutions have intrinsic worth within the social ecosystem[14] depends not only on the accumulated wisdom that underpins their stability, but also on the "at least one further" practical insight[15] and judgment of value that is required to adapt their structures to the irregularly ever-changing needs and circumstances.

In a biological ecosystem, life flows and circulates through complex and intricate patterns and channels. But these circulations do not merely reproduce the natural ecosystem, for it also evolves. In fact, it could be argued that the basic unit of evolution is not so much a species but an ecosystem – an aggregate of individuals and species linked together and interacting in intricate circulations of mutual dependency.

Like a biological ecosystem, the human good as a social ecosystem not only reproduces itself but also evolves and devolves. Both the maintenance of social systems of institutions as well as their positive transformations are the results of human beings acting in accord with the structure of ethical intentionality. Frequently our actions modify institutional patterns, sometimes in ways barely noticeable, other times in ways most dramatic. Over the long run, the accumulation of practical insights will not merely adapt, but will also gradually or dramatically transform the roles and institutions – eventually transforming even the social, economic, political, and cultural frameworks (goods of order and terminal values) that incorporate them. The judgments of value realized in individual decisions will also affect the quality of personal relations that carry the value of performing these roles in these institutional settings.

As with individual human lives, human corporate cooperation also has a kind of wholeness, a dynamic historical wholeness that is a good when it is produced by many individuals acting and interacting in accord with the structure of ethical intentionality. This dynamic wholeness is the human good writ large – the larger story (history) within which individual stories occur, from which they draw their storying resources, and to which they make their story-altering inputs.[16] Recently, it has been alleged that every human being has the fundamental right to author the story of her or his life, and therefore has the right to determine how that story ends. But neither the beginning nor the end of our lives is solely within the power of our choosing. The story we compose of our own life picks up the story of history that has been going on before our birth. Well after we are gone, what we do, including how we die, will enter into that story in ways over which we have little control. We cannot by force of will insulate the story of our own life from the larger history of humanity.

So far I have focused on the creative dynamic of history where institutions and personal relations are developed through authentic ethical intentionality. Lest the forgoing seem naively optimistic, let me emphasize that this is only the first of Lonergan's approximations to the tragedy and comedy of human history. Of course human beings also act out of bias – seemingly more often than not – in ways that short-circuit, violate, betray, and subvert the intrinsic normativity of the structure of ethical intentionality. When they do so, they introduce unintelligible and disvaluable elements into the corporate human story. Small indiscretions and acts of petty selfishness and prejudice at first introduce small distortions into the intelligible and valuable fabric of cooperative life, and are often in turn met with reprisals that only increase the disorder. Laws are passed and bureaucracies created in attempts to make sure that such infractions never happen again. However, even if these reprisals seem to make common sense, often their long-term consequences are not thoroughly considered. Some attempts to prevent future deviant behaviours can have a greater effect on stifling intelligently creative and personal responses to concrete, unforeseen situations that do arise. If so, these law and bureaucratic responses to initial infractions amplify them into more serious distortions in the good of order and personal relations. Rules and laws intended to prevent and remove small deviations from the structure of the human good can begin to make ordinary living increasingly difficult, oppressive, impossible, or absurd. As patterns become more characterized by defensive rather than by creative and cooperative patterns, they set the conditions for an acceleration of inauthentic responses, leading in the limit to the "soft tyranny" of the majority, or to more forceful forms of organized violence, terrorism, or nihilism.

So in a fuller view, the dynamics of human history form a conflicting mixture of authenticity and inauthenticity. Human history clearly is not unmitigated or inevitable progress in goodness. The wholeness of human history has a fragile goodness, where the achievements of collaborative ethical authenticity are ever threatened, degraded, and corroded by acts of inauthenticity. The course of human history has a twisted and broken goodness. As such, the strictly philosophical answer to the question of its ultimate destiny, whether goodness or nihilism will prevail, is uncertain. Whatever answer might be possible comes from Lonergan's third dynamic of recovery, and this is what he referred to as the "social function of religion."[17] This will be taken up again in chapter 13.

11.6   Summary

In the foregoing sections I have argued that to act in accord with the structure of ethical intentionality brings about several things at once. First, we constitute the human good that is our own life, the good that pertains to the sequence of activities that make up our own identity, the story and "one and only edition" of our own life. Second, while experiences, insights, feelings, judgments of value, choices, and actions constitute our own identity, they also simultaneously maintain, develop, and repair the good of the social ecosystem that is already in place – or damage and contribute to a deterioration of that good that has already been proceeding before us. In so doing, we inescapably contribute to the social good or evil and simultaneously constitute ourselves as members of that social order. Third, we also inevitably introduce intelligent and valuable innovations that gradually or dramatically transform the social ecosystem. In doing so, we help constitute the destiny of humankind as a whole, not just of our own society, and simultaneously constitute ourselves as members and participants in the grand drama of human history.[18]

In a most profound sense, to be an authentically ethical person is to take on the responsibility for receiving the living reality that one inherits, to assess its realities and values intelligently and critically, to reflect authentically about what one should do in response, and to choose how one is to pass it along to the next generation and act on those judgments of value and choices. This can happen even when individuals are not thinking explicitly about history. It happens spontaneously whenever morally converted human beings act in accord with the unrestricted notion of value, unrestricted being-in-love, and the normative scale of values. This is because actions that result from asking and answering all the further questions felt to be pertinent by a converted horizon of feelings will be just the right actions needed to make better whatever good human history has achieved so far. However, the chances that people will consistently act in such ways are slim indeed.

11.7   An Illustration: Building a Water Well in Malaya

In order to illustrate these points in a more concrete way, I draw upon Nevil Shute's novel, *A Town Like Alice*.[19] I chose this illustration because of its relative simplicity. More complex examples would require far more elaboration.

Although *A Town Like Alice* is a work of fiction, its protagonist, an Englishwoman named Jean Paget, is based upon a real person and her actual deeds during the Second World War.[20] In the novel, Paget unexpectedly receives a substantial inheritance from an uncle she barely knew. She decides to use a good portion of her new income to build a water well for the Malayan village of Kuala Telang. She explains her reasons for this decision to her solicitor by telling the story of her captivity during the war.

At the outbreak of the war, Paget was working in Malaya. She tells how she and other foreign nationals were taken prisoner by Japanese troops during their invasion. Their captors set the men to work on building a railway. Lacking a clear plan for the women and children, they forced-marched them, giving them little food or medical care. Over a period of six months they were compelled by Japanese soldiers to walk many hundreds of miles almost aimlessly, and half of the women and children perished.

The Japanese cohort guarding the women is gradually reduced to a single soldier, who eventually dies of fever at the village of Kuala Telang. The women then convince the headman of the village to let them stay and work, and he negotiates this arrangement with local occupying officials. This village becomes their refuge for the duration of the war. While there, Paget and the others observe and participate in the hard labour of the "women's work" of carrying water twice a day from a spring a mile from the village. Out of gratitude for the hospitality of the villagers, Paget decides to return to the village and to use part of her inheritance to have the well built.

The novel is a very rich narrative of many other episodes and details, but I have chosen to focus on this episode because it affords an opportunity to look closely at the concrete complexities involved in all human decisions and actions that bring about the human good.

Lonergan frequently emphasized that "the good is always concrete," and this story illustrates his point well. Paget's is not just any generalized decision. It is a decision situated with respect to very specific and concrete physical and social-cultural ecosystems and events from history. She chooses to build a very specific structure at a very specific natural and social location. The good of her actions emerges out of very particular sets of conditions that are intrinsic to its concreteness and realization. This is the case with all instances of the human good.

The building of this well depended in the first place upon a very specific natural set of conditions out of which it emerged. There had to be an aquifer beneath the village in order for the project even to be possible, and many practical insights into underground water were needed in order to know where and how to dig a well.

The specifically human dimensions came into play when human bodily movements acted upon the physical objects and natural rhythms of this natural setting. Bodily movements are among the most immediate things brought about by following the structure of ethical intentionality. Bodily movements include movements of hands, arms, and legs, but also movements of speech organs and facial muscles that communicate meanings. All this is very much in evidence in this story, as building a well requires bodily acts of probing, digging, building, and reinforcing, but also communicating and persuading people about wishes, desires, and hopes, as well as instructions for carrying out appropriate bodily actions.

Constructing a water well involves a great deal more than digging a hole with a shovel. The soil from the walls of any deep pit soon begins to loosen and collapse into the hole. It requires therefore a considerable accumulation of insights into soil and other factors in order to dig deeply enough to reach underground water while also insuring that the shaft will not collapse. In addition, some sort of device would have to be constructed in order to haul water up to the surface. Paget realizes that "well-digging is a skilled craft" involving many insights, and learns there is just one family in the vicinity with the requisite knowledge and skills. In addition to skillfully digging the well, they also have the insights and skills needed to shore up its shaft with brickwork.[21]

In terms that Lonergan develops in *Insight*, the building of this well is an instance of generalized emergent probability, where new "schemes of recurrence" arise out of prior schemes[22] – in this case, human schemes emerging out of natural schemes. At the physical level, the most important schemes of recurrence are those responsible for the replenishment of the underground aquifer. In turn, the well makes it possible for new schemes of water movement to emerge from the rhythms of the aquifer, as the villagers repeatedly draw water to the surface. Even at the physical level, therefore, a water well is more accurately understood in terms of its place in this emerging series of recurring schemes, rather than merely as a static object sitting in the middle of a village.

Yet the goods brought about by Paget's decision go considerably beyond establishing new pathways of water movement. Clearly the principal intention of her decision was to change some of the social patterns of the village. Prior to her decision, the village's recurring vital needs for water were met through the repetitive patterns of human activities carried out by the village's women. The well rendered those earlier patterns obsolete, but also set the conditions for the emergence of new patterns. For one thing, men would now become involved in the schemes of obtaining water by working the bucket. In addition, new patterns were developed for taking turns at the well. Beyond that, the well (along with a new accompanying wash house that Paget also commissioned) set the conditions for the emergences of still further new social patterns. These innovations freed great quantities of the women's time and also freed them from the physical strain and wear on their bodies that carrying water from the spring imposed. Their newly liberated time and energy became available for new kinds of social interactions, as Paget had imagined and hoped. In other words, the well provided both a time and a place where the women over and again could sit and talk while the water-drawing and washing took place.[23]

Paget's decision, therefore, eventually brought about new goods at both the physical and human levels. On the physical level, the well is the site of a new recurring scheme of water movement that emerged out of and is conditioned by the previously occurring schemes that constituted the aquifer. At the human level, new schemes of social cooperation emerged to transform the previous schemes that had constituted the life of the entire village. The life of the village was an intricate, interdependent set of recurring operations that included fishing, planting, harvesting and cooking rice, replenishing water, marrying, and begetting and rearing children, to mention but a few. The new schemes of securing water and women's gatherings were only possible in the context of the conditions provided by those other schemes. But those other patterns themselves also depended upon a constant supply of water.

All of the newly emergent schemes were instances of reality, in the sense discussed in chapter 3. According to Lonergan's account, realities are actual intelligibilities known in virtually unconditioned judgments. In the case of the Kuala Telang well, the intelligible connections among the various recurring movements of the water were provided by the laws of gravitation and hydrodynamics. But the intelligible connections among the various recurring human activities were provided by shared mutual understandings of the people involved. These new human schemes were not made regular or intelligible by natural laws alone: rather, new mutual understandings were needed to intelligibly coordinate those activities into new schemes of securing water for drinking, washing, and other vital needs. Again, new physical schemes emerge and become real once appropriate prior conditions are fulfilled through natural processes. But the human schemes became real only after some people had the practical insights and communicated them to others, who then all agreed (decided) and acted in accord with those mutual understandings. The mutual understandings grasped the intelligibilities constitutive of these new schemes. But human decisions of agreement and consequent coordinated actions – not natural processes – were required to make the intelligibilities of those human schemes of cooperation real.

Paget's own decision and actions, therefore, initiated a series of levels of emerging realities (schemes of recurrence). But of course there is yet another part of the story that has to do with the *values* of those realities. The point to building the well (and wash house) was not only the emergence of a new physical scheme or even the inauguration of new intelligible patterns of social cooperation. Most fundamentally the building of the well actualized Paget's judgments of ethical value and her decision. The actuality of the well was her concrete and particular way of expressing a value – gratitude – which itself was a response to the villagers' own earlier expressions of the values of hospitality and healing towards her and her fellow prisoners of war.

With this decision, Paget actualized herself as a person of gratitude and generosity. Hers was a decision of comparative value – one that she came to only after a period of serious reflection, which is described in some detail in the novel. At the time she learned of the inheritance, she was not married and had a very drab life as a secretary in a women's shoe and handbag factory. "I haven't got any other life," as she put it.[24] She did not think it "was a job worth doing," except for the income.[25] So she spent some time reflecting about possibilities: "If I am going to do work at anything, I want it to be really worthwhile."[26] She considered volunteering at a hospital or charitable organization or cultivating an appreciation for the fine arts. She also could have chosen to live an unchallenging life of comfort sustained by the healthy income from her inheritance. But after reflecting about the various paths she could take, she arrived at the judgment that the value of having the well built was the best course for her personally. Her felt scale of value preference formed the context for that judgment of comparative value and decision.

Her decision to build the well constituted the kind of person she would be, but simultaneously was also a decision to actualize a social value that would be independent of her own personhood. It actualized a more efficient, less onerous way of regularly meeting the village's vital needs for water. It would make "life easier for them, as they made life easier for us," as Paget put it.[27] The new roles and skills that were needed for taking turns in pulling water up from the well were actualities endowed with the social value of greater efficiency and the value of liberating women's time and strength for other worthy endeavours. But more than that, by choosing to accept the well, the village joined Paget in actualizing a new and greater valorization of the women in the village. Paget reflected carefully and deliberately about her intention to originate a small but significant transformation of the cultural value of the women: "the gift of a woman for women, and in this thing [well and wash house] the men shall do as the women say" as she put it.[28]

A few of the village women initially "looked shocked at this heresy," and worried "whether it was not impious to wish to alter arrangements that had satisfied their mothers and their grandmothers before them."[29] The women reflected together and eventually came to the value judgment that this would indeed be a good innovation. Yet Paget was also very sensitive to the cultural and gender values at stake in this village. When she met with the headman to propose the project, she followed the customs and protocols and spoke respectfully. Like the women, he too initially expressed the view that what had been good enough for their mothers and grandmothers should also be good enough for the present generation. But Paget built her case on values and recent history that were already operative in the culture of the village. In particular, she quoted to the headman from a sura in the *Qur'an*: "If ye be kind towards women and fear to do them wrong [Allah] is well acquainted with what ye do." She then interpreted, "It would be kind to let the women have their well."

The headman was persuaded, but needed to bring the proposal for deliberation among the village elders. It took them two days to come to the judgment that the new well would be a good thing, and that the innovation would not be displeasing to Allah. While all this might seem pretty insignificant on the grand order of world history, the careful deliberations by Paget, the village women, and the elders show that they understood that this proposed change somehow had far-reaching consequences. That is to say, they understood that what they were contemplating and proposing mattered and had value precisely for the story of human history.

When we look out at the great forces and movement of history, we might be tempted to say nothing we can do will change its outcome. But this is because we are trapped in our imaginations rather than engaging in self-transcendence to concretely think and evaluate the reality and value of history. We might wish and imagine that we could stop an impending war or end poverty by some action we might take. We might imagine that such actions are the only actions we could do that would affect the outcome of history. But those are just fantasies about history. In thinking this way, we would not be engaging with the reality or true value of history or with our actual decisions and actions and their consequences for the story of history.

In reality and in value, each and every human decision and action affects the story of human history. It affects the story *as a whole* – how the *whole* story turns out – not just the last episode with which the story ends. The good of that story is to be discerned in the history of the ever-changing patterns of personal relations, just as the real mission of an institution is to be discerned in the personal relations among its members and those with whom it interacts.

Because the decisions and actions of each and every human being constitute some part of that dynamic pattern of personal relations, what is at stake in each of our decisions and actions is human destiny, the story of humanity. We constitute ourselves as persons in and through our exercises and evasions of moral self-transcendence. But just as concretely, we affect the constitution of the history of personal relations within which we emerge as persons.

Therefore, the new realities of physical and human patterns, the new levels of social and cultural values and personal relations, and their contributions to the value of human history all emerged intertwined together at Kuala Telang. Just as the physical reality of the well emerged out of the conditions supplied by prior physical schemes (in conjunction with the actions of the workmen), so also the new values emerged out of the prior schemes of meaning and value that informed the life of the village. Paget's ideas, feelings, reflections, value judgments, decisions, and actions inaugurated the actualization of these realties and values, but she was not solely responsible for their emergences. In the first place, the full realization of her decision depended upon the realities and values that were already in place, which provided the conditions for the possibility of these innovations. In addition, the realities and values became actual only because other human beings (village women and elders, and the workers from outside) came to their own judgments of value, decisions, and actions that cooperated with Paget's judgments, decisions, and actions. These actualizations were the result of many acts of human cooperation that arose from the exercise of ethical intentionality by numerous people whom the story reveals to be of high degrees of moral conversion.

Before she returned to Malaya to have the well built, Paget looked back on her three years of captivity and life in the Malayan village. She said to her solicitor, "It was three years wasted, just chopped out of one's life ... At least I suppose it was. I know a lot about Malays, but that's not worth much here in England." The solicitor responded sagely, "You won't know if it is wasted until you come to the end of your life ... Perhaps not then."[30] Once the well and wash house had been built and she recognized the good of the changes she inaugurated, she tacitly accepted the wisdom of her solicitor's words. As she prepared to leave Kuala Telang for the next stage of her life, she became aware that "she was leaving three years of her life behind her, and that is never a very easy thing to do."[31] This is not the sort of thing she would have said a few months earlier. The well and the transformation of the life of the village gave meaning and value even to those three years of lost freedom and suffering. By her judgments of value, decisions, and actions – and the reciprocating decisions of others who joined with her in endorsing those values – Paget transformed those horrible years into experiences with the potential for new value. With these actions she gave a meaning and value to the sufferings she endured during the three years of captivity. Her sufferings were not only those of the physical discomforts, pain, and disease she would not have had to endure in a just, well-functioning good of order. More importantly her sufferings included having to endure in sorrow the unjust deaths of so many companions. Yet her act of building the well and all the goods that followed from it transformed those earlier sufferings from a meaningless waste into a potency out of which emerged new values that endowed the sufferings with worth. In no way was the horror and evil of sufferings given a justification. Rather, Paget was able to return goods for those evils. She was able to redeem those earlier events from the oblivion of unintelligibility and evil, and to help make them into something that played a role in the ongoing good of human history. She was able to turn those events into sources for meaning and value beyond the horrors.

Although the episode in Shute's novel is fictional, there are numerous real stories about the ways that wells or conduits to villages in developing countries dramatically transform their social lives, and especially the cultures of women.[32] The story the building of a well at Kuala Telang provides a concrete illustration of Lonergan's account of the components in the structure of the human good, and of the dynamics that are brought about when people act individually and cooperatively in accord with the structure of ethical intentionality.

Bringing about the good that being ethical intends is a matter of discerning how the good is emerging and contributing the next intelligent, critical, and ethically responsible thing needed to build up that good. But we don't make our contribution by looking at a blueprint or plan of the human good and then using it to guide our actions like a building contractor. Rather, we discern and contribute to the human good precisely by desiring it through our unrestricted notion of value, and then pursuing that desideratum through fidelity to our structure of ethical intentionality. We discern the good that we are called to bring about by asking and answering the questions that arise out of the concrete situations into which we are thrown, and doing so under the guidance of feelings of preference for the normative scale of values. Our actions are contributions to the development of the human good insofar as we are faithful to the calls of our ever further pertinent questions within a morally converted horizon of feelings.

We can discern all this at work in the story about Jean Paget's decision and its consequences. The novel illustrates the relationship between moral conversion and the structure of the human good, in the manner discussed in chapter 9, section 9.9. The narrator tells the reader that stories circulated widely in England and Malaya about Jean Paget's nobility, compassion, prudence, and strength of character under duress during her war captivity. Her decisions and actions during captivity and later in the novel reveal that her ethical focus is primarily on the third level of Lonergan's structure of the human good. This is especially revealed in her concern for personal relations not only among the women in the village but also her respect for the cultural and religious traditions that gave meaning and worth to life in the village. She changed institutional patterns by changing the operations and cooperations by which basic needs were satisfied. But satisfaction of needs was not her primary concern; her primary concern was to nurture the emergence of even more valuable personal relations out of those that had given the village its prior value orientation. Yet she wisely understood that improved personal relations are intimately bound up with an intelligibly functioning good of order, and with the reasonable satisfaction of recurring human needs. Because this kind of commitment to the human good on the third level is a key indicator of moral conversion, it is fair to say that the fictional character of Jean Paget is a representative of moral conversion.

It is possible to discern the elements of the structure and dynamics of the human good not only in fictional but also in actual human decisions and actions taken in concert with the ethical decisions and actions of others. Discerning when this happens in social and historical situations can be enhanced by an appropriate method in ethics. Lonergan's account of the structure of the human good contributes an important heuristic to such a method. Chapters 15 and 16 will explore Lonergan's contributions to a method in ethics more fully. There it will become evident that genuine practice of this method depends upon self-appropriation in the fullest sense. The next chapter, however, is devoted to the more limited goal of elaborating the heuristic structure of the human good, and examining Lonergan's claim that it is an "invariant" structure. His claim that these elements of the structure and dynamics of the human good are to be found in every instance of cooperative human relationships goes well beyond what can be established on the basis of a descriptive, illustrative story, even if that story were the actual rather than the fictional history of a single village. A different approach, an explanatory approach, is required to justify such a claim about the generality of the structure and dynamics of the human good. The next chapter therefore turns from description of the human good to an explanatory, foundational approach rooted in the very structures of ethical intentionality and human cooperation themselves.

12 The Human Good: Explanatory Foundations

12.1 Introduction

The descriptions of the various dimensions of the human good in the previous chapter raise further questions regarding its structure. First we might ask, "What is the point of this complex structure of the human good? What is it good for? What is its role in Lonergan's thought?" Again, we may well ask, "Just how universal is this structure of the human good?" Lonergan said that the structure is "invariant" across all social and cultural arrangements, which certainly implies universality. What justification can be offered in support of that claim? Again, in the earlier chapters of this book, the feelings that intend values and judgments of ethical values were shown to play prominent roles in ethical life. But just what sort of a good is a value? How does it relate to other conceptions of the good? The goodness of a value needs to be identified, as well as distinguished from and related to other kinds of goods.

This chapter addresses these questions. Their answers require a fairly technical and explanatory approach that is a departure from the descriptive approach of the preceding chapter.[1] This technical and explanatory approach is needed for several reasons. First, in chapter 11 the structure of the human good was simply presented as a given, without argument or justification. This technical and explanatory approach is needed in order to provide a justification. Second, this explanatory approach will also provide greater clarity to the meaning of the terms in the structure of the human good. Third, the discussion in this chapter will also prepare the grounds for exploring still further questions regarding the good in senses that go beyond the human good, and also for questions regarding the accuracy of Lonergan's account of the normative scale of value preference. These further questions will be taken up in the next two chapters.

12.2   The Structure of the Human Good as Heuristic

Lonergan's intention in devising his diagram of the structure of the human good (see section 11.4 of the previous chapter) was to set forth a heuristic structure. The word heuristic derives from the Greek term *heuriskein*, meaning "to discover." A heuristic structure is an aid to learning, discovering, or problem-solving. Lonergan attached great importance to the heuristic dimensions in his discussions of scientific methods and the methods of metaphysics and theology.[2]

His account of the structure of the human good extends this focus on the heuristic dimensions of human thought to the realm of ethics. The terms in his diagram of the structure of the human good offer guides and anticipations of the sorts of possible goods to be found in the realm of human affairs. When people ask, "What is the good of *that?*," they mean many different sorts of things and use the term "good" in various ways that are sometimes equivocal, conflated, conflicting, and often needlessly restricted. All too often the question is posed in an implicitly rhetorical fashion, the acceptable range of answers already taken for granted in the way the question is posed. Such rhetorical questions presuppose, for example, that things cannot be seriously considered good unless they are pleasant, fun, or morally upright, or will bring a profit, fame, power, luxurious possessions, intellectual rigour, aesthetic sublimity, or lawfulness. Each of these is a good, but none is the whole of the human good.

Lonergan's overall objective was to formulate a heuristic structure that would anticipate the broadest range of the ways in which the question, "What is the good of that?" might be answered. That heuristic was open to the possibilities of goodness beyond the human realm – the possibilities of natural and transcendent goodness, as will be shown in chapter 13. Still, his structure of the human good envisions a very wide range of goods brought about by human thought, choice, and action. His structure of the human good is, therefore, a broad and important part of his overall heuristic of the good. The diagram offers the broadest possible terms that need to be borne in mind when anyone attempts to answer objectively the question "What is the good of that?" about human affairs.[3] The story of Jean Paget and construction of the well in Kuala Telang illustrates the many dimensions of the human good that can be brought to light by using Lonergan's heuristic diagram of the structure of the human good. It can be similarly beneficial when applied to non-fictional social and historical situations as well, and thereby reveal what goods there might be, goods which would be otherwise overlooked.

Reliable heuristic guidance is especially welcome when we encounter the human condition in its messy and confusing mixture of good and evil. We encounter humanity as at once attractive, fascinating, disconcerting, disgusting, and horrifying. This encounter is made all the more difficult because along with it comes a welter of conflicting human opinions about good and evil. It is hard to know how to distinguish good from evil in what we encounter when the opinions offered about what is good and evil themselves are so conflicting.

Knowing how to discern what is good and to distinguish it from what is evil is one of the fruits of self-appropriation. That discernment is enhanced by a heuristic structure of the human good that is rooted in self-appropriation. This is what Lonergan was endeavouring to offer in his diagram. His heuristic structure brings into sharper focus the different kinds of goods to be found in the human condition, and thereby also casts important light on the different forms that human evil does take.[4]

In order to accomplish all this, this heuristic structure of the human good must have a fairly wide range of applicability. Lonergan certainly regarded the structure of the human good as transcultural. He wrote that "it can be applied to any human good [i.e., society] from the Stone age to the present time,"[5] and that it is "compatible with any stage of technological, economic, political, cultural, religious development."[6] For these reasons he claimed that this structure is "invariant."[7] However, he never presented an argument in support of this claim in *Method in Theology*. The later sections of this chapter propose a justification for his claim of invariance, by explaining the interconnections between the structure of the human good and the self-appropriation of the structure of ethical intentionality. Before taking up that explanatory effort, however, it is necessary first to embark on an extended, technical explanation of the invariance of his parallel account of the heuristic structure for metaphysics, and its derivation from cognitional structure.

12.3   Invariance of the Heuristic Structure of Proportionate Being

While Lonergan did not provide an explicit justification of the invariance of the structure of the human good anywhere in his writings, he did set forth suggestions as to how this might be done.[8] He also drew a parallel between the heuristic structure of the human good and what he called "the integral heuristic structure of proportionate being."[9]

> Just as the universe of proportionate being is a compound of potency, form, and act, because it is to be known through experience, understanding, and judgment, so the universe of [human] proportionate good is a compound of objects of desire, intelligible

orders, and values, because the good that [humanity] does intelligently and rationally is a manifold in the field of experience, ordered by intelligence, and rationally chosen.[10]

In this section we explore what he meant by the structure of proportionate being, how it can be derived from cognitional structure, and why it should be regarded as an invariant structure. In the next section we use this model to show how the structure of the human good can be similarly derived from the expanded structure of ethical intentionality. In doing so, we will also show why that structure should be regarded as invariant, and why its components should be regarded as good.

In chapter 2, we traced Lonergan's argument that the proper heuristic definition of being in the unqualified sense is the totality to be known in asking and answering all questions for intelligence and reflection: "In its full sweep, being is whatever is to be known by intelligent grasp and reasonable affirmation." But this totality can be subdivided into reality that is proportionate to human knowing and reality that transcends human knowing, where "being that is proportionate to human knowing not only is to be understood and affirmed but also is to be experienced."[11] Hence the realm of reality that is proportionate to human knowing can be defined heuristically as what is to be known by all the reasonable affirmations of the intelligent grasps of the totality of possible human experience. The realm of reality that transcends human knowing, by contrast, consists of whatever would be known in answers to questions for intelligence and reflection that go beyond human experience. (One such question, e.g., would be "Is there anything beyond possible human experience?")

Lonergan proposed that the method of metaphysics would profit by this division, and that an "integral heuristic structure" could be worked out for proportionate being.[12] By "*integral* heuristic structure," he meant the structure of "the *whole in* knowledge but not the whole *of* knowledge."[13] The whole of knowledge would be knowledge of all reality – knowledge of everything about everything. But the whole in human knowledge is just knowledge of the structure of relationships among all that could be humanly known.

12.3.1   *The Isomorphism between Human Cognition and Potency, Form, and Act*

Lonergan never provided a diagram of the integral structure of proportionate being comparable to the one he offered of the human good, but he did identify three levels in proportionate being – *potency, form, and act*[14] – that are parallel (or more precisely, isomorphic) to the fundamental acts of cognitional structure. He referred to this parallel or isomorphism as the basic "theorem" of his metaphysics.[15] In mathematical usage at least, to say that there is a theorem of isomorphism implies that there is a proof for it. Lonergan does offer an argument of sorts for his theorem, although it is terse and its significance easily overlooked. That argument such as it is runs as follows:

> It follows that *potency, form, and act* constitute a unity. For what is experienced is what is understood; and what is understood is what is affirmed. The three levels of cognitional activity yield a single knowing; for experience alone is not human knowing; experience and understanding do not suffice for knowing; only when the unconditioned is reached and affirmation or negation occurs does knowing in the proper meaning of the term arise. In like manner, the contents of the three levels of cognitional activity constitute a unity; one does not know a first proportionate being by experiencing, a second by understanding, and a third by judging; on the contrary, the three contents coalesce into a single known. Hence potency, form, and act, since they are known by experience, understanding, and judgment, are not three proportionate beings but three components in a single proportionate being.[16]

Because this argument for the three components of any entity within proportionate reality is so compact, it will be helpful to spell it out a bit. The basic outlines of the argument were already encountered in chapter 2, which reviewed Lonergan's argument that all of being is completely intelligible. Here additional nuances are introduced because of the restriction to the realm of being available to human experiencing.

The key to comprehending Lonergan's argument is to start at the top level with the act of factual judging, and to then work one's way downward towards experience. Indeed, the argument is really grounded in the very nature of the act of affirmative judging of facts. Objective affirmative judgments of fact are always unconditional answers to questions for reflection: "*Is* it so?" Acts of affirmation always assert, "Yes, it *is*." Therefore, in genuine virtually unconditioned affirmations, something or some aspect of something is known to be ("is"). Some dimension of being, of reality, is known. The *noematic* content of a *noetic* affirmative factual judgment is what Lonergan means by the metaphysical element *act*. Knowing the "isness" is knowing the *act* of a reality. Precisely because the structure of knowing includes acts of affirming, human knowing is not limited to some merely phenomenal or ideal realm; human knowing stretches past the phenomenal and the ideal to affirm and thereby know the real, the *is*. Of course a particular human affirmative judgment does not know *all* reality, *all* of what is, but each judgment of fact knows something about reality as it really is. Hence, with acts of affirming, human subjects achieve cognitional self-transcendence out of the realm of merely immanent activities into the realm of proportionate being.

This, of course, is all under the proviso that the affirmative judgments are grounded in reflective acts of understanding that genuinely grasp virtually unconditioned grounds for the affirmations. Mere assertions about facts that lack such grounds cannot be said to know what is, what is real. Still the argument is not that any particular factual proposition does or must have sufficient grounds to be judged affirmatively. Rather, the argument is that *whenever* we *do* arrive at genuinely unconditioned affirmative judgments, we do know that something is – we know *act*.

Virtually unconditioned affirmative human judgments, however, never occur in a vacuum. They always occur as the last stage of a structured series of cognitional acts. This means that there is no such thing in the order of human knowing as a pure, isolated knowing of *act* alone. Therefore, the cognitional activities of affirmative judging in effect draw with them the "it" when they affirm, "Yes, *it is* so." The "it" that is affirmed to be so is none other than the intelligibility about which a question for reflection inquired, "Is *it* so?" This means that every human act of affirming affirms the reality of some intelligible "it." When properly formulated in an explanatory fashion, that intelligibility is the *form* corresponding to the *act*.

Furthermore, human acts of understanding themselves always arise as answers to questions "What, why, where, when, how is *it*?" But the "it" referred to in this question is different from the "it" for reflection and judgment. The "it" referred to in the question for reflection is an intelligibility, whereas the "it" referred to in the question for intelligence is the *noematic* content of some *noetic* act of experiencing that gave rise to the question for intelligence. The insight that answered to that question for intelligence grasped *an* intelligibility. When the insight occurs, it might or might not be a correct understanding of *the* intelligibility of that experienced content. But once the insight (or its corrected revision) is judged to be correct, this means it *is the* intelligibility *of* the content of the experience. It is not just any insight but the insight into *this* experienced content that has been judged as correct. This intelligibility or *form* affirmed to be real is therefore simultaneously affirmed to be the real intelligibility of the content of that experience, which Lonergan calls *potency*. In this way, the content of the affirmative judgment (*act*), the intelligible content it affirms (*form*), and the experiential content (*potency*) thereby made intelligible constitute a unified compound, which together are known to be so – known to be a real entity. The pattern of relationships between *potency, form,* and *act* within a particular reality is isomorphic to the pattern of relationships between experiencing, understanding, and judging because those acts relate their contents by means of their dynamic structure.

However, the *potency*, *form*, and *act* of something real are not constituted as real by the structure of human knowing. They are constituted as real by the component of *act*. Human knowing can know that compound objectively because it is real. Human knowing can do this by subjecting its experiencing, understanding, and judging to the demands of unrestricted questioning and thereby can transcend itself to know that particular reality in its particular, actual ontological constituents of *potency*, *form*, and *act*. From all this, it follows that all that can be known by human beings – all of the realities proportionate to human knowing – have this tripartite structure of *potency*, *form*, and *act*.[17]

12.3.2 The Invariance of the Structure of Potency, Form, and Act

Furthermore, this structure has a certain kind of invariance. The invariance of the tripartite structure of proportionate beings derives from the invariance of cognitional structure. Lonergan presented an argument for the invariance of human cognitional structure in *Insight* under the heading of the impossibility of revising the reviser.[18] There he argued that any attempt to revise his account of the structure of human knowing would amount to a claim that there was something about the experiences of human knowing that Lonergan had not correctly understood. This challenge to his account, however, would involve a use of that cognitional structure itself. Any such objection would be the articulation of the judgment that a different understanding of the human cognitional experiences is the correct one or more nearly correct than Lonergan's own. In attempting to revise Lonergan's account, the reviser would be employing the basic acts of the structure itself. In other words, the objector would be involved in the "performative contradiction" of using what he or she disclaims in words.

Lonergan was quick to agree that the invariance of cognitional structure does not rule out the "possibility of the minor revisions that leave basic lines intact but attain a greater exactitude and a greater fulness of detail."[19] But the basic lines which the revision would have to leave intact are the structural relations among the acts of experiencing, questions for intelligence, insights, questions for reflection, reflective understandings of the virtually unconditioned, and judgments of fact. These alone are crucial to Lonergan's account of the invariance of human cognitional structure.

Since proportionate being is what is to be known by the cognitionally structured sequence of those acts, every reality proportionate to that structure of knowing will have the tripartite structure. So the tripartite structure of proportionate being is also invariant, since it is by definition what is to be known by human cognitional structure.

12.3.3 Further Dimensions of the Integral Heuristic Structure of Proportionate Being

While the tripartite structure of proportionate beings can therefore be said to be invariant, still the integral heuristic structure of proportionate being is not identical with the tripartite structure. The structure of proportionate being as such is the structure of the whole of what can be known by possible human experiencing, understanding, and judging. That whole does not necessarily have the same structure as the multitudes of proportionate beings that populate it. As Lonergan put it, the tripartite structure is "not an instance of an integral heuristic structure, for it does not exhaust the resources of the human mind in anticipating."[20] The tripartite structure is of the beings in the proportionate universe, but it is not necessarily the structure of the whole of all the fundamental relationships among those beings. The structure of those relations can be approached by considering other aspects of the ways that the activities of cognitional structure are related to one another.

Further components in the integral heuristic structure of proportionate being, therefore, follow from attending to other ways in which acts in the cognitional structure are related to one another. First, from the nature of negative judgments there follow heuristic anticipations of different kinds of real distinctions within proportionate being.[21] Second, basic differences among the different kinds of insights and their corresponding intelligibilities imply further distinctions within in the tripartite structure of proportionate being. The most fundamental such difference is that between explanatory insights into the relations among data, and explanatory insights into the intelligible unities of different data. This implies a differentiation of the tripartite structure into central potency, form, and act (which are heuristic anticipations of unified entities that he earlier called "things") and conjugate potency, form, and act (which anticipate what can be humanly known about the real relations among things).[22] Third, distinctions among fundamentally different kinds of explanatory relations mean that the integral heuristic structure of proportionate being must be prepared for the possibility of distinctly systematic, non-systematic, genetic, and dialectical process.[23] Fourth, because some insights will be related to others as "higher viewpoints," scientific investigations of proportionate being must therefore anticipate the possibility of distinct and even hierarchically arranged explanatory genera and species of things, events, and recurring schemes. Fifth, the integral heuristic structure of proportionate being would anticipate the possibility and even probabilities of more complex species of things and schemes emerging within genera, and developing from the potencies provided by earlier and less differentiated species.[24] Finally, Lonergan argued that proportionate being itself is dynamic ("evolving") in a manner that reflects the very dynamism of the structure of human knowing. He argued that proportionate being itself has an "upwardly but indeterminately directed dynamism" and he named that dynamism "generalized emergent probability."[25] This is the dynamic whole that provides the structural integration of all of these "metaphysical elements" taken together into the integral heuristic structure of proportionate being.

Rigorous arguments for these many details and assertions, and their claim to forming an invariant metaphysical structure, would take us too far afield for present purposes. Yet Lonergan was quite emphatic that any serious intellectual pursuit would have to be open to the possibility of all of these different aspects of reality as it endeavoured to understand correctly the universe of proportionate being. As such, he envisioned that this heuristic structure would be fruitful in bringing to light many aspects of reality that would be otherwise overlooked or mistakenly assumed to be unreal. He also proposed that the integral heuristic structure of proportionate being would prove useful in resolving deep-seated conflicts about metaphysical issues.[26]

12.4   The Structure of the Human Good as Invariant

We now turn to Lonergan's claim that the heuristic structure of the human good is also invariant. The support for this claim, I will argue, is to be found in the fact that it can be similarly derived from the structure of ethical intentionality. Lonergan intended to do something like this in *Insight* – to derive a method of ethics and an account of the good "from knowledge of the compound structure of one's knowing and doing."[27] However, he never fully realized that intention. In fact, given the way he approached ethics and the good in *Insight*, it is unlikely that he could have done so – the resources at his disposal from cognitional structure and metaphysics alone as he conceived of them at that time were not sufficient.[28] Furthermore, his new ideas after *Insight* concerning the levels of consciousness, the distinctive notion of value, feelings that intend values, and authenticity would require some revisions to the account of the compound structure of knowing and doing that he presented in *Insight*. The objective of chapters 4 through 9 of this book has been to work out the implications of Lonergan's later ideas for a revised account of that structure. This revised account now makes possible what was really not possible given the more limited resources in *Insight* – namely, to actually ground not only the structure of the human good, but to also argue for the goodness of being *in toto*. The former is the objective of the present section. The latter will be taken up in the next chapter.

12.4.1 Heuristic Definition of the Human Good

The derivation of the heuristic structure of proportionate being began with the heuristic definition of being in general. So also the derivation of the structure of the human good begins with a heuristic definition of the good in general. As was argued in chapter 8, every human being has an unrestricted desire for everything good that is revealed through our questions for value reflection, choice, and action. Therefore, just as being is defined heuristically as the objective of the pure unrestricted desire to know what is, so also the good may be defined as the objective of this unrestricted desire for the good – the unrestricted notion of value (see section 11.1 of the previous chapter).

Because this notion of value desires and intends all that is good through the totality of questions of value, it also includes whatever is humanly good. Lonergan proposed a heuristic definition for the more limited notion of the human good: "The good is human insofar as it is realized through human apprehension and choice."[29] (This corresponds to the limited heuristic definition of proportionate being as what is to be known by intelligent grasp and reasonable affirmation of the totality of possible human experience.) In what follows I will assume that by "apprehension" Lonergan here means what results from the exercise of the structure of ethical intentionality.

Clearly the unrestricted notion of the good goes beyond the notion of the human good, for there is much goodness that is not the product of human action. Human beings can affirm the goodness of what has not been humanly made. Human beings also can choose to admire, accept, endorse, praise, and love what they affirm to be of value but have not made. So the whole of the good is what is sought by human inquiry into the good, into what is of value without limit.

Conversely, in the most fundamental sense, the human good consists in what we do in our striving for the completely unrestricted good. The human good is a dynamic, "developing object and developing subject."[30] The human good is the unfolding story of human history and all the chapters written in the lives of each and every human being, the story of our corporate striving for the unrestricted good. This consists of the combined, structured efforts of striving as well as the restricted, conditional goods that are the partial attainments brought about by that striving. The human good as unrestricted striving therefore includes all the skills and forms of cooperation used to achieve the goods along the way towards the unconditional good. Hence, Lonergan's differentiation of the kinds and meanings of the good in the human realm and beyond is significant for keeping the question of the good radically open.

12.4.2 Derivation of the Heuristic Structure of the Human Good

The keys to the derivation of the structure of the human good are the connections among the activities of the structure of ethical intentionality, on the one hand, and the identity of operating and cooperating, on the other hand.

Lonergan remarked that "the human good is at once individual and social" and that his heuristic structure offered an "account of the way the two aspects combine."[31] This is reflected in the fact that his diagram integrates both aspects into a unified, more comprehensive heuristic. The first two columns in his diagram fall under the heading "Individual," with the next column entitled "Social." The link between operating and cooperating establishes the relationships among the individual and social dimensions of the structure of the human good.

We begin, therefore, with an examination of how certain elements in the heuristic structure of the human good follow from the structure of ethical intentionality as it is exercised by individuals, and then show how the remaining social elements come to light when the cooperative nature of those exercises is recognized.

12.4.3 Terminal Value, Originating Value, Orientation, Conversion, Liberty

First, then, consider how the structure of ethical intentionality bears implications for what is brought about when we perform it with fidelity. As was the case with the derivation of the heuristic structure of proportionate being from cognitional structure, we should begin at the top, so to speak. This means we should begin the derivation with what comes last in the order of ethical intentionality – the acts of deciding and acting.

It is with deciding and acting that ethical intentionality reaches a stage of completion. As a first approximation, this is what Lonergan means by *terminal values* in his diagram of the structure of the human good: "Terminal values are the values that are chosen."[32] But there is more to the matter than mere choice. Choices (and consequent actions) alone do not actualize terminal values; they do so only when our decisions and actions bring about the values that we have judged objectively to be worth actualizing. In particular, if our decisions and actions result from sustained efforts at objective self-knowledge and consequent deliberate ethical reflection and choice, then our resulting personhood is an instance of terminal value.

Our decisions, however, usually actualize more than the value of our own personhood alone. In almost every instance we bring about values that take on a life of their own that is independent of ourselves, if our decisions and actions have been based upon objective judgments of values. Then our decisions actualize terminal values that pass beyond ourselves into the constitution of the human good, in addition to actualizing the good of our own personhood.

Our personhood, however, along with the other entities that we bring into being, may or may not be instances of terminal value. We may form our personhood with little or no objective self-reflection or deliberate choice regarding the kind of life we choose to live. We may bring about events without sufficient ethical reflection, and when we do so, we contaminate the human good with the evils of unintelligibility and disvalue.

Besides the terminal values that we originate (including ourselves), we ourselves are also what Lonergan called *originating values*.[33] In *Insight*, originating value is a value that, once chosen, feeds back to the chooser in the form of enhancing or diminishing her or him as an originator of future values. As Lonergan puts it, values "are originating inasmuch as directly and explicitly or indirectly and implicitly the fact that they are chosen modifies our habitual willingness, or effective orientation in the universe, and so our contributing to the dialectical process of progress or decline."[34]

The values that we choose profoundly modify what kinds of choosers we become. What we have made of ourselves up to any point in time profoundly determines the kinds of values that we can then bring about. Originating values set the conditions for the kinds of persons, the kinds of originators of values we become. By our present and past decisions and actions we make ourselves either more or less capable of living in fidelity to our own structure of ethical intentionality. Not only our habitual valuing and willingness but also our own horizon of feelings and our existential scale of value preferences can be modified by the values and disvalues that we choose. Strictly speaking, insofar as our choices make us more effectively free to choose objective terminal values, they are instances of originating values in this sense. On the other hand, to the extent that our previous choices make us ever less capable of cooperating with the normativity of ethical intentionality, they really should be called "originating evils" or "originating disvalues."

In *Method in Theology*, Lonergan shifted to speaking of the person herself or himself as such as originating value. While the values we choose affect the kinds of valuers and choosers we become, still it is we ourselves who are the real originators of new terminal values.

Originating value has a peculiar status in Lonergan's account of the structure of the human good. Even though it is given prominence in both *Insight* and *Method in Theology*, it does not appear explicitly in Lonergan's diagram of the heuristic structure of the human good. What does appear explicitly in the diagram instead is the impact that these chosen values have on us as persons under the heading of "orientation," and he comments further that orientation is correlated with "development." These, perhaps, represent originating value in that diagram.

Orientation is embedded in our horizon of feelings, our habitual valuing, and our habitual willingness. By our present and past decisions we modify our horizons of feelings and habits of valuing and choosing. Those horizons and habits set the conditions for our future ethical reflections and choices. They dispose us as oriented towards some or all values and as towards those values with a certain scale of preference. The values that we can effectively actualize are conditioned profoundly by what we have previously made of ourselves, by our orientations. (Orientation also has a communal dimension, to which we will return later in the discussion of personal relations.)

Lonergan wrote that the most basic "orientation of the individual ... consists in the transcendental notions that both enable us and require us to advance in understanding, to judge truthfully, to respond to value."[35] This is true even when our actual judgments of value, decisions, and actions deviate occasionally or even habitually from the normativity of the orientation invited by the transcendental notions and being-in-love unconditionally. As was argued earlier, the transcendental notions and being-in-love unconditionally are always operative in every human horizon of feelings, at least marginally. Therefore, while every individual person has some particular existential orientation that effectively guides her or his deliberations and choices, the normative orientation also remains as a permanent, invariant feature of every human being's existential orientation. Bad judgments, choices, and actions register in feelings as deviations from the normative orientation. Since for so many people deviation occurs not just occasionally but with some regularity, the effective orientations manifested in their actual patterns of ethical reflection, decision, and action might better be called the evil of disorientation.

Hence while the transcendental notions are indeed at the root of all exercises of value reflecting, deciding, and acting, they become the truly effective orientations only among people who have deliberately chosen to live by them. Lonergan comments that because we "can know and choose authenticity and self-transcendence, *originating and terminating value can coincide*."[36] But clearly we can also ignore or refuse authenticity and self-transcendence. Then we as originating values are alienated from the terminal values intended by the unrestricted notion of value and unrestricted being-in-love.

That is to say, the transcendental notions of being and value and unconditional being-in-love are the effective orientations only of people who are *converted* morally as well as intellectually and religiously in Lonergan's sense. Because every human decision is a contribution to the orientation of the person doing the deciding, orientation therefore is a constant component in the structure of the human good. In addition, because the basic orientations are always to true terminal values in the unrestricted sense, *conversion* is also always an issue (if not always an achieved reality) in the human good.

On the one hand, then, originating value is the value orientation that we constitute for ourselves as we spontaneously exercise our structure of ethical intentionality. We do this either by honestly facing and responding to all the questions raised by the notion of value and unconditional being-in-love or evading their call to unrestricted goodness. On the other hand, we can also modify the kinds of choosers we will be not just by our spontaneous exercises of ethical intentionality, but even more securely if we deliberately choose the value of authentic living. Kant observes that although ordinary moral innocence is a glorious thing, "unfortunately, it does not keep very well and is easily led astray" by corrupting influences.[37] Lonergan similarly observed that the spontaneous genuineness "of the simple and honest soul" is a fine thing, but for most of us fidelity to our structure of ethical intentionality is something that has to be "won back" through self-scrutiny and ultimately through self-appropriation, the fully deliberate decision to live according to that structure.[38] This is a decision we come to if and when we realize that it is up to us to determine who we are to be. If made, it is a decision of moral conversion. This is the fullest meaning of discernment as self-appropriation, as was argued in chapter 10. Originating value as normative orientation, then, also becomes a terminal value when explicitly understood, objectively judged to be of value, chosen, and enacted in moral, religious, and intellectual conversion.

Whether as spontaneous and implicit, or as chosen and explicit, originating value as orientation is the exercise of our capacity for *liberty*. As Lonergan puts it,

> We experience our liberty as the active thrust of the subject terminating the process of deliberation by settling on one of the possible courses of action and proceeding to execute it. Now insofar as that thrust of the self regularly opts, not for the merely apparent good, but for the true good, the self thereby is achieving moral self-transcendence ... constituting [itself] as an originating value and ... bringing about terminal values.[39]

Liberty, as Lonergan understands it, therefore, is our capacity for truly actualizing in our deciding and acting the values that we have judged worthy. Liberty does entail freedom as radical contingency as was discussed in chapter 4 – the freedom of an act of deciding that is radically undetermined by anything else, including even one's own ethical judgments about the values one should choose. But liberty is not only negative freedom, as absence of other determination. More fully, liberty is the positive capacity to actualize those values that we affirm in judgments. Liberty belongs in the heuristic structure because it is absolutely indispensable to bringing about each and every instance of the human good. Without it, there could be no good in the properly human sense – the good brought about by humans. Without liberty, our actions would be fully determined by the forces and laws of the natural world. Without liberty, our belief in ourselves as agents of our own making and as agents of good in the world would be an illusion. All of our efforts at ethical reflection and deciding would be a sham. But self-appropriation in the full sense includes affirming liberty as real. "Liberty means, of course … self-determination."[40] Self-appropriation in the full sense, therefore, stands in opposition to the suggestion that liberty is an illusion.

Liberty is manifest in every decision and action that brings about any human good. It is something that we hold as a most profound and precious good, but in and of itself it is not a terminal value. It is rather a capacity that manifests itself as we actually bring about the value of ourselves and values distinct from ourselves. Those values could not be without liberty, but liberty is not one of those values. Liberty is a good, but its goodness is not the goodness of a terminal value.

Liberty in this sense is not the same as political liberty. Political liberty is a terminal value for which millions of people yearn, but a value realized in only a few very select patterns of human cooperative living. Opposed to the true value of political liberty is the disvalue of tyranny. Tyranny can be obvious and brutal, but it can also be soft and hidden – the soft tyranny found in democracy, about which de Tocqueville warned.[41] Political liberty, as with all other terminal values, is dependent upon the more fundamental meaning of liberty as the human capacity to originate and actualize values.

12.4.4 Operation, Skill, Development, Plasticity, Perfectibility

Further dimensions of the structure of the human good come into view if we now move downward one level in the structure of ethical intentionality. Judgments of value, decisions, and actions all presuppose practical insights. Practical insights grasp the intelligibilities that are at the heart of all courses of action. It is these intelligible courses of action that are judged to be, or not to be, of value.

Values are always known in judgments of value to be the value of some intelligibility. Actual values are values that some actual intelligibility is known to have. An objective judgment of fact knows the actuality of the intelligibility, while an objective judgment of value knows the value of that actual intelligibility. Possible values are the values of some intelligibility that is possible but not yet actual – or at least not yet known to be actual.

Practical insights understand the intelligibilities of possible courses of action. Our ethical reflecting and judging determines the value of these practical insights – especially once our practical insights have been modified and refined by the self-correcting cycle of further questions and answers. Practical insights, therefore, develop. Lonergan remarks that an authentic, converted orientation can only be realized and effective through *development*, and practical insights are indispensable to development in the properly human sense: "One has to acquire the skills and learning of a competent human being in some walk of life. One has to grow in sensitivity and responsiveness to values if one's humanity is to be authentic."[42]

Relying on the researches of Jean Piaget, Lonergan defines a *skill* as a "group of combinations of differentiated operations" where the term "group" has the special, technical meaning of being able to return to one's starting point unhesitatingly.[43] For example, a skilled carpenter has to be able to stop in the middle of a building project to make unexpected adjustments, and then return to the *operations* temporarily abandoned. The ability to do this sort of thing is a grouping of groups of skills, and is the index of competence and proficiency. Skill development requires the self-correcting of practical insights where bodily operations yield results and experiences that deviate from expectations, raising further questions, new insights, modified operations, and so on, until we get an intelligibly integrated group of operations that smoothly actualize the intended result, not just once but repeatedly. This is why the ability to return to a starting point is crucial to mastery of any skill.

Bodily-based skills are not the only kinds of skills that are developed in the human good. Because the human good is what is realized in the striving for the unrestricted good, that good is not restricted to vital values, nor are the requisite skills. Insofar as a skill is a grouping of differentiated operations, then the operations of ethical intentionality can also develop. In a truly fundamental way, therefore, *being ethical is a matter of sustained developing.*

It might be said that disoriented people also develop skills and feelings to live out their deviant orientations. Lonergan however understood development in a particular way that makes it difficult to apply to such cases, and he used "decline" instead to characterize such processes. Therefore development and decline are the two most fundamental orientations of both individual and communal human existence.

Lonergan thought of development as an intelligible sequence of operations of self-transformation. In a development, the operations of one stage bring about intelligibly transformed and more differentiated operations that are organized into a new stage. A person with a completely converted orientation would exhibit an undistorted, intelligible pattern of developing ethical stages from unsophisticated awkwardness to polished nobility in feeling, thinking, choosing, and acting. But when there are unresolved tensions in a person's horizon of feelings, competing orientations are operative. Reflection and action will sometimes be in conformity with the orientation of our deepest, unrestricted feelings for values, and at other times in opposition to them. Such people will pass through successive stages, but the pattern will not have the coherent intelligibility of development. Instead, the stages will form what Lonergan refers to as a "dialectical sequence," which is "a concrete unfolding of linked but opposed principles of change."[44] The opposed orientation interacts with our basic orientation to produce something analogous to a vector sum, in which neither orientation has absolute sway over the other. In the resulting sequence, our judgments of value and decisions are sometimes virtually unconditioned, but sometimes flawed. Each such decision modifies our competing orientations, so that the vector sum itself is constantly shifting in an incoherent, dialectical fashion. Perhaps, then, *dialectic* should also be included along with development in the diagram of the heuristic structure of the human good.

Since skills and their development are essential to the realization of valuable courses of action, likewise the capacities for skill formation and developmental transformation – *plasticity* and *perfectibility* – are also parts of the unfolding of the human good. Lonergan used to remark that a newborn gazelle could run fifteen minutes after its birth, but it takes a human infant a year to develop the skills required to walk. He went on to observe that the gazelle's nervous system was hard-wired to give it this survival skill, but the plasticity of the human nervous system made our legs and other body parts capable of developing and being organized into many different kinds of skills – not only running, but also kicking balls, high jumps, back flips, triple Salchows, horseback riding, yoga, and dancing, for example. I once saw a documentary about the birth defects caused by the drug thalidomide. One adult woman victim had been born without arms, but she had developed an extraordinary degree of dexterity using only her legs and feet. She could drive a specially modified car, care for her infant child, and shop in a supermarket by placing items in a shopping cart with one foot and leg while balancing on the other. That the human body has the plasticity and perfectibility needed to develop such skills is among the goods on display in the good originated by human ethical intentionality.

12.4.5 Operation, Cooperation, Good of Order, Task, Role, Institution, Particular Good

In general, practical insights assess not only physical but also human schemes of recurrence. Practical insights figure out what sort of operations and skills could bring about the intended results in that realm as well. At this point, therefore, we bring to bear the second key to derivation of the structure of the human good – the link between *operating* and *cooperating*. "To a notable extent operating is cooperating,"[45] as Lonergan remarked. Operating and cooperating are one and the same component in a course of action viewed from two different perspectives. From the perspective of the ethical subject, operating/cooperating is an action – the final component in his or her exercise of ethical intentionality. From the social perspective, one and the same action (or operation) of an individual is simultaneously an instance of cooperating, an element coordinated with the operations of others in the structure of the human good.

The rest of the components and relationships in the structure of the human good assemble around this identity of operating and cooperating. The operations of the structure of ethical intentionality of many individuals are intelligibly linked together in *cooperation*. In extremely primitive situations, a solitary person could actualize a capacity in an operation to obtain a *particular good* that meets a particular *need*. When a particular good can only be achieved by cooperating with others, however, or if it can be more easily achieved by cooperation, the direct correlation of an individual's needs, operations, and particular goods is replaced by more complex but intelligibly related indirect routes. The intelligible assembly of human acts of cooperation into these more complex routes constitute what Lonergan called a *good of order*. A good of order, he writes, "consists in an intelligible pattern of relationships that condition the fulfillment of [people's] desires with [their] contributions to the fulfillment of the desires of others and, similarly, protect [them] from the object of [their] fears in the measure that [they contribute] to warding off the objects feared by others."[46] Such patterns are to be found in every instance where two or more people cooperate to achieve some goal.

Practical insights are required in order to understand how to make one's own operations fit into the ongoing intelligible patterns of cooperation with others that constitutes the good of order. As Lonergan remarks, "In human affairs the decisive factor is what one can expect from the other fellow."[47] Understanding what is expected is an understanding of how operations of several individuals are linked to one another, as well as to needs and particular goods. Understanding what to expect, and how one's own actions will be understood, is crucial not only to fitting into a good of order that is already operating, but also to secure the cooperation of others in an innovative course of action that one judges and chooses to be worth undertaking. That success will be achieved only if others understand how to combine their operations with our own and choose to do so. In order to communicate new ways of cooperating, understanding what is currently expected and what is going on is an essential point of departure.

In any good of order that involves a significant number of people, practical insights are needed in order to grasp intelligible connections between their individual operations and skills, on the one hand, and the *tasks* assigned to a variety of *roles*, on the other. Roles, in turn, are organized into *institutions*, and the institutions into relations with one another, which constitute the intricate social ecosystem of a good of order. This social ecosystem of a good of order, this complex of intelligibly coordinated efforts, will regularly renew the supply of particular goods, on the one hand, and actualize the value of that manner of cooperative living, on the other.

The example of the Kuala Telang well illustrates abundantly just how much human cooperation is required to actualize an individual's choice of a course of action (see section 11.7 of the previous chapter). Paget's chosen course of action depended upon acts of cooperation on the part of the village women, the headman and the elders, the well diggers, and more remotely, upon people in the legal and financial institutions that provided the income derived from her uncle's will.

12.4.6 Personal Relations

Any instance of an actually functioning good of order comprises a large number of intelligibly coordinated individual courses of action. Each person will originate her or his course of action on the basis of a judgment of its value and a decision to enact it. But an individual's values become actualized in a social context only with the cooperation of others.

Earlier I said that it is only a first approximation to define terminal values as what is realized in an individual exercise of the structure of ethical intentionality. More precisely, terminal values are chosen together by a cooperating group. When cooperating people consent to the realization of a value, whether explicitly or tacitly, they simultaneously realize two values, just as individuals do: on the one hand, they realize, say, the social value of a new bridge over a river; but they also actualize the value of themselves as a community acting jointly with purpose and value.

Terminal values in the interpersonal human realm are not determined solely by a single person's decision or action alone. While we might fantasize that we have originated something of value all by ourselves, the fact of the matter is that the realization of an intelligible course of action and the value it carries is almost always a cooperative venture. Others must choose to add their operations to ours in order for a new modification in the good of order to emerge. They must judge the modification of the good of order as of value, and they must choose to accept and incorporate it into their value commitments. If the value for the sake of which they choose to cooperate in the newly modified good of order is the same as the value that motivated our own course of action, then our intended value becomes actualized in a social pattern of cooperation. But it is also possible that the group affirms and chooses the value that motivated our own choice, but does so according to a scale of values that differs from our own. For example, everyone might affirm the vital values of enhanced food supply that will be realized by building a new bridge, but the ultimate value for the person proposing the project might be to increase real estate values, while the rest of the community might accept the proposal because they have discerned it to be the right way to serve God's people, a religious value which they cherish above all else. The bridge becomes a reality in both cases, but because this had to be a cooperative undertaking, the values realized are the community's religious value constituted by its scale of values. In the end, the person for whom real estate values are ultimate does not fully participate in that actualized value of community.

When people engage in cooperative ventures because they share the same values, the sharing of those values constitutes their *personal relations.* People become accepted by a community, and come to regard their identity through membership in that community in terms of their shared judgments of value and shared decisions by which they commit to those values. Not all personal relations are positive, but all personal relations are carriers of values and disvalues. "So personal relations vary from intimacy to ignorance, from love to exploitation, from respect to contempt, from friendliness to enmity. They bind a community together or they tear it apart."[48]

Personal relations are manifested in how people treat one another. Two people can perform exactly the same roles and tasks (e.g., nurse) in the very same kind of institution (e.g., hospital) in two different cities, but they might be relating to their patients and co-workers in very different ways. Those different ways of interacting with the people involved in the same institutional patterns constitute the differences in their concrete patterns of personal relations. These patterns of personal relations constitute the different ways that institutions "feel" to people within them. What people feel are the terminal values embodied in these personal relations. The ways that people relate to one another in, say, their hospital roles usually reflect the pattern of personal relations of the local culture – say, the local municipality. One hospital will feel warm and welcoming while another will feel cold and business-like, even though both hospitals might be equally good at treating medical problems (i.e., actualizing vital values). How groups of people relate to one another while performing their institutional roles constitutes their networks of personal relations.

Personal relations originate in feelings (i.e., feeling responses that intend values), but they do not reside merely internally in sentiments. Personal relations also depend upon insights, but they do not reside in some merely idealistic realm. Personal relations reside in *how* people actually deal with one another *in doing* activities in their institutional and social settings.

Furthermore, the lived reality of personal relations is the most concrete embodiment of the terminal values of social institutions. An institution may proclaim lofty values in its mission statement, but the actuality of its mission-value is revealed in its pattern of personal relations. A group of people reveals the terminal values to which they are collectively committed in the ways that they relate to one another and to those with whom they deal outside the institution.

This is particularly true of the value of personhood. Lonergan observes that there is an intimate connection between the level of personal relations and the intelligible patterns of cooperation that occur in the institutional level of the good of order:

> The two can also be united insofar as the person emerges with *personal status* within the [good of] order. Then the order is an order between persons, and the good of order is apprehended, not so much by studying the [institutional] schemes … but by apprehending human relations … The simplest and most effective apprehension of the good of order is in the apprehension of personal relations.[49]

Lonergan's use of the phrase "personal status" here refers to how a person is actually valued in a culture, effected and constituted socially by the entire pattern of personal relations. An individual's personal value ("personal status") is implicitly defined by her or his place in a concrete, really existing pattern of relations among other persons. The meanings and values of recurring patterns of institutional interactions are what Lonergan calls cultural values.[50] Cultural values are carried in the ways that people in that culture (or subculture) relate to one another, in the pattern of their intricate and intimate personal relations. This pattern of cultural values may be expressed in stories, legends, gestures, rituals, monuments, and so on, but those expressions derive their meaning from and live on in the ongoing pattern of personal relations. The cultural valuation of a person is constituted by the cultural pattern into which she or he is thrown.

Certain values will hold the highest place in the culture of one set of personal relations, while other values will be prominent elsewhere. In one society, competition and success in business or sports will predominate, whereas *joi d'vivre* will be pre-eminent in another. Likewise, economic efficiency, love of the motherland/fatherland, or love of the proletariat can and have been extolled as the predominant values in various cultures. Other values (e.g., hard work, intellectual pursuits, artistic creativity, family affection, honesty, loyalty, modesty, generosity, etc.) rank nearer or farther away from the pre-eminent value, forming a particular culture's scale of value priorities. The pre-eminent value and its associated scale of values is to be discerned in the ways that certain people and their actions are honoured, while others are ignored, or even despised. Each culture values some people more highly than others, even when they espouse universal human rights and attest to the unconditional value (dignity) of every human being. In concrete cultural patterns of how people are actually treating each other, each person is valued more highly, or more lowly, or devalued outright, in terms of the scale of values implicit in these patterns of interpersonal regard and interaction. A person's personal value is the value bestowed upon (or denied to) that person in the particular, concrete network of personal relations within which they live.

Clearly this account of personal value and personal relations stands in some tension with the accounts of terminal value, originating value, and personal value up to this point. So far, personal value has been understood as a matter of self-origination – either spontaneous self-origination or self-origination deliberately chosen in self-appropriation and conversion – but not as the result of social construction. However, our performances of our ethical intentionality almost always occur in an interpersonal setting. The ongoing flow of experiences that form the points of departure for our exercises of moral self-transcendence overwhelmingly derive from our experiences of the actions of other human beings. We try to make sense of what they are doing and what they mean. We try to determine the right things to do in response to our estimation of the patterns of personal relations within which we operate.

Thus, while in principle personal value is the value of a person originating the meaning of her or his being through the authentic exercise of the dynamism of ethical intentionality, in fact, that originating is powerfully shaped and even dominated by some concrete cultural pattern of personal relations. No one constitutes the value of her or his personhood (her or his personal value) all alone. Rather than coming to know and value ourselves in isolation as originators of value through authentically exercising ethical intentionality, concretely we use the activities of that structure to understand, feel, and accept the personal value that is communicated about us and to us by others who share our culture.

Hence the personal value that is proper to human beings as originators of value is not always validated by the concrete personal relations in institutions and cultures. Just as individuals can and do fail to affirm or chose themselves as instances of authentic personal values, even more frequently cultures fail to communicate and cultivate personal value in its full and proper sense in and through their concrete practices of personal relations.

They may place this or that cultural ideal as the highest goal, almost completely ignoring the distinct and higher value of the person to which cultural ideals may be compared and in terms of which they may be criticized. Then there will be aberrations in the culture that lead to either overt or subtle dynamics of oppression, alienation, and *ressentiment*, which will fester and grow. The pattern of personal relations will become ever more distorted in response, and the disparity between personal value in the normative sense and the values assigned to human beings by the culture will increase, developing a social surd.

Furthermore, it is not possible to just dismiss these aberrant valuations of persons by cultures as mere illusions. Even when shamefully distorted, such valuations still enter powerfully into the constitutions of the self-valuations of the members of the culture. A certain kind of stoicism might counsel one to ignore what society and culture say and to just be oneself. But what does it mean to be oneself? No one is a *solus ipse*. Whether or not this advice is taken seriously will depend upon the personal relations that form the hearers of such counsel. Self-appropriation in the fullest sense therefore relies upon a certain kind of community to cultivate the insights, judgments, and feelings needed to arrive at this alternative evaluation, a community of conversion, of people who have already explicitly affirmed the value of being agents of ethical authenticity and have deliberately chosen to live by that affirmation.

But is such a community even possible, given the powerful influences of personal relations over one's ethical reflection and choosing? It is only possible if there is a community that includes personal relations that cannot be subjugated to the corrupting influences of biased personal relations. The possibility and actuality of such personal relations is a properly theological question. We will return to this issue in the section of chapter 13 devoted to the problem of evil and the place of religious conversion in ethics.

Finally, the phenomena of personal values reveal the deepest meaning of laws and their proper roles in society and in ethics. To a first approximation, laws are for the sake of the good of order. Laws communicate the agreed upon ways to cooperate in order to secure particular goods in order to meet particular needs. Perhaps more obviously, laws also protect those patterns of cooperation by insuring sanctions (particular fears) to deter those who would abuse the cooperative trust of others in order to satisfy their needs without making socially agreed upon contributions to the overall good of order. Beyond the first approximation, however, the fuller ethical significance of laws has to do with personal relations and terminal values. Violators of the good of order denigrate the terminal values embedded in the personal relations that form the deeper foundation of the maintenance and improvement of the good of order and its institutions. The indignation that people feel in response to those who break laws is a response to the offences against the personal relations and their embedded terminal values that are the most basic commitments of a society and ways in which its members are valued as persons.

All this is true, of course, to the extent that laws actually are genuine expressions of personal relations and terminal values of converted persons and societies. This account of the purpose of laws rooted in self-appropriation brings to light the evils of disorder and the denigration of personal relations.

12.4.7 *Needs and Particular Goods*

Further practical insights connect skills with *needs* for *particular goods*. Needs as Lonergan understood them are not limited to vital needs required to sustain human biological existence, such as needs for food, water, protection from extremes of weather, and needs for reproduction. Rather, needs "are to be understood in the broadest sense; they are not to be restricted to necessities but rather to be stretched to include wants of every kind."[51] Still, as Lonergan uses the term in his diagram of the human good, a need is for a *particular good*. According to his definition, a particular good "meets a need of a particular individual at a given place and time."[52] These kinds of needs are met at one instant, and vanish only to resurface later and be satisfied yet again. Vital needs clearly meet this definition, as do our needs for expressions of affection from our beloveds, as well as our needs for redress of injustices. But our needs for understanding and love and justice as such are not needs for something ephemeral and particular to a place and time; they are needs for enduring goods. Hence not all of our needs are for particular goods. Even when those needs are quelled for the moment, they will resurface sooner or later. On the other hand, we all have needs to understand, to know what is so and what is of value, as well as needs for social order and self-worth. While it is true that our needs for protection may be particular, our need for a just and orderly society is not for a particular good that is met once, then vanishes, and is needed again tomorrow.

12.5   Summary: The Heuristics and the Invariance of the Human Good

The early sections of this chapter argued that Lonergan formulated the structure of the human good in order to provide a heuristic guidance for discovering the various kinds of goods that are brought about when human beings act in fidelity to the norms that are intrinsic in their own structures of ethical intentionality. It also brings to light the various kinds of evils that result from failures to cooperate ethically. The fuller significance of the heuristic nature of this structure and its implications for a method in ethics will be explored further in chapter 16.

In addition, the capacity for this heuristic structure to illuminate goods and evils in a broad, transcultural diversity of human situations depends upon Lonergan's claim that it is an invariant structure. The later sections of this chapter, therefore, offered a justification of his claim. That argument for the invariance of the structure of the human good began with Lonergan's suggestion of a parallel, an isomorphism, between the way the invariant structure of proportionate being can be derived from cognitional structure, and the possibility of deriving the structure of the human good from the more encompassing structure that is involved in thinking and doing what is ethical. Further, that derivation rests upon two foundations: (1) the invariant structure of ethical intentionality present in all human beings in all times and places, and (2) the fact that almost all individual actions are *de facto* cooperative actions. Together, these two provide the grounds for the invariant relationships among the terms in the heuristic structure of the human good, which is summarized in what follows. The derivation also provides elaborations of those terms and relationships that enhance the use of the heuristic structure in investigation of particular historical societies.

The good that is brought about by each individual's decisions and actions is always already embedded in the larger comprehending structure of the human good, although this is not evident at first sight. As Lonergan put it, "because that structure is recurrent in every act of choice, it is universal on the side of the object."[53] Although the ethics of ethical intentionality at first may appear to be an individualistic ethics, in fact and more concretely it is instead a social ethics. Lonergan's account of the structure of the human good reveals the social ethical dimensions that are always already operative in our individual ethical reflections and decisions, even though it may require sophisticated discernment to recognize that this is the case.

Thus, human actions (or "*operations*") carry out decisions and are therefore the completions of each phase of our ethical intentionality. They can be operations of the human body (e.g., using hands, legs, or voices) or they can be intentional operations, such as inquiring, understanding, feeling, or judging. All such operations presuppose corresponding *capacities*, without which they could not occur. Operations can be extremely primitive, but most often they are combinations of bodily and intentional operations into intelligibly connected groupings or *skills*. Refinements of skills are brought about by *developmental* sequences of successive decisions and actions, which modify, differentiate, and integrate more primitive skills. Furthermore, just as operations depend upon capacities, so also refinements of skills depend upon the *plasticities* and *perfectibilities* required for skills to develop and not remain ossified. Skills are commonly employed to produce or secure *particular goods* that meet *needs* of many different kinds. Thus, if skills are regarded as good because they yield particular goods meeting particular needs, so also the capacities for those skills are good since they underpin operations. Likewise the developments, plasticities, and perfectibilities that make advanced skills possible are good for the same reason.

Yet most often an individual's decisions and actions explicitly or implicitly depend upon and impact the actions of others: those decisions and actions are simultaneously some form of *cooperation. Cooperations* presuppose intelligible coordinations among human decisions, actions, and skills that constitute *roles, institutions,* and *orders.* While human decisions realize these intelligible coordinations of the actions of many, they do so in order to realize values arrived at through the processes of ethical reflection and judgment that lead up to the decisions. Still such values are almost never realized by individual actions alone. Groups of individuals use their *liberty* to freely and reciprocally choose orders of institutions that they judge, explicitly or implicitly, to be worth bringing about and sustaining.

The resulting goods of order are the actualizations of *terminal values,* which are never simple or abstract, like the value of life, commerce, or art. Just as when our feelings respond to agent objects in complex webs or compositions, so also a culture's terminal values is a complex of prominent values as modulated and nuanced by auxiliary values. Terminal values of a culture are best formulated in systems of symbols and narratives. Terminal values are orders of values embodied in complex, cooperative undertakings that take place through institutions and their comprehending goods of order. Ongoing mutual decisions that sustain commitments to these terminal values arise from and reinforce fundamental *orientations* that are manifest in the *personal relations* among the cooperating actors. Finally, the orientations are authentic and the terminal values are true insofar as they proceed from judgments and decisions of *converted* persons.

All these factors are to be found in every historically existing situation where people use their structures of ethical intentionality in order to cooperate. Sometimes these factors are found in compact and undifferentiated forms in simple social arrangements; at other times they are parcelled out across many different roles and classes in highly complex societies. Yet the entire range of components in the structure of the human good must be borne in mind whenever we endeavour to answer the question "What good is it?"

Lonergan's own articulation of this invariant structure underwent considerable development over the course of his career.[54] So while the structure of the human good is invariant, any particular formulation of that structure is not necessarily invariant. Numerous further details need to be supplied in order to facilitate the scholarly study of the values and particular goods realized in various societies. Further specifications of technological, economic, social, political, cultural, and religious institutions and orders are needed to assist the study of these cooperative patterns. No doubt something better than Lonergan's own final formulation of the structure of the human good is likely to come along. So while there is ample room for improvement and refinement of Lonergan's *account* of that structure, I have endeavoured to show that these refinements would be "minor revisions that leave basic lines intact" concerning the terms and relations of the *invariant structure* that follow from cooperation and from the structure of ethical intentionality.

The next chapter endeavours to show how this structure of the human good is situated within a more comprehensive heuristic of the goodness of all being, both the finite being of the universe (i.e., proportionate being), as well as the goodness of being that transcends the universe.

13 The Notion and the Ontology of the Good

13.1 Introduction

The preceding chapter argued that in virtually every case, whenever we exercise our ethical intentionality in fidelity to our unrestricted notion of value and the normative scale of value preference, we simultaneously contribute to and commit ourselves to the intersubjective human good. But Lonergan further argued that by our ethical activity we also contribute to a goodness that is at once more subtle and more profound. Just as the individual good is situated within the larger comprehending dynamic structure of the human good, so also the human good is situated within the cosmic good that Lonergan identified as the dynamic order of proportionate being. Just as each individual decision and action is at least implicitly the realization of a social, historical good of order and terminal value, it is likewise implicitly and simultaneously the realization of a good that transcends the human good. The dynamic structure of the human good is embedded within the dynamic good of the natural universe, which in turn is grounded in a goodness that transcends all finite goods.

Clearly this implicit commitment to the cosmic and transcendent good is far from obvious. Discernment of this involvement requires the assistance of a considerable intellectual exercise. As a contribution to that exercise, this chapter explores Lonergan's arguments for the goodness of the whole world and the goodness that transcends this world. These arguments provide the bases for discerning these greater values, and for working out a more comprehensive heuristic structure that anticipates in the broadest fashion the ways in which we might answer the question, "What is the good of that?"

13.2   The Goodness of the Natural Universe

13.2.1   The Goodness of the Natural Order as a Whole

Almost everyone has some appreciation of the goodness of nature. This is already apparent when we speak of natural resources and regard the natural world as a provider of natural goods that can be used to fulfill human wants and needs. But the environmental movement and especially recent concerns about global warming and climate change have heightened our awareness that there is a goodness to the natural environment that is not exhausted by the category of natural resources. It is a goodness that is imperilled by the ways that we have been going about the business of using natural resources.

Of course the goodness envisioned in contemporary ecological concerns is not entirely new. Those who have been active in ecological movements have found great affinities with pre-modern expressions of the goodness of the natural world, frequently giving a new voice to values commonly held by members of earlier civilizations and cultures.

Lonergan also had an appreciation for the irreducible goodness of the natural universe. He argued that the commitment to that greater goodness is always implicit in every choice we make because practically all of our evaluating, choosing, and acting occurs not only in a context of other human deeds and institutions, but also in the context of an extra-human natural environment. What we do responds to and affects the natural setting. Our ethical intentionality begins in experiences that arise out of the natural environment and results in actions that modify it. Hence, when we respond to our experiences with thoughts, feelings, and actions, we are always already doing so within a context of conditions provided by the natural world. Furthermore, practically all of our decisions are carried out by our bodily movements. Hence the human goods that we bring about by the exercise of our ethical intentionality and our bodily movements are massively conditioned by the environment that nourishes and sustains our bodies.

The fact that human good builds upon and is a continuation of the conditions supplied by nature is illustrated in the story of Kuala Telang in chapter 11. Yet discerning that this is so explicitly can be facilitated by an exercise proposed by Dr. Martin Luther King, Jr. He is said to have engaged his audiences in an imaginative exercise to help them think about their ethical responsibilities to others. He asked his audiences to recall what they had for breakfast – about the different kinds of foods and beverages. He then asked them to think about how those foods reached their plates. If they did not do the cooking themselves, then who did? And, in any case, how was the energy for the cooking supplied and by whom? How was the energy delivered to the site at which the food was prepared, and who carried out the delivery? Who delivered the raw foods and beverages? Who built and repaired the roads, rails, bridges, vehicles, and pipelines that made delivery possible? And who sowed, cultivated, and harvested the plants and husbanded the animals from which the raw foodstuffs came? What financial mechanisms were involved in paying for items and reimbursing labour? By the end of the exercise, most people in the audience had become aware that they were beholden to the coordinated efforts of hundreds of people for something as simple as a single breakfast meal – a single "particular good" in Lonergan's terms.

Lonergan insists that the good is always concrete, and King's exercise brings to light what is meant by the concreteness of the human good. No human good exists apart from the conditions that make it actual. An actual value is the value of some actual intelligibility, and in the human realm actual intelligibilities are massively conditioned. In part, this is what the structure of the human good reveals. Even if we restrict the focus of our attention to a particular good, its actual goodness depends upon numerous personal relations motivating many individuals to cooperate in institutions that coordinate the performances of their capacities and skills in wide-ranging patterns. If we focus only on the fried egg sitting on the plate before us, then we are not really discerning the whole, concrete good that we are actually choosing. Unless we realize that we are choosing this egg-meal *as* made real and worthwhile by all its concrete conditions, we are not fully cognizant of the actual good we are choosing.

King's exercise can be expanded to include natural ecosystems. The complex, interconnected human operations that make a breakfast meal possible are themselves dependent upon environmental conditions. Before the foodstuffs can be harvested, transported, prepared, and financed by human actions, they have to grow in a natural environment that provides proper soil, minerals, water, atmospheric carbon dioxide and nitrogen, sunlight, and warmth. Those environmental conditions have to be replenished by natural processes, and those natural processes themselves emerged out of more primitive conditions. Before energy can be made available for transporting and cooking, it too had to be formed by natural processes that evolved over millions of years.

Lonergan's argument for the goodness of the natural world follows from these reflections on the concreteness of the human good. If we choose anything as good, we do so because we have come to know it as a value worthy of our choice through our ethical reflections and judgments of ethical value.

But what is chosen as valuable is some intelligible course of action in all its concreteness – for example, using skills appropriate to the actual concrete conditions in order to acquire a particular good. Since some of those conditions are from the pre-human realm of being, then choosing the concrete good *de facto* means also choosing those conditions as well. In their actuality, whatever we choose concretely is inextricably bound up with the conditioning human and pre-human schemes of recurrence and events that elevate their mere intelligible possibilities into virtually unconditioned intelligible realities. The actuality of both a succulent fruit (as object of human desire) and the fruit farm (as an institution in a human good of order) depends upon recurring replenishment by environmental factors (both natural and social) that lie beyond the fruit or the farm themselves. For Lonergan, the whole evolving, ongoing dynamic process of the universe of proportionate being[1] is the penultimate condition for all the events and schemes that come to be, especially our own choices to actualize intelligible courses of action and values.

Lonergan formulated this argument in the following compact form:

> If the intelligible orders of human invention are a good because they systematically assure the satisfaction of desires, then so are the intelligible orders [natural ecosystems] that underlie, condition, precede, and include [human] invention. Finally, intelligible orders and their contents as possible objects of rational choice, are values; but the universal order, which is generalized emergent probability, conditions and penetrates, corrects and develops, every particular order; and rational self-consciousness *cannot consistently choose the conditioned and reject the condition, choose the part and reject the whole, choose the consequent and reject the antecedent.* Accordingly, since [humanity] is involved in choosing and since every consistent choice, at least implicitly, is a choice of universal order, the realization of universal order is a true value.[2]

Lonergan is arguing that *if* realizing the actual, concrete value of the intelligibility embodied in any reflective human choice is good (and it will be good if chosen in fidelity to the structure of ethical intentionality by morally converted persons), *then* the actual intelligibility of the whole (which underlies and conditions the realization of that choice) is also good. As he puts it, "every consistent choice, at least implicitly, is a choice of universal order."[3] In other words, whenever we choose, our choice is a contribution to the ongoing intelligible order of proportionate being.

Lonergan calls this universal order "generalized emergent probability." This is Lonergan's understanding of evolution.[4] The wholeness of generalized emergent probability is an "upwardly but not determinately directed dynamism of proportionate being."[5] This means that this wholeness is non-systematic and open-ended, yet intelligible and therefore still a kind of order nonetheless. As Lonergan puts it, generalized emergent probability "neither denies nor minimizes such facts as entropy, cataclysm, the death that follows every birth, the extinction that threatens every survival. It offers no opinion on the ultimate fate of the universe. But it insists that the negative picture is not the whole picture."[6]

According to Lonergan's argument, by our decisions we commit ourselves to this order, this wild and untamed process of emergent probability, even when we are not explicitly aware of this. When we decide to cooperate with others in a good of order, we participate in the maintenance or emergence of humanly originated complexes of cyclical processes ("schemes of recurrence"). By means of our decisions, new events and new schemes of recurrence emerge out of those that came before and that provided the conditions for the new emergences. By our decisions, therefore, we choose to participate in this ongoing emergent process of generalized emergent probability, which embraces the whole of natural and human history. By our decisions to participate in this process of emergence, we endorse the value of its ordering of events.

In other words, Lonergan argues that every consistent human choice is in fact the choice of a good wholeness – the wholeness of what he called the universal order of proportionate being – generalized emergent probability. Seen in this light, the human good is revealed as a natural continuation of the process of generalized emergent probability that characterizes the evolution of the goodness of the natural universe.

However, human beings do not always "consistently choose." We seldom take into explicit account this larger dimension of that to which we commit ourselves when we choose. Explicitly and thematically, we usually focus only upon a part of the whole of the universal order of emergent probability – the part that would immediately satisfy our limited interests and concerns, the part that is immediately apparent in our practical insights, practical reflections, and deliberate choices. Yet implicitly and really we are always choosing that value part *as part of a whole goodness.* Without that wholeness, the chosen part, the course of action, could not be an actual, concrete good at all. It would merely be some imaginary fantasy. We may think of ourselves as choosing just this particular good in isolation, just good for ourselves, selfishly alone, with no regard for anyone or anything else. And our feelings as we make such choices might be equally self-centred, lacking in regard for the full scale of values. But whether we think and feel in this narrow way or not, actually we are choosing a specific value as it actually is, *as* conditioned.

Therefore, just as the choice of any single particular good is implicitly the valuation and choice of the human good of order that makes its realization possible, so also that same choice is simultaneously a valuation and acceptance of the natural order of generalized emergent probability that conditions the actualization of that particular good. We choose it as good because it is intelligible and the condition of what we choose as good. Hence, the choice of any conditioned course of action as good, precisely because it is conditioned by a wholeness of emerging goodness, is implicitly the choice of the goodness of that whole, whether or not the chooser is explicitly aware of this fact. By each of our ethical reflections, actions, and decisions, therefore, we are contributing to the building up of the intelligible wholeness of generalized emergent probability that includes and incorporates our action, and this is the wholeness which we are choosing and to which we are committed to by our actions.

It follows, therefore, that acting ethically in the full sense is always a matter of contributing to and promoting the development of the generalized emergent probability of proportionate being. Conversely, acting unethically always promotes its decline. This is always so, whether we explicitly think about what we are doing in that way, or not.

Cynthia Crysdale shows that it is illuminating to think of the ethics of discernment that follows from thinking of the good in terms of generalized emergent probability as an "ethic of risk," as opposed to an "ethic of control." An ethic of control attempts to guarantee good behaviour and outcomes using measures of physical or psychological force. An ethic of risk by contrast is "responsible action within the limits of bounded power" which respects the contingency and non-systematic character of the natural and human realms. As Crysdale puts it, the "goal of moral action is not complete success but creation of conditions whereby transformations [and emergence] may take place. It accepts vulnerability but undertakes risks in the name of life-affirming dignity."[7] She emphasizes that which will be the ethical risks to take has to "be discerned over and over again [intelligently, reasonably, and responsibly] in each new situation ... figuring out if this is the best way to resist" evil and injustice.[8]

13.2.2   *The Kinds of Goodness within the Natural Whole*

From this general conclusion that the whole of emergent proportionate being is good, according to Lonergan, there follows almost immediately a refinement – what mathematicians would call a corollary to the general conclusion. The corollary is: if every instance of proportionate being comprises three basic elements (potency, form, act) corresponding to the three basic cognitional acts (experiencing, understanding, judging), then the goodness of each proportionate being is likewise triply differentiated.[9] In other words, the goodness of proportionate being is subdivided into different degrees of goodness, corresponding to potency, form, and act, respectively:

> We propose to speak of a potential, formal, and actual good, where
> the potential good is identical with potential intelligibility and so
> includes but also extends beyond objects of desire, where the formal

good is identical with formal intelligibility and so includes but also
extends beyond human intelligible orders, where the actual good
is identical with actual intelligibilities and so includes but also may
extend beyond human values.[10]

Among other things, Lonergan shows that this heuristic of concrete
instances of the good casts critical light upon utilitarian and other ethical
theories, for which "the meaning of the term 'good' ... has to be the good as
experienced, and that opposite to the good there is the no less real category of
evil as experienced."[11] Lonergan argues that the proper meaning of the good
is actualized intelligibility, and that not only objects of desire but even objects
of aversion and "indifferent objects" can be potentially good – provided there
is some intelligibility that forms them into something of unconditioned value.

Again, his identification of the three components of any proportionate
good is the fundamental basis for his distinction between value and the
good. Values and actual goods are one kind of good, but not the only kind.
Particular and potential goods, goods of order and formal goods and their
various constituents, are also good. But none of these alone is the whole of
the good. Likewise values, by themselves, are not the whole of the good. It
is true that the transcendental notion of value ultimately intends goodness
in the fullest sense, and that this is the whole of all values and actual goods.
Still, by intending that whole, the notion of value also intends all the components that are related to and indispensable to actual goods/values. So
the components of the potential and formal good also are good. Still, their
goodness is distinguishable from the goodness of value.

Lonergan uses this corollary as a heuristic in developing his theory of the
integrated structural relationships among various goods. Primary among
these relationships is that having to do with the hierarchy of goods. If various potencies, forms and acts are distinguished from one another within
proportionate being in a hierarchical series of explanatory genera, then
there follow corresponding distinct, hierarchically related generic orders
of values. Further, if there really are distinct explanatory species within the
explanatory genera, then corresponding distinctions among values within
each of the distinct generic orders of values must be acknowledged.[12] We
will return to this topic in the next chapter.

13.3   Further Considerations

Lonergan's argument for the goodness of proportionate being raises several further questions. This section touches only briefly upon just a few,
namely: Is his argument anthropomorphic? Can the judgment of value of
proportionate being be made without a feeling of the value of the natural

universe? How does Lonergan's argument relate to an ethics of "natural law"? Can Lonergan's argument be made in exactly the form that he presented in *Insight*?

13.3.1 Is Lonergan's Argument Anthropomorphic?

It might be objected that Lonergan's *Insight* argument for the goodness of proportionate being is anthropomorphic. That is to say, Lonergan's argument might seem to make the goodness of the natural universe dependent upon human choice and human utility – since it rests on the claim that one cannot choose the conditioned without also choosing the conditions. The argument would seem to imply that if the universe did not condition humanly chosen and originated goods, then the universe would have no goodness intrinsic to it in itself. Hence, it might seem that Lonergan is making the goodness of the natural universe depend upon whether or not it conditions some values that human beings happen to choose.

Such, however, would not be an accurate rendering of Lonergan's argument. His argument, rather, concerns how human beings can come to affirm the goodness of the universe – not that human choices constitute that goodness. Underlying every case of human authentic human choosing is a grasp, a recognition, of the course of action as of virtually unconditioned value. If it is, then this means that all of the fulfilling conditions are indispensable contributions to the value being chosen. But more fundamentally, the grasp of a value as virtually unconditioned is a recognition of the value of oneself and one's actions as participants in a valuable "universal order," a dynamic evolving order in which one's own human action is only the most recent addition. Hence, far from making the value of the universe depend upon human choice, Lonergan's argument shows that the value of any human choice depends upon the conditioning value of the evolving universe as it extends into the ongoing story of human history.

Ultimately, then, Lonergan's argument is not anthropomorphic. It does not argue that the natural universe is good *because* of human judgment and choice; quite the contrary – the possibility of an ethically valuable human choice is substantially conditioned upon the goodness of the universe.

13.3.2 Feeling-Response to the Universe of Proportionate Being

A second consideration has to do with the role of feelings in arriving at the judgment of the goodness of the whole of proportionate being and its dynamic structure of emergent probability. The preceding chapters have argued that feelings for value play an indispensable role in the full and proper knowledge of value, and especially in arriving at judgments of ethical value. However, the argument presented in the previous sections does not invoke any felt intentions of value. In fact, at one point Lonergan seems to insist that every consideration of feelings must be excluded from the judgment of the value of the universe. He writes: "It will not be amiss to assert emphatically that the identification of being and the good bypasses human feelings and sentiments to take its stand exclusively upon intelligible order and rational value."[13]

However, the context of his statement makes clear that he has in mind only self-regarding desires and aversions regarding particular goods and evils, not the far richer realm of feelings that intend a broad scale of values. Hence, while Lonergan does not explicitly advert to them, in fact there are feelings that enter into to making a judgment of value about the order of proportionate being as a whole.

Kant famously concluded his *Critique of Practical Reason* with an encomium of just such a feeling: "Two things fill the mind with ever new and increasing admiration and reverence, the more often and more steadily one reflects on them: *the starry heavens above me and the moral law within me.*"[14]

Later, in his *Critique of Judgment,* Kant examined in greater detail the relationships among these feelings of admiration and reverence by exploring the differences between judgments regarding the beautiful and the sublime. The beautiful, he says, pertains to the purposiveness found in nature "represented as a system in accordance with laws."[15] The sublime, on the other hand, has to do with "formlessness" and "boundlessness" yet still as a "totality"[16] – what Lonergan would regard as the non-systematic process of the natural and human universe. Kant cites as examples of the sublime "bold, overhanging, and as it were threatening rocks; clouds piled up in the sky, moving with lightning flashes and thunder peals; volcanoes in all their violence of destruction; hurricanes with their track of devastation; the boundless ocean in a state of tumult; the lofty waterfall of a might river, and such like."[17] With the feeling of the sublime, Kant says, one is "not merely attracted ... but is ever being alternately repelled."[18]

It would seem that something like the feeling for the sublime would have to be involved in any "fully consistent," self-appropriated human act of choosing. Feelings of awe and even terror before the powers of nature must be ingredient in any objective judgment about the value of the emerging universe. Anyone who really understands what Lonergan means by emergent probability as the order of the universe will know that it is operative "no less in false starts and in breakdowns than in stability and progress [whose] trials will far outnumber its successes, but the trials are no less part of the program than the successes."[19] Emergent probability gives rise to the destructive violence of tsunamis and volcanoes, thermonuclear explosions in the interior of stars, and the Big Bang itself. A virtually unconditioned judgment about the goodness of proportionate being in no way

> denies or attempts to minimize pain or suffering, so it has not the slightest implication of a denial of unordered manifolds, of disorder, or of false values. For the middle term in the identification of the good with being is intelligibility. The intelligibility of this universe is to be grasped not only by direct but also by inverse insights.[20]

When we think explicitly about a universe whose intelligible order includes but rises above these massive displays of force, suffering, disorder, and evil, this certainly evokes powerful feeling responses. No judgment of value of the goodness of the natural realm could be objective if it ignored the entropy, violence, cataclysms, and extinctions that are truly part of the unfolding of generalized emergent probability.

Yet just as Kant insists that the fear and terror cannot be the determining factors for a judgment about the sublime, so also they cannot be the ultimate determining factors for a judgment about the goodness of the natural universe. Kant finds that the positive factor for a judgment of the sublime must arise because a feeling about something even grander arises out of these manifestations of the powers of nature: "The energies of the soul [are drawn] above their accustomed height and discover in us a faculty of resistance of a quite different kind, which give us courage to measure ourselves against the apparent almightiness of nature."[21] In this way Kant sought to bring together the two great feelings of admiration and respect with which he concludes his *Critique of Practical Reason.*

The feelings in support of a judgment of the value of the universe of proportionate being certainly have to include awe for human moral self-transcendence along with awe before the majesty of the natural universe. But for Lonergan, human moral self-transcendence is not isolated in the noumenal realm, separated from the phenomenal realm of the natural world, as it is for Kant. Rather, moral self-transcendence emerges out of the evolving natural universe through the same order of generalized emergent probability that embraces both. So what Kant calls the sublime would be a felt component in an even grander awe for a goodness that encompasses but surpasses both the dynamism of the universe and the self-transcendence of human thought and action.

Not many people stop and think about, let alone permit themselves to feel their efforts at, ethical living and moral self-transcendence as infinitesimal and yet indispensable participants in the cosmic unfolding of the universe of generalized emergent probability. But those who strive for self-appropriation will be led to such feelings and considerations. The judgment about the goodness of the whole of proportionate being, therefore, depends both upon such feelings and upon a sustained intellectual exploration of all of the conditions that are involved in truly being ethical.

These remarks are but meager indications of the further study that needs to be done regarding the feelings that are presupposed in a judgment about the goodness of proportionate being. Much further discussion of this topic is needed, including how this approach compares and contrasts not only with Kant's approach, but also with that of his successors. But this will have to suffice for the present.

13.3.3   *The Goodness of Proportionate Being and Natural Law Ethics*

Lonergan's argument has important implications for an ethics of natural law as well.[22] There are several long traditions of natural law ethics. Each uses some model of nature, and especially its teleological dimensions, as the basis for arguing about whether certain human actions are ethical or unethical. These traditions have been severely criticized by modern and postmodern thinkers, in part contending that what is presented as a "natural" foundation is in fact no more than some historically relativized or ideologically limited idea about nature.

But Lonergan's argument goes to the heart of certain weaknesses in natural law ethics by pointing out that the key to the goodness of nature is its virtually unconditioned intelligibility. The intelligibility of nature is a dynamic, emergent intelligibility. Because it is underpinned by unrestricted inquiry and authentic responses to the questions it poses, human fidelity to the structure of ethical intentionality partakes in this dynamic intelligibility and is in *that* precise sense "natural." This connection provides important resources for assessing the goodness of human uses and abuses of the natural environment, for thinking about "interventions" in human natural biological processes, for arriving at virtually unconditioned judgments about the natural goodness of the human process of dying, and for critically assessing the ways in which human decisions cooperate with or violate that natural goodness. However, working out the detailed implications of these suggestions for a natural law ethics is beyond the scope of this book. Here I can only point out a few of the ways that Lonergan's argument for the goodness of proportionate being can be of value in such discussions.

13.3.4   *The Inadequacy of the* Insight *Argument*

The argument presented in section 13.2.1 is a modification of the argument for the goodness of the whole of proportionate being as Lonergan presented it in *Insight*. There are two difficulties with his argument as he actually presented it. First, he argued that "the realization of universal order is a true value" because it is implicit in every consistent "rational choice" of a specifically human value.[23] In *Insight*, however, he says that a human choice can be considered rational insofar as it is "consistent with [one's] knowing."[24] The problem with this claim resides in what Lonergan meant by "knowing" at that point in the book. Up to that stage, *Insight* had only treated knowledge of facts. Knowledge of values had not been mentioned, let alone analysed prior to Lonergan's argument for the goodness of proportionate being – and it receives very little attention in the remainder of the book. So it would seem that rational choice would have to be consistent with some kind of factual knowledge rather than with knowledge of the ethical value of what one ought to do.

Lonergan certainly gives the impression that he thought it would be possible to derive an account of the good in particular and ethics in general that relied only on the account of factual knowing:

> So far our analysis has been concerned with the good in a human sense, with objects of desire, intelligible orders, terminal and originating values. But as the close relations between metaphysics and ethics suggest, it should be possible to generalize this notion and, indeed, to conceive the good as identical with the intelligibility that is intrinsic to being.[25]

But as we have seen, his account of the metaphysics of proportionate being is grounded in the self-affirmation of the cognitional structure of factual knowing. In attempting to ground an ethics (or a consequent account of the good) from factual knowing alone, Lonergan falls prey to the criticisms of Hume and Schelling that it is impossible to derive "ought" from "is," as well as to what G.E. Moore called "the naturalistic fallacy" – the fallacy of equating the good with or defining it in terms of a merely natural entity.[26]

Lonergan did provide a way in which this problem could be avoided in *Insight*. There he said that he would derive his ethics from "the compound structure of one's knowing *and doing*,"[27] and later he argued that the rationality of choice comes in response to an exigence (demand) for consistency between knowing and doing that goes beyond knowing.[28] However, he did not introduce either the idea of this exigence or anything like an articulation of the compound structure of knowing and doing until *after* he presented his argument for the goodness of proportionate being.

Lonergan thus did not provide in *Insight* a sufficient basis for his argument for the goodness of proportionate being. However, the expanded account of the structure of ethical intentionality *does* provide an ample basis for his conclusion. In this expanded account choices are made on the basis of objective knowledge of values, not facts alone. Hence, there is no violation of the naturalistic fallacy in the modified argument presented in section 13.2.1. Every "consistent" choice of an intelligible course of action known to be virtually unconditionally valuable does commit one to the goodness of the dynamic order of proportionate being, because that order is the whole in which one's chosen value arises as just a part. In chapter 15 we will return to related problems concerning Lonergan's method of ethics in *Insight* and how they, too, can be resolved by means of the expanded account of ethical intentionality.

There is a second problem with Lonergan's argument in *Insight*: he claims more than his argument establishes. His full claim is that "the good is identified with the intelligibility intrinsic to being," and that "the middle term of the identification of the good with being is intelligibility."[29] However, his argument only establishes that the good is identified with the intelligibility intrinsic to *proportionate* being (i.e., the actual, universal order of emergent probability). His argument does not establish that the entirety of being without qualification is good. To meet that difficulty we must take into account not only the question of transcendent being, but also the question of its transcendent goodness. To those issues we now turn.

13.4   The Transcendent Good

13.4.1   Transcendent Being as Ultimate Condition of Our Value Choices

Lonergan's argument can be extended still further, leading to the affirmation of the goodness of the whole of being without restriction – transcendent being as well as proportionate being.[30] In *Insight,* Lonergan seems to assume that he already achieved this when he argued that no consistent choice can choose the conditioned without also choosing the conditions, at least implicitly. Yet, in the argument that he actually presents, the only conditions that he identifies explicitly are those supplied by the underlying intelligible orders (i.e., natural and human schemes of recurrence and ecosystems) along with the dynamic wholeness of proportionate being (i.e., "the universal order, which is generalized emergent probability").[31] His argument as explicitly set forth, therefore, does not justify his claim that good is identified with the intelligibility intrinsic to the totality of being, and especially not to transcendent being.

But it is possible to refine and to extend his argument so as to achieve the full generality that he intended, for neither any reality within proportionate being nor proportionate being as a whole is self-conditioning. As Lonergan observes, "the universe of proportionate being is shot through with contingence."[32]

From the pervasiveness of contingency, other philosophies have concluded that there is nothing further to say. We live in a contingent universe devoid of any ultimate meaning or purpose, period. Lonergan asked whether another conclusion might be drawn concerning the meaning of the contingencies of the universe for human efforts to live ethically:

> To deliberate about deliberating is to ask whether any deliberating is worth while. Has "worth while" any ultimate meaning? Is moral enterprise consonant with this world? ... is the universe on our side, or are we just gamblers and, if gamblers, are we not perhaps fools, individually struggling for authenticity and collectively endeavoring to snatch progress from the ever mounting welter of decline? The questions arise and, clearly, our attitudes and our resoluteness may be profoundly affected by the answers. Does there or does there not necessarily exist a transcendent, intelligent ground of the universe? Is that ground or are we the primary instance of moral consciousness? Are cosmogenesis, biological evolution, historical process basically cognate to us as moral beings or are they indifferent and so alien to us?[33]

Lonergan's way of responding to his own question arises from one of his important claims – namely, that "the real is completely intelligible."[34] If the real is completely intelligible, then contingency cannot be the final word. If the real is completely intelligible, then there can be no ultimate, brute matters of fact – "no mere matters of fact that remain ultimately unexplained."[35]

From these observations Lonergan argues that there must then exist a being that is both self-explanatory and explanatory of everything else. This means that proportionate being cannot be the whole of being, and therefore being must include a transcendent being.[36]

Drawing upon these claims, it is possible to extend his argument about the intrinsic goodness of proportionate being to the goodness of transcendent being, and therefore, the goodness of being as a whole.

In the argument for the goodness of the whole of proportionate being, one of the crucial steps was the claim that in any act of choosing that which is grounded in a virtually unconditioned judgment of value, we are choosing as good *all* the conditions for that value along with the specific value itself, at least implicitly. In light of the further reflections about the existence of a transcendent being that is the condition for all contingent goods, we can now say that implicitly we choose it as good even more than the universal order of generalized emergent probability that conditioned the emergence of the conditions of the value we choose. In Lonergan's own words, "the actual course of generalized emergent probability is but one among a large number of other probable courses ... [that] is in fact what happens to be."[37] But if being is completely intelligible as Lonergan argued, then the actual course of the evolutionary history of the natural universe and humankind cannot be a mere matter of fact. Beyond the merely *de facto*, contingent, conditioned course of the history of proportionate being, there is the further condition that makes that process ultimately intelligible, namely, the transcendent being that is both explanatory of itself and explanatory of all the conditions of everything that is merely virtually unconditioned. The ultimate reason and value for the actual universe being and evolving in the ways that it does is its ultimate intelligibility. The transcendent being is the reason for the existence of anything and everything. It is the reason why schemes and events and things are the ways that they are, and why they come to be through generalized emergent probability rather than through some other means. Lonergan concludes, therefore, that the transcendent being "is the ground of value, and it is the ultimate cause of causes for it overcomes contingence at its deepest level."[38] The transcendent being would have to be the ultimate condition of the conditions of our ethical choices.

Therefore each consistent and objective human choice of a genuine value implicitly chooses as valuable all of its conditions – not only proportionate being as a whole, but also its ultimate intelligible source, the transcendent being. *If* our choices are unconditionally ethical and consistent, they are grounded in objective value judgments. *If* the value judgments are objective, they affirm what is genuinely of value in the context of the normative scale of values. *If* they affirm what is genuinely valuable, they affirm something as of virtually unconditioned value – as of value in and through all its fulfilling conditions. Therefore, implicitly in every genuinely ethical choice we implicitly affirm and choose the value of the transcendent being as the ultimate condition of what we choose. Hence, *if* we choose ethically and consistently, we also choose transcendent being as the ultimate condition for the actuality of generalized emergent probability, and as the ultimate condition for the choice we make that has its place within that emergent universal order. Transcendent being and its utterly transcending value therefore underlies every genuinely ethical choice. Furthermore, since the transcendent being is explanatory of itself and of everything else, this means that the reason why, the value for everything else, the ultimate intelligibility of everything else, is the unconditional goodness of the transcendent being. This means that everything that is, is shot through with the ultimate intelligibility that is unconditional goodness. The whole of being, therefore, is good.

13.4.2 Transcendent Being as Understanding and Loving

The argument offered in the previous section is also a modification of the one that Lonergan used in *Insight* to support the conclusion of the goodness of God and therefore the goodness of being in general. There he drew upon his conclusion that the goodness of all being is identical with its intelligibility. He then proceeded to argue that because the transcendent being

was completely intelligible, it was therefore also "the primary good."[39] As
we have seen, however, Lonergan's own argument for the goodness of the
whole of being is problematic; hence, his argument for the goodness of the
transcendent being is also problematic.

However, in light of the strengthened argument for the goodness of
being without restriction, it is possible to situate Lonergan's *Insight* identification of the transcendent being and transcendent good as God, where
God is conceived of as an unrestricted act of understanding. Furthermore,
we can also consider Lonergan's argument that God conceived of as an
unrestricted act of understanding is also identically an unconditional act of
loving. After placing these claims in the context of the strengthened argument above, we will also show how the more fully elaborated structure of
ethical intentionality expands Lonergan's analogical conception of God as
an unrestricted act of understanding into an analogical conception of God
as an unconditional act of understanding, valuing, choosing, and loving.

In *Insight,* Lonergan "extrapolated" an analogical conception of an "unrestricted act of understanding."[40] Any analogical conception relies upon the
basic structure of analogy:

$$A{:}B{::}C{:}X$$

In the standard paradigm for an analogy, there are four terms (A, B, C, X)
and three relations symbolized by the colons. Positing an analogy amounts
to the assertion that two of the relations are identical with one another.[41]
In the symbolized version above, the relations between A and B (symbolized by the colon between them) is the same as the relation between C
and X (likewise symbolized by the colon between them). The double colon
between B and C symbolizes the relation of identity – not the identity of B
with C, but the identity of the relations between $A|B$ and $C|X$, respectively.
In this analogy, A, B, and C are presented as knowns, while X is presented as
an unknown. Insofar as A and B are known, then their relation ($A{:}B$) is also
known. Insofar as C is also known, and its relation to X is known from $A{:}B$,
then X is known by means of this relation to C.

Lonergan uses this idea of analogy in his indirect (analogical) definition
of the unrestricted act of understanding. He approaches it as an unknown,
X, which has the same relation to the unrestricted desire to know as a single
insight has to its corresponding question. Thus,

human question for intelligence: human insight::
human unrestricted desire to know: unrestricted act of understanding

The fourth term in this analogy, the unrestricted act of understanding,
is not defined directly. This is because human insights precede and are the

basis of human formulations of definitions and concepts.[42] So in order to define an unrestricted act of understanding directly, we would have to first understand what it is to understand without limit or restriction; failing that, our conception of the unrestricted act of understanding can be only indirect, imperfect, analogical.[43]

Lonergan went on to argue that an unrestricted act of understanding would possess the essential features of a transcendent being – that is, it is both self-explanatory and explanatory of everything else.[44] That is to say, by understanding everything about everything, the unrestricted act of understanding would understand the answers to the questions about the reason for its being, how it could be, and how everything else could be made to be. This unrestricted act of understanding, he further argued, would also have the other characteristics traditionally attributed to God by classical Christian theism – it would be one, simple, eternal, the cause of all that is, and so on.[45] Lonergan also argued that because the unrestricted act of understanding would be unconditionally intelligible, it would be the primary and unconditional good, and would therefore be the condition of the goodness of all contingent goods. Finally, he also claimed that the unrestricted act of understanding would also be identically "a completely perfect act of loving."[46] This follows, he argued, from the completeness and perfection of unrestricted understanding. For, if complete and perfect loving were distinct from unrestricted understanding,

> then the primary being would be incomplete and imperfect and in need of further acts of affirming and loving to be completed and perfected. Hence, one and the same reality is at once unrestricted understanding and the primary intelligible, reflective understanding and the unconditioned, perfect affirming and the primary truth, perfect loving and the primary good.[47]

From the logic of Lonergan's argument, it follows that the unrestricted act of understanding is also unconditional loving.

Yet it is possible to offer an argument that makes more directly evident the unity of God's transcendent being, unrestricted understanding and unconditional loving as the condition for the goodness of all goods. This alternative argument follows from Lonergan's post-*Insight* realization that the unified unrestricted desire encompasses both the unrestricted notion of value as well as the unrestricted notion of being.[48] That is to say, one and the same unrestricted desire motivates and is made manifest in all questions for intelligence, for factual reflection, and for value and ethical reflection. We desire to understand, know, value, and commit ourselves to everything good about everything. On this basis it is possible to formulate another kind of analogical conception:

human question for ethical reflection: human act of choosing::
the unrestricted notion of value[49]: X

The use of *X* in the fourth position in this analogy indicates that it denotes an unknown, as was also the case with the phrase "unrestricted act of understanding" in the previous analogy. We really do not know directly at all what is meant by the phrase "unrestricted act of understanding." It is only by the indirect means provided by the other three terms in the analogy that it is possible at all to affirm even some very limited things about the unrestricted act of understanding – such as that it is one, simple, self-explanatory, and thereby explanatory of all else. But even the ability to make such limited judgments still leaves the fullness of the unrestricted act of understanding as unknown.

The same is true of whatever is denoted by *X* in the second analogy. Short of us actually understanding, valuing, and choosing everything good about everything, we could not offer a direct definition of *X*. Nevertheless, there are a few limited things that can be still said about *X*. This is what is meant by an analogical, imperfect definition.

First of all, *X* would somehow be related to the feeling of unrestricted being-in-love. Lonergan defined being-in-love in an unrestricted fashion as "the *basic* fulfilment" and "the *proper* fulfilment" of all our questioning.[50] Still, he did not define being-in-love as the *complete* fulfillment of the intentionality of all our questioning. Even though unrestricted being-in-love is present arguably in every human consciousness, nevertheless those who attend to this experience of being-in-love still have further questions about it and its implications.

On the other hand, the analogy above also situates *X* in relation to the unrestricted desire to know and value, but in such a way that *X* would have to be the *complete* fulfillment of ethical intentionality. So while unrestricted being-in-love is not exactly the *X* in question, the two are somehow closely related. Lonergan himself offers a hint as to how to think about the relation between being-in-love in an unrestricted fashion and this unknown *X*: "This view of religion is sustained when *God is conceived as the supreme fulfilment of the transcendental notions,* as supreme intelligence, truth, reality, righteousness, goodness."[51]

Lonergan's use of "supreme" as a modifier of "fulfillment" is reserved for God exclusively and unequivocally. Here he is both agreeing with the languages of religious traditions and also drawing from them evidence for his way of approaching the phenomena of religion. That is to say, the supreme and complete answer to all questions for intelligence would be supreme intelligence; to all questions for factual reflection, supreme (factual) truth and reality; to all questions for ethical value, supreme righteousness; to all questions of value whatsoever, be supreme goodness. In *Insight*, Lonergan derived the supreme goodness of God from his theorem on the goodness of being and the nature of the unrestricted act of understanding. But if we begin instead with the second analogy based on the unrestricted desire to know and value, all of the analogical predications about God follow directly from the nature of God as unconditional loving. That is to say, supreme intelligence, supreme truth, supreme reality, supreme righteousness, supreme goodness all follow because they would be contained in the *X* that is the complete answer to the whole range of questions intended in the unrestricted desire for intelligibility and truth about being and goodness.

This means, of course, that whatever else can be said of *X*, it must certainly be said to be the unrestricted act of understanding; it follows from the second analogy just as much as from the first, that there would be no unanswered questions for either intelligence or reflection in X, and therefore it would be the unrestricted act of understanding. It would understand everything about everything. It would not only be an unrestricted act of direct understanding, meeting all questions for intelligence. It would also be an unrestricted act of reflective understanding, grasping everything that is unconditionally. We human beings need to raise further pertinent questions about our limited insights before we can know whether or not those finite understandings are unconditionally correct. We need to understand under what conditions the conditioned intelligibility of our insights could reasonably be said to be real. But for an unrestricted act of understanding there would be no further questions whatsoever, pertinent or otherwise. Hence, in one and the same unrestricted act it would understand every intelligibility along with whether or not it is an unconditioned, real intelligibility.

Something similar is also the case for valuing. In the human structure of ethical intentionality, we first come to a practical insight and then ask whether or not the intelligible course of action it proposes is valuable enough for our commitment and action. We ask further pertinent questions about its ethical value because our understanding is limited and incomplete, and needs to be completed through our further value reflection. We cannot responsibly and ethically pronounce about the value of that intelligibility until we have asked and answered all the further pertinent questions about our initial understanding, correcting and refining it into a virtually unconditional correct understanding of the valuable thing to do. But an unrestricted act of understanding would always already understand everything about everything. It would have no further questions whatsoever. Hence it would always already understand both the valuable thing to do in every concrete circumstance and also the unconditional value for doing it.

Third, this analogy is not based solely on the relation of a question for ethical reflection to a judgment of value. It is based, rather, on the unified, unrestricted desire encompassing both the unrestricted notion of value as well as the unrestricted notion of being. Our unrestricted desire desires not only to know the being and value of everything about everything, but it also raises questions of choice – questions about choosing everything good. It desires the complete union with all that is good that comes only fully with choosing. This choosing should not be construed on the misleading analogy of possession, property, control, or domination. The kind of choice involved here is a choice of acceptance. Possessing everything of value is an impossibility, and if it is attempted can only lead to ruinous consequences. But accepting and embracing everything of value is possible. So the unrestricted desire to know and value would find supreme fulfillment in an unrestricted acceptance of everything good about everything. In order to do this, it would have to understand the unconditional, actual intelligibility of everything and also the value of every actual and possible intelligibility.

A term that can be appropriately used for completely unconditional acceptance is love. Love has many meanings, many of them corrupted usages. But "unconditional acceptance" is at least one meaningful way of speaking about love. This is love neither as desire, nor affect, nor mood. It is rather love as an act of choice that arises out of an unconditional being-in-love that is analogous to an affect or a mood as a felt intention of value. Unconditional being-in-love would be the unrestricted felt response to what is known in an unrestricted act of understanding, and an unconditional act of loving acceptance would be grounded in this unrestrictedly affectionate understanding and judging.

13.5   The Goodness of Being and the Problem of Evil

In the previous sections we followed Lonergan's argument for the intrinsic goodness of being. It was necessary to refine that argument in order to overcome certain limitations, but we still came to Lonergan's conclusions, namely, that being is good and that the key to the goodness of being is its intelligibility. Or, as Lonergan puts it, being and the good are convertible because of the intrinsic intelligibility of both being and the good.[52] This means that whatever is, is intelligible and therefore good.

However, before proceeding to the final point of this chapter in the next section, namely, the heuristic definition of the good in general, it is necessary to digress in order to address an obvious objection. No doubt some readers will object that it is absurd to say that whatever is, is good. It seems obvious that many things that are, are not good at all. Many things are destructive and downright evil. Poisonous snakes kill children. Tsunamis and other natural disasters kill hundreds of thousands of people. Voltaire ridiculed Leibnitz's claim that this is the best of all possible worlds. Heidegger objected to Hegel's claim that the real is the rational, and for good reasons. Lonergan seems to be making this same egregious error, and I seem to be following his bad example. Nothing it seems could be more real than the human atrocities filling every decade of the twentieth century – a century that may have been the most inhumane in the history of humanity.

13.5.1   *The Unintelligibility and Non-Value of Evil*

However, Lonergan's error is only apparent. His writings show his own horror at the evils of human history, especially the historical period of his own life when he referred to events of the twentieth century as "an earthly hell"[53] and the "monster that has stood forth in our time."[54] There is little question that his efforts in philosophy and theology were dedicated beyond all else to addressing the problem of evil. Indeed the whole of *Insight* leads up to the culminating chapter devoted to the problem of evil.

If Lonergan was therefore so keenly preoccupied with the problem of evil, how could he hold something so apparently naive, as whatever is real is good? His answer: there is something unreal about evil, and it is precisely this unreality that makes evil so hideous. This answer goes back to Lonergan's argument that "the middle term in the identification of the good with being is intelligibility."[55] Lonergan argues that evil is precisely the lack of intelligibility,[56] and thus a lack of reality. Since being is whatever is to be known in the totality of answers to questions for intelligence and factual reflection, and every question for reflection "Is it?" presupposes an intelligible "it," then if there is no intelligibility, there can be no affirmation of the being of that intelligible absence. So if evil is an absence of intelligibility, the evil *is not*.

However, not every defect of intelligibility amounts to an absolute non-existence of intelligibility. Non-intelligibility can be a relative absence, so to speak. For example, if a hawk attacks and kills a rabbit, it terminates the intelligible functioning of that creature. From the viewpoint of that rabbit, an evil has happened, and that evil is the cessation of the intelligibility and vital value that constituted its way of living. Not only rabbits but human beings also can feel the disvalue, the evil, of the death of a rabbit. But from the broader viewpoint of the whole of nature, that event is quite intelligible. Human beings can employ the methods of biological science to comprehend the intelligibility of rabbits and of hawks – and not just of an individual rabbit or hawk but of the interactions among populations of rabbits and hawks as they bring about statistical balances. These are all part and parcel of an ecosystem in which many species interact in a complex, biologically intelligible pattern. So even the destruction of the intelligibility of the life of an individual rabbit has a further intelligibility within the more comprehending intelligibility of nature, which Lonergan called generalized emergent probability.

Something similar can be said about natural disasters on much larger scales: earthquakes, volcanic eruptions, tsunamis, hurricanes, the impact of a massive asteroid, even the collision of two galaxies into one another. All these bring about massive destruction of the good, intelligible functioning of many things. Individual stars, plants, animals, and human lives are destroyed. Cosmic systems, ecosystems, and human goods of order are devastated. In every case there is an evil, because the loss of those existing intelligibilities is the destruction of something good. These evils are relative to the intelligibilities negated by the destructive forces. But these are not absolute evils. The laws of physics, chemistry, and biology can all be applied on wide scales to provide intelligible accounts of why and where and how often these events occur, and what their intelligible consequences are. All of these events occur within the more comprehending intelligible goodness of what Lonergan calls generalized emergent probability. Without generalized emergent probability itself, none of those goods could have come to be concretely or to be good at all in the first place. Their actual goodness was conditioned by the more fundamental goodness of world process – by generalized emergent probability, which includes not only the conditions and probabilities of emergence of good things and occurrences, but also of their survivals and demises.

We might imagine or wish we could extract some of the values we most cherish from the process of generalized emergent probability that brought them into being in the first place. But then we would be valuing those values merely as we imagine them, not as they truly are. There is no denying the truly lamentable loss of goodness that comes with the destruction of intelligibilities. But these evils are not absolute. There is a compensating higher intelligible goodness that explains why these losses occur. It is the terrible yet awesome intelligibility and goodness of the universe, of generalized emergent probability, that makes sense of why such losses occur. It may well require intellectual and moral conversion for someone to recognize that there is such a goodness beyond these losses, a goodness comprehended only in light of the full scale of values. Certainly, to comprehend that there is a value for the sake of which these losses occur does not make them any less painful or sorrowful. But it does remove those losses from the abyss of absolute meaninglessness.

As with natural disasters, human evil does involve the destruction of intelligibilities. Property and human fabrications are stolen or destroyed.

Intricate networks of trust and cooperation are ruined. Cultural and religious institutions once devoted to cultivating higher values are corrupted. Human beings are killed and loving patterns of personal relations are shattered.

But there are also profound differences. The most profound difference – what makes evil properly human – is the complete absence of any higher intelligible order that explains or justifies the destruction. This is because evil in the strictly human sense arises from decisions for which there is no proper value, no justifiable reason. Properly ethical decisions follow from judgments of virtually unconditioned value that are the reasons for the decisions. The judgments of value constitute the ensuing courses of action as virtually unconditional intelligibilities. But as was argued in chapter 4, human decisions are not determined or caused by judgments of value. Human decisions are radically free, and so are not determined either by natural forces or brain functioning or autonomous thought processes or even judgments of value.[57] There always remains the radical possibility of deciding not to go along with what one thinks or believes or judges to be right or wrong. When there is a failure to comply with what one knows to be the valuable thing to do, there is no reason for the decision. Instead, one is left with radical unintelligibility.[58]

This incoherence and inconsistency between one's value knowing and one's choosing is the origin of all evil in the strictly human sense. It is for this reason that there is no higher intelligibility that compensates for or explains or justifies human evil. If there were, then the higher intelligibility would either make the consequent action a purely physical or neurological matter that completely bypasses human freedom or provide the grounds for a virtually unconditioned judgment that provides the true value for the free human decision.[59] But since the focus here is upon human decisions that are freely made in violation of the person's own value knowledge of what is right and wrong, such higher intelligibilities are not in play.

This means there is a radical nothingness at the heart of human evil. There is no-thing to explain why humans decide to act in ways that go against values and reasons for acting.

However, to say that radical unintelligibility and unreality is at the root of evil human decisions is not to say that their *consequences* are unreal or in every sense unintelligible. While the deciding itself is unintelligible, still the course of action upon which it decides does have certain intelligibilities. Once the decision for which there is ultimately no value has been made, it is executed bodily – carrying away someone else's property, assaulting someone else body, pulling a trigger, or using one's body to express oneself so as to hurt another's feelings or reputation, to incite violence on the part of others, or to initiate corrupt schemes of recurrence. People need to have acquired many insights in order to be able to use their bodies in such ways, and in that limited way, their bodily actions are intelligible. Their insights and the insights of the science of physiology explain how their bodies are able to move as they do so as to carry out the chosen course of action. Everything in their course of action is intelligible, except for the decision that inaugurates the course of action itself. That decision lacks any reason or value.[60]

Likewise, the consequences initiated by the non-being of the decision can follow intelligibly from the course of action, and these consequences are all too real. Acts of robbery, rape, or murder all have intelligibly comprehensible results. The laws of physics, chemistry, biology, and psychology in combination can explain how the destruction of intelligibilities and their associated values of various kinds result from the originating bodily actions undertaken by individual human beings. Such actions predictably deprive people of their land, their access to water, meaningful work, healthcare, their savings, their voices in determining the institutional decisions that affect their lives, their psychological well-being and stability – and, ultimately, they snuff out their lives or the lives of those they love most.

All these evil consequences are real. They all follow quite intelligibly, given the bodily actions originated by human actors. But what does not follow intelligibly or with any value whatsoever is the decision that was the origin of the bodily movements and the course of action. A decision made without sufficient value and reason is radically unreal. Because there is no reason for the decision itself, it follows that *ultimately* there is no reason or value for the consequences. When decisions are unintelligible, that unintelligibility propagates and infects the consequences. The consequences accumulate to form what Lonergan called the "social surd" – a complex compound of intelligibility and unintelligibility.[61] Humans experience suffering when they encounter this compound of intelligibility and unintelligibility, and that suffering is feeling its non-value, its evil.

To say that there is an unreality to evil therefore does not mean that evil does not result in suffering. Obviously it does. This kind of suffering is suffering that is unintelligible and without value. Since in Lonergan's precise and technical sense the unintelligible is not, this means that we suffer because of the unreality. But to call evil unreal seems to denigrate people's suffering. Undeniably, their suffering is real, but what they suffer is not a reality in the sense of a virtually unconditioned intelligibility. They suffer the unintelligibility of the annihilation of something intelligible for no reason, or of being forced to undergo conditions that lack intelligibility. Their suffering is real enough and what they suffer has an immediate reality, it is ultimately unreal because it is unintelligible.[62]

This way of characterizing the unreality of evil does not sit well with what Lonergan calls the counter-position on reality.[63] That counter-position attempts to reduce reality to what is "already out there now," visible and tangible. According to this counter-position, evil is real enough and fully evident in the destroyed ruins that are out there in the world and internally in people's sufferings.

But on the position of self-appropriation, reality in the proper sense is what is known, not just by experiencing what is already out there, but also by understanding and by virtually unconditioned judgments that the understanding is correct. Whatever is only experienced but not yet understood or judged may well be a component of reality, but it is not reality itself. That people experience suffering does not therefore imply that they experience a reality. Experiences can be components of intelligible and affirmed realities, but they can also be experiences for which there is no corresponding intelligibility. As Lonergan remarks, we need inverse insights as well as direct insights in order to make sense of the full range of our experiences. In particular, "the evil of disorder is an absence of intelligibility that is to be understood only by the inverse insight that grasps its lack of intelligibility."[64]

The *experience* of suffering evil is real, but a full understanding of that suffering does not automatically imply that the *source* of that suffering is real in the full sense. The source of that suffering is unintelligible, meaningless, unreal. We know unintelligibility in limited negative judgments – "S does not have intelligibility I." These do not affirm the existence of some unintelligibility, but simply deny the existence of some intelligibility. So also we know evil, disvalue or negative value in negative judgments of value. We know this by denying that there is any finite intelligibility or value to the suffering and by denying that the events that are happening are intelligible. We judge the events to have negative values, in effect saying that they are abysses of value. We say they are absolutely evil when they lack any value whatsoever.

The unreality of evil human decisions can come about in at least two ways. The first and most obvious way is when human beings arrive at virtually unconditioned, fully objective judgments of value about a proposed course of action, but then decide in complete opposition to what they have judged. They know full well what they should (or should not) do, and they do otherwise.[65]

But there is a second, more subtle, more common, more insidious, and, in the long run, more destructive origin of evil human decisions. This has to do with decisions that are made on the basis of something other than objective, virtually unconditioned judgments of value. Such decisions may proceed from deliberations and reflections done in a horizon of feelings riddled with *ressentiment* or the four biases (dramatic, individual, group, or general), or other distortions that pervert the objective scale of values and obscure consciousness of the unrestricted notion of value and unrestricted being-in-love. Then many further pertinent questions are not raised, and of those that are raised, many go unanswered. Then courses of action that are undertaken will lack the fully corrected intelligibility that is to be discerned in judgments that truly are virtually unconditioned. Such cases involve certain degrees of ignorance. While they lack the cold-hearted deliberateness of explicitly going against what they know they should do, nevertheless, these degrees of ignorance are never fully innocent. People with good intentions often look back with regret and acknowledge that they should have known better. Sometimes this is because of their own indolence. Sometimes it is because they trusted other individuals, or even their own culture, when they should have paid attention to wispy, lingering questions about the credibility of their sources. But in all such cases, people make decisions for which there is no ultimate, justifying value. When they do, the non-value and unintelligibility of the decision propagates and infects the world, including their own lives.

Therefore, while from the natural world there is some intelligibility and good in terms of which intellectually and morally converted people can find consolation for the sorrows over losses, there is no such consoling higher good that can successfully explain away humanly originated evil.

13.5.2   The Ethics of Bringing Good Out of Evil

This account of human evil, in spite of all its sophistication, seems to leave us no better off regarding the goodness of being. It seems that human evil turns the intelligibility of the natural universe into a complex surd, a mixture of intelligibility and unintelligibility. Since the goodness of being is predicated on the basis of its intelligibility, then it seems that being cannot be wholly good because it is shot through with the radical unintelligibility that originates from evil human decisions.

Although there can be no intelligibility that explains or justifies human evil, this does not mean that the consequences of human evil cannot be made intelligible in some other way. In particular, it does not mean that subsequent human decisions and actions cannot draw good out of evil, cannot create meaning out of unintelligibility, cannot heal the injustices and build new patterns of cooperation upon the ruins of those damaged or eradicated by evil deeds, or cannot construct something that valorizes lives that were meaninglessly destroyed. Given greatness of soul, unintelligibilities can become the occasions and the potencies, so to speak, for human acts that bring about good.[66] Jean Paget's decision and the subsequent actions of others at Kuala Telang, for example, made something of astonishing value out of the horrors of her war experiences.

Lonergan's argument for the goodness of the wholeness of being, therefore, includes the possibility and indeed the actuality of good that comes out of evil, a good that makes whole what is left fractured and only partially intelligible from the viewpoint of generalized emergent probability alone. The goodness of the wholeness of being is an emerging goodness, and that emergence includes the overcoming and healing of unjustifiable suffering, destruction, disorder, and the nihilism of false values.

According to Lonergan, this bringing good out of the unintelligible morass of evil is the emergence of a "higher integration."[67] This higher integration, he says, is a new kind of good of order, a collaboration between human beings and God.[68] The foundation of this collaboration is the unconditional love of God, which endows human beings with being-in-love in an unrestricted fashion. Because the source of this overcoming is ultimately the unrestricted understanding, valuing, and love of God, this collaboration has the capacity to transform ever so gradually the unintelligibility of evil into a whole that is completely intelligible and good beyond all limitation. Such a collaboration, Lonergan writes, involves a

> dialectical attitude of will … to return good for evil. For it is only inasmuch as [humans] are willing to meet evil with good, to love their enemies, to pray for those that persecute and calumniate them, that the social surd is a potential good. It follows that love of God above all and in all so embraces the order of the universe as to love all [humans] with a self-sacrificing love.[69]

It is worth noting that Lonergan does not say that people involved in this collaboration must explicitly affirm that they are doing these things, or even that they must explicitly affirm that they are cooperating with God. Although it was argued in the previous section that God can be understood analogically as unrestricted understanding, valuing, and unconditional love, it is actions of self-sacrificing love, not professions or analogical understandings, that really are the authentic signs of membership in this collaboration. All acts truly done out of unconditional love are contributions to this collaboration. Yet, in the long run, people need to ask and answer questions about what they are doing and why, in order that they may perform acts of self-sacrificing love continuously and effectively. Among the questions will be what is really meant by unconditional love, and with whom they are in love. Intelligent and discerning answers to such questions will be needed for individuals and communities to sustain the work of this collaboration over the long haul.

An ethics of discernment grounded in the structure of ethical intentionality, therefore, opens out into a truly authentic religious ethics, which is concerned to meet the unintelligibility and disvalue of the world by discerning how to value and collaborate with God and other human beings in this work of love, of *tikkun olam*, loving repair of the world. However, further elaboration of this is the topic for another book.

13.6   The Notion of the Good and Conceptions of the Good

It is said that not only do we each have our own concept of the good, but also that we have a fundamental right to fashion our own conception of the good. Conceptions of the good in this sense are not "thin" abstract ideas but enriched "thick" ideas about the good that have resulted from answers to questions arising out of real-life situations. Conceptions of the good are not just ideas about what might be possible in situations, but those ideas as elevated into objective and compelling values by rich horizons of feelings for values and by virtually unconditioned judgments of value. These conceptions of the good, therefore, bear the stamp of the horizons of feeling within which they were born. They are the enriched and refined results of asking and answering the many questions pertinent to whether the ideas are truly worth realizing, at least as determined by the limits of a person's horizon of feeling.

Prior to conceptions of the good, then, there are the processes of ethical intentionality that produce them. Those processes may be carried out well or poorly; they may be carried out completely and thoroughly, or only partially, sporadically, and incompletely. They may faithfully follow the demanding paths of ethical inquiry, or they may succumb to biases, trends of the day, or ideologies, and brush aside further pertinent questions as annoying or threatening. They may be carried out by people who are profoundly discerning about their horizons of feeling and the self-transcending dynamics within them, or by people with shallow, superficial, or conflicted horizons of feeling that tend towards contraction. When these processes are carried through well and with discernment, all the way to virtually unconditioned judgments of value and the choices and actions that realize them, then the good is what results.

Clearly, conceptions of the good in this richer sense are the results of processes of ethical intentionality driven by the dynamisms of the pure unrestricted desire for the good, unrestricted being-in-love, and the normative scale of value preference. Before there are conceptions of the good, there is the pure wanting of what is good that is expressed in questions about what is worthwhile. It is this wanting that has to be satisfied by insights, conceptions, judgments, choices, and actions if these are to be called good. The unrestricted wanting of the good sets the norms according to which both conceptions of the good and choices are to be adjudicated as genuinely good, or as falling short of the good, or as destructive of what is good. This is so because adjudicating what is good is accomplished precisely by exercises of the structure of ethical intentionality in which hosts of further pertinent questions come forth from the unrestricted desire, each question demanding to be heard and not relenting until attention has been paid and satisfaction received.

Adjudicating what is good does not presuppose the vision of some pre-existing Idea of the Good as if in Plato's noetic heaven – as if one could look there to see what the Good really is, and then see if one's ideas and judgments conform. The primary sources of human normativity about the good are not the good as expressed in some definition, not the good as some full-blown Idea. Rather, the primary sources of normativity about the good are our unrestricted desire for and unrestricted love of everything good about everything. In human consciousness, the most fundamental "knowing" of the good is to be found in desiring, anticipating, being-in-love. That desiring and being-in-love is unlimited. That unrestricted desire and being-in-love desires and loves to know and accept everything good about every good thing.

We conclude this chapter, therefore, by returning to the point made at the beginning of chapter 11, but now hopefully with far fuller understanding. The most fundamental definition of the good is a second-order, heuristic definition. It is an anticipatory definition. It defines the good not directly, but in terms of how the good will be realized. The good will be realized by exercises of the structure of ethical intentionality that operate in converted persons, where the unrestricted notion of value, unrestricted being-in-love, and the normative scale of value preference are followed with fidelity. All other conceptions of the good derived from performances of the structure of ethical intentionality that forms the basis of this elemental heuristic definition. All other conceptions of the good are subject to its criticisms. This forms the basis of the method in ethics that will be explored in chapters 15 and 16.

14 Explanatory Genera and the Objective Scale of Values: A Preliminary Grounding

14.1 Introduction

We are now in a position to take up some fundamental questions regarding the objective normative scale of value preferences. The previous chapters explored the important role played by this scale in the ethics of discernment. Chapter 8 argued that judgments of value can be objective only to the extent that the person making them is morally converted. That is to say, there will be value objectivity only insofar as the person making these judgments operates within a horizon of feelings attuned to and oriented by the unrestricted notion of value, unrestricted being-in-love, and the normative scale of value preference. Chapter 9 drew attention to each person's particular, existential scale of value preference underlying her or his judgments of comparative value. It followed Lonergan, Scheler, and von Hildebrand in claiming that there is also a shared normative scale that "shines through" each of these individual scales. That chapter also noted the ways that Lonergan's account of that objective scale differs from those proposed by others, including Scheler and von Hildebrand.

These differences raise questions about the basis for Lonergan's account of the scale of value preference, and what sort of argument might be advanced in its favour. In this chapter, I offer one approach to answering these questions. I propose that a justification for Lonergan's account of that scale can be provided by drawing upon his notion of "explanatory genera."[1] The first sections of this chapter, therefore, are devoted to elucidating what he meant by "explanatory genera."

Chapter 9 also raised the further question of whether there might be more refined preferential scales *within* one or more of Lonergan's five generic levels of value. We are frequently confronted with questions that ask us to make value judgments and choices among two or more options, all of which fall within a single level of the scale of values. A person could be fully morally converted – could have her or his horizon of feelings fully attuned to the ascending order of vital, social, cultural, personal, and religious values – and still find no guidance whatsoever in making objective judgments of comparative value and responsible choices among the alternatives within a given level of value. I return to this problem in the penultimate section of this chapter, where I propose that Lonergan's notion of "explanatory species" can provide some guidance for thinking about this problem. In the concluding section of this chapter I also consider alternative approaches proposed by other scholars to meet the challenge of providing a grounding of Lonergan's account of the scale of values.

The extended and technical discussions in this chapter may seem to digress rather far from the subject of ethics.[2] But the digression is necessary for three reasons. First, Lonergan's claim that there is an objective scale of value preference is crucial, but it is no longer possible to give a simple argument in its favour; premises that once could have supported Lonergan's claim are no longer widely accepted. Second, his identification of the five distinct levels of that scale (vital, social, cultural, personal, and religious) is also in need of substantial support since there are contending alternatives. Third, the support I am proposing is drawn from Lonergan's discussions of explanatory genera and species. But those discussions are among the most technically demanding sections of *Insight*. There he presents an intricate argument against the "extra-scientific" assumption that modern science implies a reductionism of human consciousness and human freedom to the level of physical processes. So in order to offer support for Lonergan's claims about the objective scale of value preference, it is necessary to present this somewhat lengthy preliminary digression.

Even so, this chapter offers only a preliminary effort at establishing a basis for Lonergan's account of the objective scale of value preference. It proceeds indirectly, drawing intermediary assistance from Lonergan's explanatory genera and his theorem that "the good is identified with the intelligibility intrinsic to being."[3] Because this approach is only indirect, this means that I am deviating from the path I have followed up to now – the method of approaching ethics directly from the structure of ethical intentionality itself. I will therefore return to the question of the basis of the objective scale of values in chapter 16.

14.2   Higher Viewpoints

The next several sections explore how Lonergan's notion of explanatory genera can form the basis for his scale of value preference. In order to do so, it is necessary to first explain just what he meant by explanatory genera. Since that notion in turn rests upon his idea of higher viewpoints, we begin with that topic.

The term "higher viewpoint" is somewhat misleading, as it has nothing to do with visual standpoints. By contrast, "viewpoint" in Lonergan's terminology refers to an interconnected set of ideas that can be used in explaining data or solving problems.

Lonergan devised the idea of higher viewpoints in order to establish the possibility that two systems can be *intelligibly* related to each other as lower and higher *without* one being *logically* deducible from the other. He used the relationships between two number systems – the whole numbers and real numbers – to make his argument. The whole numbers are defined by successive operations of adding one, while the real numbers are defined as what result from the fully generalized operations of adding, subtracting, multiplying, dividing, extracting roots, and taking limits. Because these definitions are so different, there is no way of deducing statements about operations within one set of numbers from statements about the other set. In fact, from a strictly logical point of view, even the terms "number" and "adding" mean something entirely different in the two axiomatic systems.

Nevertheless, we do use exactly those same words in the whole and real number systems. Lonergan's discussion offers a reason why. Historically, whole number arithmetic came first. The activities of doing whole number arithmetic provided "a large, dynamic, virtual image" from which new insights emerged and grasped new possibilities.[4] These new insights led to new and different ways of defining and performing addition, subtraction, and other operations so that their ranges became much wider.

Even though the real numbers cannot be logically deduced from the definitions and axioms of the whole numbers, they are nevertheless intelligibly related because the ideas for the real numbers came from insights into the experiences of doing whole number arithmetic. These insights made it possible to *mirror* every operation in the whole number system with an equivalent operation newly defined in the real number system, but also to do far more – for example, to subtract a larger number from a smaller and generate a perfectly intelligible negative number, to multiply two negative numbers and get a positive number, and to extract the root of a non-perfect square number and get a legitimate irrational number, *etc.*

14.3   Higher Viewpoints, Natural Sciences, and Explanatory Genera

Later in *Insight* Lonergan reveals the importance of his idea of higher viewpoints for thinking about scientific and metaphysical issues. There he uses it to counter a prevailing set of assumptions shared by many scientists and philosophers. The first of these assumptions is that the final culmination of all scientific research will yield one, single, axiomatic scientific system that will explain all data – everything about everything.[5] The second is a metaphysical assumption thought to follow from the first, namely that there really is only one kind of entity, corresponding to the one, single science. The various versions of this metaphysical assumption, known as physicalism or materialism, differ in the details but are united around the core claim that all other qualities and properties (e.g., life, consciousness, value, personhood) are not truly distinct kinds of realities, and are ultimately reducible to combinations of the ultimate kind of reality.

Lonergan argued to the contrary that (a) it is logically possible that at the end of all scientific advance there will remain several, logically autonomous sciences, and (b) it is also likely that these sciences will be arranged in an ascending, sequential order corresponding to the idea of higher viewpoints. He suggested, as examples, that chemistry would be a higher viewpoint relative to physics, biology higher relative to chemistry, and sensitive psychology higher relative to biology.

His arguments for these two propositions derived from his account of the role that "classical heuristic method" plays in the modern natural sciences. According to Lonergan, insights and judgments concerning the true and correct sets of classical laws (or classical correlations) are ultimate objectives of classical heuristic method. These classical correlations form the basic principles or axioms or "laws" of any explanatory science and implicitly define a set of explanatory basic properties (conjugate forms) for that science. For example, in what is called the "Standard Model" of elementary particle theory in physics, a particular mathematical "group" of operations is the set of correlations that implicitly defines and relates a series of properties such as electronic charge, mass, spin, weak isospin, lepton number, and baryon number. Certain combinations of these properties serve to define the different kinds of "particles" (quarks, leptons, and bosons) and their possible interactions among, and transformations into, one another. Or again, the relations expressed in the chemical periodic table implicitly define to a first approximation the chemical properties (e.g. chemical valences) that characterize different chemical elements and their interactions in the vast range of possible chemical reactions.

Once these sets of properties have been defined they can be used to investigate and understand the processes that occur in various populations. If everything that happens in a given population can be fully comprehended by one particular science, then it is part of a larger encompassing population that Lonergan calls the "explanatory genus" that corresponds to that science.[6]

Suppose now, Lonergan continues, that one were to catalogue all the systematic processes and regular schemes of recurrence that can be deduced solely on the basis of the laws, correlations, and explanatory properties (conjugate forms) of, say, the final version of the science of chemistry.[7] Suppose further that there remain sets of chemical reactions that in fact occur regularly, but whose regularity cannot be accounted for solely within the purview of any of the systematic processes possible on the basis of the laws of chemistry alone.

He argues that this would provide the grounds for an inverse insight that the lower viewpoint of chemistry would be "insufficient because it has to regard as merely coincidental what in fact is regular."[8] This inverse insight would, in turn, motivate the search for new higher viewpoint insights that would provide intelligible explanations for the heretofore unaccounted-for regularities. These insights would be expressed in the correlations, definitions, and axioms of a new science (e.g. biology), which is not logically derivable from the laws of chemistry, but nevertheless is intelligibly related to it as a higher viewpoint.[9]

If this were truly a higher viewpoint science, then its insights would have to be able to explain how each organism sets the conditions under which the chemical reactions in its interior take place. The organism would channel chemical reactions into regular and recurrent biological patterns, and the biological insights, laws, and correlations would explain how this is done. The biological laws of this higher science would not override the laws of chemistry. Instead they would explain how each organism's organization regularly resets the concrete conditions under which the laws of chemistry operate so as to sustain properly biological functions such as obtaining nourishment, homeostasis, growth, reproduction, and so on.

When sciences and their corresponding genera are related as higher viewpoints, there is a reciprocal relationship among the levels. On the one hand, the higher biological functioning depends upon the existence of chemical molecules that it organizes into regular patterns of biochemical reactions; on the other hand, the specific chemical reactions that do occur could not happen so regularly without the organism setting the specific conditions required for their continual recurrence.

Such is a very brief sketch of Lonergan's argument. It is no more than an argument for the *possibility* of (a) a series of logically autonomous mature sciences related to one another as higher viewpoints, and (b) a corresponding hierarchy of explanatory genera. His argument does not prove that there is such a series, but it does expose the arbitrariness of metaphysical monisms such as physicalism or materialism. While it is quite legitimate to ask for further arguments to show that Lonergan's ideas are more than just possibilities (i.e., that there actually are autonomous higher viewpoint sciences and that the universe actually does display real hierarchies of explanatory genera), the same can be asked of the metaphysical monisms. What evidence is there in favour of their assumptions? Can they prove that there are no regularities that cannot be fully accounted for by the one, single science, especially since it is yet to be completed?

Although Lonergan himself did not supply the arguments that would be needed to establish his hierarchies as more than possibilities, he did hold that the differentiations of the modern sciences make it is highly likely that there are five distinct, hierarchically-related explanatory generic orders – that is, those corresponding to the successively higher viewpoints of the sciences of physics, chemistry, biology, sensitive psychology, and rational psychology.[10] For the sake of brevity, I will refer to these corresponding genera as the physical, chemical, biological, sensitive, and human. Lonergan did not argue that this is the only possible such order of explanatory higher genera. Nor did he argue that there could not be other explanatory genera intermediate between some of the levels that he proposes. Rather, he simply stated this as the most likely manifestation of a hierarchy of explanatory genera in our natural universe.

This series of genera would be scientifically explanatory, logically autonomous, serially related, hierarchically ranked, and emergent. The series of genera would be scientifically explanatory because their members would be constituted by the properties that are implicitly defined by the explanatory, classical correlations (laws) arrived at through the researches of their respective sciences. They would be logically autonomous because the laws and systems of the lower science cannot account fully for all the observed regularities, therefore requiring a higher science to introduce new higher correlations and properties that cannot be deduced from the lower ones by formal logic alone. They can only be derived by means of the novelties of higher viewpoint insights. The series of genera would be serial and hierarchical because the insights that understand, say, the strictly biological correlations and properties arise out of the experiences of puzzling regularities in chemical occurrences. The higher viewpoint insights would therefore grasp potentialities latent in the processes of the lower chemical genus – namely, their potentialities for functioning in the more comprehensive systems and operations proper to the higher biological level. Finally, the higher genera would be emergent because non-systematic, coincidental convergences of events and processes of the lower chemical genus can (eventually) accidentally set conditions for the emergence of regularly recurring processes that belong properly to the higher biological level.

14.4   A Hierarchical Scale of Natural Values

This account of explanatory higher genera also implies a hierarchy (a scale) of values. Although Lonergan himself does not draw this conclusion explicitly, he does point to this possibility in *Insight*: "Within terminal values themselves there is a hierarchy; for each is an intelligible order, but some of these orders include others, some are conditioning and others conditioned, some conditions are more general and others less."[11] The context for this passage was Lonergan's discussion of hierarchies of intelligible orders in human cooperative organizations, but the basis for the comment is so general that it also applies to hierarchies in the natural universe as well. In other words, the hierarchical relationships among the *intelligibilities* distinctive of and proper to each of the explanatory genera imply their hierarchical *value* ordering.

This value hierarchy within the natural universe follows from the principle argued in the previous chapter that identifies the good with the intelligibility of reality: "For the middle term in the identification of the good with being is intelligibility."[12] There, this principle was used to argue for a distinction among potential, formal, and actual goods because of the distinctness of their kinds of intelligibilities. That same principle can now be applied to the differences among the intelligibilities of explanatory genera, implying a corresponding hierarchy of values. The argument runs as follows: Actual values are the values of actual intelligible occurrences, processes, or things. These occurrences, processes, or things are found within one or another explanatory genus, within some population whose members share the same genus of explanatory intelligible properties. Insofar as these generic intelligibilities are ordered by higher viewpoints, this hierarchy of intelligibilities implies a corresponding hierarchy of the values. So while the actual value of each event, property, process, or thing will be unique, still those values will be related to one another hierarchically in ways that reflect the hierarchy of the genera in which they are members.

This means, therefore, that there should be a scale of value preference in ascending order of physical, chemical, biological, sensate, and human values. This also means, according to our previous discussion, that a morally converted person should have feelings for all of these levels of values, and feel them preferentially in this precise hierarchical order.

Lonergan's remark about the hierarchy of terminal values includes the phrase "some of these orders include others, some are conditioning and others conditioned, some conditions are more general and others less." This phrase offers criteria that can prove helpful in thinking about distinct levels in any value hierarchy. However, the remark can also be misleading. At first reading Lonergan seems to be saying that the lower order is the conditioning order, and the higher order is the one conditioned. After all, this seems to follow from the fact that the processes of the lower genus initially set the conditions out of which the processes of the higher genus emerge. But this would imply that the lower order is more valuable than the higher, which was clearly not Lonergan's intent.

Rather, Lonergan had in mind a different sort of conditioning/conditioned relationship. He was thinking instead of the sort of conditioning that is inaugurated *once* the regularities of the higher genus have emerged. Then *they are setting the conditions under which the lower operations are actually occurring.* For example, biological functioning determines where and how often the chemical operations will occur within an organism, and in what sequences. So the biological systems of an organism will be conditioning the occurrences of the conditioned chemical operations. This way of understanding the conditioning/conditioned relationship is employed in the next section as the basis for providing a justification for the account of the scale of values that Lonergan set forth in *Method in Theology.*

14.5   Higher Explanatory Genera and the Objective Scale of Value Preference

Clearly the catalogue of explanatory genera and values derived from *Insight* (physical, chemical, biological, sensitive, and human) does not line up with the scale value preference that appears in the *Method in Theology* (vital, social, cultural, personal, religious). In order to connect these two orders, I next endeavour to show how the *Insight* criteria for a hierarchy of values can be applied to the value categories found in the *Method in Theology* scale.

I propose that this can be accomplished by regarding the *Method* human scale of values as a further differentiation of what in *Insight* is a single, undifferentiated human level. The same principles that underlie the hierarchical ordering of the natural scale of values also apply to the ordering of the human scale. In other words, the levels of vital, social, cultural, personal, and religious values correspond to levels of intelligibility that are related via higher viewpoints in the same ways that the levels of explanatory genera in nature (physical, chemical, biological, and sensate levels) are related (i.e., conditioned and conditioning).[13]

Lonergan was able to rely upon well-established and clearly distinguished natural sciences in order to make his case in *Insight.* He was able to argue that these sciences can be related to one another by means of higher viewpoints, and therefore that their corresponding genera are logically distinct and hierarchically ordered. However, when it comes to the levels pertaining to the human scale of values, it is not possible to appeal to established human sciences, given the ongoing disagreements about the nature and classifications and even the methods of those sciences. So instead of arguing for distinctions within the human genus from distinct human sciences, I will rely instead on the notion that the operations, properties, processes, and interactions of a higher level organize, incorporate, and set the conditions for the occurrence of those of the lower level.

In the first place, then, the level of social cooperation, processes, and schemes of recurrence have specifically social forms of intelligibility. As such, they set conditions for greater regularity in the realization and maintenance of human biologically intelligible functioning. But intelligible ways of functioning cooperatively are social values, while intelligible biological functionings are vital values. Hence social values make regular what is otherwise non-systematic in the realizing of vital values such as health, strength, grace, vigour, fertility, and flourishing.[14] Chance in obtaining food is reduced even when tribal societies develop skills and organize roles into cooperative hunting and gathering ventures. Chance is further reduced in the achievement of vital values when societies develop agricultural practices and institutions. It is reduced still further when civilizations develop mutually conditioning systems of transportation, distribution, healthcare, and finance, so that the productivity of non-agricultural institutions provides financial and other resources for agricultural schemes, while the agricultural schemes provide conditions for the productivity for urban and other regions. Throughout all these social developments, regularity in realizing vital values is increased, although randomness in provision of vital values is never entirely eliminated.

Still, the values of the social institutions and processes are not reducible to the sum total of the vital values that they provide, as Lonergan observes.[15] The achievement of social schemes of cooperation is a distinct level of value in itself. The intelligible arrangements that make possible productive social cooperation are dramatically distinct from the intelligibilities of vital human bodies.[16] By engaging in the very activities of cooperating in order to stay alive and to sustain vital values, we gradually recognize and accept that cooperating itself is good, *sui generis*. Then, instead of cooperating in order to live, we live in order to cooperate and live together. We live in order to embark upon innovative, cooperative ventures. In addition, since social values can only be actualized in social institutions and arrangements in which the people playing the roles are healthy and strong enough, the social values incorporate vital values into their very actuation. Therefore, social values understood precisely as actual, concrete patterns of human cooperation, insofar as they are intelligible, integrate and set the conditions for the realization of vital values. For this very reason, intelligible social arrangements in this sense are higher values than vital values, just as the higher explanatory genus of the biological realm is of greater value than is the lower chemical realm alone.

Again, culture is a higher viewpoint relative the social. Cultural values (if they *are* values) are concrete, which means they, too, are intelligible ways of functioning cooperatively. They condition the realization of the values of social schemes of cooperation, although this is not always apparent. That they do so comes to light when social institutions and practices need to adapt to changing circumstances. Drastic social changes require sacrifices.[17] The need for sacrifices will tend to undermine the mutual understanding, trust, and the sense of belonging together that is essential to social functioning. It can confuse and make people anxious, and needed reorganizations of social arrangements will be resisted. Why should *we* change? Why shouldn't someone else make the sacrifices?

It is the function of culture to devise intelligible patterns through which to communicate values for the sake of which people will cooperate and stay together, in spite of inevitable tensions and disagreements and need for sacrifice. These cultural values transcend social functions and changes. They give people a sense of identity and "reasons of the heart" that inspire people to work out difficulties, find solutions, and adjust or replace social institutions to meet ever-changing demands. Cultural values provide the meanings of being a people that make some changes acceptable and others repugnant. Even apart from times of crisis, cultural values constantly, though less obviously, set the conditions for the maintenance of social values (i.e., social institutions and cooperative arrangements).

While authentic cultural values give people higher reasons that set the conditions for social operations and transformations, cultural disvalues are mere ideologies. Distorted cultural values give the false appearance of justifiability when distributions of the sacrifices and benefits are in fact unjust. Hence there is a need for other cultural institutions that have the capacity not merely to propagate and enforce, but also to "discover, express, validate, criticize, correct, develop and improve" cultural meanings and values.[18] Such cultural institutions, methods, and procedures make what would otherwise be a random drift or dialectically destructive decline of social changes into a sustained series of social changes that has an intelligible unity and cultural identity endowed with authentic cultural value. The regularities with which these institutions of cultural criticism function will set and reset the conditions under which human beings perform their social functions with the assurance that there is objective cultural value for what they are doing. Hence cultural values and authentic cultural institutions stand in relationship to the social values embedded in social processes and institutions as a higher genus stands to a lower one. For this reason, cultural values stand in the relation of a higher viewpoint to social values in the objective scale of value preferences.

Cultures, however, are limited. Human beings as a whole are more fundamental still, since they are the existential conditions for the discovery, discernment, expression, communication, refinement, acceptance, and practice of the cultural values that are actually put into effect. Cultural values are conditioned by the acts of experiencing, questioning, understanding, factual reflection, feeling that intends value, value reflection, value judgment, and decision of those who discern them and commit to such values. Because cultural values (along with almost all other values) are conditioned by human beings who are the agents that bring about values, personal value is a still higher level of value. As Lonergan puts it, "Personal value is the person in [his or her] self-transcendence, as loving and being loved, as originator of values in [oneself and in one's] milieu, as an inspiration and invitation to others to do likewise."[19]

Personal value is most fully realized in moral conversion, and moral conversion is conversion to all values, not just the values of one's own culture. By authentically committing oneself to follow the call of the unrestricted notion of value, people inevitably commit themselves to values beyond the limits of their own finite cultures. Whether they think of this explicitly or not, morally converted persons become citizens not only of their own polis but of the "cosmopolis" as well.[20] In other words, they become deliberate contributors not just to the realization of particular processes and practices of their own cultural values, but also to the values of the whole of human history. Implicitly, by means of their feelings, or explicitly, by means of their understandings and judgments, they realize that history sets the conditions under which cultures rise and fall. They recognize that their own deeds play an indispensable role in determining the course of history. Implicitly, if not explicitly, morally converted persons have at least a felt-awareness that their actions have consequences for the destiny of humankind. They understand that actions in the present will have profound consequences for the lives of people in the future who they will never know. Personal value is the value of individual persons as agents of the whole historical drama of human destiny that sets the conditions under which cultural, social, and vital values are realized or undermined.

Yet precisely because they are morally converted, such people tend to be realistic about values. They are not merely moral idealists or utopians. They are keenly aware that transformation of cultural values must insure the regular, just, and meaningful provision of the vital values needed to sustain human lives. They take responsibility for acting within their own particular cultural and social contexts, so as to bring about limited transformations in those institutional schemes. They commit to changing their cultural values and processes, at least minimally, in the direction of realizing personal value to a fuller degree. Still, morally converted persons cannot have such influences unless they have learned and embraced what is of deep value in their own cultures. But they take those cultural meanings, set the conditions to transform them, and incorporate them into a higher form of operating. They thereby revitalize the values of their culture, giving them a deeper grounding that appeals to the very value of being human. So far from repudiating their own vital, social, or cultural values, morally converted persons act so as to renew and deepen those values within the context provided by the higher viewpoint of personal value.

They not only realize that their own personal acts and those of others affect the outcome of human history; they also deliberately act in an effort to make human history be the historical fulfillment of personal value. They understand that their actions may draw the best in their own culture beyond itself to a fuller realization of its potential. They also are aware that their actions on behalf of personal value could also be met with hostility from what is inauthentic in their culture. But they accept the risks of doing so, and act on behalf of the higher, personal value. They are somehow aware that their efforts might sadly need to be picked up and built upon by members of some other culture more capable of renewing their own cultural institutions so as to align with the higher value of the person. But they act in hope that their work will contribute to the future, whether in their own culture or that of another.

Clearly personal value so understood has the relationship of higher viewpoint to the level of cultural value. Morally converted persons as just described know that the realization of the fullness of personal value requires the conditions of cultural and social institutions and the provision of vital values. But the full commitment to personal value that comes with moral conversion sets new conditions under which all these values will be evaluated and implemented.

Finally, religious values constitute the elevation of human history into the realization of God's value. Religious conversion is a matter of saying "Yes" to the invitations implicit in the religious experience of unconditional being-in-love. In deliberately choosing to cooperate with the invitations of unconditional love, there is the acknowledgment, at least implicitly, that human personal value is not the final or absolute originating value. Religiously converted persons recognize at least implicitly that there is an originating value even more fundamental than the originating value of the valuing, deciding, and acting human person (i.e., personal value). They recognize that the ultimate "originating value is divine light and love."[21]

Not only does the gift of grace (unrestricted being-in-love) heal and reverse biases, it also makes it possible to incorporate the free operations of human historical citizenship into the operations of realizing the infinite goodness of God's valuation of human history (sometimes misleadingly referred to as "God's plan"). What is most authentic in every religious tradition is its concern with the ultimate destiny, the ultimate value, of humanity. This is a concern that rises above any particular culture and its values. In fact, it also rises above all values that can be humanly conceived and implemented, even by morally converted persons. It is concerned with discerning the total good for the sake of which God has valued the wholeness of the order of human and indeed cosmic history. As Lonergan puts it,

> So it is that every tendency and force, every movement and change, every desire and striving is designed to bring about the order of the universe in the manner in which in fact they contribute to it; and since the order of the universe itself has been shown to be because of the perfection and excellence of the primary being and good, so all that is for the order of the universe is headed ultimately to the perfection and excellence that is its primary source and ground.[22]

Religiously converted persons recognize at least implicitly that God's love sets the conditions under which human history is to be realized. They recognize that God's meanings and values of unconditional love work through those who willingly act to realize God's meanings and value. This involves giving to social roles and cultural commitments a new organization and context with new meanings and symbols – as, for example, when *hesed* or *agape* become the criteria for the daily decisions of individuals about how to realize vital, social, cultural, and personal values. It involves embracing the personal values of freedom and dignity completely and without subjugation, but with the even more profound valuation as of them as gifts of unconditional love.

It takes a very sophisticated degree of discernment to identify and cooperate with the religious values being actualized in finite contexts of vital, social, cultural, and human personal values. How this might happen was suggested in chapter 11, where Jean Paget brought her proposal to the tribal headman and elders. Clearly she was concerned to set new conditions under which the culture of the village would now function. It is likely that she thought of those conditions within the level of personal value – elevating the personal dignity of the women of the village. But she presented her proposal in religious terms, quoting the *Qur'an*: "If ye be kind towards women and fear to do them wrong [Allah] is well acquainted with what ye do." Whether or not Paget herself was motivated by religious values in this context, it is clear that religious values did enter into the deliberations of the elders. They took two days to discern whether or not this particular undertaking would be an instance of the "kindness" that Allah wishes. This was not blind, superstitious acceptance on their part that whatever happens is Allah's will. It was, rather, an instance of discerning of what Allah wishes to be brought about, and a free and informed decision to cooperate with Allah's valuing. It is an instance of Allah conditioning the value of human history by inviting human beings to join with Allah in using their personal value in common, loving pursuit of the unconditional value that Allah offers. This kind of discernment also abounds in Jewish and Christian Scriptures as well.[23]

In this section I have endeavoured to show that the hierarchical ordering of the levels of values that Lonergan identifies in his objective scale can be understood on the analogy of the natural explanatory genera and their corresponding levels of values. The characteristics of higher viewpoint relationships that determine the hierarchical genera in the natural order likewise serve to identify and relate the levels of values in Lonergan's scale of value preferences. Like the values realized in the processes and interactions of the natural populations of explanatory genera, the higher levels in the scale of human values are autonomous, hierarchical, and emergent relative to the lower. The higher values are the goodness of the functioning orders, which set the conditions for the regular realization of the lower values.

Finally, the parallels between the value hierarchy of the natural universe and the human scale also imply a single expanded scale of value preference: physical, chemical, biological, sensate, vital, social, cultural, personal, and religious values in ascending order of preference. This is because the intelligibilities corresponding to each of these successively higher levels of values emerge from and then set conditions for the functioning of the lower orders. However, there is an openness in this expanded scale. The argument presented in this section in no way rules out the possibility of autonomous levels of value intermediate between or embedded within the levels specified here.

14.6   Value Preference within a Given Level, and Explanatory Species

Earlier we considered the problem of how to judge and choose what is better when the choice is not between values at different levels of Lonergan's scale, but among values within a given level of that scale. In this section I would like to propose that Lonergan's notion of "explanatory species" can provide some guidance here as well.

Lonergan developed his notion of explanatory species in tandem with his account of the hierarchy of explanatory genera. As we saw, the notion of a higher explanatory genus arose from problems of accounting for observed regularities that could not be explained by a lower science. Now it is one thing to develop the laws, correlations, principles, and explanatory properties that constitute a higher science; it is another thing to find the appropriate proper combinations of those properties and to apply them in such a way as to correctly explain the regularities that are actually observed in concrete circumstances. The notion of an explanatory species has to do with those regularities and the corresponding application of the combinations of properties that make them intelligible.

First, as with explanatory genus, an explanatory species is an actual, concrete population stretching across generations with characteristic interactions that recur with some regularity within a limited environmental range. In biological populations, we might tend to focus on the distinctive regularities of the physiological functions internal to the individual members of a given species. Yet just as important are the characteristic regularities in the interactions among individual organisms within the species, as well as with other entities in the environment that are not members of the species (both living and non-living). Second, different biological species are therefore defined by the distinctive, intelligible combinations of biological properties that explain both the internal and external regularities found in the characteristic behaviours of its members. Third, the regularities characteristic of a species depend upon the fulfillment of appropriate biological conditions.

Lonergan summarizes these three points, defining a biological explanatory species as "an intelligible solution to a problem of living in a given environment, where the living is a higher systematization of a controlled aggregation of aggregates of aggregates of aggregates, and the environment tends to be constituted more and more by other living things."[24]

The key to this general definition of explanatory species is that there are many possible ways to combine together the generic properties defined in each of the autonomous, higher viewpoint sciences. Each of these distinctive ways of combining the explanatory properties will be a different possible way of organizing and integrating together the regularly recurring operations of the lower genus (aggregates of aggregates). The environmental conditions will determine whether or not any particular possible combination will function successfully. The members of an explanatory species, therefore, embody a distinctive way of combining certain explanatory properties of the higher genus that successfully regularizes lower genus events and functions within a given environment. We may also add that explanatory species almost always evolve out of a prior species in a manner that Lonergan characterizes as emergent probability.

This notion of explanatory species provides a model for thinking about species of values. First, because any actual explanatory biological species is a historical population of individuals that has its unique, intelligible forms of interacting and reproducing, it is therefore also the actualization of a distinctive biological value. This follows from the theorem that identifies the good with the real on the basis of its actual intelligibility. Because each explanatory species is the actual realization of a distinctive kind of intelligibility, it is therefore also a distinctive kind of actual value.

Second, what is true of the value of each and every actual biological species is also true of every physical, chemical, and sensate species as well. The value of each such species is tied to its special, intelligible way of realizing higher-level functions by distinctive integrations of operations that pertain to the lower-level genus. These values, therefore, are tied to how they meet the challenges of regularly operating physically, chemically, or sensitively under the prevailing conditions in ways that realize the properties proper to the higher genus.

What is true of the natural values of explanatory species in the natural world is also true of species-values within each level of Lonergan's scale of values. This can be illustrated again by the story of the well in Kuala Telang. Once the well was constructed, there was a new set of environmental conditions. These new conditions set a new "problem of living," not just biologically but humanly. The "intelligible solution to a problem of living" was the pattern of cooperation for drawing and distributing water (and for washing clothes) that emerged around it. This pattern of cooperation set conditions for the exercises of bodily actions (along with the vital values of these actions) of the women who worked the well. A new species of social value emerged out of these changed conditions in the form of the community of people who adopted and participated in this new pattern of cooperation. But the new pattern also actualized new vital values (bodily hydration), as well as new cultural, personal, and religious values. These generic values were realized in ways very specific to the location – including the collection of talents and habituations of the villagers. This was a very special, possibly unique pattern of human interaction realizing these generic values in this particular population. It was, therefore, a *species* of social value.

What made this species of cooperation the right choice, within the range of different possible ways of realizing vital and social values, was its appropriateness to the circumstances. Just as a biological species is the solution to the problem of living in a specific environment, so also the right, the best way of specifically realizing a genus of values will be the one that meets the problems posed by the existing conditions. And people figure out what that value-species solution will be by asking and answering all the further questions that arise from that situation and that are guided by feelings for the generic-level in the scale of values. By following the lead of questions pertinent to that generic level of value as felt, they eventually arrive at virtually unconditioned value judgments, choices, and actions that realize a new species-value that realizes the generic value in the concrete situation.

Finally, in addition to being explanatory, integrative of lower generic operations, suited to environmental conditions, and emergent, there is a fifth property of species at the biological, sensate, and human levels: virtually all members of the species in these genera also develop. While Lonergan's discussion of development is complex, we may highlight certain features salient for the discussion of species of values within levels of the scale of value preference. The development of biological and higher species sheds light on the way that species of virtues also develop. A species-solution to issues of value often starts out vaguely, and becomes more refined as a community's thoughts and feelings develop in response to ever changing situations. Moral development manifests itself in refined, compassionate growth towards consistently hitting what Aristotle called the virtuous median of virtue. By way of contrast, lack of moral development manifests itself in rigid adherence to laws and to their applications in ways that do not take into account what is possible in concrete circumstances. On the other hand, the morally developed "great souled person" (*megalopsuchês*) is able to realize social or cultural values that are appropriate to circumstances with remarkable creativity and without the rigidity of legalism.

Lonergan's notion of explanatory species, therefore, offers a framework for thinking about the question of how to judge and decide among the various alternative courses of action that are possible within a given value level.

14.7   Alternate Approaches

Several scholars of Lonergan's thought have also wrestled with the question of the foundations of his version of the objective scale of value preference. In this section I consider one of the most prominent alternate proposals, that of Robert Doran,[25] as well as that from an anonymous source.

In addressing the question of grounding for Lonergan's account of the scale of value preference, Doran comments:

> It has always seemed obvious to me that the scale is based on the increasing degrees of self-transcendence to which one is carried or to which a community is carried in response to values at different levels. And it has also seemed right to assume that the levels of value are isomorphic with the levels of consciousness, so that vital values correspond to experience, social values to understanding, cultural values to reflection and judgment, personal values to deliberation and decision, and religious values to God's gift of love.[26]

Doran acknowledges that in fact all five levels of consciousness operate in the realization of any of the levels of values, and he rightly rules out any overly simplistic way of arguing for this isomorphism. Instead, he proposes something analogous to the relationships among levels of consciousness and the functional specialties in *Method in Theology*. That is to say, although the activities of all levels of consciousness are operative in each and every functional specialty, nevertheless each function specializes on a result proper to one or another level.[27] For example, Interpretation uses all levels of conscious operations in order to produce results proper to the level of intelligence. By analogy, Doran argues, all levels of consciousness would be involved in producing values most significantly characterized by acts and contents on one single level – for example, that understanding, judgments of fact and value, decisions, and actions are all involved in realizing vital values, even though these are values at the first level of consciousness (experiencing).

Doran may well have hit upon the proper explanation for Lonergan's scale. His approach might even be what Lonergan had in mind. Still, there are some difficulties that this approach would have to address. First and perhaps foremost, Doran's isomorphism relies upon five clearly distinguished levels of consciousness. Although I agree that there are five levels of consciousness, there is no evidence that Lonergan himself thought so at the time he was writing *Method in Theology*. To the best of my knowledge, the first time that Lonergan mentioned a fifth level was in fall 1972, after *Method in Theology* had been published.[28] Now, it is possible that Lonergan developed his formulation of the scale based on differences in experiences of his own levels of consciousness, even though he had not yet articulated this for himself with complete clarity. However, I think that he would have needed to have at least some kind of vaguely formulated understanding of the five levels of consciousness in order to think out five value levels on this basis.

A second difficulty arises with respect to the specific correspondences between the level of consciousness and the proposed correspondence with a level of values in at least two cases, if not more. Initially the correspondence between the level of experiencing and vital values seems to make sense, but consider for a moment some examples of vital values: health, strength, vitality, robustness, fertility, flourishing (along with their opposites, the disvalues of disease, weakness, lethargy, etc.). If we restrict ourselves to the data of sense and compare the acts and contents of sense experiencing with these vital values, it is difficult to discern the correspondences. Seeing colour and shape, hearing pitch and timbre, feeling the rough, smooth, painful, pleasant, hot, cold, tasting sweet, sour, salty, etc. – these are markedly different from the values revealed in feeling healthy, strong, energetic, etc. Moreover, Lonergan's two sources, Scheler and von Hildebrand (as well as Lonergan himself) *all* go to considerable lengths to emphasize the distinction between feelings-states of sensation (what I have called somatic feelings) and the intentional feelings that apprehend vital values. These considerations make it difficult to affirm without reservation a one-to-one correspondence between the conscious level of sense-experiencing, on the one hand, and the level of vital values in the scale of value preference, on the other.

The correspondence between the level of intelligent consciousness and the level of social values poses no serious difficulty, since the good of order is constituted by the complex intelligibilities that connect one person's needs with other people's actions.[29] However, Doran's way of making the connection between levels of consciousness and levels of values cannot be easily extrapolated to the next level – that of the correspondence between rational consciousness and cultural values. On the one hand, the efforts of third level conscious reflection are directed towards assembling conditions, grasping the virtually unconditioned, and making judgments of *fact*. On the other hand, while it is true that cultural values (such as the values of science and scholarship) include the practices and institutions that criticize claims about factual truths, cultural values extend beyond concern with the value of factual truths. Cultural institutions communicate, cultivate, and refine the values that make human lives, institutions, and goods of order meaningful and worth choosing. Cultures tell stories and sing songs about heroes and heroines and the values they incarnate. Cultures build monuments to great achievements of people to be emulated and to be embodied in individual deeds and in social institutions. Cultures develop universities and other institutions dedicated to criticizing claims regarding values, in addition to critiquing claims regarding facts. Indeed cultures cultivate commitments to the *value of* factual truth. It is not clear, therefore, that this broad field of cultural values can be embraced within a correspondence with the third level of consciousness.[30] They seem more appropriate to the fourth level of consciousness.

These considerations led me to propose the alternate way of supporting Lonergan's formulation of the scale of value preference that I presented earlier in this chapter. In fact, Doran himself proposed a second approach to founding the scale of values that is very close to my own. He wrote: "From below, more basic levels [of value] are required for the emergence of higher levels … whereas from above, these proportionate developments are the condition of possibility of the appropriate schemes of recurrent events at the more basic levels."[31]

Here Doran makes a very subtle but very important distinction. Others might think of conditioning in only one direction, from below: we must eat in order to work or paint or to pray. While conditioning from below certainly happens, Doran recognizes that the reverse is also true, the reciprocal form of conditioning from above. When people lose all sense of higher purpose, they abandon their plows in the fields.

Doran clearly recognizes this conditioning of the lower by the higher and illustrates his keen observation with examples from all four of the interfaces between the five levels of values. He says that while it is true that the health and strength (vital values) of a multiplicity of people are needed to implement new social organizations, once technological, economic, and political institutions are functioning actually and recurrently, they become the indispensable conditions for the effective and regular continuation of the values of health and strength of members of the society. Likewise, he notes that "the social order is a direct function of the cultural values that inform the everyday life of the community," so that the maintenance of the social order becomes crucially dependent upon continuation of cultural institutions and values. He also offers arguments and illustrations that this reciprocal relationship of the conditioning of the lower from above applies also to the relationships between cultural values and personal integrity and virtues, and between personal integrity and religious values.[32]

In Doran's second approach, what makes one level of value higher than another is its capacity, once it emerges, to operate "from above" and to set the conditions for the sustained and continued recurrence of a whole series of values at the lower levels. This does not negate the fact that the values at lower levels do provide the indispensable "materials" or conditions for the emergence of higher-level values. But it does point towards an explanatory criterion for distinguishing between lower and higher levels of values. In this chapter I have endeavoured to elaborate criteria of Doran's second approach, in hopes of providing additional support and specificity.

Finally, an anonymous reviewer of the manuscript of this book proposed a grounding that I think is quite promising and substantially correct, but one that is not without some difficulties. Still, this proposal might turn out to be the most solid approach to this question.

The reviewer wrote:

> Byrne's argument – correct as far as it goes – does not bring into clear focus the invariant analogy underlying the formulation of the scale … Proximately, it is an analogy of metaphysical structure.
>
> potency: form: act: agent:: vital: social: cultural: personal values
>
> Lonergan sets up this analogy quite clearly in his 1964/5 treatise *De redemptione* …

This argument may or may not be correct – Byrne has earlier raised a good question about whether vital values may be identified with particular goods in contradistinction to goods of order – but it seems to me undoubtedly to be the original genesis of Lonergan's scheme. Moreover, it relates (much more directly than does Byrne's argument) the preference-scale of values to the distinctions between particular goods, goods of order, and terminal values.[33]

In Article 4 ("The Comparison of Goods") of the soon-to-be-published *De Redemptione*,[34] Lonergan presents one his most extensive discussion of the three levels of the invariant structure of the human good. While he does not explicitly state the extended analogy proposed by the reviewer (i.e., potency: form: act: agent:: vital: social: cultural: personal values), it is true that the context of Lonergan's treatment there suggests strong connections among the three levels of the structure of the human good and the five levels of the scale of value preference – stronger than anywhere else that I am aware of.[35]

First, as the reviewer notes, *De Redemptione* does explicitly invoke the isomorphism between the three metaphysical elements and the three levels of the human good as discussed earlier, although here he proceeds from theological rather than philosophical grounds. Lonergan writes:

> In the light of this it becomes immediately clear that created good is composed of three elements, as it were. There is the potential element that is found in possibilities taken <u>singly</u>; second, the formal element that is discernible in a wise <u>ordering</u>; third, the actual element, or value, which consists in its commensurability to an end and hence its worthiness to be chosen.
>
> But whatever is found in any created good must necessarily be present in human goods. Clearly, particular goods belong to the potential element, the good of order to the formal element, and cultural good, by which we are led to true wisdom, to the actual element, value.[36]

Second, *De Redemptione* contains the most extensive discussion of culture by Lonergan of which I am aware. That discussion enriches his notion of culture and makes it clear that at least at that time, Lonergan was explicitly equating "cultural value" with what later he called "terminal value" in the structure of the human good. He writes, for example:

> Accordingly, since there are many possible orders ... there is a third element in the human good, which has to do with values, which aims at rendering judgment wise and will good, and which is called the cultural good.

> There is a hierarchy among these three. The good of order is ...
> superior to particular goods ... Cultural good is ... far superior to
> the good of order ...[37]

Lonergan later elaborates his reasons for the ascending hierarchy of particular goods, good of order, and cultural good. Particular goods, he observes, are those goods that meet "the requirements of living" – that is, vital goods. A good of order that would be free from disorders or injustices would provide "a constant series of particular goods." On the other hand, a cultural good, insofar as it is free of distortions and *ressentiments*, guides "wise progress toward better and better orders" and resists the forces that would lead to spirals of decline and deterioration. Cultural goods, according to *De Redemptione*, are constituted and underpinned by mutually friendly and loving interpersonal relations.

Third, *De Redemptione* also refers to the second level as that of the "social order" as well as the "good of order." This lends support to the reviewer's identification of "social value" in the scale of value preference with the "end" (i.e., good of order) of the second level in the structure of the human good. From this it would seem to follow that the "end" of the first level of the structure of the human good (i.e., particular goods) would be equated with vital values.

Fourth, Lonergan situates his discussion of the structure of the human good in *De Remeptione* within a much broader and richer context that also provides strong support for the reviewer's suggestion of integrating it with personal value. Immediately following the paragraph where he identifies the third level of the human good with culture, Lonergan writes that

> [we] are ourselves <u>instances of good originating goods</u>. By our imagination we represent to ourselves particular material goods; by inquiry, insight, and conception we set them in [a good of] order; by reflection, judgment, and will we make decisions regarding those things that we have imagined and put in order. Therefore, as originated goods are imagined, ordered, and chosen, so the originating good, as that which originates, is we ourselves, and, as that by which we originate, is the action of representing, ordering, and choosing.[38]

In other words, Lonergan explicitly situates the originating values that human persons are, as the conditioning circumstances for the realization of the first three levels of the structure of the human good. That is to say, human personal values are the higher values that originate cultural, social, and vital values.

Finally, although the reviewer did not extend the proposed analogy underlying the scale of value preference to its fifth level of religious value, that connection is made evident by the general context as well as the particulars of *De Redemptione.* The overall goal of the text is to provide a "deeper and more fruitful," albeit an imperfect, analogical interpretation of the Christian doctrine of redemption. Lonergan regards that doctrine as the affirmation of "the mystery of God's will, 'to gather up all things in Christ, things in heaven and on earth' (Ephesians 1:9–10)." In order to accomplish this objective, Lonergan says, he needs to first consider "how earthly realities are to be brought together … how the human good especially is put in order" through human collaboration.[39] Within this theological context, Lonergan emphasizes the fact that human originating value is a participation in divine goodness,[40] for divine originating value is not only the condition that makes possible finite human originating value; human originating value is also the means by which divine goodness is realized. If, then, human originating value is higher in the scale of value preference than cultural, social, and vital values because it is their condition, so also religious value (the goodness of God) is the highest in the scale of values because it is the originating condition of all other values. Thus the analogue proposed by the reviewer would become:

potency: form: act: human agent: divine agent::
vital: social: cultural: personal: religious values

The reviewer also drew attention to Lonergan's extended discussion of the social order in *De Redemptione,* where Lonergan treats the levels of domesticity, technology, economy, and politics within the second level of the human good. These are themselves arranged hierarchically, with higher (e.g., political) conditioning lower (e.g., economic) levels.[41] The reviewer wrote:

> "Social values" denote whatever goods of order, whether political, social, technological, etc., may be chosen for the sake of some values and invested with meanings … Thus technological, political, economic arrangements are "species" within the "genus" of the good of order that is chosen for the sake of a higher genus of cultural values.

This way of grounding the five levels of the invariant scale of value preference shares the overall approach that I proposed above, as well as Doran's second approach: a level of value is higher insofar as it is the level that *de facto* makes possible the continued realization of values on the lower level. However, the grounding that derives from *De Redemptione* has the advantages of both being strongly supported by Lonergan's own writings, and of adding greater and explicit specificity as to how and why the higher level grounds the lower.

There is much that is very attractive in the reviewer's proposal for the grounding of the scale of values, beginning with the way in which it situates domestic, technological, economic, and political values within a scale of preference. In addition, the proposal would tend to rule out any intermediary levels within Lonergan's five-level scale of value, and I admit that this appeals to me a great deal. In addition, it integrates the three levels of the invariant structure of the human good into the otherwise separate five levels of the scale of value preference, and this also seems correct.

However, there are a couple of difficulties with the proposal. The first was actually mentioned by the reviewer – the difficulty of identifying vital values with particular goods that I raised earlier in this section. Second, there seems to be an inconsistency in Lonergan's identification of "terminal values." While *De Redemptione* makes the explicit identification with cultural values, elsewhere he notes that civilizations can be have vital, social, or cultural values as their terminal values.[42]

These difficulties may not be insurmountable, nor may be the difficulties with Doran's suggestion of rooting the scale of value preference in the five levels of human consciousness. But for the moment I do not see a clear resolution of the difficulties. It is for this reason that I return to this question once again in chapter 16.

PART FIVE

Method in Ethics

15 Method in Ethics I: Preliminaries

Lead Kindly Light … I do not ask to see the distant scene, one step enough for me.
                                                              – John Henry Newman

A person may be apprehending symbolically a very high morality even though he seems to be apprehending nothing but the particular good.

                                                              – Bernard Lonergan, *Topics*

15.1 Ethical Intentionality as Methodical

The word "method" comes from Greek roots literally meaning the "way after" (*meta hodos*) or the "pursuit," especially the pursuit of knowledge. In colloquial speech, a method is simply a way of doing something to achieve a good result. In this sense, then, every time a human being exercises her or his structure of ethical intentionality in the attempt to work out, decide upon, and carry out a valuable course of action, he or she is being methodical – engaging in a way of doing something to achieve a good result.

When we hear the phrase "being methodical," what usually comes to mind is meticulous adherence to rules as the right way of doing things. Lonergan, however, had a different understanding of method. He defined a method as "a normative pattern of recurrent and related operations yielding cumulative and progressive results."[1] Further, he pointed out that the exercise of the fundamental structure of intentionality that guides and orients human conscious activity across the four levels of consciousness fits this definition of method. In fact, he judged this structure to be so fundamental that he called it the "transcendental method," in the sense that it is so ubiquitous that it transcends disciplinary and even cultural boundaries. We could say, then, that every exercise of ethical intentionality is a methodical practice in Lonergan's sense. For Lonergan, then, being methodical consists in carefully discerning and faithfully following the norms embedded and already stirring in the structures of cognition and ethical intentionality. In other words, being methodical is not primarily a matter of following rules. Rather, being methodical is following the immanent, self-transcending, dynamic norms that operate in the structures of our consciousnesses. Indeed, the exercise of operations in accord with these structures is the origin of all rules and of all acceptances of rules. In this sense, again, every exercise of ethical intentionality is methodical.

But this, of course, does not go far enough. We might just as well say that every human being uses the scientific method, because every human being has experiences, asks questions, gets insights, forms hypotheses, and engages in self-correcting processes in order to check out those hypotheses – which is what scientists do. This seems absurd, however, because by "scientific methods" we mean something much more specialized than such generic performance of these activities. No one without highly specialized scientific training could legitimately be said to be using a scientific method. Specialized methods therefore involve more than simply the exercise of the normative structure of human consciousness. They involve some sort of refinement of that exercise which comes from training and practice.

Hence, for a variety of reasons, method in a less generic sense involves more than the plain exercise of the native endowment of our own structure of ethical intentionality. What is needed in addition is the explicit understanding, formulation, and deliberate commitment to a more differentiated and refined practice of that structure.

In his recent book, *Doing Better: The Next Revolution in Ethics,* Tad Dunne has argued that what Lonergan called the "eight functional specialties" of theological method are already operative in ordinary exercises of human ethical intentionality.[2] In this chapter I will build upon his claim, focusing on how the more explicit appropriation of those eight functional specialties can become a most important paradigm for a more refined method in ethics. In doing so, I endeavour to take Dunne's analysis a step further. I will propose that in our ordinary exercises of ethical intentionality we always respond to ethical teachings we have received from one or another source or tradition. I will further argue that fidelity to the structure of our ethical intentionality means that we can and should engage with those sources and traditions critically. I will suggest further that Lonergan's methodical, integrated functional specialties provide the heuristic guidance needed for that critical engagement. This further refinement of our practice of ethical intentionality into the integrated eight functional specialties is what I will mean by "method in ethics," and it is intimately connected with what I have called the ethics of discernment.

While the remainder of this chapter is an explication and adaptation of Lonergan's functional specialties to the field of ethics, it cannot substitute for a careful study of the functional specialties as explained in *Method in Theology* itself. It is my hope, therefore, that the following pages lead readers to take up that text in order to more deeply appreciate the benefits of approaching ethical issues in this methodical way.

15.2   The Method of Ethics in *Insight*

Method in Theology does not make any claims to provide a model for method in ethics, but *Insight* does. In the "Preface," Lonergan wrote the following:

> As metaphysics is derived from the known structure of one's knowing, so an ethics results from knowledge of the compound structure of one's knowing and doing; and as the metaphysics, so too the ethics prolongs the initial self-criticism into an explanation of the origin of all ethical positions and into a criterion for passing judgment on each of them.[3]

Clearly a method so conceived could play the role of critically engaging sources of ethical thought and action that have been passed along to us. However, Lonergan did not actually follow the path to that method in the manner he announced in the preface. Had he done so, he would have first articulated this compound structure of structure of knowing and doing, next invited the reader to appropriate that structure for herself or himself, and only then worked out the method for evaluating all ethical positions. This was the path he did follow in working out a method for metaphysics on the basis of self-affirmation of cognitional structure, but he neglected to follow through on this path towards a method in ethics.

Instead, Lonergan's first step in his *Insight* chapter on ethics was to "work out such notions as the good, will, value, obligation."[4] Only after this did he then turn to something like an account of the structure of ethical intentionality.[5] However, he did so under the heading, "The Notion of Freedom," rather than under a heading such as "The Compound Structure of Knowing and Doing." In other words, he used the account of the compound structure of knowing and doing as the basis for his philosophical account of freedom, not as the basis of an integral heuristic structure for ethics.

Now we may well ask, "How can such ethical notions as the good, value, and obligation be 'worked out' methodically, prior to articulating and appropriating that compound structure?" I have argued in chapter 13 and elsewhere that Lonergan's analysis of the notion of the good in *Insight* suffers from a number of difficulties, but that those could have been overcome if Lonergan had invoked the unrestricted notion of value.[6] He admitted later on that he had not recognized this notion of value at the time of the writing of *Insight*, and this unquestionably affected his approach to ethics in *Insight*. In the earlier chapters of this book I have explained why I think that self-appropriation of the unrestricted notion of value would have affected his answers to the three basic ethical questions, including an account of the good. Before moving on to the question of how a full and explicit appropriation of the unrestricted notion of value and the structure of ethical intentionality affects the approach to a method in ethics, however, I offer a brief account of my understanding of what Lonergan was attempting in *Insight*.

The key notion in the *Insight* approach to ethics is what Lonergan termed the "exigence for self-consistency in knowing and doing."[7] An exigence is a demand or a requirement or a necessity. This exigence for self-consistency functions as the intrinsic norm for ethics in *Insight*. It plays the role in ethics that the detached and disinterested desire to know (i.e., the notion of being) plays in his metaphysics. But as I argued in chapter 13, a problem arises if we ask, "With just what *kind* of knowing is our doing supposed to be consistent?" It would seem that the consistency should be with our value-knowing, and especially with our knowing the moral value of what we ought to do. Unfortunately, Lonergan's discussion of that kind of knowing comes after, not before, his deployment of this notion of the exigence for consistency. The only kind of knowing that had been discussed up to that point was factual knowing – commonsense/descriptive knowing, interpersonal/dramatic knowing, scientific/explanatory knowing, knowing the reality of "things," and philosophical self-knowledge of the knower, of objectivity, and of being. No value knowing had been discussed prior to Lonergan's mention of the consistency of knowing and doing, at least not explicitly.

One possible explanation for Lonergan's approach in *Insight* is suggested by a recent paper by the late William Murnion.[8] There Murnion argues that for Aquinas, any philosophy (including ethics) must rest upon an analysis of being. This implies that, for Aquinas, "we can do good when will is functioning, in *our quest to identify* our minds *with being*" and "the match between appetite and *being as good* occurs in *reality*, insofar as appetite is gratified by the *actual* goodness of whatever it desires."[9] In other words, for Aquinas, the most fundamental quest for human beings is to "identify with being." We "identify" with being cognitionally when we become one with some aspect of being in a virtually unconditioned judgment of what is.[10] We "identify" with being, not merely cognitionally, but really, existentially ("real self-transcendence") when we choose and love "actual goodness." Murnion goes on to say that from Aquinas' perspective,

> The relation of the mind to *being as good* occurs in reality insofar as the mind [by loving] appropriates the values in themselves of the beings it actually knows ... Knowledge of the truth always supplies *a perception* of the goodness of being, even if the goodness of more particular beings is at times more immediate and compelling that that of goodness itself.[11]

This implies that without a sufficiently comprehensive heuristic notion of being, one's notion of the good will be restricted merely to the limited realm of the beings that one actually knows. Or in an even more severe impoverishment, apart from a sufficiently open notion of being, the notion of the good will contract to what one merely perceives immediately and feels intensely, lacking genuine knowledge of such things.

It would seem, therefore, that awareness of (or conversion towards) the wholeness of being is a precondition for conversion and awareness of the wholeness of the good, and that this in turn is the basis for genuine ethical knowledge and action. Murnion argues further that Lonergan, following Aquinas, developed an ethics of "self-responsibility of free will" that respects the fullness of being far better than any of the other major contending ethical traditions.

Now if Lonergan was indeed implicitly adopting something like Aquinas' position as Murnion described it, then it is possible Lonergan thought that his metaphysics would suffice as the basis for his ethics – for this would establish the "parallel and interpenetration of metaphysics and ethics."[12] There is some evidence this. In *Topics in Education* Lonergan wrote, "We will *start* from the well-known tag *ens et bonum convertuntur*, being and the good are convertible."[13] In *De redemptione* he treats the convertibility of being and the good as a kind of axiom, from which his whole account of good, evil, and redemption proceeds.[14] Both works were written only a couple of years after the completion of *Insight*. The identification of being and the good also functions as the foundational assumption, on the basis of which the *Insight* chapter on ethics unfolds.[15]

Still, at that point in Lonergan's career, the convertibility of being and the good functioned simply as an assumption for which no grounds are offered. If the "tag" derives ultimately from Aquinas's approach, Lonergan would have had to explain how Aquinas's way of making the theory of being foundational to ethics could be transposed into his own method. And while Lonergan certainly was a careful reader of Aquinas, there is no textual evidence that this portion of Aquinas's thought influenced Lonergan directly on this matter. Still, this influence is a possible explanation for the puzzling way that Lonergan proceeded in chapter 18 of *Insight*.

There is, however, textual evidence for a somewhat related way of making sense out of Lonergan's approach in *Insight*. There is at least one point in Lonergan's earlier chapters where the consistency between factual knowing and human performance is discussed at some length. This, I believe, provides a more direct clue as to how Lonergan conceived of ethics in *Insight*.

After a rich and prolonged discussion of the complexities of human development, Lonergan writes, "Genuineness is the admission of that tension into consciousness, and so it is the necessary condition of the harmonious co-operation of the conscious and unconscious components of development."[16] By "that tension" Lonergan means the tension of finality of the universe, the "upwardly but indeterminately directed dynamism of all proportionate being."[17] To be authentically human, therefore, is to ask and find intelligent and reasonable answers about how one's own knowing is related to one's own ongoing but preconscious organic development, and how both are situated within the ongoing, emerging universe of generalized emergent probability. Genuineness, in this sense,

> reveals to a man a universe of being in which he is but an item, and
> a universal order in which his desires and fears, his delight and
> anguish are but infinitesimal components in the history of mankind.
> It invites man to become intelligent and reasonable not only in
> his knowing but also in his living, to guide his actions by referring
> them, not as an animal to a habitat, but as an intelligent being to the
> intelligible context of some universal order that is or is to be … It is
> confronted with a universe of being in which it finds itself, not the
> center of reference, but an object coordinated with other objects
> and, with them, subordinated to some destiny to be discovered or
> invented, approved or disdained, accepted or repudiated.[18]

There are of course several terms in this passage that reference matters of value and not merely matters of fact – "approved or disdained, accepted or repudiated," for example. At that point in *Insight* there is no ground for addressing how such judgments of value and decisions might be made on an objective basis. Lonergan may well have been aware of this difficulty, but if he was, he did not advert to it. To all appearances, the profound challenge of genuineness that Lonergan identifies is simply a matter of consistency between one realm within proportionate being – the actualities of human development and action – and the dynamic emergent probability of proportionate being as a whole. This call for consistency is said to arise solely from the factual knowledge based largely upon self-affirmation of one's cognitional structure and its implications.

The principal implication is that to be genuinely human is to live in a way that cooperates with and promotes the intelligible movement of generalized emergent probability, which characterizes the finality of the universe. Kenneth Melchin has made this point amply in his *History, Ethics and Emergent Probability*.[19] Other things in the universe contribute to this intelligible, emerging order involuntarily. They do so automatically on the basis of their naturally given central and conjugate forms, which determine how they will function under a variety of conditions. However, human contributions do not occur automatically. The contents (i.e., conjugate forms) of properly human courses of action can only come from human acts of understanding, from insights, which precede decisions and actions. Insofar as those insights are virtually unconditioned, they ground courses of action that constitute intelligent cooperation within pre-existing schemes of recurrence, or the intelligent origination of new schemes, or new stages in developments that are more intelligently differentiated than prior stages. Moreover, when we put intelligent plans into action, we are not choosing them in isolation. Our actions build upon the circumstances that gave rise to the experiences to which our insights and choices respond. We are thereby cooperating with the intelligible, emergent dynamism of proportionate being itself, whether we think of this explicitly or not. This is the central point made in chapter 13: "Every consistent choice, at least implicitly, is a choice of universal order," and "the realization of universal order is a true value" because "self-consciousness cannot consistently choose the conditioned and reject the condition."[20] The penultimate condition for the realization of any of our courses of action is the finality of the universe, which brought about the situation out of which our action emerges and to which it responds.

Of course, people can and do *inconsistently* and selfishly choose the conditioned and reject the condition – that is to say, they choose a course of action that serves a truncated view of themselves and their world, and which therefore violates the larger intelligible dynamic trajectory of the universe and human history. Such, it would seem, is the exact opposite of genuineness – knowing who one is in the universe and history, and doing what is consistent with one's knowing of the universe of proportionate being.

This, it seems, is the kind of knowing relevant to the method of ethics in *Insight*. This interpretation is borne out in the section actually entitled "The Method of Ethics." There Lonergan proclaims that the "parallel and interpenetration of metaphysics and ethics" leads to a threefold conclusion:

> The obligatory structure of our rational self-consciousness (1) finds its materials and its basis in the products of universal finality, (2) is itself finality on the level of intelligent and rational consciousness, and (3) is finality confronted with the alternative of choosing either development and progress or decline and extinction.[21]

Hence it would seem that the principle for a method of ethics as Lonergan actually presents it in *Insight* can be formulated as follows: "Act in such a way as to be consistent with the intelligible finality of the universe of proportionate being." Expressed in this way, it bears strong resonances to one of Kant's formulations of the categorical imperative: "Act as if your maxim were to become through your will a universal law of nature."[22] In fact, in the *Insight* chapter on ethics there are strong indications that Lonergan was replying to Kant. For example, at the beginning of the chapter he writes, "The present chapter, then, sets forth not precepts but the general form of precepts."[23] Kant, of course, was likewise concerned not to set forth a code of maxims, but rather "the formula of a [maxim, which] is called an imperative."[24] We might say that for Lonergan in *Insight* the categorical imperative becomes one of consistency between knowing and doing – "Act always in such a way as to promote the intelligible emergence of proportionate being, and to reverse irrational decline."[25]

In the same chapter Lonergan addresses another of Kant's most fundamental issues – the affirmation of human freedom.[26] Melchin has argued that this is the ultimate objective of Lonergan's chapter on ethics.[27] Indeed the question implied in the title to the chapter, "The Possibility of Ethics," is a version of Kant's own question – whether a categorical imperative is possible depends on the answer to whether human beings are free.[28]

Because Lonergan departed at the outset from Kant's account of speculative or pure reason, his accounts of freedom and the form of ethical precepts also differ from those of Kant.[29] Where nature was for Kant a deterministic system governed by something like the Newtonian laws of nature, for Lonergan the universe has the "upwardly but indeterminately" dynamic intelligibility of generalized emergent probability. The questions of freedom, then, and of intelligent and rationally self-conscious action in such a universe yield answers that are significantly different from those of Kant. On the one hand, in place of a "concept of duty" formulated as a universal and necessary categorical imperative, Lonergan's norm is that of consistency between knowing and doing, which also entails fidelity to questions that arise for understanding and critical reflection. Since questions for understanding and critical reflection are often about the concrete rather than the universal, Lonergan's ethics is not tied to universalizability. On the other hand, with regard to freedom, Kant conceded deterministic control to the laws of nature in the phenomenal realm, in order to preserve freedom in a noumenal realm that lies beyond the comprehension of science and pure reason. Lonergan, on the other hand, argues that the "statistical residues" of the natural world defy complete systematic determinism. These non-systematic dimensions of the natural world are therefore open to the emergent reality of the essential freedom of human actions. But where Kant worried about the threat to freedom posed by Newtonian science, Lonergan worries about the threat to effective freedom posed by the unintelligibility and irrationality of the accumulated surds that arise both individually and socially from biases, distorted scales of values, and bad decisions.[30]

Hence it seems that Lonergan's approach to a method for ethics in *Insight* was intended at least in part as an alternative to a Kantian method for ethics. Concerning that alternative, he goes on to remark that a method of ethics so conceived pertains to all human beings because everyone possesses the exigence for consistency of such knowing and acting. Referring not just to the general form of precepts, but the ongoing generation of those precepts in the thinking of the historical sequences of individual human beings, Lonergan writes:

> Accordingly, ethical method ... can take subjects as they are; it can correct any aberration in their views by a dialectical criticism; and it can apply these corrected views to the totality of concrete objects of choice. Such a method not only sets forth precepts but also bases them on their real principles, which are not propositions or judgments but existing persons; it not only sets forth correct precepts but also provides a radical criticism for mistaken precepts; it is not content to appeal to logic for the application of precepts, for it can criticize situations as well as subjects, and it can invoke dialectical analysis to reveal how situations are to be corrected; finally, because such a method clearly grasps an unchanging dynamic structure immanent in developing subjects that deal with changing situations in correspondingly changing manners, it can steer a sane course between the relativism of mere concreteness and the legalism of remote and static generalities; and it can do so, not by good luck nor by vaguely postulating prudence, but methodically, because it takes its stand on the ever recurrent dynamic generality that is the structure of rational self-consciousness.[31]

I think that all of these elements and more from Lonergan's *Insight* method of ethics are of great importance. But as I have argued elsewhere, they are not adequately grounded in *Insight* itself. I think most, if not all, of Lonergan's claims about ethical matters in *Insight* are sublated into the fuller and more adequate conception of the method of ethics modelled on the eight functional specialties. I hope to show that this is the case in the remainder of this chapter.

15.3   Personal Decisions as Situated and Methodical

The shift in ethical method provoked by Lonergan's later thought does not reverse his position on the situatedness of human action in the finality of the universe. It does, however, place much greater emphasis on the situatedness of human action within the context of human history as the most significant part of the finality of the universe, with its ongoing transformations and deformations of meaning and value.

The need for a more differentiated and refined method in ethics becomes apparent when we reflect upon this situatedness more concretely. No exercise of ethical intentionality occurs in isolation. At a bare minimum, ethical intentionality always begins as a response to some prior set of experiences, and experiences in general are almost never our own self-creations.[32] However much we select, structure, and pattern our experiences, they always arise from events in the natural and social realms. Hence our responses of ethical intentionality are always situated within the events of the natural and social worlds.

Furthermore, by the time any of us are learned enough to read the words on this page, we have been formed in many ways. The formation of our habitual ways of thinking, feeling, valuing, deciding, and acting comes out of our responses to the words and deeds of other humans, and constitutes what sociologists and anthropologists call our "acculturation." They are the ways that we have come to habitually understand, judge, and believe facts, and to value (or disapprove) and make our own (or reject) the common-sense insights, judgments, feeling horizons, and values of our social and cultural settings. Acculturation is the way we constitute ourselves by acquiring some selection of the insights, judgments, feelings, and values of others.

In particular, the horizons of our feelings are formed through our interactions in family, social, and cultural institutions. Our horizons of feelings condition how we select and pattern our experiences, assess our situations, come up with insights into practical courses of action, and especially what we regard as pertinent further questions about those possible courses of action. It is against all of this background formation that we eventually reach our decisions and take action. This means that the concrete ways in which we exercise our ethical intentionality are also situated within the histories and biographies that influenced our formations. As Joseph Flanagan put it, "judgments of fact or value occur within a cultural context or horizon, which means that such judgments are limited by that horizon."[33]

The question of method in ethics, therefore, is a question of how well or how poorly we critically evaluate and appropriate what has been bequeathed to us by those who preceded us. Most people rely on the considerable resources of ordinary common sense. In fact it is no exaggeration to say that thinking and acting ethically would be impossible without formation in common sense. At least as Lonergan analysed it, common sense is communal and traditional, but also dynamic and innovative.[34] It is communal insofar as the contents of commonsense wisdom reside, not in any one person's consciousness, but rather are distributed throughout a community. No one person alone possesses all of the commonsense insights, judgments of fact and value, feelings, or beliefs that are needed to navigate the course of an ethical life in a community. People of common sense turn to one another for information, advice, counsel, encouragement, correction, and reprimand. Again, common sense is traditional because people rely for their ethical thinking and acting upon vast numbers of commonsense insights, judgments, feelings, and beliefs that were originated before them by particular individuals, but then communicated quickly and efficiently to those who come after. However common sense is not traditional in a static or dogmatic sense; common sense is a dynamic and innovative form of tradition. The inventories of commonsense insights, judgments of facts and values, feelings, and beliefs are always changing, because they "remain incomplete until there is added at least one further" insight,[35] judgment, feeling, or belief that meets the challenges posed by a new situation that is not completely identical with anything previously encountered. In common sense, therefore, we rely upon the inheritances of our social, cultural, and historical traditions, without being completely dominated or controlled by those acquisitions.

Nevertheless, as Lonergan observed, common sense has limits. These limits are the biases that we also inherit from our forbearers – dramatic, group, and especially general bias. These biases limit the range of further questions we are able to regard as pertinent. General bias in particular will tend to restrict the assessments by common sense to concerns that are proximate in space but especially in time. This means, among other things, that there are limitations in our commonsense capacities to take seriously what people have said and done in distant times and places as possibly relevant to the decision at hand. Hence the capacities of commonsense evaluation of the sources of our ethical evaluation and deliberation need to be supplemented by ethical method of another kind. About such a method Flanagan observes that

> the central problem in achieving authenticity as a knower and a chooser lies in distinguishing between short- and long-term cultural cycles of meaning and motives as they are operating both in the concrete and lived meanings of a culture and in the reflective and deliberative procedures of theoreticians in understanding and evaluating their own and others' lived meanings. The basic problem of

such reflecting and deliberating is to appropriate the scale of values that has been inherited from the past and is still operating.[36]

Ethical method in this sense serves a dual purpose. On the one hand, it facilitates criticism of what is biased and distorted in what we have received from the past (i.e., reverses the counter-positions). On the other hand, it also makes accessible the ethical wisdom and noble exemplars of the past that may have been lost, overlooked, underappreciated, or unfairly dismissed (i.e., promotes the positions). Encounters with these expressions of wisdom and nobility can lead us to question ourselves, our assumptions, habits, and horizons of feelings, and lead us to more authentic exercises of our ethical intentionality. This, too, is one of the objectives of a method in ethics.

15.4   Situated in a Climate of Conflict

The need for a more refined method in ethics becomes all the more evident and urgent for anyone who has pondered contemporary ethical debates. Our awareness of such debates is among the cultural influences that enter into our moments of decision. Disagreement seems to be the norm rather than the exception, whether the topic is the death penalty, abortion, assisted suicide, racism, gender discrimination, gay marriage, human embryonic stem cell research, immigration, whether or not to go to war, what the appropriate levels of risk-taking for investors are, whether any institutions are too big to fail, who should pay for healthcare and education, etc. These and many more issues all are pressing, while agreement seems all but impossible. Conflict about ethical matters is so widespread that a great many people now assume that not only is agreement impossible, but that objective answers to ethical questions simply do not exist. Ethics, it seems, is purely a matter of personal opinion. If this were true, of course, the great difficulty is how to resolve conflicting points of view. The spectres of power and violence loom as the final arbiters when all hope for objective resolution of conflict has been lost.

All this, too, is part of our situatedness, of the influences that we inherit from our social and cultural traditions of common sense. The current climate of seemingly irreconcilable conflict influences how to go about exercising our structure of ethical intentionality. We may be influenced to agree that there is no objective, ethically valuable course of action, and give up on the hard work of ethical discernment. Or we can align ourselves with one strident set of voices and dismiss as ridiculous the questions posed by contending parties. In either case, we unwittingly incorporate the conflicts into ourselves, and they inevitably distort the normativity of our ethical intentionality. Without a refined methodical way of resolving such conflicts, the exercise of ethical intentionality will seem to be naive at best, or a waste of precious time at worst.

This is not to say, of course, that everyone has abandoned all hope. Great contemporary thinkers such as Alasdair MacIntyre, John Rawls, Jürgen Habermas, Anthony Appiah, Amartya Sen, Martha Nussbaum, Charles Taylor, and many more have presented approaches to the mediation of ethical conflict in the contemporary context of a pluralism of conflicting ethical views. Without entering into a detailed debate with these important thinkers, these concluding sections endeavour to show how the ethics of discernment presented in the previous chapters can facilitate conversation and even collaboration with those whose views one opposes, and how methodical resolution of ethical conflicts might be achieved – something that Lonergan had hoped for in *Insight*.[37] In particular, I propose that the refined and differentiated method in ethics that follows from the ethics of discernment is identical with what Lonergan explains as the eight functional specialties of his *Method in Theology*. The justification for this proposal is the objective of the remainder of this chapter and the next chapter.

15.5   Method and Conflict

The problems of deep-seated conflict were foremost in Lonergan's mind when he set forth his efforts at a method in metaphysics. In *Insight*, he wrote that "the main point is that the method puts an end to mere disputation" and conflicts about metaphysical matters.[38] Later in *Method in Theology*, he was even more emphatic:

> The point to making metaphysical terms and relations not basic but derived is that a critical metaphysics results. For every term and relation there will exist a corresponding element in intentional consciousness … The importance of such a critical control will be evident to anyone familiar with the vast arid wastelands of theological controversy.[39]

What he said regarding theological controversy can easily be extended to ethical controversy as well. That Lonergan did not successfully carry out his intention to develop a method in ethics in *Insight* was perhaps providential. In my judgment, the method that is appropriate for the challenges of conflicts in ethics is the more nuanced method that he set forth fifteen years later in *Method in Theology*. There the integrated structure of the eight functional specialties addresses the complex problem of conflicting meanings.[40]

However, at first sight it does not seem that a method in theology could be sufficiently open and general to meet the problems of ethical conflict in our contemporary pluralistic society. A method in theology, it would seem, must presuppose at least the existence of a God and probably also confessional allegiance to some religious tradition and its permanent doctrines. A method in ethics so conceived, it would seem, cannot be relevant to people who cannot accept the existence of God or some particular religious affiliation. Whatever might be meant by a method in theology, then, it would seem that something else is needed to meet the challenges of ethical conflict in a pluralistic world.

It is something of a surprise, therefore, to discover that Lonergan's approach to the question of method in theology does not presuppose either the existence of God or a specific list of religious doctrines or commitment to any particular religious tradition. Instead, he came to his proposals regarding this method out of his struggles with the very general set of problems having to do with interpretation – the hermeneutic problem.[41] The problem of interpretation is in fact an interrelated set of problems – a "problematic," as Michael Buckley has called it. One of the key components in the hermeneutical problematic is that each human being brings a very particular formation to the tasks of interpreting the expressions of another (or even one's own self-expressions, as Paul Riceour has noted[42]). Personal formation comprises one's previous habits and experiences, insights, language formation, judgments of fact, horizons of feelings, scales of value preference, judgments of value, decisions, biases – as well as the particular ways that one has assimilated these from one's culture. There is nowhere to begin one's acts of interpretation except to begin with who one actually is, with the formation one actually has.

For many, this seems to imply that there can be no objective interpretation (and if this method is extended to ethics, no objective evaluation of ethical positions). Lonergan at least did not draw that conclusion, nor do I. Lonergan's great insight, of course, is that the principal sources of normativity – the unrestricted notion of value and unrestricted being-in-love – are always embedded within (though perhaps badly obscured by) the profusion of other elements in the formation of each and every person. They provide the capacities for transcending whatever limitations and biases might have accrued through acculturation, as well as from the bad decisions that are wholly one's own. Therefore, the fact that we start our interpretations and evaluations with who we are does not necessarily imply that objective interpretation and objective evaluation of one's own tradition is impossible – because who we are includes not only our biases, but also our achievements and our self-transcending dynamisms, all mixed together in unique ways. It does, however, imply that objective interpretation and evaluation will be exceedingly difficult. In some areas, such as understanding the proof of a theorem in abstract algebra, conflicts of interpretation will be minimal. But in other areas, conflicts of interpretation will abound and appear insurmountable.

The selves we bring to the task of interpretation will contain several sources of conflict. Because our cultural inheritances themselves contain conflicting judgments and feelings, we will accept some positions as our own and reject others. This means that we will be in conflict with some of the ethical views passed along to us, and will need, therefore, a methodical way of dealing with the views which we ourselves oppose. But more profoundly, the conflicts of our culture tend to produce subtle conflicts within ourselves. These are of two kinds, both of which are much more difficult to discern and to resolve than the conflicts we have with parts of cultural heritages. The first kind of conflict is thematic – conflicts between propositions that we hold simultaneously without recognizing that they are logically inconsistent. But a second kind of conflict is even more subtle and profound. These are the conflicts between the positions we hold and our very own structure of ethical intentionality itself. Some people hold with great conviction that it is bad to hold that there are objective values. But by this conviction, they themselves treat as objective their judgments of value about judgments of value. In arriving at these very acts of great conviction, these individuals are exercising their own structure of ethical intentionality in opposition to the very thing they say no one should do. This is a far more subtle but more basic kind of conflict.

Indeed, all of these kinds of conflicts between statements and performances are traceable in large measure to the conflicting tensions in the horizons of feelings. Among these conflicts the most significant are those arising from tensions between our own personal constellation of feeling preferences, on the one hand, and the normativity of the unrestricted notion of value and unrestricted being-in-love (with their implicit, objective scale of values), on the other. Unless these deep conflicts are noticed and dealt with methodically, they will persist as sources of conflicts in our interpretations. These conflicts will function as the ultimate foundation that we rely upon when we adopt one and reject others among the conflicting views that have been passed along to us by the words and deeds of others.

The chief aim of Lonergan's structure of eight interrelated components (functional specialties) is not just to arrive at objective interpretations of this or that expression of ethical positions. More fundamentally, its aim is to bring about an encounter of the interpreter with the interpreter himself or herself. The aim is to surface and draw attention to the norms already operating in one's own performance of the structure of ethical intentionality in the very work of evaluating inherited ethical positions. It is only once interpreters have truly confronted and appropriated who they are and their own internal conflicts that it becomes possible for them to have objective interpretations of the conflicting views of others about ethical matters. In the next sections I will briefly explain how Lonergan understood this integrated structure of eight functional specialties, and why it is an appropriate method for meeting the challenge of critical evaluation from a position situated in conflict.

15.6   The Eight Functional Specialties of Ethical Method

Lonergan spent most of his mature scholarly career attempting to work out the structure of an appropriate method for theology. Although originally formulated as a method for theology, Lonergan explicitly acknowledged that it had implications for all realms of human studies and human sciences.[43]

Underlying the structure of these methodical specializations is the structure of ethical intentionality itself. To each level of conscious operations in the structure of ethical intentionality there correspond two distinct scholarly specialties. Schematically, the structure looks as it does in Figure 15.1.[44]

Lonergan devotes an entire chapter to the exposition of each of these functional specialties (and two chapters to the specialty of History). Clearly, that level of detail cannot be repeated in this chapter, so the reader is referred to *Method in Theology* itself, as well as to works by Ivo Coelho, Tad Dunne, and Robert Doran for details.[45] What is possible here is to show why this further investigation would be of benefit in approaching conflicts about ethics.

Transposed into the context of ethical method, the first four of these functional specialties (Research, Interpretation, History, and Dialectic) are designed to facilitate a scholar's coming to terms with the deeds, values, and meanings that others have passed along to us. Whatever it is that others have taught, argued, and modelled about what is good and right to do – the first four specialties devote their endeavours to examining these sources. The second four specialties (Foundations, Doctrines, Systematics, and Communications) are all dedicated ultimately towards arriving at decisions regarding future courses of action – what we will pass along to posterity. This integrated structure of eight functional specialties is devoted to discerning what we will make of the past and how we incorporate it into the actions we perform which will affect the futures of the natural world, of other people, and of we ourselves.

What makes these eight divisions *specializations* of *function*, however, is that practitioners of a given division devote all of their efforts, acts of consciousness, capacities, skills, and energies to arriving at the contents proper to just one kind of act of consciousness (i.e., function) in the structure of ethical intentionality. The kind of act (and implicitly its corresponding content) is

Figure 15.1. Structure of the Eight Functional Specialties

Structure of Ethical Intentionality	Functional Specialties	
Level of Consciousness	Encountering the Past	Acting Towards the Future
Responsibility (Deciding)	Dialectic	Foundations
↑↓	↑	↓
Reasonableness (Judging)	History	Doctrines
↑↓	↑	↓
Intelligence (Understanding)	Interpretation	Systematics
↑↓	↑	↓
Attentiveness (Experiencing)	Research	Communications

designated in the left-hand column of Figure 15.1. Each kind of act and correlated content is the primary objective of each given functional specialty. Yet it takes the exercise of the entirety of ethical intentionality to deliver good work in any one of these functional specialties. In other words, specially structured acts of experiencing, inquiring, direct insights, questions for reflection and deliberation, intentional feelings, judgments of fact and value, decisions, and actions are all required to produce results in any one of the functional specialties. What distinguishes a given functional specialty is not that it exercises just one kind of act (e.g., understanding), but that it exercises all the acts in pursuit of producing results that ultimately are the contents of just one kind of act. Examples of how this is so will be presented in the next chapter.

In addition, the integrating connections among the products of these distinct specialized methods come from the dynamism of ethical intentionality itself. Just as the unrestricted notion of value and unrestricted being-in-love provide the intrinsic connections among the acts and their contents in the ordinary exercise of ethical intentionality, so also they connect the products in this more refined and differentiated exercise of that structure. The works of one functional specialty provide the materials for other functional specialties, in just the same way as the contents of one act of consciousness become sources for subsequent acts of consciousness, according to the dynamics of the structure of ethical intentionality. This bestows a double-movement upon the overall eightfold structure – the dynamisms from below upward and from above downward. These connections are symbolized by the arrows in Figure 15.1.

These reciprocal movements from below upward and above downward also operate in ordinary exercises of ethical intentionality. Up to this point, however, for the sake of simplicity I have not dwelled upon how these two movements are differentiated from one another (although Lonergan did).[46] So far I have only spoken of the tensions that the unrestricted notion of value and unrestricted being-in-love introduce into our horizons of feelings, but these two principles of our ethical intentionality do in fact have inverse and complementary dynamics. The intentionality of notion value is from our experiences of situations towards understanding and judgments of fact and value, and thence towards decisions, actions, and ultimately towards the unconditional love that embraces everything of value. But the dynamic of unrestricted being-in-love begins from that love, not as chosen but as experienced. As such, it opens up feelings for the other values that unrestricted love embraces. This opening of feelings becomes the source of wider and more refined judgments of value (including the values of critically believing and not believing others), which then seek understanding of what one has come to value initially through the ministry of love. This movement culminates in expanded openness to experiences of the world, others, and oneself that have been closed off by biases. Thus, the two dynamics organize the levels of operations of the structure of ethical intentionality into two reciprocally related patterns. Once appropriated and refined, these two dynamics form the basis for a method that can interconnect the results of eight specialized sub-methods and thereby critically evaluate a host of ethical views.

However, at the risk of prematurely complicating matters, I hasten to add that the arrows in Figure 15.1 indicate the primary, but not the only relationships among the eight specialties. There will be other reciprocities. For example, results from Foundations or Systematics can be profitably fed back to enhance the work of Interpretation or History.

In light of what has been said in the previous sections of this chapter, the crucial functional specialties are the two that correspond to the fourth level of evaluating and deciding: Dialectic and Foundations. Dialectic endeavours to identify the fundamental roots of conflicts that have permeated the prior history of claims in words and deeds about what is right and good. Foundations endeavours to spell out and appropriate the differences between what is and is not implicit in conversions to the unrestricted notion of value and unrestricted being-in-love. The functional specialties prior to Dialectic endeavour to comprehend human acts of meaning and value in all their nuances and complexities. The functional specialties following Foundations endeavour to use what has been learned through self-appropriation of the unrestricted notion of value and unconditional love in order to approve what was valuable in the past, to improve its incomplete or flawed results, and to leave aside irremediable elements, if there are any. It does so with an eye towards organizing and enacting courses of action that will have consequences for one's own future, for the futures of other human beings, and for the future of the natural universe. The next chapter will explore in greater detail these two functional specialties and their relevance for method in ethics.

It is quite significant that in Figure 15.1 there is no arrow at the juncture between Dialectic and Foundations, which would connect the upward movement of the middle column with the downward movement of the right-hand column. This is because there is no method for *producing* either free human decisions or God's free bestowal of grace or their confluence in human decisions of conversion. As Lonergan puts it, "I consider religious conversion a presupposition of moving from the first [upward] phase to the second [downward phase of the functional specialties] but I hold that conversion occurs not in the context of doing theology, but in the context of becoming religious."[47]

To this I would add that moral conversion occurs not as a product of ethical method, but in the context of striving towards and growth in being ethical. Nevertheless, if a person takes seriously the challenge of critically engaging ethical teachings that have been received, and endeavours to use the heuristic aids provided by Lonergan's eight functional specialties, this increases the likelihood that she or he will be profoundly moved in the direction of moral conversion.

Chapter 13 closed with comments about how Lonergan's approach to the question of evil raises the question of a religious dimension to the ethics of discernment. But religious dimensions are never abstract; they always are situated in some kind of a historical tradition, and historical traditions can be less or more genuinely religious in the sense proposed in chapter 13. Even people who say, "I'm spiritual but not religious," are echoing what they have heard or read from others before them, and thereby placing themselves in a kind of tradition. Lonergan claimed that religious conversion is ultimately the only standard by means of which religious traditions can be evaluated for their authenticities as well as for their inauthenticities. So he offered a method of theology to assist in discerning the differences within traditions between what is authentically and what is inauthentically religious within them.

I would argue that there is also no method for automatically producing authentic decisions for moral, intellectual, or psychic conversion. The eight methodical specialties can remove misunderstandings and lower other barriers and excuses that are obstacles to converting decisions. They can heighten tensions that favour such decisions. But the method as such provides no automatic mechanisms for producing decisions that are converting. These are matters of radical freedom, human and divine. As the next chapter endeavours to show, exercises of the functional specialties can promote, but cannot cause, the conversions that are crucial to achieving fully objective results in the method of ethics (or theology). To expect more than that of a method in ethics runs the danger of transgressing the realities of human freedom and ethical intentionality.

16 Method in Ethics II: Dialectic and Foundations

It is important for us ... to take an intelligent part in this birthing process ... A good outcome depends on a lot of cooperation with the process at the instinctual level certainly, but also through a thorough understanding of what is happening ... To make use of such a heritage, to recognize and nurture it in a new form, distinguishing it from what is to be let go, we need to understand...

> – Rosemary Luling Haughton, "Transcendence and
> the Bewilderment of Being Modern"[1]

Discovering ourselves as sinners and victims will go hand in hand with discerning authenticity and oppression in our communities of meaning. There are no shortcuts, and though there are aids to facilitate such tasks, each person and community must muddle through in its own self-correcting process of learning.

> – Cynthia S.W. Crysdale, *Embracing Travail*

16.1 Introduction

Lonergan organized the functional specialties of his method in theology into two phases: one that "encounters the past," and another that, "enlightened by the past, confronts the problems" of the present.[2] A method in ethics can be profitably organized into these two phases as well. This chapter will focus on two of the functional specialties, Dialectic and Foundations, as representatives of each of these phases, in order to illustrate how Lonergan's approach can contribute to an ethical method. This does not mean that the other six functional specialties are not of equal importance in their contributions to ethical method, as should become clear in the remainder of this chapter. Rather, these two functional specialties have been selected as representative of their phases (Dialectic for encountering the past, and Foundations for confronting problems of the present), because it is not feasible to enter here into the details of all eight functional specialties. Instead, only brief descriptions of those functional specialties are offered. Once again, the reader is encouraged to turn to *Method in Theology* itself for further details.

16.2   Critically Engaging Our Heritage: Research, Interpretation, and History

Research. Critical engagement with the ethical sources that have come down to us is the objective of the first of the two phases. Every methodical investigation begins with data from experience. Obtaining data, however, is seldom as simple a matter as just looking to see what is out there before one's eyes. In natural science, laboratory instruments must be calibrated, purified of contaminating elements, and tested before the data derived from their use can be deemed reliable for further investigation. In social science, survey questionnaires ("instruments") must be carefully prepared in order to insure reliability of the responses, and review processes have been developed to screen out unreliable or fraudulent data.

Preparation of data for humanities disciplines, including ethics and theology, poses different kinds of challenges. The primary data for ethics are data on human expressions, and especially the data of written texts. Lonergan adopted the label "Research" to designate the range of scholarly techniques that focus on preparing and authenticating the data on human expressions that are to be taken up by the seven subsequent specialties of methodical investigation. Without such authentication, Interpretation and History would arrive at unsubstantiated results.

Interpretation. Critically engaging expressions of ethical thought and behaviour from the past ultimately means evaluating them. But before we can evaluate them responsibly, we first must understand them. People understand the expressions of members of their commonsense community all the time through self-correcting processes that are underpinned by the dynamic structure of ethical intentionality. Commonsense interpretation relies upon the long-term personal acquisition of the commonsense insights, feelings, judgments, and beliefs from the community's public store. Then, when another person says something even mildly novel, understanding this expression is the relatively simple matter of "adding one or two more insights relevant to the situation or text in hand," over and above those previously acquired over a lifetime.[3] However, when ethical expressions come to us from sources other than those of our own immediate community, commonsense modes need to be supplemented by other methods. Lonergan spent much of his career working out a very general heuristic structure for the full range of human meanings based on his analysis of the structures, patterns, and differentiations of human consciousness.[4] The functional specialty, Interpretation, relies upon the guidance of these heuristics as it approaches the task of understanding these expressions and communicating that understanding to various audiences.

History. History as a reality is the process whereby we are bequeathed the resources and the corruptions that we use in exercising our structure of ethical intentionality. We not only receive written and other forms of expression from our forebears; those expressions are mediated to us by interpretations. Expressions and interpretations form historical sequences which are passed along to us and which form us. What Lonergan says about the historian can be said of each of us – namely, that we operate in the light of our "whole personal development," which is "not just [our own] but also the living on in [us] of developments that human society and culture have slowly accumulated over the centuries."[5]

Still, what we are told about the past and what actually happened often can be very different. We form feelings and evaluations in response to what we are told about the past, but what we are told about the goods or evils done in the past may be exaggerated or untrue. Evil deeds of the past may be covered over by the telling of a history, giving a better picture of a culture than it deserves. If we discover that the stories we receive are distorted, we are no longer content to live by them. Ultimately, we are not satisfied merely with edifying stories. We desire histories that are true. We wish to know, therefore, whether what has come down to us is an authentic communication and adaptation of an original ethical vision, or whether it is somehow a betrayal of that vision.

The methodical specialty of History in Lonergan's sense therefore makes a substantial contribution to the critical appropriation of our ethical heritage. History as Lonergan understands it "is a functional specialty that aims at settling matters of fact by appealing to empirical evidence" about human meanings.[6] Knowing the factual history of our ethical heritage takes us beyond the manipulations of opinion, rhetoric, propaganda, and ideology. Lonergan quotes historian Carl Becker regarding the value of critical history: "It prepares us to live more humanely in the present and to meet rather than foretell the future."[7]

What Lonergan says about history in *Method in Theology* can be supplemented in light of the preceding chapters of this book. The general heuristic of the human, natural, and transcendent good, along with the scale of value preferences, can be used to assist historical investigation in analysing the various kinds of goods and evils as they develop and decline in authors, texts, deeds, institutions, societies, and cultures.[8] The methodical work of History, therefore, makes crucial contributions towards purifying and enriching our inherited resources, in order that we may better draw upon them as we respond to our contemporary situations.

16.3 Dialectic

Critical engagement with ethical expressions reaches its culmination in the functional specialty of Dialectic. Important as they are, the contributions of Research, Interpretation, and History are limited. Beyond knowing matters of fact, there lies the "task of passing judgments on the values and disvalues offered us by the past," which pertains to the further specialties of Dialectic and Foundations.[9]

Dialectic presupposes the indispensable contributions of the three prior functional specialties and places them into a wider and deeper context. Dialectic therefore plays a crucial role in critically appropriating and discerning what our heritage has bequeathed to us. We wish to know whether what has been bequeathed is good and worthy of emulation, improvement, and dissemination – or whether it is tarnished, corrupted, or perhaps toxic, to be corrected, discouraged, or perhaps quarantined. Lonergan devised Dialectic as a method for making such evaluations. Its primary task is "to add to the interpretation that understands a further interpretation that appreciates ... [and] to add to the history that grasps what was going forward a history that evaluates achievements, that discerns good and evil."[10] These are the essential contributions of Dialectic over and above the results produced by the three prior methodical specialties.

No doubt many will object that evaluation of past achievements is not the proper task of any kind of scholarly work. Along with Max Weber, they will insist that scholarship (*Wissenschaft*) must limit itself to objective facts, and that subjective opinions about values lie outside its boundaries.[11] In response, Lonergan himself quoted historians, such as Friedrich Meinecke and Carl Becker, who held that "the value of history is ... moral" insofar as it leads to "deepening the sympathies and fortifying the will."[12] He also offered the works of Jacob Burkhardt as examples of this evaluative kind of history.

As a further response to the objection, I would refer to the earlier chapters of this book, which presented a case for the possibility of objective judgments of value. Objectivity in the realm of values is parallel to objectivity in the realm of facts. Both depend upon fidelity to the call of unrestricted questioning – whether questions about what truly is, or questions about what is truly valuable. Objectivity in the realm of values also depends upon a normatively oriented horizon of feelings. Objectivity depends, in short, upon a person who is intellectually, religiously, and morally converted, and who thinks out of and lives out the normativity intrinsic to those conversions. Dialectic therefore raises to the level of a scholarly method what is already immanent and operative in the ordinary thinking and living of authentic human beings. Appreciative interpretations and evaluative histories can be the proper work of scholarship, therefore, if these sources of objectivity are recognized and addressed methodically. This is the point to Dialectic as Lonergan conceived of it. Dialectic becomes methodical by taking as its sources the critical, scholarly studies of researchers, interpreters, and historians, and by bringing the sources of objective evaluation into play.

However, Lonergan's functionally specialized method of adding evaluative interpretations and histories runs up against a problem. As methodical and specialized, Dialectic must rely upon the works of scholars engaged in Research, Interpretation, and History.[13] Yet the results put forth by different scholars can and do conflict with one another. Thus in order to be able to use them as bases for evaluations, those conflicts need to be identified, comprehended, and resolved in some fashion.

Lonergan opens his chapter on Dialectic, therefore, with the declaration that its purpose is to deal with conflicts. As a first step, he proposes procedures for distinguishing among different kinds of conflicts. Some conflicts are familiar (such as those between people who play different roles in their societies, which he ascribes to different sets of commonsense insights), while some come to light through his intentionality analysis (such as those arising from differentiations of consciousness or different stages of meaning).[14] The preliminary procedures in the methodical practice of Dialectic, therefore, are devoted to clarifying these different kinds of conflicts.[15]

Yet these preliminary procedures are intended to set the stage for the primary objective of Dialectic, namely engaging the most fundamental of kinds of conflicts – those that arise because of the presence or absence of the three conversions (intellectual, moral, and religious, to which we may also add psychic).

In order to meet the challenges of these deeper kinds of conflicts, the method of Dialectic follows two precepts: "develop positions; reverse counter-positions."[16] By "positions," Lonergan means statements that are not merely logically consistent with other statements, but are also consistent with the actual performance of the structured activities of cognitional structure. By extension, we may speak of positions as statements that are consistent with the more encompassing structure of ethical intentionality. A statement such as "Objectivity in matters of fact and value is possible" would be an example of a position. Counter-positions are statements that are inconsistent with the exercise of ethical intentionality. For example, the assertion "It is always bad to make value judgments" would be of a counter-position, since the person making the statement is exercising the very activity she or he condemns.[17]

Lack of conversion itself can lead to various kinds of dialectical conflicts. So, for example, Lonergan claims that both empiricism and idealism result from the absence of intellectual conversion in the full sense. But their statements do not conflict solely with the statements of Lonergan's critical realism. The claims of empiricists and idealists will also conflict with one another, precisely because of the ways that their commitments about knowing, objectivity, and reality deviate from cognitional structure and its implications. Similarly, I would suggest that the conflicts between utilitarians and deontologists on ethical matters arise from horizons that are both lacking in moral conversion in the full sense. For example, utilitarians tend to focus on goods of the first level of the structure of the human good, while deontologists tend to focus on personal value in the scale of values. Moral conversion situates the goodness of both within the larger contexts of the whole structure of the human good and the entire scale of values.

By taking on the tasks of developing positions and reversing counter-positions, Dialectical scholars would themselves be making value judgments and taking decisive stands. They would take a stand whenever they pronounce that some claim by a predecessor is either a position or a counter-position. As Lonergan observes, when dialecticians develop positions and reverse counter-positions they will "be presenting an idealized version of the past, something *better* than was the reality."[18] Even more obviously, they also make value judgments and decisions when they take a stand as to what of value was moving forward in history on the basis of those dialectically refined results.

Once again, this might sound as though Lonergan has given up on objectivity. Giving a scholarly account of the past as better than it really was – rather than just as it really was – just seems purely subjective. It seems worse than merely an idealized account. It seems, rather, like an idealistic projection fulfilling the wishes of the investigator, rather than facing the cold, hard facts of human reality. Or perhaps Lonergan's method is in reality a disguised and perhaps a self-deluded effort to promote some social or cultural or ideological or religious agenda.[19]

Lonergan was well aware of these problems, and he approached them with something even more subtle in mind. Dialectic in his sense situates interpretations and histories in a larger context. Just as the historian takes the results of interpreters and the critical evaluation of witnesses as sources to be woven together into a correct narrative of what was going forward, so also the dialectician takes the interpretations and histories that have been written and places them into a still larger and more complex context. The moto of critical history has been *Sitz im Leben* – the injunction to comprehend the meanings of expressions properly by understanding and situating them in the context of their original, lived, social, cultural, and historical settings. But there is a subtle oversight in this approach. What exactly is the "historical setting" of an expression? Contextualizing meanings *Sitz im Leben* is indispensable as far as it goes, but it excessively restricts the contexts within which expressions are to be understood. All social and cultural contexts are themselves situated within the context of history itself. The penultimate setting and context of the meaning of any expression therefore is history itself, and Lonergan devoted much of his career to developing a philosophical and heuristic account of history. Rather than *Sitz im Leben*, then, the slogan would be revised in Lonergan's context to read *Sitz in die Geschichte*.

This does not mean, however, that the dialectician must first have some Hegelian or God's-eye understanding of the whole of history (*Geschichte*), and then force the meaning of a text or a historical period into that preconceived whole. Rather, the dialectician accomplishes this task of situating expressions within the context of history itself while being led in the dark by the very dynamics constantly used by human beings as they constitute the unfolding of history itself – that is, the dialectician receives from her or his predecessors their best scholarly efforts, takes their conflicts as the starting point, and then uses the structure of ethical intentionality in order to trace the origins of those conflicts back to positions or counter-positions. In doing so, the dialectician adds what was missing from the accounts he or she receives and thereby transforms the received meanings into something "better than it really was." The dialectician makes his or her methodical contribution to the gradual construction of History, the process of piecing together meanings and resolving of conflicts that has been going on in history and in scholarship, and which will continue for many generations to come.

In a different context, Paul Griffiths has made a similar point. Commenting on the biblical book *The Song of Songs*, Griffiths writes,

> None of this means that all versions [interpretations] are equally good ... But it is no simple matter to discriminate the good from the less so. This is because there are many variables at play ... Some versions die and some live; some enter deeply into the corporate and individual life of the Lord's people and some remain on the margins or fall dead-born from the press. Fortunately, those who offer a version of a commentary do not need to worry very much about this. They need only do their work thoughtfully, attentively, prayerfully, and with love.[20]

In the context of the present discussion of method in ethics, we might echo Griffiths by saying, "The dialecticians do not need to worry about the unknown totality of the story of history. They need only do their work methodically, attentively, intelligently, reasonably, responsibly, and with love." This means applying their structure of ethical intentionality to the scholarly work they receive, guided by the unrestricted notion of value, unrestricted being-in-love, and the normative scale of value preference. This is the work of discernment as performed by a scholar of Dialectic.

It is therefore quite appropriate for the dialectician to present a version of a limited historical episode as "better than it really was," because history as a whole is better than any of its limited epochs. Some historians regard power as the reality upon which historical studies should be focused. For Lonergan on the other hand, history is about the reality of the advances and declines in intelligibility, goodness, and love.

As was argued in chapter 13, generalized emergent probability, human history included, is good because it is intelligible. Its intelligibility includes but goes beyond all the violence and social evil that is so obvious in history. As Lonergan remarks, positions and counter-positions "are to be understood as opposed moments in an ongoing process. They are to be apprehended in their proper dialectical character."[21] The process Lonergan speaks of is generalized emergent probability, which incorporates the dialectical movements of progress, decline, and redemption. It is a process which can transform even the counter-positions and the great damages they beget into contributions to a surpassing value. It is for this reason that Lonergan can hold that the most objective thing a dialectician can do is to remove the meaning or a historical period from its seemingly isolated *Sitz im Leben* context and reveal it as an irreplaceable component in the larger value of *Geschichte* as a whole. In doing so, the Dialectician passes along the resources of the past in profoundly refined forms that can used profitably in the building up of the good of generalized emergent probability.

It is not a failure of objectivity, therefore, when a converted scholar transforms Research, Interpretations, and Histories by completing them through the evaluative method of Dialectic. Still, we may ask, where are these converted scholars to be found, or how are they to be trained? Lonergan's answer is, in the very work of doing Dialectic itself. While conversions certainly do happen without the methodological assistance of Dialectic, committed engagement in the heuristic structure and hard work of Dialectic still has the capacity to promote the conversions. This is because Dialectic, along with Research, Interpretation, and History, brings about personal encounters between scholars and those who came before them. The purpose of Dialectic, then, is "to bring conflicts to light, and to provide a technique that objectifies subjective differences and promotes conversion."[22] Lonergan continues:

> The purpose of dialectic is to invite the reader to an encounter, a personal encounter, with the originating and traditional and interpreting and history-writing persons of the past in their divergences ... understanding texts is relevant to the dialectic that invites or challenges the [scholar] to conversion.[23]

Insofar as the work of one's predecessors was the product of exercises of converted ethical intentionality, it has the power to inspire emulation and thereby challenge the dialectician (and other scholars) to aspire to higher standards. Insofar as the work of predecessors is lacking in conversion, it will heighten tensions in the scholar that will inspire the quest for their proper resolution, which comes only in conversion. Such inspiration comes about because a human being's "deepest need and most prized achievement is authenticity,"[24] and because human feelings respond to such examples with apprehensions of their values.

It is noteworthy that Lonergan said "promote" and "invite" and "challenge" conversion, not "produce" conversion. No method in Lonergan's sense can produce results automatically. While results depend upon the sincere and sustained efforts of practitioners under the guidance of sophisticated heuristic structures, there always remains a non-systematic dimension to the relationship between these methods and their results. The eight methodical specialties are neither automatic nor foolproof. All that these methods can do is increase the probability of results; they cannot guarantee results. This contingency of results is especially pronounced in the case of Dialectic. This is because the conversions come about only through radically free acts of human choice.[25] Conversion "occurs only inasmuch as [one] discovers what is unauthentic in [oneself] and turns away from it, inasmuch as [one] discovers what the fullness of human authenticity can be and embraces it with [one's] whole being."[26] Dialectic and the other functional specialties can foster genuine human encounters[27] and thereby increase the likelihood of such discoveries and decisions, but only the individual person can freely take the final step.

Hence Dialectic

> will not be automatically efficacious, it will provide the open-minded, the serious, the sincere with the occasion to ask themselves some basic questions, first, about others but eventually, even about themselves. It will make conversion a topic and thereby promote it ... conversion

commonly is a slow process of maturation. It is finding out for oneself and in oneself what it is to be intelligent, to be reasonable, to be responsible, to love. Dialectic contributes to that end by pointing out ultimate differences, by offering the example of others that differ radically from oneself, by providing the occasions for a reflection, a self-scrutiny that can lead to a new understanding of oneself and one's destiny.[28]

Lonergan further proposes that this process will be accelerated when the results of dialecticians themselves become the inputs for subsequent exercises of Dialectic by later scholars.[29] This means that the results will improve because this self-reflective repetition of Dialectic will tend to promote the further growth in conversion among dialecticians themselves.

Notice that there is no requirement that people must first prove to some unnamed authority they are converted before they receive a license to practise Dialectic. People just engage in Dialectic, and those who are converted or become converted in the process will produce results that come to be esteemed as the most valuable by people who are converted, just as for Aristotle dialecticians who possess *euphuia* are best able to select the dialectical option that is most in harmony with the love of truth and goodness.

Converted people, just because they are converted, will be able to discern positions and counter-positions on the basis of the fundamental commitments that they themselves have made to intelligibility, truth, reality, goodness, and unconditional love. Making and especially sustaining these fundamental commitments, and drawing upon them to engage in the method of Dialectic more effectively, is greatly enhanced by explicitly thematizing those fundamental commitments well. But even without sophisticated articulation, when such people engage in Research, Interpretation, and History directly, or when they reflect on these results of others and endeavour to build upon them and to choose as their own the values they have discerned in those prior results in Dialectic, they will do so with a normativity that cannot be fully captured in rules.

It is only through the movement towards cognitional and moral self-transcendence, in which the theologian [or ethicist] overcomes his own conflicts, that he can hope to discern the ambivalence at work in others and the measure in which they resolved their problems. Only through such discernment can he hope to appreciate all that has been intelligent, true, and good in the past even in the lives and the thought of opponents. Only through such discernment can he come to acknowledge all that was misinformed, misunderstood, mistaken, evil even in those

with whom he is allied. Further, however, this action is reciprocal. Just as it is one's own self-transcendence that enables one to
know others accurately and to judge them fairly, so inversely it
is through knowledge and appreciation of others that we come
to know ourselves and to fill out and refine our apprehension of
values.[30]

Lonergan himself makes explicit the intimate connection between a method
of functional specialization and an ethics of discernment.

The positive work of Dialectic is done by people who *are* converted, not
necessarily people who can give a coherent and polished account of what
conversion is. That is the work of Foundations.

16.4   Responsible Initiative for the Future: Policy, Planning, and Execution

The second phase of method in ethics takes a stand and confronts the
problems of the present. Critical evaluation of the sources to be employed
in the present is primarily the task of the first four functional specialties:
Research, Interpretation, History, and Dialectic. Commitment and action
(and especially the actions of teaching and persuading others), rather
than critical evaluation, is the principal objective of the second four
methodical specialties (Foundations, Doctrines, Systematics, Communications). Lonergan himself observed that the structure of the last three
methodical specialties could be adapted from the field of theology to
"policy making, planning and execution" in cooperative ventures to promote the human good and heal the damage done by evil.[31] The use of this
second phase of structured specialties can make personal and especially
group ethical action more methodical and less haphazard. This work will
be greatly enhanced if it employs the products of Foundations (i.e., its
"basic categories"). While Lonergan attributes the work of developing
positions and reversing counter-positions to Dialectic, in fact most of the
nitty-gritty details of that work are taken up by the functional specialties of Doctrines, Systematics, and Communications (as policy, planning,
and execution). This is where persons and groups really appropriate a
tradition as their own and work to improve it – or to reject it in part or
whole. In particular, the general heuristic structure of the good that is
developed in Foundations can be used by these last three functional specialties. It provides a structure for deliberating individually and commu-
nally about what sorts of goods are called for and possible in the present
situation. It may be that new skills are required to make new particular
goods available. Or it may be that new institutions are needed. Or it may

be that a conversion of personal relations towards higher terminal values is necessary before any meaningful reform of institutions could be possible. The value of the work of the latter three methodical specialties, therefore, will depend upon how well they have taken into account the works of Foundations.

16.5   Foundations

The basic task of Foundations is to clarify the conversions and their implications. The conversions themselves derive their authenticity from the fundamental structured relationships that occur repeatedly among the acts of consciousness of each and every human being. Hence, to speak of the conversions as foundational is to speak of people who have come to correctly understand, to value, and to commit themselves to living and thinking in accord with those normative structures. In other words, converted people are people committed to discernment as the standard of their ethical thinking and acting. Such people are not perfect, but they have decisively committed themselves to overcoming whatever biases and *ressentiments* they may harbour and that impede their living and thinking authentically. They commit themselves, however fragilely, to discerning daily how to be intelligent and reasonable thinkers and to be responsible and loving valuers, choosers, and actors.

This means that the Foundations clarifies the conversions and their implications by clarifying the structure of ethical intentionality and its implications. It does so by providing what Lonergan calls "basic categories."[32] These basic categories spell out the key characteristics of the structures of cognition and ethical intentionality, as well as their most fundamental implications. The method for articulating these categories is in fact discernment as self-appropriation.

> If categories are to be derived, there is needed a base from which they are derived. The base … is the attending, inquiring, reflecting, deliberating subject … and the structure within which the operations occur. The subject in question is not any general or abstract or theoretical subject; it is in each case the particular [person] who happens to be doing [the operations].[33]

Lonergan devoted much of his career to working out such basic categories, especially his own accounts of the three conversions themselves. In addition, his own contributions to Foundations include posing and answering the three questions regarding cognitional structure, factual objectivity, and reality. His contributions also include the following accounts: the methods of the empirical sciences and their implications for a generalized emergent probability and a method for metaphysics; the implications of cognitional structure for knowledge about God; the transcendental notion of value and the structure of the human good; the structure of human history; the functions, realms, carriers, and stages of meaning; and the scale of value preference. All these are examples of the work of "thematizing and objectifying" and working out the implications of the conversions.[34] I have already explored how Lonergan addressed most of these topics in various places in this book, so it is unnecessary to repeat them here.

In addition, I have endeavoured in this book to offer my own contributions to the work of Foundations, expanding upon Lonergan's work by formulating three questions for ethics that parallel Lonergan's three questions for knowing, and also by offering accounts of the structure of ethical intentionality, how intentional feelings respond to various agent objects and intend various values, the horizons of intentional feelings and their tensions, the grasp of the virtually unconditioned that grounds objective judgments of value and the role of horizons of feelings in reaching such judgments and the decisions that follow from them, the role of the scale of value preference in moral conversion, and how the structure of the good can be derived from the structure of ethical intentionality. I hope that these examples illuminate what is meant by Foundations as a functional specialty, and its relevance to method in ethics. In no way should it be assumed that the work of Foundations ended with Lonergan, and certainly not with my own contributions. Foundations, like the other seven functional specialties, is an ongoing method anticipating future contributions.

Although Lonergan himself presented basic descriptions of the three conversions in the chapter in *Method in Theology* devoted to Dialectic, technically this is the work of the specialty of Foundations. Conversions and the structures of consciousness which underlie them can be understood well or poorly. While conversions can and do influence how people evaluate, decide, and act even if their conversions are not explicitly thematized, still methodically articulating just what one understands by conversion has several positive benefits. First, it can strengthen the conversions themselves by identifying and clarifying them. Second, articulating a conversion helps one sort out confusions that can make counter-positional proposals of others seem positional. Third, the effectiveness of the other functional specialties will be greatly enhanced if they draw upon the explicit clarifications provided by Foundations. This is most obvious in the case of Dialectic, whose task is to discern when conflicts arise from the differences between conversion and its absence, and between the positions and counter-positions that ensue from conversion or its lack. In similar fashion, clarifications produced by Foundations will assist those engaged in the other functional specialties in being more attentive and faithful to what it means to be operating as a converted scholar in those specialized lines of investigation. This means that the relationships among the eight functional specialties need not be a one-way street, simply from Research towards Communications. There is instead a mutual interdependence among the methodical specialties. In particular, the practice of each of them will be enhanced if they draw upon the categories as provided by Foundations.

Fourth and finally, articulating conversion exposes the limits and flaws of one's own self-understanding of conversion to the recommendations and criticisms of others who are taking the topic of conversion seriously. There is not now, and I hope never will be, any certification process that credentials a person for the practice of Foundations. No doubt many unconverted people will believe themselves converted and will proceed to articulate basic categories and implications that derive from their deviations from the authentic normativity of the unrestricted notions of intelligence, reasonableness, value, responsibility, and unconditional love. The only real check on such deviations is the response by others who are converted. Such responses are not only the work of Foundations, but also involve Research, Interpretation, History, and Dialectic, as applied reflexively to the expressions of those purporting to do the work of Foundations.

At the root of Lonergan's method of eight functional specialties, therefore, there is a profound hopefulness. It is a hopefulness that "the converted will find one another" because every human being's "deepest need and most prized achievement is authenticity."[35]

While the ineliminable human aspiration for authenticity is a ground for such hopefulness, for Lonergan as a Christian theologian there is also a far deeper ground for such hopefulness in the power of unconditional love that is God's grace. This hopefulness is intrinsic to a Christian and more generally to a religious view of history. The conviction that love is stronger than all other forces – such as self-centredness, greed, violence, power, hatred, nihilism, or political and economic forces – this itself is grounded in conversion. To say this is a religious view is to say that the power of unconditional love has been and always will continue to motivate the repair and leavening of a world that often seems destined for ultimate nothingness. (That this is also a genuinely realistic view has been argued to some extent in chapter 13).

All this is true independently of a method in ethics. Method in ethics makes any efforts to be ethical more methodical, and therefore improves the ways that people draw upon ethical traditions. Method in ethics makes more effective what has been happening and will continue to happen through the agency of converted people in transforming history. The special contribution of Foundations to this methodical transformation is to make "conversion a topic and thereby promote it," to move the discussion of the presence or absence of conversion in ethical endeavours to the forefront, to ever correct and refine a tradition's understanding of the good and the right, and to promote honest and decisive valuing and commitment to living in fidelity to those conversions.

Since much of what is proper to the work of Foundations in the method in ethics has been set forth earlier in this book, I will only dwell on one topic here – the Foundations of the normative scale of value preference. In chapter 14, I offered an indirect effort at establishing a basis for Lonergan's account of the objective scale of value preference – that is to say, I argued from the cognitional facts of higher viewpoints and the possibility of higher viewpoints in the empirical sciences to the ontological structure of a hierarchy of explanatory genera, and from there to an objective hierarchy of values. That indirect approach must be regarded as merely provisional and inadequate. Taking Lonergan literally, the ground of ethical objectivity, and especially the ground of the normative scale of value preference, is and can only be morally converted human beings. This means that articulating the proper and correct normative scale of values is something that only morally converted human beings can do. It means the hard work of discerning that normative scale by beginning with the glimpses that "shine through" one's own existential scale of values. Moreover, people endeavouring to discern this normative scale of values cannot do this work in isolation. They can achieve such articulations only in communal dialogue with others who are intelligent and serious about these questions of value. They will do it by methodically including in their discernment the ethical expressions in words and deeds of others from very distant places, times, and cultures. They will consider accounts of the proper priorities of value that are different from their own. They will use the first four methodical specialties to set up their discernment of what is converted and what is unconverted among conflicting accounts of value preferences. They will correct their own original assumptions about higher and lower values as a result of their encounters with the thoughts and deeds of others. They will offer increasingly more accurate categories to express how they have come to understand and embrace the proper ordering of values. Sometimes this will mean changing their own formulations of that scale. Sometimes it will involve the humbling recognition that their own felt value priorities are truncated or distorted. Such recognition will lead them into the hard work of personal reform. In the end, however, refined formulations of the proper scale of value preference, probably something close to Lonergan's own, will gradually emerge from the work of practitioners of Foundations on the topic of the scale of values.

16.6   Conclusion

This book endeavours to show the importance of Lonergan's work for the field of ethics. I suggest that discernment is at the heart of this importance, and that discernment is equivalent to what Lonergan calls self-appropriation. Discernment as self-appropriation begins with increased attentiveness to what is moving in our consciousness as we engage in ethical reflections, decisions, and actions. I propose that it is most important to pay attention to the stirring of questions and feelings that intend values and the tensions among those feelings, and to endeavour to discern the sources of these tensions in the unrestricted notion of value and unrestricted being-in-love.

Yet discernment requires more than attentiveness to these experiences of the dynamics of consciousness; it also requires gaining some insights into this new, vast, field of stirrings in consciousness. It further requires testing those insights with ever further questions so as to reach truly correct understandings of those dynamics – understanding the role of those dynamics in reaching objective judgments of facts and of values and authentic ethical decisions. Discernment also means correctly understanding other dynamics, especially those that violate unrestricted valuing and loving, and understanding how these differ from the dynamics that lead to authentically ethical decisions and actions.

Discernment as self-appropriation goes beyond even correctly understanding the dynamics that provide norms for authentic ethical thought, choice, and action. Discernment also includes recognizing feelings and questions about how one is to respond to such knowledge about oneself.

Discerning the structure of ethical intentionality, therefore, leads up to questions of decision for or against conversion, not to join a religious or political group, but to abide by the ethical norms already operating in one's own consciousness through questions and tensions among feelings for values.

None of this is easy. Many things compete for our attention, and distract us from dwelling with our questions and feelings. It takes commitment, perseverance, and practice to achieve this heightened sensitivity to these dynamics in our consciousness, and a community that can support, enlighten, and encourage one in such efforts.

This book attempts to provide a small contribution for those wishing to engage in self-appropriation of their own structure of ethical intentionality. It endeavours to work out some of the major implications that follow from knowledge of and commitment to that structure of ethical intentionality, including some heuristic structures and methods. Still, this book is only a beginning. It is my hope that the reader will build upon what can be gleaned from this book, and will better understand, criticize, and evaluate the array of ethical opinions on the important issues of our day, and will be better able to respond in ways that they individually are called to bring about what is good.

Notes

Preface

1 Bernard Lonergan, "The Subject," in *A Second Collection*, ed. William F.J. Ryan and Bernard J. Tyrrell (Philadelphia: The Westminster Press, 1974), 83; cited hereafter as "The Subject."

Introduction

1 Bernard Lonergan, *Insight: A Study of Human Understanding*, vol. 3 of *Collected Works of Bernard Lonergan*, ed. Frederick E. Crowe and Robert M. Doran (Toronto: University of Toronto Press, 1992); cited hereafter as *Insight*.
2 *Insight*, 23. See also page 618. Lonergan's approach to ethics in *Insight* is treated in chapter 15, section 15.2 of this book.
3 Bernard Lonergan, *Method in Theology* (New York: Herder and Herder, 1972); cited hereafter as *MT*.
4 *Insight*, 13. Lonergan's insistence on the experiment as "not public but private" in this passage will raise justifiable objections from contemporary philosophers. For the moment I will simply reply that Lonergan's words here must be taken with more than a grain of salt. I will return to this problem in chapter 3, section 3.4.

1 Discernment and Self-Appropriation

1 Self-appropriation is the exploration of ethical intentionality by means of ethical intentionality. This will be explored in detail in the subsequent chapters in this book.

2 *Rhetoric*, I.1, 1355a16–18; translation by James Allen, to whom I am indebted for this reference. Allen explores the connection between dialectic and rhetoric in his "Aristotle on the Value of 'Probability,' Persuasiveness, and Verisimilitude in Rhetorical Argument," in *Probabilities, Hypotheticals and Counterfactuals in Ancient Greek Thought*, ed. V. Wohl (New York: Cambridge University Press, 2014), 47–64. Although this passage seems to apply to rhetoric rather than dialectic, Aristotle explains that persuasion is a kind of demonstration, that all demonstrations are kinds of deductions, and that "deductions of all kinds are ... the business of dialectic" (I.1, 1355a5–9).

3 C.D.C. Reeve, "Aristotle's Philosophical Method," in *The Oxford Handbook of Aristotle*, ed. Christopher Shields (New York: Oxford University Press, 2012), 150; cited hereafter as Reeve, "Aristotle's Philosophical Method." I am indebted to Reeve for the account of dialectic and *euphuia* presented in this section.

4 Ibid., 157–9.

5 Aristotle, *Topics*, VIII 14 163b9–16. Reeve initially translates *krinousi* as "judge" but subsequently as "discern."

6 Reeve, "Aristotle's Philosophical Method," 166, quoting *Topics*, VIII 14 163b9–12.

7 In the Loeb Classical Library edition, E.S. Forster, for example, translates it as "natural ability"; see Aristotle, *Topica*, trans. E.S. Foster (Cambridge, MA: Harvard University Press, 1966), 735. See also Henry George Liddell and Robert Scott et al., *A Greek-English Lexicon: A New Edition* (New York: Oxford University Press, 1940).

8 Reeve, "Aristotle's Philosophical Method," 167.

9 1 *Corinthians* 14:29. Paul, it should be noted, does not use the same Greek word as Aristotle to express this idea of discernment.

10 1 *Thessalonians* 5:21.

11 *Romans* 12:2.

12 I.e., discerning "what is good and acceptable and perfect" (1 *Corinthians* 2:15).

13 *Romans* 5:5.

14 1 *Corinthians* 12:4.

15 *Romans* 12:6–8 and 1 *Corinthians* 12:8–10.

16 See David M. Stanley, SJ, *A Modern Scriptural Approach to the Spiritual Exercises* (Chicago: The Institute of Jesuit Sources, 1967), 156; cited hereafter as Stanley, *A Modern Scriptural Approach*.

17 David M. Stanley, SJ, *Boasting in the Lord: The Phenomenon of Prayer in Saint Paul* (New York: The Paulist Press, 1973), 131; cited hereafter as Stanley, *Boasting in the Lord*. See also his *The Call to Discipleship: The Spiritual Exercises with the Gospel of St. Mark* (London: The Way, 1982), 76.

18 Stanley, *Boasting in the Lord*, 130.

19 Stanley, *A Modern Scriptural Approach*, 156.

20 1 *Corinthians* 8:4.

21 See Joseph A. Fitzmyer, SJ, *Spiritual Exercises Based on Paul's Epistle to the Romans* (Grand Rapids, MI: William B. Eerdmans, 1995), 190.

22 Thirty days is the recommended period for the Ignatian spiritual exercises. This is how men contemplating life as a Jesuit begin the discernment of their vocations. However, Ignatius recognized that not everyone, especially lay people, would be able to leave their commitments for thirty days, and so made provision for adaptations to meet the life situations of such people – usually called "19th Annotation Retreats." See David L. Fleming, SJ, *The Spiritual Exercises of Saint Ignatius: A Literal Translation and A Contemporary Reading* (St. Louis, MO: Institute of Jesuit Sources, 1978), 16 [19]; cited hereafter as Fleming, *Ignatius*. (It is customary to use numbers in square brackets to refer to paragraphs of *The Spiritual Exercises*, first published in Latin in 1548, from the Spanish *Autograph*, first written down sometime around 1522–4.)

23 As cited in Jules J. Toner, SJ, *Discerning God's Will: Ignatius of Loyola's Teaching on Christian Decision Making* (St. Louis, MO: Institute of Jesuit Sources, 1991), 33, emphasis as in the text; cited hereafter as Toner, *God's Will*. I am indebted to J. Michael Stebbins for referring me to Toner's scholarly works.

24 Toner, *God's Will*, 15.

25 Aristotle, *Nicomachean Ethics*, trans. Martin Ostwald (Englewood Cliffs, NJ: Prentice Hall, 1962), 4, I.2 1094a17–18, and 8 I.5 1095b15–35; cited hereafter as Aristotle, *NE*.

26 Toner, *God's Will*, 26–7.

27 Ibid., 26.

28 Ibid., 29.

29 Ibid., 18.

30 Toner argues that there are two distinct yet interrelated dimensions to Ignatius' notion of discernment: discernment of spirits and discernment of God's will. Toner devoted a separate book to each of these.

31 On the misleading impressions created by calling these "rules," see Jules J. Toner, SJ, *A Commentary on Saint Ignatius' Rules for the Discernment of Spirits: A Guide to the Principles and Practices* (St. Louis, MO: Institute of Jesuit Sources, 1982), 9; cited hereafter as Toner, *Spirits*.

32 Toner, *Spirits*, 12; see also 43.

33 Toner, *God's Will*, 103. According to Toner, *elección* should not be translated as "choice" or "decision" because it is a larger process that includes choice as its culminating moment.

34 Fleming, *Ignatius*, 106 [177]; Toner, *God's Will*, 170.

35 Fleming, *Ignatius*, 106 [177]; Toner, *God's Will*, 161–2.

36 Toner, *God's Will*, 169–70.

37 Toner, *Spirits*, 79.

38 Ibid., 84.

39 Fleming, *Ignatius*, 206 [316]. See also Toner, *Spirits*, 24, 81–121, 283–90.

40 Toner, *Spirits*, 123–5. See especially Fleming, *Ignatius*, 206 [317].

41 Fleming, *Ignatius*, 214 [330]; Toner, *Spirits*, 216.

42 Toner, *Sprits*, 251.

43 Toner, *Spirits*, 29. See also Fleming, *Ignatius*, 218 [336].

44 Toner, *Spirits*, 30 [336]. See especially Toner's detailed analysis, 243–56. Of special importance is the fifth rule in the second week; Toner, *Spirits*, 28 [333].

45 Toner, *Spirits*, 25 [318].

46 Ibid., 239.

47 Toner, *Spirits*, 49. See Fleming, *Ignatius*, 204 [214–15].

48 Toner, *Spirits*, 54.

49 *Insight*, 327 and 732. The word does, however, feature prominently and repeatedly in an important passage in his *Method in Theology*. See the epigraph to this chapter.

50 Robert M. Doran, "Lonergan's Ethics and Ignatian Election," *Lonergan Resource* 2008, 6; retrieved from http://www.lonerganresource.com/pdf/books/1/33%20-%20Lonergan's%20Ethics%20and%20Ignatian%20Election.pdf. See also his "Ignatian Themes in the Thought of Bernard Lonergan: Revisiting a Topic that Deserves Further Reflection," *Lonergan Workshop* 19 (2006): 83–106.

51 Cynthia S.W. Crysdale, *Embracing Travail: Retrieving the Cross Today* (New York: Continuum, 1999), 78; cited hereafter as Crysdale, *Embracing Travail*.

52 Ibid., 71, emphasis added.

53 "Bernard Lonergan to Thomas O'Malley," *Method: Journal of Lonergan Studies* 20 (2002): 81–2.

54 For details of how conceptualism proved a barrier to Lonergan's full appropriation of his experiences of grace, see Pierre Lambert, Charlotte Tansey, and Cathleen Going (eds.), *Caring about Meaning* (Montreal: Thomas More Institute, 1982), 144–5; and Gordon Rixon, "Bernard Lonergan and Mysticism," *Theological Studies* 62 (2001): 480–5.

55 Bernard Lonergan, "Grace and the Spiritual Exercises of St. Ignatius," *Method: Journal of Lonergan Studies* 21 (2003): 89–99; cited hereafter as "Grace and the Spiritual Exercises." The editor's comments accompanying these "notes" suggest that they were probably written between 1947 and 1953, possibly for a lecture to a group of Jesuits that never actually took place (see 100–5).

56 Ibid.

57 Ibid., 89. Lonergan regarded conceptualism as one of the greatest aberrations in the philosophy of history, and dedicated much of his work to reversing its influences.

58 Bernard Lonergan, *Understanding and Being: The Halifax Lectures on Insight,* vol. 5 of *Collected Works of Bernard Lonergan,* ed. Elizabeth A. Morelli and Mark D. Morelli, revised and augmented by Frederick E. Crowe with the

collaboration of Elizabeth A. Morelli, Mark D. Morelli, Robert M. Doran, and Thomas V. Daly (Toronto: University of Toronto Press, 1990), 17, emphasis added; hereafter cited as *U&B*.

59 See for example Doran, "Lonergan's Ethics and Ignatian Election."

60 See Joseph Flanagan, *The Quest for Self-Knowledge: An Essay in Lonergan's Philosophy* (Toronto: University of Toronto Press, 1997), 8–15; cited hereafter as Flanagan, *The Quest.*

61 Immanuel Kant, *Grounding for the Metaphysics of Morals*, trans. James W. Ellington (Indianapolis, IN: Hackett, 1981), 16–17 <405–6>; cited hereafter as Kant, *GMM.*

62 See William A. Mathews, *Lonergan's Quest: A Study of Desire in the Authoring of* INSIGHT (Toronto: University of Toronto Press, 2005), 43–8, 54–8; cited hereafter as Mathews, *Lonergan's Quest.* See especially Mark D. Morelli, *At the Threshold of the Halfway House: A Study of Bernard Lonergan's Encounter with John Alexander Stewart* (Chestnut Hill, MA: Lonergan Institute at Boston College, 2007).

63 See especially *Insight*, 753–70.

2 Objectivity and Factual Knowing

1 Bernard Lonergan, "Cognitional Structure," in vol. 4 of *Collected Works of Bernard Lonergan*, ed. Frederick E. Crowe and Robert M. Doran (Toronto: University of Toronto Press, 1988), 220; hereafter referred to as *CS.*

2 *MT*, 38.

3 There are many ways of drawing a distinction between ethical and moral values. For Aristotle, moral virtues have to do with proper habitual dispositions regarding one's emotions and action, while ethics has to do with the larger sphere of human self-constitution (*praxis*) that includes thinking well and one's relations with other human beings. For Kant, morality has to do with universalized duty, while for Hegel the ethical order (*Sittlichkeit*) is the condition for the emergence of individuals who internalize universal Kantian morality. For the present I will use the terms "moral" and "ethical" interchangeably. My own way of drawing the distinctions between them is indebted to the work of Brian Cronin, and will be presented in chapter 9.

4 *MT*, 25. See also his *A Second Collection*, ed. William F.J. Ryan and Bernard J. Tyrrell (Philadelphia: The Westminster Press, 1974), 203, and *Philosophical and Theological Papers: 1965–1980*, vol. 17 of *Collected Works of Bernard Lonergan*, ed. Robert C. Croken and Robert M. Doran (Toronto: University of Toronto Press, 2004), 4, 76; cited hereafter as *PTP: 1965–1980.*

5 Lonergan of course had good reasons for choosing *Insight* as his title. Among these is the fact that the neglect of insight in scholastic philosophy led to "conceptualism" – a style of thinking that regards concepts as the proper

and even sole objects of acts of understanding. Lonergan attributed many of the faults of scholastic and post-scholastic philosophy to this dominance of conceptualism. His endeavour to restore proper emphasis upon the prior and foundational act of *intelligere* (insight or understanding) was indeed the cornerstone of all of his subsequent philosophical and theological achievements.

6 *Insight*, 3–4.

7 Ibid., 34, emphasis added. The passage can be read as referring either to the pre-linguistic tension of inquiry behind a particular linguistic expression of "Why?" or it can also be read as referring to the even more fundamental and completely comprehensive pure unrestricted desire to know.

8 *CS*, 206.

9 Ibid., 207. Indeed, Lonergan insists that human knowing is a "formally dynamic structure" in which not only is each of the conscious acts active (dynamic), but in addition the very structuring together of these acts itself is also dynamic. This is a crucial feature of the structure of ethical intentionality as well. See chapter 4.

10 Lonergan does use such terminology, for example, in his *Topics in Education*, vol. 10 of *Collected Works of Bernard Lonergan*, ed. Frederick E. Crowe and Robert M. Doran (Toronto: University of Toronto Press, 1993), 82–8; cited hereafter as *Topics*.

11 This does *not* mean that *every* activity in the flow of our stream of consciousness must be somehow related to other activities *via* this structure of consciousness. Many of our acts of consciousness are random thoughts, not contributing to any integrated set of activities that makes up an instance of genuine human cognition (i.e., knowing). The assertion only means that in genuine instances of knowing, the activities do not merely succeed one another. They are related to one another in the form of this structure.

12 Richard Kearney, *The Wake of the Imagination* (New York: Routledge, 1998).

13 Augustine, *Confessions*, trans. R.S. Pine-Coffin (New York: Viking Penguin, 1961), X.1–26, cited hereafter as Augustine, *Confessions*; Henri Bergson, *Matter and Memory* (London: G. Allen and Co., 1913).

14 Robert Bellah et al., *Habits of the Heart: Individualism and Community* (Berkeley: University of California Press, 1985), 153; cited hereafter as Bellah et al., *Habits*.

15 *Insight*, 204–14.

16 Ibid., 212–14. See also chapter 5, sections 5.3 and 5.5, of this book.

17 See, for example, *Insight*, 106. Chapter 4 will take up the further kinds of questions, beyond cognitional, that have to do with valuing and deciding. The modifiers "for intelligence" and "for reflection" may suggest a variety of meanings – for example, "questions for reflection on the assigned readings for today's class" or even for "reflection on one's life." However, Lonergan uses

these modifiers in very specific ways. The intent of this chapter is to make clear those precise meanings, and the reader is advised to ignore other misleading connotations of those terms.

18 See *Insight*, 380, 407. More precisely, it is their structural location in relation to the fuller set of cognitional activities (including understanding, reflecting, and judging) that constitutes some acts *as* acts of experiencing. In turn, the activities of understanding, reflecting, and judging themselves are constituted by their relationships to inquiries as well as to the other activities. The terms in the whole nexus or structure are "implicitly defined" through the pattern of relationships to one another. See *Insight*, 36–7, 357–8.

19 See *Insight*, 209.

20 In particular, Lonergan prided himself on rediscovering that for Aquinas "insight is into phantasms (images)" rather than into concepts. See, for example, *Insight*, 31–3. See also Bernard Lonergan, *Verbum: Word and Idea in Aquinas*, vol. 2 of *Collected Works of Bernard Lonergan*, ed. Frederick E. Crowe and Robert M. Doran (Toronto: University of Toronto Press, 1997), 39n126; see also 168–79, 194–7; hereafter cited as *Verbum*.

21 *Insight*, 3.

22 John Read, *Through Alchemy to Chemistry* (New York: Harper and Row, 1963), 179–80.

23 He says, for example, "We have devoted so much care to working out in general the difference between noesis ... and noema, because apprehending and mastering this difference are of the greatest import for phenomenology." Edmund Husserl, *Ideas for a Pure Phenomenology and Phenomenological Philosophy: First Book: General Introduction to Pure Phenomenology*, trans. Daniel O. Dahlstrom (Indianapolis, IN: Hackett, 2014), 192.

24 *Insight*, 15.

25 Ibid., 44.

26 Ibid., 441.

27 Ibid., 28.

28 "Is it so?" is but one way of expressing linguistically this form of inquiry. Some other forms of expression are "Is it real?," "Is it the case?," and "Is it true?" In all cases, the "it" is the intelligible content of some insight. An argument for the fundamental equivalence of these various linguistic forms is beyond the goal of this chapter. See, however, *Insight*, 413, 513, 575–6.

29 *Ibid.*, 305.

30 For Lonergan's general account of reflective understanding and "the virtually unconditioned," see *Insight*, 305–6; for his account of some of the extended complexities, see 307–16.

31 See, for example, Amir D. Aczel, *Fermat's Last Theorem: Unlocking the Secret of an Ancient Mathematical Problem* (New York: Four Walls Eight Windows, 1996).

32 *Insight*, 304–6.

33 Ibid., 305.

34 The use of the quotation marks around the word "knowing" here is intended
to indicate that they are partial "knowings" ("knowing in a loose or generic
sense") as opposed to Lonergan's full, strict sense of human knowing (see *CS*,
207). Human knowing in that full sense always rests upon the entire, structured
sequence of acts of consciousness culminating in reasonable judgments.
"Knowings" in less than that full sense lack the culminating element of
judgment. While it is possible that both a link and fulfillment of conditions can
be known in the full sense as affirmed propositions, in general both the link and
the conditions will be "known" in "a more rudimentary state" (*Insight*, 305–6).

35 *Insight*, 308–12.

36 Ibid., 3.

37 Ibid., 441.

38 Ibid., 308–12.

39 The question of whether or not the reader does in fact actually perform these
acts of consciousness in this dynamic structure is the topic of chapter 3.

40 In *Insight*, 399–409, Lonergan sets forth a more complex account of
objectivity – in terms of a principal notion of objectivity plus three partial
notions (experiential, normative, and absolute). In interests of space, I
must forego any detailed discussion of this more complex treatment. The
normative and absolute dimensions of the notion of objectivity are treated
implicitly throughout the section. The principal notion of objectivity puts
knowledge of self and knowledge of the other on the same footing, and
undermines any privileging of "interior" self-knowledge as prior to, and a
foundation of knowledge of, an "exterior" other.

41 *MT*, 292; see also 265.

42 *CS*, 211, emphasis added.

43 Ibid., 213.

44 I use the term "problematic" rather than "problem" to convey that this is not
one isolated problem, but a complex and interconnected set of problems. I
am indebted for this use of the term to Michael J. Buckley, SJ.

45 This is what Lonergan meant by normative objectivity; *Insight*, 404–5.

46 *CS*, 211, 213.

47 This is what Lonergan meant by absolute objectivity; *Insight*, 402–4.

48 Ibid., 372.

49 Ibid., 373.

50 See Jerome Miller, *In the Throe of Wonder: Intimations of the Sacred in a Post-
Modern World* (Albany: State University of New York Press, 1992).

51 *Insight*, 375–6.

52 Ibid., 375.

53 The problem of sustaining criticism of value issues, as well as ontological
issues, will be discussed in the next chapter.

54 *Insight*, 373.

55 Lonergan presents long analyses of various strategies for interfering with the unrestricted desire to know – the various forms of biases, as he calls them. See *Insight*, 214–27, 244–57.

56 *MT*, 157.

57 See *Insight*, 214–27, 244–67.

58 Ibid., 206.

59 Ibid., 276–9.

60 See, for example, *MT*, 241. The notion of intellectual conversion will be discussed further in chapter 2, section 2.6.2, and chapter 8.

61 As Lonergan rightly notes, "the conditions for the prospective judgment are fulfilled when there are no further pertinent questions. Note that it is not enough to say that the conditions are fulfilled when no further questions occur to me" (*Insight*, 309).

62 For purposes of simplicity, I have omitted discussion of the more complicated question of what is known in a negative judgment. In other words, what do we know when we judge that some intelligible content is not? While sometimes negative judgments simply amount to knowledge that something is not, Lonergan's more nuanced answer is that frequently we know distinctions and differences within reality. See *Insight*, 513–14.

63 See *Insight*, 523.

64 Lonergan introduces his technical terminology of "positions" and "counter-positions" regarding what is real in *Insight*, 413.

65 Ibid., 22.

66 In speaking of the attitudes of ordinary pragmatic people, I do not intend to also include the positions of the philosophers known as pragmatists. For at least some of these philosophers, there can be no direct access to reality from within reasoning as pragmatic-discursive. For the most extreme of these, truth and reality are no more and no less than what pragmatic-discursive reasoning arrives at.

67 The notion of intellectual conversion will be discussed further in chapter 8.

68 Lonergan refers to the "borrowed contents" of judging; see *Insight*, 300–1.

69 *Verbum*, 192.

70 See Morelli, *At the Threshold of the Halfway House*, and Mathews, *Lonergan's Quest*, 57–71.

71 See *CS*, 218.

72 Ibid.

73 *Insight*, 44.

74 Ibid., 523, 695. Lonergan's fuller account of reality – being – includes distinctions between transcendent and proportionate being, as well as the distinctions among several features of proportionate being that can be analyzed heuristically. However, these further distinctions will be taken up in chapter 13 in their relations to the structure of the human good.

75 *Insight*, 309, emphasis added.

3 Self-Appropriation, Part I

1 *Insight*, 769–70.
2 Ibid., 13
3 *MT*, 168, 246–7, 252.
4 *Insight*, 13. See also 11.
5 Ibid., 343.
6 Ibid., 343–4. On what Lonergan means by "concrete and intelligible unity-identity-whole," see *Insight*, 270–5.
7 *U&B*, 3.
8 Bernard Lonergan, "Christ as Subject: A Reply," in vol. 4 of *Collected Works of Bernard Lonergan*, ed. Frederick E. Crowe and Robert M. Doran (Toronto: University of Toronto Press, 1988), 162–6.
9 See *Insight*, 406–7.
10 Ibid., 3.
11 *CS*, 208.
12 Jürgen Habermas, *Philosophical Discourse of Modernity* (Cambridge, MA: MIT Press, 1987), 296.
13 It would take us too far afield here to discuss the criticisms Habermas, Foucault, and others have levelled against the power-motivations behind the discourses that have structured modern notions of subjectivity, and the ways in which self-affirmation in Lonergan's sense would respond to those criticisms.
14 See Norwood Russell Hanson, *Patterns of Discovery* (Cambridge: Cambridge University Press, 1969), 4–30.
15 *Insight*, 96.
16 See ibid., 351–2.
17 Ibid., 406–7.
18 See chapter 2, section 2.4.4. For Lonergan's rejection of "introspection," see *Insight*, 344.
19 Paul Ricoeur, *Oneself as Another*, trans. Kathleen Blamey (Chicago: University of Chicago Press, 1992), 11. Ricoeur proceeds to trace Nietzsche's critique and its difficulties, in part making it clear that Nietzsche regards all mediation as distorting (e.g., see 14). In this way, it appears that Nietzsche's critique operates with an unexamined assumption that objectivity is possible only if there could be immediate contact with the "already out there now," an immediacy which never happens in human thought or linguistic performance. If, however, objectivity is not immediate contact with the already out there, but is a matter of "an unrestricted intention and an unconditioned result," then the generality of Nietzsche's critique must be reconsidered. But this would take us too far afield here.
20 *Insight*, 344, emphasis added.
21 *MT*, 7n2.

22 See, for example, Patrick H. Byrne, "Lonergan's Philosophy of the Natural Sciences and Christian Faith in *Insight*," in *Going Beyond Essentialism: Bernard J. F. Lonergan, an Atypical Neo-Scholastic*, ed. Cloe Taddei-Ferretti (Naples, Italy: Nella sede dell'Istituto, 2012), 81–99.

23 Peter Beer, SJ, *An Introduction to Bernard Lonergan* (Victoria, Australia: Sid Harta, 2010); Brian Cronin, C.S.Sp., *Foundations of Philosophy: Lonergan's Cognitional Theory and Epistemology* (Nairobi, Kenya: Consolata Institute of Philosophy, 1999) (first Internet edition at http://www.lonergan.org/online_books/cronin/table_of_contents.htm); Flanagan, *The Quest*; Mark D. Morelli, *Self-Posession: Being at Home in Conscious Performance* (Chestnut Hill, MA: The Lonergan Institute, 2015).

24 But offering in-depth exercises in heightening experiences of the cognitional activities is not possible here, as it would add even much more length to this already-lengthy book.

25 See *U&B*, 14–17.

26 *Insight*, 18.

27 Ibid., 12–13, 348. See also 11–14, 22, 350–1.

28 Ibid., 590.

29 Ibid., 5.

30 Ibid., 359–60.

31 Ibid., 13.

4 The Structure of Ethical Intentionality

1 *Insight*, 641.

2 Ibid., 23; see also 641.

3 Yet it is possible to infer what he likely thought about it at that time from his discussions of practical insight, practical reflection, and decision. See *Insight*, 632–9.

4 Bernard Lonergan, "Healing and Creating in History," in *A Third Collection*, ed. Frederick E. Crowe, SJ (New York: Paulist Press, 1985), 106; cited hereafter as "H&CH."

5 Flanagan, *The Quest*, 197, with a variant formulation at 223–4.

6 I will use "choosing" and "deciding" interchangeably, which is to say I will use both terms interchangeably to refer to one and the same act of consciousness. Likewise with "choice" and "decision."

7 *MT*, 53. Strictly speaking, being responsible also includes and incorporates the other three transcendental precepts: Be attentive. Be intelligent. Be reasonable. Later Lonergan added "Be loving" as the fifth transcendental precept, which sublates the other four.

8 Lonergan's own use of the exact phrase "intentional responses to value" appears in *MT*, 38, but is implicit in the fuller elaboration on pages 30–1.

See Dietrich von Hildebrand, *Christian Ethics* (New York: David McKay, 1953), 191ff; cited hereafter as von Hildebrand, *CE*.

9 Strictly speaking, the acts of factual cognition are also structured by affective intentional responses to value, although Lonergan did not explicitly advert to this fact in his essay "Cognitional Structure." The patterning of our experiences does take place under the auspices of our "interests and concerns" which flow from our feelings and our decisions. Likewise, when we make responsible decisions about which lines of inquiry we will pursue in the immediate future, and which must be deferred, these decisions are also profoundly informed by our feelings for values.

10 For a complementary list of ethical questions, see Brian Cronin, *Value Ethics: A Lonergan Perspective* (Nairobi, Kenya: Consolata Institute of Philosophy, 2006), 129–30; cited hereafter as Cronin, *Value Ethics*.

11 Bernard Lonergan, "Faith and Beliefs," in *PTP: 1965–1980*, 37; cited hereafter as "Faith and Beliefs."

12 Jane Jacobs, *The Death and Life of Great American Cities* (New York: The Modern Library, 1993), 7–8.

13 *Insight*, 201.

14 Ibid., 197–9.

15 See Arrhenius, "On the Influence of Carbonic Acid in the Air upon the Temperatures of the Ground," *Philosophical Magazine and Journal of Science* 5, vol. 41 (April 1896): 237–76. Available at http://www.rsc.org/images/Arrhenius1896_tcm18-173546.pdf

16 *MT*, 241. See also "Faith and Beliefs," 36–7.

17 Cronin, *Value Ethics*, 139–40.

18 For a parallel treatment of ethical reflection and value judgments, see Cronin, *Value Ethics*, 187–93. While I am essentially in agreement with most of Cronin's account, I differ in at least two respects. The first is minor; I have preferred to use the term "reflective understanding of ethical value as virtually unconditioned" in place of his phrase "deliberative insight" (where he follows Michael Vertin). Deliberation implies decision as its outcome, whereas reflections leading to reflective understandings of a value judgment as virtually unconditioned can extend to values other than the values of decisions to be made. Cronin himself discusses several such examples (191–3). The second difference is more substantial, and it has to do with the role played in value and ethical reflection by feelings as intentional responses. On those differences, see section 4.6.1 and chapters 5–10 of this book, and compare Cronin, *Value Ethics*, 245–50.

19 Although I have presented the "should" and "worthwhile" questions with the subject "I," it should not be assumed that this is an individualistic, solitary enterprise. Frequently we ask, "Is it worthwhile for us to do it?" and "Should we do it?" Chapters 11–13 explore the interpersonal situatedness of our acts

of ethical intentionality. To introduce that discussion here would disrupt the continuity of the overview of the structure of ethical intentionality being presented. For the moment, it should be noted that even when we ask, "Should we do it?," it is our own individual acts of deliberating and deciding that determine whether or not we speak the words of this question to others, and whether or not we enter into verbal discussion of the merits of the joint course of action, and, ultimately, it is our own acts of deliberating and deciding that determine whether or not we join in the joint action.

20 Lonergan remarked, "Judgments of value differ in content but not in structure from judgments of fact" (*MT*, 37).

21 *Insight*, 633.

22 Ibid., 729–30. We will return to the analysis of believing as such in section 4.8.

23 Ibid., 633–4.

24 See *Verbum*, 56–7 and 76–7.

25 See Mark J. Doorley, *The Place of the Heart in Lonergan's Ethics* (Lanham, MD: University Press of America, 1996), 1–15.

26 See chapter 5, section 5.3.

27 *MT*, 37.

28 Ibid., 30–1.

29 No doubt some will object that it is possible to have it both ways – that, for example, one can choose to earn great wealth and to be generous. Stated in this abstract fashion, these of course are not incompatible alternatives for choice, although the concrete realities tend to make it rather difficult to do both proficiently. Be that as it may, the question for choice is always some concrete value delivered by the judgment of value – "To consent to the value of pursuing wealth at this time in these ways – or refusing the value of pursuing wealth at this time in these ways." Neither of these choices excludes choices about being generous, but refusing this precise value judgment does in fact exclude consenting to it.

30 *MT*, 240.

31 See chapter 2, section 2.5.5.

32 René Descartes, "Second Meditation," *Discourse on Method and Meditations*, trans. Donald A. Cress (Indianapolis, IN: Hackett, 1980), 62.

33 See *Insight*, 476–8 and 494–504.

34 Ibid., 636–45.

35 Lonergan discusses these habits of choosing under the heading of "willingness." See *Insight*, 621–2.

36 Ibid., 636–9 and 643–5.

37 Ibid., 650–3.

38 Human choice in this life, of course, also presupposes the vast networks of pre-conscious neurological and biological acts that condition the functioning of the conscious structure.

39 The topic of comparative value judgments will be explored in chapter 9.

40 *Insight*, 729–30. Notice that unlike chapter 18, here Lonergan explicitly identifies the act of reflective understanding, the judgment of value, and the decision.

41 That is to say, when you attend to the experiences of your acts of believing, do you discover yourself to have performed an infinite regress before arriving at your act of believing? This is an example of the kind of thing that is involved in the more comprehensive meaning of self-appropriation. We will return to this topic in chapter 10.

5 Kinds of Feelings

1 After this book was completed, I discovered that Robert J. Solomon proposed a similar division of feelings in his *The Passions: Emotions and the Meaning of Life* (Indianapolis, IN: Hackett, 1993), especially 60, 68–88, and 96–7; cited hereafter as Solomon, *Passions*. Solomon prefers "passions" or "emotions" to "feelings" or "affects," respectively, and argues that the word "feelings" should be reserved solely to designate what I have called "somatic feelings." Although I agree with much of what Solomon has written, there are also notable differences between his approach and my own. It would be too great a diversion at this point to examine those differences.

2 *MT*, 30.

3 von Hildebrand, *CE*, 191ff.

4 Max Scheler, *Formalism in Ethics and Non-Formal Ethics of Values*, trans. Manfred S. Frings and Roger L. Funk (Evanstone, IL: Northwestern University Press, 1973), 255–9; cited hereafter as Scheler, *Formalism/Values*.

5 Scheler, *Formalism/Values*, 90–3.

6 von Hildebrand, *CE*, 191.

7 On the relationship between *noetic* and *noematic*, see chapter 2, section 2.4.2.

8 *MT*, 30, emphasis added.

9 As Scheler's example reveals, intentional feelings respond to and combine with somatic feelings to yield important feeling complexes that, in large part, are what we call the "experiences of embodiment." This is explored in more detail in chapter 6.

10 See *MT*, 66–7.

11 See *Insight*, 492–3.

12 Because cnidarians lack a central nervous system – having instead nerve nets – it is uncertain that they actually have consciousness of feelings. The point here, however, is that differentiations of somatic feelings ultimately derive from structures originally correlated with touch.

13 *MT*, 30.

14 von Hildebrand, *CE*, 191.

15 Ibid.
16 *Insight*, 412–15.
17 *Topics*, 83–5.
18 *Insight*, 214–19.
19 See also ibid., 496.
20 Given the objectives of this book, it is impossible to discuss the wide range
   of scientific research that correlates neurophysiological functioning with
   somatic feelings. This chapter can only acknowledge this work, and argue
   for some claims that run counter to some of the extra-scientific, reductionist
   claims made by some of these researchers.
21 See Lonergan's comments on this; *Insight*, 608–9.
22 Solomon proposes a similar division of feelings ("passions" or "emotions," as
   he prefers). See Solomon, *Passions* 70–2.
23 Aristotle, *NE*, 20–1, 1099a7–21. Since virtuous actions are the meaning of
   happiness, and this is what everyone desires (4, 1094a19), pleasures taken in
   virtuous deed would be at least partial satisfactions of the desire for happiness.
24 Augustine, *Confessions*, 21 [I.1].
25 Martin Heidegger, *Being and Time*, trans. John Maquarrie and Edward
   Robinson (Oxford: Blackwell, 1962), 172.
26 Robert Doran, "Two Ways of Being Conscious: The Notion of Psychic
   Conversion," *Method: Journal of Lonergan Studies* 3 (2012): 11.

6 Feelings as Intentional Responses and Horizons of Feelings

1 *MT*, 31.
2 I am here assuming a very obtuse spectator who has neither affects nor even
  questions about the value of what he sees taking place in the sporting event.
  Questions of value, after all, are one kind of desire – a desire for value answers.
3 Most often Lonergan uses only the phrase "intentional responses" for this
  category of feelings, but he also does use the entire phrase "intentional
  responses to values" (*MT*, 38).
4 *MT*, 30.
5 Ibid., 31, emphasis added.
6 Ibid., emphasis added. The second sentence continues, "… about evils
  to be lamented or remedied, about the good that can, might, must be
  accomplished." I omitted this part of the sentence (which clearly does speak
  of feelings in relation to values and disvalues) in order to emphasize the
  fact that Lonergan also speaks of non-values as objects of feelings as well.
  For the moment, I am prescinding from the further complications raised by
  Lonergan's remarks that certain questions also intend values; see *MT*, 34.
  On this, see section 6.5.
7 von Hildebrand, *CE*, 191.

8 See especially ibid., 191–2, which shows that von Hildebrand conceives intentionality in general on the model of "knowing as taking a look": "Perception is necessarily a perception *of something* extraneous to my mind."

9 See *Insight*, 413. See also chapter 2 of this book.

10 Michael Vertin was the first to draw upon Lonergan's *Verbum* distinctions among the objects of insights in order to clarify the nature of feelings as intentional responses in "Judgments of Value for the Later Lonergan," *Method: Journal of Lonergan Studies* 13 (1995): 232–3. For a further discussion of this topic, see Patrick H. Byrne, "Feelings as Intentional, Feelings as Responses, and Value Judgments," in *Lonergan's Legacy: Ethics and Religion*, special issue of *Theoforum*, ed. Mary Beth Yount and Kenneth Melchin, forthcoming.

11 See Ibid., 88, 138–51, 173–80.

12 Ibid., 149.

13 Ibid., 150.

14 Ibid., 172.

15 Ibid., 174–5.

16 Ibid., 175. Lonergan also argues that Aquinas also uses *quidditas sive natura rei materialis* and "universal" to designate this purely intelligible object.

17 Ibid., 173. See also *Insight*, 3.

18 *Verbum*, 150, emphasis added.

19 See *Insight*, 402–4.

20 *Verbum*, 185. See also *Insight*, 431–2, especially note 2.

21 *Verbum*, 186.

22 Aristotle, *NE*, V.8, 1135b28–9.

23 *MT*, 245.

24 Scheler, *Formalism/Values*, 35.

25 Ibid., 68.

26 See chapter 5, section 5.2.

27 *Insight*, 706.

28 See, for example, "feelings respond *to* values" (*MT*, 31, emphasis added).

29 *MT*, 61.

30 Ibid., 64.

31 *Topics*, 218.

32 *MT*, 63–4.

33 See *Insight*, 316–17.

34 For fuller discussion, see chapter 11.

35 Bill Kinser and Neil Kleinman, *The Dream that Was No More a Dream* (New York: Harper and Row, 1969), 13.

36 It is almost always the case that distortions in feelings result in distorted judgments of fact as well.

37 See, for instance, Amanda Szabo-Reed, Florence Breslin, et al., "Brain Function Predictors and Outcome of Weight Loss and Weight Loss Maintenance,"

Contemporary Clinical Trials 40 (19 December 2014), published online at
http://www.contemporaryclinicaltrials.com/article/S1551-7144(14)00193-
1/abstract, for their discussion of the observed complex neurophysiological
hunger response to the simple sight of food.

38 While particular questions for intelligence only indirectly intend the
intelligibilities that will be directly intended by the insights that satisfy
the tensions of inquiry, the unrestricted desire to know is the immediate
relation to being for humans. Both particular questions as well as particular
insights and judgments gradually and incrementally mediate our immediate
relationship of being into a growing understanding and knowledge of
being. But while for humans the immediate relationship to being is through
the unrestricted desire to know, this is not yet a direct intention of being.
The direct intention of being is to be attained only in an unrestricted act of
understanding that understands everything about everything.

39 For the discussion of judgments and decisions of comparative value, see
chapter 9.

40 See Robert A. Caro, *The Power Broker: Robert Moses and the Fall of New York*
(New York: Random House, 1974).

41 Lonergan also uses the term "horizon" in this way, although not
specifically with regard to feelings as intentional responses. See, for
example, *MT*, 235–7.

42 *MT*, 31.

43 This actually did happen in 2002 when Dr. David C. Arndt left Mt. Auburn
Hospital in Cambridge, Massachusetts, in the middle of surgery to carry
out a banking transaction. See "Surgeon Who Left Operation to Run an
Errand Is Suspended," *New York Times*, 9 August 2002, http://www.nytimes.
com/2002/08/09/us/surgeon-who-left-an-operation-to-run-an-errand-is-
suspended.html

44 *MT*, 32.

45 Max Scheler, *Ressentiment*, ed. Lewis A. Coser, trans. William W. Holdheim (New
York: Schoken Books, 1961), 53–5; cited hereafter as Scheler, *Ressentiment.*

7 Feelings and Value Reflection

1 *Insight*, 308.

2 See ibid., 501, 633–4.

3 Jane Austen, *Pride and Prejudice* (New York: Bantam Books, 1981), 52; cited
hereafter as Austen, *P&P.*

4 Ibid., 96.

5 Ibid., 142.

6 That pride can be a genuine virtue is difficult for most contemporary people to
accept. Virtuous pride is not to be confused with vices such as haughtiness or

conceitedness, and Jane Austen was well aware of the differences. On pride as a virtue and the deviations from it, see Aristotle, *NE*, IV.3, 1123a34–1125a35.

7 Strictly speaking, Elizabeth did raise a new question for value judgment – "Is marriage to Darcy worthwhile for me?" – and she responded to it negatively. However, the sequel provides a much clearer example of how a new question emerges out of habitual valuing.

8 Austen, *P&P*, 153.

9 Ibid., 71–2.

10 Ibid., 153.

11 Ibid., 155, emphasis in the original.

12 Ibid., 156.

13 Augustine, *Confessions*, X.33.

14 See chapter 5, section 5.7.

15 See Alexis de Tocqueville, *Democracy in America*, trans. George Lawrence (Garden City, NY: Anchor Books, 1969), hereafter cited as de Tocqueville, *Democracy*; Bellah et al., *Habits*; Robert Putnam, *Bowling Alone: The Collapse and Revival of American Community* (New York: Simon and Schuster, 2000); see also his earlier study, *Making Democracy Work: Civic Traditions in Modern Italy* (Princeton, NJ: Princeton University Press, 1994).

16 See, for example, Alasdair MacIntyre, *After Virtue* (Notre Dame, IN: University of Notre Dame Press, 1981), 23–4.

17 *Insight*, 309.

18 See also ibid., 634.

19 See chapter 2, section 2.4.4.

20 Jane Austen, *Northanger Abbey* (New York: Bantam Books, 1985). This episode and all quotes are taken from chapter 11.

21 Ibid., 66–7.

22 In chapter 11, following Lonergan, I argue that values are always concrete. This means that each new authentic decision actualizes a new, concrete value. In this case, the trial called for the actualization of a new value, a new instance of the value of justice. While our trial did not create a dramatically innovative new departure in the realm of justice as is portrayed, for example, in Aescyleus' *Eumenides*, it was nevertheless an instance of value not previously actualized concretely.

23 Recall that "What should I do?" is a compact formulation of three closely related questions: "What could I do?," "Is it worthwhile for me to do it?," and "Should I do it?"

24 See, for example, Eugene T. Gendlin, *Focusing* (New York: Bantam Books, 1981).

25 The goods that are brought about by performance of ethical intentionality will be explored in greater detail in chapters 11 and 12.

26 See *Insight*, 642.

27 As Aristotle puts it, "making [*poesis*] aims at an end distinct from the act
    of making, whereas in doing [*praxis*] the end cannot be other than the act
    itself; doing well is in itself the end" (Aristotle, *NE*, VI.5, 1140b 5–6).
28 *Insight*, 624.
29 On the habitual dimensions of our ethical behaviour, see *Insight*, 621–4 and
    643–7; for our unethical habitualities, see 653–6.
30 St. Paul, *Romans*, 7:18–19.
31 See Michael Vertin, "Judgments of Value for the Later Lonergan," *Method:
    Journal of Lonergan Studies* 13 (1995): 221–48, and "Deliberative Insight
    Revisited," unpublished lecture delivered at the West Coast Methods
    Institute, Loyola Marymount University, 28–30 April 2011, communicated
    by the author, cited hereafter as Vertin, "Judgments," and Vertin, "Insight,"
    respectively. The earlier article tends to focus more on values of possible
    decisions to be made, while the later one focuses on judgments of value
    about realities already actualized. This distinction is not hard and fast, as
    Vertin envisions a deliberative process "that terminates in a decision to
    enjoy the actual value" (Vertin, "Judgments," 239), and presumably for this
    reason regards both as *deliberative* insights. While I do agree that there are
    indeed profound decisions to accept the values of actualities not of one's
    own making, I also contend that there are value reflective processes that
    simply terminate in judgments of value without any immediate necessity of a
    decision to accept those values. See also Vertin, "Insight," n11.
32 Vertin, "Judgments," 231. The context of this remark makes it clear that
    "*affective* cognition" means a feeling that is an intentional response to value.
33 More precisely, "the condition to which the link connects the hypothetically
    true judgment of value is not simply experiential data but, more narrowly,
    the data of consciousness that are my positive feelings toward the reality
    whose value I am wondering about; and the fulfillment of that condition is
    my concrete experience of those feelings" (Vertin, "Insight," 9).
34 Vertin, "Judgments," 232–3.
35 See chapter 10.
36 Vertin "Judgments," 235 and 243, and Vertin, "Insight," 7–8 and 11.
37 Vertin "Insight," 13.
38 See chapter 4, section 4.7.

8 Horizons of Feelings, Conversion, and Objectivity

1 Max Weber, "Science as a Vocation," in *From Max Weber: Essays in Sociology*, ed.
   Hans H. Gerth and C. Wright Mills (New York: Oxford University Press, 1946),
   129–56. The subtleties of Weber's own account of the fact/value distinction
   are not always appreciated by all who cite him in support of their views.
2 *Insight*, 523; also 413.

3 See also Flanagan, *The Quest*, 199–201.

4 See ibid., 200, 212.

5 See ibid., 208–9. Lonergan remarks that even a decisive commitment to what he calls moral conversion "falls far short of moral perfection" unless it is followed up by a great many further decisions. "Deciding is one thing, doing is another. One has yet to uncover and root out one's individual, group, and general bias ... One has to keep scrutinizing one's intentional responses to values and their implicit scales of preference. One has to listen to criticism and to protest. One has to remain ready to learn from others. For moral knowledge is the proper possession only of morally good men and, until one has merited that title, one has still to advance and learn" (*MT*, 240).

6 *MT*, 32. See further 32–4 for Lonergan's appreciation of the richness and complexity of what I have called "horizons of feeling."

7 Ibid., 34.

8 "The Subject," 82.

9 *Insight*, 348–52.

10 *MT*, 34.

11 Ibid., 36.

12 Ibid., 38, 104, 233, 241–2, 289, 338.

13 *Insight*, 373.

14 *MT*, 105–6.

15 For the sake of clarity, it is worth paraphrasing the point made in an earlier footnote in chapter 6. Particular questions of value only indirectly intend the values that will be directly known in the judgments of value that properly resolve the tensions of those questions. Moreover, the unrestricted notion of value is our immediate relation to the wholeness of the good, the totality of value, for humans. The series of particular questions, as well as particular judgments of value, gradually and incrementally mediate our immediate relationship to the totality of value through growth in knowledge and performance of value. But while for humans the immediate relationship to the totality of value is through the unrestricted desire to know, this is not yet a direct intention of the totality of value. Only a "basic," direct intention of value is attained in the dynamic state of being-in-love in an unrestricted fashion, but it is unconditionally attained only in the unity of an unrestricted act of valuing and loving everything good about every good thing, which is unique to God.

16 *MT*, 106.

17 Ibid., 105–6.

18 Ibid., 106.

19 *PTP: 1965–1980*, 22–3.

20 See Frederick E. Crowe, "Lonergan's Universalist View of Religion," *Method: Journal of Lonergan Studies* 12 (1994): 147–79.

21 *MT*, 32.

22 Regarding the notion of orientation, see ibid., 51–2.

23 See *Insight*, 476–84 for a more precise discussion.

24 Ibid., 242.

25 See, for example, *MT*, 237–8.

26 See section 8.3.4.

27 See, for example, *MT*, 121–2.

28 Ibid., 238–44.

29 See Robert M. Doran, *Theology and the Dialectics of History* (Toronto: University of Toronto Press, 2001), 42–63, 211–94, 630–56; cited hereafter as Doran, *TDH*.

30 See chapter 3.

31 *MT*, 238.

32 Ibid., 240.

33 Ibid., 241.

34 Ibid., 116.

35 Ibid., 106.

36 Ibid., 240.

37 Doran, *TDH*, 248.

38 *MT*, 38.

39 Chapter 7, section 7.5.

40 "The Subject," 83.

41 See, for example, "The Subject," and Bernard Lonergan, *Phenomenology and Logic: The Boston College Lectures on Mathematical Logic and Existentialism*, vol. 18 of *Collected Works of Bernard Lonergan*, ed. Philip J. McShane (Toronto: University of Toronto Press, 2001).

42 "The Subject," 83.

43 Crysdale, *Embracing Travail*, 138.

44 *MT*, 241–2.

45 This raises the question of whether or not moral conversion entails religious conversion – since religious value is included in the whole of values. This question will be addressed in chapter 9, section 9.5, once the issue of the scale of value preference has been discussed more fully.

46 *MT*, 38.

47 Judgments of comparative value and their corresponding scales of value will be taken up in further detail in chapter 9.

48 Elizabeth Murray has also argued for "a negative and a positive dimension" to moral conversion. See her "Conscience and Passion: Moral Conversion as Self-Transcendence," in *2014 Proceedings of the American Catholic Philosophical Association*, vol. 88 (Charlottesville, VA: Philosophy Documentation Center, forthcoming), cited hereafter as Murray, "Conscience and Passion." Her analysis draws upon Lonergan's remarks regarding two levels in his structure of the human good. Her analysis will be considered more fully in chapter 9, section 9.8.

49 *MT*, 31.

50 Ibid., 32.

51 Ibid., 240. We will return to the stages of development of moral conversion in chapter 11, section 11.6. There the connection between the levels in the structure of the human good and the stages of moral conversion will be explored. At the lowest stage, what Lonergan called "particular goods" function as the highest goods for human choice. Particular goods include, but go beyond, objects of somatic pleasure and comfort, and particular ills include, but go beyond, objects of somatic pain and disturbance.

52 *MT*, 240.

53 Ibid., 292; see also 265.

54 Augustine, *Confessions*, VII.12. See also, "evil is nothing but the removal of good until finally nothing good remains" (III.7).

55 Ibid., VII.12–13.

56 Ibid., VII.18.

57 Rosemary Haughton, *The Transformation of Man: A Study of Conversion and Community* (Springfield, IL: Templegate, 1980), 38.

58 Fyodor Dostoevsky, epilogue to *Crime and Punishment*, trans. Constance Garnett (NY: Random House, Inc., 1994), 2.628.

59 Austen, *P&P*, 276–7.

60 *MT*, 64.

61 Ibid., 66–7.

62 Doran, "Two Ways of Being Conscious," 1–18.

9 Judgments of Comparative Value

1 *MT*, 36.

2 Robert Nisbet, *The Quest for Community* (London: Oxford University Press, 1953), 212, quoting vol. 2 of Hegel's *Aesthetics*. See also Robert R. Williams, *Hegel's Ethics of Recognition* (Berkeley: University of California Press, 1997), 348.

3 *Insight*, 468–9; see also 195.

4 George Eliot, *Middlemarch* (New York: Bantam Books, 1992), 267; cited hereafter as Eliot, *Middlemarch*.

5 Ibid., 267.

6 Ibid., 538.

7 Ibid., 591.

8 Ibid., 595.

9 Ibid., 762.

10 See Max Scheler, "*Ordo Amoris*," in *Selected Philosophical Essays* (Evanston, IL: Northwestern University Press, 1973), 98–135.

11 Scheler, *Ressentiment*, 58.

12 Ibid., 73.

13 Ibid., 77, emphasis added.

14 For a more detailed discussion, see Patrick H. Byrne, "Which Scale of Value Preference? Lonergan, Scheler, von Hildebrand and Doran," in *Meaning and History in Systematic Theology: Essays in Honor of Robert M. Doran, S.J.*, ed. John Dadosky (Milwaukee, WI: Marquette University Press, 2009), 19–49.

15 *MT*, 31.

16 A fuller critical engagement with the host of other formulations of scales of value priority falls to a much larger scholarly project that would be facilitated by the method of ethics that is explored in the final chapters of this book.

17 Scheler, *Formalism/Values*, 100.

18 Ibid., 103–110.

19 Ibid., 108. Lonergan of course assigns a much higher (cultural) value to scientific/explanatory knowledge, because for him it is not reducible to its technological applications in "controlling" nature.

20 Ibid., 93.

21 See, for example, von Hildebrand, *CE*, 237, 239.

22 Ibid., 64–71.

23 Ibid., 40, 43.

24 Ibid., 40.

25 Ibid., 136.

26 *MT*, 31.

27 Ibid. See chapters 11 and 12 for a fuller discussion of "the good of order."

28 *MT*, 32.

29 Flanagan, *The Quest*, 202.

30 *MT*, 32.

31 See also his *De Redemptione*, soon to be published in volume 9 of *Collected Works of Bernard Lonergan*, translated and edited by Robert J. Doran and Jeremy Wilkins, cited hereafter as *De Redemptione Draft*. I am grateful to Robert Doran, SJ, for making this draft available to me.

32 *Insight*, 261.

33 *MT*, 104.

34 Cronin, *Value Ethics*, 164. See also Patrick H. Byrne, "Moral Value, Personal Value and History," *Lonergan Workshop* 25 (2013): 13–52.

35 See Flanagan, *The Quest*, 200–1.

36 Even the personal value of another person is realized in some of our choices and courses of action, as when we stand up for the dignity of another person or love that person unconditionally. This will be explored further in the next chapter.

37 Scheler also makes this distinction, but does not integrate it with the self-transcending dynamism of ethical inquiry and responses that I have developed here and in chapter 7. See Scheler, *Formalism/Values*, 27–9.

38 Beginning with Kant, modern ethical and political philosophy has attempted to ground the supreme value of personhood in respect. While this is an important development in the history of ethics, it would require a separate study to adequately argue the insufficiency of this approach.

39 See Max Scheler, *The Nature of Sympathy*, trans. Peter Heath (New Brunswick, NJ: Transaction, 2008), 70–1.

40 I am grateful to Fred Lawrence for making this clear to me. See also Flanagan, *The Quest*, 203–4.

41 *MT*, 350.

42 Ibid., 105–6.

43 Gregory Boyle, *Tattoos on the Heart: The Power of Boundless Compassion* (New York: Free Press, 2010), 87.

44 Tad Dunne, *Doing Better: The Next Revolution in Ethics* (Milwaukee, WI: Marquette University Press, 2010), 33.

45 *Insight*, 343.

46 See also von Hildebrand, *CE*, 222.

47 Ibid., 222–3.

48 Max Scheler acknowledges this when he speaks of the endurance of a value apart from changing vicissitudes: "When we execute the act of loving a person (on the basis of his personal value) … [the] *phenomenon of endurance* is implicit in both the [personal] *value* to which we are directed and the experienced value of the *act of love*" (Scheler, *Formalism/Values*, 91). It should be noted, however, that Scheler makes it sound as though there is a form of consciousness of personal value that somehow pre-exists acts of love, rather than human acts of love being the acts that bring to consciousness personal value precisely as lovely.

49 This is a level that does not appear explicitly in Lonergan's scale of values (see *MT*, 31), or even in von Hildebrand's scale. It does however appear in Scheler's scale. See section 9.4.1 above.

50 Something like this seems to follow from Scheler's statement: "A positive value ought to be and a negative value ought not to be" (Scheler, *Formalism/Values*, 82). If value *A* is higher than *B*, and if time does not permit the realization of both, it seems to follow that *A* should be chosen over *B* just because it is higher. See also pp. 26–30.

51 On Lonergan's understanding of sublation, see *MT*, 316; also 241.

52 Ibid., 31.

53 Scheler, *Formalism/Values*, 89, emphasis is Scheler's own.

54 Ibid., 87, emphasis is Scheler's own.

55 Ibid., 89–90, emphasis is Scheler's own.

56 *MT*, 115.

57 There is also an important, second role that reason plays in evaluating and in authentic moral living. This is the role played by experiencing, inquiring,

understanding, reflecting, and judging in comparing our actual scale of preference to *the* normative scale of preference. Reason will not "make" us choose the authentic scale of values over our own degenerate scale and cannot by itself produce any conversion. But reason is needed in order to clarify and to present and to effectively communicate *the* scale and *why* it is the scale. What one chooses to do in response to such presentations and communications is the most radical exercise of freedom, and radical freedom cannot ultimately be caused even by reason.

58 See *Insight*, 214–22 and 244–51.

59 I am grateful to my students for pressing me to think through this issue.

60 For but one of numerous examples, see Bellah et al., *Habits*, 3–8. Of course, by "personal values" Lonergan does *not* mean individualism – that something is of value merely because an individual arbitrarily chooses it. Rather, he means the values that pertain to persons *qua* "originating values" (*MT*, 51, and *Insight*, 601).

61 See also chapter 8, section 8.3.3 of this book.

62 *U&B*, 234.

63 Murray, "Conscience and Passion," 4.

64 For details, see chapters 11 and 12.

65 Murray, "Conscience and Passion," 11.

66 See chapters 11 and 12.

67 Murray, "Conscience and Passion," 16.

68 On feelings as self-transcending see, *MT*, 37–41.

69 Ibid., 285.

70 See chapter 14.

71 *MT*, 240; see also 110.

72 See chapters 15 and 16.

73 A scale is intact, of course, when religious conversion as well as moral conversion is operative; religious conversion is the existential foundation for the level of religious values being properly preferred in one's own individual scale of value preference.

10 Self-Appropriation, Part II

1 Kant, *GMM*, 9 <397>.

2 Aristotle, *NE*, II.1 1103a17–18. This phrase is frequently translated as "moral virtue," although there is no distinction between "ethical" and "moral" in Aristotle's terminology.

3 Ibid., II.1 1103a1.

4 Ibid., II.1 1103b14–23.

5 Ibid., II.6.

6 Ibid., I.3 1094b14–17.

7 Ibid., II.3 1105b4–9.

8 See Patrick H. Byrne, "*Phronêsis* and Commonsense Judgment: Aristotle and Lonergan on Moral Wisdom," *Virtues and Virtue Theories: Proceedings of the American Catholic Philosophical Association* 71 (1997): 163–77.

9 Kant, *GMM*, 9 and 14–16 <397 and 401–4>.

10 See "On a Supposed Right to Lie Because of Philanthropic Concerns," Kant, *GMM*, 63–67, <425–30>.

11 In some cases, of course, we may objectively judge that there is more than one possible course of action that would be valuable for us to do, though this is less frequent than is usually supposed. In such cases, one still has to choose among the options, since it is not possible to do them all, and it is not ethical to do none. In the end, the structure of ethical intentionality shifts, then, to ask, "Among the several possible ethically worthwhile things to do, which one should I do, since I know I must choose one?" Here very subtle gradations in our scale of values come forward to guide these ethical reflections and deliberations.

12 See chapters 11 and 12.

13 These steps are outlined by Martin Luther King Jr. in his "Letter from a Birmingham Jail," in James M. Washington (ed.), *A Testament of Hope: The Essential Writings and Speeches of Martin Luther King, Jr.* (San Francisco: HarperCollins, 1991), 289–302.

14 I am grateful to Christopher Berger for pointing out the importance of including these remarks on civil disobedience.

15 A method for approaching the critical evaluation of laws and institutions will be considered in chapters 15 and 16.

16 For a much more complete and especially insightful study of Lonergan's understanding of authenticity in comparison with the influential accounts offered by Martin Heidegger and Charles Taylor, see Brian J. Braman, *Meaning and Authenticity: Bernard Lonergan and Charles Taylor on the Drama of Authentic Human Existence* (Toronto: University of Toronto Press, 2008).

17 *CS*, 208.

18 *MT*, 38.

19 *Insight*, 461.

20 *MT*, 38.

21 Friedrich Nietzsche, *Beyond Good and Evil*, in *The Basic Writings of Nietzsche*, trans. and ed. Walter Kaufmann (New York: The Modern Library, 1968), 279.

22 *Topics*, 217.

23 *Insight*, 3.

24 See Flanagan, *The Quest*, 199.

25 See chapters 11 and 13.

26 See chapter 4, section 4.2.

27 It is for this reason that Flanagan emphasizes the importance of
   understanding feelings. See Flanagan, *The Quest*, 199.

11 The Human Good Described

1 *Insight*, 374.
2 Ibid., 372 and 384.
3 Ibid., 628. For details, see *Topics*, 33–41, and *MT*, 47–52.
4 "The Subject," 83.
5 Cronin, *Value Ethics*, 164, and Byrne, "Moral Value, Personal Value and History."
6 The surd within an individual's life is parallel to what Lonergan refers to as
   "the social surd." See *Insight*, 255–7.
7 Bernard Lonergan, *Grace and Freedom: Operative Grace in the Thought of St.
   Thomas Aquinas*, vol. 1 of *Collected Works of Bernard Lonergan*, ed. Frederick
   E. Crowe and Robert M. Doran (Toronto: University of Toronto Press,
   2000); *Insight*, chapter 20; Bernard Lonergan, "The Supernatural Order"
   [translation of *De Ente Supernaturali: Supplementum schematicum*], trans.
   Michael G. Shields, in vol. 19 of *Collected Works of Bernard Lonergan*, ed.
   Robert M. Doran and H. Daniel Monsour (Toronto: University of Toronto
   Press, 2011), 53–255. For the development, see J. Michael Stebbins, *The
   Divine Initiative: Grace, World-Order and Human Freedom in the Early Writings of
   Bernard Lonergan* (Toronto: University of Toronto Press, 1995).
8 *MT*, 48.
9 I am using the terms "social ecosystem" or "ethical ecosystem" in place of
   the traditional phrase "the common good." This is because "the common
   good" is all too frequently thought of in an abstract way, as a concept or
   plan, whereas "ecosystem" emphasizes the complex and concrete patterns
   of interdependence that make up every instance of the human good life
   in common. Also, "ecosystem" at least implies situatedness in an ongoing
   evolutionary process (see next section), whereas "the common good" tends
   to be thought of in a timeless fashion. Jane Jacobs objected to the phrase
   "the common good" because it reminded her of the way Robert Moses
   planned the "good" for the citizens of New York City, a "good" that became
   an all-too-real nightmare. See Jacobs, response to Byrne, *Ethics in Making a
   Living*, ed. Fred Lawrence (Chico, CA: Scholars Press, 1989), 186–7.
10 See *Insight*, 234–44.
11 *MT*, 48–52. A series of provisional versions of the structure of the human
   good stretch from Lonergan's essay "Finality, Love, Marriage," in vol. 4 of
   Collected Works of Bernard Lonergan, 17–52, through to *Insight*, 619–21, and
   Topics 33–43.
12 *Topics*, 28–78.
13 Ibid., 33.

14 On the intrinsic worth of institutions, especially as cultural inheritances, see Hugh Heclo, *On Thinking Institutionally* (Boulder, CO: Paradigm, 2008).

15 *Insight*, 199.

16 See Flanagan, *The Quest*, 222.

17 *MT*, 52. See "H&CH," 100–9.

18 See Flanagan, *The Quest*, 224, 229.

19 Nevil Shute, *A Town Like Alice* (New York: Ballentine Books, 1950); cited hereafter as Shute, *TLA*.

20 The novel's protagonist was based on Carry Geysel (Mrs. J.G. Geysel-Vonck) who was part of a group of about 80 Dutch civilians taken prisoner by Japanese forces at Padang, Dutch East Indies, in 1942. Shute, *TLA*, 279.

21 Ibid., 109–10.

22 *Insight*, 142, 234–5. See also chapter 13, section 13.2.

23 Shute, *TLA*, 107.

24 Ibid., 18.

25 Ibid., 27.

26 Ibid., 29.

27 Ibid., 99.

28 Ibid., 107.

29 Ibid.

30 Ibid., 98.

31 Ibid., 113.

32 See, for example, *Gender, Water and Development*, ed. Anne Coles and Tina Wallace (New York: Berg, 2005), and Kuntala Lahiri-Dutt (ed.), *Fluid Bonds: Views on Gender and Water* (Calcutta, India: Stree, 2006).

12 The Human Good: Explanatory Foundations

1 On Lonergan's way of distinguishing between description and explanation, see *Insight*, 188.

2 See Ibid., chapters 2 and 14. In particular: "A heuristic notion, then, is the notion of an unknown content, and it is determined by anticipating the type of act through which the unknown would become known. A heuristic structure is an ordered set of heuristic notions," 417. See also *MT*, chapters 1 and 5.

3 Lonergan criticized as too limited one traditional way of defining the good derived from Aristotle as "*id quod omnia appetunt* (what everything seeks or runs after)" (*Topics*, 28). See also his *De Redemptione Draft*.

4 See *Topics*, 43–8.

5 Ibid., 39.

6 MT, 52.

7 *Topics*, 41.

8 See, for example, ibid., 41–3.

9 *Insight*, 416.

10 Ibid., 626; see also 619.

11 Ibid., 416. See also *U&B*, 195.

12 Implicitly, this also means that another method would have to be developed in order to approach questions about transcendent being. That might be called the "method of extrapolation" (*Insight*, 659) or the "method of analogy" (*U&B*). This method approaches questions about transcendent being by way of their analogical relationships to certain aspects of proportionate being that *can* be known directly through the exercise of human cognitional structure.

13 *Insight*, 416, emphasis added.

14 For the sake of clarity I will temporarily use italics for Lonergan's metaphysical elements *potency*, *form*, and *act* during the explication of his argument for the isomorphism of the acts of knowing and the realities known.

15 *Insight*, 470, 757; see also 509–11 for a statement of the centrality of this "necessary isomorphism" to his metaphysics.

16 Ibid., 457, emphasis added.

17 Strictly speaking, what Lonergan means by "potency, form, and act" is more nuanced than this. For one thing, Lonergan recognized that a proper and productive account of the structure of proportionate being had to be done in the context of the explanatory understanding. This brings about important nuances in the rigorous definitions of potency, form, and act. See *Insight*, 457. However, the technical details of the proper definitions would prove too lengthy a diversion from the objective of this chapter.

18 Ibid., 359–60.

19 Ibid., 359.

20 Ibid., 417.

21 Ibid., 513–14.

22 Ibid., 460–3.

23 Ibid., 509–10.

24 Ibid., 280–3, 287–92, 463–7. We return to this topic in more exacting detail in chapter 14.

25 See *Insight*, 460–73, 478, and 487 for details.

26 Ibid., 504–11, 544–52.

27 Ibid., 23.

28 See chapter 15. See also Patrick H. Byrne, "The Goodness of Being in Lonergan's *Insight*," *American Catholic Philosophical Quarterly* (2007): 43–72.

29 *Topics*, 32. Chapter 13 will endeavour to show how this heuristic of the human good is integrated into a more comprehensive heuristic structure that anticipates the natural and transcendent good as well.

30 Ibid., chapters 2–4.

31 *MT*, 47.

32 Ibid., 51.

33 Ibid. See also *Insight*, 624.
34 *Insight*, 624.
35 *MT*, 51.
36 Ibid., emphasis added.
37 Kant, *GMM*, 16 <405>.
38 *Insight*, 500.
39 *MT*, 50.
40 Ibid.
41 de Tocqueville, *Democracy*, 690–3.
42 *MT*, 51.
43 See ibid., 27–30, for a fuller discussion.
44 *Insight*, 242.
45 *MT*, 48.
46 *Insight*, 238.
47 Ibid., 248.
48 *MT*, 50.
49 *Topics*, 41, emphasis added.
50 *MT*, 39.
51 Ibid., 48.
52 Ibid.
53 *Insight*, 627.
54 Compare, for example, *Insight*, 237–9, 619–21; *Topics*, 33–41; *MT*, 47–52; and Bernard Lonergan, *The Triune God: Systematics*, vol. 12 of *Collected Works of Bernard Lonergan*, trans. Michael G. Shileds, ed. Robert M. Doran and H. Daniel Monsour (Toronto: University of Toronto Press, 2007), 492–3.

13 The Notion and the Ontology of the Good

1 *Insight*, 628.
2 Ibid., 628–9, emphasis added.
3 Ibid., 629.
4 Lonergan developed his account of emergent probability based solely on results from classical and statistical methods (*Insight*, 144–51). *Generalized* emergent probability includes the results from genetic (487) and dialectical methods as well. However, discussing the details of this generalization would require too great a digression at this point.
5 *Insight*, 497; see also 656. Lonergan's comment is actually about "finality," which is more general than generalized emergent probability, because its characteristics are based upon cognitional structure as such, rather than upon particular manifestations of cognitional structure in particular scientific methods.
6 *Insight*, 472.

7 Crysdale, *Embracing Travail,* 42–3. See Also Patrick H. Byrne, "On Taking Responsibility for the Indeterminate Future," *Phenomenology and the Understanding of Human Destiny,* vol. 1, *Current Continental Research,* ed. Stephen Skousgaard (Pittsburgh, PA: Center for Advanced Research in Phenomenology, 1981), 229–38.

8 Crysdale, *Embracing Travail,* 50, 57–8.

9 See chapter 12 in this volume.

10 *Insight,* 628.

11 Ibid., 629.

12 On Lonergan's account of potency, form, and act see *Insight,* 456–67; on his triple subdivision of the good, see 628–30; see also Lonergan, "The Role of the Catholic University in the Modern World," vol. 4 of *Collected Works of Bernard Lonergan,* ed. Frederick E. Crowe and Robert M. Doran (Toronto: University of Toronto Press, 1988), 108.

13 *Insight,* 629.

14 Immanuel Kant, *Critique of Practical Reason,* ed. and trans. Mary Gregor (New York: Cambridge University Press, 1997), 133 <162>, emphasis in the original.

15 Immanuel Kant, *Critique of Judgment,* trans. J.H. Bernard (New York: Hafner Press, 1951), 84 <246>; cited hereafter as Kant, *CJ.*

16 Ibid., 82 <244>.

17 Ibid., 100 <261>.

18 Ibid., 83 <245>.

19 *Insight,* 474.

20 Ibid., 630.

21 Kant, *CJ,* 100–1 <261>.

22 See especially R.J. Snell, *The Perspective of Love: Natural Law in a New Mode* (Eugene, OR: Pickwick Publications, 2014).

23 *Insight,* 628–9.

24 Ibid., 636.

25 Ibid., 628.

26 George Edward Moore, *Principia Ethica* (Cambridge: Cambridge University Press, 1959), 9–15.

27 *Insight,* 23, emphasis added.

28 Ibid., 636–7.

29 Ibid., 629–30.

30 Regarding Lonergan's differentiation of proportionate and transcendent being, see *Insight,* 663. See also his *U&B,* 195, 202.

31 *Insight,* 628–9.

32 Ibid., 679.

33 *MT,* 102–3.

34 *Insight,* 695. See chapter 2 in this volume.

35 *Insight,* 679.

36 Lonergan distinguishes between the transcendent being of God, and other transcendent realities, such as divine grace. While mindful of and in agreement with Lonergan's distinction, I am prescinding from it here in order to avoid a lengthy digression at this point in the argument. Regarding transcendent realities that are distinct from God, see *Insight,* chap. 20. See also Bernard Lonergan, "The Supernatural Order," *Early Latin Theology,* vol. 19 of *Collected Works of Bernard Lonergan,* ed. Robert M. Doran and H. Daniel Mansour, trans. Michael G. Shields (Toronto: University of Toronto Press, 2011), 52–255, and Michael J. Stebbins, *The Divine Initiative: Grace, World-Order, and Human Freedom in the Early Writings of Bernard Lonergan* (Toronto: University of Toronto Press, 1995).

37 *Insight,* 677.

38 Ibid., 679–80.

39 Ibid., 681.

40 Ibid., 664–7.

41 Positing an analogy does not mean that all of the relations of *A* to *B* are identical with all the relations of *C* to *X.* The analogy only claims that *A* and *B* share at least one relation in common with *C* and *X.*

42 See *Verbum,* 45–57.

43 *MT,* 339.

44 *Insight,* 678.

45 Ibid., 680–92.

46 Ibid., 681.

47 Ibid., 681–2.

48 *MT,* 12.

49 In order to state this analogy in a manageable form, I have used "the unrestricted notion of value" as an abbreviation for "the unified unrestricted desire that encompasses both the unrestricted notion of value as well as the unrestricted notion of being."

50 *MT,* 105–6.

51 Ibid., 111, emphasis added.

52 *Topics,* 27; *Insight,* 570, 630.

53 Bernard Lonergan, "Philosophy of History," unpublished essay from the 1930s. Bernard Lonergan Archive, http://www.bernardlonergan.com/pdf/71309DTE030.pdf. Thanks to John Volk for this reference.

54 *MT,* 40.

55 *Insight,* 630.

56 Ibid., 690–1.

57 Ibid., 644.

58 Ibid., 644, 690.

59 Ibid., 689–90.

60 Lonergan speaks of the *consequences* of the evil decision as "moral evils," but calls the nihilism of the valueless decision itself "basic sins." *Insight*, 689–90.
61 *Insight*, 255.
62 For an especially illuminating discussion of the destructive consequences that result from the counter-positional assumption that evil *is* intelligible, see Crysdale, *Embracing Travail*, 147–9.
63 *Insight*, 412–14. See also chapters 5, 6, and 8 in this volume.
64 Ibid., 709.
65 Ibid., 689–90.
66 Ibid., 630.
67 Ibid., 719.
68 Ibid., 740–1.
69 Ibid., 721–2.

14 Explanatory Genera and the Objective Scale of Values

1 Lonergan himself points in this direction in his discussion of the hierarchy of terminal values (*Insight*, 625). Regarding explanatory genera, see *Insight* 280–3, 463–4.
2 Therefore the reader might find it helpful to go first directly to section 14.5 in order to see the point to this digression, and then return to the technical discussions presented in sections 14.2–4.
3 *Insight*, 629.
4 Ibid., 41.
5 Ibid., 280.
6 Ibid., 280–2. Lonergan uses "explanatory" in contrast to "descriptive," where the former has to do with understanding things intrinsically through their interactions with one another, as opposed to their merely superficial appearances to our sensations and needs. See ibid., 102–4.
7 For present purposes, systematic processes can be understood as a certain class of combinations of operations based upon the insights into classical laws of a science. For example, a chemical reaction or transformation is a chemical operation made possible by the laws of chemistry. For Lonergan's more detailed account of systematic processes of operations, and the account of the alternative possibilities of non-systematic processes, see *Insight*, 70–6.
8 Ibid., 281.
9 A rigorous development of this relationship between, say, the lower science and genus of chemistry and the higher level would have to take up how the lower-level operations are "mirrored" in the higher level. That higher level would have to be called something like "biological-chemistry" (rather than "biochemistry," which already has a different meaning). The rigorous development would have to show how what are called "chemical

reactions" in the science of chemistry would be included and mirrored in the science of biological-chemistry. But those reactions would actually be defined differently in the higher viewpoint of biological-chemistry than in chemistry – differences in definition among reactions taking place within living organisms rather than in test-tubes or corpses. However, this kind of rigorous development is beyond the scope of this book. See *Insight* 280–4.

10 Ibid., 280–1.

11 Ibid., 625. Lonergan suggests the relevance of this hierarchy for ethics: "The division and the hierarchy of values reveal how the dynamic exigence of rational self-consciousness for self-consistency unfolds into a body of moral precepts concretely operative in a moral consciousness" – that is, precepts concerning what is objectively preferable (ibid.).

12 Ibid., 630.

13 There is, of course, one very significant difference. While each of the higher viewpoints of physical, chemical, biological, sensate, and human defines a distinct genus of things as well as conjugates, the higher viewpoints within the human level do not define distinct things separated into genera of vital, social, cultural, personal, and religious entities. There is only a single human genus of persons, who participate in these distinct levels of values. This is because the defining features of the human genus are the unrestricted notion of value and being-in-love in an unrestricted fashion. All the higher viewpoints of the scale of values arise out of and are made actual by these sources of human apprehension and choice of values. On the technical meaning of Lonergan's use of the term "thing" as defined by its explanatory attributes and the relationships among things and emergent generic levels, see *Insight*, 270–3 and 284–7.

14 See *MT*, 31.

15 Ibid.

16 It is difficult to understand why Lonergan speaks only of *social* values, without distinguishing among technological, economic, and political values. He seems to have some such hierarchy of human schemes in *Insight*, 234–5. Perhaps these should be differentiated as distinct levels of value within the less differentiated notion of social value.

17 See *De Redemptione Draft*, 169–70.

18 *MT*, 32.

19 Ibid. See also *Insight*, 624–5.

20 See *Insight*, 266.

21 *MT*, 116.

22 *Insight*, 688; see also 721.

23 For example, Walter Brueggemann has argued that the prophets endeavour to change the imaginative conditions under which the people of Israel act – often with what seems like futile efforts. He argues further that the

original Mosaic community involved a dramatic reorientation of economic and political institutions under the supreme value of "the freedom of God," and that the Prophetic movement and Jesus Christ continually endeavoured to call the people of Israel back to that supreme value. See his *The Prophetic Imagination*, 2nd ed. (Minneapolis, MN: The Fortress Press, 2001).

24 *Insight*, 290. For technical details, see 287–90 and 463–7.

25 Brian Cronin has also endorsed Doran's approach to explaining Lonergan's scale of value preference in his *Value Ethics*, 144.

26 Robert M. Doran, *What is Systematic Theology?* (Toronto: University of Toronto Press, 2005), 181; hereafter cited as Doran, *WST*. See also Doran, *TDH*, 88.

27 See chapter 15.

28 See Bernard Lonergan, *Philosophy of God, and Theology* (Philadelphia: The Westminster Press, 1973), 38. Although published in 1973, the remark came in an informal response to a question after a lecture in fall 1972. For a comprehensive survey of Lonergan's single reference to a fifth level published during his lifetime, along with numerous unpublished remarks regarding a fifth level, see Michael Vertin, "Lonergan on Consciousness: Is There a Fifth Level?," *Method: Journal of Lonergan Studies* 12 (1994): 1–36. My own response to Vertin can be found in "Consciousness: Levels, Sublations and the Subject as Subject," *Method: Journal of Lonergan Studies* 13 (1995): 131–50.

29 *Insight*, 238–9.

30 In a personal conversation, Doran told me his own thinking on this third-level correspondence arose from Lonergan's own comments, where he himself drew a connection between culture and the development on the third level of reflective consciousness (*Topics*, 54–8). However, these remarks were delivered during a course and clearly show signs of being from an unfinished, transitional stage of Lonergan's thinking. He also gave these lectures prior to the major breakthrough whereby he discerned the distinctness of the transcendental notion of value, and thereby recognized the clear differentiation between the third and fourth levels of consciousness. I do not believe that Lonergan would have adhered to this same analysis of culture after that breakthrough.

31 Doran, *WST*, 190. See also *TDH*, 89.

32 Doran, *WST*, 190.

33 From an anonymous review for the publisher of an earlier manuscript of this book.

34 *De Redemptione* was written as a "supplement" or appendix to Lonergan's text, *De Verbo Incarnato* (*DVI*), which he used in his courses at the Gregorian University, Rome, between 1960 and 1964. *DVI* was published in three editions for the course, but the supplement, *De Redemptione*, was not. The exact dating of *De Redemptione* is somewhat uncertain, but is more probably 1958 than 1964/65 as the anonymous reviewer claimed. See John Volk,

"Lonergan on the Historical Causality of Christ: An Interpretation of the Redemption: A Supplement to De Verbo Incarnato" (PhD dissertation, Marquette University, Milwaukee, WI, 2011), 5–7.

35 I owe a debt of gratitude to the reviewer for drawing my attention to this text and these connections.

36 *De Redemptione Draft*, 169, emphasis in the original.

37 Ibid., 170.

38 Ibid., emphasis in the original.

39 Ibid., 152.

40 Ibid., 153.

41 Ibid., 158, 162. See also *Insight*, 233–4.

42 *Topics*, 42.

15 Method in Ethics I

1 *MT*, 4.

2 Tad Dunne, *Doing Better: The Next Revolution in Ethics* (Milwaukee, WI: Marquette University Press, 2010); hereafter cited as Dunne, *Doing Better*.

3 *Insight*, 23; see also 618.

4 Ibid., 618.

5 Ibid., 631–9.

6 Patrick H. Byrne, "The Goodness of Being in Lonergan's *Insight*," *American Catholic Philosophical Quarterly* (2007): 43–72.

7 *Insight*, 622.

8 William E. Murnion, "Telling the Truth and Doing Good: A Key to the Infrastructure of Modern Philosophy," *The Lonergan Review*, forthcoming; typescript version that accompanied his presentation at the Lonergan Workshop Conference, Boston College, Chestnut Hill, MA, 19 June 2014; cited henceforth as Murnion, "Truth and Good."

9 Murnion, "Truth and Good," 1 and 11, respectively, emphases added.

10 Lonergan esteemed Aquinas and Aristotle for the discovery that "knowing is by identity," over against the theory of "knowing by confrontation," which, he claimed, derived from Plato. See *Verbum*, 192–9.

11 Murnion, "Truth and Good," 3.

12 *Insight*, 626. A thorough explanation of this suggestion would be tangential to this chapter, and will have to be deferred to another time.

13 *Topics*, 27, emphasis added.

14 *De Redemptione Draft*.

15 To be more precise, the fundamental assumption is "As being is intelligible and one, so also it is good" (*Insight*, 619), "the good as identical with the intelligibility that is intrinsic to being" (*Insight*, 628). See also 576, 529–30.

16 Ibid., 502.

17 Ibid., 501.

18 Ibid., 498.

19 Kenneth R. Melchin, *History, Ethics and Emergent Probability: Ethics, Society and History in the Work of Bernard Lonergan* (Lanham, MD: University Press of America, 1987), especially 191–9. See also his "History, Ethics, and Emergent Probability," *Lonergan Workshop* 7 (1988), 269–94.

20 *Insight*, 629.

21 Ibid., 626.

22 Kant, *GMM*, 30 <421>.

23 *Insight*, 618.

24 Kant, *GMM*, 24 <413>.

25 Or, equivalently, in the post-*Insight* context for ethics, the general form of maxims becomes the following: Be attentive; Be intelligent; Be reasonable; Be responsible; Be loving.

26 *Insight*, 636–56.

27 Kenneth R. Melchin, "Ethics in *Insight*," *Lonergan Workshop* 8 (1990): 135–47.

28 Kant, *GMM*, 27–9 <417–20>, 49–61 <446–63>.

29 "Is there a meaning to the word 'ought'? Our answer differs from the Kantian answer, for if we agree in affirming a categorical imperative, we disagree inasmuch as we derive it wholly from speculative intelligence and reason" (*Insight*, 623–4). For Lonergan, the source of the meaning of "ought" is the exigence for consistency between knowing and doing. He holds that this exigence is to be known in the "speculative" self-affirming judgments of fact. However, we have already discussed the difficulties of deriving ought from judgments of fact, whether speculative, self-affirming, or otherwise.

30 *Insight*, 643–56.

31 Ibid., 627–8.

32 The exceptions would be experiences that come from constructions of our own imagination. In the extreme, of course, preference for imaginary experiences over sense experiences leads to madness.

33 Flanagan, *The Quest*, 207.

34 Lonergan's most focused and detailed analysis is of common sense "as intellectual" – that is to say, of the role of insights and the self-correcting dynamics of intelligence as they operate in the commonsense mode (see *Insight*, 196–269). The character of commonsense judgments of facts and value, beliefs, and commonsense feelings as responses to value do not receive nearly the same detailed attention.

35 *Insight*, 199.

36 Flanagan, *The Quest*, 223.

37 *Insight*, 627–8.

38 Ibid., 548.

39 *MT*, 343.

40 Ibid., 235ff.

41 See Ivo Coelho, *Hermeneutics and Method: The Universal Viewpoint in Bernard Lonergan* (Toronto: University of Toronto Press, 2001); cited hereafter as Coelho, *H&M*.

42 Paul Ricoeur, *Oneself as Another* (Chicago: University of Chicago Press, 1992).

43 *MT*, 364–6.

44 In order to avoid repeating cumbersome phrases such as "the functional specialty of history," and in order to distinguish Lonergan's technical meanings of those words from other common meanings, I will capitalize the names of the eight functional specialties by capitalizing the first letter (e.g., History).

45 See Coelho, *H&M*; Doran, *TDH*.

46 Bernard Lonergan, "Healing and Creating in History," in *A Third Collection*, ed. Frederick E. Crowe, SJ (New York: Paulist Press, 1985), 106.

47 *MT*, 170.

16 Method in Ethics II

1 Rosemary Luling Haughton, "Transcendence and the Bewilderment of Being Modern," in *A Catholic Modernity?*, ed. James L. Heft (New York: Oxford University Press, 1999), 77–8. Lulling Haughton's full quotation continues, "we need to understand at least a little about what myth is." The context of her statement reveals that her concerns are very close to those of Lonergan's method.

2 *MT*, 133.

3 Ibid., 159. See also *Insight*, 199.

4 See Coelho, *H&M*.

5 *MT*, 223.

6 Ibid., 232.

7 Ibid., 245.

8 Scheler also recognized the heuristic value of the scale of values for sociological and historical investigations. See Scheler, "*Ordo Amoris*," 98–9.

9 *MT*, 233.

10 Ibid., 246.

11 See chapter 8.

12 *MT*, 245.

13 Lonergan even claims that "specialized research" will also be affected by the conversions or the lack thereof. See ibid., 246–7.

14 See ibid., 257–62.

15 Lonergan identifies and describes these procedures: *Assembly, Completion, Comparison, Reduction, Classification,* and *Selection*. See ibid., 249–50.

16 Ibid., 249.

17 For further illustrations, see *MT*, 253–66, and *Insight*, 413–14.

18 *MT*, 251, emphasis added to illustrate the implicit judgment of value. By way of contrast, says Lonergan, when this effort is made by someone lacking in conversion, the result will "present the past as worse than it really was" (ibid.). For examples that indicate what Lonergan would mean by evaluative history that "is better than it really was," see Bernard Lonergan, *The Way to Nicea: The Dialectical Development of Trinitarian Theology,* trans. Conn O'Donovan (Philadelphia: The Westminster Press, 1976).

19 *MT*, 232.

20 Paul J. Griffiths, *Song of Songs* (Grand Rapids, MI: Brazos Press, 2011), xxviii.

21 *MT*, 252.

22 Ibid., 235.

23 Ibid., 168; see also 253–4.

24 Ibid., 254.

25 Converting decisions also depend upon effects of divine grace in important ways. See chapter 1. But neither truly free human decisions nor truly gratuitous acts of God can be produced by any method.

26 *MT*, 271.

27 Ibid., 247.

28 Ibid., 253.

29 Ibid., 250.

30 Ibid., 252–3.

31 Ibid., 365.

32 In *MT*, Lonergan distinguishes basic categories into general and special. Ibid., 285–291.

33 Ibid., 286.

34 Ibid., 130–1.

35 Ibid., 254.